The Best in Science Fiction

The Best in Science Fiction

Winners and Nominees
of the Major Awards in Science Fiction

AUREL GUILLEMETTE

SCOLAR
PRESS

Published by
Scolar Press
Gower House
Croft Road
Aldershot
Hants GU11 3HR
England

humra

Ashgate Publishing Company
Old Post Road
Brookfield
Vermont 05036
USA

British Library Cataloguing-in-Publication data.

Guillemette, Aurel
  Best in Science Fiction: Winners and
  Nominees of the Major Awards in Science
  Fiction
  I. Title
  016.823

ISBN 1 85928 005 6

Printed in Great Britain at the University Press, Cambridge

Dedicated

to the staff of the

MERRIL COLLECTION OF
SCIENCE FICTION, SPECULATION & FANTASY
40 St. George Street, 2nd Floor
Toronto, Ontario (Canada) M5S 2E4

With thanks for their professionalism,
dedication to the art form, and support,
without which this project could not
have been completed

Contents

Introduction

This book contains the winners and nominees of the major science fiction awards. Readers will find this information useful in several ways.

- Collectors will be able to build a library of the best in science fiction, not only the rarest of issues.

- Readers will be able to select from the best novels, shorter works or non-fiction reference texts.

- Students of science fiction will be able to study the development of trends and tastes by following the selection process of the awards.

HOW TO USE THIS BOOK

This book is divided into different sections, each of which presents the information as follows:

Section A lists all the major awards alphabetically. You may wish to compare the winners and nominees of the major awards in a particular year in order to ascertain the prevailing tastes for that year. Most awards are given for works published in the preceding year, however, the Nebula is given for works published in the award-year. Each list is preceded by a short description of the award.

Section B lists all the authors in alphabetical order, whether they are award-winners or nominees. This is particularly useful for readers searching for a particular title when only the author's name is known, or in locating a list of works by a favourite author.

Section C lists alphabetically all the titles of works which have won or been nominated. This is useful for readers seeking a particular title, or to discover for which award(s) a title has received a win or nomination.

Section D lists award winners only, by year. This clearly indicates trends, while multiple-award winners are easily identified.

Section E applies a weighting system to all titles, based on winning or being a nominee, and on the importance of the award (i.e. the Hugo carries a higher weighting than a Clarke award).

Some titles may have received multiple wins or nominations, thus the weight shown is a combined-weight for all appearances. The titles with the highest combined-weights are listed within several categories such as novels, shorter works, collections and anthologies, horror and fantasies.

Section F lists 'The Best' from Section E, in chronological order.

THE SELECTION OF AWARDS

Some of the awards, such as the Hugo, Nebula and World Fantasy awards, require no justification. They are universally recognized as the major awards in the field.

There are two major criteria for the inclusion of the remaining awards. First, these awards must have longevity, that is, they must have been presented for at least five years.

Second, the method of selection must clearly indicate a wide pooling of opinion, or at least a selection body of recognized stature within the science fiction community. Thus the two magazine awards, Locus and Science Fiction Chronicle, are voted on by a considerable readership, whose vote is often larger than the Hugos or Nebulas. Other awards, such as the Clarkes, Campbell or Crook awards, are awarded by panels of respected authors and critics.

Many awards are not considered major because they are given as prizes in literary contests. These untested works cannot be judged at the same level with those competing for Hugos and Nebulas. Others are awarded by a single individual or by a group with special interests, for example: feminist literature, first-time women writers, works that promote libertarian philosophy, etc.

Finally, foreign-language awards are not included, though non-North American awards in the English language, such as the Ditmar (Australia) and British awards, are.

CATEGORIES

Most award committees or organizations present awards in a number of categories, such as: novels, novellas, novelettes, short stories, anthology or collection, non-fiction. For a listing of all categories, please consult the list of abbreviations which follows the section-identifier page at the beginning of each section in this book.

The awards listed only refer to the literary categories. They do not include awards for illustrations, audio or video materials, special recognition awards, or non-literary categories.

TITLE SOURCES

It is often the practice to indicate the printing history or reference to the publisher/publication where a title first appeared. This has not been included with this text for two reasons: first, the extra information would have greatly increased the extent of the text. Second and more importantly, many of the shorter works appeared in magazines, and back-issues are often difficult to locate. Since most of the award-winners and nominees have been anthologized, often included in 'Year's Best' or Hugo and Nebula Winners' annual series, we would refer you to those sources.

Part A MAJOR SCIENCE FICTION AWARDS

Winners and Nominees

This section describes all the major science fiction awards, in alphabetical order and lists all of the award winners and nominees in each category. While most awards are given for works published in the previous year, the Nebula Award is given to works published in the same year.

A full description of all abbreviations used within these listings can be found on the next page.

SECTION A: AWARDS (Alphabetically)

HEADINGS:

CAT	T I T L E	AW W/N Y	A U T H O R

EXPLANATIONS:

CAT = Category (length and type)

1 Novel	2 Novella	3 Novellette
4 Short Story	5 1-Author Collection	6 Collection/Anthology
7 Non-Fiction	8 Series	9 First Novel
10 Horror	11 Fantasy Novel	12 Magazine Article
13 Original Anthology	14 Reprint Anthology	

LENGTH OF WORK (from Locus Reader Awards)	
Novel	40,000 + words
Novella	17,500 - 40,000
Novellette	7,500 - 17,500
Short Story	up to 7,500

AW = Award

AUR	Aurora (Casper)
BFA	British Fantasy
BSF	British Science Fiction
CLA	Arthur C. Clarke
COM	Compton Crook
DAV	Davis Publications
DIC	Dick
DIT	Ditmar
HUG	Hugo
IFA	International Fantasy
JUP	Jupiter
JWC	J W Campbell
LOC	Locus Magazine
NEB	Nebula
SFC	SF Chronicle Magazine
STO	Bram Stoker
WFA	World Fantasy

W/N = winner or nominee

Y   = year award presented

CASPER and AURORA AWARDS

The Casper Awards (The Canadian Hugos) were created in 1980, and are awarded annually at CanVention, the Canadian National Science Fiction Convention, to recognize achievements by Canadian writers. The award is chosen by a mail vote of the the convention's attending and supporting membership. Nomination forms and ballots are distributed by the CanVention committee through the national science fiction newsletter, MLR, fanzines, clubs, amateur press associations, and other conventions.

The awards began with a single presentation, usually for lifetime contribution, but were reorganized in 1984 to honor best novel, short fiction, and other categories. The prize takes the form of a statuette of Coeurl, the alien creature from Canadian SF author A.E. van Vogt's story, "Black Destroyer", and was created by Michael Spencer.

Beginning in 1991, the awards were renamed the Aurora Awards.

CAT	T I T L E	AW W/N Y	A U T H O R
1	Judgement of Dragons	AUR-W 82	GOTLIEB, Phyllis
1	Friendly Aliens	AUR-N 82	COLOMBO, Robert
1	Imaro	AUR-N 82	SAUDERS, Charles
7	Visions From the Edge	AUR-N 82	BELL, John
1	Journey to Apriloth	AUR-W 85	KERNAGHAN, Eileen
1	Maple Leaf Rag	AUR-W 86	SPENCER, Garth
4	Yadjine et la Mort	AUR-W 86	SERMINE, Daniel
1	Wandering Fire, The	AUR-W 87	KAY, Guy Gavriel
1	Hidden Place, A	AUR-N 87	WILSON, Robert Charles
1	Lifter	AUR-N 87	KILLIAN, Crawford
1	Yarrow	AUR-N 87	de LINT, Charles
4	La Carte du Tendre	AUR-W 87	VONARBURG, Elisabeth
1	Jack the Giant Killer	AUR-W 88	de LINT, Charles
4	Les Crabes de Venus	AUR-W 88	BERGERON, Alain
1	Mona Lisa Overdrive	AUR-W 89	GIBSON, William
4	Sleeping in a Box	AUR-W 89	DORSEY, Candas Jane
1	West of January	AUR-W 90	DUNCAN, Dave
4	Carpe Diem	AUR-W 90	KERNAGHAN, Eileen
1	Tigana	AUR-W 91	KAY, Guy Gavriel
4	Muffin Explains Technology to the World	AUR-W 91	GARDNER, James Alan
1	Golden Fleece	AUR-W 92	SAWYER, Robert J
4	Breaking Ball	AUR-W 92	SKEET, Michael
4	Niche, A	AUR-W 92	WATTS, Peter

BRITISH FANTASY AWARDS

The British Fantasy Awards are presented annually by the British
Fantasy Society to honor the best fantasy works of the year. The prize
was established in 1971 in memory of August Darleth, the well-known
writer, editor, and publisher of Arkham House. The physical award
consists of a statuette of the Lovecraftian god Cthulhu, fashioned of
white ivory on a wood base.

   Associational awards in various categories have also been
presented by the Society, and take the same physical form as the novel
award. The Icarus Award, given each year to the most promising
newcomer to the field (the British equivalent of the John W. Campbell
Award), was established in 1987 (1988).

   Year presented for previously published year.

CAT	TITLE	AW W/N Y	AUTHOR
1	Knight of the Swords, The	BFA-W 73	MOORCOCK, Michael
1	King of the Swords, The	BFA-W 74	MOORCOCK, Michael
1	Hrolf Kraki's Saga	BFA-W 75	ANDERSON, Poul
4	Sticks	BFA-W 75	WAGNER, Karl Edward
1	Hollow Lands, The	BFA-W 76	MOORCOCK, Michael
1	Dragon and the George, The	BFA-W 77	DICKSON, Gordon R
4	Two Suns Setting	BFA-W 77	WAGNER, Karl Edward
1	Spell for Chameleon, A	BFA-W 78	ANTHONY, Piers
4	In the Bag	BFA-W 78	CAMPBELL, Ramsey
1	Chronicles o/Thomas Covenant t/Unbeleive	BFA-W 79	DONALDSON, Stephen R
1	Dying of the Light	BFA-N 79	MARTIN, George R R
1	Gloriana	BFA-N 79	MOORCOCK, Michael
1	Quest of the White Witch, The	BFA-N 79	LEE, Tanith
1	Road to Corley, The	BFA-N 79	COWPER, Richard
4	Jeffty is Five	BFA-W 79	ELLISON, Harlan
4	Big Spell, The	BFA-N 79	REAVES, Michael
4	Changer of Names, The	BFA-N 79	CAMPBELL, Ramsey
4	Lady in White, The	BFA-N 79	DONALDSON, Stephen R
4	Within the Walls of Tyre	BFA-N 79	BISHOP, Michael
1	Death's Master	BFA-W 80	LEE, Tanith
1	Harpist in the Wind	BFA-N 80	McKILLIP, Patricia
1	Sorcerer's Son	BFA-N 80	EISENSTEIN, Phyllis
4	Button Molder, The	BFA-W 80	LEIBER, Fritz
4	First Make Them Mad	BFA-N 80	COLE, Adrian
4	Red As Blood	BFA-N 80	LEE, Tanith

CAT	T I T L E	AW W/N Y	A U T H O R
1	To Wake the Dead	BFA-W 81	CAMPBELL, Ramsey
1	Firestarter	BFA-N 81	KING, Stephen
1	Kill The Dead	BFA-N 81	LEE, Tanith
1	Storm of Wings, A	BFA-N 81	HARRISON, M John
1	Wounded Land, The	BFA-N 81	DONALDSON, Stephen R
4	Stains	BFA-W 81	AICKMAN, Robert
4	Crouch End	BFA-N 81	KING, Stephen
4	House of the Temple, The	BFA-N 81	LUMLEY, Brian
4	Late Shift, The	BFA-N 81	ETCHISON, Dennis
1	Cujo	BFA-W 82	KING, Stephen
4	Dark Country, The	BFA-W 82	ETCHISON, Dennis
4	Do the Dead Sing?	BFA-W 82	KING, Stephen
4	Coin of the Realm	BFA-N 82	GRANT, Charles L
4	Fairy Tale	BFA-N 82	DANN, Jack
6	Elsewhere	BFA-W 82	WINDLING, Terri
6	Fantasy Annual 4	BFA-N 82	CARR, Terry
6	Shadows 4	BFA-N 82	GRANT, Charles L
6	Tales From the Nightside	BFA-N 82	GRANT, Charles L
6	Whispers 3	BFA-N 82	SCHIFF, Stuart David
1	Sword of the Lichtor, The	BFA-W 83	WOLFE, Gene
1	In Viriconium	BFA-N 83	HARRISON, M John
1	Psycho II	BFA-N 83	BLOCH, Robert
4	Breathing Method, The	BFA-W 83	KING, Stephen
4	Apt Pupil	BFA-N 83	KING, Stephen
4	Name and Number	BFA-N 83	LUMLEY, Brian
1	Floating Dragons	BFA-W 84	STRAUB, Peter
4	Neither Brute Nor Human	BFA-W 84	WAGNER, Karl Edward
1	Ceremonies, The	BFA-W 85	KLEIN, T E D
4	Forbidden, The	BFA-W 85	BARKER, Clive
1	Ragged Astronauts, The	BFA-W 86	SHAW, Bob
4	Kaeti and the Hangman	BFA-W 86	ROBERTS, Keith
1	It	BFA-W 87	KING, Stephen
4	Olympic Runner, The	BFA-W 87	ETCHISON, Dennis
1	Hungry Moon, The	BFA-W 88	CAMPBELL, Ramsey
1	Aegypt	BFA-N 88	CROWLEY, John
1	Bones of the Moon	BFA-N 88	CARROLL, Jonathan
1	Valley of Lights	BFA-N 88	GALLAGHER, Stephen
1	Weaveworld	BFA-N 88	BARKER, Clive

BRITISH FANTASY AWARDS

CAT	T I T L E	AW W/N Y	A U T H O R
4	Leaks	BFA-W 88	TEM, Steve Rasnic
4	Another World	BFA-N 88	CAMPBELL, Ramsey
4	Fat Face	BFA-N 88	SHEA, Michael
4	Friend's Best Man	BFA-N 88	CARROLL, Jonathan
4	Wound, The	BFA-N 88	TUTTLE, Lisa
1	Influence, The	BFA-W 89	CAMPBELL, Ramsey
4	Fruiting Bodies	BFA-W 89	LUMLEY, Brian
1	Carrion Comfort	BFA-W 90	SIMMONS, Dan
4	On t/Far Side of t/Cadillac Desert w/Dea	BFA-W 90	LANSDALE, Joe R
1	Outside the Dog Museum	BFA-W 91	CARROLL, Jonathan
1	Count of Eleven, The	BFA-N 91	CAMPBELL, Ramsey
1	Summer of Night	BFA-N 91	SIMMONS, Dan
4	Dark Land, The	BFA-W 91	SMITH, Michael Marshall
4	Boo Hoo Forest	BFA-N 91	PAVEY, Jack
4	Flipping	BFA-N 91	SILVA, David
6	Darklands	BFA-W 91	BOYLE, Nicholson
6	Borderlands	BFA-N 91	MONTELEONE, Thomas F
6	Dark Voices	BFA-N 91	SUTTON, David
1	Midnight Sun	BFA-W 92	CAMPBELL, Ramsey
4	Man Who Drew Cats, The	BFA-W 92	SMITH, Michael Marshall
6	Best New Horror	BFA-W 92	JONES, Stephen

BRITISH SCIENCE FICTION ASSOCIATION AWARD

The BSFA Awards are nominated by members of the British Science Fiction Association (BSFA). A panel of judges, including members of the BSFA, The International Science Policy Foundation, and the Science Fiction Foundation, make the final decision. Presentations are made annually at England's National Science Fiction Convention, held around Easter, usually in April. The physical award is an engraved plaque on a wooden shield. When the awards where first established in 1969, they were presented only for the best novel. Following a reorganization in 1979, they now recognize the best science fiction works in four categories: novel, short fiction, media presentation, and artist, for works first published or presented in the United Kingdom during the preceding calendar year.

CAT	TITLE	AW W/N Y	AUTHOR
1	Stand on Zanzibar	BSF-W 70	BRUNNER, John
1	Jagged Orbit, The	BSF-W 71	BRUNNER, John
1	Moment of Eclipse, The	BSF-W 72	ALDISS, Brian W
1	Rendezvous with Rama	BSF-W 74	CLARKE, Arthur C
7	Billion Year Spree	BSF-W 74	ALDISS, Brian W
1	Orbitsville	BSF-W 75	SHAW, Bob
1	Brontomek?	BSF-W 77	CONEY, Michael G
7	Pictorial History of Science Fiction, A	BSF-W 77	KYLE, David A
1	Jonah Kit, The	BSF-W 78	WATSON, Ian
1	Unlimited Dream Company, The	BSF-W 80	BALLARD, J G
1	A.K.A.: A Cosmic Tale	BSF-N 80	SWIGART, Rob
1	Blind Voices	BSF-N 80	REAMY, Tom
1	Fountains of Paradise, The	BSF-N 80	CLARKE, Arthur C
1	On Wings of Song	BSF-N 80	DISCH, Thomas M
4	Palely Loitering	BSF-W 80	PRIEST, Christopher
4	Camps	BSF-N 80	DANN, Jack
4	Crossing Into Cambodia	BSF-N 80	MOORCOCK, Michael
4	Prose Bowl	BSF-N 80	MALZBERG, Barry N
4	Sex Pirates of the Blood Asteroid	BSF-N 80	LANGFORD, David
1	Timescape	BSF-W 81	BENFORD, Gregory
1	Beyond the Blue Event Horizon	BSF-W 81	POHL, Frederik
1	Engine Summer	BSF-N 81	CROWLEY, John
1	Molly Zero	BSF-N 81	ROBERTS, Keith
1	Transfigurations	BSF-N 81	BISHOP, Michael
1	World Between, A	BSF-N 81	SPINRAD, Norman
4	Brave Little Toaster, The	BSF-N 81	DISCH, Thomas M
4	Ink Imp, The	BSF-N 81	LAMMING, R M
4	Lordly Ones, The	BSF-N 81	ROBERTS, Keith
4	Rautavaara's Case	BSF-N 81	DICK, Philip K
4	Web of the Magi, The	BSF-N 81	COWPER, Richard
4	World SF Convention of 2080, The	BSF-N 81	WATSON, Ian

BRITISH SCIENCE FICTION ASSOCIATION AWARD

CAT	TITLE	AW W/N Y	AUTHOR
1	Shadow of the Torturer, The	BSF-W 82	WOLFE, Gene
1	Affirmation, The	BSF-N 82	PRIEST, Christopher
1	Hello America	BSF-N 82	BALLARD, J G
1	Where Time Winds Blow	BSF-N 82	HOLDSTOCK, Robert
4	Mythago Wood	BSF-W 82	HOLDSTOCK, Robert
4	Cage for Death, A	BSF-N 82	WATSON, Ian
4	Checkout, The	BSF-N 82	ROBERTS, Keith
4	Killing Thought, The	BSF-N 82	SHAVER, Edward
4	Treading the Maze	BSF-N 82	TUTTLE, Lisa
1	Helliconia Spring	BSF-W 83	ALDISS, Brian W
1	Divine Invasion, The	BSF-N 83	DICK, Philip K
1	Little Big	BSF-N 83	CROWLEY, John
1	No Enemy But Time	BSF-N 83	BISHOP, Michael
1	Sword of the Lichtor, The	BSF-N 83	WOLFE, Gene
4	Kitemaster	BSF-W 83	ROBERTS, Keith
4	Dissemblers, The	BSF-N 83	KILWORTH, Garry
4	Myths of the Near Future	BSF-N 83	BALLARD, J G
4	Overture to a Midsummer Night's Dream	BSF-N 83	CARTER, Angela
4	Third Test, The	BSF-N 83	WEINER, Andrew
1	Tik-Tok	BSF-W 84	SLADEK, John
1	Cat Karina	BSF-N 84	CONEY, Michael G
1	Citadel of the Autarch, The	BSF-N 84	WOLFE, Gene
1	Golden Witchbreed	BSF-N 84	GENTLE, Mary
1	Helliconia Spring	BSF-N 84	ALDISS, Brian W
4	After Images	BSF-W 84	EDWARDS, Malcolm
4	Calling All Gumdrops	BSF-N 84	SLADEK, John
4	Flash Kid, The	BSF-N 84	BRADFIELD, Scott
4	Tithonian Factor, The	BSF-N 84	COWPER, Richard
1	Mythago Wood	BSF-W 85	HOLDSTOCK, Robert
1	Empire of the Sun	BSF-N 85	BALLARD, J G
1	Glamour, The	BSF-N 85	PRIEST, Christopher
1	Neuromancer	BSF-N 85	GIBSON, William
1	Nights At the Circus	BSF-N 85	CARTER, Angela
4	Unconquered Country, The	BSF-W 85	RYMAN, Geoff
4	Man Who Painted the Dragon Griaule, The	BSF-N 85	SHEPARD, Lucius
4	Object of the Attack, The	BSF-N 85	BALLARD, J G
4	Spiral Winds	BSF-N 85	KILWORTH, Garry
4	Unmistakably the Finest	BSF-N 85	BRADFIELD, Scott
1	Helliconia Winter	BSF-W 86	ALDISS, Brian W
1	Anubis Gates, The	BSF-N 86	POWERS, Tim
1	Free, Live Free	BSF-N 86	WOLFE, Gene
1	Kiteworld	BSF-N 86	ROBERTS, Keith
1	Warrior Who Carried Life, The	BSF-N 86	RYMAN, Geoff

BRITISH SCIENCE FICTION ASSOCIATION AWARD

CAT	TITLE	AW W/N Y	AUTHOR
4	Cube Root	BSF-W 86	LANGFORD, David
4	Kitemistress	BSF-N 86	ROBERTS, Keith
4	O' Happy Day	BSF-N 86	RYMAN, Geoff
4	People of the Precipice	BSF-N 86	WATSON, Ian
6	Young Man's Journey to Viriconium, A	BSF-N 86	HARRISON, M John
1	Ragged Astronauts, The	BSF-W 87	SHAW, Bob
1	Blood Music	BSF-N 87	BEAR, Greg
1	Count Zero	BSF-N 87	GIBSON, William
1	Queen of the States	BSF-N 87	SAXTON, Josephine
1	Schismatrix	BSF-N 87	STERLING, Bruce
4	Kaeti and the Hangman	BSF-W 87	ROBERTS, Keith
4	And He Not Busy Being Born	BSF-N 87	STABLEFORD, Brian
4	Jangling Geordie's Hole	BSF-N 87	WATSON, Ian
4	Winter Market, The	BSF-N 87	GIBSON, William
1	Grianne	BSF-W 88	ROBERTS, Keith
4	Love Sickness	BSF-W 88	RYMAN, Geoff
1	Pyramids	BSF-W 90	PRATCHETT, Terry
4	In Transition	BSF-W 90	TUTTLE, Lisa
1	Take Back Plenty	BSF-W 91	GREENLAND, Colin
1	Difference Engine, The	BSF-N 91	GIBSON, William
1	Hyperion	BSF-N 91	SIMMONS, Dan
1	Rats and Gargoyles	BSF-N 91	GENTLE, Mary
1	Use of Weapons	BSF-N 91	BANKS, Iain M
4	Original Dr. Shade, The	BSF-W 91	NEWMAN, Kim
4	Axiomatic	BSF-N 91	EGAN, Greg
4	Death of Cassandra Quebec, The	BSF-N 91	BROWN, Eric
4	Learning To Be Me	BSF-N 91	EGAN, Greg
4	Phargean Effect, The	BSF-N 91	BROWN, Eric
4	Winning	BSF-N 91	McDONALD, Ian
1	Fall of Hyperion, The	BSF-W 92	SIMMONS, Dan
1	Architecture of Desire, The	BSF-N 92	GENTLE, Mary
1	Eternal Light	BSF-N 92	McAULEY, Paul J
4	Bad Timing	BSF-W 92	BROWN, Molly
4	Floating Dogs	BSF-N 92	McDONALD, Ian
4	Nothing Special	BSF-N 92	GREENLAND, Colin

ARTHUR C CLARKE AWARD

For the best paperback book of the previous year, published in Great Britain.

CAT	TITLE	AW W/N Y	AUTHOR
1	Handmaid's Tale, The	CLA-W 87	ATWOOD, Margaret
1	Eon	CLA-N 87	BEAR, Greg
1	Escape Plans	CLA-N 87	JONES, Gwyneth
1	Green Eyes	CLA-N 87	SHEPARD, Lucius
1	Memory of Whiteness, The	CLA-N 87	ROBINSON, Kim Stanley
1	Queen of the States	CLA-N 87	SAXTON, Josephine
1	Ragged Astronauts, The	CLA-N 87	SHAW, Bob
1	Stars in My Pocket Like Grains of Sand	CLA-N 87	DELANY, Samuel R
1	Sea and Summer, The	CLA-W 88	TURNER, George
1	Aegypt	CLA-N 88	CROWLEY, John
1	Ancient of Days	CLA-N 88	BISHOP, Michael
1	Fiasco	CLA-N 88	LEM, Stanislaw
1	Grianne	CLA-N 88	ROBERTS, Keith
1	Memoirs of An Invisible Man	CLA-N 88	SAINT, H F
1	Replay	CLA-N 88	GRIMWOOD, Ken
1	Unquenchable Fire	CLA-W 89	POLLACK, Richard
1	Empire of Fear, The	CLA-N 89	STABLEFORD, Brian
1	Kairos	CLA-N 89	JONES, Gwyneth
1	Life During Wartime	CLA-N 89	SHEPARD, Lucius
1	Philip K Dick Is Dead Alas	CLA-N 89	BISHOP, Michael
1	Rumours of Spring	CLA-N 89	GRANT, Richard
1	Whores of Babylon	CLA-N 89	WATSON, Ian
1	Children of the Garden	CLA-W 90	RYMAN, Geoff
1	Child Across the Sky, A	CLA-N 90	CARROLL, Jonathan
1	Desolation Road	CLA-N 90	McDONALD, Ian
1	Ivory: Legend Past & Future	CLA-N 90	RESNICK, Mike
1	Mask For The General, A	CLA-N 90	GOLDSTEIN, Lisa
1	Neverness	CLA-N 90	ZINDELL, David
1	Soldiers of Paradise	CLA-N 90	PAUL, Park
1	Take Bake Plenty	CLA-W 91	GREENLAND, Colin
1	Farewell Horizontal	CLA-N 91	JETER, K W
1	Rats and Gargoyles	CLA-N 91	GENTLE, Mary
1	Red Spider, White Web	CLA-N 91	MISHA
1	The City, Not Long After	CLA-N 91	MURPHY, Pat
1	Use of Weapons	CLA-N 91	BANKS, Iain M
1	Synners	CLA-W 92	CADIGAN, Pat
1	Eternal Light	CLA-N 92	McAULEY, Paul J
1	Hyperion Cantos	CLA-N 92	SIMMONS, Dan
1	Raft	CLA-N 92	BAXTER, Stephen M
1	Subterranean Gallery	CLA-N 92	RUSSO, Richard Paul
1	White Queen	CLA-N 92	JONES, Gwyneth

COMPTON CROOK AWARD

The Compton N. Crook/Stephen Tall Memorial Award is voted upon and given by the Baltimore Science Fiction Society (Baltimore SFS), for the best first novel of science fiction from the previous year. The name honors the memory of SF writer Crook, who wrote under the name Stephen Tall.

The prize consists of $500 and a certificate presented annually at Balticon.

CAT	TITLE	AW W/N Y	AUTHOR
1	Courtship Rite	COM-W 83	KINGSBURY, Donald
1	War for Eternity, The	COM-W 84	ROWLEY, Christopher
1	Emergence	COM-W 85	PALMER, David R
1	Infinity's Web	COM-W 86	FINCH, Sheila
1	Doomsday Effect, The	COM-W 87	WREN, Thomas
1	Crosstime Engineer, The	COM-N 87	FRANKOWSKI, Leo
1	Game of Fox and Lion, The	COM-N 87	CHASE, Robert R
1	Hidden Place, A	COM-N 87	WILSON, Charles
1	Shards of Honor	COM-N 87	BUJOLD, Lois McMaster
1	After the Zap	COM-N 88	ARMSTRONG, Michael
1	In Conquest Born	COM-N 88	FRIEDMAN, C S
1	Liege-Killer	COM-N 88	HINZ, Christopher
1	War For the Oaks	COM-N 88	BULL, Emma
1	Sheepfarmer's Daughter	COM-W 89	MOON, Elizabeth
1	Dragon Prince	COM-N 89	RAWN, Melanie
1	Heavenly Horse From the Outermost West	COM-N 89	STANTON, Mary
1	Leaves of October, The	COM-N 89	SAKERS, Don
1	Shining Falcon, The	COM-W 90	SHERMAN, Josepha
1	In the Net of Dreams	COM-N 91	SIMMONS, Wm Mark
1	Interior of Life, The	COM-N 91	BLAKE, Katherine
1	Reefsong	COM-W 92	SEVERANCE, Carol
1	Ground Ties	COM-N 92	FANCHER, Jane
1	In the Dark Lands	COM-N 92	SAGARA, Michelle

DAVIS READERS' AWARDS

The Davis Readers Awards are given annually by Analog Science
Fiction/Science Fact Magazine, and Isaac Asimov's Science Fiction
Magazine (IASFM), both issued by Davis publications, through polls
taken of those publications' readers. The physical prize consists of
$200 and a certificate.

The year awarded is for the previous calendar year publication.

CAT	TITLE	AW W/N Y	AUTHOR
2	Spice Pogrom	DAV-W 87	WILLIS, Connie
3	Eifelheim	DAV-W 87	FLYNN, Michael F
3	Prisoner of Chillon	DAV-W 87	KELLY, James Patrick
4	Phreak Encounter	DAV-W 87	ALLEN, Roger MacBride
4	Robot Dreams	DAV-W 87	ASIMOV, Isaac
12	Long Stern Case: Speculative Exercise	DAV-W 87	COOK, Rick
2	Mother Goddess of the World	DAV-W 88	ROBINSON, Kim Stanley
3	Gift, The	DAV-W 88	FORDE, Pat
3	Rachel in Love	DAV-W 88	MURPHY, Pat
4	Why I Left Harry's All-Night Hamburgers	DAV-W 88	WATT-EVANS, Lawrence
4	Love Song of Laura Morrison, The	DAV-W 88	OLTOIN, Jerry
12	Nanotechnology	DAV-W 88	PETERSON, Chris
2	Last of the Winnebagos, The	DAV-W 89	WILLIS, Connie
2	Surfacing	DAV-N 89	WILLIAMS, Walter Jon
2	Scalehunter's Beautiful Daughter, The	DAV-N 89	SHEPARD, Lucius
3	Dowser	DAV-W 89	CARD, Orson Scott
3	Sanctuary	DAV-W 89	WHITE, James
3	Guz's Place	DAV-N 89	PERPER, Timothy
3	Hob, The	DAV-N 89	MOFFATT, Judith
3	Peaches For Mad Molly	DAV-N 89	GOULD, Stephen
3	Under the Covenant Stars	DAV-N 89	BARNES, John
4	Circus Horse, The	DAV-W 89	BECHTEL, Amy
4	Midwinter's Tale, A	DAV-W 89	SWANWICK, Michael
4	Christmas Without Rodney	DAV-N 89	ASIMOV, Isaac
4	Frame of Reference	DAV-N 89	KRAUS, Stephen
4	Ripples in the Dirac Sea	DAV-N 89	LANDIS, Geoffrey A
4	Siren	DAV-N 89	AUSTIN, A J
12	An Introduction to Psychohistory	DAV-W 89	FLYNN, Michael F
12	24th Century Medicine	DAV-N 89	DONALDSON, Thomas
12	Extrat'l Intel & t/Interdict Hypothesis	DAV-N 89	FOGG, Martyn J
2	Touch of Lavender, A	DAV-W 90	LINDHOLM, Megan
3	Labyrinth	DAV-W 90	BUJOLD, Lois McMaster
3	Loch Moose Monster, The	DAV-W 90	KAGAN, Janet
4	Windwagon Smith and the Martians	DAV-W 90	WATT-EVANS, Lawrence
4	Happy Dead, The	DAV-W 90	BECHTEL, Amy
12	Ape-Man Within Us, The	DAV-W 90	de CAMP, L Sprague

DAVIS READERS' AWARDS

CAT	TITLE	AW W/N Y	AUTHOR
2	Mr. Boy	DAV-W 91	KELLY, James Patrick
2	Weatherman	DAV-W 91	BUJOLD, Lois McMaster
3	Getting the Bugs Out	DAV-W 91	KAGAN, Janet
4	VRM-547	DAV-W 91	THOMPSON, W R
4	Bears Discover Fire	DAV-W 91	BISSON, Terry
12	Sixty Astounding Years	DAV-W 91	FLYNN, Michael F

PHILIP K DICK AWARD

The Philip K. Dick Memorial Award was created by Thomas M. Disch, David Hartwell, and Charles N. Brown shortly after Dick's death, to honor the Best American Original SF Paperback Book of the year. The prize is awarded annually by the Philadelphia SF Society at Norwescon and consists of a cash prize of $1,000 for first prize and $500 for second. Both prizes come with a certificate, a gold logo for first, silver for second.

A five-person jury comprises each year's panel: each juror names his/her successor for the following year. There is always at least one academic and one editor on the panel, in addition to working SF and fantasy authors. The award is administered by four directors: David Hartwell, Paul O. Williams, Algis Budrys, and Russell Galen. Prize monies are obtained by soliciting contributions from original paperback publishers.

CAT	TITLE	AW W/N Y	AUTHOR
1	Software	DIC-W 83	RUCKER, Rudy
1	Aurelia	DIC-N 83	LAFFERTY, R A
1	Prometheus Man, The	DIC-N 83	NELSON, Ray F
1	Roderick	DIC-N 83	SLADEK, John
1	Waiting for the Barbarians	DIC-N 83	COETZEE, J M
1	Anubis Gates, The	DIC-W 84	POWERS, Tim
1	Benefits	DIC-N 84	FAIRBAIRNS, Zoe
1	Floating Gods, The	DIC-N 84	HARRISON, M John
1	Millenium	DIC-N 84	VARLEY, John
1	Tea With The Black Dragon	DIC-N 84	MacAVOY, R A
1	Zen Gun, The	DIC-N 84	BAYLEY, Barrington J
1	Neuromancer	DIC-W 85	GIBSON, William
1	Alchemists, The	DIC-N 85	GRAVEL, Geary
1	Emergence	DIC-N 85	PALMER, David R
1	Frontera	DIC-N 85	SHINER, Lewis
1	Green Eyes	DIC-N 85	SHEPARD, Lucius
1	Them Bones	DIC-N 85	WALDROP, Howard
1	Voyager in Night	DIC-N 85	CHERRYH, C J
1	Wild Shore, The	DIC-N 85	ROBINSON, Kim Stanley
1	Dinner at Deviant's Place	DIC-W 86	POWERS, Tim
1	Enterprise	DIC-N 86	KUBE-McDOWELL, Michael P
1	Knight Moves	DIC-N 86	WILLIAMS, Walter Jon
1	Remaking of Sigmund Freud, The	DIC-N 86	MALZBERG, Barry N
1	Saraband of Lost Time	DIC-N 86	GRANT, Richard
1	Terrarium	DIC-N 86	SANDERS, Scott Russell
1	Timeservers, The	DIC-N 86	GRIFFIN, Russell
1	Homunculus	DIC-W 87	BLAYLOCK, James P
1	Artificial Things	DIC-N 87	FOWLER, Karen Joy
1	Hercules Text, The	DIC-N 87	McDEVITT, Jack
1	Hidden Place, A	DIC-N 87	WILSON, Robert Charles

PHILIP K DICK AWARD

CAT	TITLE	AW W/N Y	AUTHOR
1	Strange Toys	DIC-W 88	GEARY, Patricia
1	Dark Seeker	DIC-N 88	JETER, K W
1	Dover Beach	DIC-N 88	BOWKER, Richard
1	Life During Wartime	DIC-N 88	SHEPARD, Lucius
1	Memories	DIC-N 88	McQUAY, Mike
1	Midplayers	DIC-N 88	CADIGAN, Pat
1	Wetware	DIC-W 89	RUCKER, Rudy
1	400 Billion Stars	DIC-N 89	McCAULEY, Paul J
1	Becoming Alien	DIC-N 89	ORE, Rebecca Brown
1	Neon Lotus	DIC-N 89	LAIDLAW, Marc
1	Orphan of Creation	DIC-N 89	ALLEN, Roger MacBride
1	Rendezvous	DIC-N 89	SMITH, D Alexander
1	Subturranean Gallery	DIC-W 90	RUSSO, Richard Paul
1	Being Alien	DIC-N 90	ORE, Rebecca Brown
1	Fearful Symmetry, A	DIC-N 90	LUCENO, James
1	Heritage of Flight	DIC-N 90	SHWARTZ, Susan
1	Infinity Hold	DIC-N 90	LONGYEAR, Barry
1	On My Way To Paradise	DIC-N 90	WOLVERTON, Dave
1	Points of Departure	DIC-W 91	MURPHY, Pat
1	Clarke County, Space	DIC-N 91	STEELE, Allan
1	Oxygen Barons	DIC-N 91	FEELEY, Gregory
1	Schizogenic Man, The	DIC-N 91	HARRIS, Raymond
1	Winterlong	DIC-N 91	HAND, Elizabeth
1	King of the Morning, Queen of Day	DIC-W 92	McDONALD, Ian
1	Bone Dance	DIC-N 92	BULL, Emma
1	Bridge of Years	DIC-N 92	WILSON, Robert Charles
1	Cipher, The	DIC-N 92	KOJA, Kathe
1	Mojo and the Pickle Jar	DIC-N 92	BELL, Douglas

DITMAR AWARDS (Australia)

The Ditmars (the Australian equivalent of the Hugos) were created in
1969 by Dick Jensen, Terry Dowling, Merv Binns, and others on the
committee of that year's Australian National Science Fiction
Convention. After much argument over the name of the award, Jensen
suggested the Scandinavian form of his own name, Ditmar, as a joke;
much to his astonishment, the name was adopted. Jensen then put up the
money to make the first trophies.

The award is administered by the organizing committee of each
annual Australian National SF Convention. Theoretically, all works
nominated should have first become available in Australia in the year
prior to the awards ceremony, but in reality, works have been nominated
up to ten years after their first appearance there; also, some of the
nominated works have been only marginally fantastic. Categories have
changed frequently from convention to convention.

The William Atheling, Jr. Award (referred to as the Atheling
Award) is given for best nonfiction work in science fiction and fantasy
fields. Atheling was a pseudonym of the late SF writer, James Blish
(1921-1975).

The only awards listed below are for the International Award.

CAT	T I T L E	AW W/N Y	A U T H O R
1	Camp Concentration	DIT-W 69	DISCH, Thomas M
1	Cosmicomics	DIT-W 70	CALVINO, Italo
1	Ringworld	DIT-W 72	NIVEN, Larry
1	Gods Themselves, The	DIT-W 73	ASIMOV, Isaac
1	Protector	DIT-W 75	NIVEN, Larry
1	Forever War, The	DIT-W 76	HALDEMAN, Joe
1	Space Machine, The	DIT-W 77	PRIEST, Christopher
1	Simarillion, The	DIT-W 78	TOLKIEN, J R R
1	White Dragon, The	DIT-W 79	McCAFFREY, Anne
1	Hitchhiker's Guide to the Galaxy, The	DIT-W 80	ADAMS, Douglas
1	Timescape	DIT-W 81	BENFORD, Gregory
1	Affirmation, The	DIT-W 82	PRIEST, Christopher
1	Riddley Walker	DIT-W 83	HOBAN, Russell
1	Neuromancer	DIT-W 85	GIBSON, William
1	Compass Rose, The	DIT-W 86	LeGUIN, Ursula K
1	Seventh Son	DIT-W 89	CARD, Orson Scott

HUGO AWARDS

The first Science Fiction Achievement Awards, nicknamed the Hugos (after Hugo Gernsback) were given out at the Philadelphia World Science Fiction Convention of 1953.

From the first, the winners were picked by popular vote, unlike many other awards which are chosen by a panel.

Before 1959, there were no nominees, and only one ballot was sent out before the convention.

Categories have been expanded and modified substantially since they were first introduced. Today, it is usual to award winners in approximately ten categories.

There were no awards given in 1954, but awards were made without interruption beginning in 1955.

The first John W. Campbell Award, for best new writer, while not a Hugo, was given in 1973. In 1974, the Gandalf Award, for Grand Master of Fantasy, was first presented. The Gandalf is not a Hugo.

It is an honour to be nominated for a Hugo. Only ties get duplicate awards. The "Australian" ballot is used to assure a majority winner without a run-off. The voter is asked to mark all nominees by number, indicating a first, second, third, etc... choices. "On the first count only first-place votes are counted. At the end of the count, the nominee with the fewest votes is dropped and the second choices of his supporters are distributed between the remaining nominees. This is repeated until the leading nominee has over 50% of the vote" (Progress Report #3, St. Louiscon).

HUGO AWARD

CAT	TITLE	AW W/N Y	AUTHOR
1	Demolished Man	HUG-W 53	BESTER, Alfred
	No awards presented	54	
1	They'd Rather Be Right	HUG-W 55	CLIFTON, Mark
3	Darfsteller, The	HUG-W 55	MILLER, Walter M Jr
4	Allamagoosa	HUG-W 55	RUSSELL, Eric Frank
1	Double Star	HUG-W 56	HEINLEIN, Robert A
3	Exploration Team	HUG-W 56	LEINSTER, Murray
4	Star, The	HUG-W 56	CLARKE, Arthur C
1	Big Time, The	HUG-W 58	LEIBER, Fritz
4	Or All The Seas With Oysters	HUG-W 58	DAVIDSON, Avram
1	Case of Conscience, A	HUG-W 59	BLISH, James
1	Enemy Stars, The	HUG-N 59	ANDERSON, Poul
1	Have Space Suit-Will Travel	HUG-N 59	HEINLEIN, Robert A
1	Immortality Inc	HUG-N 59	SHECKLEY, Robert
1	Who	HUG-N 59	BUDRYS, Algis
3	Big Front Yard, The	HUG-W 59	SIMAK, Clifford D
3	Captivity	HUG-N 59	HENDERSON, Zenna
3	Deskful of Girls, A	HUG-N 59	LEIBER, Fritz
3	Miracle Workers	HUG-N 59	VANCE, Jack
3	Rat in the Skull	HUG-N 59	PHILLIPS, Rog
3	Reap the Dark Tide (Shark Ship)	HUG-N 59	KORNBLUTH, Cyril M
3	Second Game (Cosmic Checkmate)	HUG-N 59	MacLEAN, Katherine
3	Unwilling to School	HUG-N 59	ASHWELL, Pauline
4	Hell-Bound Train, That	HUG-W 59	BLOCH, Robert
4	Advent of Channel Twelve, The	HUG-N 59	KORNBLUTH, Cyril M
4	Edge of the Sea, The	HUG-N 59	BUDRYS, Algis
4	Men Who Murdered Mohammed, The	HUG-N 59	BESTER, Alfred
4	Nine Yards of Other Cloth	HUG-N 59	WELLMAN, Manly Wade
4	Rump-Titty-Titty-Tum-TAH-Tee	HUG-N 59	LEIBER, Fritz
4	Space to Swing a Cat	HUG-N 59	MULLEN, Stanley
4	Theory of Rocketry	HUG-N 59	KORNBLUTH, Cyril M
4	They've Been Working On...	HUG-N 59	BAKER, Anton Lee
4	Triggerman	HUG-N 59	BONE, J F
1	Starship Troopers	HUG-W 60	HEINLEIN, Robert A
1	Brain Twister	HUG-N 60	PHILLIPS, Mark
1	Deathworld	HUG-N 60	HARRISON, Harry
1	Genetic General (Dorsai)	HUG-N 60	DICKSON, Gordon R
1	High Crusade, The	HUG-N 60	ANDERSON, Poul
1	Pirates of Zan	HUG-N 60	LEINSTER, Murray
1	Sirens of Titan, The	HUG-N 60	VONNEGUT, Kurt Jr

CAT	TITLE	AW W/N Y	AUTHOR
4	Flowers for Algernon	HUG-W 60	KEYES, Daniel
4	Alley Man, The	HUG-N 60	FARMER, Philip Jose
4	Cat and Mouse	HUG-N 60	WILLIAMS, Ralph
4	Man Who Lost the Sea	HUG-N 60	STURGEON, Theodore
4	Pi Man, The	HUG-N 60	BESTER, Alfred
1	Canticle for Leibowitz	HUG-W 61	MILLER, Walter M Jr
1	Deathworld	HUG-N 61	HARRISON, Harry
1	Fall of Moondust, A	HUG-N 61	CLARKE, Arthur C
1	High Crusade, The	HUG-N 61	ANDERSON, Poul
1	Rogue Moon	HUG-N 61	BUDRYS, Algis
1	Venus Pluz X	HUG-N 61	STURGEON, Theodore
4	Longest Voyage, The	HUG-W 61	ANDERSON, Poul
4	Lost Kafoozalum, The	HUG-N 61	ASHWELL, Pauline
4	Need	HUG-N 61	STURGEON, Theodore
4	Open to Me, My Sister (My Sis's Brother)	HUG-N 61	FARMER, Philip Jose
1	Stranger in a Strange Land	HUG-W 62	HEINLEIN, Robert A
1	Dark Universe	HUG-N 62	GALOUYE, Daniel F
1	Planet of t/Damned (Sense of Obligation)	HUG-N 62	HARRISON, Harry
1	Second Ending	HUG-N 62	WHITE, James
1	Sword of Aldones(10): Darkover	HUG-N 62	BRADLEY, Marion Zimmer
1	Time is the Simplest Thing (Fisherman)	HUG-N 62	SIMAK, Clifford D
4	Hothouse Series, The	HUG-W 62	ALDISS, Brian W
4	Lion Loose	HUG-N 62	SCHMITZ, James H
4	Monument	HUG-N 62	BIGGLE, Lloyd Jr
4	Scylla's Daughter	HUG-N 62	LEIBER, Fritz
4	Status Quo	HUG-N 62	REYNOLDS, Mack
1	Man in the High Castle, The	HUG-W 63	DICK, Philip K
1	Fall of Moondust, A	HUG-N 63	CLARKE, Arthur C
1	Little Fuzzy	HUG-N 63	PIPER, H Beam
1	Sword of Aldones(10): Darkover	HUG-N 63	BRADLEY, Marion Zimmer
1	Sylva	HUG-N 63	VERCORS
1	Witch World	HUG-N 63	NORTON, Andre
4	Dragon Masters, The	HUG-W 63	VANCE, Jack
4	Myrrha	HUG-N 63	JENNINGS, Gary
4	Unholy Grail, The	HUG-N 63	LEIBER, Fritz
4	When You Care, When You Love	HUG-N 63	STURGEON, Theodore
4	Where is the Bird of Fire?	HUG-N 63	SWANN, Thomas Burnett
1	Way Station (Here Gather Stars)	HUG-W 64	SIMAK, Clifford D
1	Cat's Cradle	HUG-N 64	VONNEGUT, Kurt Jr
1	Dune World	HUG-N 64	HERBERT, Frank
1	Dying Earth	HUG-N 64	VANCE, Jack
1	Glory Road	HUG-N 64	HEINLEIN, Robert A
1	Witch World	HUG-N 64	NORTON, Andre
4	No Truce with Kings	HUG-W 64	ANDERSON, Poul
4	Code Three	HUG-N 64	RAPHAEL, Rick
4	Rose for Ecclesiastes, A	HUG-N 64	ZELAZNY, Roger
4	Savage Pellucidar	HUG-N 64	BURROUGHS, Edgar Rice

CAT	TITLE	AW W/N Y	AUTHOR
1	Wanderer, The	HUG-W 65	LEIBER, Fritz
1	Davy	HUG-N 65	PANGBORN, Edgar
1	Planet Buyer, The	HUG-N 65	SMITH, Cordwainer
1	Whole Man, The	HUG-N 65	BRUNNER, John
4	Soldier, Ask Not	HUG-W 65	DICKSON, Gordon R
4	Little Dog Gone	HUG-N 65	YOUNG, Robert F
4	Once A Cop	HUG-N 65	RAPHAEL, Rick
1	Dune	HUG-W 66	HERBERT, Frank
1	Babel-17	HUG-N 66	DELANY, Samuel R
1	Moon is a Harsh Mistress	HUG-N 66	HEINLEIN, Robert A
1	Skylark Dusquenes	HUG-N 66	SMITH, E E "Doc"
1	Squares of the City, The	HUG-N 66	BRUNNER, John
4	Repent Harlequin...	HUG-W 66	ELLISON, Harlan
8	Foundation	HUG-W 66	ASIMOV, Isaac
8	Foundation Trilogy	HUG-W 66	ASIMOV, Isaac
1	Moon is a Harsh Mistress	HUG-W 67	HEINLEIN, Robert A
1	Babel-17	HUG-N 67	DELANY, Samuel R
1	Day of the Minotaur	HUG-N 67	BURNETT, Thomas
1	Flowers for Algernon	HUG-N 67	KEYES, Daniel
1	Thorns	HUG-N 67	SILVERBERG, Robert
1	Too Many Magicians	HUG-N 67	GARRETT, Randall
1	Witches of Karres	HUG-N 67	SCHMITZ, James H
3	Last Castle, The	HUG-W 67	VANCE, Jack
3	Alchemist, The	HUG-N 67	HARNESS, Charles L
3	Apology to Inky	HUG-N 67	GREEN, Robert M Jr
3	Call Him Lord	HUG-N 67	DICKSON, Gordon R
3	Eskimo Invasion, The	HUG-N 67	HOWARD, Hayden
3	For A Breath I Tarry	HUG-N 67	ZELAZNY, Roger
3	Manor of Roses, The	HUG-N 67	BURNETT, Thomas
3	Ornament of His Profession, An	HUG-N 67	HARNESS, Charles L
3	This Moment of the Storm	HUG-N 67	ZELAZNY, Roger
4	Neutron Star, The	HUG-W 67	NIVEN, Larry
4	Comes Now the Power	HUG-N 67	ZELAZNY, Roger
4	Delusion for a Dragon Slayer	HUG-N 67	ELLISON, Harlan
4	Light of Other Days	HUG-N 67	SHAW, Bob
4	Man In His Time	HUG-N 67	ALDISS, Brian W
4	Mr. Jester	HUG-N 67	SABERHAGEN, Fred
4	Rat Race	HUG-N 67	JONES, Raymond F
4	Secret Place, The	HUG-N 67	McKENNA, Richard
1	Lord of Light	HUG-W 68	ZELAZNY, Roger
1	Butterfly Kid, The	HUG-N 68	ANDERSON, Chester
1	Chton	HUG-N 68	ANTHONY, Piers
1	Einstein Intersection	HUG-N 68	DELANY, Samuel R

HUGO AWARD

CAT	TITLE	AW W/N Y	AUTHOR
2	Riders of the Purple Wage	HUG-W 68	FARMER, Philip Jose
2	Weyr Search	HUG-W 68	McCAFFREY, Anne
2	Damnation Alley	HUG-N 68	ZELAZNY, Roger
2	Hawksbill Station	HUG-N 68	SILVERBERG, Robert
2	Star Pit, The	HUG-N 68	DELANY, Samuel R
3	Gonna Roll Those Bones	HUG-W 68	LEIBER, Fritz
3	Faith of Our Fathers	HUG-N 68	DICK, Philip K
3	Pretty Maggie Moneyeyes	HUG-N 68	ELLISON, Harlan
3	Wizard's World	HUG-N 68	NORTON, Andre
4	I Have no Mouth..	HUG-W 68	ELLISON, Harlan
4	Aye, and Gomorrah	HUG-N 68	DELANY, Samuel R
4	Jigsaw Man, The	HUG-N 68	NIVEN, Larry
1	Stand on Zanzibar	HUG-W 69	BRUNNER, John
1	Macroscope	HUG-N 69	ANTHONY, Piers
1	Nova	HUG-N 69	DELANY, Samuel R
1	Past Master	HUG-N 69	LAFFERTY, R A
1	Picnic on Paradise	HUG-N 69	RUSS, Joanna
1	Rite of Passage	HUG-N 69	PANSHIN, Alexei
2	Nightwings	HUG-W 69	SILVERBERG, Robert
2	Dragonrider	HUG-N 69	McCAFFREY, Anne
2	Hawk Among the Sparrows	HUG-N 69	McLAUGHLIN, Dean
2	Lines of Power	HUG-N 69	DELANY, Samuel R
3	Sharing of Flesh, The	HUG-W 69	ANDERSON, Poul
3	Getting Through University	HUG-N 69	ANTHONY, Piers
3	Mother to the World	HUG-N 69	WILSON, Richard
3	Total Environment	HUG-N 69	ALDISS, Brian W
4	Beast t/Shouted Love a/t/Heart o/t/World	HUG-W 69	ELLISON, Harlan
4	All the Myriad Ways	HUG-N 69	NIVEN, Larry
4	Dance of the Changer and the Three, The	HUG-N 69	CARR, Terry
4	Masks	HUG-N 69	KNIGHT, Damon
4	Steiger Effect, The	HUG-N 69	CURTIS, Betsy
1	Left Hand of Darkness	HUG-W 70	LEGUIN, Ursula K
1	Bug Jack Barron	HUG-N 70	SPINRAD, Norman
1	Macroscope	HUG-N 70	ANTHONY, Piers
1	Slaughterhouse-Five	HUG-N 70	VONNEGUT, Kurt Jr
1	Up the Line	HUG-N 70	SILVERBERG, Robert
2	Ship of Shadows	HUG-W 70	LEIBER, Fritz
2	Boy and His Dog, A	HUG-N 70	ELLISON, Harlan
2	Dramatic Mission	HUG-N 70	McCAFFREY, Anne
2	To Jorslem	HUG-N 70	SILVERBERG, Robert
2	We All Die Naked	HUG-N 70	BLISH, James
4	Time Considered as a Helix..	HUG-W 70	DELANY, Samuel R
4	Deeper Than the Darkness	HUG-N 70	BENFORD, Gregory
4	Not Long Before the End	HUG-N 70	NIVEN, Larry
4	Passengers	HUG-N 70	SILVERBERG, Robert
4	Winter's King	HUG-N 70	LeGUIN, Ursula K

CAT	TITLE	AW W/N Y	AUTHOR
1	Ringworld	HUG-W 71	NIVEN, Larry
1	Starlight	HUG-N 71	CLEMENT, Hal
1	Tau Zero	HUG-N 71	ANDERSON, Poul
1	Tower of Glass, The	HUG-N 71	SILVERBERG, Robert
1	Year of the Quiet Sun	HUG-N 71	TUCKER, Wilson
2	Ill Met in Lankhmar	HUG-W 71	LEIBER, Fritz
2	Beastchild	HUG-N 71	KOONTZ, Dean R
2	Region Between, The	HUG-N 71	ELLISON, Harlan
2	Snow Women, The	HUG-N 71	LEIBER, Fritz
2	Thing in the Stone, The	HUG-N 71	SIMAK, Clifford D
2	World Outside, The	HUG-N 71	SILVERBERG, Robert
4	Slow Sculpture	HUG-W 71	STURGEON, Theodore
4	Brillo	HUG-N 71	BOVA, Ben
4	Continued on Next Rock	HUG-N 71	LAFFERTY, R A
4	In the Queue	HUG-N 71	LAUMER, Keith
4	Jean Dupres	HUG-N 71	DICKSON, Gordon R
1	To Your Scattered Bodies Go	HUG-W 72	FARMER, Philip Jose
1	Dragonquest	HUG-N 72	McCAFFREY, Anne
1	Jack of Shadows	HUG-N 72	ZELAZNY, Roger
1	Lathe of Heaven, The	HUG-N 72	LeGUIN, Ursula K
1	Time of Changes, A	HUG-N 72	SILVERBERG, Robert
1	World Inside, The	HUG-N 72	SILVERBERG, Robert
2	Queen of Air and Darkness, The	HUG-W 72	ANDERSON, Poul
2	Dread Empire	HUG-N 72	BRUNNER, John
2	Fourth Profession	HUG-N 72	NIVEN, Larry
2	Meeting With Medusa, A	HUG-N 72	CLARKE, Arthur C
2	Special Kind of Morning	HUG-N 72	DOZOIS, Gardner R
4	Inconstant Moon	HUG-W 72	NIVEN, Larry
4	All the Last Wars at Once	HUG-N 72	EFFINGER, George Alec
4	Autumn Land, The	HUG-N 72	SIMAK, Clifford D
4	Bear With the Knot on His Tail, The	HUG-N 72	TALL, Stephen
4	Sky	HUG-N 72	LAFFERTY, R A
4	Vaster Than Empires and More Slow	HUG-N 72	LeGUIN, Ursula K
1	Gods Themselves, The	HUG-W 73	ASIMOV, Isaac
1	Book of Skulls, The	HUG-N 73	SILVERBERG, Robert
1	Choice of Gods, A	HUG-N 73	SIMAK, Clifford D
1	Dying Inside	HUG-N 73	SILVERBERG, Robert
1	There Will be Time	HUG-N 73	ANDERSON, Poul
1	When Harlie Was One	HUG-N 73	GERROLD, David
2	Word for World is Forest, The	HUG-W 73	LeGUIN, Ursula K
2	Fifth Head of Cerberus, The	HUG-N 73	WOLFE, Gene
2	Gold at the Starbow's End, The	HUG-N 73	POHL, Frederik
2	Hero	HUG-N 73	HALDEMAN, Joe
2	Mercenary, The	HUG-N 73	POURNELLE, Jerry

HUGO AWARD

CAT	TITLE	AW W/N Y	AUTHOR
3	Goat Song	HUG-W 73	ANDERSON, Poul
3	Basilisk	HUG-N 73	ELLISON, Harlan
3	Kingdom By the Sea, A	HUG-N 73	DOZOIS, Gardner
3	Painwise	HUG-N 73	TIPTREE, James Jr
3	Patron of the Arts	HUG-N 73	ROTSLER, William
4	Eurema's Dam	HUG-W 73	LAFFERTY, R A
4	Meeting, The	HUG-W 73	POHL, Frederik
4	And I Awoke & Found Me Here t/Cold Hill'	HUG-N 73	TIPTREE, James Jr
4	When It Changed	HUG-N 73	RUSS, Joanna
4	When We Went to See the End of the World	HUG-N 73	SILVERBERG, Robert
1	Rendezvous with Rama	HUG-W 74	CLARKE, Arthur C
1	Man Who Folded Himself, The	HUG-N 74	GERROLD, David
1	People of the Wind, The	HUG-N 74	ANDERSON, Poul
1	Protector	HUG-N 74	NIVEN, Larry
1	Time Enough For Love	HUG-N 74	HEINLEIN, Robert A
2	Girl Who was Plugged In, The	HUG-W 74	TIPTREE, James Jr
2	Chains of the Sea	HUG-N 74	DOZOIS, Gardner
2	Death and Designation Among the Asadi	HUG-N 74	BISHOP, Michael
2	Death of Doctor Island, The	HUG-N 74	WOLFE, Gene
2	White Otters of Childhood, The	HUG-N 74	BISHOP, Michael
3	Deathbird, The	HUG-W 74	ELLISON, Harlan
3	City on the Sand, The	HUG-N 74	EFFINGER, George Alec
3	He Fell Into a Dark Hole	HUG-N 74	POURNELLE, Jerry
3	Love Is the Plan, the Plan Is Death	HUG-N 74	TIPTREE, James Jr
3	Of Mist, and Grass, and Sand	HUG-N 74	McINTYRE, Vonda N
4	Ones Who Walk Away from Omelas	HUG-W 74	LeGUIN, Ursula K
4	Construction Shack	HUG-N 74	SIMAK, Clifford D
4	Wings	HUG-N 74	McINTYRE, Vonda N
4	With Morning Comes Mistfall	HUG-N 74	MARTIN, George R R
1	Dispossessed, The	HUG-W 75	LEGUIN, Ursula K
1	Fire Time	HUG-N 75	ANDERSON, Poul
1	Flow My Tears, The Policeman Said	HUG-N 75	DICK, Philip K
1	Inverted World, The	HUG-N 75	PRIEST, Christopher
1	Mote in God's Eye, The	HUG-N 75	NIVEN, Larry
2	Song For Lya, A	HUG-W 75	MARTIN, George R R
2	Assault on a City	HUG-N 75	VANCE, Jack
2	Born With the Dead	HUG-N 75	SILVERBERG, Robert
2	Riding the Torch	HUG-N 75	SPINRAD, Norman
2	Strangers	HUG-N 75	DOZOIS, Gardner
3	Adrift, Just off t/Islets of Langerhans	HUG-W 75	ELLISON, Harlan
3	After the Dreamtime	HUG-N 75	LUPOFF, Richard A
3	Brother to Dragons, A	HUG-N 75	WILHELM, Kate
3	Extreme Prejudice	HUG-N 75	POURNELLE, Jerry
3	Midnight by the Morphy Watch	HUG-N 75	LEIBER, Fritz
3	Nix Olypica	HUG-N 75	WALLING, William
3	That Thou Art Mindful of Him	HUG-N 75	ASIMOV, Isaac

CAT	T I T L E	AW W/N Y	A U T H O R
4	Hole Man, The	HUG-W 75	NIVEN, Larry
4	Cathadonian Odyssey	HUG-N 75	BISHOP, Michael
4	Day Before the Revolution, The	HUG-N 75	LeGUIN, Ursula K
4	Four-Hour Fugue, The	HUG-N 75	BESTER, Alfred
4	Schwartz Between the Galaxies	HUG-N 75	SILVERBERG, Robert
1	Forever War, The	HUG-W 76	HALDEMAN, Joe
1	Computer Connection, The	HUG-N 76	BESTER, Alfred
1	Doorways in the Sand	HUG-N 76	ZELAZNY, Roger
1	Inferno	HUG-N 76	NIVEN, Larry
1	Stochastic Man, The	HUG-N 76	SILVERBERG, Robert
2	Home is the Hangman	HUG-W 76	ZELAZNY, Roger
2	ARM	HUG-N 76	NIVEN, Larry
2	Custodians, The	HUG-N 76	COWPER, Richard
2	Silen Eyes of Time, The	HUG-N 76	BUDRYS, Algis
2	Storms of Windhaven, The	HUG-N 76	MARTIN, George R R
3	Borderland of Sol, The	HUG-N 76	NIVEN, Larry
3	New Atlantis, The	HUG-N 76	LeGUIN, Ursula K
3	San Diego Lightfoot Sue	HUG-N 76	REAMY, Tom
3	Tinker	HUG-N 76	POURNELLE, Jerry
3	...and Seven Times Never Kill Man	HUG-N 76	MARTIN, George R R
4	Catch That Zeppelin	HUG-W 76	LEIBER, Fritz
4	Child of All Ages	HUG-N 76	PLAUGER, P J
4	Croatoan	HUG-N 76	ELLISON, Harlan
4	Doing Lennon	HUG-N 76	BENFORD, Gregory
4	Rogue Tomato	HUG-N 76	BISHOP, Michael
4	Sail the Tide of Mourning	HUG-N 76	LUPOFF, Richard A
1	Where Late the Sweet Birds Sang	HUG-W 77	WILHELM, Kate
1	Children of Dune	HUG-N 77	HERBERT, Frank
1	Man Plus	HUG-N 77	POHL, Frederik
1	Mindbridge	HUG-N 77	HALDEMAN, Joe
1	Shadrach in the Furnace	HUG-N 77	SILVERBERG, Robert
2	By Any Other Name	HUG-W 77	ROBINSON, Spider
2	Houston, Houston. Do You Read?	HUG-W 77	TIPTREE, James Jr
2	Piper at the Gates of Dawn	HUG-N 77	COWPER, Richard
2	Samurai and the Willows, The	HUG-N 77	BISHOP, Michael
3	Bicentennial Man, The	HUG-W 77	ASIMOV, Isaac
3	Diary of the Rose, The	HUG-N 77	LeGUIN, Ursula K
3	Gotta Sing, Gotta Dance	HUG-N 77	VARLEY, John
3	Phantom of Kansas, The	HUG-N 77	VARLEY, John
4	Tricentennial	HUG-W 77	HALDEMAN, Joe
4	Crowd of Shadows, A	HUG-N 77	GRANT, Charles L
4	Custom Fitting	HUG-N 77	WHITE, James
4	I See You	HUG-N 77	KNIGHT, Damon

HUGO AWARD

CAT	TITLE	AW W/N Y	AUTHOR
1	Gateway	HUG-W 78	POHL, Frederik
1	Dying of the Light	HUG-N 78	MARTIN, George R R
1	Forbidden Tower (4): Darkover	HUG-N 78	BRADLEY, Marion Zimmer
1	Lucifer's Hammer	HUG-N 78	NIVEN, Larry
1	Time Storm	HUG-N 78	DICKSON, Gordon R
2	Stardance	HUG-W 78	ROBINSON, Spider & Jeanne
2	Aztecs	HUG-N 78	McINTYRE, Vonda N
2	In the Hall of the Martian Kings	HUG-N 78	VARLEY, John
2	Snark in the Night, A	HUG-N 78	BENFORD, Gregory
2	Wonderful Secret, The	HUG-N 78	LAUMER, Keith
3	Eyes of Amber	HUG-W 78	VINGE, Joan D
3	Ender's Game	HUG-N 78	CARD, Orson Scott
3	Ninth Symphony of Ludwig v/Beethoven...	HUG-N 78	SCHOLZ, Carter
3	Prismatica	HUG-N 78	DELANY, Samuel R
3	Screwfly Solution, The	HUG-N 78	SHELDON, Raccoona
4	Jeffty is Five	HUG-W 78	ELLISON, Harlan
4	Air Raid	HUG-N 78	VARLEY, John
4	Dog Day Evening	HUG-N 78	ROBINSON, Spider
4	Lauralyn	HUG-N 78	GARRETT, Randall
4	Time-Sharing Angel	HUG-N 78	TIPTREE, James Jr
1	Dreamsnake	HUG-W 79	McINTYRE, Vonda N
1	Blind Voices	HUG-N 79	REAMY, Tom
1	Faded Sun, The: Kesrith	HUG-N 79	CHERRYH, C J
1	Up the Walls of the World	HUG-N 79	TIPTREE, James Jr
1	White Dragon, The	HUG-N 79	McCAFFREY, Anne
2	Persistence of Vision, The	HUG-W 79	VARLEY, John
2	Enemies of the System	HUG-N 79	ALDISS, Brian W
2	Fireship	HUG-N 79	VINGE, Joan D
2	Seven American Nights	HUG-N 79	WOLFE, Gene
2	Watched, The	HUG-N 79	PRIEST, Christopher
3	Hunter's Moon	HUG-W 79	ANDERSON, Poul
3	Barbie Murders, The	HUG-N 79	VARLEY, John
3	Devil You Don't Know	HUG-N 79	ING, Dean
3	Man Who Had No Idea, The	HUG-N 79	DISCH, Thomas M
3	Mikal's Songbird	HUG-N 79	CARD, Orson Scott
4	Cassandra	HUG-W 79	CHERRYH, C J
4	Count the Clock That Tells the Time	HUG-N 79	ELLISON, harlan
4	Stone	HUG-N 79	BRYANT, Edward
4	Very Slow Time Machine, The	HUG-N 79	WATSON, Ian
4	View From a Height	HUG-N 79	VINGE, Joan D
1	Fountains of Paradise, The	HUG-W 80	CLARKE, Arthur C
1	Harpist in the Wind	HUG-N 80	McKILLIP, Patricia
1	JEM	HUG-N 80	POHL, Frederik
1	On Wings of Song	HUG-N 80	DISCH, Thomas M
1	Titan	HUG-N 80	VARLEY, John

CAT	TITLE	AW W/N Y	AUTHOR
2	Enemy Mine	HUG-W 80	LONGYEAR, Barry
2	Battle of the Abaco Reefs, The	HUG-N 80	SCHENCK, Hilbert
2	Ker Plop	HUG-N 80	REYNOLDS, Ted
2	Moon Goddess and the Son, The	HUG-N 80	KINGSBURY, Donald
2	Songhouse	HUG-N 80	CARD, Orson Scott
3	Sandkings	HUG-W 80	MARTIN, George R R
3	Fireflood and Other Stories	HUG-N 80	McINTYRE, Vonda N
3	Homecoming	HUG-N 80	LONGYEAR, Barry
3	Locusts, The	HUG-N 80	NIVEN, Larry
3	Options	HUG-N 80	VARLEY, John
3	Palely Loitering	HUG-N 80	PRIEST, Christopher
4	Way of Cross and Dragon, The	HUG-W 80	MARTIN, George R R
4	Can These Bones Live?	HUG-N 80	REYNOLDS, Ted
4	Daisy, in the Sun	HUG-N 80	WILLIS, Connie
4	giANTS	HUG-N 80	BRYANT, Edward
4	Unaccompanied Sonata	HUG-N 80	CARD, Orson Scott
7	Science Fiction Encyclopedia, The	HUG-W 80	NICHOLS, Peter
7	Barlowe's Guide to Extraterrestials	HUG-N 80	BARLOWE, Wayne D
7	In Memory Yet Green	HUG-N 80	ASIMOV, Isaac
7	Language of the Night, The	HUG-N 80	LeGUIN, Ursula K
7	Wonderworks	HUG-N 80	DONNING, Whelan
1	Snow Queen, The	HUG-W 81	VINGE, Joan D
1	Beyond the Blue Event Horizon	HUG-N 81	POHL, Frederik
1	Lord Valentine's Castle	HUG-N 81	SILVERBERG, Robert
1	Ringworld Engineers, The	HUG-N 81	NIVEN, Larry
1	Wizard	HUG-N 81	VARLEY, John
2	Lost Dorsai	HUG-W 81	DICKSON, Gordon R
2	All the Lies That Are My Life	HUG-N 81	ELLISON, Harlan
2	Brave Little Toaster, The	HUG-N 81	DISCH, Thomas M
2	Nightflyers	HUG-N 81	MARTIN, George R R
2	One-Wing	HUG-N 81	TUTTLE, Lisa
3	Cloak and the Staff, The	HUG-W 81	DICKSON, Gordon R
3	Autopsy, The	HUG-N 81	SHEA, Michael
3	Beatnik Bayou	HUG-N 81	VARLEY, John
3	Lordly Ones, The	HUG-N 81	ROBERTS, Keith
3	Savage Planet, The	HUG-N 81	LONGYEAR, Barry
3	Ugly Chickens, The	HUG-N 81	WALDROP, Howard
4	Grotto of the Dancing Bear, The	HUG-W 81	SIMAK, Clifford D
4	Cold Hands	HUG-N 81	DUNTEMANN, Jeff
4	Guardian	HUG-N 81	DUNTEMANN, Jeff
4	Our Lady of the Sauropods	HUG-N 81	SILVERBERG, Robert
4	Spidersong	HUG-N 81	PETREY, Susan C
7	Cosmos	HUG-W 81	SAGAN, Carl
7	DiFate's Catalog of S Fiction Hardware	HUG-N 81	DiFATE, Vincent
7	Dream Makers	HUG-N 81	PLATT, Charles
7	In Joy Still Felt	HUG-N 81	ASIMOV, Isaac
7	Warhoon 28 Walter A Willis	HUG-N 81	BERGERON, Richard

CAT	T I T L E	AW W/N Y	A U T H O R
1	Downbelow Station	HUG-W 82	CHERRYH, C J
1	Claw of the Conciliator, The	HUG-N 82	WOLFE, Gene
1	Little Big	HUG-N 82	CROWLEY, John
1	Many-Colored Land, The	HUG-N 82	MAY, Julian
1	Project Pope	HUG-N 82	SIMAK, Clifford D
2	Saturn Game, The	HUG-W 82	ANDERSON, Poul
2	Blue Champagne	HUG-N 82	VARLEY, John
2	Emergence	HUG-N 82	PALMER, David R
2	In the Western Tradition	HUG-N 82	EISENSTEIN, Phyllis
2	True Names	HUG-N 82	VINGE, Vernor
2	With Thimbles, With Forks and Hope	HUG-N 82	WILHELM, Kate
3	Unicorn Variations	HUG-W 82	ZELAZNY, Roger
3	Fire When It Comes, The	HUG-N 82	GODWIN, Parke
3	Guardians	HUG-N 82	MARTIN, George R R
3	Quickening, The	HUG-N 82	BISHOP, Michael
3	Thermals of August, The	HUG-N 82	BRYANT, Edward
4	Pusher, The	HUG-W 82	VARLEY, John
4	Absent Thee From Felicity Awhile	HUG-N 82	SUCHARITKUL, Somtow
4	Quiet, The	HUG-N 82	FLORANCE-GUTHRIDGE, George
4	Woman the Unicorn Loved, The	HUG-N 82	WOLFE, Gene
7	Danse Macabre	HUG-W 82	KING, Stephen
7	After Man	HUG-N 82	DIXON, Dougal
7	Anatomy of Wonder 2nd	HUG-N 82	BARRON, Neil
7	Art of Leo and Diane Dillon, The	HUG-N 82	PREISS, Byron
7	Grand Tour, The	HUG-N 82	MILLER, Ron
1	Foundation's Edge	HUG-W 83	ASIMOV, Isaac
1	2010: Odyssey Two	HUG-N 83	CLARKE, Arthur C
1	Courtship Rite	HUG-N 83	KINGSBURY, Donald
1	Friday	HUG-N 83	HEINLEIN, Robert A
1	Pride of Chanur, The	HUG-N 83	CHERRYH, C J
1	Sword of the Lichtor, The	HUG-N 83	WOLFE, Gene
2	Souls	HUG-W 83	RUSS, Joanna
2	Another Orphan	HUG-N 83	KESSEL, John
2	Brainchild	HUG-N 83	DELANEY, Joseph H
2	Postman, The	HUG-N 83	BRIN, David
2	To Leave a Mark	HUG-N 83	ROBINSON, Kim Stanley
2	Unsound Variations	HUG-N 83	MARTIN, George R R
3	Firewatch	HUG-W 83	WILLIS, Connie
3	Aquila	HUG-N 83	SUCHARITKUL, Somtow
3	Nightlife	HUG-N 83	EISENSTEIN, Phyllis
3	Pawn's Gambit	HUG-N 83	ZAHN, Timothy
3	Swarm	HUG-N 83	STERLING, Bruce

CAT	TITLE	AW W/N Y	AUTHOR
4	Melancholy Elephants	HUG-W 83	ROBINSON, Spider
4	Boy Who Waterskied Forever, The	HUG-N 83	TIPTREE, James Jr
4	Ike at the Mike	HUG-N 83	WALDROP, Howard
4	Spider Rose	HUG-N 83	STERLING, Bruce
4	Sur	HUG-N 83	LeGUIN, Ursula K
7	Isaac Asimov: The Foundations of SF	HUG-W 83	GUNN, James E
7	Engines of the Night, The	HUG-N 83	MALZBERG, Barry N
7	Fear Itself:T/Horror Fiction of S King	HUG-N 83	UNDERWOOD, Tim
7	Reader's Guide to Fantasy, A	HUG-N 83	SEARLES, Baird
7	World of the Dark Crystal, The	HUG-N 83	FROUD, Brian
1	Startide Rising	HUG-W 84	BRIN, David
1	Millenium	HUG-N 84	VARLEY, John
1	Moreta	HUG-N 84	McCAFFREY, Anne
1	Robots of Dawn	HUG-N 84	ASIMOV, Isaac
1	Tea With the Black Dragon	HUG-N 84	MacAVOY, R A
2	Cascade Point	HUG-W 84	ZAHN, Timothy
2	Hardfought	HUG-N 84	BEAR, Greg
2	Hurricane Claude	HUG-N 84	SCHENCK, Hilbert
2	In the Face of My Enemy	HUG-N 84	DELANEY, Joseph H
2	Seeking	HUG-N 84	PALMER, David R
3	Blood Music	HUG-W 84	BEAR, Greg
3	Black Air	HUG-N 84	ROBINSON, Kim Stanley
3	Monkey Treatment, The	HUG-N 84	BEAR, Greg
3	Sidon in the Mirror, The	HUG-N 84	WILLIS, Connie
3	Slow Birds	HUG-N 84	WATSON, Ian
4	Speech Sounds	HUG-W 84	BUTLER, Octavia E
4	Geometry of Narrative, The	HUG-N 84	SCHENCK, Hilbert
4	Peacemaker, The	HUG-N 84	DOZOIS, Gardner
4	Servant of the People	HUG-N 84	POHL, Frederik
4	Wong's Lost and Found Emporium	HUG-N 84	WU, William F
7	Encyclopedia of SF and Fantasy #3	HUG-W 84	TUCK, Donald H
7	Dream Makers Vol 2	HUG-N 84	PLATT, Charles
7	Fantastic Art of Rowena	HUG-N 84	MORRILL, Rowena
7	High Kings, The	HUG-N 84	CHANT, Joy
7	Staying Alive: A Writer's Guide	HUG-N 84	SPINRAD, Norman
1	Neuromancer	HUG-W 85	GIBSON, William
1	Emergence	HUG-N 85	PALMER, David R
1	Integral Trees, The	HUG-N 85	NIVEN, Larry
1	Job: A Comedy of Justice	HUG-N 85	HEINLEIN, Robert A
1	Peace War, The	HUG-N 85	VINGE, Vernor
2	Press Enter	HUG-W 85	VARLEY, John
2	Cyclops	HUG-N 85	BRIN, David
2	Elementals	HUG-N 85	LANDIS, Geoffrey A
2	Summer Solstice	HUG-N 85	HARNESS, Charles L
2	Valentina	HUG-N 85	DELANEY, Joseph H

CAT	TITLE	AW W/N Y	AUTHOR
3	Bloodchild	HUG-W 85	BUTLER, Octavia E
3	Blued Moon	HUG-N 85	WILLIS, Connie
3	Lucky Strike, The	HUG-N 85	ROBINSON, Kim Stanley
3	Man Who Painted the Dragon Griaule, The	HUG-N 85	SHEPARD, Lucius
3	Return to the Fold	HUG-N 85	ZAHN, Timothy
3	Silicon Muse	HUG-N 85	SCHENCK, Hilbert
3	Wigher, The	HUG-N 85	VINICOFF, Eric
4	Crystal Spheres, The	HUG-W 85	BRIN, David
4	Aliens Who Knew, I Mean Everything, The	HUG-N 85	EFFINGER, George Alec
4	Ridge Running	HUG-N 85	ROBINSON, Kim Stanley
4	Rory	HUG-N 85	GOULD, Steven
4	Salvador	HUG-N 85	SHEPARD, Lucius
4	Symphony for a Lost Traveler	HUG-N 85	KILLOUGH, Lee
7	Wonder's Child: My Life in S Fiction	HUG-W 85	WILLIAMSON, Jack
7	Dune Encyclopedia, The	HUG-N 85	McNELLY, Willis E Dr.
7	Faces of Science Fiction, The	HUG-N 85	PERRET, Patti
7	In t/Heart Or In t/Head:Essay T/Travel	HUG-N 85	TURNER, George
7	Sleepless Nights in the Procrustean Bed:	HUG-N 85	ELLISON, Harlan
1	Ender's Game	HUG-W 86	CARD, Orson Scott
1	Blood Music	HUG-N 86	BEAR, Greg
1	Cuckoo's Egg	HUG-N 86	CHERRYH, C J
1	Emergence	HUG-N 86	PALMER, David R
1	Footfall	HUG-N 86	NIVEN, Larry
1	Postman, The	HUG-N 86	BRIN, David
2	24 Views of Mount Fuji by Hokusai	HUG-W 86	ZELAZNY, Roger
2	Green Mars	HUG-N 86	ROBINSON, Kim Stanley
2	Only Neat Thing to Do, The	HUG-N 86	TIPTREE, James Jr
2	Sailing to Byzantium	HUG-N 86	SILVERBERG, Robert
2	Scapegoat, The	HUG-N 86	CHERRYH, C J
3	Paladin of the Lost Hour	HUG-W 86	ELLISON, Harlan
3	Dogfight	HUG-N 86	SWANWICK, Michael
3	Fringe, The	HUG-N 86	CARD, Orson Scott
3	Gift From the Graylanders, A	HUG-N 86	BISHOP, Michael
3	Portraits of His Children	HUG-N 86	MARTIN, George R R
4	Fermi and Frost	HUG-W 86	POHL, Frederik
4	Dinner in Audoghast	HUG-N 86	STERLING, Bruce
4	Flying Saucer Rock and Roll	HUG-N 86	WALDROP, Howard
4	Hong's Bluff	HUG-N 86	WU, William F
4	Snow	HUG-N 86	CROWLEY, John
7	Science Made Stupid	HUG-W 86	WELLER, Tom
7	An Edge in My Voice	HUG-N 86	ELLISON, Harlan
7	Benchmarks: Galaxy Bookshelf	HUG-N 86	BUDRYS, Algis
7	Faces of Fear: Encount W/t/Creat Mod Hor	HUG-N 86	WINTER, Douglas E
7	John W Campbell Letters Vol 1, The	HUG-N 86	CHAPDELAINE, Perry A Sr.
7	Pale Shadow of Science, The	HUG-N 86	ALDISS, Brian W

CAT	TITLE	AW W/N Y	AUTHOR
1	Speaker for the Dead	HUG-W 87	CARD, Orson Scott
1	Black Genesis	HUG-N 87	HUBBARD, L Ron
1	Count Zero	HUG-N 87	GIBSON, William
1	Marooned in Real Time	HUG-N 87	VINGE, Vernor
1	Ragged Astronauts, The	HUG-N 87	SHAW, Bob
2	Gilgamesh in the Outback	HUG-W 87	SILVERBERG, Robert
2	Eifelheim	HUG-N 87	FLYNN, Michael F
2	Escape from Kathmandu	HUG-N 87	ROBINSON, Kim Stanley
2	R & R	HUG-N 87	SHEPARD, Lucius
2	Spice Pogrom	HUG-N 87	WILLIS, Connie
3	Permafrost	HUG-W 87	ZELAZNY, Roger
3	Barbarian Princess, The	HUG-N 87	VINGE, Vernor
3	Hatrack River	HUG-N 87	CARD, Orson Scott
3	Thor Meets Captain America	HUG-N 87	BRIN, David
3	Winter Market, The	HUG-N 87	GIBSON, William
4	Tangents	HUG-W 87	BEAR, Greg
4	Boy Who Plaited Manes, The	HUG-N 87	SPRINGER, Nancy
4	Rat	HUG-N 87	KELLY, James Patrick
4	Robot Dreams	HUG-N 87	ASIMOV, Isaac
4	Still Life	HUG-N 87	GARNETT, David
7	Trillion Year Spree	HUG-W 87	ALDISS, Brian W
7	Dark Knight Returns, The	HUG-N 87	MILLER, Frank
7	Industrial Light & Magic: Special Effect	HUG-N 87	SMITH, Thomas G
7	Only Apparently Real: World of P K Dick	HUG-N 87	WILLIAMS, Paul
7	Science Fiction in Print 1985	HUG-N 87	BROWN, Charles N
1	Uplift War, The	HUG-W 88	BRIN, David
1	Forge of God, The	HUG-N 88	BEAR, Greg
1	Seventh Son	HUG-N 88	CARD, Orson Scott
1	Urth of the New Sun, The	HUG-N 88	WOLFE, Gene
1	When Gravity Fails	HUG-N 88	EFFINGER, George Alec
2	Eye for Eye	HUG-W 88	CARD, Orson Scott
2	Blind Geometer, The	HUG-N 88	ROBINSON, Kim Stanley
2	Forest of Time, The	HUG-N 88	FLYNN, Michael F
2	Mother Goddess of the World	HUG-N 88	ROBINSON, Kim Stanley
2	Secret Sharer, The	HUG-N 88	SILVERBERG, Robert
3	Buffalo Gals, Won't You Come Out Tonight	HUG-W 88	LeGUIN, Ursula K
3	Dinausaurs	HUG-N 88	WILLIAMS, Walter Jon
3	Dream Baby	HUG-N 88	McALLISTER, Bruce
3	FLowers of Edo	HUG-N 88	STERLING, Bruce
3	Rachel in Love	HUG-N 88	MURPHY, Pat
4	Why I Left Harry's All-Night Hamburgers	HUG-W 88	WATT-EVANS, Lawrence
4	Angel	HUG-N 88	CADIGAN, Pat
4	Cassandra's Photographs	HUG-N 88	GOLDSTEIN, Lisa
4	Faithful Companion, The	HUG-N 88	FOWLER, Karen Joy
4	Forever Yours, Anna	HUG-N 88	WILHELM, Kate
4	Night of the Cooters	HUG-N 88	WALDROP, Howard

CAT	T I T L E	AW W/N Y	A U T H O R
7	Michael Whelan's Works of Wonder	HUG-W 88	WHELAN, Michael
7	Anatomy of Wonder 3rd	HUG-N 88	BARRON, Neil
7	Battle of Brasil, The	HUG-N 88	MATHEWS, Jack
7	Imagination: Art & Techn of David Cherry	HUG-N 88	CHERRY, David A
7	SF, Fantasy & Horror 1986	HUG-N 88	BROWN, Charles N
1	Cyteen	HUG-W 89	CHERRYH, C J
1	Falling Free	HUG-N 89	BUJOLD, Lois McMaster
1	Guardsman, The	HUG-N 89	BEESE, P J
1	Islands in the Net	HUG-N 89	STERLING, Bruce
1	Mona Lisa Overdrive	HUG-N 89	GIBSON, William
1	Red Prophet	HUG-N 89	CARD, Orson Scott
2	Last of the Winnebagos, The	HUG-W 89	WILLIS, Connie
2	Calvin Coolidge Home for Dead Comedians	HUG-N 89	DENTON, Bradley
2	Journals of the Plague Years, The	HUG-N 89	SPINRAD, Norman
2	Scalehunter's Beautiful Daughter, The	HUG-N 89	SHEPARD, Lucius
2	Surfacing	HUG-N 89	WILLIAMS, Walter Jon
3	Schrodinger's Kitten	HUG-W 89	EFFINGER, George Alec
3	Do Ya, Do Ya, Wanna Dance	HUG-N 89	WALDROP, Howard
3	Function of Dream Sleep, The	HUG-N 89	ELLISON, Harlan
3	Ginny Sweethips' Flying Circus	HUG-N 89	BARRETT, Neal Jr
3	Peaches for Mad Molly	HUG-N 89	GOULD, Stephen
4	Kirinyaga	HUG-W 89	RESNICK, Mike
4	Fort Moxie Branch, The	HUG-N 89	McDEVITT, Jack
4	Giving Plague, The	HUG-N 89	BRIN, David
4	Our Neural Chernobyl	HUG-N 89	STERLING, Bruce
4	Ripples in the Dirac Sea	HUG-N 89	LANDIS, Geoffrey A
4	Stable Strategies for Middle Management	HUG-N 89	GUNN, Eileen
7	Motion of Light in Water, The: Sex & SF	HUG-W 89	DELANY, Samuel R
7	Biog Dictionary of SF & Fantasy Artists	HUG-N 89	WEINBERG, Robert
7	First Maitz	HUG-N 89	MAITZ, Don
7	New Encyclopedia of Science Fiction, The	HUG-N 89	GUNN, James E
7	Science Fiction, Fantasy and Horror	HUG-N 89	BROWN, Charles N
1	Hyperion	HUG-W 90	SIMMONS, Dan
1	Boat of a Million Years	HUG-N 90	ANDERSON, Poul
1	Fire in the Sun, A	HUG-N 90	EFFINGER, George Alec
1	Grass	HUG-N 90	TEPPER, Sheri S
1	Prentice Alvin	HUG-N 90	CARD, Orson Scott
2	Mountains of Mourning, The	HUG-W 90	BUJOLD, Lois McMaster
2	Father of Stones, The	HUG-N 90	SHEPARD, Lucius
2	Time-Out	HUG-N 90	WILLIS, Connie
2	Tiny Tango	HUG-N 90	MOFFETT, Judith
2	Touch of Lavender, A	HUG-N 90	LINDHOLM, Megan

CAT	TITLE	AW W/N Y	AUTHOR
3	Enter a Soldier, Later Enter Another	HUG-W 90	SILVERBERG, Robert
3	At the Rialto	HUG-N 90	WILLIS, Connie
3	Dogwalker	HUG-N 90	CARD, Orson Scott
3	Everything but Honor	HUG-N 90	EFFINGER, George Alec
3	For I Have Touched the Sky	HUG-N 90	RESNICK, Mike
3	Prince of Oranges, The	HUG-N 90	KRESS, Nancy
4	Boobs	HUG-W 90	CHARNAS, Suzy McKee
4	Computer Friendly	HUG-N 90	GUNN, Eileen
4	Dori Bangs	HUG-N 90	STERLING, Bruce
4	Edge of the World, The	HUG-N 90	SWANWICK, Michael
4	Lost Boys	HUG-N 90	CARD, Orson Scott
4	Return of William Proxmire, The	HUG-N 90	NIVEN, Larry
7	World Beyond the Hill, The	HUG-W 90	PANSHIN, Alexei and Cory
7	Astounding Days	HUG-N 90	CLARKE, Arthur C
7	Dancing at the Edge of the World	HUG-N 90	LeGUIN, Ursula K
7	Grumbles from the Grave	HUG-N 90	HEINLEIN, Robert A
7	Harlan Ellison's Watching	HUG-N 90	ELLISON, Harlan
7	Noreascon Three Souvenir Book	HUG-N 90	THOKAR, Greg
1	Vor Game, The	HUG-W 91	BUJOLD, Lois McMaster
1	Earth	HUG-N 91	BRIN, David
1	Fall of Hyperion, The	HUG-N 91	SIMMONS, Dan
1	Queen of Angels	HUG-N 91	BEAR, Greg
1	Quiet Pools, The	HUG-N 91	KUBE-McDOWELL, Michael P
2	Hemingway Hoax, The	HUG-W 91	HALDEMAN, Joe
2	Bones	HUG-N 91	MURPHY, Pat
2	Bully!	HUG-N 91	RESNICK, Mike
2	Fool to Believe	HUG-N 91	CADIGAN, Pat
2	Short, Sharp, Shock, A	HUG-N 91	ROBINSON, Kim Stanley
3	Manamouki, The	HUG-W 91	RESNICK, Mike
3	Braver Thing, A	HUG-N 91	SHEFFIELD, Charles
3	Coon Rolled Down and Ruptured...	HUG-N 91	HUGH, Dafydd A B
3	Dr. Pak's Preschool	HUG-N 91	BRIN, David
3	Over the Long Haul	HUG-N 91	SOUKUP, Martha
3	Shobie's Story, The	HUG-N 91	LeGUIN, Ursula K
3	Tower of Babylon	HUG-N 91	CHIANG, Ted
4	Bears Discover Fire	HUG-W 91	BISSON, Terry
4	Cibola	HUG-N 91	WILLIS, Connie
4	Godspeed	HUG-N 91	SHEFFIELD, Charles
4	Utility Man, The	HUG-N 91	REED, Robert
4	VRM-547	HUG-N 91	THOMPSON, W R
7	How to Write Science Fiction and Fantasy	HUG-W 91	CARD, Orson Scott
7	Bury My Heart at W.H. Smiths	HUG-N 91	ALDISS, Brian W
7	Hollywood Gothic	HUG-N 91	SKAL, David J
7	Science Fiction in the Real World	HUG-N 91	SPINRAD, Norman
7	SFWA Handbook: The Prof Writer's Guide	HUG-N 91	RUSCH, Kristine Kathryn

HUGO AWARD

CAT	T I T L E	AW W/N Y	A U T H O R
1	Barrayar	HUG-W 92	BUJOLD, Lois McMaster
1	All the Weyrs of Pern	HUG-N 92	McCAFFREY, Anne
1	Bone Dance	HUG-N 92	BULL, Emma
1	Stations of the Tide	HUG-N 92	SWANWICK, Michael
1	Summer Queen, The	HUG-N 92	VINGE, Joan D
1	Xenocide	HUG-N 92	CARD, Orson Scott
2	Beggars in Spain	HUG-W 92	KRESS, Nancy
2	And Wild For To Hold	HUG-N 92	KRESS, Nancy
2	Gallery of His Dreams, The	HUG-N 92	RUSCH, Kristine Kathryn
2	Griffin's Egg	HUG-N 92	SWANWICK, Michael
2	Jack	HUG-N 92	WILLIS, Connie
3	Gold	HUG-W 92	ASIMOV, Isaac
3	Dispatches from the Revolution	HUG-N 92	CADIGAN, Pat
3	Fin de Cycle	HUG-N 92	WALDROP, Howard
3	Miracle	HUG-N 92	WILLIS, Connie
3	Understand	HUG-N 92	CHIANG, Ted
4	Walk in the Sun, A	HUG-W 92	LANDIS, Geoffrey A
4	Buffalo	HUG-N 92	KESSEL, John
4	Dog's Life	HUG-N 92	SOUKUP, Martha
4	In the Late Cretaceous	HUG-N 92	WILLIS, Connie
4	One Perfect Morning, With Jackals	HUG-N 92	RESNICK, Mike
4	Press Ann	HUG-N 92	BISSON, Terry
4	Winter Solstice	HUG-N 92	RESNICK, Mike
7	World of Charles Addams, The	HUG-W 92	ADDAMS, Charles
7	Bakery Men Don't See Cookbook, The	HUG-N 92	GOMOLL, et al
7	Clive Barker's Shawows in Eden	HUG-N 92	JONES, Stephen
7	Science-Fantasy Publishers, The	HUG-N 92	CHALKER, Jack
7	SF: The Early Years	HUG-N 92	BLEILER, Everett F

INTERNATIONAL FANTASY AWARDS

The International Fantasy Awards were created by four British Sf
personalities - Leslie Flood, John Beynon Harris, G. Ken Chapman, and
Frankk A. Cooper - at the 1951 British Science Fiction Convention. The
awards were selected by an international panel (including the four
above named), and honored works of fantastic literature and nonfiction
books of interest to the field. Among the sometime judges were:
Judith Merril, Anthony Boucher, P. Schuyler Miller, Groff Conklin,
Basil Davenport, E. J. (Ted) Carnell, and others.

After 1952 the awards were presented at a special dinner party.
The Non-fiction category was dropped in 1954, and the Fiction awards
were ultimately discontinued in 1958. The IFA was the first major
award created specifically to honor fantastic literature, and has
maintained the most consistent historical reputation for excellence
and critical discernment.

Year given is for publication in previous calendar year.

CAT	T I T L E	AW W/N Y	A U T H O R
1	Earth Abides	IFA-W 51	STEWART, George R
7	Conquest of Space	IFA-W 51	LEY, Willy
1	Fancies and Goodnights	IFA-W 52	COLLIER, John
1	Day of the Triffids, The	IFA-N 52	WYNDHAM, John
1	Illustrated Man, The	IFA-N 52	BRADBURY, Ray
7	Exploration of Space	IFA-W 52	CLARKE, Arthur C
7	Dragons in Amber	IFA-N 52	LEY, Willy
7	Rockets,Jets,Guided Missls & Spaceships	IFA-N 52	COGGINS, Jack
1	City	IFA-W 53	SIMAK, Clifford D
1	Player Piano	IFA-N 53	VONNEGUT, Kurt Jr
1	Takeoff	IFA-N 53	KORNBLUTH, Cyril M
7	Lands Beyond	IFA-W 53	LEY, Willy
1	More Than Human	IFA-W 54	STURGEON, Theodore
1	Demolished Man	IFA-N 54	BESTER, Alfred
1	Mirror for Observers, A	IFA-W 55	PANGBORN, Edgar
1	Mission of Gravity	IFA-N 55	CLEMENT, Hal
1	Lord of the Rings - Trilogy	IFA-W 57	TOLKIEN, J R R

JUPITER Awards

The Jupiter Awards were presented by the ISFHE (Instructors of Science Fiction in Higher Eduction), an organization of SF teachers with 105 members (1975) worldwide. Membership was open to those who taught at high school level.

The award was first presented in 1974 but was discontinued in 1979.

CAT	TITLE	AW W/N Y	AUTHOR
1	Rendezvous with Rama	JUP-W 74	CLARKE, Arthur C
1	Gravity's Rainbow	JUP-N 74	PYNCHON, Thomas
1	Herovit's World	JUP-N 74	MALZBERG, Barry N
1	Man Who Folded Himself, The	JUP-N 74	GERROLD, David
1	Time Enough For Love	JUP-N 74	HEINLEIN, Robert A
2	Feast of St. Dionysus, The	JUP-W 74	SILVERBERG, Robert
2	Chains of the Sea	JUP-N 74	DOZOIS, Gardner
2	Hellhound Project, The	JUP-N 74	GOULART, Ron
2	In The Problem Pit	JUP-N 74	POHL, Frederik
2	Magic Striptease, The	JUP-N 74	GARRETT, George
2	Quincux of Time, The	JUP-N 74	BLISH, James
3	Deathbird, The	JUP-W 74	ELLISON, Harlan
3	Death of Doctor Island, The	JUP-N 74	WOLFE, Gene
3	Everyday Life in the Later Roman Empire	JUP-N 74	DISCH, Thomas M
3	Flash Crowd	JUP-N 74	NIVEN, Larry
3	Girl Who Was Plugged In, The	JUP-N 74	TIPTREE, James Jr
3	Survivability	JUP-N 74	TUNING, William
3	Who Steals My Purse	JUP-N 74	BRUNNER, John
4	Supplicant in Space, A	JUP-W 74	SHECKLEY, Robert
4	Days of Grass, Days of Straw	JUP-N 74	LAFFERTY, R A
4	Direction of the Road	JUP-N 74	LeGUIN, Ursula K
4	Of Mist, and Grass, and Sand	JUP-N 74	McINTYRE, Vonda N
4	Ones Who Walk Away from Omelas	JUP-N 74	LeGUIN, Ursula K
4	Shark	JUP-N 74	BRYANT, Edward
4	Thing of Beauty, A	JUP-N 74	SPINRAD, Norman
4	Village, The	JUP-N 74	WILHELM, Kate
1	Dispossessed, The	JUP-W 75	LeGUIN, Ursula K
1	All Times Possible	JUP-N 75	EKLUND, Gordon
1	Company of Glory, The	JUP-N 75	PANGBORN, Edgar
1	Mote in God's Eye, The	JUP-N 75	NIVEN, Larry
1	Norstilia	JUP-N 75	SMITH, Cordwainer
2	Riding the Torch	JUP-W 75	SPINRAD, Norman
2	Assault on a City	JUP-N 75	VANCE, Jack
2	Born With the Dead	JUP-N 75	SILVERBERG, Robert
2	Song for Lya, A	JUP-N 75	MARTIN, George R R
2	Strangers	JUP-N 75	DOZOIS, Gardner
3	Seventeen Virgins	JUP-W 75	VANCE, Jack
3	Horrus Errand, The	JUP-N 75	COCHRANE, William C
3	If the Stars are Gods	JUP-N 75	EKLUND, Gordon
3	Tin Soldier	JUP-N 75	VINGE, Joan D
3	Women Men Don't See	JUP-N 75	TIPTREE, James Jr

CAT	TITLE	AW W/N Y	AUTHOR
4	Day Before the Revolution, The	JUP-W 75	LeGUIN, Ursula K
4	An Old Fashioned Girl	JUP-N 75	RUSS, Joanna
4	Blue Butter	JUP-N 75	STURGEON, Theodore
4	Engine at Heartsprings Center, The	JUP-N 75	ZELAZNY, Roger
4	Sleeping Dogs	JUP-N 75	ELLISON, Harlan
1	Where Late the Sweet Birds Sang	JUP-W 77	WILHELM, Kate
2	Houston, Houston, Do You Read?	JUP-W 77	TIPTREE, James Jr
3	Diary of the Rose, The	JUP-W 77	LeGUIN, Ursula K
4	I See You	JUP-W 77	KNIGHT, Damon
1	Heritage of Stars	JUP-W 78	SIMAK, Clifford D
2	In the Hall of the Martian Kings	JUP-W 78	VARLEY, John
3	Time Storm	JUP-W 78	DICKSON, Gordon R
4	Jeffty is Five	JUP-W 78	ELLISON, Harlan

JOHN W CAMPBELL MEMORIAL AWARD and THEODORE STURGEON MEMORIAL AWARD

The John W. Cambell Jr. Memorial Award honors the best science fiction novel of the preceding year, and is given in memory of the well-known science fiction writer and editor, one of the founding fathers of moders SF.

The award is chosen by an international panel of SF professionals, and is presented annuually by administrator James E. Gunn, at the University of Kansas, Lawrence, Kansas. The prize consists of a large iron ring perched on a tall wooden base bearing a name plate. The trophy was designed by Eldon Tefft. This award should not be confused with the John W. Campbell Jr. (Hugo) Award for best new author of the year.

In 1987 a companion award, The Theodore Sturgeon Award, was created to honor the best science fiction short story (under 17,500 words) published during the prevcious calendar year in English.

CAT	TITLE	AW W/N Y	AUTHOR
1	Beyond Apollo	JWC-W 73	MALZBERG, Barry N
1	Listeners, The	JWC-N 73	WOLFE, Gene
1	Rendezvous with Rama	JWC-W 74	CLARKE, Arthur C
1	Malevil	JWC-W 74	MERLE, Robert
1	Green Gene, The	JWC-N 74	DICKINSON, Peter
1	Embedding, The	JWC-N 74	WATSON, Ian
7	Cosmic Connection, The	JWC-W 74	SAGAN, Carl
1	Flow My Tears, The Policeman Said	JWC-W 75	DICK, Philip K
1	Dispossessed, The	JWC-N 75	LeGUIN, Ursula K
1	Alteration, The	JWC-W 77	AMIS, Kingsley
1	Man Plus	JWC-N 77	POHL, Frederik
1	Where Late the Sweet Birds Sang	JWC-N 77	WILHELM, Kate
1	Gateway	JWC-W 78	POHL, Frederik
1	Gloriana	JWC-W 79	MOORCOCK, Michael
1	Altered States	JWC-W 79	CHAYEFSKY, Paddy
1	...And Having Writ	JWC-W 79	BENSEN, Donald R
1	On Wings of Song	JWC-W 80	DISCH, Thomas M
1	Engine Summer	JWC-W 80	CROWLEY, John
1	Unlimited Dream Company, The	JWC-W 80	BALLARD, J G
1	Timescape	JWC-W 81	BENFORD, Gregory
1	Dreaming Dragon, The	JWC-N 81	BRODERICK, Damien
1	Shadow of the Torturer, The	JWC-N 81	WOLFE, Gene
1	Riddley Walker	JWC-W 82	HOBAN, Russell
1	Helliconia Spring	JWC-W 83	ALDISS, Brian W
1	No Enemy But Time	JWC-N 83	BISHOP, Michael

CAT	TITLE	AW W/N Y	AUTHOR
1	Citadel of the Autarch, The	JWC-W 84	WOLFE, Gene
1	Birth of t/People's Republ of Antarctica	JWC-N 84	BATCHELOR, John C
1	Tik-Tok	JWC-N 84	SLADEK, John
1	Years of the City, The	JWC-W 85	POHL, Frederik
1	Green Eyes	JWC-N 85	SHEPARD, Lucius
1	Neuromancer	JWC-N 85	GIBSON, William
1	Postman, The	JWC-W 86	BRIN, David
1	Blood Music	JWC-N 86	BEAR, Greg
1	Galapagos	JWC-N 86	VONNEGUT, Kurt Jr
1	Kiteworld	JWC-N 86	ROBERTS, Keith
1	Door Into Ocean	JWC-W 87	SLONCZEWSKI, Joan
1	Speaker for the Dead	JWC-N 87	CARD, Orson Scott
1	This Is the Way The World Ends	JWC-N 87	MORROW, James
4	Surviving	JWC-W 87	MOFFETT, Judith
4	Elephant	JWC-N 87	PALWICK, Susan
4	Grave Angels, The	JWC-N 87	KEARNS, Richard
4	Lions Are Asleep This Night, The	JWC-N 87	WALDROP, Howard
4	Pretty Boy Crossover	JWC-N 87	CADIGAN, Pat
1	Lincoln's Dreams	JWC-W 88	WILLIS, Connie
1	Sea In Summer, The	JWC-N 88	TURNER, George
1	Unconquered Country, The	JWC-N 88	RYMAN, Geoff
4	Rachel in Love	JWC-W 88	MURPHY, Pat
4	Buffalo Gals, Won't You Come Out Tonight	JWC-N 88	LeGUIN, Ursula K
4	Dinosaurs	JWC-N 88	WILLIAMS, Walter Jon
4	Evening and the Morning and the Night	JWC-N 88	BUTLER, Octavia E
4	Gift, The	JWC-N 88	FORDE, Pat
4	Heroics	JWC-N 88	KELLY, James Patrick
1	Islands in the Net	JWC-W 89	STERLING, Bruce
1	Dragon's Dawn	JWC-N 89	McCAFFREY, Anne
1	Gold Coast, The	JWC-N 89	ROBINSON, Kim Stanley
4	Schrodinger's Kitten	JWC-W 89	EFFINGER, George Alec
4	Do Ya, Do Ya, Wanna Dance	JWC-N 89	WALDROP, Howard
4	Stairs	JWC-N 89	BARRETT, Neil Jr
1	Child Garden, The	JWC-W 90	RYMAN, Geoff
1	Farewell Horizontal	JWC-N 90	JETER, K W
1	Good News From Outer Space	JWC-N 90	KESSEL, John
4	Edge of the World, The	JWC-W 90	SWANWICK, Michael
4	Dori Bangs	JWC-N 90	STERLING, Bruce
4	Silver Lady and the Fortyish Man, The	JWC-N 90	LINDHOLM, Megan

CAMPBELL / STURGEON AWARDS

CAT	TITLE	AW W/N Y	AUTHOR
1	Pacific Edge	JWC-W 91	ROBINSON, Kim Stanley
1	Only Begotten Daughter	JWC-N 91	MORROW, James
1	Queen of Angels	JWC-N 91	BEAR, Greg
4	Bears Discover Fire	JWC-W 91	BISSON, Terry
4	Episodes of the Argo	JWC-N 91	LAFFERTY, R A
4	My Advice to the Civilized	JWC-N 91	BARNES, John
1	Buddy Holly is Alive & Well On Ganymede	JWC-W 92	DENTON, Bradley
1	Difference Engine, The	JWC-N 92	GIBSON, William
1	Silicon Man, The	JWC-N 92	PLATT, Charles
1	Stations of the Tide	JWC-N 92	SWANWICK, Michael
1	Woman of the Iron People, A	JWC-N 92	ARNASON, Eleanor
4	Buffalo	JWC-W 92	KESSEL, John
4	Happy Man, The	JWC-N 92	LETHEM, Jonathan
4	Ma Qui	JWC-N 92	BRENNERT, Alan

LOCUS MAGAZINE AWARDS

The Locus Awards were created by Charles N. Brown, publisher and editor
of Locus, The Newspaper of the Science Fiction Field, and are voted
upon annually by the readers of that publication. No physical award
was presented originally, and the physical shape of the award has
varied considerably from year to year.

CAT	T I T L E	AW W/N Y	A U T H O R
1	Ringworld	LOC-W 71	NIVEN, Larry
1	And Chaos Died	LOC-N 71	RUSS, Joanna
1	Downward to the Earth	LOC-N 71	SILVERBERG, Robert
1	Fourth Mansions	LOC-N 71	LAFFERTY, R A
1	Tower of Glass, The	LOC-N 71	SILVERBERG, Robert
1	Year of the Quiet Sun	LOC-N 71	TUCKER, Wilson
4	Region Between, The	LOC-W 71	ELLISON, Harlan
4	Beastchild	LOC-N 71	KOONTZ, Dean R
4	Continued on Next Rock	LOC-N 71	LAFFERTY, R A
4	In the Queue	LOC-N 71	LAUMER, Keith
4	Slow Sculpture	LOC-N 71	STURGEON, Theodore
4	Snow Women, The	LOC-N 71	LEIBER, Fritz
6	Science Fiction Hall of Fame Vol 1	LOC-W 71	SILVERBERG, Robert
6	900 Grandmothers	LOC-N 71	LAFFERTY, R A
6	Orbit 6	LOC-N 71	KNIGHT, Damon
6	Orbit 7	LOC-N 71	KNIGHT, Damon
6	Quark 1	LOC-N 71	DELANY, Samuel R
6	World's Best Science Fiction: 1970	LOC-N 71	WOLHEIM, Donald H
1	Lathe of Heaven, The	LOC-W 72	LeGUIN, Ursula K
1	Dragonquest	LOC-N 72	McCAFFREY, Anne
1	Jack of Shadows	LOC-N 72	ZELAZNY, Roger
1	Time of Changes, A	LOC-N 72	SILVERBERG, Robert
1	To Your Scattered Bodies Go	LOC-N 72	FARMER, Philip Jose
4	Queen of Air and Darkness, The	LOC-W 72	ANDERSON, Poul
4	All the Last Wars at Once	LOC-N 72	EFFINGER, George Alec
4	Autumn Land, The	LOC-N 72	SIMAK, Clifford D
4	Meeting With Medusa, A	LOC-N 72	CLARKE, Arthur C
4	Wheels	LOC-N 72	THURSTON, Robert
13	Universe 1	LOC-W 72	CARR, Terry
13	Clarion 1	LOC-N 72	WILSON, Robin Scott
13	Infinity 2	LOC-N 72	HOSKINS, Robert
13	New Dimensions 1	LOC-N 72	SILVERBERG, Robert
13	Protostars	LOC-N 72	GERROLD, David
14	World's Best Science Fiction: 1971	LOC-W 72	WOLHEIM, Donald H
14	Driftglass	LOC-N 72	DELANY, Samuel R
14	Hugo Winners Vol 2	LOC-N 72	ASIMOV, Isaac
14	New Worlds of Fantasy 3rd ed	LOC-N 72	CARR, Terry
14	Sturgeon is Alive and Well	LOC-N 72	STURGEON, Theodore

CAT	TITLE	AW W/N Y	AUTHOR
1	Gods Themselves, The	LOC-W 73	ASIMOV, Isaac
1	Book of Skulls, The	LOC-N 73	SILVERBERG, Robert
1	Choice of Gods, A	LOC-N 73	SIMAK, Clifford D
1	Dying Inside	LOC-N 73	SILVERBERG, Robert
1	Sheep Look Up, The	LOC-N 73	BRUNNER, John
1	When Harlie Was One	LOC-N 73	GERROLD, David
2	Gold at the Starbow's End, The	LOC-W 73	POHL, Frederik
2	Fifth Head of Cerberus, The	LOC-N 73	WOLFE, Gene
2	Hero	LOC-N 73	HALDEMAN, Joe
2	Midsummer Century	LOC-N 73	BLISH, James
2	With t/Bentfin Boomer Boys on Little Old	LOC-N 73	LUPOFF, Richard A
2	Word for World is Forest, The	LOC-N 73	LeGUIN, Ursula K
4	Basilisk	LOC-W 73	ELLISON, Harlan
4	And I Awoke & Found Me Here t/Cold Hill'	LOC-N 73	TIPTREE, James Jr
4	Goat Song	LOC-N 73	ANDERSON, Poul
4	Kingdom by the Sea, A	LOC-N 73	DOZOIS, Gardner
4	Patron of the Arts	LOC-N 73	ROTSLER, William
4	When It Changed	LOC-N 73	RUSS, Joanna
13	Again, Dangerous Visions	LOC-W 73	ELLISON, Harlan
13	New Dimensions 2	LOC-N 73	SILVERBERG, Robert
13	Nova 2	LOC-N 73	HARRISON, Harry
13	Orbit 10	LOC-N 73	KNIGHT, Damon
13	Orbit 11	LOC-N 73	KNIGHT, Damon
13	Universe 2	LOC-N 73	CARR, Terry
14	Best Science Fiction of the Year: 1972	LOC-W 73	CARR, Terry
14	1972 Annual World's Best SF	LOC-N 73	WOLHEIM, Donald H
14	Alpha Three	LOC-N 73	SILVERBERG, Robert
14	Early Asimov, The	LOC-N 73	ASIMOV, Isaac
14	Gold at the Starbow's End, The	LOC-N 73	POHL, Frederik
14	Science Fiction Argosy, A	LOC-N 73	KNIGHT, Damon
1	Rendezvous with Rama	LOC-W 74	CLARKE, Arthur C
1	Man Who Folded Himself, The	LOC-N 74	GERROLD, David
1	People of the Wind, The	LOC-N 74	ANDERSON, Poul
1	Protector	LOC-N 74	NIVEN, Larry
1	Time Enough For Love	LOC-N 74	HEINLEIN, Robert A
1	Trullion Alastor	LOC-N 74	VANCE, Jack
2	Death of Doctor Island, The	LOC-W 74	WOLFE, Gene
2	Chains of the Sea	LOC-N 74	DOZOIS, Gardner
2	Defenseless Dead, The	LOC-N 74	NIVEN, Larry
2	Feast of St. Dionysus, The	LOC-N 74	SILVERBERG, Robert
2	Sketches Among the Ruins of My Mind	LOC-N 74	FARMER, Philip Jose
2	White Otters of Childhood, The	LOC-N 74	BISHOP, Michael
4	Deathbird, The	LOC-W 74	ELLISON, Harlan
4	Girl Who Was Plugged In, The	LOC-N 74	TIPTREE, James Jr
4	Love is the Plan, the Plan is Death	LOC-N 74	TIPTREE, James Jr
4	Ms Found in an Abandoned Time Machine	LOC-N 74	SILVERBERG, Robert
4	Of Mist, and Grass, and Sand	LOC-N 74	McINTYRE, Vonda N
4	Ones Who Walk Away from Omelas	LOC-N 74	LeGUIN, Ursula K

CAT	TITLE	AW W/N Y	AUTHOR
13	Astounding	LOC-W 74	HARRISON, Harry
13	Alien Condition, The	LOC-N 74	GOLDIN, Stephen
13	An Exaltation of Stars	LOC-N 74	CARR, Terry
13	New Dimensions 3	LOC-N 74	SILVERBERG, Robert
13	Orbit 12	LOC-N 74	KNIGHT, Damon
13	Universe 3	LOC-N 74	CARR, Terry
14	Best Science Fiction of the Year # 2	LOC-W 74	CARR, Terry
14	1973 Annual World's Best SF	LOC-N 74	WOLHEIM, Donald A
14	Jupiter	LOC-N 74	POHL, Frederik
14	Science Fiction Hall of Fame Vol 2a & 2b	LOC-N 74	BOVA, Ben
14	Ten Thousand Light Years From Home	LOC-N 74	TIPTREE, James Jr
14	Those Who Can	LOC-N 74	WILSON, Robin Scott
1	Dispossessed, The	LOC-W 75	LeGUIN, Ursula K
1	Flow My Tears, The Policeman Said	LOC-N 75	DICK, Philip K
1	Godwhale, The	LOC-N 75	BASS, T J
1	Inverted World, The	LOC-N 75	PRIEST, Christopher
1	Mote in God's Eye, The	LOC-N 75	NIVEN, Larry
1	Unsleeping Eye, The	LOC-N 75	COMPTON, D G
2	Born with the Dead	LOC-W 75	SILVERBERG, Robert
2	Assault on a City	LOC-N 75	VANCE, Jack
2	Marathon Photograph, The	LOC-N 75	SIMAK, Clifford D
2	Riding the Torch	LOC-N 75	SPINRAD, Norman
2	Song for Lya, A	LOC-N 75	MARTIN, George R R
2	Strangers	LOC-N 75	DOZOIS, Gardner
3	Adrift, Just off t/Islets of Langerhans	LOC-W 75	ELLISON, Harlan
3	I'm Looking for Kadak	LOC-N 75	ELLISON, Harlan
3	On Venus, Have We Got A Rabbi	LOC-N 75	TENN, William
3	Pre-Persons, The	LOC-N 75	DICK, Philip K
3	That Thou Art Mindful of Him	LOC-N 75	ASIMOV, Isaac
3	Twig	LOC-N 75	DICKSON, Gordon R
4	Day Before the Revolution, The	LOC-W 75	LeGUIN, Ursula K
4	Author of the Acacia Seeds, The	LOC-N 75	LeGUIN, Ursula K
4	Engine at Heartsprings Center, The	LOC-N 75	ZELAZNY, Roger
4	Four-Hour Fugue, The	LOC-N 75	BESTER, Alfred
4	Hole Man, The	LOC-N 75	NIVEN, Larry
4	Schwartz Between The Galaxies	LOC-N 75	SILVERBERG, Robert
13	Universe 4	LOC-W 75	CARR, Terry
13	New Dimensions 4	LOC-N 75	SILVERBERG, Robert
13	Orbit 14	LOC-N 75	KNIGHT, Damon
13	Stellar 1	LOC-N 75	del REY, Judy-Lynn
13	Threads of Time	LOC-N 75	SILVERBERG, Robert
13	Wandering Stars	LOC-N 75	DANN, Jack
14	Before the Golden Age	LOC-W 75	ASIMOV, Isaac
14	1974 Annual World's Best SF	LOC-N 75	WOLHEIM, Donald A
14	Alpha 5	LOC-N 75	SILVERBERG, Robert
14	Best From F&SF: 25th Anniversary	LOC-N 75	FERMAN, Ed
14	Best Science Fiction of the Year # 3	LOC-N 75	CARR, Terry
14	Nebula Award Stories 9	LOC-N 75	WILHELM, Kate

CAT	TITLE	AW W/N Y	AUTHOR
1	Forever War, The	LOC-W 76	HALDEMAN, Joe
1	Computer Connection, The	LOC-N 76	BESTER, Alfred
1	Dhalgren	LOC-N 76	DELANY, Samuel R
1	Imperial Earth	LOC-N 76	CLARKE, Arthur C
1	Shockwave Rider, The	LOC-N 76	BRUNNER, John
1	Stochastic Man, The	LOC-N 76	SILVERBERG, Robert
2	Storms of Windhaven, The	LOC-W 76	MARTIN, George R R
2	ARM	LOC-N 76	NIVEN, Larry
2	Borderland of Sol, The	LOC-N 76	NIVEN, Larry
2	Custodians, The	LOC-N 76	COWPER, Richard
2	Home is the Hangman	LOC-N 76	ZELAZNY, Roger
2	Silent Eyes of Time, The	LOC-N 76	BUDRYS, Algis
3	New Atlantis, The	LOC-W 76	LeGUIN, Ursula K
3	Down to a Sunless Sea	LOC-N 76	SMITH, Cordwainer
3	For A Single Yesterday	LOC-N 76	MARTIN, George R R
3	Galaxy Called Rome, A	LOC-N 76	MALZBERG, Barry N
3	Retrograde Summer	LOC-N 76	VARLEY, John
3	...and Seven Times Never Kill Man	LOC-N 76	MARTIN, George R R
4	Croatoan	LOC-W 76	ELLISON, Harlan
4	Child of All Ages	LOC-N 76	PLAUGER, P J
4	Doing Lennon	LOC-N 76	BENFORD, Gregory
4	Mother Trip, The	LOC-N 76	POHL, Frederik
4	Sail the Tide of Mourning	LOC-N 76	LUPOFF, Richard A
4	Sierra Maestra	LOC-N 76	SPINRAD, Norman
5	Epoch	LOC-W 76	ELWOOD, Roger
5	Best From Orbit 1-10	LOC-N 76	KNIGHT, Damon
5	Best Science Fiction of the Year # 4	LOC-N 76	CARR, Terry
5	Final Stage	LOC-N 76	FERMAN, Ed
5	New Atlantis, The	LOC-N 76	SILVERBERG, Robert
5	New Dimensions 5	LOC-N 76	SILVERBERG, Robert
6	Wind's Twelve Quarters	LOC-W 76	LeGUIN, Ursula K
6	Best of Cordwainer Smith, The	LOC-N 76	SMITH, Cordwainer
6	Best of Henry Kuttner, The	LOC-N 76	KUTTNER, Henry
6	Deathbird Stories	LOC-N 76	ELLISON, Harlan
6	Tales of Known Space	LOC-N 76	NIVEN, Larry
6	Warm Worlds and Otherwise	LOC-N 76	TIPTREE, James Jr
1	Where Late the Sweet Birds Sang	LOC-W 77	WILHELM, Kate
1	Children of Dune	LOC-N 77	HERBERT, Frank
1	Man Plus	LOC-N 77	POHL, Frederik
1	Mindbridge	LOC-N 77	HALDEMAN, Joe
1	Shadrach in the Furnace	LOC-N 77	SILVERBERG, Robert
1	World Out of Time, A	LOC-N 77	NIVEN, Larry
2	Samurai and the Willows, The	LOC-W 77	BISHOP, Michael
2	Anvil of Jove, The	LOC-N 77	BENFORD, Gregory
2	Eyeflash Miracles, The	LOC-N 77	WOLFE, Gene
2	Houston, Houston, Do You Read?	LOC-N 77	TIPTREE, James Jr
2	Piper at the Gates of Dawn	LOC-N 77	COWPER, Richard
2	Weather War	LOC-N 77	COCHRANE, William E

LOCUS MAGAZINE AWARDS

CAT	TITLE	AW W/N Y	AUTHOR
3	Bicentennial Man, The	LOC-W 77	ASIMOV, Isaac
3	Diary of the Rose, The	LOC-N 77	LeGUIN, Ursula K
3	Gotta Sing, Gotta Dance	LOC-N 77	VARLEY, John
3	Hertford Manuscript, The	LOC-N 77	COWPER, Richard
3	Phantom of Kansas, The	LOC-N 77	VARLEY, John
3	Psychologist Who Would'nt Do Awful Thing	LOC-N 77	TIPTREE, James Jr
4	Tricentennial	LOC-W 77	HALDEMAN, Joe
4	Crowd of Shadows, A	LOC-N 77	GRANT, Charles L
4	Custom Fitting	LOC-N 77	WHITE, James
4	Death of Princes, The	LOC-N 77	LEIBER, Fritz
4	I See You	LOC-N 77	KNIGHT, Damon
4	Seeing	LOC-N 77	ELLISON, Harlan
5	Song for Lya, A	LOC-W 77	MARTIN, George R R
5	Best of Damon Knight, The	LOC-N 77	KNIGHT, Damon
5	Bicentennial Man, The	LOC-N 77	ASIMOV, Isaac
5	Light Fantastic, The	LOC-N 77	BESTER, Alfred
5	Star Light, Star Bright	LOC-N 77	BESTER, Alfred
5	Worlds of Fritz Leiber, The	LOC-N 77	LEIBER, Fritz
14	Best Science Fiction of the Year # 5	LOC-W 77	CARR, Terry
14	Future Power	LOC-N 77	DANN, Jack
14	New Dimensions 6	LOC-N 77	SILVERBERG, Robert
14	Orbit 18	LOC-N 77	KNIGHT, Damon
14	Stellar 2	LOC-N 77	Del REY, Judy-Lynn
14	Universe 6	LOC-N 77	CARR, Terry
1	Gateway	LOC-W 78	POHL, Frederik
1	In the Ocean of the Night	LOC-N 78	BENFORD, Gregory
1	Michaelmas	LOC-N 78	BUDRYS, Algis
1	Opiuchi Hotline, The	LOC-N 78	VARLEY, John
1	Time Storm	LOC-N 78	DICKSON, Gordon R
2	Stardance	LOC-W 78	ROBINSON, Spider
2	Auk House	LOC-N 78	SIMAK, Clifford D
2	Aztecs	LOC-N 78	McINTYRE, Vonda N
2	Mars Ship, The	LOC-N 78	THURSTON, Robert
2	Snark in the Night, A	LOC-N 78	BENFORD, Gregory
4	Jeffty is Five	LOC-W 78	ELLISON, Harlan
4	Air Raid	LOC-N 78	BOEM, Herb (Varley, John)
4	Eyes of Amber	LOC-N 78	VINGE, Joan D
4	Rite of Spring, A	LOC-N 78	LEIBER, Fritz
4	Screwfly Solution, The	LOC-N 78	SHELDON, Raccoona
11	Silmarillion	LOC-W 78	TOLKIEN, J R R
11	Chronicles o/Thomas Covenant t/Unbeleive	LOC-N 78	DONALDSON, Stephen R
11	Our Lady of Darkness	LOC-N 78	LEIBER, Fritz
11	Shining, The	LOC-N 78	KING, Stephen
11	Sword of Shannara, The	LOC-N 78	BROOKS, Terry

CAT	T I T L E	AW W/N Y	A U T H O R
1	Dreamsnake	LOC-W 79	McINTYRE, Vonda N
1	Blind Voices	LOC-N 79	REAMY, Tom
1	Colony	LOC-N 79	BOVA, Ben
1	Faded Sun, The: Kesrith	LOC-N 79	CHERRYH, C J
1	White Dragon, The	LOC-N 79	McCAFFREY, Anne
2	Persistence of Vision, The	LOC-W 79	VARLEY, John
2	Fireship	LOC-N 79	VINGE, Joan D
2	Old Folks At Home	LOC-N 79	BISHOP, Michael
2	Seven American Nights	LOC-N 79	WOLFE, Gene
2	Watched, The	LOC-N 79	PRIEST, Christopher
3	Barbie Murders, The	LOC-W 79	VARLEY, John
3	Devil You Don't Know	LOC-N 79	ING, Dean
3	Hunter's Moon	LOC-N 79	ANDERSON, Poul
3	Mikal's Songbird	LOC-N 79	CARD, Orson Scott
3	Swanilda's Song	LOC-N 79	POHL, Frederik
4	Count the Clock That Tells the Time	LOC-W 79	ELLISON, Harlan
4	Hiss of Dragon, A	LOC-N 79	BENFORD, Gregory
4	Stone	LOC-N 79	BRYANT, Edward
4	View From A Height	LOC-N 79	VINGE, Joan D
4	Virra	LOC-N 79	CARR, Terry
5	Earth Book of Stormgate, The	LOC-N 79	ANDERSON, Poul
5	Infinite Dreams	LOC-N 79	HALDEMAN, Joe
5	Still I Persist in Wondering	LOC-N 79	PANGBORN, Edgar
5	Strange Wine	LOC-N 79	ELLISON, Harlan
6	Best Science Fiction of the Year # 7	LOC-W 79	CARR, Terry
6	1978 Annual World's Best SF	LOC-N 79	WOLHEIM, Donald A
6	New Dimensions 8	LOC-N 79	SILVERBERG, Robert
6	Stellar 4	LOC-N 79	del REY, Judy-Lynn
6	Universe 8	LOC-N 79	CARR, Terry
7	Way the Future Was, The	LOC-W 79	POHL, Frederik
7	Encyclopedia of SF and Fantasy #2	LOC-N 79	TUCK, Donald H
7	Fantasia: A Jack Vance Bibliography	LOC-N 79	LEVACK
7	Index to SF Anthologies and Collections	LOC-N 79	CONTENTO, William
7	SF and Heroic Fantasy Index	LOC-N 79	WELLS, Stuart W III
1	Titan	LOC-W 80	VARLEY, John
1	Fountains of Paradise, The	LOC-N 80	CLARKE, Arthur C
1	JEM	LOC-N 80	POHL, Frederik
1	On Wings of Song	LOC-N 80	DISCH, Thomas M
1	Stardance	LOC-N 80	ROBINSON, Spider
2	Enemy Mine	LOC-W 80	LONGYEAR, Barry
2	Battle of the Abaco Reefs, The	LOC-N 80	SCHENCK, Hilbert
2	Mars Masked	LOC-N 80	POHL, Frederik
2	Palely Loitering	LOC-N 80	PRIEST, Christopher
2	Songhouse	LOC-N 80	CARD, Orson Scott

CAT	TITLE	AW W/N Y	AUTHOR
3	Sandkings	LOC-W 80	MARTIN, George R R
3	Fireflood and Other Stories	LOC-N 80	McINTYRE, Vonda N
3	Galatea Galante	LOC-N 80	BESTER, Alfred
3	Options	LOC-N 80	VARLEY, John
3	Out There Where the Big Ships Go	LOC-N 80	COWPER, Richard
4	Way of Cross and Dragon, The	LOC-W 80	MARTIN, George R R
4	giANTS	LOC-N 80	BRYANT, Edward
4	Quietus	LOC-N 80	CARD, Orson Scott
4	Redeemer	LOC-N 80	BENFORD, Gregory
4	War Beneath the Tree	LOC-N 80	WOLFE, Gene
5	Convergent Series	LOC-W 80	NIVEN, Larry
5	Eyes of Amber	LOC-N 80	VINGE, Joan D
5	Fireflood and Other Stories	LOC-N 80	McINTYRE, Vonda N
5	Riverworlds and Other Stories	LOC-N 80	FARMER, Philip Jose
5	Stars Are the Styx, The	LOC-N 80	STURGEON, Theodore
6	Universe 9	LOC-W 80	CARR, Terry
6	Amazons!	LOC-N 80	SALMONSON, Jessica Amanda
6	Best of New Dimensions	LOC-N 80	SILVERBERG, Robert
6	Best Science Fiction of the Year # 8	LOC-N 80	CARR, Terry
6	Chrysalis 3	LOC-N 80	TORGESON, Roy
7	Science Fiction Encyclopedia, The	LOC-W 80	NICHOLS, Peter
7	In Memory Yet Green	LOC-N 80	ASIMOV, Isaac
7	Language of the Night, The	LOC-N 80	LeGUIN, Ursula K
7	Reader's Guide to SF, A	LOC-N 80	SEARLES, Baird
7	World of SF 1926-76	LOC-N 80	del REY, Lester
11	Harpist in the Wind	LOC-W 80	McKILLIP, Patricia
11	Castle Roogna	LOC-N 80	ANTHONY, Piers
11	Dead Zone, The	LOC-N 80	KING, Stephen
11	Merman's Children, The	LOC-N 80	ANDERSON, Poul
11	Tales of Neveryon	LOC-N 80	DELANY, Samuel R
1	Snow Queen, The	LOC-W 81	VINGE, Joan D
1	Beyond The Blue Event Horizon	LOC-N 81	POHL, Frederik
1	Ringworld Engineers, The	LOC-N 81	NIVEN, Larry
1	Timescape	LOC-N 81	BENFORD, Gregory
1	Wizard	LOC-N 81	VARLEY, John
2	Nightflyers	LOC-W 81	MARTIN, George R R
2	Autopsy, The	LOC-N 81	SHEA, Michael
2	Dangerous Games	LOC-N 81	RANDALL, Marta
2	Patchwork Girl, The	LOC-N 81	NIVEN, Larry
2	Web of the Magi, The	LOC-N 81	COWPER, Richard
3	Brave Little Toaster, The	LOC-W 81	DISCH, Thomas M
3	Beatnik Bayou	LOC-N 81	VARLEY, John
3	Strata	LOC-N 81	BRYANT, Edward
3	Ugly Chickens, The	LOC-N 81	WALDROP, Howard
3	Way Station, The	LOC-N 81	KING, Stephen

CAT	T I T L E	AW W/N Y	A U T H O R
4	Grotto of the Dancing Bear, The	LOC-W 81	SIMAK, Clifford D
4	Bug House	LOC-N 81	TUTTLE, Lisa
4	Last Answer, The	LOC-N 81	ASIMOV, Isaac
4	Our Lady of the Sauropods	LOC-N 81	SILVERBERG, Robert
4	Window	LOC-N 81	LEMAN, Bob
5	Barbie Murders, The	LOC-W 81	VARLEY, John
5	Island of Dr. Death, The	LOC-N 81	WOLFE, Gene
5	Last Defender of Camelot	LOC-N 81	ZELAZNY, Roger
5	San Diego Lightfoot Sue	LOC-N 81	REAMY, Tom
5	Shatterday	LOC-N 81	ELLISON, Harlan
6	Magazine of Fant & SF: A 30 Yr Retrospec	LOC-W 81	FERNAN, Edward L
6	Arbor House Treasury of Modern SF	LOC-N 81	SILVERBERG, Robert
6	Best Science Fiction of the Year # 9	LOC-N 81	CARR, Terry
6	Dark Forces	LOC-N 81	McCAULEY, Kirby
6	Tales of the Vulgar Unicorn	LOC-N 81	ASPRIN, Robert Lynn
7	In Joy Still Felt	LOC-W 81	ASIMOV, Isaac
7	Cosmos	LOC-N 81	SAGAN, Carl
7	Dream Makers	LOC-N 81	PLATT, Charles
7	Jack Vance	LOC-N 81	UNDERWOOD, Tim
7	SF and Fantasy Authors	LOC-N 81	CURREY, L W
9	Dragon's Eggs	LOC-W 81	FORWARD, Dr. Robert L
9	Beyond Rejection	LOC-N 81	LEIBER, Fritz
9	Gates of Heaven, The	LOC-N 81	PREUSS, Paul
9	Orphan, The	LOC-N 81	STALLMAN, Robert
9	Sundiver	LOC-N 81	BRIN, David
11	Lord Valentine's Castle	LOC-W 81	SILVERBERG, Robert
11	Changeling	LOC-N 81	ZELAZNY, Roger
11	Northern Girl, The	LOC-N 81	LYNN, Elizabeth A
11	Shadow of the Torturer, The	LOC-N 81	WOLFE, Gene
11	Wounded Land, The	LOC-N 81	DONALDSON, Stephen R
1	Many Colored Land, The	LOC-W 82	MAY, Julian
1	Downbelow Station	LOC-N 82	CHERRYH, C J
1	Dream Park	LOC-N 82	NIVEN, Larry
1	Project Pope	LOC-N 82	SIMAK, Clifford D
1	Windhaven	LOC-N 82	MARTIN, George R R
2	Blue Champagne	LOC-W 82	VARLEY, John
2	Desert of Stolen Dreams, The	LOC-N 82	SILVERBERG, Robert
2	In the Western Tradition	LOC-N 82	EISENSTEIN, Phyllis
2	Saturn Game, The	LOC-N 82	ANDERSON, Poul
2	With Delicate Mad Hands	LOC-N 82	TIPTREE, James Jr
3	Guardians	LOC-W 82	MARTIN, George R R
3	Haunted Tower, The	LOC-N 82	CHERRYH, C J
3	Out of Everywhere	LOC-N 82	TIPTREE, James Jr
3	Thermals of August, The	LOC-N 82	BRYANT, Edward
3	Unicorn Variations	LOC-N 82	ZELAZNY, Roger

LOCUS MAGAZINE AWARDS

CAT	T I T L E	AW W/N Y	A U T H O R
4	Pusher, The	LOC-W 82	VARLEY, John
4	Needle Men, The	LOC-N 82	MARTIN, George R R
4	Only Death, The	LOC-N 82	CHERRYH, C J
4	Remembering Melody	LOC-N 82	MARTIN, George R R
4	Serpent's Teeth	LOC-N 82	ROBINSON, Spider
5	Sandkings	LOC-W 82	MARTIN, George R R
5	Gene Wolfe's Book of Days	LOC-N 82	WOLFE, Gene
5	Lord Darcy Investigates	LOC-N 82	GARRETT, Randall
5	Particle Theory	LOC-N 82	BRYANT, Edward
5	Sunfall	LOC-N 82	CHERRYH, C J
6	Shadows of Sanctuary	LOC-W 82	ASPRIN, Robert Lynn
6	Best Science Fiction of the Year #10	LOC-N 82	CARR, Terry
6	Flashing Swords #5	LOC-N 82	CARTER, Lin
6	New Voices 4	LOC-N 82	MARTIN, George R R
6	Universe 11	LOC-N 82	CARR, Terry
7	Danse Macabre	LOC-W 82	KING, Stephen
7	After Man	LOC-N 82	DIXON, Dougal
7	Anatomy of Wonder 2nd	LOC-N 82	BARRON, Neil
7	Art of Leo and Diane Dillon, The	LOC-N 82	PREISS, Byron
7	Grand Tour, The	LOC-N 82	MILLER, Ron
9	Starship and Haiku	LOC-W 82	SOMTOW, S P
9	At the Eye of the Ocean	LOC-N 82	SCHENCK, Hilbert
9	Breaking of Northwall, The	LOC-N 82	WILLIAMS, Paul O
9	Radix	LOC-N 82	ATTANASIO, A A
9	War Games	LOC-N 82	HANSEN, Karl
11	Claw of the Conciliator, The	LOC-W 82	WOLFE, Gene
11	Captive, The	LOC-N 82	STALLMAN, Robert
11	Changing Land, The	LOC-N 82	ZELAZNY, Roger
11	Little Big	LOC-N 82	CROWLEY, John
11	War Hounds and the World's Pain, The	LOC-N 82	MOORCOCK, Michael
1	Foundation's Edge	LOC-W 83	ASIMOV, Isaac
1	2010: Odyssey Two	LOC-N 83	CLARKE, Arthur C
1	Courtship Rite	LOC-N 83	KINGSBURY, Donald
1	Friday	LOC-N 83	HEINLEIN, Robert A
1	Helliconia Spring	LOC-N 83	ALDISS, Brian W
1	Pride of Chanur, The	LOC-N 83	CHERRYH, C J
2	Souls	LOC-W 83	RUSS, Joanna
2	Horrible Imaginings (Death)	LOC-N 83	LEIBER, Fritz
2	Postman, The	LOC-N 83	BRIN, David
2	Thesme and the Ghayrog	LOC-N 83	SILVERBERG, Robert
2	Unsound Variations	LOC-N 83	MARTIN, George R R
3	Djinn, No Chaser	LOC-W 83	ELLISON, Harlan
3	Firewatch	LOC-N 83	WILLIS, Connie
3	High Steel	LOC-N 83	HALDEMAN, Joe
3	Myth of the Near Future	LOC-N 83	BALLARD, J G
3	Willow	LOC-N 83	CHERRYH, C J

CAT	T I T L E	AW W/N Y	A U T H O R
4	Sur	LOC-W 83	LeGUIN, Ursula K
4	Boy Who Waterskied Forever, The	LOC-N 83	TIPTREE, James Jr
4	God's Hooks	LOC-N 83	WALDROP, Howard
4	Melancholy Elephants	LOC-N 83	ROBINSON, Spider
4	Spider Rose	LOC-N 83	STERLING, Bruce
5	Compass Rose, The	LOC-W 83	LeGUIN, Ursula K
5	Different Seasons	LOC-N 83	KING, Stephen
5	Dilvish Be Damned	LOC-N 83	ZELAZNY, Roger
5	Majipoor Chronicle	LOC-N 83	SILVERBERG, Robert
5	Stalking the Nightmare	LOC-N 83	ELLISON, Harlan
6	Best Science Fiction of the Year #11	LOC-W 83	CARR, Terry
6	Fantasy Annual 5	LOC-N 83	CARR, Terry
6	Perpetual Light	LOC-N 83	RYAN, Alan
6	Storm Season	LOC-N 83	ASPRIN, Robert Lynn
6	Universe 12	LOC-N 83	CARR, Terry
7	Engines of the Night, The	LOC-W 83	MALZBERG, Barry N
7	Fear Itself:T/Horror Fiction of S King	LOC-N 83	UNDERWOOD, Tim
7	Isaac Asimov: The Foundations of SF	LOC-N 83	GUNN, James E
7	Reader's Guide to Fantasy, A	LOC-N 83	SEARLES, Baird
7	World of the Dark Crystal, The	LOC-N 83	FROUD, Brian
9	Courtship Rite	LOC-W 83	KINGSBURY, Donald
9	Dreamrider	LOC-N 83	MIESEL, Sandra
9	Lady of Light	LOC-N 83	PAXSON, Diana
9	Red Magician, The	LOC-N 83	GOLDSTEIN, Lisa
9	Windhover Tapes, The	LOC-N 83	NORWOOD, Warren
11	Sword of the Lichtor, The	LOC-W 83	WOLFE, Gene
11	Citadel of the Autarch, The	LOC-N 83	WOLFE, Gene
11	Fevre Dream	LOC-N 83	MARTIN, George R R
11	One Tree, The	LOC-N 83	DONALDSON, Stephen R
11	Transmigration of Timothy Archer, The	LOC-N 83	DICK, Philip K
1	Startide Rising	LOC-W 84	BRIN, David
1	Helliconia Summer	LOC-N 84	ALDISS, Brian W
1	Millenium	LOC-N 84	VARLEY, John
1	Moreta: Dragonlady of Pern	LOC-N 84	McCAFFREY, Anne
1	Robots of Dawn	LOC-N 84	ASIMOV, Isaac
1	Void Captain's Tale, The	LOC-N 84	SPINRAD, Norman
2	Her Habiline Husband	LOC-W 84	BISHOP, Michael
2	Cascade Point	LOC-N 84	ZAHN, Timothy
2	Hardfought	LOC-N 84	BEAR, Greg
2	Homefaring	LOC-N 84	SILVERBERG, Robert
2	Seeking	LOC-N 84	PALMER, David R
3	Monkey Treatment, The	LOC-W 84	MARTIN, George R R
3	Black Air	LOC-N 84	ROBINSON, Kim Stanley
3	Blood Music	LOC-N 84	BEAR, Greg
3	Slow Birds	LOC-N 84	WATSON, Ian
3	Street Meat	LOC-N 84	SPINRAD, Norman

LOCUS MAGAZINE AWARDS

CAT	TITLE	AW W/N Y	AUTHOR
4	Beyond the Dead Reef	LOC-W 84	TIPTREE, James Jr
4	Peacemaker, The	LOC-N 84	DOZOIS, Gardner
4	Servant of the People	LOC-N 84	POHL, Frederik
4	Speech Sounds	LOC-N 84	BUTLER, Octavia E
4	Spending A Day at the Lottery Fair	LOC-N 84	POHL, Frederik
5	Unicorn Variations	LOC-W 84	ZELAZNY, Roger
5	Red As Blood	LOC-N 84	LEE, Tanith
5	Sentinel, The	LOC-N 84	CLARKE, Arthur C
5	Wind From A Burning Woman	LOC-N 84	BEAR, Greg
5	Zanzibar Cat, The	LOC-N 84	RUSS, Joanna
6	Best Science Fiction of the Year #12	LOC-W 84	CARR, Terry
6	1983 Annual World's Best SF	LOC-N 84	WOLHEIM, Donald A
6	Face of Chaos	LOC-N 84	ASPRIN, Robert Lynn
6	Universe 13	LOC-N 84	CARR, Terry
6	Whispers 4	LOC-N 84	SCHIFF, Stuart David
7	Dream Makers Vol 2	LOC-W 84	PLATT, Charles
7	Encyclopedia of SF and Fantasy #3	LOC-N 84	TUCK, Donald H
7	Fantastic Art of Rowena	LOC-N 84	MORRILL, Rowena
7	High Kings, The	LOC-N 84	CHANT, Joy
7	Staying Alive: A Writer's Guide	LOC-N 84	SPINRAD, Norman
9	Tea with the Black Dragon	LOC-W 84	MacAVOY, R A
9	Blackcollar, The	LOC-N 84	ZAHN, Timothy
9	King's Blood Four	LOC-N 84	TEPPER, Sheri S
9	Rumor of Angels, A	LOC-N 84	KELLOGG, M Bradley
9	Starrigger	LOC-N 84	de CHANCLE, John
11	Mists of Avalon, The	LOC-N 84	BRADLEY, Marion Zimmer
11	Anubis Gates, The	LOC-N 84	POWERS, Tim
11	Armageddon Rag, The	LOC-N 84	MARTIN, George R R
11	Lyonesse	LOC-N 84	VANCE, Jack
11	White Gold Wielder	LOC-N 84	DONALDSON, Stephen R
1	Integral Trees, The	LOC-W 85	NIVEN, Larry
1	Across The Sea of Suns	LOC-N 85	BENFORD, Gregory
1	Chanur's Venture	LOC-N 85	CHERRYH, C J
1	Demon	LOC-N 85	VARLEY, John
1	Heechee Rendezvous	LOC-N 85	POHL, Frederik
1	Stars in My Pocket Like Grains of Sand	LOC-N 85	DELANY, Samuel R
2	Press Enter	LOC-W 85	VARLEY, John
2	Ballad of the Flexible Bullet, The	LOC-N 85	KING, Stephen
2	Blister, The	LOC-N 85	POHL, Frederik
2	Scapegoat, The	LOC-N 85	CHERRYH, C J
2	Traveler's Tale, A	LOC-N 85	SHEPARD, Lucius
2	Trinity	LOC-N 85	KRESS, Nancy

LOCUS MAGAZINE AWARDS

CAT	T I T L E	AW W/N Y	A U T H O R
3	Bloodchild	LOC-W 85	BUTLER, Octavia E
3	Blued Moon	LOC-N 85	WILLIS, Connie
3	Kindly Isle, The	LOC-N 85	POHL, Frederik
3	Lucky Strike, The	LOC-N 85	ROBINSON, Kim Stanley
3	Man Whp Painted the Dragon Griaule, The	LOC-N 85	SHEPARD, Lucius
3	With A Little Help From Her Friends	LOC-N 85	BISHOP, Michael
4	Salvador	LOC-W 85	SHEPARD, Lucius
4	Aliens Who Knew, I Mean Everything, The	LOC-N 85	EFFINGER, George Alec
4	Bright Burning Tiger	LOC-N 85	LEE, Tanith
4	Cabin on the Coast, A	LOC-N 85	WOLFE, Gene
4	Crystal Spheres, The	LOC-N 85	BRIN, David
4	Ridge Running	LOC-N 85	ROBINSON, Kim Stanley
5	Ghost Light, The	LOC-W 85	LEIBER, Fritz
5	Extra(ordinary) People	LOC-N 85	RUSS, Joanna
5	One Winter in Eden	LOC-N 85	BISHOP, Michael
5	Pohlstars	LOC-N 85	POHL, Frederik
5	Tamastara	LOC-N 85	LEE, Tanith
5	Years of the City, The	LOC-N 85	POHL, Frederik
6	Light Years and Dark	LOC-W 85	BISHOP, Michael
6	1984 Annual World's Best SF	LOC-N 85	WOLHEIM, Donald A
6	Best Science Fiction of the Year #13	LOC-N 85	CARR, Terry
6	Universe 14	LOC-N 85	CARR, Terry
6	Wings of Omen	LOC-N 85	ASPRIN, Robert Lynn
6	Year's Best Science Fiction, 1st	LOC-N 85	DOZOIS, Gardner
7	Sleepless Nights in the Procrustean Bed:	LOC-W 85	ELLISON, Harlan
7	Age of Wonders: Exploring t/World of SF	LOC-N 85	HARTWELL, David G
7	Atlas of Pern, The	LOC-N 85	FONSTAD, Karen Wynn
7	Dune Encyclopedia, The	LOC-N 85	McNELLY, Willis E Dr.
7	Faces of Science Fiction, The	LOC-N 85	PERRET, Patti
7	Wonder's Child: My Life in S Fiction	LOC-N 85	WILLIAMSON, Jack
9	Wild Shore, The	LOC-W 85	ROBINSON, Kim Stanley
9	Emergence	LOC-N 85	PALMER, David R
9	Green Eyes	LOC-N 85	SHEPARD, Lucius
9	Neuromancer	LOC-N 85	GIBSON, William
9	Them Bones	LOC-N 85	WALDROP, Howard
9	Valentina: Soul in Sapphire	LOC-N 85	DELANEY, Joseph H
11	Job: A Comedy of Justice	LOC-W 85	HEINLEIN, Robert A
11	Damiano's Lute	LOC-N 85	MacAVOY, R A
11	Gilgamesh, The King	LOC-N 85	SILVERBERG, Robert
11	Infinity Concerto, The	LOC-N 85	BEAR, Greg
11	Raphael	LOC-N 85	MacAVOY, R A
11	Talisman, The	LOC-N 85	KING, Stephen

LOCUS MAGAZINE AWARDS

CAT	T I T L E	AW W/N Y	A U T H O R
1	Postman, The	LOC-W 86	BRIN, David
1	Cat Who Walks Through Walls, The	LOC-N 86	HEINLEIN, Robert A
1	Ender's Game	LOC-N 86	CARD, Orson Scott
1	Footfall	LOC-N 86	NIVEN, Larry
1	Helliconia Winter	LOC-N 86	ALDISS, Brian W
1	Robots and Empire	LOC-N 86	ASIMOV, Isaac
2	Only Neat Thing To Do, The	LOC-W 86	TIPTREE, James Jr
2	24 Views of Mount Fuji by Hokusai	LOC-N 86	ZELAZNY, Roger
2	Green Mars	LOC-N 86	ROBINSON, Kim Stanley
2	Plague Star, The	LOC-N 86	MARTIN, George R R
2	Sailing to Byzantium	LOC-N 86	SILVERBERG, Robert
2	Scapegoat, The	LOC-N 86	CHERRYH, C J
3	Paladin of the Lost Hour	LOC-W 86	ELLISON, Harlan
3	Dogfight	LOC-N 86	SWANWICK, Michael
3	Fringe, The	LOC-N 86	CARD, Orson Scott
3	Jaguar Hunter, The	LOC-N 86	SHEPARD, Lucius
3	Portraits of His Children	LOC-N 86	MARTIN, George R R
3	Under Siege	LOC-N 86	MARTIN, George R R
4	With Virgil Oddum at the East Pole	LOC-W 86	ELLISON, Harlan
4	Dinner in Audoghast	LOC-N 86	STERLING, Bruce
4	Fermi and Frost	LOC-N 86	POHL, Frederik
4	Mengele	LOC-N 86	SHEPARD, Lucius
4	Snow	LOC-N 86	CROWLEY, John
4	Time's Rub	LOC-N 86	BENFORD, Gregory
5	Skeleton Crew	LOC-W 86	KING, Stephen
5	Clive Barker's Books of Blood, Vols 4-6	LOC-N 86	BARKER, Clive
5	Fire Watch	LOC-N 86	WILLIS, Connie
5	Limits	LOC-N 86	NIVEN, Larry
5	Melancholy Elephants	LOC-N 86	ROBINSON, Spider
5	Nightflyers	LOC-N 86	MARTIN, George R R
6	Medea: Harlan's World	LOC-W 86	ELLISON, Harlan
6	Best Science Fiction of the Year #14	LOC-N 86	CARR, Terry
6	Imaginary Lands	LOC-N 86	McKINLEY, Robin
6	Thieve's World #7: The Dead of Winter	LOC-N 86	ASPRIN, Robert Lynn
6	Universe 15	LOC-N 86	CARR, Terry
6	Year's Best Science Fiction, 2nd	LOC-N 86	DOZOIS, Gardner
7	Benchmarks: Galaxy Bookshelf	LOC-W 86	BUDRYS, Algis
7	Faces of Fear: Encount W/t/Creat Mod Hor	LOC-N 86	WINTER, Douglas E
7	Novels of Philip K Dick, The	LOC-N 86	ROBINSON, Kim Stanley
7	Pale Shadow of Science, The	LOC-N 86	ALDISS, Brian W
7	Science Fiction: The 100 Best Novels	LOC-N 86	PRINGLE, David
7	Science Made Stupid	LOC-N 86	WELLER, Tom

CAT	T I T L E	AW W/N Y	A U T H O R
9	Contact	LOC-W 86	SAGAN, Carl
9	Cats Have No Lord	LOC-N 86	SHETTERLEY, Will
9	Emprise	LOC-N 86	KUBE-McDOWELL, Michael P
9	In the Drift	LOC-N 86	SWANWICK, Michael
9	Summer Tree, The	LOC-N 86	KAY, Guy Gavriel
9	Tailchaser's Song	LOC-N 86	WILLIAMS, Tad
11	Trumps of Doom	LOC-W 86	ZELAZNY, Roger
11	Book of Kells, The	LOC-N 86	MacAVOY, R A
11	Dragonsbane	LOC-N 86	HAMBLY, Barbara
11	King's Justice, The	LOC-N 86	KURTZ, Katherine
11	Lyonesse: The Green Pearl	LOC-N 86	VANCE, Jack
11	Vampire Lestat, The	LOC-N 86	RICE, Anne
1	Speaker for the Dead	LOC-W 87	CARD, Orson Scott
1	Chanur's Homecoming	LOC-N 87	CHERRYH, C J
1	Count Zero	LOC-N 87	GIBSON, William
1	Foundation and Earth	LOC-N 87	ASIMOV, Isaac
1	Handmaid's Tale, The	LOC-N 87	ATWOOD, Margaret
1	Heart of the Comet	LOC-N 87	BENFORD, Gregory
2	R & R	LOC-W 87	SHEPARD, Lucius
2	Collision	LOC-N 87	TIPTREE, James Jr
2	Escape From Kathmandu	LOC-N 87	ROBINSON, Kim Stanley
2	Gilgamesh in the Outback	LOC-N 87	SILVERBERG, Robert
2	Spice Pogrom	LOC-N 87	WILLIS, Connie
2	Tango Charlie and Foxtrot Romeo	LOC-N 87	VARLEY, John
3	Thor Meets Captain America	LOC-W 87	BRIN, David
3	Glass Flower, The	LOC-N 87	MARTIN, George R R
3	Hatrack River	LOC-N 87	CARD, Orson Scott
3	Of Space-Time and the River	LOC-N 87	BENFORD, Gregory
3	Permafrost	LOC-N 87	ZELAZNY, Roger
3	Winter Market, The	LOC-N 87	GIBSON, William
4	Robot Dreams	LOC-W 87	ASIMOV, Isaac
4	Alien Grafitti	LOC-N 87	BISHOP, Michael
4	Boy Who Plaited Manes, The	LOC-N 87	SPRINGER, Nancy
4	Down and Out in the Year 2000	LOC-N 87	ROBINSON, Kim Stanley
4	Rat	LOC-N 87	KELLY, James Patrick
4	Tangents	LOC-N 87	BEAR, Greg
5	Blue Champagne	LOC-W 87	VARLEY, John
5	Burning Chrome	LOC-N 87	GIBSON, William
5	Howard Who?	LOC-N 87	WALDROP, Howard
5	River of Time, The	LOC-N 87	BRIN, David
5	Tuf Voyaging	LOC-N 87	MARTIN, George R R
5	Visible Light	LOC-N 87	CHERRYH, C J
6	Year's Best Science Fiction, 3rd	LOC-W 87	DOZOIS, Gardner
6	Afterlives	LOC-N 87	SARGENT, Pamela
6	Best Science Fiction of the Year #15	LOC-N 87	CARR, Terry
6	Mirrorshades: The Cyberpunk Anthology	LOC-N 87	STERLING, Bruce
6	Universe 16	LOC-N 87	CARR, Terry
6	Wild Cards	LOC-N 87	MARTIN, George R R

LOCUS MAGAZINE AWARDS

CAT	T I T L E	AW W/N Y	A U T H O R
7	Trillion Year Spree	LOC-W 87	ALDISS, Brian W
7	Industrial Light & Magic: Special Effect	LOC-N 87	SMITH, Thomas G
7	John W Campbell Letters Vol 1, The	LOC-N 87	CHAPDELAINE, Perry A Sr.
7	Only Apparently Real: World of P K Dick	LOC-N 87	WILLIAMS, Paul
7	Penguin Encycl of Horror & Supernatural	LOC-N 87	SULLIVAN, Jack
7	Science Fiction in Print 1985	LOC-N 87	BROWN, Charles N
9	Hercules Text, The	LOC-W 87	McDEVITT, Jack
9	Crosstime Engineer, The	LOC-N 87	FRANKOWSKI, Leo
9	Hidden Place, A	LOC-N 87	WILSON, Robert Charles
9	No Safe Place	LOC-N 87	MOROZ, Anne
9	Shards of Honor	LOC-N 87	BUJOLD, Lois McMaster
9	Wrack & Roll	LOC-N 87	DENTON, Bradley
11	Soldier of the Mist	LOC-W 87	WOLFE, Gene
11	Blood of Amber	LOC-N 87	ZELAZNY, Roger
11	Folk of the Air, The	LOC-N 87	BEAGLE, Peter S
11	Goodbody	LOC-N 87	STURGEON, Theodore
11	It	LOC-N 87	KING, Stephen
11	Twisting The Rope	LOC-N 87	MacAVOY, R A
1	Uplift War, The	LOC-W 88	BRIN, David
1	Annals of the HeeChee, The	LOC-W 88	POHL, Frederik
1	Forge of God, The	LOC-N 88	BEAR, Greg
1	Life During Wartime	LOC-N 88	SHEPARD, Lucius
1	Urth of the New Sun, The	LOC-N 88	WOLFE, Gene
1	When Gravity Fails	LOC-N 88	EFFINGER, George Alec
2	Secret Sharer, The	LOC-W 88	SILVERBERG, Robert
2	Blind Geometer, The	LOC-N 88	ROBINSON, Kim Stanley
2	Eye for Eye	LOC-N 88	CARD, Orson Scott
2	Glass Cloud	LOC-N 88	KELLY, James Patrick
2	Mother Goddess of the World	LOC-N 88	ROBINSON, Kim Stanley
2	Superwine	LOC-N 88	TURTLEDOVE, Harry
3	Rachel in Love	LOC-W 88	MURPHY, Pat
3	America	LOC-N 88	CARD, Orson Scott
3	Buffalo Gals, Won't You Come Out Tonight	LOC-N 88	LeGUIN, Ursula K
3	Dream Baby	LOC-N 88	McALLISTER, Bruce
3	Flowers of Edo	LOC-N 88	STERLING, Bruce
3	Shades	LOC-N 88	SHEPARD, Lucius
4	Angel	LOC-W 88	CADIGAN, Pat
4	Delta Sly Honey	LOC-N 88	SHEPARD, Lucius
4	Faithful Companion at Forty, The	LOC-N 88	FOWLER, Karen Joy
4	Glassblower's Dragon, The	LOC-N 88	SHEPARD, Lucius
4	In the Midst of Life	LOC-N 88	TIPTREE, James Jr
4	Why I Left Harry's All-Night Hamburgers	LOC-N 88	WATT-EVANS, Lawrence
5	Jaguar Hunter, The	LOC-W 88	SHEPARD, Lucius
5	All About Str'ge Monsters F/Recent Past	LOC-N 88	WALDROP, Howard
5	And the Gods Laughed	LOC-N 88	BROWN, Fredric
5	Collected Stories of Philip K Dick, The	LOC-N 88	DICK, Philip K
5	Essential Ellison, The	LOC-N 88	ELLISON, Harlan
5	Portraits of His Children	LOC-N 88	MARTIN, George R R

CAT	TITLE	AW W/N Y	AUTHOR
6	Year's Best Science Fiction, 4th	LOC-W 88	DOZOIS, Gardner
6	Best SF and Fantasy of the Year #16	LOC-N 88	CARR, Terry
6	Dark Descent, The	LOC-N 88	HARTWELL, David G
6	In the Field of Fire	LOC-N 88	DANN, Jeanne van Buren
6	Universe 17	LOC-N 88	CARR, Terry
6	Worlds of Wonder	LOC-N 88	SILVERBERG, Robert
7	Watchmen	LOC-W 88	MOORE, Alan
7	Anatomy of Wonder 3rd	LOC-N 88	BARRON, Neil
7	Culture Made Stupid	LOC-N 88	WELLER, Tom
7	Michael Whelan's Works of Wonder	LOC-N 88	WHELAN, Michael
7	SF, Fantasy & Horror 1986	LOC-N 88	BROWN, Charles N
7	Wizardry and Wild Romance	LOC-N 88	MOORCOCK, Michael
9	War for the Oaks	LOC-W 88	BULL, Emma
9	Arrows of the Queen	LOC-N 88	LACKEY, Mercedes
9	In Conquest Born	LOC-N 88	FRIEDMAN, C S
9	Liege-Killer	LOC-N 88	HINZ, Christopher
9	Mindplayers	LOC-N 88	CADIGAN, Pat
9	Net, The	LOC-N 88	MacGREGOR, Loren J
11	Seventh Son	LOC-W 88	CARD, Orson Scott
11	Aegypt	LOC-N 88	CROWLEY, John
11	Lincoln's Dreams	LOC-N 88	WILLIS, Connie
11	On Stranger Tides	LOC-N 88	POWERS, Tim
11	Sign of Chaos	LOC-N 88	ZELAZNY, Roger
11	Weaveworld	LOC-N 88	BARKER, Clive
1	Cyteen	LOC-W 89	CHERRYH, C J
1	Eternity	LOC-N 89	BEAR, Greg
1	Gold Coast, The	LOC-N 89	ROBINSON, Kim Stanley
1	Islands in the Net	LOC-N 89	STERLING, Bruce
1	Mona Lisa Overdrive	LOC-N 89	GIBSON, William
1	Prelude to Foundation	LOC-N 89	ASIMOV, Isaac
2	Scalehunter's Beautiful Daughter, The	LOC-W 89	SHEPARD, Lucius
2	Color of Neanderthal Eyes, The	LOC-N 89	TIPTREE, James Jr
2	Journals of the Plague Years, The	LOC-N 89	SPINRAD, Norman
2	Last of the Winnebagos, The	LOC-N 89	WILLIS, Connie
2	Surfacing	LOC-N 89	WILLIAMS, Walter Jon
2	We Are for the Dark	LOC-N 89	SILVERBERG, Robert
3	Function of Dream Sleep, The	LOC-W 89	ELLISON, Harlan
3	Do Ya, Do Ya, Wanna Dance	LOC-N 89	WALDROP, Howard
3	Dowser	LOC-N 89	CARD, Orson Scott
3	Earth Doth Like a Snake Renew, The	LOC-N 89	TIPTREE, James Jr
3	Glacier	LOC-N 89	ROBINSON, Kim Stanley
3	Schrodinger's Kitten	LOC-N 89	EFFINGER, George Alec
4	Eidolons	LOC-W 89	ELLISON, Harlan
4	Giving Plague, The	LOC-N 89	BRIN, David
4	Kirinyaga	LOC-N 89	RESNICK, Mike
4	Midwinter's Tale, A	LOC-N 89	SWANWICK, Michael
4	Wild, Wild Horses	LOC-N 89	WALDROP, Howard
4	Year's Best Science Fiction, 5th	LOC-N 89	DOZOIS, Gardner

LOCUS MAGAZINE AWARDS

CAT	TITLE	AW W/N Y	AUTHOR
5	Angry Candy	LOC-W 89	ELLISON, Harlan
5	Crown of Stars	LOC-N 89	TIPTREE, James Jr
5	Empire Dreams	LOC-N 89	McDONALD, Ian
5	John the Balladeer	LOC-N 89	WELLMAN, Manly Wade
5	Knight and the Knave of Swords, The	LOC-N 89	LEIBER, Fritz
5	Other Americas	LOC-N 89	SPINRAD, Norman
6	Full Spectrum	LOC-W 89	ARONICA, Lou
6	Man-Kzin Wars, The	LOC-N 89	NIVEN, Larry
6	Terry's Universe	LOC-N 89	MEECHAM, Beth
6	Wild Cards IV: Aces Abroad	LOC-N 89	MARTIN, George R R
6	Year's Best Fantasy and Horror 1st	LOC-N 89	DATLOW, Ellen
6	Youthful Folly	LOC-N 89	SHEPARD, Lucius
7	First Maitz	LOC-W 89	MAITZ, Don
7	Bare Bones:Convers'ns on Terror w/S King	LOC-N 89	UNDERWOOD, Tim
7	Bio of an Ogre:Autobiog of Piers Anthony	LOC-N 89	ANTHONY, Piers
7	Motion of Light in Water, The: Sex & SF	LOC-N 89	DELANY, Samuel R
7	New Encyclopedia of Science Fiction, The	LOC-N 89	GUNN, James E
7	Strokes: Essays and Reviews 1966-1986	LOC-N 89	CLUTE, John
9	Desolation Road	LOC-W 89	McDONALD, Ian
9	Armageddon Blues, The	LOC-N 89	MORAN, Daniel Keys
9	Dragon Prince	LOC-N 89	RAWN, Melanie
9	Metrophage	LOC-N 89	KADREY, Richard
9	Sheepfarmer's Daughter	LOC-N 89	MOON, Elizabeth
9	Walkabout Woman	LOC-N 89	ROESSNER, Michaela
10	Those Who Hunt the Night	LOC-W 89	HAMBLY, Barbara
10	Faerie Tale	LOC-N 89	FEIST, Raymond E
10	Koko	LOC-N 89	STRAUB, Peter
10	Queen of the Damned	LOC-N 89	RICE, Anne
10	Silence of the Lambs, The	LOC-N 89	HARRIS, Thomas
10	Stinger	LOC-N 89	McCAMMON, Robert R
11	Red Prophet	LOC-W 89	CARD, Orson Scott
11	King of the Murgos	LOC-N 89	EDDINGS, David
11	Last Coin, The	LOC-N 89	BLAYLOCK, James P
11	Paladin, The	LOC-N 89	CHERRYH, C J
11	There Are Doors	LOC-N 89	WOLFE, Gene
11	Unicorn Mountain	LOC-N 89	BISHOP, Michael
1	Hyperion	LOC-W 90	SIMMONS, Dan
1	Boat of A Million Years	LOC-N 90	ANDERSON, Poul
1	Fire in the Sun, A	LOC-N 90	EFFINGER, George Alec
1	Grass	LOC-N 90	TEPPER, Sheri S
1	RAMA II	LOC-N 90	CLARKE, Arthur C
1	Rimrunners	LOC-N 90	CHERRYH, C J
1	Tides of Light	LOC-N 90	BENFORD, Gregory

CAT	T I T L E	AW W/N Y	A U T H O R
2	Father of Stones, The	LOC-W 90	SHEPARD, Lucius
2	Dozen Tough Jobs, A	LOC-N 90	WALDROP, Howard
2	Labyrinth	LOC-N 90	BUJOLD, Lois McMaster
2	Mountains of Mourning, The	LOC-N 90	BUJOLD, Lois McMaster
2	Pageant Wagon	LOC-N 90	CARD, Orson Scott
2	Time-Out	LOC-N 90	WILLIS, Connie
2	Tiny Tango	LOC-N 90	MOFFETT, Judith
3	Dogwalker	LOC-W 90	CARD, Orson Scott
3	At the Rialto	LOC-N 90	WILLIS, Connie
3	Bound For Glory	LOC-N 90	SHEPARD, Lucius
3	Enter a Soldier, Later Enter Another	LOC-N 90	SILVERBERG, Robert
3	For I Have Touched the Sky	LOC-N 90	RESNICK, Mike
3	Price of Oranges, The	LOC-N 90	KRESS, Nancy
3	Sisters	LOC-N 90	BEAR, Greg
4	Lost Boys	LOC-W 90	CARD, Orson Scott
4	Year's Best Science Fiction, 6th	LOC-W 90	DOZOIS, Gardner
4	Boobs	LOC-N 90	CHARNAS, Suzy McKee
4	Dilemna	LOC-N 90	WILLIS, Connie
4	Dori Bangs	LOC-N 90	STERLING, Bruce
4	Edge of the World, The	LOC-N 90	SWANWICK, Michael
4	Power and the Passion, The	LOC-N 90	CADIGAN, Pat
4	Privacy	LOC-N 90	BRIN, David
5	Patterns	LOC-W 90	CADIGAN, Pat
5	Borders of Infinity	LOC-N 90	BUJOLD, Lois McMaster
5	Crystal Express	LOC-N 90	STERLING, Bruce
5	Endangered Species	LOC-N 90	WOLFE, Gene
5	Folk on the Fringe, The	LOC-N 90	CARD, Orson Scott
5	Frost and Fire	LOC-N 90	ZELAZNY, Roger
5	Tangents	LOC-N 90	BEAR, Greg
6	Blood is Not Enough	LOC-N 90	DATLOW, Ellen
6	Foundations's Friends	LOC-N 90	GREENBERG, Martin A
6	Full Spectrum 2	LOC-N 90	ARONICA, Lou
6	Razored Saddles	LOC-N 90	LANSDALE, Joe R
6	What Might Have Been Vol 2	LOC-N 90	BENFORD, Gregory
6	Year's Best Fantasy and Horror 2nd	LOC-N 90	DATLOW, Ellen
7	Grumbles From the Grave	LOC-W 90	HEINLEIN, Robert A
7	Astounding Days	LOC-N 90	CLARKE, Arthur C
7	Dancing at the Edge of the World	LOC-N 90	LeGUIN, Ursula K
7	Divine Invasions	LOC-N 90	SUTIN, Lawrence
7	Giger's Alien	LOC-N 90	GIGER, H R
7	SF, Fantasy & Horror 1988	LOC-N 90	BROWN, Charles N
7	World Beyond the Hill, The	LOC-N 90	PANSHIN, Alexei
9	Orbital Decay	LOC-W 90	STEELE, Allan
9	Laying the Music to Rest	LOC-N 90	SMITH, Dean Wesley
9	On My Way to Paradise	LOC-N 90	WOLVERTON, Dave
9	Strange Invasion	LOC-N 90	KANDEL, Michael
9	Sunglasses After Dark	LOC-N 90	COLLINS, Nancy A
9	Tides of God, The	LOC-N 90	REYNOLDS, Ted

CAT	TITLE	AW W/N Y	AUTHOR
10	Carrion Comfort	LOC-W 90	SIMMONS, Dan
10	Dark Half, The	LOC-N 90	KING, Stephen
10	Geek Love	LOC-N 90	DUNN, Katherine
10	Great and Secret Show	LOC-N 90	BARKER, Clive
10	Midnight	LOC-N 90	KOONTZ, Dean R
10	Wolf's Hour, The	LOC-N 90	McCAMMON, Robert R
11	Prentice Alvin	LOC-W 90	CARD, Orson Scott
11	Dream Baby	LOC-N 90	McALLISTER, Bruce
11	Lyonesse: Madouc	LOC-N 90	VANCE, Jack
11	Rusalka	LOC-N 90	CHERRYH, C J
11	Soldier of Arete	LOC-N 90	WOLFE, Gene
11	Stress of Her Regard, The	LOC-N 90	POWERS, Tim
11	White Jenna	LOC-N 90	YOLEN, Jane
1	Fall of Hyperion, The	LOC-W 91	SIMMONS, Dan
1	Difference Engine, The	LOC-N 91	GIBSON, William
1	Earth	LOC-N 91	BRIN, David
1	Jurassic Park	LOC-N 91	CRICHTON, Michael
1	Queen of Angels	LOC-N 91	BEAR, Greg
1	Quiet Pools, The	LOC-N 91	KUBE-McDOWELL, Michael P
1	Redshift Rendezvous	LOC-N 91	STITH, John E
1	Vor Game, The	LOC-N 91	BUJOLD, Lois McMaster
1	Voyage to the Red Planet	LOC-N 91	BISSON, Ted
2	Short, Sharp, Shock, A	LOC-W 91	ROBINSON, Kim Stanley
2	Year's Best Science Fiction, 7th	LOC-W 91	DOZOIS, Gardner
2	Bones	LOC-N 91	MURPHY, Pat
2	Bully!	LOC-N 91	RESNICK, Mike
2	Fool to Believe	LOC-N 91	CADIGAN, Pat
2	Heads	LOC-N 91	BEAR, Greg
2	Hemingway Hoax, The	LOC-N 91	HALDEMAN, Joe
2	Kalimantan	LOC-N 91	SHEPARD, Lucius
2	Lion Time in Timbuctoo	LOC-N 91	SILVERBERG, Robert
2	Mr. Boy	LOC-N 91	KELLY, James Patrick
2	Skull City	LOC-N 91	SHEPARD, Lucius
2	Weatherman	LOC-N 91	BUJOLD, Lois McMaster
3	Entropy's Bed at Midnight	LOC-W 91	SIMMONS, Dan
3	Braver Thing, A	LOC-N 91	SHEFFIELD, Charles
3	Coon Rolled Down and Ruptured...	LOC-N 91	HUGH, Dafydd ab
3	Dr. Pak's Preschool	LOC-N 91	BRIN, David
3	Shobie's Story, The	LOC-N 91	LeGUIN, Ursula K
3	Tower of Babylon	LOC-N 91	CHIANG, Ted
4	Bears Discover Fire	LOC-W 91	BISSON, Terry
4	Cibola	LOC-N 91	WILLIS, Connie
4	First Time, The	LOC-N 91	JETER, K W
4	Godspeed	LOC-N 91	SHEFFIELD, Charles
4	Lieserl	LOC-N 91	FOWLER, Karen Joy
4	Love and Sex Among the Vertebrates	LOC-N 91	MURPHY, Pat
4	Utility Man, The	LOC-N 91	REED, Robert
4	VRM-547	LOC-N 91	THOMPSON, W R

CAT	TITLE	AW W/N Y	AUTHOR
5	Maps in a Mirror	LOC-W 91	CARD, Orson Scott
5	Four Past Midnight	LOC-N 91	KING, Stephen
5	Her Smoke Rose Up Forever	LOC-N 91	TIPTREE, James Jr
5	Leiber Chronicles, The	LOC-N 91	LEIBER, Fritz
5	N-Space	LOC-N 91	NIVEN, Larry
5	Prayers to Broken Stones	LOC-N 91	SIMMONS, Dan
6	1990 Annual World's Best SF	LOC-N 91	WOLHEIM, Donald A
6	Alien Sex	LOC-N 91	DATLOW, Ellen
6	Great SF Stories #21, The	LOC-N 91	ASIMOV, Isaac
6	Nebula Awards #24	LOC-N 91	BISHOP, Michael
6	Universe 1	LOC-N 91	CARR, Terry
6	Year's Best Fantasy and Horror 3rd	LOC-N 91	DATLOW, Ellen
7	SFWA Handbook: The Prof Writer's Guide	LOC-W 91	RUSCH, Kristine Kathryn
7	Bury My Heart at W.H. Smiths	LOC-N 91	ALDISS, Brian W
7	Hollywood Gothic	LOC-N 91	SKAL, David J
7	How to Write Science Fiction and Fantasy	LOC-N 91	CARD, Orson Scott
7	Science Fiction in the Real World	LOC-N 91	SPINRAD, Norman
9	In the Country of The Blind	LOC-W 91	FLYNN, Michael F
9	An Abyss of Light	LOC-N 91	O'NEAL, Kathleen M
9	Arachne	LOC-N 91	MASON, Lisa
9	Black Snow Days	LOC-N 91	O'KEEFE, Claudia
9	Golden Fleece	LOC-N 91	SAWYER, Robert J
9	Wintersong	LOC-N 91	HAND, Elizabeth
10	Witching Hour, The	LOC-W 91	RICE, Anne
10	Mary Reilly	LOC-N 91	MARTIN, Valerie
10	Moon Dance	LOC-N 91	SOMTOW, S P
10	Stand, The: The Complete, Uncut Edition	LOC-N 91	KING, Stephen
10	Tempter	LOC-N 91	COLLINS, A
10	Werewolves of London	LOC-N 91	STABLEFORD, Brian
11	Tehanu: The Last Book of Earthsea	LOC-W 91	LeGUIN, Ursula K
11	Eye of the World, The	LOC-N 91	JORDON, Robert
11	Good Omens	LOC-N 91	PRATCHETT, Terry
11	Only Begotten Daughter	LOC-N 91	MORROW, James
11	Thomas the Rhymer	LOC-N 91	KUSHNER, Ellen
11	Tigana	LOC-N 91	KAY, Guy Gavriel
1	Barrayar	LOC-W 92	BUJOLD, Lois McMaster
1	All the Weyrs of Pern	LOC-N 92	McCAFFREY, Anne
1	Bone Dance	LOC-N 92	BULL, Emma
1	Stations of the Tide	LOC-N 92	SWANWICK, Michael
1	Summer Queen, The	LOC-N 92	VINGE, Joan D
1	Xenocide	LOC-N 92	CARD, Orson Scott
2	Gallery of His Dreams, The	LOC-W 92	RUSCH, Kristine Kathryn
2	And Wild For To Hold	LOC-N 92	KRESS, Nancy
2	Beggars in Spain	LOC-N 92	KRESS, Nancy
2	Griffin's Egg	LOC-N 92	SWANWICK, Michael
2	Jack	LOC-N 92	WILLIS, Connie
2	Star of the Sea	LOC-N 92	ANDERSON, Poul

CAT	TITLE	AW W/N Y	AUTHOR
3	All Dracula's Children	LOC-W 92	SIMMONS, Dan
3	Black Glass	LOC-N 92	FOWLER, Karen Joy
3	Fin de Cycle	LOC-N 92	WALDROP, Howard
3	Gold	LOC-N 92	ASIMOV, Isaac
3	Matter's End	LOC-N 92	BENFORD, Gregory
3	Miracle	LOC-N 92	WILLIS, Connie
4	Buffalo	LOC-W 92	KESSEL, John
4	Angels in Love	LOC-N 92	KOJA, Kathe
4	Daughter Earth	LOC-N 92	MORROW, James
4	In the Late Cretaceous	LOC-N 92	WILLIS, Connie
4	Press Ann	LOC-N 92	BISSON, Terry
4	Vinland the Dream	LOC-N 92	ROBINSON, Kim Stanley
4	Year's Best Science Fiction, 8th	LOC-N 92	DOZOIS, Gardner
5	Night of the Cooters: More Neat Stories	LOC-W 92	WALDROP, Howard
5	Best of James H. Schmitz, The	LOC-N 92	SCHMITZ, James H
5	Gravity's Angels	LOC-N 92	SWANWICK, Michael
5	Mirabile	LOC-N 92	KAGAN, Janet
5	Playgrounds of the Mind	LOC-N 92	NIVEN, Larry
5	Remaking History	LOC-N 92	ROBINSON, Kim Stanley
6	Full Spectrum 3	LOC-W 92	ARONICA, Lou
6	Man-Kzin Wars IV	LOC-N 92	NIVEN, Larry
6	What Might Have Been Vol 3: Alt Wars	LOC-N 92	BENFORD, Gregory
6	Whisper of Blood, A	LOC-N 92	DATLOW, Ellen
6	Year's Best Fantasy and Horror 4th	LOC-N 92	DATLOW, Ellen
7	SF: The Early Years	LOC-W 92	BLEILER, Everett F
7	Clive Barker's Shadows in Eden	LOC-N 92	JONES, Stephen
7	Griffin & Sabine	LOC-N 92	BANTOCK, Nick
7	Pish, Posh, Said Hieronymous Bosch	LOC-N 92	DILLON, Leo
7	SF, Fantasy & Horror 1990	LOC-N 92	BROWN, Charles N
7	World of Charles Addams, The	LOC-N 92	ADDAMS, Charles
8	Cipher, The	LOC-W 92	KOJA, Kathe
8	Alien Blues	LOC-N 92	HIGHTOWER, Lynn S
8	Carve the Sky	LOC-N 92	JABLOKOV, Alexander
8	Halo	LOC-N 92	MADDOX, Tom
8	Raft	LOC-N 92	BAXTER, Stephen M
8	White Mists of Power, The	LOC-N 92	RUSCH, Kristine Kathryn
10	Summer of Night	LOC-W 92	SIMMONS, Dan
10	Blood Price	LOC-N 92	HUFF, Tanya
10	Dark Towers III, The: The Waste Lands	LOC-N 92	KING, Stephen
10	Imajica	LOC-N 92	BARKER, Clive
10	In the Blood	LOC-N 92	COLLINS, Nancy A
10	M.D., The	LOC-N 92	DISCH, Thomas M
11	Beauty	LOC-W 92	TEPPER, Sheri S
11	Eight Skilled Gentlemen	LOC-N 92	HUGHART, Barry
11	Hereafter Gang, The	LOC-N 92	BARRETT, Neal Jr
11	King of the Morning, Queen of Day	LOC-N 92	McDONALD, Ian
11	Little Country, The	LOC-N 92	de LINT, Charles
11	Rainbow Abyss, The	LOC-N 92	HAMBLY, Barbara

NEBULA AWARDS

These awards were presented annually by the Science Fiction Writers of America (SFWA). Founded by Damon Knight, the SFWA is composed of about 500 members, including most of the major writers.

SFWA members nominate throughout the year and a cumulative list is supplied periodically to the membership. Early the following year, a vote my mail is held. In some years, two ballots were used, the first included all nominees, then, a second run-off ballot. Beginning in 1974, a committee reviews the nominations and decides on which stories are to appear upon the single ballot.

In order to raise funds, the SFWA has created a series of anthologies. The series consists of Nebula winners with runners-up and are selected by each anthology's editor; because of length and commercial considerations, the winning novel is excluded.

In comparing Nebula and Hugo Awards, it must be noted that a different dating system is used. The Nebula Awards are presented approximately six months before the Hugo Awards and are dated according to the year in which the stories were published rather than the year in which the awards are actually given. For the Hugo Awards, the reverse is true.

While there is a major difference in the method of selecting winners of both these awards, there is a surprising level of similarity between them. There is no question that the Nebula, along with the Hugo are the premiere awards in Science Fiction.

NEBULA AWARDS

CAT	TITLE	AW W/N Y	AUTHOR
1	Hospital Station	NEB-N 62	WHITE, James
1	Davy	NEB-N 64	PANGBORN, Edgar
1	Nova Express	NEB-N 64	BURROUGHS, William S
1	Dune	NEB-W 65	HERBERT, Frank
1	All Flesh is Grass	NEB-N 65	SIMAK, Clifford D
1	Clone, The	NEB-N 65	THOMAS, Theodore L
1	Doctor Bloodmoney	NEB-N 65	DICK, Philip K
1	Escape Orbit	NEB-N 65	WHITE, James
1	Genocides, The	NEB-N 65	DISCH, Thomas M
1	Nova Express	NEB-N 65	BURROUGHS, William S
1	Plague of Demons, A	NEB-N 65	LAUMER, Keith
1	Rogue Dragon	NEB-N 65	DAVIDSON, Avram
1	Ship Sailed the Time Stream	NEB-N 65	EDMONDSON, G C
1	Star Fox	NEB-N 65	ANDERSON, Poul
1	Three Stigmata Palmer Eldritch	NEB-N 65	DICK, Philip K
2	He Who Shapes	NEB-W 65	ZELAZNY, Roger
2	Saliva Tree	NEB-W 65	ALDISS, Brian W
2	Ballad of Beta-2	NEB-N 65	DELANY, Samuel R
2	Mercuryman, The	NEB-N 65	MacAPP, C C
2	On the Storm Planet	NEB-N 65	SMITH, Cordwainer
2	Research Alpha	NEB-N 65	VAN VOGT, A E
2	Rogue Dragon	NEB-N 65	DAVIDSON, Avram
2	Under Two Moons	NEB-N 65	POHL, Frederik
3	Doors of His Face...	NEB-W 65	ZELAZNY, Roger
3	102 H-Bombs	NEB-N 65	DISCH, Thomas M
3	Adventure of the Extraterrestrial	NEB-N 65	REYNOLDS, Mack
3	At The Institute	NEB-N 65	KAGAN, Norman
3	Decision Makers, The	NEB-N 65	GREEN, Joseph
3	Earth Merchants, The	NEB-N 65	KAGAN, Norman
3	Four Ghosts in Hamlet	NEB-N 65	LEIBER, Fritz
3	Goblin Night	NEB-N 65	SCHMITZ, James H
3	Half a Loaf	NEB-N 65	FITZPATRICK, R C
3	Laugh Along With Franz	NEB-N 65	KAGAN, Norman
3	Life of Your Time, The	NEB-N 65	KARAGEORGE, Michael
3	Maiden Voyage	NEB-N 65	SCHUTZ, J W
3	Masculine Revolt, The	NEB-N 65	TENN, William
3	Masque of the Red Shift	NEB-N 65	SABERHAGEN, Fred
3	Planet of Forgetting	NEB-N 65	SCHMITZ, James H
3	Shall We Have a Little Talk?	NEB-N 65	SHECKLEY, Robert
3	Shipwrecked Hotel, The	NEB-N 65	BLISH, James
3	Small One	NEB-N 65	McCARTY, E Clayton
3	Vanishing Point	NEB-N 65	BRAND, Jonathan

NEBULA AWARDS

CAT	TITLE	AW W/N Y	AUTHOR
4	Repent Harlequin, Said the Ticktockman	NEB-W 65	ELLISON, Harlan
4	Balance Ecology	NEB-N 65	SCHMITZ, James H
4	Becalmed in Hell	NEB-N 65	NIVEN, Larry
4	Better Mousehold, A	NEB-N 65	PANGBORN, Edgar
4	Better Than Ever	NEB-N 65	KIRS, Alex
4	Calling Dr. Clockwork	NEB-N 65	GOULART, Ron
4	Come to Venus Melancholy	NEB-N 65	DISCH, Thomas M
4	Computers Don't Argue	NEB-N 65	DICKSON, Gordon R
4	Cyclops	NEB-N 65	LEIBER, Fritz
4	Devil Car	NEB-N 65	ZELAZNY, Roger
4	Eight Billion, The	NEB-N 65	WILSON, Richard
4	Eyes Do More Than See	NEB-N 65	ASIMOV, Isaac
4	Few Kindred Spirits, A	NEB-N 65	CHRISTOPHER, John
4	Founding Father	NEB-N 65	ASIMOV, Isaac
4	Games	NEB-N 65	BARTHELME, Donald
4	Good New Days, The	NEB-N 65	LEIBER, Fritz
4	House the Blakeneys Built, The	NEB-N 65	DAVIDSON, Avram
4	In Our Block	NEB-N 65	LAFFERTY, R A
4	Inside Man	NEB-N 65	GOLD, H L
4	Keep Them Happy	NEB-N 65	ROHRER, Robert
4	Leader For Yesterday, A	NEB-N 65	REYNOLDS, Mack
4	Lord Moon	NEB-N 65	BEAUCLERK, Jane
4	Mischief Maker, The	NEB-N 65	OLIN, Richard
4	Of One Mind	NEB-N 65	DURHAM, James
4	Over the River and Through the Trees	NEB-N 65	SIMAK, Clifford D
4	Peacock King, The	NEB-N 65	WHITE, Ted
4	Slow Tuesday Night	NEB-N 65	LAFFERTY, R A
4	Souvenir	NEB-N 65	BALLARD, J G
4	Though A Sparrow Fall	NEB-N 65	NICHOLS, Scott
4	Uncollected Works	NEB-N 65	CARTER, Lin
4	Wrong-Way Street	NEB-N 65	NIVEN, Larry
1	Babel-17	NEB-W 66	DELANY, Samuel R
1	Flowers for Algernon	NEB-W 66	KEYES, Daniel
1	Moon is a Harsh Mistress	NEB-N 66	HEINLEIN, Robert A
2	Last Castle, The	NEB-W 66	VANCE, Jack
2	Alchemist, The	NEB-N 66	HARNESS, Charles L
2	Clash of Star Kings	NEB-N 66	DAVIDSON, Avram
3	Call Him Lord	NEB-W 66	SPENCER, W
3	An Ornament to His Profession	NEB-W 66	HARNESS, Charles L
3	Apology to Inky	NEB-N 66	GREEN, Robert M Jr
3	Eskimo Invasion, The	NEB-N 66	HOWARD, Hayden
3	Moment of the Storm, This	NEB-N 66	ZELAZNY, Roger
4	Secret Place, The	NEB-W 66	McKENNA, Richard
4	Light of Other Days	NEB-N 66	SHAW, Bob
4	Man In His Time	NEB-N 66	ALDISS, Brian W

CAT	T I T L E	AW W/N Y	A U T H O R
1	Einstein Intersection	NEB-W 67	DELANY, Samuel R
1	Chton	NEB-N 67	ANTHONY, Piers
1	Eskimo Invasion, The	NEB-N 67	HOWARD, Hayden
1	Lord of Light	NEB-N 67	ZELAZNY, Roger
1	Productions of Time	NEB-N 67	BRUNNER, John
1	Thorns	NEB-N 67	SILVERBERG, Robert
2	Behold the Man	NEB-W 67	MOORCOCK, Michael
2	Hawksbill Station	NEB-N 67	SILVERBERG, Robert
2	If All Men Were Brothers Would You Let..	NEB-N 67	STURGEON, Theodore
2	Riders of the Purple Wage	NEB-N 67	FARMER, Philip Jose
2	Weyr Search	NEB-N 67	McCAFFREY, Anne
3	Gonna Roll Those Bones	NEB-W 67	LEIBER, Fritz
3	Flatlander	NEB-N 67	NIVEN, Larry
3	Keys to December, The	NEB-N 67	ZELAZNY, Roger
3	Mortal Mountain, The	NEB-N 67	ZELAZNY, Roger
3	Pretty Maggie Moneyeyes	NEB-N 67	ELLISON, Harlan
4	Aye, and Gomorrah	NEB-W 67	DELANY, Samuel R
4	Answering Service	NEB-N 67	LEIBER, Fritz
4	Baby, You Were Great	NEB-N 67	WILHELM, Kate
4	Doctor, The	NEB-N 67	THOMAS, Theodore L
4	Driftglass	NEB-N 67	DELANY, Samuel R
4	Earthwoman	NEB-N 67	BRETNOR, Reginald
1	Rite of Passage	NEB-W 68	PANSHIN, Alexei
1	Black Easter	NEB-N 68	BLISH, James
1	Do Androids Dream of Electric Sheep?	NEB-N 68	DICK, Philip K
1	Masks of Time, The	NEB-N 68	SILVERBERG, Robert
1	Past Master	NEB-N 68	LAFFERTY, R A
1	Stand on Zanzibar	NEB-N 68	BRUNNER, John
2	Dragonrider	NEB-W 68	McCAFFREY, Anne
2	Day Beyond Forever, The	NEB-N 68	LAUMER, Keith
2	Hawk Among The Sparrows	NEB-N 68	McLAUGHLIN, Dean
2	Lines of Power	NEB-N 68	DELANY, Samuel R
2	Nightwings	NEB-N 68	SILVERBERG, Robert
3	Mother of the World	NEB-W 68	WILSON, Richard
3	Final War	NEB-N 68	O'DONNELL, K M
3	Guerilla Trees, The	NEB-N 68	HOLLIS, H H
3	Listeners, The	NEB-N 68	GUNN, James E
3	Once There Was a Giant	NEB-N 68	LAUMER, Keith
3	Sharing of Flesh, The	NEB-N 68	ANDERSON, Poul
3	Total Environment	NEB-N 68	ALDISS, Brian W
4	Planners, The	NEB-W 68	WILHELM, Kate
4	Dance of the Changer and the Three, The	NEB-N 68	CARR, Terry
4	Idiot's Mate	NEB-N 68	TAYLOR, Robert
4	Kyrie	NEB-N 68	ANDERSON, Poul
4	Masks	NEB-N 68	KNIGHT, Damon
4	Sword Game	NEB-N 68	HOLLIS, H H

NEBULA AWARDS

CAT	TITLE	AW W/N Y	AUTHOR
1	Left Hand of Darkness, The	NEB-W 69	LEGUIN, Ursula K
1	Age of the Pussyfoot	NEB-N 69	POHL, Frederik
1	Bug Jack Barrow	NEB-N 69	SPINRAD, Norman
1	Isle of the Dead	NEB-N 69	ZELAZNY, Roger
1	Jagged Orbit, The	NEB-N 69	BRUNNER, John
1	Slaughterhouse-Five	NEB-N 69	VONNEGUT, Kurt Jr
1	Up the Line	NEB-N 69	SILVERBERG, Robert
2	Boy and His Dog, A	NEB-W 69	ELLISON, Harlan
2	Dramatic Mission	NEB-N 69	McCAFFREY, Anne
2	Probable Cause	NEB-N 69	HARNESS, Charles L
2	Ship of Shadows	NEB-N 69	LEIBER, Fritz
2	To Jorslem	NEB-N 69	SILVERBERG, Robert
3	Time Considered as a Helix...	NEB-W 69	DELANY, Samuel R
3	Big Flash, The	NEB-N 69	SPINRAD, Norman
3	Deeper Than the Darkness	NEB-N 69	BENFORD, Gregory
3	Nine Lives	NEB-N 69	LeGUIN, Ursula K
4	Passengers	NEB-W 69	SILVERBERG, Robert
4	Last Flight of Dr. Ain, The	NEB-N 69	TIPTREE, James Jr
4	Man Who Learned Loving, The	NEB-N 69	STURGEON, Theodore
4	Not Long Before the End	NEB-N 69	NIVEN, Larry
4	Shattered Like a Glass Goblin	NEB-N 69	ELLISON, Harlan
1	Ringworld	NEB-W 70	NIVEN, Larry
1	And Chaos Died	NEB-N 70	RUSS, Joanna
1	Fourth Mansions	NEB-N 70	LAFFERTY, R A
1	Steel Crocodile, The	NEB-N 70	COMPTON, D G
1	Tower of Glass, The	NEB-N 70	SILVERBERG, Robert
1	Year of the Quiet Sun	NEB-N 70	TUCKER, Wilson
2	Ill Met in Lankhmar	NEB-W 70	LEIBER, Fritz
2	April Fool's Day Forever	NEB-N 70	WILHELM, Kate
2	Fatal Fulfillment, The	NEB-N 70	ANDERSON, Poul
2	Region Between, The	NEB-N 70	ELLISON, Harlan
2	Thing in the Stone, The	NEB-N 70	SIMAK, Clifford D
3	Slow Sculpture	NEB-W 70	STURGEON, Theodore
3	Asian Shores	NEB-N 70	DISCH, Thomas M
3	Continued on Next Rock	NEB-N 70	LAFFERTY, R A
3	Dear Aunt Annie	NEB-N 70	EKLUND, Gordon
3	Second Inquisition, The	NEB-N 70	RUSS, Joanna
3	Shaker Revival	NEB-N 70	JONAS, Gerald
4	By the Falls	NEB-N 70	HARRISON, Harry
4	Cold Night Dark With Snow, A	NEB-N 70	WILHELM, Kate
4	Creation of Bennie Good, The	NEB-N 70	SALLIS, James
4	Dream at Noonday, A	NEB-N 70	DOZOIS, Gardner
4	Entire and Perfect Chrysolite	NEB-N 70	LAFFERTY, R A
4	In the Queue	NEB-N 70	LAUMER, Keith
4	Island of Dr. Death, The	NEB-N 70	WOLFE, Gene

NEBULA AWARDS

CAT	TITLE	AW W/N Y	AUTHOR
1	Time of Changes, A	NEB-W 71	SILVERBERG, Robert
1	Byworlder	NEB-N 71	ANDERSON, Poul
1	Devil is Dead, The	NEB-N 71	LAFFERTY, R A
1	Half Past Human	NEB-N 71	BASS, T J
1	Lathe of Heaven, The	NEB-N 71	LEGUIN, Ursula K
1	Margaret and I	NEB-N 71	WILHELM, Kate
2	Missing Man, The	NEB-W 71	MacLEAN, Katherine
2	Being There	NEB-N 71	KOSINSKI, Jerry
2	God House, The	NEB-N 71	ROBERTS, Keith
2	Infinity Box, The	NEB-N 71	WILHELM, Kate
2	Plastic Abyss, The	NEB-N 71	WILHELM, Kate
3	Queen of Air and Darkness, The	NEB-W 71	ANDERSON, Poul
3	Encounter, The	NEB-N 71	WILHELM, Kate
3	Mount Charity	NEB-N 71	PANGBORN, Edgar
3	Poor Man, Beggar Man	NEB-N 71	RUSS, Joanna
3	Special Kind of Morning	NEB-N 71	DOZOIS, Gardner
4	Good News from the Vatican	NEB-W 71	SILVERBERG, Robert
4	Heathen God	NEB-N 71	ZEBROWSKI, George
4	Horse of Air	NEB-N 71	DOZOIS, Gardner
4	Last Ghost, The	NEB-N 71	GOLDIN, Stephen
1	Gods Themselves, The	NEB-W 72	ASIMOV, Isaac
1	Book of Skulls, The	NEB-N 72	SILVERBERG, Robert
1	Dying Inside	NEB-N 72	SILVERBERG, Robert
1	Iron Dream, The	NEB-N 72	SPINRAD, Norman
1	Sheep Look Up, The	NEB-N 72	BRUNNER, John
1	What Entropy Means to Me	NEB-N 72	EFFINGER, George Alec
1	When Harlie Was One	NEB-N 72	GERROLD, David
2	Meeting with Medusa, A	NEB-W 72	CLARKE, Arthur C
2	Fifth Head of Cerberus, The	NEB-N 72	WOLFE, Gene
2	Gold at the Starbow's End, The	NEB-N 72	POHL, Frederik
2	Son of the Morning	NEB-N 72	GOTLIEB, Phyllis
2	With t/Bentfin Boomer Boys on Little Old	NEB-N 72	LUPOFF, Richard A
2	Word for World is Forest, The	NEB-N 72	LeGUIN, Ursula K
3	Goat Song	NEB-W 72	ANDERSON, Poul
3	Animal Fair, The	NEB-N 72	BESTER, Alfred
3	Basilisk	NEB-N 72	ELLISON, Harlan
3	Funeral, The	NEB-N 72	WILHELM, Kate
3	In the Deadlands	NEB-N 72	GERROLD, David
3	Kingdom By the Sea, A	NEB-N 72	DOZOIS, Gardner
3	Patron of the Arts	NEB-N 72	ROTSLER, William
4	When it Changed	NEB-W 72	RUSS, Joanna
4	Against the Lafayette Escadrille	NEB-N 72	WOLFE, Gene
4	And I Awoke & Found Me Here t/Cold Hill'	NEB-N 72	TIPTREE, James Jr
4	On the Downhill Side	NEB-N 72	ELLISON, Harlan
4	Shaffery Among the Immortals	NEB-N 72	POHL, Frederik

NEBULA AWARDS

CAT	TITLE	AW W/N Y	AUTHOR
1	Rendezvous with Rama	NEB-W 73	CLARKE, Arthur C
1	Gravity's Rainbow	NEB-N 73	PYNCHON, Thomas
1	Man Who Folded Himself, The	NEB-N 73	GERROLD, David
1	People of the Wind, The	NEB-N 73	ANDERSON, Poul
1	Time Enough For Love	NEB-N 73	HEINLEIN, Robert A
2	Death of Doctor Island, The	NEB-W 73	WOLFE, Gene
2	Chains of the Sea	NEB-N 73	DOZOIS, Gardner
2	Death and Designation Among the Asadi	NEB-N 73	BISHOP, Michael
2	Junction	NEB-N 73	DANN, Jack
2	White Otters of Childhood, The	NEB-N 73	BISHOP, Michael
3	Of Mist, and Grass, and Sand	NEB-W 73	McINTYRE, Vonda N
3	Case and the Dreamer	NEB-N 73	STURGEON, Theodore
3	Deathbird, The	NEB-N 73	ELLISON, Harlan
3	Girl Who Was Plugged In, The	NEB-N 73	TIPTREE, James Jr
4	Love is the Plan, the Plan is Death	NEB-W 73	TIPTREE, James Jr
4	How I Lost the Second World War and ...	NEB-N 73	WOLFE, Gene
4	Shark	NEB-N 73	BRYANT, Edward
4	Thing of Beauty, A	NEB-N 73	SPINRAD, Norman
4	Wings	NEB-N 73	McINTYRE, Vonda N
4	With Morning Comes Mistfall	NEB-N 73	MARTIN, George R R
1	Dispossessed, The	NEB-W 74	LEGUIN, Ursula K
1	334	NEB-N 74	DISCH, Thomas M
1	Flow My Tears, The Policeman Said	NEB-N 74	DICK, Philip K
1	Godwhale, The	NEB-N 74	BASS, T J
2	Born with the Dead	NEB-N 74	SILVERBERG, Robert
2	On the Street of the Serpents	NEB-N 74	BISHOP, Michael
2	Song For Lya, A	NEB-N 74	MARTIN, George R R
3	If the Stars are Gods	NEB-W 74	BENFORD and EKLUND
3	Rest Is Silence, The	NEB-N 74	GRANT, Charles L
3	Twilla	NEB-N 74	REAMY, Tom
4	Day Before the Revolution, The	NEB-W 74	LEGUIN, Ursula K
4	After King Kong Fell	NEB-N 74	FARMER, Philip Jose
4	Engine at Heartsprings Center, The	NEB-N 74	ZELAZNY, Roger

NEBULA AWARDS

CAT	TITLE	AW W/N Y	AUTHOR
1	Forever War, The	NEB-W 75	HALDEMAN, Joe
1	Autumn Angels	NEB-N 75	COVER, Arthur B
1	Birthgrave, The	NEB-N 75	LEE, Tanith
1	Computer Connection, The	NEB-N 75	BESTER, Alfred
1	Dhalgren	NEB-N 75	DELANY, Samuel R
1	Doorways in the Sand	NEB-N 75	ZELAZNY, Roger
1	Embedding, The	NEB-N 75	WATSON, Ian
1	Exile Waiting, The	NEB-N 75	McINTYRE, Vonda N
1	Female Man, The	NEB-N 75	RUSS, Joanna
1	Funeral For Eyes of Fire, A	NEB-N 75	BISHOP, Michael
1	Guernica Night	NEB-N 75	MALZBERG, Barry N
1	Heritage Hastur (9):Darkover	NEB-N 75	BRADLEY, Marion Zimmer
1	Invisible Cities	NEB-N 75	CALVINO, Italo
1	Midsummer Tempest, A	NEB-N 75	ANDERSON, Poul
1	Missing Man, The	NEB-N 75	MacLEAN, Katherine
1	Mote In God's Eye, The	NEB-N 75	NIVEN, Larry
1	Ragtime	NEB-N 75	DOCTOROW, E L
1	Stochastic Man, The	NEB-N 75	SILVERBERG, Robert
2	Home is the Hangman	NEB-W 75	ZELAZNY, Roger
2	Momentary Taste of Being, A	NEB-N 75	TIPTREE, James Jr
2	Storms of Windhaven, The	NEB-N 75	TUTTLE, Lisa
2	Sunrise West	NEB-N 75	CARLSON, William K
3	San Diego Lightfoot Sue	NEB-W 75	REAMY, Tom
3	Bleeding Man, The	NEB-N 75	STRETE, Craig
3	Blooded on Arachne	NEB-N 75	BISHOP, Michael
3	Custodians, The	NEB-N 75	COWPER, Richard
3	Dybbuk Dolls, The	NEB-N 75	DANN, Jack
3	Final Sighting of Fion Mac Cumhaill, The	NEB-N 75	GARRETT, Randall
3	Galaxy Called Rome, A	NEB-N 75	MALZBERG, Barry N
3	New Atlantis, The	NEB-N 75	LeGUIN, Ursula K
3	Polly Charms, The Sleeping Woman	NEB-N 75	DAVIDSON, Avram
3	Retrograde Summer	NEB-N 75	VARLEY, John
3	Warlord of Saturn's Moons, The	NEB-N 75	ARNASON, Eleanor
4	Catch That Zeppelin	NEB-W 75	LEIBER, Fritz
4	Attachment	NEB-N 75	EISENSTEIN, Phyllis
4	Child of All Ages	NEB-N 75	PLAUGER, P J
4	Doing Lennon	NEB-N 75	BENFORD, Gregory
4	Find the Lady	NEB-N 75	FISK, Nicholas
4	Growing Up in Edge City	NEB-N 75	POHL, Frederik
4	Sail the Tide of Mourning	NEB-N 75	LUPOFF, Richard A
4	Scraping of the Bones, A	NEB-N 75	BUDRYS, Algis
4	Shatterday	NEB-N 75	ELLISON, Harlan
4	Time Deer	NEB-N 75	STRETE, Craig
4	Utopia of a Tired Man	NEB-N 75	BORGES, Jorge Luis
4	White Creatures	NEB-N 75	BENFORD, Gregory
4	White Wolf Calling	NEB-N 75	GRANT, Charles L

CAT	TITLE	AW W/N Y	AUTHOR
1	Man Plus	NEB-W 76	POHL, Frederik
1	Inferno	NEB-N 76	NIVEN, Larry
1	Islands	NEB-N 76	RANDALL, Marta
1	Shadrach in the Furnace	NEB-N 76	SILVERBERG, Robert
1	Triton	NEB-N 76	DELANY, Samuel R
1	Where Late the Sweet Birds Sang	NEB-N 76	WILHELM, Kate
2	Houston, Houston. Do you read?	NEB-W 76	TIPTREE, James Jr
2	Eyeflash Miracles, The	NEB-N 76	WOLFE, Gene
2	Piper at the Gates of Dawn	NEB-N 76	COWPER, Richard
2	Samurai and the Willows, The	NEB-N 76	BISHOP, Michael
3	Bicentennial Man, The	NEB-W 76	ASIMOV, Isaac
3	Custer's Last Jump	NEB-N 76	UTLEY, Steven
3	Diary of the Rose, The	NEB-N 76	LeGUIN, Ursula K
3	His Hour Upon the Stage	NEB-N 76	CARRINGTON, Grant
4	Crowd of Shadows, A	NEB-W 76	GRANT, Charles L
4	Back to the Stone Age	NEB-N 76	SAUNDERS, Jake
4	Death's a Ware That Will Not Keep	NEB-N 76	MONTELEONE, Thomas F
4	Mary Margaret Road-Grader	NEB-N 76	WALDROP, Howard
4	Stone Circle	NEB-N 76	TUTTLE, Lisa
4	Tricentennial	NEB-N 76	HALDEMAN, Joe
1	Gateway	NEB-W 77	POHL, Frederik
1	Cirque	NEB-N 77	CARR, Terry
1	In the Ocean of the Night	NEB-N 77	BENFORD, Gregory
1	Moonstar Odyssey	NEB-N 77	GERROLD, David
1	Sword of the Demon	NEB-N 77	LUPOFF, Richard A
2	Stardance	NEB-W 77	ROBINSON, Spider & Jeanne
2	Aztecs	NEB-N 77	McINTYRE, Vonda N
3	Screwfly Solution, The	NEB-W 77	SHELDON, Raccoona(Tiptree)
3	Ninth Symphony of Ludwig v/Beethoven...	NEB-N 77	SCHOLZ, Carter
3	Particle Theory	NEB-N 77	BRYANT, Edward
3	Rite of Spring, A	NEB-N 77	LEIBER, Fritz
3	Stone City, The	NEB-N 77	MARTIN, George R R
4	Jeffty is Five	NEB-W 77	ELLISON, Harlan
4	Air Raid	NEB-N 77	VARLEY, John
4	Camera Obscura	NEB-N 77	MONTELEONE, Thomas F
4	Kibakusha Gallery, The	NEB-N 77	BRYANT, Edward
4	Tin Woodsman	NEB-N 77	BAILEY, Dennis
1	Dreamsnake	NEB-W 78	McINTYRE, Vonda N
1	Blind Voices	NEB-N 78	REAMY, Tom
1	Faded Sun, The: Kesrith	NEB-N 78	CHERRYH, C J
1	Kalki	NEB-N 78	VIDAL, Gore
1	Strangers	NEB-N 78	DOZOIS, Gardner
2	Persistence of Vision, The	NEB-W 78	VARLEY, John
2	Seven American Nights	NEB-N 78	WOLFE, Gene

CAT	TITLE	AW W/N Y	AUTHOR
3	Glow of Candles, a Unicorn's Eye, A	NEB-W 78	GRANT, Charles L
3	Devil You Don't Know	NEB-N 78	ING, Dean
3	Mikal's Songbird	NEB-N 78	CARD, Orson Scott
4	Stone	NEB-W 78	BRYANT, Edward
4	Cassandra	NEB-N 78	CHERRYH, C J
4	Quiet Revolution For Death	NEB-N 78	DANN, Jack
1	Fountains of Paradise, The	NEB-W 79	CLARKE, Arthur C
1	JEM	NEB-N 79	POHL, Frederik
1	Juniper Time	NEB-N 79	WILHELM, Kate
1	On Wings of Song	NEB-N 79	DISCH, Thomas M
1	Road to Corlay, The	NEB-N 79	COWPER, Richard
1	Titan	NEB-N 79	VARLEY, John
2	Enemy Mine	NEB-W 79	LONGYEAR, Barry
2	Battle of the Abaco Reefs, The	NEB-N 79	SCHENCK, Hilbert
2	Fireship	NEB-N 79	VINGE, Joan D
2	Mars Masked	NEB-N 79	POHL, Frederik
2	Story Writer, The	NEB-N 79	WILSON, Richard
2	Tale of Gorgik, The	NEB-N 79	DELANY, Samuel R
3	Sandkings	NEB-W 79	MARTIN, George R R
3	Angel of Death, The	NEB-N 79	SHEA, Michael
3	Camps	NEB-N 79	DANN, Jack
3	Options	NEB-N 79	VARLEY, John
3	Ways of Love, The	NEB-N 79	ANDERSON, Poul
4	giANTS	NEB-W 79	BRYANT, Edward
4	Extraordinary Voyages of Amelie Bertrand	NEB-N 79	RUSS, Joanna
4	Red As Blood	NEB-N 79	LEE, Tanith
4	Unaccompanied Sonata	NEB-N 79	CARD, Orson Scott
4	Vernalfest	NEB-N 79	BISHOP, Michael
4	Way of Cross and Dragon, The	NEB-N 79	MARTIN, George R R
1	Timescape	NEB-W 80	BENFORD, Gregory
1	Beyond the Blue Event Horizon	NEB-N 80	POHL, Frederik
1	Mockingbird	NEB-N 80	TEVIS, Walter
1	Orphan, The	NEB-N 80	STALLMAN, Robert
1	Shadow of the Torturer, The	NEB-N 80	WOLFE, Gene
1	Snow Queen, The	NEB-N 80	VINGE, Joan D
2	Unicorn Tapestry	NEB-W 80	CHARNAS, Suzy McKee
2	Autopsy, The	NEB-N 80	SHEA, Michael
2	Brave Little Toaster, The	NEB-N 80	DISCH, Thomas M
2	Dangerous Games	NEB-N 80	RANDALL, Marta
2	Lost Dorsai	NEB-N 80	DICKSON, Gordon R
2	There Beneath the Silky Trees...	NEB-N 80	DAVIDSON, Avram
3	Ugly Chickens, The	NEB-W 80	WALDROP, Howard
3	Beatnik Bayou	NEB-N 80	WALDROP, Howard
3	Feast of St. Janis, The	NEB-N 80	SWANWICK, Michael
3	Ginungagap	NEB-N 80	VARLEY, John
3	Strata	NEB-N 80	BRYANT, Edward
3	Way Station, The	NEB-N 80	KING, Stephen

NEBULA AWARDS

CAT	TITLE	AW W/N Y	AUTHOR
4	Grotto of the Dancing Bear, The	NEB-W 80	SIMAK, Clifford D
4	Secrets of the Heart	NEB-N 80	GRANT, Charles L
4	Sunday Visit, A	NEB-N 80	STRETE, Craig
4	War Beneath the Tree	NEB-N 80	WOLFE, Gene
4	Window	NEB-N 80	LEMAN, Bob
1	Claw of the Conciliator, The	NEB-W 81	WOLFE, Gene
1	Little Big	NEB-N 81	CROWLEY, John
1	Many-Colored Land, The	NEB-N 81	MAY, Julian
1	Radix	NEB-N 81	ATTANASIO, A A
1	Riddley Walker	NEB-N 81	HOBAN, Russell
1	Vampire Tapestry, The	NEB-N 81	CHARNAS, Suzy McKee
2	Saturn Game, The	NEB-W 81	ANDERSON, Poul
2	Amnesia	NEB-N 81	DANN, Jack
2	In the Western Tradition	NEB-N 81	EISENSTEIN, Phyllis
2	Swarmer, Skimmer	NEB-N 81	BENFORD, Gregory
2	True Names	NEB-N 81	VINGE, Vernor
2	Winter Beach, The	NEB-N 81	WILHELM, Kate
3	Quickening, The	NEB-W 81	BISHOP, Michael
3	Fire When it Comes, The	NEB-N 81	GODWIN, Parke
3	Lirios: A Tale of The Quuintana Roo	NEB-N 81	TIPTREE, James Jr
3	Mummer Kiss	NEB-N 81	SWANWICK, Michael
3	Sea Changeling	NEB-N 81	BROXON, Midlred Downey
3	Thermals of August, The	NEB-N 81	BRYANT, Edward
4	Bone Flute, The	NEB-W 81	TUTTLE, Lisa
4	Disciples	NEB-N 81	DOZOIS, Gardner
4	Going Under	NEB-N 81	DANN, Jack
4	Johny Mnemonic	NEB-N 81	GIBSON, William
4	Pusher, The	NEB-N 81	VARLEY, John
4	Quiet, The	NEB-N 81	FLORANCE-GUTHRIDGE, George
4	Venice Drowned	NEB-N 81	ROBINSON, Kim Stanley
4	Zeke Timothy	NEB-N 81	SULLIVAN, Robert
1	No Enemy But Time	NEB-W 82	BISHOP, Michael
1	Foundation's Edge	NEB-N 82	ASIMOV, Isaac
1	Friday	NEB-N 82	HEINLEIN, Robert A
1	Helliconia Spring	NEB-N 82	ALDISS, Brian W
1	Sword of the Lichtor, The	NEB-N 82	WOLFE, Gene
1	Transmigration of Timothy Archer, The	NEB-N 82	DICK, Philip K
2	Another Orphan	NEB-W 82	KESSEL, John
2	Horrible Imaginings (Death)	NEB-N 82	LEIBER, Fritz
2	Moon of Ice	NEB-N 82	LINAWEAVER, Brad
2	Souls	NEB-N 82	RUSS, Joanna
2	Unsound Variations	NEB-N 82	MARTIN, George R R
3	Fire Watch	NEB-W 82	WILLIS, Connie
3	Burning Chrome	NEB-N 82	GIBSON, William
3	Mystery of the Young Gentleman, The	NEB-N 82	RUSS, Joanna
3	Myths of the Near Future	NEB-N 82	BALLARD, J G
3	Swarm	NEB-N 82	STERLING, Bruce
3	Understanding Human Behavior	NEB-N 82	DISCH, Thomas M

CAT	TITLE	AW W/N Y	AUTHOR
4	Letter From the Clearys, A	NEB-W 82	WILLIS, Connie
4	Corridors	NEB-N 82	MALZBERG, Barry N
4	God's Hooks	NEB-N 82	WALDROP, Howard
4	High Steel	NEB-N 82	HALDEMAN, Jack C
4	Petra	NEB-N 82	BEAR, Greg
4	Pope of the Chimps, The	NEB-N 82	SILVERBERG, Robert
1	Startide Rising	NEB-W 83	BRIN, David
1	Against Infinity	NEB-N 83	BENFORD, Gregory
1	Citadel of the Autarch, The	NEB-N 83	WOLFE, Gene
1	Lyonesse	NEB-N 83	VANCE, Jack
1	Tea With the Black Dragon	NEB-N 83	MacAVOY, R A
1	Void Captain's Tale, The	NEB-N 83	SPINRAD, Norman
2	Hardfought	NEB-W 83	BEAR, Greg
2	Esterhazy and the Autogondola-Invention	NEB-N 83	DAVIDSON, Avram
2	Gospel According to Gamaliel-Crucis, The	NEB-N 83	BISHOP, Michael
2	Her Habiline Husband	NEB-N 83	BISHOP, Michael
2	Homefaring	NEB-N 83	SILVERBERG, Robert
2	Transit	NEB-N 83	McINTYRE, Vonda N
3	Blood Music	NEB-W 83	BEAR, Greg
3	Black Air	NEB-N 83	ROBINSON, Kim Stanley
3	Blind Shemmy	NEB-N 83	DANN, Jack
3	Cicada Queen	NEB-N 83	STERLING, Bruce
3	Monkey Treatment, The	NEB-N 83	MARTIN, George R R
3	Sidon in the Mirror, The	NEB-N 83	WILLIS, Connie
3	Slow Birds	NEB-N 83	WATSON, Ian
4	Peacemaker, The	NEB-W 83	DOZOIS, Gardner
4	Cryptic	NEB-N 83	McDEVITT, Jack
4	Geometry of Narrative, The	NEB-N 83	SCHENCK, Hilbert
4	Ghost Town	NEB-N 83	OLIVER, Chad
4	Her Furry Face	NEB-N 83	KENNEDY, Leigh
4	Wong's Lost and Found Emporium	NEB-N 83	WU, William F
1	Neuromancer	NEB-W 84	GIBSON, William
1	Frontera	NEB-N 84	SHINER, Lewis
1	Integral Trees, The	NEB-N 84	NIVEN, Larry
1	Job: A Comedy of Justice	NEB-N 84	HEINLEIN, Robert A
1	Man Who Melted, The	NEB-N 84	DANN, Jack
1	Wild Shore, The	NEB-N 84	ROBINSON, Kim Stanley
2	Press Enter	NEB-W 84	VARLEY, John
2	Greening of Bed-Stuy, The	NEB-N 84	POHL, Frederik
2	Marrow Death	NEB-N 84	SWANWICK, Michael
2	Traveler's Tale, A	NEB-N 84	SHEPARD, Lucius
2	Trinity	NEB-N 84	KRESS, Nancy
3	Bloodchild	NEB-W 84	BUTLER, Octavia E
3	Bad Medicine	NEB-N 84	DANN, Jack
3	Lucky Strike, The	NEB-N 84	ROBINSON, Kim Stanley
3	Man WHo Painted the Dragon Griaule, The	NEB-N 84	SHEPARD, Lucius
3	Saint Theresa of the Aliens	NEB-N 84	KELLY, James Patrick
3	Trojan Horse	NEB-N 84	SWANWICK, Michael

NEBULA AWARDS

CAT	T I T L E	AW W/N Y	A U T H O R
4	Morning Child	NEB-W 84	DOZOIS, Gardner
4	Aliens Who Knew, I Mean Everything, The	NEB-N 84	EFFINGER, George Alec
4	Cabin on the Coast, A	NEB-N 84	WOLFE, Gene
4	Eichman Variations, The	NEB-N 84	ZEBROWSKI, George
4	Salvador	NEB-N 84	SHEPARD, Lucius
4	Sunken Gardens	NEB-N 84	STERLING, Bruce
6	Young Doctor Esterhazy	NEB-N 84	DAVIDSON, Avram
1	Ender's Game	NEB-W 85	CARD, Orson Scott
1	Blood Music	NEB-N 85	BEAR, Greg
1	Dinner at Deviant's Palace	NEB-N 85	POWERS, Tim
1	Helliconia Winter	NEB-N 85	ALDISS, Brian W
1	Postman, The	NEB-N 85	BRIN, David
1	Remaking of Sigmund Freud, The	NEB-N 85	MALZBERG, Barry N
1	Schismatrix	NEB-N 85	STERLING, Bruce
2	Sailing To Byzantium	NEB-W 85	SILVERBERG, Robert
2	24 Views of Mount Fuji by Hokusai	NEB-N 85	ZELAZNY, Roger
2	Gorgon, The	NEB-N 85	WILHELM, Kate
2	Green Days in Brunei	NEB-N 85	STERLING, Bruce
2	Only Neat Thing To Do, The	NEB-N 85	TIPTREE, James Jr
3	Portraits of His Children	NEB-W 85	MARTIN, George R R
3	Dogfight	NEB-N 85	SWANWICK, Michael
3	Fringe, The	NEB-N 85	CARD, Orson Scott
3	Gift From the Graylanders, A	NEB-N 85	BISHOP, Michael
3	Jaguar Hunter, The	NEB-N 85	SHEPARD, Lucius
3	Paladin of the Lost Hour	NEB-N 85	ELLISON, Harlan
3	Rockabye Baby	NEB-N 85	SYKES, S C
4	Out of All Them Bright Stars	NEB-W 85	KRESS, Nancy
4	Flying Saucer Rock and Roll	NEB-N 85	WALDROP, Howard
4	Gods of Mars, The	NEB-N 85	DOZOIS, Gardner
4	Heirs of the Perisphere	NEB-N 85	WALDROP, Howard
4	Hong's Bluff	NEB-N 85	WU, William F
4	More Than The Sum of His Parts	NEB-N 85	HALDEMAN, Joe
4	Paper Dragons	NEB-N 85	BLAYLOCK, James P
4	Snow	NEB-N 85	CROWLEY, John
1	Speaker for the Dead	NEB-W 86	CARD, Orson Scott
1	Count Zero	NEB-N 86	GIBSON, William
1	Free, Live Free	NEB-N 86	WOLFE, Gene
1	Handmaid's Tale, The	NEB-N 86	ATWOOD, Margaret
1	Journal of Nicholas the American	NEB-N 86	KENNEDY, L
1	This is the Way the World Ends	NEB-N 86	MORROW, James
2	R & R	NEB-W 86	SHEPARD, Lucius
2	Dydeetown Girl	NEB-N 86	WILSON, F Paul
2	Escape from Kathmandu	NEB-N 86	ROBINSON, Kim Stanley
2	Gilgamesh in the Outback	NEB-N 86	SILVERBERG, Robert
2	Newton Sleep	NEB-N 86	BENFORD, Gregory

CAT	T I T L E	AW W/N Y	A U T H O R
3	Girl Who Fell Into the Sky, The	NEB-W 86	WILHELM, Kate
3	Aymara	NEB-N 86	SHEPARD, Lucius
3	Hatrack River	NEB-N 86	CARD, Orson Scott
3	Listening to Brahms	NEB-N 86	CHARNAS, Suzy McKee
3	Permafrost	NEB-N 86	ZELAZNY, Roger
3	Surviving	NEB-N 86	MOFFETT, Judith
3	Winter Market, The	NEB-N 86	GIBSON, William
4	Tangents	NEB-W 86	BEAR, Greg
4	Boy Who Plaited Manes, The	NEB-N 86	SPRINGER, Nancy
4	Lions Are Asleep This Night, The	NEB-N 86	WALDROP, Howard
4	Pretty Boy Crossover	NEB-N 86	CADIGAN, Pat
4	Rat	NEB-N 86	KELLY, James Patrick
4	Robot Dreams	NEB-N 86	ASIMOV, Isaac
1	Falling Woman, The	NEB-W 87	MURPHY, Pat
1	Forge of God, The	NEB-N 87	BEAR, Greg
1	Soldier of the Mist	NEB-N 87	WOLFE, Gene
1	Uplift War, The	NEB-N 87	BRIN, David
1	Vergil in Averno	NEB-N 87	DAVIDSON, Avram
1	When Gravity Fails	NEB-N 87	EFFINGER, George Alec
2	Geometer Blind, The	NEB-W 87	ROBINSON, Kim Stanley
2	Fugue State	NEB-N 87	FORD, John M
2	Secret Sharer, The	NEB-N 87	SILVERBERG, Robert
2	Tiger Sweater, The	NEB-N 87	ROBERTS, Keith
2	Unconquered Country, The	NEB-N 87	RYMAN, Geoff
2	Witness	NEB-N 87	WILLIAMS, John
3	Rachel in Love	NEB-W 87	MURPHY, Pat
3	Buffalo Gals, Won't You Come Out Tonight	NEB-N 87	LeGUIN, Ursula K
3	Dream Baby	NEB-N 87	McALLISTER, Bruce
3	Evening and the Morning and the Night	NEB-N 87	BUTLER, Octavia E
3	FLowers of Edo	NEB-N 87	STERLING, Bruce
3	Schwarzschild Radius	NEB-N 87	WILLIS, Connie
4	Forever Yours, Anna	NEB-W 87	WILHELM, Kate
4	Angel	NEB-N 87	CADIGAN, Pat
4	Cassandra's Photographs	NEB-N 87	GOLDSTEIN, Lisa
4	Faithful Companion, The	NEB-N 87	FOWLER, Karen Joy
4	Kid Charlemagne	NEB-N 87	FILIPPO, Paul Di
4	Temple to a Minor Goddess	NEB-N 87	SHWARTZ, Susan
4	Why I Left Harry's All-Night Hamburgers	NEB-N 87	WATT-EVANS, Lawrence
1	Falling Free	NEB-W 88	BUJOLD, Lois McMaster
1	Deserted Cities of the Heart	NEB-N 88	SHINER, Lewis
1	Drowning Towers	NEB-N 88	TURNER, George
1	Great Sky River	NEB-N 88	BENFORD, Gregory
1	Mona Lisa Overdrive	NEB-N 88	GIBSON, William
1	Red Prophet	NEB-N 88	CARD, Orson Scott
1	Urth of the New Sun, The	NEB-N 88	WOLFE, Gene

CAT	TITLE	AW W/N Y	AUTHOR
2	Last of the Winnebagos, The	NEB-W 88	WILLIS, Connie
2	Calvin Coolidge Home for Dead Comedians	NEB-N 88	DENTON, Bradley
2	Devil's Arithmetic, The	NEB-N 88	YOLEN, Jane
2	Journals of the Plague Years, The	NEB-N 88	SPINRAD, Norman
2	Scalehunter's Beautiful Daughter, The	NEB-N 88	SHEPARD, Lucius
2	Surfacing	NEB-N 88	WILLIAMS, Walter Jon
3	Ochrodinger's Kitten	NEB-W 88	EFFINGER, George Alec
3	Do Ya, Do Ya, Wanna Dance	NEB-N 88	WALDROP, Howard
3	Ginny Sweethips' Flying Circus	NEB-N 88	BARRETT, Neal Jr
3	Hob, The	NEB-N 88	MOFFETT, Judith
3	Kirinyaga	NEB-N 88	RESNICK, Mike
3	Peaches for Mad Molly	NEB-N 88	GOULD, Stephen
3	Unfinished Portrait of the King of Pain	NEB-N 88	McDONALD, Ian
4	Bible Stories For Adults #17 The Deluge	NEB-W 88	MORROW, James
4	Color Winter, The	NEB-N 88	POPKES, Steven
4	Dead Men on TV	NEB-N 88	MURPHY, Pat
4	Fort Maxie Branch, The	NEB-N 88	McDEVITT, Jack
4	Mrs. Shummel Exits a Winner	NEB-N 88	KESSEL, John
4	Voices of the Kill	NEB-N 88	DISCH, Thomas M
1	Healers War, The	NEB-W 89	SCARBOROUGH, Elizabeth
1	Boat of a Million Years	NEB-N 89	ANDERSON, Poul
1	Good News From Outer Space	NEB-N 89	KESSEL, John
1	Ivory: Legend Past & Future	NEB-N 89	RESNICK, Mike
1	Prentice Alvin	NEB-N 89	CARD, Orson Scott
1	Sister Light, Sister Dark	NEB-N 89	YOLEN, Jane
2	Mountains of Mourning, The	NEB-W 89	BUJOLD, Lois McMaster
2	Dozen Tough Jobs, A	NEB-N 89	WALDROP, Howard
2	Great Works of Time	NEB-N 89	CROWLEY, John
2	Marid Changes His Mind	NEB-N 89	EFFINGER, George Alec
2	Tiny Tango	NEB-N 89	MOFFETT, Judith
2	Touch of Lavender, A	NEB-N 89	LINDHOLM, Megan
3	At the Rialto	NEB-W 89	WILLIS, Connie
3	Enter a Soldier, Later Enter Another	NEB-N 89	SILVERBERG, Robert
3	Fast Cars	NEB-N 89	RUSCH, Kristine Kathryn
3	For I Have Touched the Sky	NEB-N 89	RESNICK, Mike
3	Silver Lady and the Fortyish Man, The	NEB-N 89	LINDHOLM, Megan
3	Sisters	NEB-N 89	BEAR, Greg
4	Ripples in the Dirac Sea	NEB-W 89	LANDIS, Geoffrey A
4	Adinkra Cloth, The	NEB-N 89	ADRIDGE, Mary
4	Boobs	NEB-N 89	CHARNAS, Suzy McKee
4	Dori Bangs	NEB-N 89	STERLING, Bruce
4	Lost Boys	NEB-N 89	CARD, Orson Scott
4	Omnatidium Miniatures	NEB-N 89	BISHOP, Michael

NEBULA AWARDS

CAT	TITLE	AW W/N Y	AUTHOR
1	Tehanu: The Last Book of Earthsea	NEB-W 91	LeGUIN, Ursula K
1	Fall of Hyperion, The	NEB-N 91	SIMMONS, Dan
1	Mary Reilly	NEB-N 91	MARTIN, Valerie
1	Only Begotten Daughter	NEB-N 91	MORROW, James
1	Redshift Rendezvous	NEB-N 91	STITH, John E
1	White Jenna	NEB-N 91	YOLEN, Jane
2	Bones	NEB-N 91	MURPHY, Pat
2	Bully!	NEB-N 91	RESNICK, Mike
2	Fool to Believe	NEB-N 91	CADIGAN, Pat
2	Hemingway Hoax, The	NEB-N 91	HALDEMAN, Joe
2	Mr. Boy	NEB-N 91	KELLY, James Patrick
2	Weatherman	NEB-N 91	BUJOLD, Lois McMaster
3	1/72 nd Scale	NEB-N 91	MacLEOD, Ian
3	Coon Rolled Down and Ruptured...	NEB-N 91	HUGH, Dafydd ab
3	Loose Cannon	NEB-N 91	SHWARTZ, Susan
3	Manamouki, The	NEB-N 91	RESNICK, Mike
3	Over the Long Haul	NEB-N 91	SOUKUP, Martha
3	Shobie's Story, The	NEB-N 91	LeGUIN, Ursula K
3	Time For Every Purpose, A	NEB-N 91	RUSCH, Kristine Kathryn
3	Tower of Babylon	NEB-N 91	CHIANG, Ted
4	Bears Discover Fire	NEB-N 91	BISSON, Terry
4	Before I Wake	NEB-N 91	ROBINSON, Kim Stanley
4	Lieserl	NEB-N 91	FOWLER, Karen Joy
4	Love and Sex Among the Vertebrates	NEB-N 91	MURPHY, Pat
4	Power and the Passion, The	NEB-N 91	CADIGAN, Pat
4	Story Child	NEB-N 91	RUSCH, Kristine Kathryn
1	Stations of the Tide	NEB-W 92	SWANWICK, Michael
1	Barrayar	NEB-N 92	BUJOLD, Lois McMaster
1	Bone Dance	NEB-N 92	BULL, Emma
1	Difference Engine, The	NEB-N 92	GIBSON, William
1	Orbital Resonance	NEB-N 92	BARNES, John
1	Synners	NEB-N 92	CADIGAN, Pat
2	Beggars in Spain	NEB-W 92	KRESS, Nancy
2	Apartheid,Superstr'gs & Modercai Thubana	NEB-N 92	BISHOP, Michael
2	Bully!	NEB-N 92	RESNICK, Mike
2	Gallery of His Dreams, The	NEB-N 92	RUSCH, Kristine Kathryn
2	Jack	NEB-N 92	WILLIS, Connie
2	Man Opening a Door	NEB-N 92	ASH, Paul
3	Guide Dog	NEB-W 92	CONNER, Mike
3	All-consuming, The	NEB-N 92	SHEPARD, Lucius
3	Black Glass	NEB-N 92	FOWLER, Karen Joy
3	Gate of Faces	NEB-N 92	ALDRIDGE, Ray
3	Getting Real	NEB-N 92	SHWARTZ, Susan
3	Happy Man, The	NEB-N 92	LETHEM, Jonathan
3	Standing in Line with Mister Jimmy	NEB-N 92	KELLY, James Patrick

NEBULA AWARDS

CAT	T I T L E	AW W/N Y	A U T H O R
4	Ma Qui	NEB-W 92	BRENNERT, Alan
4	Buffalo	NEB-N 92	KESSEL, John
4	Button and What You Know, The	NEB-N 92	STEWART, W Gregory
4	Dark, The	NEB-N 92	FOWLER, Daren Joy
4	Dog's Life	NEB-N 92	SOUKUP, Martha
4	They're Made Out of Meat	NEB-N 92	BISSON, Terry

SCIENCE FICTION CHRONICLE AWARDS

The Science Fiction Chronicle Awards are sponsored by the magazine
Science Fiction Chronicle, and its editor, Andrew Porter, and, like the
Locus Awards, are voted upon by readers of the magazine.

CAT	TITLE	AW W/N Y	AUTHOR
1	Claw of the Conciliator, The	SFC-W 82	WOLFE, Gene
2	In the Western Tradition	SFC-W 82	EISENSTEIN, Phyllis
3	Mummer Kiss	SFC-W 82	SWANWICK, Michael
4	Pusher, The	SFC-W 82	VARLEY, John
1	Sword of the Lichtor, The	SFC-W 83	WOLFE, Gene
1	2010: Odyssey Two	SFC-N 83	CLARKE, Arthur C
1	Foundation's Edge	SFC-N 83	ASIMOV, Isaac
2	Souls	SFC-W 83	RUSS, Joanna
2	Another Orphan	SFC-N 83	KESSEL, John
2	Horrible Imaginings (Death)	SFC-N 83	LEIBER, Fritz
3	Fire Watch	SFC-W 83	WILLIS, Connie
3	Understanding Human Behavior	SFC-W 83	DISCH, Thomas M
3	Burning Chrome	SFC-N 83	GIBSON, William
4	Petra	SFC-W 83	BEAR, Greg
4	Letter From the Clearys, A	SFC-N 83	WILLIS, Connie
4	Sur	SFC-N 83	LeGUIN, Ursula K
1	Anubis Gates, The	SFC-W 84	POWERS, Tim
1	Citadel of the Autarch, The	SFC-N 84	WOLFE, Gene
1	Helliconia Summer	SFC-N 84	ALDISS, Brian W
1	Startide Rising	SFC-N 84	BRIN, David
2	Her Habiline Husband	SFC-W 84	BISHOP, Michael
2	Hardfought	SFC-N 84	BEAR, Greg
2	Homefaring	SFC-N 84	SILVERBERG, Robert
3	Black Air	SFC-W 84	ROBINSON, Kim Stanley
3	Blind Shemmy	SFC-N 84	DANN, Jack
3	Blood Music	SFC-N 84	BEAR, Greg
4	Peacemaker, The	SFC-W 84	DOZOIS, Gardner
4	Brothers	SFC-N 84	COWPER, Richard
4	Her Furry Face	SFC-N 84	KENNEDY, Leigh
1	Neuromancer	SFC-W 85	GIBSON, William
1	Integral Trees, The	SFC-N 85	NIVEN, Larry
1	Wild Shore, The	SFC-N 85	ROBINSON, Kim Stanley
2	Press Enter	SFC-W 85	VARLEY, John
2	Traveler's Tale, A	SFC-N 85	SHEPARD, Lucius
2	Trinity	SFC-N 85	KRESS, Nancy

CAT	T I T L E	AW W/N Y	A U T H O R
3	Bloodchild	SFC-W 85	BUTLER, Octavia E
3	Lucky Strike, The	SFC-N 85	ROBINSON, Kim Stanley
3	Man Who Painted the Dragon Griaule, The	SFC-N 85	SHEPARD, Lucius
4	Salvador	SFC-W 85	SHEPARD, Lucius
4	Aliens Who Knew, I Mean Everything, The	SFC-N 85	EFFINGER, George Alec
4	Morning Child	SFC-N 85	DOZOIS, Gardner
1	Ender's Game	SFC-W 86	CARD, Orson Scott
1	Helliconia Winter	SFC-N 86	ALDISS, Brian W
1	Postman, The	SFC-N 86	BRIN, David
2	Only Neat Thing to Do, The	SFC-W 86	TIPTREE, James Jr
2	Green Mars	SFC-N 86	ROBINSON, Kim Stanley
2	Sailing to Byzantium	SFC-N 86	SILVERBERG, Robert
3	Portraits of His Children	SFC-W 86	MARTIN, George R R
3	Dogfight	SFC-N 86	SWANWICK, Michael
3	Paladin of the Lost Hour	SFC-N 86	ELLISON, Harlan
4	Paper Dragons	SFC-W 86	BLAYLOCK, James P
4	Fermi and Frost	SFC-N 86	POHL, Frederik
4	Time's Rub	SFC-N 86	BENFORD, Gregory
1	Speaker for the Dead	SFC-W 87	CARD, Orson Scott
1	Count Zero	SFC-N 87	GIBSON, William
1	Handmaid's Tale, The	SFC-N 87	ATWOOD, Margaret
2	R & R	SFC-W 87	SHEPARD, Lucius
2	Escape From Kathmandu	SFC-N 87	ROBINSON, Kim Stanley
2	Gilgamesh in the Outback	SFC-N 87	SILVERBERG, Robert
3	Aymara	SFC-W 87	SHEPARD, Lucius
3	Hatrack River	SFC-N 87	CARD, Orson Scott
3	Thor Meets Captain America	SFC-N 87	BRIN, David
3	Winter Market, The	SFC-N 87	GIBSON, William
4	Pretty Boy Crossover	SFC-W 87	CADIGAN, Pat
4	Rat	SFC-N 87	KELLY, James Patrick
4	Robot Dreams	SFC-N 87	ASIMOV, Isaac
4	Tangents	SFC-N 87	BEAR, Greg
1	Urth of the New Sun, The	SFC-W 88	WOLFE, Gene
1	Swordpoint	SFC-N 88	KUSHNER, Ellen
1	When Gravity Fails	SFC-N 88	EFFINGER, George Alec
2	Secret Sharer, The	SFC-W 88	SILVERBERG, Robert
2	Blind Geometer, The	SFC-N 88	ROBINSON, Kim Stanley
2	Tale of Rumor and Desire, The	SFC-N 88	DELANY, Samuel R
3	Evening and the Morning and the Night	SFC-W 88	BUTLER, Octavia E
3	Rachel in Love	SFC-N 88	MURPHY, Pat
3	Schwarzschild Radius	SFC-N 88	SHWARTZ, Susan

SCIENCE FICTION CHRONICLE

CAT	TITLE	AW W/N Y	AUTHOR
4	Circular Library of Stones	SFC-W 88	EMSHWILLER, Carol
4	Angel	SFC-N 88	CADIGAN, Pat
4	Forever Yours, Anna	SFC-N 88	WILHELM, Kate
1	Cyteen	SFC-W 89	CHERRYH, C J
1	Islands in the Net	SFC-N 89	STERLING, Bruce
1	Ivory: Legend Past & Future	SFC-N 89	RESNICK, Mike
2	Last of the Winnebagos, The	SFC-W 89	WILLIS, Connie
2	Journals of the Plague Years, The	SFC-N 89	SPINRAD, Norman
2	Scalehunter's Beautiful Daughter, The	SFC-N 89	SHEPARD, Lucius
3	Schrodinger's Kitten	SFC-W 89	EFFINGER, George Alec
3	Do Ya, Do Ya, Wanna Dance	SFC-N 89	WALDROP, Howard
3	Glacier	SFC-N 89	ROBINSON, Kim Stanley
4	Kirinyaga	SFC-W 89	RESNICK, Mike
4	Our Neural Chernobyl	SFC-N 89	STERLING, Bruce
4	Ripples in the Dirac Sea	SFC-N 89	LANDIS, Geoffrey A
1	Fire in the Sun, A	SFC-W 90	EFFINGER, George Alec
1	Boat of a Million Years	SFC-N 90	ANDERSON, Poul
1	Hyperion	SFC-N 90	SIMMONS, Dan
2	Mountains of Mourning, The	SFC-W 90	BUJOLD, Lois McMaster
2	Father of Stones, The	SFC-N 90	SHEPARD, Lucius
2	Great Work of Time	SFC-N 90	CROWLEY, John
3	For I Have Touched the Sky	SFC-W 90	RESNICK, Mike
3	At the Rialto	SFC-N 90	WILLIS, Connie
3	Everything But Honor	SFC-N 90	CARD, Orson Scott
4	Dori Bangs	SFC-W 90	STERLING, Bruce
4	Boobs	SFC-N 90	CHARNAS, Suzy McKee
4	Lost Boys	SFC-N 90	CARD, Orson Scott
1	Earth	SFC-N 91	BRIN, David
1	Fall of Hyperion, The	SFC-N 91	SIMMONS, Dan
1	Vor Game, The	SFC-N 91	BUJOLD, Lois McMaster
2	Bully!	SFC-N 91	RESNICK, Mike
2	Hemingway Hoax, The	SFC-N 91	HALDEMAN, Joe
2	Short, Sharp, Shock, A	SFC-N 91	ROBINSON, Kim Stanley
3	Braver Thing, A	SFC-N 91	SHEFFIELD, Charles
3	Manamouki, The	SFC-N 91	RESNICK, Mike
3	Tower of Babylon	SFC-N 91	CHIANG, Ted
4	Bears Discover Fire	SFC-N 91	BISSON, Terry
4	Cibola	SFC-N 91	WILLIS, Connie
4	Godspeed	SFC-N 91	SHEFFIELD, Charles

SCIENCE FICTION CHRONICLE

CAT	TITLE	AW W/N Y	AUTHOR
1	All the Weyrs of Pern	SFC-N 92	McCAFFREY, Anne
1	Barrayar	SFC-N 92	BUJOLD, Lois McMaster
1	Stations of the Tide	SFC-N 92	SWANWICK, Michael
2	Beggars in Spain	SFC-N 92	KRESS, Nancy
2	Griffin's Egg	SFC-N 92	SWANWICK, Michael
2	Jack	SFC-N 92	WILLIS, Connie
3	Gate of Faces	SFC-N 92	ALDRIDGE, Ray
3	History of the 20th Century, A	SFC-N 92	ROBINSON, Kim Stanley
3	What Continues, What Fails	SFC-N 92	BRIN, David
4	Dream Cargoes	SFC-N 92	BALLARD, J G
4	One Perfect Morning, With Jackals	SFC-N 92	RESNICK, Mike
4	Vinland the Dream	SFC-N 92	ROBINSON, Kim Stanley

BRAM STOKER AWARD

The Bram Stoker Award was the first modern American award to recognize outstanding achievement in horror and dark fantasy. The Stoker Awards are chosen annually by active members of The Horror Writers of America (HWA). Each participant votes for two winners in each category, designating "first" and "second" on the ballot. The votes are then counted by an outside agency.

The physical prize, designed by Stephen M. Kirk, brother of science fiction artist Tim Kirk, consists of a minitiature gothic mansion eight inches high, decorated with gargoyles, skeletons, and creeping vines. The front door of the mansion opens to reveal the winner's name and category.

Year given for previous year publication.

CAT	TITLE	AW W/N Y	AUTHOR
1	Misery	STO-W 88	KING, Stephen
1	Swan Song	STO-W 88	McCAMMON, Robert R
1	Ash Wednesday	STO-N 88	WILLIAMSON, Chet
1	Live Girls	STO-N 88	GARTON, Ray
1	Unassigned Territory	STO-N 88	NUNN, Ken
3	Boy Who Came Back From the Grave, The	STO-W 88	RODGERS, Alan
3	Pear-Shaped Man, The	STO-W 88	MARTIN, George R R
3	Pamela's Get	STO-N 88	SCHOW, David J
3	Resurrec Tech	STO-N 88	SOMTOW, S P
4	Deep End, The	STO-W 88	McCAMMON, Robert R
4	Day-Tay-Vao	STO-N 88	WILSON, F Paul
4	Friend's Best Man	STO-N 88	CARROLL, Jonathan
4	This Old Man	STO-N 88	GRANT, Charles L
4	Traps	STO-N 88	WILSON, F Paul
6	Essential Ellison, The	STO-W 88	ELLISON, Harlan
6	All About Str'ge Monsters F/Recent Past	STO-N 88	WALDROP, Howard
6	Midnight Pleasures	STO-N 88	BLOCH, Robert
6	Scared Stiff, Tales of Sex & Death	STO-N 88	CAMPBELL, Ramsey
6	Why Not You and I?	STO-N 88	WAGNER, Karl Edward
7	Mary Shelley	STO-W 88	SPARKS, Muriel
7	Joe Bob Goes Back to the Drive-in	STO-N 88	BRIGGS, Joe Bob
7	Zombies That Ate Pittsburgh	STO-N 88	GAGNE, Paul A
9	Manse, The	STO-W 88	CANTRELL, Lisa W
9	Damnation Game, The	STO-N 88	BARKER, Clive
9	Excavation	STO-N 88	TEM, Steve Rasnic
9	Harvest Bride, The	STO-N 88	RICHARDS, Torvy
9	Slob	STO-N 88	MILLER, Rex
1	Silence of the Lambs, The	STO-W 89	HARRIS, Thomas
1	Black Wind	STO-N 89	WILSON, F Paul
1	Drive-in, The	STO-N 89	LANSDALE, Joe R
1	Flesh	STO-N 89	LAYMON, Richard
1	Queen of the Damned	STO-N 89	RICE, Anne
1	Stinger	STO-N 89	McCAMMON, Robert R

STOKER AWARDS

CAT	TITLE	AW W/N Y	AUTHOR
3	Orange Is For Anguish, Blue For Insanity	STO-W 89	MORRELL, David
3	Function of Dream Sleep, The	STO-N 89	ELLISON, Harlan
3	Horrorshow	STO-N 89	FARRIS, John
3	Juniper Tree, The	STO-N 89	STRAUB, Peter
3	Night Flier, The	STO-N 89	KING, Stephen
3	Skin Trade, The	STO-N 89	MARTIN, George R R
4	Night They Missed the Horror Show, The	STO-W 89	LANSDALE, Joe R
4	Jack's Decline	STO-N 89	SHEPARD, Lucius
4	Music of the Dark Time, The	STO-N 89	WILLIAMSON, Chet
4	Nobody Lives There Now	STO-N 89	ORLOCK, Carol
4	She's A Yng Thing & C'not Leave H/Mother	STO-N 89	ELLISON, Harlan
4	Thing At the Top of the Stairs, The	STO-N 89	BRADBURY, Ray
6	Charles Beaumont: Selected Stories	STO-W 89	BEAUMONT, Charles
6	Angry Candy	STO-N 89	ELLISON, Harlan
6	Blood and Water and Other Tales	STO-N 89	McGRATH, Patrick
6	Blood Kiss, The	STO-N 89	ETCHISON, Dennis
6	Scare Tactics	STO-N 89	FARRIS, John
6	Toynbee Convector, The	STO-N 89	BRADBURY, Ray
9	Suiting, The	STO-W 89	WILDE, Kelley
9	Cities of the Dead	STO-N 89	PAINE, Michael
9	Deliver Us From Evil	STO-N 89	HARRIS, Alan Lee
9	Demon Night	STO-N 89	STRACZYNSKI, J Michael
9	Fear Book	STO-N 89	BYRNE, John L
9	Resurrection Inc.	STO-N 89	ANDERSON, Kevin J
1	Carrion Comfort	STO-W 90	SIMMONS, Dan
1	Geek Love	STO-N 90	DUNN, Katherine
1	In A Dark Stream	STO-N 90	GRANT, Charles L
1	Midnight	STO-N 90	KOONTZ, Dean R
1	Wolf's Hour, The	STO-N 90	McCAMMON, Robert R
2	On t/Far Side of t/Cadillac Desert w/Dea	STO-W 90	LANSDALE, Joe R
2	At First Just Ghostly	STO-N 90	WAGNER, Karl Edward
2	Confession of St James, The	STO-N 90	WILLIAMSON, Chet
2	Phantom	STO-N 90	RUSCH, Kristine Kathryn
4	Eat Me	STO-W 90	McCAMMON, Robert R
4	Bodies and Heads	STO-N 90	TEM, Steve Rasnic
4	Each Night, Each Year	STO-N 90	PTACEK, Kathryn
4	Last Sad Love..., A	STO-N 90	BRYANT, Edward
6	Richard Matheson: Collected Stories	STO-W 90	MATHESON, Richard
6	Blue World and Other Stories	STO-N 90	McCAMMON, Robert R
6	By Bizarre Hands	STO-N 90	LANSDALE, Joe R
6	Patterns	STO-N 90	CADIGAN, Pat
6	Soft and Others	STO-N 90	WILSON, F Paul
6	Yore Skin's Jes' Soft'n' Purty, He Said	STO-N 90	WILLIAMSON, Chet

STOKER AWARDS

CAT	TITLE	AW W/N Y	AUTHOR
7	Harlan Ellison's Watching	STO-W 90	ELLISON, Harlan
7	Amer Vampires:Fans,Victims,Practicioners	STO-N 90	DRESSER, Norine
7	Horror: A Connoisseur's Guide	STO-N 90	WOLF, Leonard
7	Horror: The 100 Best Books	STO-N 90	JONES, Stephen
7	H.P. Lovecraft	STO-N 90	CANNON, Peter
9	Sunglasses After Dark	STO-W 90	COLLINS, Nancy A
9	Dwelling, The	STO-N 90	ELLIOT, Tom
9	Goat Dance	STO-N 90	CLEGG, Douglas
9	Laying the Music to Rest	STO-N 90	SMITH, Dean Wesley
9	Lilith Factor, The	STO-N 90	PAIVA, Jean
1	Mine	STO-W 91	McCAMMON, Robert R
1	Funland	STO-N 91	LAYMON, Richard
1	Reign	STO-N 91	WILLIAMSON, Chet
1	Savage Season	STO-N 91	LANSDALE, Joe R
2	Stephen	STO-W 91	MASSIE, Elizabeth
2	Bestseller	STO-N 91	BLUMLEIN, Michael
2	Entropy's Bed at Midnight	STO-N 91	SIMMONS, Dan
2	Langoliers, The	STO-N 91	KING, Stephen
2	Pelts	STO-N 91	WILSON, F Paul
4	Calling, The	STO-W 91	SILVA, David
4	Back Windows	STO-N 91	TEM, Steve Rasnic
4	But You'll Never Follow Me	STO-N 91	WAGNER, Karl Edward
4	From the Papers of Helmut Hecher	STO-N 91	WILLIAMSON, Chet
4	Loneliest Number, The	STO-N 91	BRYANT, Edward
6	Four Past Midnight	STO-W 91	KING, Stephen
6	Brains of Rats, The	STO-N 91	BLUMLEIN, Michael
6	Houses Without Doors	STO-N 91	STRAUB, Peter
6	Prayers to Broken Stones	STO-N 91	SIMMONS, Dan
7	Dark Dreamers	STO-W 91	WIATER, Stanley
7	Hollywood Gothic	STO-N 91	SKAL, David J
7	Horror Literature: A Reader's Guide	STO-N 91	BARRON, Neil
7	Joe Bob Goes Back to the Drive-in	STO-N 91	BRIGGS, Joe Bob
7	Weird Tale, The	STO-N 91	JOSHI, S T
9	Revelation, The	STO-W 91	LITTLE, Bentley
9	Blood of the Children	STO-N 91	RODGERS, Alan
9	Dark Father	STO-N 91	PICCIRILLI, Tom
9	Nightblood	STO-N 91	MARTINDALE, T Chris
1	Boy's Life	STO-W 92	McCAMMON, Robert R
1	Dark Towers III, The: The Waste Lands	STO-N 92	KING, Stephen
1	M.D., The	STO-N 92	DISCH, Thomas M
1	Needful Things	STO-N 92	KING, Stephen
1	Summer of Night	STO-N 92	SIMMONS, Dan
2	Beautiful Uncut Hair of Graves	STO-W 92	MORRELL, David
2	Advocates	STO-N 92	CHARNAS, Suzy McKee
2	Death Leaves an Echo	STO-N 92	de LINT, Charles
2	Fetish	STO-N 92	BRYANT, Edward
2	Magpie	STO-N 92	GALLAGHER, Stephen

CAT	TITLE	AW W/N Y	AUTHOR
4	Lady Madonna	STO-W 92	HOLDER, Nancy
4	Ash of Memory, The Dust of Desire, The	STO-N 92	BRITE, Poppy Z
4	Braile Encyclopedia, The	STO-N 92	MORRISON, Grant
4	Love Doll: A Fable	STO-N 92	LANSDALE, Joe R
4	Richard's Head	STO-N 92	SARRANTONIO, Al
4	Wolf Winter	STO-N 92	O'CALLAGHAN, Maxine
5	Prayers to Broken Stones	STO-W 92	SIMMONS, Dan
5	Author's Choice Monthly #24	STO-N 92	WILLIAMSON, J N
5	Sexpunks and Savage Sagas	STO-N 92	SUTPHIN, Richard
5	Walking Nightmares	STO-N 92	CAMPBELL, Ramsey
7	Clive Barker's Shadows of Eden	STO-W 92	JONES, Stephen
7	Prism of the Night: Biography Anne Rice	STO-N 92	RAMSLAND, Katherine
7	Shape Under t/Street:Compl Encycl S King	STO-N 92	SPIGNESI, Stephen J
7	Vampires Among Us	STO-N 92	GUILLEN, Rosemary Ellen
9	Cipher, The	STO-W 92	KOJA, Kathe
9	Prodigal	STO-W 92	TEM, Melanie
9	Unearthed	STO-N 92	McCONNELL, Ashley
9	Wilderness	STO-N 92	DANVERS, Dennis
9	Winter Scream	STO-N 92	CURRY, Chris

WORLD FANTASY AWARD

The World Fantasy Award (also called the Howard Award) consists of a misshapen metal bust of H(oward) P(hillips) Lovecraft designed by artist Grahan Wilson. Attending and supporting members of the World Fantasy Convention are eligible to nominate potential winners, the final decision being made by a panel of judges. Only living persons are eligible. Presentations are made annually at the World Fantasy Convention.

CAT	TITLE	AW W/N Y	AUTHOR
1	Forgotten Beast of Eld	WFA-W 75	McKILLIP, Patricia
1	Merlin's Ring	WFA-N 75	MUNN, H Warner
1	Midsummer Tempest, A	WFA-N 75	ANDERSON, Poul
2	Pages From A Young Girl's Diary	WFA-W 75	AICKMAN, Robert
2	Events at Poroth Farm	WFA-N 75	KLEIN, T E D
2	Farmer's Tale, A	WFA-N 75	LANIER, Sterling
2	Sticks	WFA-N 75	WAGNER, Karl Edward
5	Worse Things Waiting	WFA-W 75	WELLMAN, Manly Wade
5	From Earth's Pillow	WFA-N 75	COPPER, Basil
1	Bid Time Return	WFA-W 76	MATHESON, Richard
1	Salem's Lot	WFA-N 76	KING, Stephen
2	Belsen Express	WFA-W 76	LEIBER, Fritz
2	Barrow Troll, The	WFA-N 76	DRAKE, David
2	Born of the Winds	WFA-N 76	LUMLEY, Brian
2	Ghastly Priest Doth Reign, The	WFA-N 76	WELLMAN, Manly Wade
5	Enquiries of Dr Eszterhazy	WFA-W 76	DAVIDSON, Avram
5	Deathbird Stories	WFA-N 76	ELLISON, Harlan
5	Early Long, The	WFA-N 76	LONG, Frank Belknap
5	Far Lands, Other Days	WFA-N 76	PRICE, E Hoffman
1	Doctor Rat	WFA-W 77	KOTZWINKLE, William
1	Acts of King Arthur & His Noble Knights	WFA-N 77	STEINBECK, John
1	Dark Crusade	WFA-N 77	WAGNER, Karl Edward
1	Doll Who Ate His Mother, The	WFA-N 77	CAMPBELL, Ramsey
1	Dragon and the George, The	WFA-N 77	DICKSON, Gordon R
1	Sailor on the Seas of Fate, The	WFA-N 77	MOORCOCK, Michael
2	There's A Long, Long Trail A-Winding	WFA-W 77	KIRK, Russell
2	Companion, The	WFA-N 77	CAMPBELL, Ramsey
2	Dark Wings	WFA-N 77	LEIBER, Fritz
2	It Only Comes Out At Night	WFA-N 77	ETCHISON, Dennis
2	Two Suns Setting	WFA-N 77	WAGNER, Karl Edward
2	What Is Life	WFA-N 77	SHECKLEY, Robert
6	Frights	WFA-W 77	McCAULEY, Kirby
6	Cinnabar	WFA-N 77	BRYANT, Edward
6	Flashing Swords #3	WFA-N 77	CARTER, Lin
6	Height of the Scream, The	WFA-N 77	CAMPBELL, Ramsey
6	Long After Midnight	WFA-N 77	BRADBURY, Ray
6	Superhorror	WFA-N 77	CAMPBELL, Ramsey

WORLD FANTASY AWARD

CAT	TITLE	AW W/N Y	AUTHOR
1	Our Lady of Darkness	WFA-W 78	LEIBER, Fritz
1	Chronicles o/Thomas Covenant t/Unbeleive	WFA-N 78	DONALDSON, Stephen R
1	Hour of the Oxrun Dead, The	WFA-N 78	GRANT, Charles L
4	Bagful of Dreams	WFA-N 78	VANCE, Jack
4	Jeffty is Five	WFA-N 78	ELLISON, Harlan
4	Loveman's Comeback	WFA-N 78	CAMPBELL, Ramsey
4	Manatee Gal, Ain't Ya Comin' Out Tonight	WFA-N 78	DAVIDSON, Avram
4	When All the Children Call My Name	WFA-N 78	GRANT, Charles L
6	Murgunstrumm and Others	WFA-W 78	CAVE, Hugh B
6	Cold Chills	WFA-N 78	BLOCH, Robert
6	Swords and Ice Magic	WFA-N 78	LEIBER, Fritz
6	Whispers	WFA-N 78	SCHIFF, Stuart David
6	Year's Best Horror Stories # 5	WFA-N 78	PAGE, Gerald W
1	Gloriana	WFA-W 79	MOORCOCK, Michael
1	Black Castle, The	WFA-N 79	DANIELS, Lee
1	Night's Master	WFA-N 79	LEE, Tanith
1	Sound At Midnight, The	WFA-N 79	GRANT, Charles L
1	Stand, The	WFA-N 79	KING, Stephen
4	Naples	WFA-N 79	DAVIDSON, Avram
4	Good Night's Sleep, A	WFA-N 79	DAVIDSON, Avram
4	Hear Me Now, Sweet Abbey Rose	WFA-N 79	GRANT, Charles L
4	Magic Goes Away, The	WFA-N 79	NIVEN, Larry
4	Within the Walls of Tyre	WFA-N 79	BISHOP, Michael
6	Shadows	WFA-W 79	GRANT, Charles L
6	Heroes and Horror	WFA-N 79	LEIBER, Fritz
6	Night Shift	WFA-N 79	KING, Stephen
6	Night Winds	WFA-N 79	WAGNER, Karl Edward
6	Redward, Edward Papers, The	WFA-N 79	DAVIDSON, Avram
6	Year's Best Horror Stories # 6	WFA-N 79	PAGE, Gerald W
1	Watchtower	WFA-N 80	LYNN, Elizabeth A
1	Dancers of Arun, The	WFA-N 80	LYNN, Elizabeth A
1	Dark Bright Water, The	WFA-N 80	WRIGHTSON, Patricia
1	Harpist in the Wind	WFA-N 80	McKILLIP, Patricia
1	Last Call of Morning, The	WFA-N 80	GRANT, Charles L
1	Palace, The	WFA-N 80	YARBRO, Chelsea Quinn
4	Macintosth Willy	WFA-N 80	CAMPBELL, Ramsey
4	Women Who Loved the Moon	WFA-N 80	LYNN, Elizabeth A
4	Button Molder, The	WFA-N 80	LEIBER, Fritz
4	Petey	WFA-N 80	KLEIN, T E D
4	Saturday's Shadow	WFA-N 80	NOLAN, William F
4	Year's Finest Fantasy Vol 2	WFA-N 80	CARR, Terry
6	Amazons!	WFA-N 80	SALMONSON, Jessica Amanda
6	Nightmares	WFA-N 80	GRANT, Charles L
6	Shadows 2	WFA-N 80	GRANT, Charles L
6	Thieve's World	WFA-N 80	ASPRIN, Robert Lynn
6	Whispers 2	WFA-N 80	SCHIFF, Stuart David

CAT	T I T L E	AW W/N Y	A U T H O R
1	Shadow of the Torturer, The	WFA-W 81	WOLFE, Gene
1	Ariosto	WFA-N 81	YARBRO, Chelsea Quinn
1	Firelord	WFA-N 81	GODWIN, Parke
1	Mist, The	WFA-N 81	KING, Stephen
1	Shadow Land	WFA-N 81	STRAUB, Peter
4	Ugly Chickens, The	WFA-W 81	WALDROP, Howard
4	Cabin 33	WFA-N 81	YARBRO, Chelsea Quinn
4	Children of the Kingdom	WFA-N 81	KLEIN, T E D
4	Unicorn Tapestry	WFA-N 81	CHARNAS, Suzy McKee
6	Dark Forces	WFA-W 81	McCAULEY, Kirby
6	Dragons of Light	WFA-N 81	CARD, Orson Scott
6	Mummy! A Chrestomathy of Crypt-ology	WFA-N 81	PRONZINI, Bill
6	New Terrors 1	WFA-N 81	CAMPBELL, Ramsey
6	Shadows 3	WFA-N 81	GRANT, Charles L
6	Shatterday	WFA-N 81	ELLISON, Harlan
1	Little Big	WFA-W 82	CROWLEY, John
1	Claw of the Conciliator, The	WFA-N 82	WOLFE, Gene
1	Nameless, The	WFA-N 82	CAMPBELL, Ramsey
1	War Hounds and the World's Pain, The	WFA-N 82	MOORCOCK, Michael
1	White Hotel, The	WFA-N 82	THOMAS, D M
2	Fire When It Comes, The	WFA-W 82	GODWIN, Parke
2	Ealdwood	WFA-N 82	CHERRYH, C J
2	Mythago Wood	WFA-N 82	HOLDSTOCK, Robert
2	River of Night's Dreaming	WFA-N 82	WAGNER, Karl Edward
4	Dark Country, The	WFA-W 82	ETCHISON, Dennis
4	Do the Dead Sing?	WFA-W 82	KING, Stephen
4	Coin of the Reallm	WFA-N 82	GRANT, Charles L
4	Fairy Tale	WFA-N 82	DANN, Jack
6	Elsewhere	WFA-W 82	WINDLING, Terri
6	Fantasy Annual 4	WFA-N 82	CARR, Terry
6	Shadows 4	WFA-N 82	GRANT, Charles L
6	Tales From the Nightside	WFA-N 82	GRANT, Charles L
6	Whispers 3	WFA-N 82	SCHIFF, Stuart David
1	Nifft the Lean	WFA-W 83	SHEA, Michael
1	Fevre Dream	WFA-N 83	MARTIN, George R R
1	Nestling, The	WFA-N 83	GRANT, Charles L
1	Phantom	WFA-N 83	TESSIER, Thomas
1	Sword of the Lichtor, The	WFA-N 83	WOLFE, Gene
2	Beyond All Measure	WFA-W 83	WAGNER, Karl Edward
2	Confess the Seasons	WFA-W 83	GRANT, Charles L
2	Breathing Method, The	WFA-N 83	KING, Stephen
2	Horrible Imaginings (Death)	WFA-N 83	LEIBER, Fritz
2	Night's Swift Dragons	WFA-N 83	GRANT, Charles L

CAT	TITLE	AW W/N Y	AUTHOR
4	Gorgon, The	WFA-W 83	LEE, Tanith
4	Deathtracks	WFA-N 83	ETCHISON, Dennis
4	Firestorm	WFA-N 83	TEM, Steve Rasnic
4	Gorgon, The	WFA-N 83	LEE, Tanith
4	Man Who Met Picasso, The	WFA-N 83	SWANWICK, Michael
4	Petra	WFA-N 83	BEAR, Greg
6	Nightmare Seasons	WFA-W 83	GRANT, Charles L
1	Dragon Waiting, The	WFA-W 84	FORD, John M
1	Armageddon Rag, The	WFA-N 84	MARTIN, George R R
1	Lyonesse	WFA-N 84	VANCE, Jack
1	Pet Sematary	WFA-N 84	KING, Stephen
1	Tea With The Black Dragon	WFA-N 84	MacAVOY, R A
1	Wandering Unicorn, The	WFA-N 84	LAINEZ, Manuel Mujica
2	Black Air	WFA-W 84	ROBINSON, Kim Stanley
2	Lurking Duck, The	WFA-N 84	BAKER, Scott
2	Monkey's Bride, The	WFA-N 84	BISHOP, Michael
2	Nung Dimittis	WFA-N 84	LEE, Tanith
2	Red Hawk, The	WFA-N 84	LYNN, Elizabeth A
4	Elle Est Trois	WFA-W 84	LEE, Tanith
4	Hundred Year Christmas	WFA-N 84	MORRELL, David
4	Into Whose Hands	WFA-N 84	WAGNER, Karl Edward
4	Silent Cradle	WFA-N 84	KENNEDY, Leigh
4	Solitario's Eyes	WFA-N 84	SHEPARD, Lucius
4	Wong's Lost and Found Emporium	WFA-N 84	WU, William F
6	High Spirits	WFA-W 84	DAVIES, Robinson
6	Dodd, Mead Gallery of Horrors, The	WFA-N 84	GRANT, Charles L
6	Red As Blood	WFA-N 84	LEE, Tanith
6	Shadows 6	WFA-N 84	GRANT, Charles L
6	Tales of Wonder	WFA-N 84	YOLEN, Jane
1	Bridge of Birds	WFA-W 85	HUGHART, Barry
1	Mythago Wood	WFA-W 85	HOLDSTOCK, Robert
1	Archer's Goon	WFA-N 85	JONES, Diana Wynne
1	Ceremonies, The	WFA-N 85	KLEIN, T E D
1	Talisman, The	WFA-N 85	STRAUB, Peter
2	Unconquered Country, The	WFA-W 85	RYMAN, Geoff
2	Ballad of the Flexible Bullet, The	WFA-N 85	KING, Stephen
2	In The Sumerian Marshes	WFA-N 85	PEARLE, Gerald
2	Jacqueline Ess: Her Will and Testament	WFA-N 85	BARKER, Clive
2	Man Who Painted the Dragon Griaule, The	WFA-N 85	SHEPARD, Lucius
4	Bones Wizard, The	WFA-W 85	RYAN, Alan
4	Still Life With Scorpion	WFA-W 85	BAKER, Scott
4	Bad Medicine	WFA-N 85	DANN, Jack
4	Nightcrawlers	WFA-N 85	McCAMMON, Robert R

WORLD FANTASY AWARD

CAT	TITLE	AW W/N Y	AUTHOR
6	Clive Barker's Books of Blood, Vols 1-3	WFA-W 85	BARKER, Clive
6	Fire When It Comes, The	WFA-N 85	GODWIN, Parke
6	Masques	WFA-N 85	WILLIAMSON, J N
6	Night Visions 1	WFA-N 85	RYAN, Alan
6	Songbird of Pain, The	WFA-N 85	KILWORTH, Garry
6	Viriconium Nights	WFA-N 85	HARRISON, M John
1	Song of Kali	WFA-W 86	SIMMONS, Dan
1	Damnation Game, The	WFA-N 86	BARKER, Clive
1	Dream Years, The	WFA-N 86	GOLDSTEIN, Lisa
1	Illywacker	WFA-N 86	CAREY, Peter
1	Vampire Lestat, The	WFA-N 86	RICE, Anne
1	Winter King	WFA-N 86	HAZEL, Paul
2	Nadelman's God	WFA-W 86	KLEIN, T E D
2	Dare I Eat A Peach	WFA-N 86	YARBRO, Chelsea Quinn
2	Dead Image	WFA-N 86	MORRELL, David
2	Flight	WFA-N 86	DICKINSON, Peter
2	Gorgon Field, The	WFA-N 86	WILHELM, Kate
4	Paper Dragons	WFA-W 86	BLAYLOCK, James P
4	Jaguar Hunter, The	WFA-N 86	SHEPARD, Lucius
4	Return of the Dust Vampire	WFA-N 86	FARBER, Sharon
4	Slovo Stove, The	WFA-N 86	DAVIDSON, Avram
6	Imaginary Lands	WFA-W 86	McKINLEY, Robin
6	Black Venus	WFA-N 86	CARTER, Angela
6	Clive Barker's Books of Blood, Vols 4-6	WFA-N 86	BARKER, Clive
6	Dragonfields	WFA-N 86	YOLEN, Jane
6	Feary	WFA-N 86	WINDLING, Terri
6	Night Visions 2	WFA-N 86	GRANT, Charles L
6	Skeleton Crew	WFA-N 86	KING, Stephen
6	Whispers 5	WFA-N 86	SCHIFF, Stuart David
1	Perfume	WFA-W 87	SUSKIND, Patrick
1	It	WFA-N 87	KING, Stephen
1	Pet, The	WFA-N 87	GRANT, Charles L
1	Soldier of the Mist	WFA-N 87	WOLFE, Gene
1	Strangers	WFA-N 87	KOONTZ, Dean R
1	Talking Man	WFA-N 87	BISSON, Terry
1	Tricksters, The	WFA-N 87	MAHY, Margaret
2	Hatrack River	WFA-W 87	CARD, Orson Scott
2	Chance	WFA-N 87	WILLIS, Connie
2	Hellhound Heart	WFA-N 87	BARKER, Clive
2	Night Moves	WFA-N 87	POWERS, Tim
2	Night Seasons, The	WFA-N 87	WILLIAMSON, J N

CAT	TITLE	AW W/N Y	AUTHOR
4	Red Light	WFA-W 87	SCHOW, David J
4	Boy Who Plaited Manes, The	WFA-N 87	SPRINGER, Nancy
4	Brains of Rats, The	WFA-N 87	BLUMLEIN, Michael
4	End of the Whole Mess, The	WFA-N 87	KING, Stephen
4	Pain	WFA-N 87	STRIEBER, Whitley
4	Rise and Fall of Father Alex, The	WFA-N 87	NAEGELE, Amyas
4	They're Coming For You	WFA-N 87	DANIELS, Les
4	Tight Little Stitches in Dead Man's Back	WFA-N 87	LANSDALE, Joe R
6	Tales of the Quintana Roo	WFA-W 87	TIPTREE, James Jr
6	Black Wine	WFA-N 87	WINTER, Douglas E
6	Cutting Edge	WFA-N 87	ETCHISON, Dennis
6	Dreams of Dark and Light	WFA-N 87	LEE, Tanith
6	Liavek: The Players of Luck	WFA-N 87	SHETTERLEY, Will
6	Merlin's Booke	WFA-N 87	YOLEN, Jane
6	Night Visions 3	WFA-N 87	MARTIN, George R R
1	Replay	WFA-W 88	GRIMWOOD, Ken
1	Aegypt	WFA-N 88	CROWLEY, John
1	Misery	WFA-N 88	KING, Stephen
1	On Stranger Tides	WFA-N 88	POWERS, Tim
1	Seventh Son	WFA-N 88	CARD, Orson Scott
1	Swan Song	WFA-N 88	McCAMMON, Robert R
1	Weaveworld	WFA-N 88	BARKER, Clive
2	Buffalo Gals, Won't You Come Out Tonight	WFA-W 88	LeGUIN, Ursula K
2	Best Friends	WFA-N 88	McCAMMON, Robert R
2	Boy Who Came Back From the Dead, The	WFA-N 88	RODGERS, Alan
2	Hypothetical Lizard, A	WFA-N 88	MOORE, Alan
2	Nesting Instinct	WFA-N 88	BAKER, Scott
2	Pear-Shaped Man, The	WFA-N 88	MARTIN, George R R
2	Shades	WFA-N 88	SHEPARD, Lucius
4	Friend's Best Man	WFA-W 88	CARROLL, Jonathan
4	Angel	WFA-N 88	CADIGAN, Pat
4	Hogfoot Right and Bird-Hands	WFA-N 88	KILWORTH, Garry
4	In The House of Gingerbread	WFA-N 88	WOLFE, Gene
4	Pamela's Get	WFA-N 88	SCHOW, David J
4	Splatter: A Cautionary Tale	WFA-N 88	WINTER, Douglas E
5	Jaguar Hunter, The	WFA-W 88	SHEPARD, Lucius
5	Night Sorceries	WFA-N 88	LEE, Tanith
5	Polyphemus	WFA-N 88	SHEA, Michael
5	Scared Stiff, Tales of Sex & Death	WFA-N 88	CAMPBELL, Ramsey
5	Why Not You and I?	WFA-N 88	WAGNER, Karl Edward
6	Architecture of Fear	WFA-N 88	CRAMER, Kathryn
6	Dark Descent, The	WFA-N 88	HARTWELL, David G
6	In the Field of Fire	WFA-N 88	DANN, Jeanne van Buren
6	Masques II	WFA-N 88	WILLIAMSON, J N
6	Night Visions 4	WFA-N 88	Dark Harvest
6	Other Edens	WFA-N 88	EVANS, Christopher
6	Year's Best Horror Stories #15	WFA-N 88	WAGNER, Karl Edward

WORLD FANTASY AWARD

CAT	TITLE	AW W/N Y	AUTHOR
1	Koko	WFA-W 89	STRAUB, Peter
1	Drive-in, The	WFA-N 89	LANSDALE, Joe R
1	Fade	WFA-N 89	CORMIER, Robert
1	Last Coin, The	WFA-N 89	BLAYLOCK, James P
1	Silence of the Lambs, The	WFA-N 89	HARRIS, Thomas
1	Sleeping in Flame	WFA-N 89	CARROLL, Jonathan
2	Skin Trade, The	WFA-W 89	MARTIN, George R R
2	Devil's Arithmetic, The	WFA-N 89	YOLEN, Jane
2	Gardener, The	WFA-N 89	TEPPER, Sheri S
2	Scalehunter's Beautiful Daughter, The	WFA-N 89	SHEPARD, Lucius
4	Winter Solstice, Camelot Station	WFA-W 89	FORD, John M
4	Life of Buddha	WFA-N 89	SHEPARD, Lucius
4	Metastasis	WFA-N 89	SIMMONS, Dan
4	Night They Missed the Horror Show, The	WFA-N 89	LANSDALE, Joe R
5	Angry Candy	WFA-N 89	ELLISON, Harlan
5	Blood Kiss, The	WFA-N 89	ETCHISON, Dennis
5	Cabal	WFA-N 89	BARKER, CLive
5	Charles Beaumont: Selected Stories	WFA-N 89	ANKER, Roger
5	Knight and the Knave of Swords, The	WFA-N 89	LEIBER, Fritz
5	Storeys From The Old Hotel	WFA-N 89	WOLFE, Gene
6	Year's Best Fantasy and Horror 1st	WFA-N 89	DATLOW, Ellen
6	Night Visions 6	WFA-N 89	ANON
6	Prime Evil	WFA-N 89	WINTER, Douglas E
6	Silver Scream	WFA-N 89	SCHOW, David J
1	Lyonesse: Madouc	WFA-W 90	VANCE, Jack
1	Carrion Comfort	WFA-N 90	SIMMONS, Dan
1	Child Across the Sky, A	WFA-N 90	CARROLL, Jonathan
1	In A Dark Dream	WFA-N 90	GRANT, Charles L
1	Soldier of Arete	WFA-N 90	WOLFE, Gene
1	Stress of Her Regard, The	WFA-N 90	POWERS, Tim
2	Great Works of Time	WFA-W 90	CROWLEY, John
2	Apartheid,Superstr'gs & Modercai Thubana	WFA-N 90	BISHOP, Michael
2	Dozen Tough Jobs, A	WFA-N 90	WALDROP, Howard
2	Father of Stones, The	WFA-N 90	SHEPARD, Lucius
2	On t/Far Side of t/Cadillac Desert w/Dea	WFA-N 90	LANSDALE, Joe R
4	Illusionist, The	WFA-W 90	MILLHAUSER, Steven
4	Edge of the World, The	WFA-N 90	SWANWICK, Michael
4	Last Sad Love..., A	WFA-N 90	BRYANT, Edward
4	Mr. Fiddlehead	WFA-N 90	CARROLL, Jonathan
4	Varicose Worms	WFA-N 90	BAKER, Scott
5	Richard Matheson: Collected Stories	WFA-W 90	MATHESON, Richard
5	Blue World and Other Stories	WFA-N 90	McCAMMON, Robert R
5	By Bizarre Hands	WFA-N 90	LANSDALE, Joe R
5	Harlan Ellison's Watching	WFA-N 90	ELLISON, Harlan
5	Novelty	WFA-N 90	CROWLEY, John

CAT	TITLE	AW W/N Y	AUTHOR
6	Year's Best Fantasy and Horror 2nd	WFA-W 90	DATLOW, Ellen
6	Blood is Not Enough	WFA-N 90	DATLOW, Ellen
6	Book of the Dead	WFA-N 90	SKIPP, John
6	Razored Saddles	WFA-N 90	LANSDALE, Joe R
6	Yore Skin's Jes' Soft'n' Purty, He Said	WFA-N 90	WILLIAMSON, Chet
1	Only Begotten Daughter	WFA-W 91	MORROW, James
1	Thomas the Rhymer	WFA-W 91	KUSHNER, Ellen
1	Good Omens	WFA-N 91	PRATCHETT, Terry
1	Mary Reilly	WFA-N 91	MARTIN, Valerie
1	Tigana	WFA-N 91	KAY, Guy Gavriel
2	Bones	WFA-W 91	MURPHY, Pat
2	Barrens, The	WFA-N 91	WILSON, F Paul
2	Black Cocktail	WFA-N 91	CARROLL, Jonathan
2	Hemingway Hoax, The	WFA-N 91	HALDEMAN, Joe
4	Midsummer Night's Dream, A	WFA-W 91	GAIMAN, Neil
4	Bears Discover Fire	WFA-N 91	BISSON, Terry
4	Last Feast of Harlequin, The	WFA-N 91	LIGOTTI, Thomas
4	Stephen	WFA-N 91	MASSIE, Elizabeth
5	Start of the End of It All...	WFA-W 91	EMSHWILLER, Carol
5	Brains of Rats, The	WFA-N 91	BLUMLEIN, Michael
5	Houses Without Doors	WFA-N 91	STRAUB, Peter
5	Leiber Chronicles, The	WFA-N 91	LEIBER, Fritz
5	Prayers to Broken Stones	WFA-N 91	SIMMONS, Dan
6	Best New Horror	WFA-W 91	JONES, Stephen
6	Alien Sex	WFA-N 91	DATLOW, Ellen
6	Borderlands	WFA-N 91	MONTELEONE, Thomas F
6	Dark Voices 2	WFA-N 91	SUTTON, David
6	Walls of Fear	WFA-N 91	CRAMER, Kathryn
6	Year's Best Fantasy and Horror 4th	WFA-N 91	DATLOW, Ellen
1	Boy's Life	WFA-W 92	McCAMMON, Robert R
1	Bone Dance	WFA-N 92	BULL, Emma
1	Hunting the Ghost Dancer	WFA-N 92	ATTANASIO, A A
1	Little Country, The	WFA-N 92	de LINT, Charles
1	Outside the Dog Museum	WFA-N 92	CARROLL, Jonathan
1	Paper Grail, The	WFA-N 92	BLAYLOCK, James P
2	Gallery of His Dreams, The	WFA-N 92	RUSCH, Kristine Kathryn
2	Gwidion and the Dragon	WFA-N 92	CHERRYH, C J
2	Our Lady of the Harbour	WFA-N 92	de LINT, Charles
2	Pavilion of Frozen Women, The	WFA-N 92	SOMTOW, S P
2	Ragthorn, The	WFA-N 92	HOLDSTOCK, Robert
2	To Become A Sorcerer	WFA-N 92	SCHWEITZER, Darrell
4	Better Boy	WFA-N 92	BLAYLOCK, James P
4	Conjure Man, The	WFA-N 92	de LINT, Charles
4	Pity the Monsters	WFA-N 92	de LINT, Charles
4	Somewhere Doors, The	WFA-N 92	CHAPPELL, Fred

WORLD FANTASY AWARD

CAT	TITLE	AW W/N Y	AUTHOR
5	Bone Forest, The	WFA-N 92	HOLDSTOCK, Robert
5	Ends of the Earth, The	WFA-N 92	SHEPARD, Lucius
5	Grimscribe: His Lives and Works	WFA-N 92	LIGOTTI, Thomas
5	Lafferty in Orbit	WFA-N 92	LAFFERTY, R A
5	More Shapes Than One	WFA-N 92	CHAPPELL, Fred
5	Night of the Cooters: More Neat Stories	WFA-N 92	WALDROP, Howard
6	After t/King:Stories Honor of Tolkien	WFA-N 92	GREENBERG, Martin H
6	Famous Fantastic Mysteries	WFA-N 92	DZIEMIANOWICZ, Stefan R
6	Final Shadows	WFA-N 92	GRANT, Charles L
6	When The Music is Over	WFA-N 92	SHINER, Lewis
6	Whisper of Blood, A	WFA-N 92	DATLOW, Ellen
6	Year's Best Fantasy and Horror 4th	WFA-N 92	DATLOW, Ellen

Part B   MAJOR SCIENCE FICTION AWARDS

Authors Listed Alphabetically

The authors are listed alphabetically along with their winning or nominated works. This is particularly useful for readers who wish to locate a particular title but are only certain of the author's name, or to obtain a listing of the important works of a favourite author.

A full description of all abbreviations used within these listings can be found on the next page.

SECTION B: AUTHORS (Alphabetically)

HEADINGS:

AUTHOR		
CAT	TITLE	AW W/N Y

EXPLANATIONS:

CAT = Category (length and type)

1	Novel	2	Novella	3	Novellette
4	Short Story	5	1-Author Collection	6	Collection/Anthology
7	Non-Fiction	8	Series	9	First Novel
10	Horror	11	Fantasy Novel	12	Magazine Article
13	Original Anthology	14	Reprint Anthology		

LENGTH OF WORK	(from Locus Reader Awards)
Novel	40,000 + words
Novella	17,500 - 40,000
Novellette	7,500 - 17,500
Short Story	up to 7,500

AW = Award

AUR	Aurora (Casper)
BFA	British Fantasy
BSF	British Science Fiction
CLA	Arthur C. Clarke
COM	Compton Crook
DAV	Davis Publications
DIC	Dick
DIT	Ditmar
HUG	Hugo
IFA	International Fantasy
JUP	Jupiter
JWC	J W Campbell
LOC	Locus Magazine
NEB	Nebula
SFC	SF Chronicle Magazine
STO	Bram Stoker
WFA	World Fantasy

W/N = winner or nominee

Y = year award presented

AUTHORS - Alphabetically

AUTHOR		
CAT	T I T L E	AW W/N Y
ADAMS, Douglas		
1	Hitchhiker's Guide to the Galaxy, The	DIT-W 80
ADDAMS, Charles		
7	World of Charles Addams, The	HUG-W 92
7	World of Charles Addams, The	LOC-N 92
ADRIDGE, Mary		
4	Adinkra Cloth, The	NEB-N 89
2	Pages From A Young Girl's Diary	WFA-W 75
4	Stains	BFA-W 81
ALDISS, Brian W		
7	Billion Year Spree	BSF-W 74
7	Bury My Heart at W.H. Smiths	LOC-N 91
7	Bury My Heart at W.H. Smiths	HUG-N 91
2	Enemies of the System	HUG-N 79
1	Helliconia Spring	JWC-W 83
1	Helliconia Spring	NEB-N 82
1	Helliconia Spring	LOC-N 83
1	Helliconia Spring	BSF-N 84
1	Helliconia Spring	BSF-W 83
1	Helliconia Summer	SFC-N 84
1	Helliconia Summer	LOC-N 84
1	Helliconia Winter	NEB-N 85
1	Helliconia Winter	BSF-W 86
1	Helliconia Winter	LOC-N 86
1	Helliconia Winter	SFC-N 86
4	Hothouse Series, The	HUG-W 62
4	Man In His Time	HUG-N 67
4	Man In His Time	NEB-N 66
1	Moment of Eclipse, The	BSF-W 72
7	Pale Shadow of Science, The	HUG-N 86
7	Pale Shadow of Science, The	LOC-N 86
2	Saliva Tree	NEB-W 65
3	Total Environment	NEB-N 68
3	Total Environment	HUG-N 69
7	Trillion Year Spree	HUG-W 87
7	Trillion Year Spree	LOC-W 87

AUTHORS - Alphabetically

CAT	A U T H O R	
	T I T L E	AW W/N Y
	ALDRIDGE, Ray	
3	Gate of Faces	NEB-N 92
3	Gate of Faces	SFC-N 92
	ALLEN, Roger MacBride	
1	Orphan of Creation	DIC-N 89
4	Phreak Encounter	DAV-W 87
	AMIS, Kingsley	
1	Alteration, The	JWC-W 77
	ANDERSON, Chester	
1	Butterfly Kid, The	HUG-N 68
	ANDERSON, Kevin J	
9	Resurrection Inc.	STO-N 89
	ANDERSON, Poul	
1	Boat of a Million Years	SFC-N 90
1	Boat of a Million Years	HUG-N 90
1	Boat of a Million Years	LOC-N 90
1	Boat of a Million Years	NEB-N 89
1	Byworlder	NEB-N 71
5	Earth Book of Stormgate, The	LOC-N 79
1	Enemy Stars, The	HUG-N 59
2	Fatal Fulfillment, The	NEB-N 70
1	Fire Time	HUG-N 75
4	Goat Song	LOC-N 73
3	Goat Song	HUG-W 73
3	Goat Song	NEB-W 72
1	High Crusade, The	HUG-N 60
1	High Crusade, The	HUG-N 61
1	Hrolf Kraki's Saga	BFA-W 75
3	Hunter's Moon	HUG-W 79
3	Hunter's Moon	LOC-N 79
4	Kyrie	NEB-N 68
4	Longest Voyage, The	HUG-W 61
11	Merman's Children, The	LOC-N 80

CAT	T I T L E	AW W/N Y
A U T H O R		

ANDERSON, Poul   Continued...

CAT	TITLE	AW W/N Y
1	Midsummer Tempest, A	NEB-N 75
1	Midsummer Tempest, A	WFA-N 75
4	No Truce with Kings	HUG-W 64
1	People of the Wind, The	NEB-N 73
1	People of the Wind, The	HUG-N 74
1	People of the Wind, The	LOC-N 74
2	Queen of Air and Darkness, The	HUG-W 72
4	Queen of Air and Darkness, The	LOC-W 72
3	Queen of Air and Darkness, The	NEB-W 71
2	Saturn Game, The	NEB-W 81
2	Saturn Game, The	HUG-W 82
2	Saturn Game, The	LOC-N 82
3	Sharing of Flesh, The	NEB-N 68
3	Sharing of Flesh, The	HUG-W 69
1	Star Fox	NEB-N 65
2	Star of the Sea	LOC-N 92
1	Tau Zero	HUG-N 71
1	There Will be Time	HUG-N 73
3	Ways of Love, The	NEB-N 79

ANKER, Roger

| 5 | Charles Beaumont: Selected Stories | WFA-N 89 |

ANON

| 6 | Night Visions 6 | WFA-N 89 |

ANTHONY, Piers

7	Bio of an Ogre:Autobiog of Piers Anthony	LOC-N 89
11	Castle Roogna	LOC-N 80
1	Chton	NEB-N 67
1	Chton	HUG-N 68
3	Getting Through University	HUG-N 69
1	Macroscope	HUG-N 70
1	Macroscope	HUG-N 69
1	Spell for Chameleon, A	BFA-W 78

ARMSTRONG, Michael

| 1 | After the Zap | COM-N 88 |

AUTHOR		
CAT	T I T L E	AW W/N Y
ARNASON, Eleanor		
3	Warlord of Saturn's Moons, The	NEB-N 75
1	Woman of the Iron People, A	JWC-N 92
ARONICA, Lou		
6	Full Spectrum	LOC-W 89
6	Full Spectrum 2	LOC-N 90
6	Full Spectrum 3	LOC-W 92
ASH, Paul		
2	Man Opening a Door	NEB-N 92
ASHWELL, Pauline		
4	Lost Kafoozalum, The	HUG-N 61
3	Unwilling to School	HUG-N 59
ASIMOV, Isaac		
14	Before the Golden Age	LOC-W 75
5	Bicentennial Man, The	LOC-N 77
3	Bicentennial Man, The	LOC-W 77
3	Bicentennial Man, The	NEB-W 76
3	Bicentennial Man, The	HUG-W 77
4	Christmas Without Rodney	DAV-N 89
14	Early Asimov, The	LOC-N 73
4	Eyes Do More Than See	NEB-N 65
8	Foundation	HUG-W 66
1	Foundation and Earth	LOC-N 87
8	Foundation Trilogy	HUG-W 66
1	Foundation's Edge	SFC-N 83
1	Foundation's Edge	NEB-N 82
1	Foundation's Edge	LOC-W 83
1	Foundation's Edge	HUG-W 83
4	Founding Father	NEB-N 65
1	Gods Themselves, The	LOC-W 73
1	Gods Themselves, The	NEB-W 72
1	Gods Themselves, The	HUG-W 73
1	Gods Themselves, The	DIT-W 73
3	Gold	LOC-N 92
3	Gold	HUG-W 92

CAT	TITLE	AW W/N Y
	A U T H O R	

ASIMOV, Isaac   Continued...

CAT	TITLE	AW W/N Y
6	Great SF Stories #21, The	LOC-N 91
14	Hugo Winners Vol 2	LOC-N 72
7	In Joy Still Felt	HUG-N 81
7	In Joy Still Felt	LOC-W 81
7	In Memory Yet Green	LOC-N 80
7	In Memory Yet Green	HUG-N 80
4	Last Answer, The	LOC-N 81
1	Prelude to Foundation	LOC-N 89
4	Robot Dreams	HUG-N 87
4	Robot Dreams	DAV-W 87
4	Robot Dreams	NEB-N 86
4	Robot Dreams	LOC-W 87
4	Robot Dreams	SFC-N 87
1	Robots and Empire	LOC-N 86
1	Robots of Dawn	LOC-N 84
1	Robots of Dawn	HUG-N 84
3	That Thou Art Mindful of Him	HUG-N 75
3	That Thou Art Mindful of Him	LOC-N 75

ASPRIN, Robert Lynn

CAT	TITLE	AW W/N Y
6	Face of Chaos	LOC-N 84
6	Shadows of Sanctuary	LOC-W 82
6	Storm Season	LOC-N 83
6	Tales of the Vulgar Unicorn	LOC-N 81
6	Thieve's World	WFA-N 80
6	Thieve's World #7: The Dead of Winter	LOC-N 86
6	Wings of Omen	LOC-N 85

ATTANASIO, A A

CAT	TITLE	AW W/N Y
1	Hunting the Ghost Dancer	WFA-N 92
1	Radix	NEB-N 81
9	Radix	LOC-N 82

ATWOOD, Margaret

CAT	TITLE	AW W/N Y
1	Handmaid's Tale, The	LOC-N 87
1	Handmaid's Tale, The	CLA-W 87
1	Handmaid's Tale, The	NEB-N 86
1	Handmaid's Tale, The	SFC-N 87

AUTHOR		
CAT	T I T L E	AW W/N Y
AUSTIN, A J		
4	Siren	DAV-N 89
BAILEY, Dennis		
4	Tin Woodsman	NEB-N 77
BAKER, Anton Lee		
4	They've Been Working On...	HUG-N 59
BAKER, Scott		
2	Lurking Duck, The	WFA-N 84
2	Nesting Instinct	WFA-N 88
4	Still Life With Scorpion	WFA-W 85
4	Varicose Worms	WFA-N 90
BALLARD, J G		
4	Dream Cargoes	SFC-N 92
1	Empire of the Sun	BSF-N 85
1	Hello America	BSF-N 82
3	Myths of the Near Future	LOC-N 83
3	Myths of the Near Future	NEB-N 82
4	Myths of the Near Future	BSF-N 83
4	Object of the Attack, The	BSF-N 85
4	Souvenir	NEB-N 65
1	Unlimited Dream Company, The	JWC-N 80
1	Unlimited Dream Company, The	BSF-W 80
BANKS, Iain M		
1	Use of Weapons	CLA-N 91
1	Use of Weapons	BSF-N 91
BANTOCK, Nick		
7	Griffin & Sabine	LOC-N 92

AUTHORS - Alphabetically

	A U T H O R	
CAT	T I T L E	AW W/N Y
BARKER, Clive		
5	Cabal	WFA-N 89
6	Clive Barker's Books of Blood, Vols 1-3	WFA-W 85
5	Clive Barker's Books of Blood, Vols 4-6	LOC-N 86
6	Clive Barker's Books of Blood, Vols 4-6	WFA-N 86
1	Damnation Game, The	WFA-N 86
9	Damnation Game, The	STO-N 88
4	Forbidden, The	BFA-W 85
10	Great and Secret Show	LOC-N 90
2	Hellhound Heart	WFA-N 87
10	Imajica	LOC-N 92
2	Jacqueline Ess: Her Will and Testament	WFA-N 85
1	Weaveworld	BFA-N 88
11	Weaveworld	LOC-N 88
1	Weaveworld	WFA-N 88
BARLOWE, Wayne D		
7	Barlowe's Guide to Extraterrestials	HUG-N 80
BARNES, John		
4	My Advice to the Civilized	JWC-N 91
1	Orbital Resonance	NEB-N 92
3	Under the Covenant Stars	DAV-N 89
BARRETT, Neal Jr		
3	Ginny Sweethips' Flying Circus	NEB-N 88
3	Ginny Sweethips' Flying Circus	HUG-N 89
11	Hereafter Gang, The	LOC-N 92
4	Stairs	JWC-N 89
BARRON, Neil		
7	Anatomy of Wonder 2nd	HUG-N 82
7	Anatomy of Wonder 2nd	LOC-N 82
7	Anatomy of Wonder 3rd	LOC-N 88
7	Anatomy of Wonder 3rd	HUG-N 88
7	Horror Literature: A Reader's Guide	STO-N 91
BARTHELME, Donald		
4	Games	NEB-N 65

AUTHORS - Alphabetically

AUTHOR		
CAT	T I T L E	AW W/N Y
BASS, T J		
1	Godwhale, The	NEB-N 74
1	Godwhale, The	LOC-N 75
1	Half Past Human	NEB-N 71
BATCHELOR, John C		
1	Birth of t/People's Republ of Antarctica	JWC-N 84
BAXTER, Stephen M		
1	Raft	CLA-N 92
8	Raft	LOC-N 92
BAYLEY, Barrington J		
1	Zen Gun, The	DIC-N 84
BEAGLE, Peter S		
11	Folk of the Air, The	LOC-N 87
BEAR, Greg		
1	Blood Music	NEB-N 85
1	Blood Music	HUG-N 86
1	Blood Music	BSF-N 87
1	Blood Music	JWC-N 86
3	Blood Music	NEB-W 83
3	Blood Music	SFC-N 84
3	Blood Music	HUG-W 84
3	Blood Music	LOC-N 84
1	Eon	CLA-N 87
1	Eternity	LOC-N 89
1	Forge of God, The	LOC-N 88
1	Forge of God, The	NEB-N 87
1	Forge of God, The	HUG-N 88
2	Hardfought	LOC-N 84
2	Hardfought	NEB-W 83
2	Hardfought	SFC-N 84
2	Hardfought	HUG-N 84
2	Heads	LOC-N 91
11	Infinity Concerto, The	LOC-N 85

AUTHORS - Alphabetically

AUTHOR		
CAT	TITLE	AW W/N Y
BEAR, Greg Continued...		
3	Monkey Treatment, The	HUG-N 84
4	Petra	NEB-N 82
4	Petra	SFC-W 83
4	Petra	WFA-N 83
1	Queen of Angels	HUG-N 91
1	Queen of Angels	LOC-N 91
1	Queen of Angels	JWC-N 91
3	Sisters	LOC-N 90
3	Sisters	NEB-N 89
4	Tangents	SFC-N 87
4	Tangents	NEB-W 86
4	Tangents	LOC-N 87
5	Tangents	LOC-N 90
4	Tangents	HUG-W 87
5	Wind From A Burning Woman	LOC-N 84
BEAUCLERK, Jane		
4	Lord Moon	NEB-N 65
BEAUMONT, Charles		
6	Charles Beaumont: Selected Stories	STO-W 89
BECHTEL, Amy		
4	Circus Horse, The	DAV-W 89
4	Happy Dead, The	DAV-W 90
BEESE, P J		
1	Guardsman, The	HUG-N 89
BELL, Douglas		
1	Mojo and the Pickle Jar	DIC-N 92
BELL, John		
7	Visions From the Edge	AUR-N 82

AUTHOR		
CAT	**T I T L E**	**AW W/N Y**
BENFORD, Gregory		
1	Across The Sea of Suns	LOC-N 85
1	Against Infinity	NEB-N 83
2	Anvil of Jove, The	LOC-N 77
3	Deeper Than the Darkness	NEB-N 69
4	Deeper Than the Darkness	HUG-N 70
4	Doing Lennon	LOC-N 76
4	Doing Lennon	NEB-N 75
4	Doing Lennon	HUG-N 76
1	Great Sky River	NEB-N 88
1	Heart of the Comet	LOC-N 87
4	Hiss of Dragon, A	LOC-N 79
3	If the Stars are Gods	NEB-W 74
1	In the Ocean of the Night	LOC-N 78
1	In the Ocean of the Night	NEB-N 77
3	Matter's End	LOC-N 92
2	Newton Sleep	NEB-N 86
3	Of Space-Time and the River	LOC-N 87
4	Redeemer	LOC-N 80
2	Snark in the Night, A	LOC-N 78
2	Snark in the Night, A	HUG-N 78
2	Swarmer, Skimmer	NEB-N 81
1	Tides of Light	LOC-N 90
1	Timescape	NEB-W 80
1	Timescape	JWC-W 81
1	Timescape	LOC-N 81
1	Timescape	BSF-W 81
1	Timescape	DIT-W 81
4	Time's Rub	LOC-N 86
4	Time's Rub	SFC-N 86
6	What Might Have Been Vol 2	LOC-N 90
6	What Might Have Been Vol 3: Alt Wars	LOC-N 92
4	White Creatures	NEB-N 75
BENSEN, Donald R		
1	...And Having Writ	JWC-N 79
BERGERON, Alain		
4	Les Crabes des Venus	AUR-W 88

A U T H O R		
CAT	**T I T L E**	**AW W/N Y**
BERGERON, Richard		
7	Warhoon 28 Walter A Willis	HUG-N 81
BESTER, Alfred		
3	Animal Fair, The	NEB-N 72
1	Computer Connection, The	LOC-N 76
1	Computer Connection, The	NEB-N 75
1	Computer Connection, The	HUG-N 76
1	Demolished Man	HUG-W 53
1	Demolished Man	IFA-N 54
4	Four-Hour Fugue, The	HUG-N 75
4	Four-Hour Fugue, The	LOC-N 75
3	Galatea Galante	LOC-N 80
5	Light Fantastic, The	LOC-N 77
4	Men Who Murdered Mohammed, The	HUG-N 59
4	Pi Man, The	HUG-N 60
5	Star Light, Star Bright	LOC-N 77
BIGGLE, Lloyd Jr		
4	Monument	HUG-N 62
BISHOP, Michael		
4	Alien Grafitti	LOC-N 87
1	Ancient of Days	CLA-N 88
2	Apartheid,Superstr'gs & Modercai Thubana	NEB-N 92
2	Apartheid,Superstr'gs & Modercai Thubana	WFA-N 90
3	Blooded on Arachne	NEB-N 75
4	Cathadonian Odyssey	HUG-N 75
2	Death and Designation Among the Asadi	HUG-N 74
2	Death and Designation Among the Asadi	NEB-N 73
1	Funeral For Eyes of Fire, A	NEB-N 75
3	Gift From the Graylanders, A	NEB-N 85
3	Gift From the Graylanders, A	HUG-N 86
2	Gospel According to Gamaliel Crucis, The	NEB-N 83
2	Her Habiline Husband	SFC-W 84
2	Her Habiline Husband	NEB-N 83
2	Her Habiline Husband	LOC-W 84
6	Light Years and Dark	LOC-W 85
2	Monkey's Bride, The	WFA-N 84
6	Nebula Awards #24	LOC-N 91

AUTHOR		
CAT	T I T L E	AW W/N Y

BISHOP, Michael   Continued...

CAT	TITLE	AW W/N Y
1	No Enemy But Time	NEB-W 82
1	No Enemy But Time	BSF-N 83
1	No Enemy But Time	JWC-N 83
2	Old Folks At Home	LOC-N 79
4	Omnatidium Miniatures	NEB-N 89
2	On the Street of the Serpents	NEB-N 74
5	One Winter in Eden	LOC-N 85
1	Philip K Dick Is Dead Alas	CLA-N 89
3	Quickening, The	HUG-N 82
3	Quickening, The	NEB-W 81
4	Rogue Tomato	HUG-N 76
2	Samurai and the Willows, The	NEB-N 76
2	Samurai and the Willows, The	LOC-W 77
2	Samurai and the Willows, The	HUG-N 77
1	Transfigurations	BSF-N 81
11	Unicorn Mountain	LOC-N 89
4	Vernalfest	NEB-N 79
2	White Otters of Childhood, The	LOC-N 74
2	White Otters of Childhood, The	HUG-N 74
2	White Otters of Childhood, The	NEB-N 73
3	With A Little Help From Her Friends	LOC-N 85
4	Within the Walls of Tyre	BFA-N 79
4	Within the Walls of Tyre	WFA-N 79

BISSON, Ted

CAT	TITLE	AW W/N Y
1	Voyage to the Red Planet	LOC-N 91

BISSON, Terry

CAT	TITLE	AW W/N Y
4	Bears Discover Fire	JWC-W 91
4	Bears Discover Fire	NEB-N 91
4	Bears Discover Fire	WFA-N 91
4	Bears Discover Fire	HUG-W 91
4	Bears Discover Fire	LOC-W 91
4	Bears Discover Fire	DAV-W 91
4	Bears Discover Fire	SFC-N 91
4	Press Ann	LOC-N 92
4	Press Ann	HUG-N 92
1	Talking Man	WFA-N 87
4	They're Made Out of Meat	NEB-N 92

AUTHORS - Alphabetically

AUTHOR		
CAT	TITLE	AW W/N Y
BLAKE, Katherine		
1	Interior of Life, The	COM-N 91
BLAYLOCK, James P		
4	Better Boy	WFA-N 92
1	Homunculus	DIC-W 87
11	Last Coin, The	LOC-N 89
1	Last Coin, The	WFA-N 89
4	Paper Dragons	SFC-W 86
4	Paper Dragons	WFA-W 86
4	Paper Dragons	NEB-N 85
1	Paper Grail, The	WFA-N 92
BLEILER, Everett F		
7	SF: The Early Years	HUG-N 92
7	SF: The Early Years	LOC-W 92
BLISH, James		
1	Black Easter	NEB-N 68
1	Case of Conscience, A	HUG-W 59
2	Midsummer Century	LOC-N 73
2	Quincux of Time, The	JUP-N 74
3	Shipwrecked Hotel, The	NEB-N 65
2	We All Die Naked	HUG-N 70
BLOCH, Robert		
6	Cold Chills	WFA-N 78
4	Hell-Bound Train, That	HUG-W 59
6	Midnight Pleasures	STO-N 88
1	Psycho II	BFA-N 83
BLUMLEIN, Michael		
2	Bestseller	STO-N 91
6	Brains of Rats, The	STO-N 91
4	Brains of Rats, The	WFA-N 87
5	Brains of Rats, The	WFA-N 91

AUTHOR		
CAT	T I T L E	AW W/N Y
BOEM, Herb (Varley, John)		
4	Air Raid	LOC-N 78
BONE, J F		
4	Triggerman	HUG-N 59
BORGES, Jorge Luis		
4	Utopia of a Tired Man	NEB-N 75
BOVA, Ben		
4	Brillo	HUG-N 71
1	Colony	LOC-N 79
14	Science Fiction Hall of Fame Vol 2a & 2b	LOC-N 74
BOWKER, Richard		
1	Dover Beach	DIC-N 88
BOYLE, Nicholson		
6	Darklands	BFA-W 91
BRADBURY, Ray		
1	Illustrated Man, The	IFA-N 52
6	Long After Midnight	WFA-N 77
4	Thing At the Top of the Stairs, The	STO-N 89
6	Toynbee Convector, The	STO-N 89
BRADFIELD, Scott		
4	Flash Kid, The	BSF-N 84
4	Unmistakably the Finest	BSF-N 85
BRADLEY, Marion Zimmer		
1	Forbidden Tower (4): Darkover	HUG-N 78
1	Heritage Hastur (9):Darkover	NEB-N 75
11	Mists of Avalon, The	LOC-W 84
1	Sword of Aldones(10): Darkover	HUG-N 62
1	Sword of Aldones(10): Darkover	HUG-N 63

AUTHOR		
CAT	T I T L E	AW W/N Y
BRAND, Jonathan		
3	Vanishing Point	NEB-N 65
BRENNERT, Alan		
4	Ma Qui	NEB-W 92
4	Ma Qui	JWC-N 92
BRETNOR, Reginald		
4	Earthwoman	NEB-N 67
BRIGGS, Joe Bob		
7	Joe Bob Goes Back to the Drive-in	STO-N 88
7	Joe Bob Goes Back to the Drive-in	STO-N 91
BRIN, David		
4	Crystal Spheres, The	LOC-N 85
4	Crystal Spheres, The	HUG-W 85
2	Cyclops	HUG-N 85
3	Dr. Pak's Preschool	LOC-N 91
3	Dr. Pak's Preschool	HUG-N 91
1	Earth	HUG-N 91
1	Earth	LOC-N 91
1	Earth	SFC-N 91
4	Giving Plague, The	HUG-N 89
4	Giving Plague, The	LOC-N 89
1	Postman, The	LOC-W 86
1	Postman, The	SFC-N 86
1	Postman, The	NEB-N 85
1	Postman, The	HUG-N 86
2	Postman, The	LOC-N 83
1	Postman, The	JWC-W 86
2	Postman, The	HUG-N 83
4	Privacy	LOC-N 90
5	River of Time, The	LOC-N 87
1	Startide Rising	LOC-W 84
1	Startide Rising	SFC-N 84
1	Startide Rising	NEB-W 83
1	Startide Rising	HUG-W 84
9	Sundiver	LOC-N 81

AUTHOR		
CAT	T I T L E	AW W/N Y
BRIN, David Continued...		
3	Thor Meets Captain America	LOC-W 87
3	Thor Meets Captain America	SFC-N 87
3	Thor Meets Captain America	HUG-N 87
1	Uplift War, The	LOC-W 88
1	Uplift War, The	NEB-N 87
1	Uplift War, The	HUG-W 88
3	What Continues, What Fails	SFC-N 92
BRITE, Poppy Z		
4	Ash of Memory, The Dust of Desire, The	STO-N 92
BRODERICK, Damien		
1	Dreaming Dragon, The	JWC-N 81
BROOKS, Terry		
11	Sword of Shannara, The	LOC-N 78
BROWN, Charles N		
7	Science Fiction, Fantasy and Horror	HUG-N 89
7	Science Fiction in Print 1985	HUG-N 87
7	Science Fiction in Print 1985	LOC-N 87
7	SF, Fantasy & Horror 1986	HUG-N 88
7	SF, Fantasy & Horror 1986	LOC-N 88
7	SF, Fantasy & Horror 1988	LOC-N 90
7	SF, Fantasy & Horror 1990	LOC-N 92
BROWN, Eric		
4	Death of Cassandra Quebec, The	BSF-N 91
4	Phargean Effect, The	BSF-N 91
BROWN, Fredric		
5	And the Gods Laughed	LOC-N 88
BROWN, Molly		
4	Bad Timing	BSF-W 92

	A U T H O R	
CAT	T I T L E	AW W/N Y
	BROXON, Midlred Downey	
3	Sea Changeling	NEB-N 81
	BRUNNER, John	
2	Dread Empire	HUG-N 72
1	Jagged Orbit, The	BSF-W 71
1	Jagged Orbit, The	NEB-N 69
1	Productions of Time	NEB-N 67
1	Sheep Look Up, The	LOC-N 73
1	Sheep Look Up, The	NEB-N 72
1	Shockwave Rider, The	LOC-N 76
1	Squares of the City, The	HUG-N 66
1	Stand on Zanzibar	HUG-W 69
1	Stand on Zanzibar	NEB-N 68
1	Stand on Zanzibar	BSF-W 70
3	Who Steals My Purse	JUP-N 74
1	Whole Man, The	HUG-N 65
	BRYANT, Edward	
6	Cinnabar	WFA-N 77
2	Fetish	STO-N 92
4	giANTS	NEB-W 79
4	giANTS	LOC-N 80
4	giANTS	HUG-N 80
4	Kibakusha Gallery, The	NEB-N 77
4	Last Sad Love..., A	WFA-N 90
4	Last Sad Love..., A	STO-N 90
4	Loneliest Number, The	STO-N 91
5	Particle Theory	LOC-N 82
3	Particle Theory	NEB-N 77
4	Shark	JUP-N 74
4	Shark	NEB-N 73
4	Stone	HUG-N 79
4	Stone	NEB-W 78
4	Stone	LOC-N 79
3	Strata	LOC-N 81
3	Strata	NEB-N 80
3	Thermals of August, The	LOC-N 82
3	Thermals of August, The	HUG-N 82
3	Thermals of August, The	NEB-N 81

AUTHOR		
CAT	**T I T L E**	**AW W/N Y**
BUDRYS, Algis		
7	Benchmarks: Galaxy Bookshelf	LOC-W 86
7	Benchmarks: Galaxy Bookshelf	HUG-N 86
4	Edge of the Sea, The	HUG-N 59
1	Michaelmas	LOC-N 78
1	Rogue Moon	HUG-N 61
4	Scraping of the Bones, A	NEB-N 75
2	Silent Eyes of Time, The	HUG-N 76
2	Silent Eyes of Time, The	LOC-N 76
1	Who	HUG-N 59
BUJOLD, Lois McMaster		
1	Barrayar	SFC-N 92
1	Barrayar	NEB-N 92
1	Barrayar	LOC-W 92
1	Barrayar	HUG-W 92
5	Borders of Infinity	LOC-N 90
1	Falling Free	HUG-N 89
1	Falling Free	NEB-W 88
3	Labyrinth	DAV-W 90
2	Labyrinth	LOC-N 90
2	Mountains of Mourning, The	LOC-N 90
2	Mountains of Mourning, The	NEB-W 89
2	Mountains of Mourning, The	HUG-W 90
2	Mountains of Mourning, The	SFC-W 90
9	Shards of Honor	LOC-N 87
1	Shards of Honor	COM-N 87
1	Vor Game, The	SFC-N 91
1	Vor Game, The	HUG-W 91
1	Vor Game, The	LOC-N 91
2	Weatherman	NEB-N 91
2	Weatherman	DAV-W 91
2	Weatherman	LOC-N 91
BULL, Emma		
1	Bone Dance	WFA-N 92
1	Bone Dance	LOC-N 92
1	Bone Dance	HUG-N 92
1	Bone Dance	DIC-N 92
1	Bone Dance	NEB-N 92
9	War For the Oaks	LOC-W 88
1	War For the Oaks	COM-N 88

AUTHORS - Alphabetically

AUTHOR		
CAT	T I T L E	AW W/N Y
BURNETT, Thomas		
1	Day of the Minotaur	HUG-N 67
3	Manor of Roses, The	HUG-N 67
BURROUGHS, Edgar Rice		
4	Savage Pellucidar	HUG-N 64
BURROUGHS, William S		
1	Nova Express	NEB-N 65
1	Nova Express	NEB-N 64
BUTLER, Octavia E		
3	Bloodchild	LOC-W 85
3	Bloodchild	NEB-W 84
3	Bloodchild	HUG-W 85
3	Bloodchild	SFC-W 85
4	Evening and the Morning and the Night	JWC-N 88
3	Evening and the Morning and the Night	SFC-W 88
3	Evening and the Morning and the Night	NEB-N 87
4	Speech Sounds	HUG-W 84
4	Speech Sounds	LOC-N 84
BYRNE, John L		
9	Fear Book	STO-N 89
CADIGAN, Pat		
4	Angel	SFC-N 88
4	Angel	WFA-N 88
4	Angel	HUG-N 88
4	Angel	LOC-W 88
4	Angel	NEB-N 87
3	Dispatches from the Revolution	HUG-N 92
2	Fool to Believe	LOC-N 91
2	Fool to Believe	NEB-N 91
2	Fool to Believe	HUG-N 91
1	Midplayers	DIC-N 88
9	Mindplayers	LOC-N 88
6	Patterns	STO-N 90
5	Patterns	LOC-W 90

AUTHOR		
CAT	**T I T L E**	**AW W/N Y**
CADIGAN, Pat Continued...		
4	Power and the Passion, The	NEB-N 91
4	Power and the Passion, The	LOC-N 90
4	Pretty Boy Crossover	JWC-N 87
4	Pretty Boy Crossover	NEB-N 86
4	Pretty Boy Crossover	SFC-W 87
1	Synners	NEB-N 92
1	Synners	CLA-W 92
CALVINO, Italo		
1	Cosmicomics	DIT-W 70
1	Invisible Cities	NEB-N 75
CAMPBELL, Ramsey		
4	Another World	BFA-N 88
4	Changer of Names, The	BFA-N 79
2	Companion, The	WFA-N 77
1	Count of Eleven, The	BFA-N 91
1	Doll Who Ate His Mother, The	WFA-N 77
6	Height of the Scream, The	WFA-N 77
1	Hungry Moon, The	BFA-W 88
4	In the Bag	BFA-W 78
1	Influence, The	BFA-W 89
4	Loveman's Comeback	WFA-N 78
4	Macintosth Willy	WFA-W 80
1	Midnight Sun	BFA-W 92
1	Nameless, The	WFA-N 82
6	New Terrors 1	WFA-N 81
CAMPBELL, Ramsey		
5	Scared Stiff, Tales of Sex & Death	WFA-N 88
6	Scared Stiff, Tales of Sex & Death	STO-N 88
6	Superhorror	WFA-N 77
1	To Wake the Dead	BFA-W 81
5	Walking Nightmares	STO-N 92
CANNON, Peter		
7	H.P. Lovecraft	STO-N 90

AUTHOR		
CAT	T I T L E	AW W/N Y
CANTRELL, Lisa W		
9	Manse, The	STO-W 88
CARD, Orson Scott		
3	America	LOC-N 88
3	Dogwalker	LOC-W 90
3	Dogwalker	HUG-N 90
3	Dowser	DAV-W 89
3	Dowser	LOC-N 89
6	Dragons of Light	WFA-N 81
1	Ender's Game	NEB-W 85
1	Ender's Game	SFC-W 86
1	Ender's Game	HUG-W 86
1	Ender's Game	LOC-N 86
3	Ender's Game	HUG-N 78
3	Everything But Honor	SFC-N 90
2	Eye for Eye	LOC-N 88
2	Eye for Eye	HUG-W 88
5	Folk on the Fringe, The	LOC-N 90
3	Fringe, The	LOC-N 86
3	Fringe, The	NEB-N 85
3	Fringe, The	HUG-N 86
3	Hatrack River	NEB-N 86
3	Hatrack River	HUG-N 87
3	Hatrack River	LOC-N 87
2	Hatrack River	WFA-W 87
3	Hatrack River	SFC-N 87
7	How to Write Science Fiction and Fantasy	LOC-N 91
7	How to Write Science Fiction and Fantasy	HUG-W 91
4	Lost Boys	NEB-N 89
4	Lost Boys	SFC-N 90
4	Lost Boys	HUG-N 90
4	Lost Boys	LOC-W 90
5	Maps in a Mirror	LOC-W 91
3	Mikal's Songbird	NEB-N 78
3	Mikal's Songbird	HUG-N 79
3	Mikal's Songbird	LOC-N 79
2	Pageant Wagon	LOC-N 90
11	Prentice Alvin	LOC-W 90
1	Prentice Alvin	HUG-N 90
1	Prentice Alvin	NEB-N 89
4	Quietus	LOC-N 80

AUTHOR		
CAT	T I T L E	AW W/N Y
CARD, Orson Scott Continued...		
1	Red Prophet	NEB-N 88
1	Red Prophet	HUG-N 89
11	Red Prophet	LOC-W 89
1	Seventh Son	WFA-N 88
11	Seventh Son	LOC-W 88
1	Seventh Son	DIT-W 89
1	Seventh Son	HUG-N 88
2	Songhouse	HUG-N 80
2	Songhouse	LOC-N 80
1	Speaker for the Dead	HUG-W 87
1	Speaker for the Dead	NEB-W 86
1	Speaker for the Dead	LOC-W 87
1	Speaker for the Dead	JWC-N 87
1	Speaker for the Dead	SFC-W 87
4	Unaccompanied Sonata	NEB-N 79
4	Unaccompanied Sonata	HUG-N 80
1	Xenocide	HUG-N 92
1	Xenocide	LOC-N 92
CAREY, Peter		
1	Illywacker	WFA-N 86
CARLSON, William K		
2	Sunrise West	NEB-N 75
CARR, Terry		
13	An Exaltation of Stars	LOC-N 74
14	Best Science Fiction of the Year # 2	LOC-W 74
14	Best Science Fiction of the Year # 3	LOC-N 75
5	Best Science Fiction of the Year # 4	LOC-N 76
14	Best Science Fiction of the Year # 5	LOC-W 77
6	Best Science Fiction of the Year # 7	LOC-W 79
6	Best Science Fiction of the Year # 8	LOC-N 80
6	Best Science Fiction of the Year # 9	LOC-N 81
6	Best Science Fiction of the Year #10	LOC-N 82
6	Best Science Fiction of the Year #11	LOC-W 83
6	Best Science Fiction of the Year #12	LOC-W 84
6	Best Science Fiction of the Year #13	LOC-N 85
6	Best Science Fiction of the Year #14	LOC-N 86

	A U T H O R	
CAT	T I T L E	AW W/N Y
CARR, Terry	Continued...	
6	Best Science Fiction of the Year #15	LOC-N 87
14	Best Science Fiction of the Year: 1972	LOC-W 73
6	Best SF and Fantasy of the Year #16	LOC-N 88
1	Cirque	NEB-N 77
4	Dance of the Changer and the Three, The	NEB-N 68
4	Dance of the Changer and the Three, The	HUG-N 69
6	Fantasy Annual 4	WFA-N 82
6	Fantasy Annual 4	BFA-N 82
6	Fantasy Annual 5	LOC-N 83
14	New Worlds of Fantasy 3rd ed	LOC-N 72
6	Universe 1	LOC-N 91
13	Universe 1	LOC-W 72
13	Universe 2	LOC-N 73
13	Universe 3	LOC-N 74
13	Universe 4	LOC-W 75
14	Universe 6	LOC-N 77
6	Universe 8	LOC-N 79
6	Universe 9	LOC-W 80
6	Universe 11	LOC-N 82
6	Universe 12	LOC-N 83
6	Universe 13	LOC-N 84
6	Universe 14	LOC-N 85
6	Universe 15	LOC-N 86
6	Universe 16	LOC-N 87
6	Universe 17	LOC-N 88
4	Virra	LOC-N 79
4	Year's Finest Fantasy Vol 2	WFA-N 80
CARRINGTON, Grant		
3	His Hour Upon the Stage	NEB-N 76
CARROLL, Jonathan		
2	Black Cocktail	WFA-N 91
1	Bones of the Moon	BFA-N 88
1	Child Across the Sky, A	WFA-N 90
1	Child Across the Sky, A	CLA-N 90
4	Friend's Best Man	WFA-W 88
4	Friend's Best Man	BFA-N 88
4	Friend's Best Man	STO-N 88
4	Mr. Fiddlehead	WFA-N 90

AUTHOR		
CAT	TITLE	AW W/N Y
CARROLL, Jonathan Continued...		
1	Outside the Dog Museum	WFA-N 92
1	Outside the Dog Museum	BFA-W 91
1	Sleeping in Flame	WFA-N 89
CARTER, Angela		
6	Black Venus	WFA-N 86
1	Nights At the Circus	BSF-N 85
4	Overture to a Midsummer Night's Dream	BSF-N 83
CARTER, Lin		
6	Flashing Swords #3	WFA-N 77
6	Flashing Swords #5	LOC-N 82
4	Uncollected Works	NEB-N 65
CAVE, Hugh B		
6	Murgunstrumm and Others	WFA-W 78
CHALKER, Jack		
7	Science-Fantasy Publishers, The	HUG-N 92
CHANT, Joy		
7	High Kings, The	LOC-N 84
7	High Kings, The	HUG-N 84
CHAPDELAINE, Perry A Sr.		
7	John W Campbell Letters Vol 1, The	HUG-N 86
7	John W Campbell Letters Vol 1, The	LOC-N 87
CHAPPELL, Fred		
5	More Shapes Than One	WFA-N 92
4	Somewhere Doors, The	WFA-N 92

	A U T H O R	
CAT	T I T L E	AW W/N Y
	CHARNAS, Suzy McKee	
2	Advocates	STO-N 92
4	Boobs	NEB-N 89
4	Boobs	LOC-N 90
4	Boobs	SFC-N 90
4	Boobs	HUG-W 90
3	Listening to Brahms	NEB-N 86
2	Unicorn Tapestry	NEB-W 80
4	Unicorn Tapestry	WFA-N 81
1	Vampire Tapestry, The	NEB-N 81
	CHASE, Robert R	
1	Game of Fox and Lion, The	COM-N 87
	CHAYEFSKY, Paddy	
1	Altered States	JWC-N 79
	CHERRY, David A	
7	Imagination: Art & Techn of David Cherry	HUG-N 88
	CHERRYH, C J	
4	Cassandra	NEB-N 78
4	Cassandra	HUG-W 79
1	Chanur's Homecoming	LOC-N 87
1	Chanur's Venture	LOC-N 85
1	Cuckoo's Egg	HUG-N 86
1	Cyteen	HUG-W 89
1	Cyteen	SFC-W 89
1	Cyteen	LOC-W 89
1	Downbelow Station	HUG-W 82
1	Downbelow Station	LOC-N 82
2	Ealdwood	WFA-N 82
1	Faded Sun, The: Kesrith	NEB-N 78
1	Faded Sun, The: Kesrith	LOC-N 79
1	Faded Sun, The: Kesrith	HUG-N 79
2	Gwidion and the Dragon	WFA-N 92
3	Haunted Tower, The	LOC-N 82
4	Only Death, The	LOC-N 82
11	Paladin, The	LOC-N 89

CAT	AUTHOR	AW W/N Y
	T I T L E	

CHERRYH, C J   Continued...

CAT	TITLE	AW W/N Y
1	Pride of Chanur, The	HUG-N 83
1	Pride of Chanur, The	LOC-N 83
1	Rimrunners	LOC-N 90
11	Rusalka	LOC-N 90
2	Scapegoat, The	HUG-N 86
2	Scapegoat, The	LOC-N 85
2	Scapegoat, The	LOC-N 86
5	Sunfall	LOC-N 82
5	Visible Light	LOC-N 87
1	Voyager in Night	DIC-N 85
3	Willow	LOC-N 83

CHIANG, Ted

CAT	TITLE	AW W/N Y
3	Tower of Babylon	LOC-N 91
3	Tower of Babylon	NEB-N 91
3	Tower of Babylon	HUG-N 91
3	Tower of Babylon	SFC-N 91
3	Understand	HUG-N 92

CHRISTOPHER, John

CAT	TITLE	AW W/N Y
4	Few Kindred Spirits, A	NEB-N 65

CLARKE, Arthur C

CAT	TITLE	AW W/N Y
1	2010: Odyssey Two	LOC-N 83
1	2010: Odyssey Two	SFC-N 83
1	2010: Odyssey Two	HUG-N 83
7	Astounding Days	HUG-N 90
7	Astounding Days	LOC-N 90
7	Exploration of Space	IFA-W 52
1	Fall of Moondust, A	HUG-N 61
1	Fall of Moondust, A	HUG-N 63
1	Fountains of Paradise, The	HUG-W 80
1	Fountains of Paradise, The	BSF-N 80
1	Fountains of Paradise, The	LOC-N 80
1	Fountains of Paradise, The	NEB-W 79
1	Imperial Earth	LOC-N 76
4	Meeting With Medusa, A	LOC-N 72
2	Meeting With Medusa, A	HUG-N 72
2	Meeting with Medusa, A	NEB-W 72

AUTHORS - Alphabetically

	AUTHOR	
CAT	T I T L E	AW W/N Y
CLARKE, Arthur C Continued...		
1	RAMA II	LOC-N 90
1	Rendezvous with Rama	JUP-W 74
1	Rendezvous with Rama	BSF-W 74
1	Rendezvous with Rama	LOC-W 74
1	Rendezvous with Rama	HUG-W 74
1	Rendezvous with Rama	JWC-W 74
1	Rendezvous with Rama	NEB-W 73
5	Sentinel, The	LOC-N 84
4	Star, The	HUG-W 56
CLEGG, Douglas		
9	Goat Dance	STO-N 90
CLEMENT, Hal		
1	Mission of Gravity	IFA-N 55
1	Starlight	HUG-N 71
CLIFTON, Mark		
1	They'd Rather Be Right	HUG-W 55
CLUTE, John		
7	Strokes: Essays and Reviews 1966-1986	LOC-N 89
COCHRANE, William C		
3	Horrus Errand, The	JUP-N 75
2	Weather War	LOC-N 77
COETZEE, J M		
1	Waiting for the Barbarians	DIC-N 83
COGGINS, Jack		
7	Rockets,Jets,Guided Missls & Spaceships	IFA-N 52
COLE, Adrian		
4	First Make Them Mad	BFA-N 80

AUTHOR		
CAT	T I T L E	AW W/N Y
COLLIER, John		
1	Fancies and Goodnights	IFA-W 52
COLLINS, A		
10	Tempter	LOC-N 91
COLLINS, Nancy A		
10	In the Blood	LOC-N 92
9	Sunglasses After Dark	STO-W 90
9	Sunglasses After Dark	LOC-N 90
COLOMBO, Robert		
1	Friendly Aliens	AUR-N 82
COMPTON, D G		
1	Steel Crocodile, The	NEB-N 70
1	Unsleeping Eye, The	LOC-N 75
CONEY, Michael G		
1	Brontomek?	BSF-W 77
1	Cat Karina	BSF-N 84
CONNER, Mike		
3	Guide Dog	NEB-W 92
CONTENTO, William		
7	Index to SF Anthologies and Collections	LOC-N 79
COOK, Rick		
12	Long Stern Case: Speculative Exercise	DAV-W 87
COPPER, Basil		
5	From Earth's Pillow	WFA-N 75

AUTHORS - Alphabetically

AUTHOR		
CAT	TITLE	AW W/N Y
CORMIER, Robert		
1	Fade	WFA-N 89
COVER, Arthur B		
1	Autumn Angels	NEB-N 75
COWPER, Richard		
4	Brothers	SFC-N 84
2	Custodians, The	LOC-N 76
3	Custodians, The	NEB-N 75
2	Custodians, The	HUG-N 76
3	Hertford Manuscript, The	LOC-N 77
3	Out There Where the Big Ships Go	LOC-N 80
2	Piper at the Gates of Dawn	LOC-N 77
2	Piper at the Gates of Dawn	NEB-N 76
2	Piper at the Gates of Dawn	HUG-N 77
1	Road to Corlay, The	NEB-N 79
1	Road to Corlay, The	BFA-N 79
4	Tithonian Factor, The	BSF-N 84
2	Web of the Magi, The	LOC-N 81
4	Web of the Magi, The	BSF-N 81
CRAMER, Kathryn		
6	Architecture of Fear	WFA-N 88
6	Walls of Fear	WFA-N 91
CRICHTON, Michael		
1	Jurassic Park	LOC-N 91
CROWLEY, John		
1	Aegypt	BFA-N 88
1	Aegypt	WFA-N 88
1	Aegypt	CLA-N 88
11	Aegypt	LOC-N 88
1	Engine Summer	BSF-N 81
1	Engine Summer	JWC-N 80
2	Great Works of Time	SFC-N 90
2	Great Works of Time	WFA-W 90
2	Great Works of Time	NEB-N 89

AUTHORS - Alphabetically

	AUTHOR	
CAT	TITLE	AW W/N Y
	CROWLEY, John Continued...	
1	Little Big	HUG-N 82
11	Little Big	LOC-N 82
1	Little Big	NEB-N 81
1	Little Big	BSF-N 83
1	Little Big	WFA-W 82
5	Novelty	WFA-N 90
4	Snow	HUG-N 86
4	Snow	NEB-N 85
4	Snow	LOC-N 86
	CURREY, L W	
7	SF and Fantasy Authors	LOC-N 81
	CURRY, Chris	
9	Winter Scream	STO-N 92
	CURTIS, Betsy	
4	Steiger Effect, The	HUG-N 69
	DANIELS, Lee	
1	Black Castle, The	WFA-N 79
	DANIELS, Les	
4	They're Coming For You	WFA-N 87
	DANN, Jack	
2	Amnesia	NEB-N 81
3	Bad Medicine	NEB-N 84
4	Bad Medicine	WFA-N 85
3	Blind Shemmy	SFC-N 84
3	Blind Shemmy	NEB-N 83
4	Camps	BSF-N 80
3	Camps	NEB-N 79
3	Dybbuk Dolls, The	NEB-N 75
4	Fairy Tale	WFA-N 82
4	Fairy Tale	BFA-N 82

AUTHOR		
CAT	T I T L E	AW W/N Y
DANN, Jack	**Continued...**	
14	Future Power	LOC-N 77
4	Going Under	NEB-N 81
2	Junction	NEB-N 73
1	Man Who Melted, The	NEB-N 84
4	Quiet Revolution For Death	NEB-N 78
13	Wandering Stars	LOC-N 75
DANN, Jeanne van Buren		
6	In the Field of Fire	LOC-N 88
6	In the Field of Fire	WFA-N 88
DANVERS, Dennis		
9	Wilderness	STO-N 92
Dark Harvest		
6	Night Visions 4	WFA-N 88
DATLOW, Ellen		
6	Alien Sex	LOC-N 91
6	Alien Sex	WFA-N 91
6	Blood is Not Enough	LOC-N 90
6	Blood is Not Enough	WFA-N 90
6	Whisper of Blood, A	LOC-N 92
6	Whisper of Blood, A	WFA-N 92
6	Year's Best Fantasy and Horror 1st	WFA-W 89
6	Year's Best Fantasy and Horror 1st	LOC-N 89
6	Year's Best Fantasy and Horror 2nd	LOC-N 90
6	Year's Best Fantasy and Horror 2nd	WFA-W 90
6	Year's Best Fantasy and Horror 3rd	LOC-N 91
6	Year's Best Fantasy and Horror 4th	LOC-N 92
6	Year's Best Fantasy and Horror 4th	WFA-N 91
6	Year's Best Fantasy and Horror 4th	WFA-N 92
DAVIDSON, Avram		
2	Clash of Star Kings	NEB-N 66
5	Enquiries of Dr Eszterhazy	WFA-W 76
2	Esterhazy and the Autogondola-Invention	NEB-N 83
4	Good Night's Sleep, A	WFA-N 79

AUTHOR		
CAT	T I T L E	AW W/N Y
DAVIDSON, Avram Continued...		
4	House the Blakeneys Built, The	NEB-N 65
4	Manatee Gal, Ain't Ya Comin' Out Tonight	WFA-N 78
4	Naples	WFA-W 79
4	Or All The Seas With Oysters	HUG-W 58
3	Polly Charms, The Sleeping Woman	NEB-N 75
6	Redward, Edward Papers, The	WFA-N 79
2	Rogue Dragon	NEB-N 65
1	Rogue Dragon	NEB-N 65
4	Slovo Stove, The	WFA-N 86
2	There Beneath the Silky Trees...	NEB-N 80
1	Vergil in Averno	NEB-N 87
6	Young Doctor Esterhazy	NEB-N 84
DAVIES, Robinson		
6	High Spirits	WFA-W 84
de CAMP, L Sprague		
12	Ape-Man Within Us, The	DAV-W 90
de CHANCLE, John		
9	Starrigger	LOC-N 84
de LINT, Charles		
4	Conjure Man, The	WFA-N 92
2	Death Leaves an Echo	STO-N 92
1	Jack the Giant Killer	AUR-W 88
1	Little Country, The	WFA-N 92
11	Little Country, The	LOC-N 92
2	Our Lady of the Harbour	WFA-N 92
4	Pity the Monsters	WFA-N 92
1	Yarrow	AUR-N 87
del REY, Judy-Lynn		
13	Stellar 1	LOC-N 75
14	Stellar 2	LOC-N 77
6	Stellar 4	LOC-N 79

AUTHORS - Alphabetically

CAT	A U T H O R	
	T I T L E	AW W/N Y
del REY, Lester		
7	World of SF 1926-76	LOC-N 80
DELANEY, Joseph H		
2	Brainchild	HUG-N 83
2	In the Face of My Enemy	HUG-N 84
2	Valentina	HUG-N 85
9	Valentina: Soul in Sapphire	LOC-N 85
DELANY, Samuel R		
4	Aye, and Gomorrah	HUG-N 68
4	Aye, and Gomorrah	NEB-W 67
1	Babel-17	HUG-N 67
1	Babel-17	NEB-W 66
1	Babel-17	HUG-N 66
2	Ballad of Beta-2	NEB-N 65
1	Dhalgren	NEB-N 75
1	Dhalgren	LOC-N 76
14	Driftglass	LOC-N 72
4	Driftglass	NEB-N 67
1	Einstein Intersection	NEB-W 67
1	Einstein Intersection	HUG-N 68
2	Lines of Power	NEB-N 68
2	Lines of Power	HUG-N 69
7	Motion of Light in Water, The: Sex & SF	LOC-N 89
7	Motion of Light in Water, The: Sex & SF	HUG-W 89
1	Nova	HUG-N 69
3	Prismatica	HUG-N 78
6	Quark 1	LOC-N 71
2	Star Pit, The	HUG-N 68
1	Stars in My Pocket Like Grains of Sand	CLA-N 87
1	Stars in My Pocket Like Grains of Sand	LOC-N 85
2	Tale of Gorgik, The	NEB-N 79
2	Tale of Rumor and Desire, The	SFC-N 88
11	Tales of Neveryon	LOC-N 80
4	Time Considered as a Helix...	HUG-W 70
3	Time Considered as a Helix...	NEB-W 69
1	Triton	NEB-N 76

AUTHORS - Alphabetically

AUTHOR		
CAT	TITLE	AW W/N Y
DENTON, Bradley		
1	Buddy Holly is Alive & Well On Ganymede	JWC-W 92
2	Calvin Coolidge Home for Dead Comedians	NEB-N 88
2	Calvin Coolidge Home for Dead Comedians	HUG-N 89
9	Wrack & Roll	LOC-N 87
DICK, Philip K		
5	Collected Stories of Philip K Dick, The	LOC-N 88
1	Divine Invasion, The	BSF-N 83
1	Do Androids Dream of Electric Sheep?	NEB-N 68
1	Doctor Bloodmoney	NEB-N 65
3	Faith of Our Fathers	HUG-N 68
1	Flow My Tears, The Policeman Said	HUG-N 75
1	Flow My Tears, The Policeman Said	NEB-N 74
1	Flow My Tears, The Policeman Said	JWC-W 75
1	Flow My Tears, The Policeman Said	LOC-N 75
1	Man in the High Castle, The	HUG-W 63
3	Pre-Persons, The	LOC-N 75
4	Rautavaara's Case	BSF-N 81
1	Three Stigmata Palmer Eldritch	NEB-N 65
11	Transmigration of Timothy Archer, The	LOC-N 83
1	Transmigration of Timothy Archer, The	NEB-N 82
DICKINSON, Peter		
2	Flight	WFA-N 86
1	Green Gene, The	JWC-N 74
DICKSON, Gordon R		
3	Call Him Lord	HUG-N 67
3	Cloak and the Staff, The	HUG-W 81
4	Computers Don't Argue	NEB-N 65
1	Dragon and the George, The	WFA-N 77
1	Dragon and the George, The	BFA-W 77
1	Genetic General (Dorsai)	HUG-N 60
4	Jean Dupres	HUG-N 71
2	Lost Dorsai	NEB-N 80
2	Lost Dorsai	HUG-W 81
4	Soldier, Ask Not	HUG-W 65
1	Time Storm	HUG-N 78
1	Time Storm	LOC-N 78
3	Time Storm	JUP-W 78
3	Twig	LOC-N 75

AUTHORS - Alphabetically

AUTHOR		
CAT	TITLE	AW W/N Y
DiFATE, Vincent		
7	DiFate's Catalog of S Fiction Hardware	HUG-N 81
DILLON, Leo		
7	Pish, Posh, Said Hieronymous Bosch	LOC-N 92
DISCH, Thomas M		
3	102 H-Bombs	NEB-N 65
1	334	NEB-N 74
3	Asian Shores	NEB-N 70
2	Brave Little Toaster, The	NEB-N 80
2	Brave Little Toaster, The	HUG-N 81
3	Brave Little Toaster, The	LOC-W 81
4	Brave Little Toaster, The	BSF-W 81
1	Camp Concentration	DIT-W 69
4	Come to Venus Melancholy	NEB-N 65
3	Everyday Life in the Later Roman Empire	JUP-N 74
1	Genocides, The	NEB-N 65
3	Man Who Had No Idea, The	HUG-N 79
10	M.D., The	LOC-N 92
1	M.D., The	STO-N 92
1	On Wings of Song	HUG-N 80
1	On Wings of Song	LOC-N 80
1	On Wings of Song	NEB-N 79
1	On Wings of Song	JWC-W 80
1	On Wings of Song	BSF-N 80
3	Understanding Human Behavior	NEB-N 82
3	Understanding Human Behavior	SFC-W 83
4	Voices of the Kill	NEB-N 88
DIXON, Dougal		
7	After Man	HUG-N 82
7	After Man	LOC-N 82
DOCTOROW, E L		
1	Ragtime	NEB-N 75

AUTHOR		
CAT	T I T L E	AW W/N Y
DONALDSON, Stephen R		
1	Chronicles o/Thomas Covenant t/Unbeleive	WFA-N 78
11	Chronicles o/Thomas Covenant t/Unbeleive	LOC-N 78
1	Chronicles o/Thomas Covenant t/Unbeleive	BFA-W 79
4	Lady in White, The	BFA-N 79
11	One Tree, The	LOC-N 83
11	White Gold Wielder	LOC-N 84
1	Wounded Land, The	BFA-N 81
11	Wounded Land, The	LOC-N 81
DONALDSON, Thomas		
12	24th Century Medicine	DAV-N 89
DONNING, Whelan		
7	Wonderworks	HUG-N 80
DORSEY, Candas Jane		
4	Sleeping in a Box	AUR-W 89
DOZOIS, Gardner		
2	Chains of the Sea	JUP-N 74
2	Chains of the Sea	HUG-N 74
2	Chains of the Sea	LOC-N 74
2	Chains of the Sea	NEB-N 73
4	Disciples	NEB-N 81
4	Dream at Noonday, A	NEB-N 70
4	Gods of Mars, The	NEB-N 85
4	Horse of Air	NEB-N 71
4	Kingdom By the Sea, A	LOC-N 73
3	Kingdom By the Sea, A	HUG-N 73
3	Kingdom By the Sea, A	NEB-N 72
4	Morning Child	SFC-N 85
4	Morning Child	NEB-W 84
4	Peacemaker, The	HUG-N 84
4	Peacemaker, The	LOC-N 84
4	Peacemaker, The	NEB-W 83
4	Peacemaker, The	SFC-W 84
3	Special Kind of Morning	NEB-N 71
2	Special Kind of Morning	HUG-N 72

CAT	TITLE	AW W/N Y
	A U T H O R	
	DOZOIS, Gardner Continued...	
1	Strangers	NEB-N 78
2	Strangers	HUG-N 75
2	Strangers	LOC-N 75
2	Strangers	JUP-N 75
6	Year's Best Science Fiction, 1st	LOC-N 85
6	Year's Best Science Fiction, 2nd	LOC-N 86
6	Year's Best Science Fiction, 3rd	LOC-W 87
6	Year's Best Science Fiction, 4th	LOC-W 88
4	Year's Best Science Fiction, 5th	LOC-N 89
4	Year's Best Science Fiction, 6th	LOC-W 90
2	Year's Best Science Fiction, 7th	LOC-W 91
4	Year's Best Science Fiction, 8th	LOC-N 92
	DRAKE, David	
2	Barrow Troll, The	WFA-N 76
	DRESSER, Norine	
7	Amer Vampires:Fans,Victims,Practicioners	STO-N 90
	DUNCAN, Dave	
1	West of January	AUR-W 90
	DUNN, Katherine	
10	Geek Love	LOC-N 90
1	Geek Love	STO-N 90
	DUNTEMANN, Jeff	
4	Cold Hands	HUG-N 81
4	Guardian	HUG-N 81
	DURHAM, James	
4	Of One Mind	NEB-N 65
	DZIEMIANOWICZ, Stefan R	
6	Famous Fantastic Mysteries	WFA-N 92

A U T H O R		
CAT	T I T L E	AW W/N Y
EDDINGS, David		
11	King of the Murgos	LOC-N 89
EDMONDSON, G C		
1	Ship Sailed the Time Stream	NEB-N 65
EDWARDS, Malcolm		
4	After Images	BSF-W 84
EFFINGER, George Alec		
4	Aliens Who Knew, I Mean Everything, The	NEB-N 84
4	Aliens Who Knew, I Mean Everything, The	LOC-N 85
4	Aliens Who Knew, I Mean Everything, The	SFC-N 85
4	Aliens Who Knew, I Mean Everything, The	HUG-N 85
4	All the Last Wars at Once	LOC-N 72
4	All the Last Wars at Once	HUG-N 72
3	City on the Sand, The	HUG-N 74
3	Everything but Honor	HUG-N 90
1	Fire in the Sun, A	HUG-N 90
1	Fire in the Sun, A	SFC-W 90
1	Fire in the Sun, A	LOC-N 90
2	Marid Changes His Mind	NEB-N 89
3	Schrodinger's Kitten	NEB-W 88
3	Schrodinger's Kitten	SFC-W 89
3	Schrodinger's Kitten	LOC-N 89
3	Schrodinger's Kitten	HUG-W 89
4	Schrodinger's Kitten	JWC-W 89
1	What Entropy Means to Me	NEB-N 72
1	When Gravity Fails	HUG-N 88
1	When Gravity Fails	NEB-N 87
1	When Gravity Fails	LOC-N 88
1	When Gravity Fails	SFC-N 88
EGAN, Greg		
4	Axiomatic	BSF-N 91
4	Learning To Be Me	BSF-N 91

CAT	TITLE	AW W/N Y
	A U T H O R	

EISENSTEIN, Phyllis

CAT	TITLE	AW W/N Y
4	Attachment	NEB-N 75
2	In the Western Tradition	SFC-W 82
2	In the Western Tradition	HUG-N 82
2	In the Western Tradition	LOC-N 82
2	In the Western Tradition	NEB-N 81
3	Nightlife	HUG-N 83
1	Sorcerer's Son	BFA-N 80

EKLUND, Gordon

CAT	TITLE	AW W/N Y
1	All Times Possible	JUP-N 75
3	Dear Aunt Annie	NEB-N 70
3	If the Stars are Gods	JUP-N 75

ELLIOT, Tom

CAT	TITLE	AW W/N Y
9	Dwelling, The	STO-N 90

ELLISON, Harlan

CAT	TITLE	AW W/N Y
3	Adrift, Just off t/Islets of Langerhans	HUG-W 75
3	Adrift, Just off t/Islets of Langerhans	LOC-W 75
13	Again, Dangerous Visions	LOC-W 73
2	All the Lies That Are My Life	HUG-N 81
7	An Edge in My Voice	HUG-N 86
6	Angry Candy	STO-N 89
5	Angry Candy	LOC-W 89
5	Angry Candy	WFA-N 89
3	Basilisk	NEB-N 72
4	Basilisk	LOC-W 73
3	Basilisk	HUG-N 73
4	Beast t/Shouted Love a/t/Heart o/t/World	HUG-W 69
2	Boy and His Dog, A	HUG-N 70
2	Boy and His Dog, A	NEB-W 69
4	Count the Clock That Tells the Time	HUG-N 79
4	Count the Clock That Tells the Time	LOC-W 79
4	Croatoan	LOC-W 76
4	Croatoan	HUG-N 76
4	Deathbird, The	LOC-W 74
3	Deathbird, The	JUP-W 74
3	Deathbird, The	NEB-N 73
3	Deathbird, The	HUG-W 74

	A U T H O R	
CAT	T I T L E	AW W/N Y
	ELLISON, Harlan Continued...	
6	Deathbird Stories	LOC-N 76
5	Deathbird Stories	WFA-N 76
4	Delusion for a Dragon Slayer	HUG-N 67
3	Djinn, No Chaser	LOC-W 83
4	Eidolons	LOC-W 89
5	Essential Ellison, The	LOC-N 88
6	Essential Ellison, The	STO-W 88
3	Function of Dream Sleep, The	STO-N 89
3	Function of Dream Sleep, The	HUG-N 89
3	Function of Dream Sleep, The	LOC-W 89
7	Harlan Ellison's Watching	HUG-N 90
7	Harlan Ellison's Watching	STO-W 90
5	Harlan Ellison's Watching	WFA-N 90
4	I Have no Mouth Yet I Must Scream	HUG-W 68
3	I'm Looking for Kadak	LOC-N 75
4	Jeffty is Five	JUP-W 78
4	Jeffty is Five	HUG-W 78
4	Jeffty is Five	WFA-N 78
4	Jeffty is Five	BFA-W 79
4	Jeffty is Five	NEB-W 77
4	Jeffty is Five	LOC-W 78
6	Medea: Harlan's World	LOC-W 86
4	On the Downhill Side	NEB-N 72
3	Paladin of the Lost Hour	SFC-N 86
3	Paladin of the Lost Hour	NEB-N 85
3	Paladin of the Lost Hour	HUG-W 86
3	Paladin of the Lost Hour	LOC-W 86
3	Pretty Maggie Moneyeyes	NEB-N 67
3	Pretty Maggie Moneyeyes	HUG-N 68
2	Region Between, The	HUG-N 71
2	Region Between, The	NEB-N 70
4	Region Between, The	LOC-W 71
4	Repent Harlequin..	NEB-W 65
4	Repent Harlequin...	HUG-W 66
4	Seeing	LOC-N 77
5	Shatterday	LOC-N 81
4	Shatterday	NEB-N 75
6	Shatterday	WFA-N 81
4	Shattered Like a Glass Goblin	NEB-N 69
4	She's A Yng Thing & C'not Leave H/Mother	STO-N 89
4	Sleeping Dogs	JUP-N 75

AUTHOR		
CAT	TITLE	AW W/N Y
ELLISON, Harlan	**Continued...**	
7	Sleepless Nights in the Procrustean Bed:	HUG-N 85
7	Sleepless Nights in the Procrustean Bed:	LOC-W 85
5	Stalking the Nightmare	LOC-N 83
5	Strange Wine	LOC-N 79
4	With Virgil Oddum at the East Pole	LOC--W 86
ELWOOD, Roger		
5	Epoch	LOC-W 76
EMSHWILLER, Carol		
4	Circular Library of Stones	SFC-W 88
5	Start of the End of It All...	WFA-W 91
ETCHISON, Dennis		
5	Blood Kiss, The	WFA-N 89
6	Blood Kiss, The	STO-N 89
6	Cutting Edge	WFA-N 87
4	Dark Country, The	BFA-W 82
4	Dark Country, The	WFA-W 82
4	Deathtracks	WFA-N 83
2	It Only Comes Out At Night	WFA-N 77
4	Late Shift, The	BFA-N 81
4	Olympic Runner, The	BFA-W 87
EVANS, Christopher		
6	Other Edens	WFA-N 88
FAIRBAIRNS, Zoe		
1	Benefits	DIC-N 84
FANCHER, Jane		
1	Ground Ties	COM-N 92
FARBER, Sharon		
4	Return of the Dust Vampire	WFA-N 86

AUTHOR		
CAT	TITLE	AW W/N Y
FARMER, Philip Jose		
4	After King Kong Fell	NEB-N 74
4	Alley Man, The	HUG-N 60
4	Open to Me, My Sister (My Sis's Brother)	HUG-N 61
2	Riders of the Purple Wage	HUG-W 68
2	Riders of the Purple Wage	NEB-N 67
5	Riverworlds and Other Stories	LOC-N 80
2	Sketches Among the Ruins of My Mind	LOC-N 74
1	To Your Scattered Bodies Go	HUG-W 72
1	To Your Scattered Bodies Go	LOC-N 72
FARRIS, John		
3	Horrorshow	STO-N 89
6	Scare Tactics	STO-N 89
FEELEY, Gregory		
1	Oxygen Barons	DIC-N 91
FEIST, Raymond E		
10	Faerie Tale	LOC-N 89
FERMAN, Ed		
14	Best From F&SF: 25th Anniversary	LOC-N 75
5	Final Stage	LOC-N 76
6	Magazine of Fant & SF: A 30 Yr Retrospec	LOC-W 81
FILIPPO, Paul Di		
4	Kid Charlemagne	NEB-N 87
FINCH, Sheila		
1	Infinity's Web	COM-W 86
FISK, Nicholas		
4	Find the Lady	NEB-N 75

AUTHORS - Alphabetically

AUTHOR		
CAT	T I T L E	AW W/N Y
FITZPATRICK, R C		
3	Half a Loaf	NEB-N 65
FLORANCE-GUTHRIDGE, George		
4	Quiet, The	HUG-N 82
4	Quiet, The	NEB-N 81
FLYNN, Michael F		
12	An Introduction to Psychohistory	DAV-W 89
2	Eifelheim	HUG-N 87
3	Eifelheim	DAV-W 87
2	Forest of Time, The	HUG-N 88
9	In the Country of The Blind	LOC-W 91
12	Sixty Astounding Years	DAV-W 91
FOGG, Martyn J		
12	Extrat'l Intel & t/Interdict Hypothesis	DAV-N 89
FONSTAD, Karen Wynn		
7	Atlas of Pern, The	LOC-N 85
FORD, John M		
1	Dragon Waiting, The	WFA-W 84
2	Fugue State	NEB-N 87
4	Winter Solstice, Camelot Station	WFA-W 89
FORDE, Pat		
4	Gift, The	JWC-N 88
3	Gift, The	DAV-W 88
FORWARD, Dr. Robert L		
9	Dragon's Eggs	LOC-W 81

AUTHOR		
CAT	T I T L E	AW W/N Y
FOWLER, Karen Joy		
1	Artificial Things	DIC-N 87
3	Black Glass	LOC-N 92
3	Black Glass	NEB-N 92
4	Dark, The	NEB-N 92
4	Faithful Companion, The	NEB-N 87
4	Faithful Companion, The	HUG-N 88
4	Faithful Companion at Forty, The	LOC-N 88
4	Lieserl	LOC-N 91
4	Lieserl	NEB-N 91
FRANKOWSKI, Leo		
1	Crosstime Engineer, The	COM-N 87
9	Crosstime Engineer, The	LOC-N 87
FRIEDMAN, C S		
1	In Conquest Born	COM-N 88
9	In Conquest Born	LOC-N 88
FROUD, Brian		
7	World of the Dark Crystal, The	LOC-N 83
7	World of the Dark Crystal, The	HUG-N 83
GAGNE, Paul A		
7	Zombies That Ate Pittsburgh	STO-N 88
GAIMAN, Neil		
4	Midsummer Night's Dream, A	WFA-W 91
GALLAGHER, Stephen		
2	Magpie	STO-N 92
1	Valley of Lights	BFA-N 88
GALOUYE, Daniel F		
1	Dark Universe	HUG-N 62

A U T H O R		
CAT	T I T L E	AW W/N Y
GARDNER, James Alan		
4	Muffin Explains Technology to the World	AUR-W 91
GARNETT, David		
4	Still Life	HUG-N 87
GARRETT, George		
2	Magic Striptease, The	JUP-N 74
GARRETT, Randall		
3	Final Sighting of Fion Mac Cumhaill, The	NEB-N 75
4	Lauralyn	HUG-N 78
5	Lord Darcy Investigates	LOC-N 82
1	Too Many Magicians	HUG-N 67
GARTON, Ray		
1	Live Girls	STO-N 88
GEARY, Patricia		
1	Strange Toys	DIC-W 88
GENTLE, Mary		
1	Architecture of Desire, The	BSF-N 92
1	Golden Witchbreed	BSF-N 84
1	Rats and Gargoyles	CLA-N 91
1	Rats and Gargoyles	BSF-N 91
GERROLD, David		
3	In the Deadlands	NEB-N 72
1	Man Who Folded Himself, The	HUG-N 74
1	Man Who Folded Himself, The	JUP-N 74
1	Man Who Folded Himself, The	LOC-N 74
1	Man Who Folded Himself, The	NEB-N 73
1	Moonstar Odyssey	NEB-N 77
13	Protostars	LOC-N 72
1	When Harlie Was One	HUG-N 73
1	When Harlie Was One	NEB-N 72
1	When Harlie Was One	LOC-N 73

	A U T H O R	
CAT	T I T L E	AW W/N Y

	GIBSON, William	
5	Burning Chrome	LOC-N 87
3	Burning Chrome	NEB-N 82
3	Burning Chrome	SFC-N 83
1	Count Zero	HUG-N 87
1	Count Zero	LOC-N 87
1	Count Zero	BSF-N 87
1	Count Zero	SFC-N 87
1	Count Zero	NEB-N 86
1	Difference Engine, The	JWC-N 92
1	Difference Engine, The	BSF-N 91
1	Difference Engine, The	LOC-N 91
1	Difference Engine, The	NEB-N 92
4	Johny Mnemonic	NEB-N 81
1	Mona Lisa Overdrive	LOC-N 89
1	Mona Lisa Overdrive	AUR-W 89
1	Mona Lisa Overdrive	NEB-N 88
1	Mona Lisa Overdrive	HUG-N 89
1	Neuromancer	BSF-N 85
1	Neuromancer	DIC-W 85
1	Neuromancer	HUG-W 85
9	Neuromancer	LOC-N 85
1	Neuromancer	SFC-W 85
1	Neuromancer	DIT-W 85
1	Neuromancer	JWC-N 85
1	Neuromancer	NEB-W 84
3	Winter Market, The	HUG-N 87
3	Winter Market, The	SFC-N 87
3	Winter Market, The	LOC-N 87
4	Winter Market, The	BSF-N 87
3	Winter Market, The	NEB-N 86

	GIGER, H R	
7	Giger's Alien	LOC-N 90

	GODWIN, Parke	
3	Fire When it Comes, The	NEB-N 81
6	Fire When It Comes, The	WFA-N 85
2	Fire When It Comes, The	WFA-W 82
3	Fire When It Comes, The	HUG-N 82
1	Firelord	WFA-N 81

	A U T H O R	
CAT	T I T L E	AW W/N Y
GOLD, H L		
4	Inside Man	NEB-N 65
GOLDIN, Stephen		
13	Alien Condition, The	LOC-N 74
4	Last Ghost, The	NEB-N 71
GOLDSTEIN, Lisa		
4	Cassandra's Photographs	NEB-N 87
4	Cassandra's Photographs	HUG-N 88
1	Dream Years, The	WFA-N 86
1	Mask For The General, A	CLA-N 90
9	Red Magician, The	LOC-N 83
GOMOLL, et al		
7	Bakery Men Don't See Cookbook, The	HUG-N 92
GOTLIEB, Phyllis		
1	Judgement of Dragons	AUR-W 82
2	Son of the Morning	NEB-N 72
GOULART, Ron		
4	Calling Dr. Clockwork	NEB-N 65
2	Hellhound Project, The	JUP-N 74
GOULD, Stepehn		
3	Peaches for Mad Molly	HUG-N 89
3	Peaches for Mad Molly	NEB-N 88
3	Peaches for Mad Molly	DAV-N 89
4	Rory	HUG-N 85
GRANT, Charles L		
4	Coin of the Realm	WFA-N 82
4	Coin of the Realm	BFA-N 82
2	Confess the Seasons	WFA-W 83

AUTHOR		
CAT	TITLE	AW W/N Y
GRANT, Charles L Continued...		
4	Crowd of Shadows, A	NEB-W 76
4	Crowd of Shadows, A	LOC-N 77
4	Crowd of Shadows, A	HUG-N 77
6	Dodd, Mead Gallery of Horrors, The	WFA-N 84
6	Final Shadows	WFA-N 92
3	Glow of Candles, a Unicorn's Eye, A	NEB-W 78
4	Hear Me Now, Sweet Abbey Rose	WFA-N 79
1	Hour of the Oxrun Dead, The	WFA-N 78
1	In A Dark Dream	WFA-N 90
1	In A Dark Stream	STO-N 90
1	Last Call of Morning, The	WFA-N 80
1	Nestling, The	WFA-N 83
6	Night Visions 2	WFA-N 86
6	Nightmare Seasons	WFA-W 83
6	Nightmares	WFA-N 80
2	Night's Swift Dragons	WFA-N 83
1	Pet, The	WFA-N 87
3	Rest Is Silence, The	NEB-N 74
4	Secrets of the Heart	NEB-N 80
6	Shadows	WFA-W 79
6	Shadows 2	WFA-N 80
6	Shadows 3	WFA-N 81
6	Shadows 4	BFA-N 82
6	Shadows 4	WFA-N 82
6	Shadows 6	WFA-N 84
1	Sound At Midnight, The	WFA-N 79
6	Tales From the Nightside	WFA-N 82
6	Tales From the Nightside	BFA-N 82
4	This Old Man	STO-N 88
4	When All the Children Call My Name	WFA-N 78
4	White Wolf Calling	NEB-N 75
GRANT, Richard		
1	Rumours of Spring	CLA-N 89
1	Saraband of Lost Time	DIC-N 86
GRAVEL, Geary		
1	Alchemists, The	DIC-N 85

AUTHORS - Alphabetically

AUTHOR		
CAT	TITLE	AW W/N Y
	GREEN, Joseph	
3	Decision Makers, The	NEB-N 65
	GREEN, Robert M Jr	
3	Apology to Inky	NEB-N 66
3	Apology to Inky	HUG-N 67
	GREENBERG, Martin H	
6	After t/King:Stories Honor of Tolkien	WFA-N 92
6	Foundations's Friends	LOC-N 90
	GREENLAND, Colin	
4	Nothing Special	BSF-N 92
1	Take Back Plenty	BSF-W 91
1	Take Back Plenty	CLA-W 91
	GRIFFIN, Russell	
1	Timeservers, The	DIC-N 86
	GRIMWOOD, Ken	
1	Replay	WFA-W 88
1	Replay	CLA-N 88
	GUILLEN, Rosemary Ellen	
7	Vampires Among Us	STO-N 92
	GUNN, Eileen	
4	Computer Friendly	HUG-N 90
4	Stable Strategies for Middle Management	HUG-N 89
	GUNN, James E	
7	Isaac Asimov: The Foundations of SF	HUG-W 83
7	Isaac Asimov: The Foundations of SF	LOC-N 83
3	Listeners, The	NEB-N 68
7	New Encyclopedia of Science Fiction, The	LOC-N 89
7	New Encyclopedia of Science Fiction, The	HUG-N 89

AUTHOR		
CAT	T I T L E	AW W/N Y
HALDEMAN, Joe		
1	Forever War, The	LOC-W 76
1	Forever War, The	HUG-W 76
1	Forever War, The	NEB-W 75
1	Forever War, The	DIT-W 76
2	Hemingway Hoax, The	HUG-W 91
2	Hemingway Hoax, The	LOC-N 91
2	Hemingway Hoax, The	NEB-N 91
2	Hemingway Hoax, The	SFC-N 91
2	Hemingway Hoax, The	WFA-N 91
2	Hero	LOC-N 73
2	Hero	HUG-N 73
3	High Steel	LOC-N 83
4	High Steel	NEB-N 82
5	Infinite Dreams	LOC-N 79
1	Mindbridge	HUG-N 77
1	Mindbridge	LOC-N 77
4	More Than The Sum of His Parts	NEB-N 85
4	Tricentennial	NEB-N 76
4	Tricentennial	LOC-W 77
4	Tricentennial	HUG-W 77
HAMBLY, Barbara		
11	Dragonsbane	LOC-N 86
11	Rainbow Abyss, The	LOC-N 92
10	Those Who Hunt the Night	LOC-W 89
HAND, Elizabeth		
1	Wintersong	DIC-N 91
9	Wintersong	LOC-N 91
HANSEN, Karl		
9	War Games	LOC-N 82
HARNESS, Charles L		
2	Alchemist, The	NEB-N 66
3	Alchemist, The	HUG-N 67
3	An Ornament to His Profession	NEB-N 66
3	Ornament of His Profession, An	HUG-N 67

AUTHOR		
CAT	T I T L E	AW W/N Y
HARNESS, Charles L Continued...		
2	Probable Cause	NEB-N 69
2	Summer Solstice	HUG-N 85
HARRIS, Alan Lee		
9	Deliver Us From Evil	STO-N 89
HARRIS, Raymond		
1	Schizogenic Man, The	DIC-N 91
HARRIS, Thomas		
1	Silence of the Lambs, The	WFA-N 89
10	Silence of the Lambs, The	LOC-N 89
1	Silence of the Lambs, The	STO-W 89
HARRISON, Harry		
13	Astounding	LOC-W 74
4	By the Falls	NEB-N 70
1	Deathworld	HUG-N 61
1	Deathworld	HUG-N 60
13	Nova 2	LOC-N 73
1	Planet of t/Damned (Sense of Obligation)	HUG-N 62
HARRISON, M John		
1	Floating Gods, The	DIC-N 84
1	In Viriconium	BFA-N 83
1	Storm of Wings, A	BFA-N 81
6	Viriconium Nights	WFA-N 85
6	Young Man's Journey to Viriconium, A	BSF-N 86
HARTWELL, David G		
7	Age of Wonders: Exploring t/World of SF	LOC-N 85
6	Dark Descent, The	LOC-N 88
6	Dark Descent, The	WFA-N 88
HAZEL, Paul		
1	Winter King	WFA-N 86

AUTHOR		
CAT	TITLE	AW W/N Y
HEINLEIN, Robert A		
1	Cat Who Walks Through Walls, The	LOC-N 86
1	Double Star	HUG-W 56
1	Friday	HUG-N 83
1	Friday	HUG-N 83
1	Friday	LOC-N 83
1	Friday	NEB-N 82
1	Glory Road	HUG-N 64
7	Grumbles From the Grave	LOC-W 90
7	Grumbles From the Grave	HUG-N 90
1	Have Space Suit-Will Travel	HUG-N 59
1	Job: A Comedy of Justice	NEB-N 84
1	Job: A Comedy of Justice	HUG-N 85
11	Job: A Comedy of Justice	LOC-W 85
1	Moon is a Harsh Mistress, The	HUG-N 66
1	Moon is a Harsh Mistress, The	NEB-N 66
1	Moon is a Harsh Mistress, The	HUG-N 67
1	Starship Troopers	HUG-W 60
1	Stranger in a Strange Land	HUG-W 62
1	Time Enough For Love	LOC-N 74
1	Time Enough For Love	JUP-N 74
1	Time Enough For Love	HUG-N 74
1	Time Enough For Love	NEB-N 73
HENDERSON, Zenna		
3	Captivity	HUG-N 59
HERBERT, Frank		
1	Children of Dune	LOC-N 77
1	Children of Dune	HUG-N 77
1	Dune	HUG-W 66
1	Dune	NEB-W 65
1	Dune World	HUG-N 64
HIGHTOWER, Lynn S		
8	Alien Blues	LOC-N 92
HINZ, Christopher		
1	Liege-Killer	COM-N 88
9	Liege-Killer	LOC-N 88

AUTHORS - Alphabetically

CAT	T I T L E	AW W/N Y
A U T H O R		
HOBAN, Russell		
1	Riddley Walker	NEB-N 81
1	Riddley Walker	JWC-W 82
1	Riddley Walker	DIT-W 83
HOLDER, Nancy		
4	Lady Madonna	STO-W 92
HOLDSTOCK, Robert		
5	Bone Forest, The	WFA-N 92
1	Mythago Wood	WFA-W 85
4	Mythago Wood	BSF-W 82
2	Mythago Wood	WFA-N 82
1	Mythago Wood	BSF-W 85
2	Ragthorn, The	WFA-N 92
1	Where Time Winds Blow	BSF-N 82
HOLLIS, H H		
3	Guerilla Trees, The	NEB-N 68
4	Sword Game	NEB-N 68
HOSKINS, Robert		
13	Infinity 2	LOC-N 72
HOWARD, Hayden		
3	Eskimo Invasion, The	NEB-N 66
3	Eskimo Invasion, The	HUG-N 67
1	Eskimo Invasion, The	NEB-N 67
HUBBARD, L Ron		
1	Black Genesis	HUG-N 87
HUFF, Tanya		
10	Blood Price	LOC-N 92

CAT	TITLE	AW W/N Y
AUTHOR		
HUGH, Dafydd ab		
3	Coon Rolled Down and Ruptured...	LOC-N 91
3	Coon Rolled Down and Ruptured...	NEB-N 91
3	Coon Rolled Down and Ruptured...	HUG-N 91
HUGHART, Barry		
1	Bridge of Birds	WFA-W 85
11	Eight Skilled Gentlemen	LOC-N 92
ING, Dean		
3	Devil You Don't Know	HUG-N 79
3	Devil You Don't Know	LOC-N 79
3	Devil You Don't Know	NEB-N 78
JABLOKOV, Alexander		
8	Carve the Sky	LOC-N 92
JENNINGS, Gary		
4	Myrrha	HUG-N 63
JETER, K W		
1	Dark Seeker	DIC-N 88
1	Farewell Horizontal	JWC-N 90
1	Farewell Horizontal	CLA-N 91
4	First Time, The	LOC-N 91
JONAS, Gerald		
3	Shaker Revival	NEB-N 70
JONES, Diana Wynne		
1	Archer's Goon	WFA-N 85
JONES, Gwyneth		
1	Escape Plans	CLA-N 87
1	Kairos	CLA-N 89
1	White Queen	CLA-N 92

AUTHORS - Alphabetically

	A U T H O R	
CAT	**T I T L E**	**AW W/N Y**
	JONES, Raymond F	
4	Rat Race	HUG-N 67
	JONES, Stephen	
6	Best New Horror	WFA-W 91
6	Best New Horror	BFA-W 92
7	Clive Barker's Shadows in Eden	LOC-N 92
7	Clive Barker's Shadows in Eden	STO-W 92
7	Clive Barker's Shawows in Eden	HUG-N 92
7	Horror: The 100 Best Books	STO-N 90
	JORDON, Robert	
11	Eye of the World, The	LOC-N 91
	JOSHI, S T	
7	Weird Tale, The	STO-N 91
	KADREY, Richard	
9	Metrophage	LOC-N 89
	KAGAN, Janet	
3	Getting the Bugs Out	DAV-W 91
3	Loch Moose Monster, The	DAV-W 90
5	Mirabile	LOC-N 92
	KAGAN, Norman	
3	At The Institute	NEB-N 65
3	Earth Merchants, The	NEB-N 65
3	Laugh Along With Franz	NEB-N 65
	KANDEL, Michael	
9	Strange Invasion	LOC-N 90
	KARAGEORGE, Michael	
3	Life of Your Time, The	NEB-N 65

AUTHORS - Alphabetically

AUTHOR		
CAT	T I T L E	AW W/N Y
KAY, Guy Gavriel		
9	Summer Tree, The	LOC-N 86
1	Tigana	WFA-N 91
1	Tigana	AUR-W 91
11	Tigana	LOC-N 91
1	Wandering Fire, The	AUR-W 87
KEARNS, Richard		
4	Grave Angels, The	JWC-N 87
KELLOGG, M Bradley		
9	Rumor of Angels, A	LOC-N 84
KELLY, James Patrick		
2	Glass Cloud	LOC-N 88
4	Heroics	JWC-N 88
2	Mr. Boy	LOC-N 91
2	Mr. Boy	DAV-W 91
2	Mr. Boy	NEB-N 91
3	Prisoner of Chillon	DAV-W 87
4	Rat	HUG-N 87
4	Rat	LOC-N 87
4	Rat	SFC-N 87
4	Rat	NEB-N 86
KELLY, James Patrick		
3	Saint Theresa of the Aliens	NEB-N 84
3	Standing in Line with Mister Jimmy	NEB-N 92
KENNEDY, L		
1	Journal of Nicholas the American	NEB-N 86
KENNEDY, Leigh		
4	Her Furry Face	NEB-N 83
4	Her Furry Face	SFC-N 84
4	Silent Cradle	WFA-N 84

CAT	T I T L E	AW W/N Y
AUTHOR		
KERNAGHAN, Eileen		
4	Carpe Diem	AUR-W 90
1	Journey to Apriloth	AUR-W 85
KESSEL, John		
2	Another Orphan	HUG-N 83
2	Another Orphan	NEB-W 82
2	Another Orphan	SFC-N 83
4	Buffalo	JWC-W 92
4	Buffalo	HUG-N 92
4	Buffalo	NEB-N 92
4	Buffalo	LOC-W 92
1	Good News From Outer Space	NEB-N 89
1	Good News From Outer Space	JWC-N 90
4	Mrs. Shummel Exits a Winner	NEB-N 88
KEYES, Daniel		
1	Flowers for Algernon	NEB-W 66
1	Flowers for Algernon	HUG-N 67
4	Flowers for Algernon	HUG-W 60
KILLIAN, Crawford		
1	Lifter	AUR-N 87
KILLOUGH, Lee		
4	Symphony for a Lost Traveler	HUG-N 85
KILWORTH, Garry		
4	Dissemblers, The	BSF-N 83
4	Hogfoot Right and Bird-Hands	WFA-N 88
6	Songbird of Pain, The	WFA-N 85
4	Spiral Winds	BSF-N 85
KING, Stephen		
4	Apt Pupil	BFA-N 83
2	Ballad of the Flexible Bullet, The	WFA-N 85
2	Ballad of the Flexible Bullet, The	LOC-N 85

	A U T H O R	
CAT	T I T L E	AW W/N Y
	KING, Stephen Continued...	
4	Breathing Method, The	BFA-W 83
2	Breathing Method, The	WFA-N 83
4	Crouch End	BFA-N 81
1	Cujo	BFA-W 82
7	Danse Macabre	LOC-W 82
7	Danse Macabre	HUG-W 82
10	Dark Half, The	LOC-N 90
10	Dark Towers III, The: The Waste Lands	LOC-N 92
1	Dark Towers III, The: The Waste Lands	STO-N 92
11	Dead Zone, The	LOC-N 80
5	Different Seasons	LOC-N 83
4	Do the Dead Sing?	BFA-W 82
4	Do the Dead Sing?	WFA-W 82
4	End of the Whole Mess, The	WFA-N 87
1	Firestarter	BFA-N 81
5	Four Past Midnight	LOC-N 91
6	Four Past Midnight	STO-W 91
1	It	BFA-W 87
11	It	LOC-N 87
1	It	WFA-N 87
2	Langoliers, The	STO-N 91
1	Misery	STO-W 88
1	Misery	WFA-N 88
1	Mist, The	WFA-N 81
1	Needful Things	STO-N 92
3	Night Flier, The	STO-N 89
6	Night Shift	WFA-N 79
1	Pet Sematary	WFA-N 84
1	Salem's Lot	WFA-N 76
11	Shining, The	LOC-N 78
5	Skeleton Crew	LOC-W 86
6	Skeleton Crew	WFA-N 86
1	Stand, The	WFA-N 79
10	Stand, The: The Complete, Uncut Edition	LOC-N 91
11	Talisman, The	LOC-N 85
3	Way Station, The	LOC-N 81
3	Way Station, The	NEB-N 80

AUTHORS - Alphabetically

	A U T H O R	
CAT	**T I T L E**	**AW W/N Y**
	KINGSBURY, Donald	
1	Courtship Rite	HUG-N 83
1	Courtship Rite	COM-W 83
1	Courtship Rite	HUG-N 83
9	Courtship Rite	LOC-W 83
1	Courtship Rite	LOC-N 83
2	Moon Goddess and the Son, The	HUG-N 80
	KIRK, Russell	
2	There's A Long, Long Trail A-Winding	WFA-W 77
	KIRS, Alex	
4	Better Than Ever	NEB-N 65
	KLEIN, T E D	
1	Ceremonies, The	WFA-N 85
1	Ceremonies, The	BFA-W 85
4	Children of the Kingdom	WFA-N 81
2	Events at Poroth Farm	WFA-N 75
2	Nadelman's God	WFA-W 86
4	Petey	WFA-N 80
	KNIGHT, Damon	
5	Best From Orbit 1-10	LOC-N 76
5	Best of Damon Knight, The	LOC-N 77
4	I See You	HUG-N 77
4	I See You	LOC-N 77
4	I See You	JUP-W 77
4	Masks	NEB-N 68
4	Masks	HUG-N 69
6	Orbit 6	LOC-N 71
6	Orbit 7	LOC-N 71
13	Orbit 10	LOC-N 73
13	Orbit 11	LOC-N 73
13	Orbit 12	LOC-N 74
13	Orbit 14	LOC-N 75
14	Orbit 18	LOC-N 77
14	Science Fiction Argosy, A	LOC-N 73

AUTHOR		
CAT	T I T L E	AW W/N Y
KOJA, Kathe		
4	Angels in Love	LOC-N 92
8	Cipher, The	LOC-W 92
9	Cipher, The	STO-W 92
1	Cipher, The	DIC-N 92
KOONTZ, Dean R		
4	Beastchild	LOC-N 71
2	Beastchild	HUG-N 71
1	Midnight	STO-N 90
10	Midnight	LOC-N 90
1	Strangers	WFA-N 87
KORNBLUTH, Cyril M		
4	Advent of Channel Twelve, The	HUG-N 59
3	Reap the Dark Tide (Shark Ship)	HUG-N 59
1	Takeoff	IFA-N 53
4	Theory of Rocketry	HUG-N 59
KOSINSKI, Jerry		
2	Being There	NEB-N 71
KOTZWINKLE, William		
1	Doctor Rat	WFA-W 77
KRAUS, Stephen		
4	Frame of Reference	DAV-N 89
KRESS, Nancy		
2	And Wild For To Hold	LOC-N 92
2	And Wild For To Hold	HUG-N 92
2	Beggars in Spain	HUG-W 92
2	Beggars in Spain	SFC-N 92
2	Beggars in Spain	NEB-W 92
2	Beggars in Spain	LOC-N 92
4	Out of All Them Bright Stars	NEB-W 85

AUTHOR		
CAT	T I T L E	AW W/N Y
KRESS, Nancy Continued...		
3	Prince of Oranges, The	LOC-N 90
3	Prince of Oranges, The	HUG-N 90
2	Trinity	SFC-N 85
2	Trinity	NEB-N 84
2	Trinity	LOC-N 85
KUBE-McDOWELL, Michael P		
9	Emprise	LOC-N 86
1	Enterprise	DIC-N 86
1	Quiet Pools, The	HUG-N 91
1	Quiet Pools, The	LOC-N 91
KURTZ, Katherine		
11	King's Justice, The	LOC-N 86
KUSHNER, Ellen		
1	Swordpoint	SFC-N 88
11	Thomas the Rhymer	LOC-N 91
1	Thomas the Rhymer	WFA-W 91
KUTTNER, Henry		
6	Best of Henry Kuttner, The	LOC-N 76
KYLE, David A		
7	Pictorial History of Science Fiction, A	BSF-W 77
LACKEY, Mercedes		
9	Arrows of the Queen	LOC-N 88
LAFFERTY, R A		
6	900 Grandmothers	LOC-N 71
1	Aurelia	DIC-N 83
4	Continued on Next Rock	HUG-N 71
3	Continued on Next Rock	NEB-N 70
4	Continued on Next Rock	LOC-N 71

CAT	T I T L E	AW W/N Y
A U T H O R		

LAFFERTY, R A   Continued...

CAT	T I T L E	AW W/N Y
4	Days of Grass, Days of Straw	JUP-N 74
1	Devil is Dead, The	NEB-N 71
4	Entire and Perfect Chrysolite	NEB-N 70
4	Episodes of the Argo	JWC-N 91
4	Eurema's Dam	HUG-W 73
1	Fourth Mansions	LOC-N 71
1	Fourth Mansions	NEB-N 70
4	In Our Block	NEB-N 65
5	Lafferty in Orbit	WFA-N 92
1	Past Master	NEB-N 68
1	Past Master	HUG-N 69
4	Sky	HUG-N 72
4	Slow Tuesday Night	NEB-N 65

LAIDLAW, Marc

CAT	T I T L E	AW W/N Y
1	Neon Lotus	DIC-N 89

LAINEZ, Manuel Mujica

CAT	T I T L E	AW W/N Y
1	Wandering Unicorn, The	WFA-N 84

LAMMING, R M

CAT	T I T L E	AW W/N Y
4	Ink Imp, The	BSF-N 81

LANDIS, Geoffrey A

CAT	T I T L E	AW W/N Y
2	Elementals	HUG-N 85
4	Ripples in the Dirac Sea	HUG-N 89
4	Ripples in the Dirac Sea	NEB-W 89
4	Ripples in the Dirac Sea	DAV-N 89
4	Ripples in the Dirac Sea	SFC-N 89
4	Walk in the Sun, A	HUG-W 92

LANGFORD, David

CAT	T I T L E	AW W/N Y
4	Cube Root	BSF-W 86
4	Sex Pirates of the Blood Asteroid	BSF-N 80

LANIER, Sterling

CAT	T I T L E	AW W/N Y
2	Farmer's Tale, A	WFA-N 75

CAT	TITLE	AW W/N Y
	A U T H O R	

LANSDALE, Joe R

CAT	TITLE	AW W/N Y
5	By Bizarre Hands	WFA-N 90
6	By Bizarre Hands	STO-N 90
1	Drive-in, The	STO-N 89
1	Drive-in, The	WFA-N 89
4	Love Doll: A Fable	STO-N 92
4	Night They Missed the Horror Show, The	WFA-N 89
4	Night They Missed the Horror Show, The	STO-W 89
2	On t/Far Side of t/Cadillac Desert w/Dea	STO-W 90
4	On t/Far Side of t/Cadillac Desert w/Dea	BFA-W 90
2	On t/Far Side of t/Cadillac Desert w/Dea	WFA-N 90
6	Razored Saddles	LOC-N 90
6	Razored Saddles	WFA-N 90
1	Savage Season	STO-N 91
4	Tight Little Stitches in Dead Man's Back	WFA-N 87

LAUMER, Keith

CAT	TITLE	AW W/N Y
2	Day Beyond Forever, The	NEB-N 68
4	In the Queue	NEB-N 70
4	In the Queue	LOC-N 71
4	In the Queue	HUG-N 71
3	Once There Was a Giant	NEB-N 68
1	Plague of Demons, A	NEB-N 65
2	Wonderful Secret, The	HUG-N 78

LAYMON, Richard

CAT	TITLE	AW W/N Y
1	Flesh	STO-N 89
1	Funland	STO-N 91

LEE, Tanith

CAT	TITLE	AW W/N Y
1	Birthgrave, The	NEB-N 75
4	Bright Burning Tiger	LOC-N 85
1	Death's Master	BFA-W 80
6	Dreams of Dark and Light	WFA-N 87
4	Elle Est Trois	WFA-W 84
4	Gorgon, The	WFA-W 83
4	Gorgon, The	WFA-N 83
1	Kill The Dead	BFA-N 81
5	Night Sorceries	WFA-N 88
1	Night's Master	WFA-N 79
2	Nung Dimittis	WFA-N 84

AUTHOR		
CAT	T I T L E	AW W/N Y

LEE, Tanith   Continued...

1	Quest of the White Witch, The	BFA-N 79
6	Red As Blood	WFA-N 84
5	Red As Blood	LOC-N 84
4	Red As Blood	BFA-N 80
4	Red As Blood	NEB-N 79
5	Tamastara	LOC-N 85

LeGUIN, Ursula K

4	Author of the Acacia Seeds, The	LOC-N 75
3	Buffalo Gals, Won't You Come Out Tonight	HUG-W 88
3	Buffalo Gals, Won't You Come Out Tonight	LOC-N 88
4	Buffalo Gals, Won't You Come Out Tonight	JWC-N 88
2	Buffalo Gals, Won't You Come Out Tonight	WFA-W 88
3	Buffalo Gals, Won't You Come Out Tonight	NEB-N 87
5	Compass Rose, The	LOC-W 83
1	Compass Rose, The	DIT-W 86
7	Dancing at the Edge of the World	LOC-N 90
7	Dancing at the Edge of the World	HUG-N 90
4	Day Before the Revolution, The	LOC-W 75
4	Day Before the Revolution, The	HUG-N 75
4	Day Before the Revolution, The	JUP-W 75
4	Day Before the Revolution, The	NEB-W 74
3	Diary of the Rose, The	NEB-N 76
3	Diary of the Rose, The	JUP-W 77
3	Diary of the Rose, The	HUG-N 77
3	Diary of the Rose, The	LOC-N 77
4	Direction of the Road	JUP-N 74
1	Dispossessed, The	NEB-W 74
1	Dispossessed, The	JUP-W 75
1	Dispossessed, The	JWC-N 75
1	Dispossessed, The	HUG-W 75
1	Dispossessed, The	LOC-W 75
7	Language of the Night, The	LOC-N 80
7	Language of the Night, The	HUG-N 80
1	Lathe of Heaven, The	LOC-W 72
1	Lathe of Heaven, The	NEB-N 71
1	Lathe of Heaven, The	HUG-N 72
1	Left Hand of Darkness	HUG-W 70
1	Left Hand of Darkness	NEB-W 69
3	New Atlantis, The	HUG-N 76
3	New Atlantis, The	LOC-W 76
3	New Atlantis, The	NEB-N 75

	A U T H O R	
CAT	T I T L E	AW W/N Y
LeGUIN, Ursula K	Continued...	
3	Nine Lives	NEB-N 69
4	Ones Who Walk Away from Omelas	LOC-N 74
4	Ones Who Walk Away from Omelas	HUG-W 74
4	Ones Who Walk Away from Omelas	JUP-N 74
3	Shobie's Story, The	NEB-N 91
3	Shobie's Story, The	HUG-N 91
3	Shobie's Story, The	LOC-N 91
4	Sur	LOC-W 83
4	Sur	SFC-N 83
4	Sur	HUG-N 83
11	Tehanu: The Last Book of Earthsea	LOC-W 91
1	Tehanu: The Last Book of Earthsea	NEB-W 91
4	Vaster Than Empires and More Slow	HUG-N 72
6	Wind's Twelve Quarters	LOC-W 76
4	Winter's King	HUG-N 70
2	Word for World is Forest, The	HUG-W 73
2	Word for World is Forest, The	LOC-N 73
2	Word for World is Forest, The	NEB-N 72
LEIBER, Fritz		
4	Answering Service	NEB-N 67
2	Belsen Express	WFA-W 76
9	Beyond Rejection	LOC-N 81
1	Big Time, The	HUG-W 58
4	Button Molder, The	WFA-N 80
4	Button Molder, The	BFA-W 80
4	Catch That Zeppelin	HUG-W 76
4	Catch That Zeppelin	NEB-W 75
4	Cyclops	NEB-N 65
2	Dark Wings	WFA-N 77
4	Death of Princes, The	LOC-N 77
3	Deskful of Girls, A	HUG-N 59
3	Four Ghosts in Hamlet	NEB-N 65
5	Ghost Light, The	LOC-W 85
3	Gonna Roll Those Bones	NEB-W 67
3	Gonna Roll Those Bones	HUG-W 68
4	Good New Days, The	NEB-N 65
6	Heroes and Horror	WFA-N 79
2	Horrible Imaginings (Death)	NEB-N 82
2	Horrible Imaginings (Death)	WFA-N 83
2	Horrible Imaginings (Death)	LOC-N 83
2	Horrible Imaginings (Death)	SFC-N 83

CAT	TITLE	AW W/N Y
	A U T H O R	

LEIBER, Fritz   Continued...

CAT	TITLE	AW W/N Y
2	Ill Met in Lankhmar	HUG-W 71
2	Ill Met in Lankhmar	NEB-W 70
5	Knight and the Knave of Swords, The	WFA-N 89
5	Knight and the Knave of Swords, The	LOC-N 89
5	Leiber Chronicles, The	WFA-N 91
5	Leiber Chronicles, The	LOC-N 91
3	Midnight by the Morphy Watch	HUG-N 75
1	Our Lady of Darkness	WFA-W 78
11	Our Lady of Darkness	LOC-N 78
3	Rite of Spring, A	NEB-N 77
4	Rite of Spring, A	LOC-N 78
4	Rump-Titty-Titty-Tum-TAH-Tee	HUG-N 59
4	Scylla's Daughter	HUG-N 62
2	Ship of Shadows	NEB-N 69
2	Ship of Shadows	HUG-W 70
4	Snow Women, The	LOC-N 71
2	Snow Women, The	HUG-N 71
6	Swords and Ice Magic	WFA-N 78
4	Unholy Grail, The	HUG-N 63
1	Wanderer, The	HUG-W 65
5	Worlds of Fritz Leiber, The	LOC-N 77

LEINSTER, Murray

CAT	TITLE	AW W/N Y
3	Exploration Team	HUG-W 56
1	Pirates of Zan	HUG-N 60

LEM, Stanislaw

CAT	TITLE	AW W/N Y
1	Fiasco	CLA-N 88

LEMAN, Bob

CAT	TITLE	AW W/N Y
4	Window	LOC-N 81
4	Window	NEB-N 80

LETHEM, Jonathan

CAT	TITLE	AW W/N Y
4	Happy Man, The	JWC-N 92
3	Happy Man, The	NEB-N 92

CAT	AUTHOR TITLE	AW W/N Y
LEVACK		
7	Fantasia: A Jack Vance Bibliography	LOC-N 79
LEY, Willy		
7	Conquest of Space	IFA-W 51
7	Dragons in Amber	IFA-N 52
7	Lands Beyond	IFA-W 53
LIGOTTI, Thomas		
5	Grimscribe: His Lives and Works	WFA-N 92
4	Last Feast of Harlequin, The	WFA-N 91
LINAWEAVER, Brad		
2	Moon of Ice	NEB-N 82
LINDHOLM, Megan		
4	Silver Lady and the Fortyish Man, The	JWC-N 90
3	Silver Lady and the Fortyish Man, The	NEB-N 89
2	Touch of Lavender, A	NEB-N 89
2	Touch of Lavender, A	DAV-W 90
2	Touch of Lavender, A	HUG-N 90
LITTLE, Bentley		
9	Revelation, The	STO-W 91
LONG, Frank Belknap		
5	Early Long, The	WFA-N 76
LONGYEAR, Barry		
2	Enemy Mine	HUG-W 80
2	Enemy Mine	NEB-W 79
2	Enemy Mine	LOC-W 80
3	Homecoming	HUG-N 80
1	Infinity Hold	DIC-N 90
3	Savage Planet, The	HUG-N 81

	A U T H O R	
CAT	T I T L E	AW W/N Y
	LUCENO, James	
1	Fearful Symmetry, A	DIC-N 90
	LUMLEY, Brian	
2	Born of the Winds	WFA-N 76
4	Fruiting Bodies	BFA-W 89
4	House of the Temple, The	BFA-N 81
4	Name and Number	BFA-N 83
	LUPOFF, Richard A	
3	After the Dreamtime	HUG-N 75
4	Sail the Tide of Mourning	NEB-N 75
4	Sail the Tide of Mourning	HUG-N 76
4	Sail the Tide of Mourning	LOC-N 76
1	Sword of the Demon	NEB-N 77
2	With t/Bentfin Boomer Boys on Little Old	LOC-N 73
2	With t/Bentfin Boomer Boys on Little Old	NEB-N 72
	LYNN, Elizabeth A	
1	Dancers of Arun, The	WFA-N 80
11	Northern Girl, The	LOC-N 81
2	Red Hawk, The	WFA-N 84
1	Watchtower	WFA-W 80
4	Women Who Loved the Moon	WFA-W 80

AUTHORS - Alphabetically

MacAPP, C C		
2	Mercuryman, The	NEB-N 65

MacAVOY, R A		
11	Book of Kells, The	LOC-N 86
11	Damiano's Lute	LOC-N 85
11	Raphael	LOC-N 85
1	Tea With the Black Dragon	HUG-N 84
1	Tea With The Black Dragon	DIC-N 84
1	Tea With The Black Dragon	WFA-N 84
9	Tea with the Black Dragon	LOC-W 84
1	Tea With the Black Dragon	NEB-N 83
11	Twisting The Rope	LOC-N 87

MacGREGOR, Loren J		
9	Net, The	LOC-N 88

MacLEAN, Katherine		
2	Missing Man, The	NEB-W 71
1	Missing Man, The	NEB-N 75
3	Second Game (Cosmic Checkmate)	HUG-N 59

MacLEOD, Ian		
3	1/72 nd Scale	NEB-N 91

MADDOX, Tom		
8	Halo	LOC-N 92

MAHY, Margaret		
1	Tricksters, The	WFA-N 87

MAITZ, Don		
7	First Maitz	HUG-N 89
7	First Maitz	LOC-W 89

MALZBERG, Barry N		
1	Beyond Apollo	JWC-W 73
4	Corridors	NEB-N 82
7	Engines of the Night, The	HUG-N 83
7	Engines of the Night, The	LOC-W 83

AUTHOR		
CAT	T I T L E	AW W/N Y
MALZBERG, Barry N Continued...		
3	Galaxy Called Rome, A	NEB-N 75
3	Galaxy Called Rome, A	LOC-N 76
1	Guernica Night	NEB-N 75
1	Herovit's World	JUP-N 74
4	Prose Bowl	BSF-N 80
1	Remaking of Sigmund Freud, The	DIC-N 86
1	Remaking of Sigmund Freud, The	NEB-N 85
MARTIN, George R R		
11	Armageddon Rag, The	LOC-N 84
1	Armageddon Rag, The	WFA-N 84
1	Dying of the Light	BFA-N 79
1	Dying of the Light	HUG-N 78
11	Fevre Dream	LOC-N 83
1	Fevre Dream	WFA-N 83
3	For A Single Yesterday	LOC-N 76
3	Glass Flower, The	LOC-N 87
3	Guardians	HUG-N 82
3	Guardians	LOC-W 82
3	Monkey Treatment, The	NEB-N 83
3	Monkey Treatment, The	LOC-W 84
4	Needle Men, The	LOC-N 82
6	New Voices 4	LOC-N 82
6	Night Visions 3	WFA-N 87
5	Nightflyers	LOC-N 86
2	Nightflyers	LOC-W 81
2	Nightflyers	HUG-N 81
2	Pear-Shaped Man, The	WFA-N 88
3	Pear-Shaped Man, The	STO-W 88
2	Plague Star, The	LOC-N 86
3	Portraits of His Children	HUG-N 86
5	Portraits of His Children	LOC-N 88
3	Portraits of His Children	NEB-W 85
3	Portraits of His Children	LOC-N 86
3	Portraits of His Children	SFC-W 86
4	Remembering Melody	LOC-N 82
3	Sandkings	LOC-W 80
3	Sandkings	HUG-W 80
5	Sandkings	LOC-W 82
3	Sandkings	NEB-W 79
3	Skin Trade, The	STO-N 89
2	Skin Trade, The	WFA-W 89

	A U T H O R	
CAT	T I T L E	AW W/N Y
MARTIN, George R R Continued...		
2	Song For Lya, A	NEB-N 74
2	Song for Lya, A	JUP-N 75
5	Song for Lya, A	LOC-W 77
2	Song for Lya, A	LOC-N 75
2	Song For Lya, A	HUG-W 75
3	Stone City, The	NEB-N 77
2	Storms of Windhaven, The	LOC-W 76
2	Storms of Windhaven, The	HUG-N 76
5	Tuf Voyaging	LOC-N 87
3	Under Siege	LOC-N 86
2	Unsound Variations	LOC-N 83
2	Unsound Variations	NEB-N 82
2	Unsound Variations	HUG-N 83
4	Way of Cross and Dragon, The	HUG-W 80
4	Way of Cross and Dragon, The	NEB-N 79
4	Way of Cross and Dragon, The	LOC-W 80
6	Wild Cards	LOC-N 87
6	Wild Cards IV: Aces Abroad	LOC-N 89
1	Windhaven	LOC-N 82
4	With Morning Comes Mistfall	HUG-N 74
4	With Morning Comes Mistfall	NEB-N 73
3	...and Seven Times Never Kill Man	LOC-N 76
3	...and Seven Times Never Kill Man	HUG-N 76
MARTIN, Valerie		
1	Mary Reilly	NEB-N 91
10	Mary Reilly	LOC-N 91
1	Mary Reilly	WFA-N 91
MARTINDALE, T Chris		
9	Nightblood	STO-N 91
MASON, Lisa		
9	Arachne	LOC-N 91
MASSIE, Elizabeth		
2	Stephen	STO-W 91
4	Stephen	WFA-N 91

A U T H O R		
CAT	T I T L E	AW W/N Y
MATHESON, Richard		
1	Bid Time Return	WFA-W 76
6	Richard Matheson: Collected Stories	STO-W 90
5	Richard Matheson: Collected Stories	WFA-W 90
MATHEWS, Jack		
7	Battle of Brasil, The	HUG-N 88
MAY, Julian		
1	Many Colored Land, The	LOC-W 82
1	Many-Colored Land, The	NEB-N 81
1	Many-Colored Land, The	HUG-N 82
McALLISTER, Bruce		
3	Dream Baby	NEB-N 87
3	Dream Baby	LOC-N 88
3	Dream Baby	HUG-N 88
11	Dream Baby	LOC-N 90
McAULEY, Paul J		
1	Eternal Light	CLA-N 92
1	Eternal Light	BSF-N 92
McCAFFREY, Anne		
1	All the Weyrs of Pern	LOC-N 92
1	All the Weyrs of Pern	SFC-N 92
1	All the Weyrs of Pern	HUG-N 92
1	Dragonquest	LOC-N 72
1	Dragonquest	HUG-N 72
2	Dragonrider	HUG-N 69
2	Dragonrider	NEB-W 68
1	Dragon's Dawn	JWC-N 89
2	Dramatic Mission	HUG-N 70
2	Dramatic Mission	NEB-N 69
1	Moreta	HUG-N 84
1	Moreta: Dragonlady of Pern	LOC-N 84
2	Weyr Search	HUG-W 68
2	Weyr Search	NEB-N 67

AUTHOR		
CAT	TITLE	AW W/N Y
McCAFFREY, Anne Continued...		
1	White Dragon, The	DIT-W 79
1	White Dragon, The	HUG-N 79
1	White Dragon, The	LOC-N 79
McCAMMON, Robert R		
2	Best Friends	WFA-N 88
6	Blue World and Other Stories	STO-N 90
5	Blue World and Other Stories	WFA-N 90
1	Boy's Life	WFA-W 92
1	Boy's Life	STO-W 92
4	Deep End, The	STO-W 88
4	Eat Me	STO-W 90
1	Mine	STO-W 91
4	Nightcrawlers	WFA-N 85
10	Stinger	LOC-N 89
1	Stinger	STO-N 89
1	Swan Song	WFA-N 88
1	Swan Song	STO-W 88
10	Wolf's Hour, The	LOC-N 90
1	Wolf's Hour, The	STO-N 90
McCARTY, E Clayton		
3	Small One	NEB-N 65
McCAULEY, Kirby		
6	Dark Forces	WFA-W 81
6	Dark Forces	LOC-N 81
6	Frights	WFA-W 77
McCAULEY, Paul J		
1	400 Billion Stars	DIC-N 89
McCONNELL, Ashley		
9	Unearthed	STO-N 92

AUTHOR		
CAT	T I T L E	AW W/N Y
McDEVITT, Jack		
4	Cryptic	NEB-N 83
4	Fort Maxie Branch, The	NEB-N 88
4	Fort Moxie Branch, The	HUG-N 89
1	Hercules Text, The	DIC-N 87
9	Hercules Text, The	LOC-W 87
McDONALD, Ian		
9	Desolation Road	LOC-W 89
1	Desolation Road	CLA-N 90
5	Empire Dreams	LOC-N 89
4	Floating Dogs	BSF-N 92
11	King of the Morning, Queen of Day	LOC-N 92
1	King of the Morning, Queen of Day	DIC-W 92
3	Unfinished Portrait of the King of Pain	NEB-N 88
4	Winning	BSF-N 91
McGRATH, Patrick		
6	Blood and Water and Other Tales	STO-N 89
McINTYRE, Vonda N		
2	Aztecs	HUG-N 78
2	Aztecs	NEB-N 77
2	Aztecs	LOC-N 78
1	Dreamsnake	LOC-W 79
1	Dreamsnake	NEB-W 78
1	Dreamsnake	HUG-W 79
1	Exile Waiting, The	NEB-N 75
3	Fireflood and Other Stories	LOC-N 80
5	Fireflood and Other Stories	LOC-N 80
3	Fireflood and Other Stories	HUG-N 80
4	Of Mist, and Grass, and Sand	JUP-N 74
3	Of Mist, and Grass, and Sand	NEB-W 73
4	Of Mist, and Grass, and Sand	LOC-N 74
3	Of Mist, and Grass, and Sand	HUG-N 74
2	Transit	NEB-N 83
4	Wings	NEB-N 73
4	Wings	HUG-N 74

AUTHORS - Alphabetically

CAT	T I T L E	AW W/N Y
	A U T H O R	
McKENNA, Richard		
4	Secret Place, The	HUG-N 67
4	Secret Place, The	NEB-W 66
McKILLIP, Patricia		
1	Forgotten Beast of Eld	WFA-W 75
1	Harpist in the Wind	BFA-N 80
11	Harpist in the Wind	LOC-W 80
1	Harpist in the Wind	HUG-N 80
1	Harpist in the Wind	WFA-N 80
McKINLEY, Robin		
6	Imaginary Lands	WFA-W 86
6	Imaginary Lands	LOC-N 86
McLAUGHLIN, Dean		
2	Hawk Among the Sparrows	HUG-N 69
2	Hawk Among The Sparrows	NEB-N 68
McNELLY, Dr. Willis E		
7	Dune Encyclopedia, The	HUG-N 85
7	Dune Encyclopedia, The	LOC-N 85
McQUAY, Mike		
1	Memories	DIC-N 88
MEECHAM, Beth		
6	Terry's Universe	LOC-N 89
MERLE, Robert		
1	Malevil	JWC-W 74
MIESEL, Sandra		
9	Dreamrider	LOC-N 83

CAT	TITLE	AW W/N Y
	A U T H O R	
	MILLER, Frank	
7	Dark Knight Returns, The	HUG-N 87
	MILLER, Rex	
9	Slob	STO-N 88
	MILLER, Ron	
7	Grand Tour, The	HUG-N 82
7	Grand Tour, The	LOC-N 82
	MILLER, Walter M Jr	
1	Canticle for Leibowitz	HUG-W 61
3	Darfsteller, The	HUG-W 55
	MILLHAUSER, Steven	
4	Illusionist, The	WFA-W 90
	MISHA	
1	Red Spider, White Web	CLA-N 91
	MOFFATT, Judith	
3	Hob, The	DAV-N 89
3	Hob, The	NEB-N 88
3	Surviving	NEB-N 86
4	Surviving	JWC-W 87
2	Tiny Tango	NEB-N 89
2	Tiny Tango	HUG-N 90
2	Tiny Tango	LOC-N 90
	MONTELEONE, Thomas F	
6	Borderlands	BFA-N 91
6	Borderlands	WFA-N 91
4	Camera Obscura	NEB-N 77
4	Death's a Ware That Will Not Keep	NEB-N 76

AUTHOR		
CAT	TITLE	AW W/N Y
MOON, Elizabeth		
9	Sheepfarmer's Daughter	LOC-N 89
1	Sheepfarmer's Daughter	COM-W 89
MOORCOCK, Michael		
2	Behold the Man	NEB-W 67
4	Crossing Into Cambodia	BSF-N 80
1	Gloriana	WFA-W 79
1	Gloriana	BFA-N 79
1	Gloriana	JWC-W 79
1	Hollow Lands, The	BFA-N 76
1	King of the Swords, The	BFA-W 74
1	Knight of the Swords, The	BFA-W 73
1	Sailor on the Seas of Fate, The	WFA-N 77
11	War Hounds and the World's Pain, The	LOC-N 82
1	War Hounds and the World's Pain, The	WFA-N 82
7	Wizardry and Wild Romance	LOC-N 88
MOORE, Alan		
2	Hypothetical Lizard, A	WFA-N 88
7	Watchmen	LOC-W 88
MORAN, Daniel Keys		
9	Armageddon Blues, The	LOC-N 89
MOROZ, Anne		
9	No Safe Place	LOC-N 87
MORRELL, David		
2	Beautiful Uncut Hair of Graves	STO-W 92
2	Dead Image	WFA-N 86
4	Hundred Year Christmas	WFA-N 84
3	Orange Is For Anguish, Blue For Insanity	STO-W 89
MORRILL, Rowena		
7	Fantastic Art of Rowena	LOC-N 84
7	Fantastic Art of Rowena	HUG-N 84

AUTHOR		
CAT	TITLE	AW W/N Y
MORRISON, Grant		
4	Braile Encyclopedia, The	STO-N 92
MORROW, James		
4	Bible Stories For Adults #17 The Deluge	NEB-W 88
4	Daughter Earth	LOC-N 92
1	Only Begotten Daughter	NEB-N 91
1	Only Begotten Daughter	JWC-N 91
11	Only Begotten Daughter	LOC-N 91
1	Only Begotten Daughter	WFA-W 91
1	This is the Way the World Ends	NEB-N 86
1	This Is the Way The World Ends	JWC-N 87
MULLEN, Stanley		
4	Space to Swing a Cat	HUG-N 59
MUNN, H Warner		
1	Merlin's Ring	WFA-N 75
MURPHY, Pat		
2	Bones	NEB-N 91
2	Bones	HUG-N 91
2	Bones	WFA-W 91
2	Bones	LOC-N 91
4	Dead Men on TV	NEB-N 88
1	Falling Woman, The	NEB-W 87
4	Love and Sex Among the Vertebrates	NEB-N 91
4	Love and Sex Among the Vertebrates	LOC-N 91
1	Points of Departure	DIC-W 91
3	Rachel in Love	DAV-W 88
4	Rachel in Love	JWC-W 88
3	Rachel in Love	LOC-W 88
3	Rachel in Love	HUG-N 88
3	Rachel in Love	SFC-N 88
3	Rachel in Love	NEB-W 87
1	The City, Not Long After	CLA-N 91
NAEGELE, Amyas		
4	Rise and Fall of Father Alex, The	WFA-N 87

	A U T H O R	
CAT	T I T L E	AW W/N Y
	NELSON, Ray F	
1	Prometheus Man, The	DIC-N 83
	NEWMAN, Kim	
4	Original Dr. Shade, The	BSF-W 91
	NICHOLS, Peter	
7	Science Fiction Encyclopedia, The	LOC-W 80
7	Science Fiction Encyclopedia, The	HUG-W 80
	NICHOLS, Scott	
4	Though A Sparrow Fall	NEB-N 65
	NIVEN, Larry	
4	All the Myriad Ways	HUG-N 69
2	ARM	HUG-N 76
2	ARM	LOC-N 76
4	Becalmed in Hell	NEB-N 65
2	Borderland of Sol, The	LOC-N 76
3	Borderland of Sol, The	HUG-W 76
5	Convergent Series	LOC-W 80
2	Defenseless Dead, The	LOC-N 74
1	Dream Park	LOC-N 82
3	Flash Crowd	JUP-N 74
3	Flatlander	NEB-N 67
1	Footfall	HUG-N 86
1	Footfall	LOC-N 86
2	Fourth Profession	HUG-N 72
4	Hole Man, The	LOC-N 75
4	Hole Man, The	HUG-W 75
4	Inconstant Moon	HUG-W 72
1	Inferno	NEB-N 76
1	Inferno	HUG-N 76
1	Integral Trees, The	HUG-N 85
1	Integral Trees, The	LOC-W 85
1	Integral Trees, The	SFC-N 85
1	Integral Trees, The	NEB-N 84
4	Jigsaw Man, The	HUG-N 68
5	Limits	LOC-N 86
3	Locusts, The	HUG-N 80

AUTHOR		
CAT	T I T L E	AW W/N Y
NIVEN, Larry	Continued...	
1	Lucifer's Hammer	HUG-N 78
4	Magic Goes Away, The	WFA-N 79
6	Man-Kzin Wars, The	LOC-N 89
6	Man-Kzin Wars IV	LOC-N 92
1	Mote in God's Eye, The	NEB-N 75
1	Mote in God's Eye, The	JUP-N 75
1	Mote in God's Eye, The	HUG-N 75
1	Mote in God's Eye, The	LOC-N 75
4	Neutron Star, The	HUG-W 67
4	Not Long Before the End	HUG-N 70
4	Not Long Before the End	NEB-N 69
5	N-Space	LOC-N 91
2	Patchwork Girl, The	LOC-N 81
5	Playgrounds of the Mind	LOC-N 92
1	Protector	DIT-W 75
1	Protector	LOC-N 74
1	Protector	HUG-N 74
4	Return of William Proxmire, The	HUG-N 90
1	Ringworld	NEB-W 70
1	Ringworld	LOC-W 71
1	Ringworld	DIT-W 72
1	Ringworld	HUG-W 71
1	Ringworld Engineers, The	HUG-N 81
1	Ringworld Engineers, The	LOC-N 81
6	Tales of Known Space	LOC-N 76
1	World Out of Time, A	LOC-N 77
4	Wrong-Way Street	NEB-N 65
NOLAN, William F		
4	Saturday's Shadow	WFA-N 80
NORTON, Andre		
1	Witch World	HUG-N 64
1	Witch World	HUG-N 63
3	Wizard's World	HUG-N 68
NORWOOD, Warren		
9	Windhover Tapes, The	LOC-N 83

AUTHORS - Alphabetically

CAT	A U T H O R T I T L E	AW W/N Y
	NUNN, Ken	
1	Unassigned Territory	STO-N 88
	OLIN, Richard	
4	Mischief Maker, The	NEB-N 65
	OLIVER, Chad	
4	Ghost Town	NEB-N 83
	OLTOIN, Jerry	
4	Love Song of Laura Morrison, The	DAV-W 88
	ORE, Rebecca Brown	
1 1	Being Alien Becoming Alien	DIC-N 90 DIC-N 89
	ORLOCK, Carol	
4	Nobody Lives There Now	STO-N 89
	O'CALLAGHAN, Maxine	
4	Wolf Winter	STO-N 92
	O'DONNELL, K M	
3	Final War	NEB-N 68
	O'KEEFE, Claudia	
9	Black Snow Days	LOC-N 91
	O'NEAL, Kathleen M	
9	An Abyss of Light	LOC-N 91
	PAGE, Gerald W	
6 6	Year's Best Horror Stories # 5 Year's Best Horror Stories # 6	WFA-N 78 WFA-N 79

AUTHOR		
CAT	T I T L E	AW W/N Y
PAINE, Michael		
9	Cities of the Dead	STO-N 89
PAIVA, Jean		
9	Lilith Factor, The	STO-N 90
PALMER, David R		
1	Emergence	COM-W 85
2	Emergence	HUG-N 82
1	Emergence	HUG-N 86
1	Emergence	DIC-N 85
1	Emergence	HUG-N 85
9	Emergence	LOC-N 85
2	Seeking	HUG-N 84
2	Seeking	LOC-N 84
PALWICK, Susan		
4	Elephant	JWC-N 87
PANGBORN, Edgar		
4	Better Mousehold, A	NEB-N 65
1	Company of Glory, The	JUP-N 75
1	Davy	NEB-N 64
1	Davy	HUG-N 65
1	Mirror for Observers, A	IFA-W 55
3	Mount Charity	NEB-N 71
5	Still I Persist in Wondering	LOC-N 79
PANSHIN, Alexei		
1	Rite of Passage	NEB-W 68
1	Rite of Passage	HUG-N 69
7	World Beyond the Hill, The	LOC-N 90
7	World Beyond the Hill, The	HUG-W 90
PAUL, Park		
1	Soldiers of Paradise	CLA-N 90

AUTHORS - Alphabetically

AUTHOR		
CAT	TITLE	AW W/N Y
PAVEY, Jack		
4	Boo Hoo Forest	BFA-N 91
PAXSON, Diana		
9	Lady of Light	LOC-N 83
PEARLE, Gerald		
2	In The Sumerian Marshes	WFA-N 85
PERPER, Timothy		
3	Guz's Place	DAV-N 89
PERRET, Patti		
7	Faces of Science Fiction, The	LOC-N 85
7	Faces of Science Fiction, The	HUG-N 85
PETERSON, Chris		
12	Nanotechnology	DAV-W 88
PETREY, Susan C		
4	Spidersong	HUG-N 81
PHILLIPS, Mark		
1	Brain Twister	HUG-N 60
PHILLIPS, Rog		
3	Rat in the Skull	HUG-N 59
PICCIRILLI, Tom		
9	Dark Father	STO-N 91
PIPER, H Beam		
1	Little Fuzzy	HUG-N 63

CAT	TITLE	AW W/N Y
AUTHOR		

PLATT, Charles

CAT	TITLE	AW W/N Y
7	Dream Makers	LOC-N 81
7	Dream Makers	HUG-N 81
7	Dream Makers Vol 2	HUG-N 84
7	Dream Makers Vol 2	LOC-W 84
1	Silicon Man, The	JWC-N 92

PLAUGER, P J

CAT	TITLE	AW W/N Y
4	Child of All Ages	LOC-N 76
4	Child of All Ages	HUG-N 76
4	Child of All Ages	NEB-N 75

POHL, Frederik

CAT	TITLE	AW W/N Y
1	Age of the Pussyfoot	NEB-N 69
1	Annals of the HeeChee, The	LOC-N 88
1	Beyond the Blue Event Horizon	NEB-N 80
1	Beyond the Blue Event Horizon	HUG-N 81
1	Beyond the Blue Event Horizon	BSF-N 81
1	Beyond the Blue Event Horizon	LOC-N 81
2	Blister, The	LOC-N 85
4	Fermi and Frost	SFC-N 86
4	Fermi and Frost	HUG-W 86
4	Fermi and Frost	LOC-N 86
1	Gateway	LOC-W 78
1	Gateway	HUG-W 78
1	Gateway	NEB-W 77
1	Gateway	JWC-W 78
2	Gold at the Starbow's End, The	LOC-W 73
14	Gold at the Starbow's End, The	LOC-N 73
2	Gold at the Starbow's End, The	NEB-N 72
2	Gold at the Starbow's End, The	HUG-N 73
2	Greening of Bed-Stuy, The	NEB-N 84
4	Growing Up in Edge City	NEB-N 75
1	Heechee Rendezvous	LOC-N 85
2	In The Problem Pit	JUP-N 74
1	JEM	HUG-N 80
1	JEM	LOC-N 80
1	JEM	NEB-N 79
14	Jupiter	LOC-N 74
3	Kindly Isle, The	LOC-N 85

AUTHOR		
CAT	T I T L E	AW W/N Y
POHL, Frederik	Continued...	
1	Man Plus	JWC-N 77
1	Man Plus	NEB-W 76
1	Man Plus	LOC-N 77
1	Man Plus	HUG-N 77
2	Mars Masked	LOC-N 80
2	Mars Masked	NEB-N 79
4	Meeting, The	HUG-W 73
4	Mother Trip, The	LOC-N 76
5	Pohlstars	LOC-N 85
4	Servant of the People	HUG-N 84
4	Servant of the People	LOC-N 84
4	Shaffery Among the Immortals	NEB-N 72
4	Spending A Day at the Lottery Fair	LOC-N 84
3	Swanilda's Song	LOC-N 79
2	Under Two Moons	NEB-N 65
7	Way the Future Was, The	LOC-W 79
5	Years of the City, The	LOC-N 85
1	Years of the City, The	JWC-W 85
POLLACK, Richard		
1	Unquenchable Fire	CLA-W 89
POPKES, Steven		
4	Color Winter, The	NEB-N 88
POURNELLE, Jerry		
3	Extreme Prejudice	HUG-N 75
3	He Fell Into a Dark Hole	HUG-N 74
2	Mercenary, The	HUG-N 73
3	Tinker	HUG-N 76
POWERS, Tim		
11	Anubis Gates, The	LOC-N 84
1	Anubis Gates, The	SFC-W 84
1	Anubis Gates, The	BSF-N 86
1	Anubis Gates, The	DIC-W 84
1	Dinner at Deviant's Place	NEB-N 85
1	Dinner at Deviant's Place	DIC-W 86

AUTHOR		
CAT	TITLE	AW W/N Y
POWERS, Tim Continued...		
2	Night Moves	WFA-N 87
11	On Stranger Tides	LOC-N 88
1	On Stranger Tides	WFA-N 88
1	Stress of Her Regard, The	WFA-N 90
11	Stress of Her Regard, The	LOC-N 90
PRATCHETT, Terry		
1	Good Omens	WFA-N 91
11	Good Omens	LOC-N 91
1	Pyramids	BSF-W 90
PREISS, Byron		
7	Art of Leo and Diane Dillon, The	HUG-N 82
7	Art of Leo and Diane Dillon, The	LOC-N 82
PREUSS, Paul		
9	Gates of Heaven, The	LOC-N 81
PRICE, E Hoffman		
5	Far Lands, Other Days	WFA-N 76
PRIEST, Christopher		
1	Affirmation, The	DIT-W 82
1	Affirmation, The	BSF-N 82
1	Glamour, The	BSF-N 85
1	Inverted World, The	HUG-N 75
1	Inverted World, The	LOC-N 75
3	Palely Loitering	HUG-N 80
2	Palely Loitering	LOC-N 80
4	Palely Loitering	BSF-W 80
1	Space Machine, The	DIT-W 77
2	Watched, The	LOC-N 79
2	Watched, The	HUG-N 79
PRINGLE, David		
7	Science Fiction: The 100 Best Novels	LOC-N 86

AUTHOR		
CAT	T I T L E	AW W/N Y
PRONZINI, Bill		
6	Mummy! A Chrestomathy of Crypt-ology	WFA-N 81
PTACEK, Kathryn		
4	Each Night, Each Year	STO-N 90
PYNCHON, Thomas		
1	Gravity's Rainbow	NEB-N 73
1	Gravity's Rainbow	JUP-N 74
RAMSLAND, Katherine		
7	Prism of the Night: Biography Anne Rice	STO-N 92
RANDALL, Marta		
2	Dangerous Games	NEB-N 80
2	Dangerous Games	LOC-N 81
1	Islands	NEB-N 76
RAPHAEL, Rick		
4	Code Three	HUG-N 64
4	Once A Cop	HUG-N 65
RAWN, Melanie		
9	Dragon Prince	LOC-N 89
1	Dragon Prince	COM-N 89
REAMY, Tom		
1	Blind Voices	NEB-N 78
1	Blind Voices	LOC-N 79
1	Blind Voices	BSF-N 80
1	Blind Voices	HUG-N 79
5	San Diego Lightfoot Sue	LOC-N 81
3	San Diego Lightfoot Sue	HUG-N 76
3	San Diego Lightfoot Sue	NEB-W 75
3	Twilla	NEB-N 74

AUTHOR		
CAT	TITLE	AW W/N Y
REAVES, Michael		
4	Big Spell, The	BFA-N 79
REED, Robert		
4	Utility Man, The	HUG-N 91
4	Utility Man, The	LOC-N 91
RESNICK, Mike		
2	Bully!	SFC-N 91
2	Bully!	NEB-N 91
2	Bully!	HUG-N 91
2	Bully!	LOC-N 91
2	Bully!	NEB-N 92
3	For I Have Touched the Sky	HUG-N 90
3	For I Have Touched the Sky	SFC-W 90
3	For I Have Touched the Sky	NEB-N 89
3	For I Have Touched the Sky	LOC-N 90
1	Ivory: Legend Past & Future	CLA-N 90
1	Ivory: Legend Past & Future	NEB-N 89
1	Ivory: Legend Past & Future	SFC-N 89
3	Kirinyaga	NEB-N 88
4	Kirinyaga	LOC-N 89
4	Kirinyaga	SFC-W 89
4	Kirinyaga	HUG-W 89
3	Manamouki, The	NEB-N 91
3	Manamouki, The	SFC-N 91
3	Manamouki, The	HUG-W 91
4	One Perfect Morning, With Jackals	SFC-N 92
4	One Perfect Morning, With Jackals	HUG-N 92
4	Winter Solstice	HUG-N 92
REYNOLDS, Mack		
3	Adventure of the Extraterrestrial	NEB-N 65
4	Leader For Yesterday, A	NEB-N 65
4	Status Quo	HUG-N 62
REYNOLDS, Ted		
4	Can These Bones Live?	HUG-N 80
2	Ker Plop	HUG-N 80
9	Tides of God, The	LOC-N 90

AUTHOR		
CAT	TITLE	AW W/N Y
RICE, Anne		
1	Queen of the Damned	STO-N 89
10	Queen of the Damned	LOC-N 89
1	Vampire Lestat, The	WFA-N 86
11	Vampire Lestat, The	LOC-N 86
10	Witching Hour, The	LOC-W 91
RICHARDS, Torvy		
9	Harvest Bride, The	STO-N 88
ROBERTS, Keith		
4	Checkout, The	BSF-N 82
2	God House, The	NEB-N 71
1	Grianne	CLA-N 88
1	Grianne	BSF-W 88
4	Kaeti and the Hangman	BFA-W 86
4	Kaeti and the Hangman	BSF-W 87
4	Kitemaster	BSF-W 83
4	Kitemistress	BSF-N 86
1	Kiteworld	BSF-N 86
1	Kiteworld	JWC-N 86
4	Lordly Ones, The	BSF-N 81
3	Lordly Ones, The	HUG-N 81
1	Molly Zero	BSF-N 81
2	Tiger Sweater, The	NEB-N 87
ROBINSON, Kim Stanley		
4	Before I Wake	NEB-N 91
3	Black Air	NEB-N 83
3	Black Air	LOC-N 84
3	Black Air	SFC-W 84
2	Black Air	WFA-W 84
3	Black Air	HUG-N 84
2	Blind Geometer, The	HUG-N 88
2	Blind Geometer, The	SFC-N 88
2	Blind Geometer, The	LOC-N 88
4	Down and Out in the Year 2000	LOC-N 87
2	Escape from Kathmandu	LOC-N 87
2	Escape from Kathmandu	NEB-N 86
2	Escape from Kathmandu	SFC-N 87
2	Escape from Kathmandu	HUG-N 87

AUTHOR		
CAT	**T I T L E**	**AW W/N Y**
	ROBINSON, Kim Stanley Continued...	
2	Geometer Blind, The	NEB-W 87
3	Glacier	SFC-N 89
3	Glacier	LOC-N 89
1	Gold Coast, The	LOC-N 89
1	Gold Coast, The	JWC-N 89
2	Green Mars	HUG-N 86
2	Green Mars	SFC-N 86
2	Green Mars	LOC-N 86
3	History of the 20th Century, A	SFC-N 92
3	Lucky Strike, The	LOC-N 85
3	Lucky Strike, The	SFC-N 85
3	Lucky Strike, The	HUG-N 85
3	Lucky Strike, The	NEB-N 84
1	Memory of Whiteness, The	CLA-N 87
2	Mother Goddess of the World	DAV-W 88
2	Mother Goddess of the World	HUG-N 88
2	Mother Goddess of the World	LOC-N 88
7	Novels of Philip K Dick, The	LOC-N 86
1	Pacific Edge	JWC-W 91
5	Remaking History	LOC-N 92
4	Ridge Running	HUG-N 85
4	Ridge Running	LOC-N 85
2	Short, Sharp, Shock, A	LOC-W 91
2	Short, Sharp, Shock, A	SFC-N 91
2	Short, Sharp, Shock, A	HUG-N 91
2	To Leave a Mark	HUG-N 83
4	Venice Drowned	NEB-N 81
4	Vinland the Dream	LOC-N 92
4	Vinland the Dream	SFC-N 92
1	Wild Shore, The	NEB-N 84
9	Wild Shore, The	LOC-W 85
1	Wild Shore, The	DIC-N 85
1	Wild Shore, The	SFC-N 85
	ROBINSON, Spider	
2	By Any Other Name	HUG-W 77
4	Dog Day Evening	HUG-N 78
4	Melancholy Elephants	LOC-N 83
4	Melancholy Elephants	HUG-W 83
5	Melancholy Elephants	LOC-N 86
4	Serpent's Teeth	LOC-N 82

	A U T H O R	
CAT	T I T L E	AW W/N Y
ROBINSON, Spider	Continued...	
2	Stardance	LOC-W 78
1	Stardance	LOC-N 80
2	Stardance	HUG-W 78
2	Stardance	NEB-W 77
RODGERS, Alan		
9	Blood of the Children	STO-N 91
2	Boy Who Came Back From the Dead, The	WFA-N 88
3	Boy Who Came Back From the Grave, The	STO-W 88
ROESSNER, Michaela		
9	Walkabout Woman	LOC-N 89
ROHRER, Robert		
4	Keep Them Happy	NEB-N 65
ROTSLER, William		
3	Patron of the Arts	HUG-N 73
3	Patron of the Arts	NEB-N 72
4	Patron of the Arts	LOC-N 73
ROWLEY, Christopher		
1	War for Eternity, The	COM-W 84
RUCKER, Rudy		
1	Software	DIC-W 83
1	Wetware	DIC-W 89
RUSCH, Kristine Kathryn		
3	Fast Cars	NEB-N 89
2	Gallery of His Dreams, The	HUG-N 92
2	Gallery of His Dreams, The	LOC-W 92
2	Gallery of His Dreams, The	NEB-N 92
2	Gallery of His Dreams, The	WFA-N 92
2	Phantom	STO-N 90

AUTHOR		
CAT	TITLE	AW W/N Y
RUSCH, Kristine Kathryn Continued...		
7	SFWA Handbook: The Prof Writer's Guide	LOC-W 91
7	SFWA Handbook: The Prof Writer's Guide	HUG-N 91
4	Story Child	NEB-N 91
3	Time For Every Purpose, A	NEB-N 91
8	White Mists of Power, The	LOC-N 92
RUSS, Joanna		
4	An Old Fashioned Girl	JUP-N 75
1	And Chaos Died	NEB-N 70
1	And Chaos Died	LOC-N 71
4	Extraordinary Voyages of Amelie Bertrand	NEB-N 79
5	Extra(ordinary) People	LOC-N 85
1	Female Man, The	NEB-N 75
3	Mystery of the Young Gentleman, The	NEB-N 82
1	Picnic on Paradise	HUG-N 69
3	Poor Man, Beggar Man	NEB-N 71
3	Second Inquisition, The	NEB-N 70
2	Souls	HUG-W 83
2	Souls	NEB-N 82
2	Souls	SFC-W 83
2	Souls	LOC-W 83
4	When It Changed	LOC-N 73
4	When It Changed	NEB-W 72
4	When It Changed	HUG-N 73
5	Zanzibar Cat, The	LOC-N 84
RUSSELL, Eric Frank		
4	Allamagoosa	HUG-W 55
RUSSO, Richard Paul		
1	Subterranean Gallery	CLA-N 92
1	Subterranean Gallery	DIC-W 90
RYAN, Alan		
4	Bones Wizard, The	WFA-W 85
6	Night Visions 1	WFA-N 85
6	Perpetual Light	LOC-N 83

AUTHORS - Alphabetically

	AUTHOR	
CAT	TITLE	AW W/N Y
RYMAN, Geoff		
1	Child Garden, The	JWC-W 90
1	Children of the Garden	CLA-W 90
4	Love Sickness	BSF-W 88
4	O' Happy Day	BSF-N 86
4	Unconquered Country, The	BSF-W 85
2	Unconquered Country, The	NEB-N 87
1	Unconquered Country, The	JWC-N 88
2	Unconquered Country, The	WFA-W 85
1	Warrior Who Carried Life, The	BSF-N 86
SABERHAGEN, Fred		
3	Masque of the Red Shift	NEB-N 65
4	Mr. Jester	HUG-N 67
SAGAN, Carl		
9	Contact	LOC-W 86
7	Cosmic Connection, The	JWC-W 74
7	Cosmos	HUG-W 81
7	Cosmos	LOC-N 81
SAGARA, Michelle		
1	In the Dark Lands	COM-N 92
SAINT, H F		
1	Memoirs of An Invisible Man	CLA-N 88
SAKERS, Don		
1	Leaves of October, The	COM-N 89
SALLIS, James		
4	Creation of Bennie Good, The	NEB-N 70
SALMONSON, Jessica Amanda		
6	Amazons!	WFA-W 80
6	Amazons!	LOC-N 80

CAT	AUTHOR	AW W/N Y
	TITLE	
	SANDERS, Scott Russell	
1	Terrarium	DIC-N 86
	SARGENT, Pamela	
6	Afterlives	LOC-N 87
	SARRANTONIO, Al	
4	Richard's Head	STO-N 92
	SAUDERS, Charles	
1	Imaro	AUR-N 82
	SAUNDERS, Jake	
4	Back to the Stone Age	NEB-N 76
	SAWYER, Robert J	
9	Golden Fleece	LOC-N 91
1	Golden Fleece	AUR-W 92
	SAXTON, Josephine	
1	Queen of the States	BSF-N 87
1	Queen of the States	CLA-N 87
	SCARBOROUGH, Elizabeth	
1	Healers War, The	NEB-W 89
	SCHENCK, Hilbert	
9	At the Eye of the Ocean	LOC-N 82
2	Battle of the Abaco Reefs, The	NEB-N 79
2	Battle of the Abaco Reefs, The	LOC-N 80
2	Battle of the Abaco Reefs, The	HUG-N 80
4	Geometry of Narrative, The	HUG-N 84
4	Geometry of Narrative, The	NEB-N 83
2	Hurricane Claude	HUG-N 84
3	Silicon Muse	HUG-N 85

CAT	TITLE	AW W/N Y
AUTHOR		

CAT	TITLE	AW W/N Y
SCHIFF, Stuart David		
6	Whispers	WFA-N 78
6	Whispers 2	WFA-N 80
6	Whispers 3	BFA-N 82
6	Whispers 3	WFA-N 82
6	Whispers 4	LOC-N 84
6	Whispers 5	WFA-N 86
SCHMITZ, James H		
4	Balance Ecology	NEB-N 65
5	Best of James H. Schmitz, The	LOC-N 92
3	Goblin Night	NEB-N 65
4	Lion Loose	HUG-N 62
3	Planet of Forgetting	NEB-N 65
1	Witches of Karres	HUG-N 67
SCHOLZ, Carter		
3	Ninth Symphony of Ludwig v/Beethoven...	HUG-N 78
3	Ninth Symphony of Ludwig v/Beethoven...	NEB-N 77
SCHOW, David J		
3	Pamela's Get	STO-N 88
4	Pamela's Get	WFA-N 88
4	Red Light	WFA-W 87
6	Silver Scream	WFA-N 89
SCHUTZ, J W		
3	Maiden Voyage	NEB-N 65
SCHWEITZER, Darrell		
2	To Become A Sorcerer	WFA-N 92
SEARLES, Baird		
7	Reader's Guide to Fantasy, A	LOC-N 83
7	Reader's Guide to Fantasy, A	HUG-N 83
7	Reader's Guide to SF, A	LOC-N 80

AUTHORS - Alphabetically

	A U T H O R	
CAT	T I T L E	AW W/N Y
SERMINE, Daniel		
4	Yadjine et la Mort	AUR-W 86
SEVERANCE, Carol		
1	Reefsong	COM-W 92
SHAVER, Edward		
4	Killing Thought, The	BSF-N 82
SHAW, Bob		
4	Light of Other Days	NEB-N 66
4	Light of Other Days	HUG-N 67
1	Orbitsville	BSF-W 75
1	Ragged Astronauts, The	BFA-W 86
1	Ragged Astronauts, The	BSF-W 87
1	Ragged Astronauts, The	HUG-N 87
1	Ragged Astronauts, The	CLA-N 87
SHEA, Michael		
3	Angel of Death, The	NEB-N 79
2	Autopsy, The	LOC-N 81
3	Autopsy, The	HUG-N 81
2	Autopsy, The	NEB-N 80
4	Fat Face	BFA-N 88
1	Nifft the Lean	WFA-W 83
5	Polyphemus	WFA-N 88
SHECKLEY, Robert		
1	Immortality Inc	HUG-N 59
3	Shall We Have a Little Talk?	NEB-N 65
4	Supplicant in Space, A	JUP-W 74
2	What Is Life	WFA-N 77
SHEFFIELD, Charles		
3	Braver Thing, A	LOC-N 91
3	Braver Thing, A	SFC-N 91
3	Braver Thing, A	HUG-N 91

AUTHOR		
CAT	T I T L E	AW W/N Y
SHEFFIELD, Charles Continued...		
4	Godspeed	LOC-N 91
4	Godspeed	HUG-N 91
4	Godspeed	SFC-N 91
SHELDON, Raccoona		
4	Screwfly Solution, The	LOC-N 78
3	Screwfly Solution, The	NEB-W 77
3	Screwfly Solution, The	HUG-N 78
SHEPARD, Lucius		
3	All-consuming, The	NEB-N 92
3	Aymara	NEB-N 86
3	Aymara	SFC-W 87
3	Bound For Glory	LOC-N 90
4	Delta Sly Honey	LOC-N 88
5	Ends of the Earth, The	WFA-N 92
2	Father of Stones, The	LOC-W 90
2	Father of Stones, The	HUG-N 90
2	Father of Stones, The	WFA-N 90
2	Father of Stones, The	SFC-N 90
4	Glassblower's Dragon, The	LOC-N 88
9	Green Eyes	LOC-N 85
1	Green Eyes	JWC-N 85
1	Green Eyes	DIC-N 85
1	Green Eyes	CLA-N 87
4	Jack's Decline	STO-N 89
5	Jaguar Hunter, The	LOC-W 88
3	Jaguar Hunter, The	LOC-N 86
4	Jaguar Hunter, The	WFA-N 86
3	Jaguar Hunter, The	NEB-N 85
5	Jaguar Hunter, The	WFA-W 88
2	Kalimantan	LOC-N 91
1	Life During Wartime	CLA-N 89
1	Life During Wartime	LOC-N 88
1	Life During Wartime	DIC-N 88
4	Life of Buddha	WFA-N 89

	A U T H O R	
CAT	T I T L E	AW W/N Y

SHEPARD, Lucius   Continued...

CAT	TITLE	AW W/N Y
3	Man Who Painted the Dragon Griaule, The	HUG-N 85
3	Man Who Painted the Dragon Griaule, The	NEB-N 84
3	Man Who Painted the Dragon Griaule, The	SFC-N 85
4	Man Who Painted the Dragon Griaule, The	BSF-N 85
2	Man Who Painted the Dragon Griaule, The	WFA-N 85
3	Man Who Painted the Dragon Griaule, The	LOC-N 85
4	Mengele	LOC-N 86
2	R & R	NEB-W 86
2	R & R	SFC-W 87
2	R & R	HUG-N 87
2	R & R	LOC-W 87
4	Salvador	HUG-N 85
4	Salvador	NEB-N 84
4	Salvador	SFC-W 85
4	Salvador	LOC-W 85
2	Scalehunter's Beautiful Daughter, The	NEB-N 88
2	Scalehunter's Beautiful Daughter, The	WFA-N 89
2	Scalehunter's Beautiful Daughter, The	DAV-N 89
2	Scalehunter's Beautiful Daughter, The	LOC-W 89
2	Scalehunter's Beautiful Daughter, The	HUG-N 89
2	Scalehunter's Beautiful Daughter, The	SFC-N 89
3	Shades	LOC-N 88
2	Shades	WFA-N 88
2	Skull City	LOC-N 91
4	Solitario's Eyes	WFA-N 84
2	Traveler's Tale, A	LOC-N 85
2	Traveler's Tale, A	SFC-N 85
2	Traveler's Tale, A	NEB-N 84
6	Youthful Folly	LOC-N 89

SHERMAN, Josepha

CAT	TITLE	AW W/N Y
1	Shining Falcon, The	COM-W 90

SHETTERLEY, Will

CAT	TITLE	AW W/N Y
9	Cats Have No Lord	LOC-N 86
6	Liavek: The Players of Luck	WFA-N 87

AUTHORS - Alphabetically

AUTHOR		
CAT	T I T L E	AW W/N Y
	SHINER, Lewis	
1	Deserted Cities of the Heart	NEB-N 88
1	Frontera	DIC-N 85
1	Frontera	NEB-N 84
6	When The Music is Over	WFA-N 92
	SHWARTZ, Susan	
3	Getting Real	NEB-N 92
1	Heritage of Flight	DIC-N 90
3	Loose Cannon	NEB-N 91
3	Schwarzschild Radius	SFC-N 88
4	Temple to a Minor Goddess	NEB-N 87
	SILVA, David	
4	Calling, The	STO-W 91
4	Flipping	BFA-N 91
	SILVERBERG, Robert	
14	Alpha 5	LOC-N 75
14	Alpha Three	LOC-N 73
6	Arbor House Treasury of Modern SF	LOC-N 81
6	Best of New Dimensions	LOC-N 80
1	Book of Skulls, The	NEB-N 72
1	Book of Skulls, The	HUG-N 73
1	Book of Skulls, The	LOC-N 73
2	Born With the Dead	HUG-N 75
2	Born With the Dead	JUP-N 75
2	Born With the Dead	LOC-W 75
2	Born With the Dead	NEB-W 74
2	Desert of Stolen Dreams, The	LOC-N 82
1	Downward to the Earth	LOC-N 71
1	Dying Inside	LOC-N 73
1	Dying Inside	NEB-N 72
1	Dying Inside	HUG-N 73
3	Enter a Soldier, Later Enter Another	LOC-N 90
3	Enter a Soldier, Later Enter Another	HUG-W 90
3	Enter a Soldier, Later Enter Another	NEB-N 89
2	Feast of St. Dionysus, The	JUP-W 74
2	Feast of St. Dionysus, The	LOC-N 74
11	Gilgamesh, The King	LOC-N 85

AUTHOR		
CAT	T I T L E	AW W/N Y
SILVERBERG, Robert Continued...		
2	Gilgamesh in the Outback	NEB-N 86
2	Gilgamesh in the Outback	SFC-N 87
2	Gilgamesh in the Outback	HUG-W 87
2	Gilgamesh in the Outback	LOC-N 87
4	Good News from the Vatican	NEB-W 71
2	Hawksbill Station	NEB-N 67
2	Hawksbill Station	HUG-N 68
2	Homefaring	LOC-N 84
2	Homefaring	SFC-N 84
2	Homefaring	NEB-N 83
2	Lion Time in Timbuctoo	LOC-N 91
11	Lord Valentine's Castle	LOC-W 81
1	Lord Valentine's Castle	HUG-N 81
5	Majipoor Chronicle	LOC-N 83
1	Masks of Time, The	NEB-N 68
4	Ms Found in an Abandoned Time Machine	LOC-N 74
5	New Atlantis, The	LOC-N 76
13	New Dimensions 1	LOC-N 72
13	New Dimensions 2	LOC-N 73
13	New Dimensions 3	LOC-N 74
13	New Dimensions 4	LOC-N 75
5	New Dimensions 5	LOC-N 76
14	New Dimensions 6	LOC-N 77
6	New Dimensions 8	LOC-N 79
2	Nightwings	NEB-N 68
2	Nightwings	HUG-W 69
4	Our Lady of the Sauropods	LOC-N 81
4	Our Lady of the Sauropods	HUG-N 81
4	Passengers	NEB-W 69
4	Passengers	HUG-N 70
4	Pope of the Chimps, The	NEB-N 82
2	Sailing to Byzantium	HUG-N 86
2	Sailing to Byzantium	LOC-N 86
2	Sailing To Byzantium	NEB-W 85
2	Sailing to Byzantium	SFC-N 86
4	Schwartz Between the Galaxies	HUG-N 75
4	Schwartz Between The Galaxies	LOC-N 75
6	Science Fiction Hall of Fame Vol 1	LOC-W 71
2	Secret Sharer, The	SFC-W 88
2	Secret Sharer, The	NEB-N 87
2	Secret Sharer, The	LOC-W 88
2	Secret Sharer, The	HUG-N 88

	A U T H O R	
CAT	T I T L E	AW W/N Y
	SILVERBERG, Robert Continued...	
1	Shadrach in the Furnace	LOC-N 77
1	Shadrach in the Furnace	HUG-N 77
1	Shadrach in the Furnace	NEB-N 76
1	Stochastic Man, The	HUG-N 76
1	Stochastic Man, The	NEB-N 75
1	Stochastic Man, The	LOC-N 76
2	Thesme and the Ghayrog	LOC-N 83
1	Thorns	NEB-N 67
1	Thorns	HUG-N 67
13	Threads of Time	LOC-N 75
1	Time of Changes, A	LOC-N 72
1	Time of Changes, A	NEB-W 71
1	Time of Changes, A	HUG-N 72
2	To Jorslem	HUG-N 70
2	To Jorslem	NEB-N 69
1	Tower of Glass, The	NEB-N 70
1	Tower of Glass, The	LOC-N 71
1	Tower of Glass, The	HUG-N 71
1	Up the Line	HUG-N 70
1	Up the Line	NEB-N 69
2	We Are for the Dark	LOC-N 89
4	When We Went to See the End of the World	HUG-N 73
1	World Inside, The	HUG-N 72
2	World Outside, The	HUG-N 71
6	Worlds of Wonder	LOC-N 88
	SIMAK, Clifford D	
1	All Flesh is Grass	NEB-N 65
2	Auk House	LOC-N 78
4	Autumn Land, The	LOC-N 72
4	Autumn Land, The	HUG-N 72
3	Big Front Yard, The	HUG-W 59
1	Choice of Gods, A	LOC-N 73
1	Choice of Gods, A	HUG-N 73
1	City	IFA-W 53
4	Construction Shack	HUG-N 74
4	Grotto of the Dancing Bear, The	NEB-W 80
4	Grotto of the Dancing Bear, The	LOC-W 81
4	Grotto of the Dancing Bear, The	HUG-W 81
1	Heritage of Stars	JUP-W 78
2	Marathon Photograph, The	LOC-N 75
4	Over the River and Through the Trees	NEB-N 65

CAT	T I T L E	AW W/N Y
A U T H O R		

	A U T H O R	
CAT	T I T L E	AW W/N Y
SIMAK, Clifford D Continued...		
1	Project Pope	HUG-N 82
1	Project Pope	LOC-N 82
2	Thing in the Stone, The	HUG-N 71
2	Thing in the Stone, The	NEB-N 70
1	Time is the Simplest Thing (Fisherman)	HUG-N 62
1	Way Station (Here Gather Stars)	HUG-W 64
SIMMONS, Dan		
3	All Dracula's Children	LOC-W 92
1	Carrion Comfort	WFA-N 90
10	Carrion Comfort	LOC-W 90
1	Carrion Comfort	BFA-W 90
1	Carrion Comfort	STO-W 90
2	Entropy's Bed at Midnight	STO-N 91
3	Entropy's Bed at Midnight	LOC-W 91
1	Fall of Hyperion, The	BSF-W 92
1	Fall of Hyperion, The	HUG-N 91
1	Fall of Hyperion, The	NEB-N 91
1	Fall of Hyperion, The	LOC-W 91
1	Fall of Hyperion, The	SFC-N 91
1	Hyperion	SFC-N 90
1	Hyperion	BSF-N 91
1	Hyperion	HUG-W 90
1	Hyperion	LOC-W 90
1	Hyperion Cantos	CLA-N 92
4	Metastasis	WFA-N 89
5	Prayers to Broken Stones	STO-W 92
6	Prayers to Broken Stones	STO-N 91
5	Prayers to Broken Stones	WFA-N 91
5	Prayers to Broken Stones	LOC-N 91
1	Song of Kali	WFA-W 86
10	Summer of Night	LOC-W 92
1	Summer of Night	STO-N 92
1	Summer of Night	BFA-N 91
SIMMONS, Wm Mark		
1	In the Net of Dreams	COM-N 91

CAT	TITLE	AW W/N Y
AUTHOR		
SKAL, David J		
7	Hollywood Gothic	STO-N 91
7	Hollywood Gothic	LOC-N 91
7	Hollywood Gothic	HUG-N 91
SKEET, Michael		
4	Breaking Ball	AUR-W 92
SKIPP, John		
6	Book of the Dead	WFA-N 90
SLADEK, John		
4	Calling All Gumdrops	BSF-N 84
1	Roderick	DIC-N 83
1	Tik-Tok	JWC-N 84
1	Tik-Tok	BSF-W 84
SLONCZEWSKI, Joan		
1	Door Into Ocean	JWC-W 87
SMITH, Cordwainer		
6	Best of Cordwainer Smith, The	LOC-N 76
3	Down to a Sunless Sea	LOC-N 76
1	Norstilia	JUP-N 75
2	On the Storm Planet	NEB-N 65
1	Planet Buyer, The	HUG-N 65
SMITH, D Alexander		
1	Rendezvous	DIC-N 89
SMITH, Dean Wesley		
9	Laying the Music to Rest	LOC-N 90
9	Laying the Music to Rest	STO-N 90
SMITH, E E "Doc"		
1	Skylark Dusquenes	HUG-N 66

	AUTHOR	
CAT	TITLE	AW W/N Y
	SMITH, Michael Marshall	
4	Dark Land, The	BFA-W 91
4	Man Who Drew Cats, The	BFA-W 92
	SMITH, Thomas G	
7	Industrial Light & Magic: Special Effect	HUG-N 87
7	Industrial Light & Magic: Special Effect	LOC-N 87
	SOMTOW, S P	
10	Moon Dance	LOC-N 91
2	Pavilion of Frozen Women, The	WFA-N 92
3	Resurrec Tech	STO-N 88
9	Starship and Haiku	LOC-W 82
	SOUKUP, Martha	
4	Dog's Life	NEB-N 92
4	Dog's Life	HUG-N 92
3	Over the Long Haul	NEB-N 91
3	Over the Long Haul	HUG-N 91
	SPARKS, Muriel	
7	Mary Shelley	STO-W 88
	SPENCER, Garth	
1	Maple Leaf Rag	AUR-W 86
	SPENCER, W	
3	Call Him Lord	NEB-W 66
	SPIGNESI, Stephen J	
7	Shape Under t/Street:Compl Encycl S King	STO-N 92

AUTHOR		
CAT	T I T L E	AW W/N Y
SPINRAD, Norman		
3	Big Flash, The	NEB-N 69
1	Bug Jack Barrow	NEB-N 69
1	Bug Jack Barrow	HUG-N 70
1	Iron Dream, The	NEB-N 72
2	Journals of the Plague Years, The	NEB-N 88
2	Journals of the Plague Years, The	HUG-N 89
2	Journals of the Plague Years, The	LOC-N 89
2	Journals of the Plague Years, The	SFC-N 89
5	Other Americas	LOC-N 89
2	Riding the Torch	JUP-W 75
2	Riding the Torch	LOC-N 75
2	Riding the Torch	HUG-N 75
7	Science Fiction in the Real World	LOC-N 91
7	Science Fiction in the Real World	HUG-N 91
4	Sierra Maestra	LOC-N 76
7	Staying Alive: A Writer's Guide	HUG-N 84
7	Staying Alive: A Writer's Guide	LOC-N 84
3	Street Meat	LOC-N 84
4	Thing of Beauty, A	JUP-N 74
4	Thing of Beauty, A	NEB-N 73
1	Void Captain's Tale, The	NEB-N 83
1	Void Captain's Tale, The	LOC-N 84
1	World Between, A	BSF-N 81
SPRINGER, Nancy		
4	Boy Who Plaited Manes, The	NEB-N 86
4	Boy Who Plaited Manes, The	WFA-N 87
4	Boy Who Plaited Manes, The	HUG-N 87
4	Boy Who Plaited Manes, The	LOC-N 87
STABLEFORD, Brian		
4	And He Not Busy Being Born	BSF-N 87
1	Empire of Fear, The	CLA-N 89
10	Werewolves of London	LOC-N 91
STALLMAN, Robert		
11	Captive, The	LOC-N 82
9	Orphan, The	LOC-N 81
1	Orphan, The	NEB-N 80

AUTHOR		
CAT	TITLE	AW W/N Y
STANTON, Mary		
1	Heavenly Horse From the Outermost West,	COM-N 89
STEELE, Allan		
1	Clarke County, Space	DIC-N 91
9	Orbital Decay	LOC-W 90
STEINBECK, John		
1	Acts of King Arthur & His Noble Knights	WFA-N 77
STERLING, Bruce		
3	Cicada Queen	NEB-N 83
5	Crystal Express	LOC-N 90
4	Dinner in Audoghast	LOC-N 86
4	Dinner in Audoghast	HUG-N 86
4	Dori Bangs	HUG-N 90
4	Dori Bangs	SFC-W 90
4	Dori Bangs	LOC-N 90
4	Dori Bangs	JWC-N 90
4	Dori Bangs	NEB-N 89
3	FLowers of Edo	HUG-N 88
3	Flowers of Edo	LOC-N 88
3	FLowers of Edo	NEB-N 87
2	Green Days in Brunei	NEB-N 85
1	Islands in the Net	HUG-N 89
1	Islands in the Net	LOC-N 89
1	Islands in the Net	SFC-N 89
1	Islands in the Net	JWC-W 89
6	Mirrorshades: The Cyberpunk Anthology	LOC-N 87
4	Our Neural Chernobyl	SFC-N 89
4	Our Neural Chernobyl	HUG-N 89
1	Schismatrix	NEB-N 85
1	Schismatrix	BSF-N 87
4	Spider Rose	LOC-N 83
4	Spider Rose	HUG-N 83
4	Sunken Gardens	NEB-N 84
3	Swarm	HUG-N 83
3	Swarm	NEB-N 82

AUTHOR		
CAT	T I T L E	AW W/N Y
STEWART, George R		
1	Earth Abides	IFA-W 51
STEWART, W Gregory		
4	Button and What You Know, The	NEB-N 92
STITH, John E		
1	Redshift Rendezvous	LOC-N 91
1	Redshift Rendezvous	NEB-N 91
STRACZYNSKI, J Michael		
9	Demon Night	STO-N 89
STRAUB, Peter		
1	Floating Dragons	BFA-W 84
6	Houses Without Doors	STO-N 91
5	Houses Without Doors	WFA-N 91
3	Juniper Tree, The	STO-N 89
10	Koko	LOC-N 89
1	Koko	WFA-W 89
1	Shadow Land	WFA-N 81
1	Talisman, The	WFA-N 85
STRETE, Craig		
3	Bleeding Man, The	NEB-N 75
4	Sunday Visit, A	NEB-N 80
4	Time Deer	NEB-N 75
STRIEBER, Whitley		
4	Pain	WFA-N 87
STURGEON, Theodore		
4	Blue Butter	JUP-N 75
3	Case and the Dreamer	NEB-N 73
11	Goodbody	LOC-N 87
2	If All Men Were Brothers Would You Let..	NEB-N 67

AUTHOR		
CAT	T I T L E	AW W/N Y
STURGEON, Theodore	Continued...	
4	Man Who Learned Loving, The	NEB-N 69
4	Man Who Lost the Sea	HUG-N 60
1	More Than Human	IFA-W 54
4	Need	HUG-N 61
4	Slow Sculpture	HUG-W 71
4	Slow Sculpture	LOC-N 71
3	Slow Sculpture	NEB-W 70
5	Stars Are the Styx, The	LOC-N 80
14	Sturgeon is Alive and Well	LOC-N 72
1	Venus Pluz X	HUG-N 61
4	When You Care, When You Love	HUG-N 63
SUCHARITKUL, Somtow		
4	Absent Thee From Felicity Awhile	HUG-N 82
3	Aquila	HUG-N 83
SULLIVAN, Jack		
7	Penguin Encycl of Horror & Supernatural	LOC-N 87
SULLIVAN, Robert		
4	Zeke Timothy	NEB-N 81
SUSKIND, Patrick		
1	Perfume	WFA-W 87
SUTIN, Lawrence		
7	Divine Invasions	LOC-N 90
SUTPHIN, Richard		
5	Sexpunks and Savage Sagas	STO-N 92
SUTTON, David		
6	Dark Voices	BFA-N 91
6	Dark Voices 2	WFA-N 91

	A U T H O R	
CAT	T I T L E	AW W/N Y
	SWANN, Thomas Burnett	
4	Where is the Bird of Fire?	HUG-N 63
	SWANWICK, Michael	
3	Dogfight	HUG-N 86
3	Dogfight	SFC-N 86
3	Dogfight	LOC-N 86
3	Dogfight	NEB-N 85
4	Edge of the World, The	HUG-N 90
4	Edge of the World, The	JWC-W 90
4	Edge of the World, The	LOC-N 90
4	Edge of the World, The	WFA-N 90
3	Feast of St. Janis, The	NEB-N 80
5	Gravity's Angels	LOC-N 92
2	Griffin's Egg	SFC-N 92
2	Griffin's Egg	HUG-N 92
2	Griffin's Egg	LOC-N 92
9	In the Drift	LOC-N 86
4	Man Who Met Picasso, The	WFA-N 83
2	Marrow Death	NEB-N 84
4	Midwinter's Tale, A	LOC-N 89
4	Midwinter's Tale, A	DAV-W 89
3	Mummer Kiss	NEB-N 81
3	Mummer Kiss	SFC-W 82
1	Stations of the Tide	SFC-N 92
1	Stations of the Tide	LOC-N 92
1	Stations of the Tide	NEB-W 92
1	Stations of the Tide	JWC-N 92
1	Stations of the Tide	HUG-N 92
3	Trojan Horse	NEB-N 84
	SWIGART, Rob	
1	A.K.A.: A Cosmic Tale	BSF-N 80
	SYKES, S C	
3	Rockabye Baby	NEB-N 85
	TALL, Stephen	
4	Bear With the Knot on His Tail, The	HUG-N 72

	A U T H O R	
CAT	T I T L E	AW W/N Y
	TAYLOR, Robert	
4	Idiot's Mate	NEB-N 68
	TEM, Melanie	
9	Prodigal	STO-W 92
	TEM, Steve Rasnic	
4	Back Windows	STO-N 91
4	Bodies and Heads	STO-N 90
9	Excavation	STO-N 88
4	Firestorm	WFA-N 83
4	Leaks	BFA-W 88
	TENN, William	
3	Masculine Revolt, The	NEB-N 65
3	On Venus, Have We Got A Rabbi	LOC-N 75
	TEPPER, Sheri S	
11	Beauty	LOC-W 92
2	Gardener, The	WFA-N 89
1	Grass	LOC-N 90
1	Grass	HUG-N 90
9	King's Blood Four	LOC-N 84
	TESSIER, Thomas	
1	Phantom	WFA-N 83
	TEVIS, Walter	
1	Mockingbird	NEB-N 80
	THOKAR, Greg	
7	Noreascon Three Souvenir Book	HUG-N 90
	THOMAS, D M	
1	White Hotel, The	WFA-N 82

AUTHORS - Alphabetically

AUTHOR		
CAT	T I T L E	AW W/N Y
THOMAS, Theodore L		
1	Clone, The	NEB-N 65
4	Doctor, The	NEB-N 67
THOMPSON, W R		
4	VRM-547	DAV-W 91
4	VRM-547	LOC-N 91
4	VRM-547	HUG-N 91
THURSTON, Robert		
2	Mars Ship, The	LOC-N 78
4	Wheels	LOC-N 72
TIPTREE, James Jr		
4	And I Awoke & Found Me Here t/Cold Hill'	HUG-N 73
4	And I Awoke & Found Me Here t/Cold Hill'	LOC-N 73
4	And I Awoke & Found Me Here t/Cold Hill'	NEB-N 72
4	Beyond the Dead Reef	LOC-W 84
4	Boy Who Waterskied Forever, The	LOC-N 83
4	Boy Who Waterskied Forever, The	HUG-N 83
2	Collision	LOC-N 87
2	Color of Neanderthal Eyes, The	LOC-N 89
5	Crown of Stars	LOC-N 89
3	Earth Doth Like a Snake Renew, The	LOC-N 89
3	Girl Who Was Plugged In, The	JUP-N 74
4	Girl Who Was Plugged In, The	LOC-N 74
3	Girl Who Was Plugged In, The	NEB-N 73
2	Girl Who Was Plugged In, The	HUG-W 74
5	Her Smoke Rose Up Forever	LOC-N 91
2	Houston, Houston, Do You Read?	LOC-N 77
2	Houston, Houston, Do You Read?	JUP-W 77
2	Houston, Houston. Do You read?	NEB-W 76
2	Houston, Houston. Do You Read?	HUG-W 77
4	In the Midst of Life	LOC-N 88
4	Last Flight of Dr. Ain, The	NEB-N 69
3	Lirios: A Tale of The Quuintana Roo	NEB-N 81
3	Love is the Plan, the Plan is Death	HUG-N 74
4	Love is the Plan, the Plan is Death	NEB-W 73
4	Love is the Plan, the Plan is Death	LOC-N 74
2	Momentary Taste of Being, A	NEB-N 75

CAT	T I T L E	AW W/N Y
AUTHOR		

TIPTREE, James Jr   Continued...

CAT	TITLE	AW W/N Y
2	Only Neat Thing To Do, The	SFC-W 86
2	Only Neat Thing To Do, The	LOC-W 86
2	Only Neat Thing To Do, The	NEB-N 85
2	Only Neat Thing To Do, The	HUG-N 86
3	Out of Everywhere	LOC-N 82
3	Painwise	HUG-N 73
3	Psychologist Who Would'nt Do Awful Thing	LOC-N 77
6	Tales of the Quintana Roo	WFA-W 87
14	Ten Thousand Light Years From Home	LOC-N 74
4	Time-Sharing Angel	HUG-N 78
1	Up the Walls of the World	HUG-N 79
6	Warm Worlds and Otherwise	LOC-N 76
2	With Delicate Mad Hands	LOC-N 82
3	Women Men Don't See	JUP-N 75

TOLKIEN, J R R

1	Lord of the Rings - Trilogy	IFA-W 57
11	Silmarillion	LOC-W 78
1	Simarillion, The	DIT-W 78

TORGESON, Roy

| 6 | Chrysalis 3 | LOC-N 80 |

TUCK, Donald H

7	Encyclopedia of SF and Fantasy #2	LOC-N 79
7	Encyclopedia of SF and Fantasy #3	LOC-N 84
7	Encyclopedia of SF and Fantasy #3	HUG-W 84

TUCKER, Wilson

1	Year of the Quiet Sun	HUG-N 71
1	Year of the Quiet Sun	LOC-N 71
1	Year of the Quiet Sun	NEB-N 70

TUNING, William

| 3 | Survivability | JUP-N 74 |

AUTHORS - Alphabetically

CAT	T I T L E	AW W/N Y
A U T H O R		

TURNER, George

CAT	TITLE	AW W/N Y
1	Drowning Towers	NEB-N 88
7	In t/Heart Or In t/Head:Essay T/Travel	HUG-N 85
1	Sea In Summer, The	CLA-W 88
1	Sea In Summer, The	JWC-N 88

TURTLEDOVE, Harry

CAT	TITLE	AW W/N Y
2	Superwine	LOC-N 88

TUTTLE, Lisa

CAT	TITLE	AW W/N Y
4	Bone Flute, The	NEB-W 81
4	Bug House	LOC-N 81
4	In Transition	BSF-W 90
2	One-Wing	HUG-N 81
4	Stone Circle	NEB-N 76
2	Storms of Windhaven, The	NEB-N 75
4	Treading the Maze	BSF-N 82
4	Wound, The	BFA-N 88

UNDERWOOD, Tim

CAT	TITLE	AW W/N Y
7	Bare Bones:Convers'ns on Terror w/S King	LOC-N 89
7	Fear Itself:T/Horror Fiction of S King	LOC-N 83
7	Fear Itself:T/Horror Fiction of S King	HUG-N 83
7	Jack Vance	LOC-N 81

UTLEY, Steven

CAT	TITLE	AW W/N Y
3	Custer's Last Jump	NEB-N 76

VAN VOGT, A E

CAT	TITLE	AW W/N Y
2	Research Alpha	NEB-N 65

VANCE, Jack

CAT	TITLE	AW W/N Y
2	Assault on a City	HUG-N 75
2	Assault on a City	LOC-N 75
2	Assault on a City	JUP-N 75
4	Bagful of Dreams	WFA-N 78
4	Dragon Masters, The	HUG-W 63
1	Dying Earth	HUG-N 64

AUTHOR		
CAT	TITLE	AW W/N Y
VANCE, Jack	Continued...	
2	Last Castle, The	NEB-W 66
3	Last Castle, The	HUG-W 67
1	Lyonesse	WFA-N 84
11	Lyonesse	LOC-N 84
1	Lyonesse	NEB-N 83
11	Lyonesse: Madouc	LOC-N 90
1	Lyonesse: Madouc	WFA-W 90
11	Lyonesse: The Green Pearl	LOC-N 86
3	Miracle Workers	HUG-N 59
3	Seventeen Virgins	JUP-W 75
1	Trullion Alastor	LOC-N 74
VARLEY, John		
4	Air Raid	HUG-N 78
4	Air Raid	NEB-N 77
3	Barbie Murders, The	HUG-N 79
3	Barbie Murders, The	LOC-W 79
5	Barbie Murders, The	LOC-W 81
3	Beatnik Bayou	LOC-N 81
3	Beatnik Bayou	HUG-N 81
5	Blue Champagne	LOC-W 87
2	Blue Champagne	LOC-W 82
2	Blue Champagne	HUG-N 82
1	Demon	LOC-N 85
3	Ginungagap	NEB-N 80
3	Gotta Sing, Gotta Dance	HUG-N 77
3	Gotta Sing, Gotta Dance	LOC-N 77
2	In the Hall of the Martian Kings	HUG-N 78
2	In the Hall of the Martian Kings	JUP-W 78
1	Millenium	DIC-N 84
1	Millenium	LOC-N 84
1	Millenium	HUG-N 84
1	Opiuchi Hotline, The	LOC-N 78
3	Options	LOC-N 80
3	Options	NEB-N 79
3	Options	HUG-N 80
2	Persistence of Vision, The	HUG-W 79
2	Persistence of Vision, The	NEB-W 78
2	Persistence of Vision, The	LOC-W 79
3	Phantom of Kansas, The	HUG-N 77
3	Phantom of Kansas, The	LOC-N 77

	A U T H O R	
CAT	**T I T L E**	**AW W/N Y**
	VARLEY, John Continued...	
2	Press Enter	SFC-W 85
2	Press Enter	LOC-W 85
2	Press Enter	NEB-W 84
2	Press Enter	HUG-W 85
4	Pusher, The	LOC-W 82
4	Pusher, The	SFC-W 82
4	Pusher, The	HUG-W 82
4	Pusher, The	NEB-N 81
3	Retrograde Summer	LOC-N 76
3	Retrograde Summer	NEB-N 75
2	Tango Charlie and Foxtrot Romeo	LOC-N 87
1	Titan	HUG-N 80
1	Titan	NEB-N 79
1	Titan	LOC-W 80
1	Wizard	HUG-N 81
1	Wizard	LOC-N 81
	VERCORS	
1	Sylva	HUG-N 63
	VIDAL, Gore	
1	Kalki	NEB-N 78
	VINGE, Joan D	
4	Eyes of Amber	LOC-N 78
5	Eyes of Amber	LOC-N 80
3	Eyes of Amber	HUG-W 78
2	Fireship	NEB-N 79
2	Fireship	LOC-N 79
2	Fireship	HUG-N 79
1	Snow Queen, The	HUG-W 81
1	Snow Queen, The	NEB-N 80
1	Snow Queen, The	LOC-N 81
1	Summer Queen, The	LOC-N 92
1	Summer Queen, The	HUG-N 92
3	Tin Soldier	JUP-N 75
4	View From A Height	HUG-N 79
4	View From A Height	LOC-N 79

AUTHOR		
CAT	T I T L E	AW W/N Y
VINGE, Vernor		
3	Barbarian Princess, The	HUG-N 87
1	Marooned in Real Time	HUG-N 87
1	Peace War, The	HUG-N 85
2	True Names	NEB-N 81
2	True Names	HUG-N 82
VINICOFF, Eric		
3	Wigher, The	HUG-N 85
VONARBURG, Elisabeth		
4	La Carte du Tendre	AUR-W 87
VONNEGUT, Kurt Jr		
1	Cat's Cradle	HUG-N 64
1	Galapagos	JWC-N 86
1	Player Piano	IFA-N 53
1	Sirens of Titan, The	HUG-N 60
1	Slaughterhouse-Five	NEB-N 69
1	Slaughterhouse-Five	HUG-N 70
WAGNER, Karl Edward		
2	At First Just Ghostly	STO-N 90
2	Beyond All Measure	WFA-W 83
4	But You'll Never Follow Me	STO-N 91
1	Dark Crusade	WFA-N 77
4	Into Whose Hands	WFA-N 84
4	Neither Brute Nor Human	BFA-W 84
6	Night Winds	WFA-N 79
2	River of Night's Dreaming	WFA-N 82
2	Sticks	WFA-N 75
4	Sticks	BFA-W 75
4	Two Suns Setting	BFA-W 77
2	Two Suns Setting	WFA-N 77
5	Why Not You and I?	WFA-N 88
6	Why Not You and I?	STO-N 88
6	Year's Best Horror Stories #15	WFA-N 88

AUTHOR		
CAT	T I T L E	AW W/N Y
WALDROP, Howard		
6	All About Str'ge Monsters F/Recent Past	STO-N 88
5	All About Str'ge Monsters F/Recent Past	LOC-N 88
3	Beatnik Bayou	NEB-N 80
3	Do Ya, Do Ya, Wanna Dance	SFC-N 89
3	Do Ya, Do Ya, Wanna Dance	HUG-N 89
3	Do Ya, Do Ya, Wanna Dance	NEB-N 88
4	Do Ya, Do Ya, Wanna Dance	JWC-N 89
3	Do Ya, Do Ya, Wanna Dance	LOC-N 89
2	Dozen Tough Jobs, A	WFA-N 90
2	Dozen Tough Jobs, A	NEB-N 89
2	Dozen Tough Jobs, A	LOC-N 90
3	Fin de Cycle	LOC-N 92
3	Fin de Cycle	HUG-N 92
4	Flying Saucer Rock and Roll	NEB-N 85
4	Flying Saucer Rock and Roll	HUG-N 86
4	God's Hooks	LOC-N 83
4	God's Hooks	NEB-N 82
4	Heirs of the Perisphere	NEB-N 85
5	Howard Who?	LOC-N 87
4	Ike at the Mike	HUG-N 83
4	Lions Are Asleep This Night, The	JWC-N 87
4	Lions Are Asleep This Night, The	NEB-N 86
4	Mary Margaret Road-Grader	NEB-N 76
4	Night of the Cooters	HUG-N 88
5	Night of the Cooters: More Neat Stories	WFA-N 92
5	Night of the Cooters: More Neat Stories	LOC-W 92
9	Them Bones	LOC-N 85
1	Them Bones	DIC-N 85
3	Ugly Chickens, The	HUG-N 81
4	Ugly Chickens, The	WFA-W 81
3	Ugly Chickens, The	LOC-N 81
3	Ugly Chickens, The	NEB-W 80
4	Wild, Wild Horses	LOC-N 89
WALLING, William		
3	Nix Olypica	HUG-N 75

AUTHOR		
CAT	T I T L E	AW W/N Y
WATSON, Ian		
4	Cage for Death, A	BSF-N 82
1	Embedding, The	NEB-N 75
1	Embedding, The	JWC-N 74
4	Jangling Geordie's Hole	BSF-N 87
1	Jonah Kit, The	BSF-W 78
4	People of the Precipice	BSF-N 86
3	Slow Birds	NEB-N 83
3	Slow Birds	LOC-N 84
3	Slow Birds	HUG-N 84
4	Very Slow Time Machine, The	HUG-N 79
1	Whores of Babylon	CLA-N 89
4	World SF Convention of 2080, The	BSF-N 81
WATTS, Peter		
4	Niche, A	AUR-W 92
WATT-EVANS, Lawrence		
4	Why I Left Harry's All-Night Hamburgers	DAV-W 88
4	Why I Left Harry's All-Night Hamburgers	NEB-N 87
4	Why I Left Harry's All-Night Hamburgers	LOC-N 88
4	Why I Left Harry's All-Night Hamburgers	HUG-W 88
4	Windwagon Smith and the Martians	DAV-W 90
WEINBERG, Robert		
7	Biog Dictionary of SF & Fantasy Artists	HUG-N 89
WEINER, Andrew		
4	Third Test, The	BSF-N 83
WELLER, Tom		
7	Culture Made Stupid	LOC-N 88
7	Science Made Stupid	HUG-W 86
7	Science Made Stupid	LOC-N 86

	A U T H O R	
CAT	T I T L E	AW W/N Y
WELLMAN, Manly Wade		
2	Ghastly Priest Doth Reign, The	WFA-N 76
5	John the Balladeer	LOC-N 89
4	Nine Yards of Other Cloth	HUG-N 59
5	Worse Things Waiting	WFA-W 75
WELLS, Stuart W III		
7	SF and Heroic Fantasy Index	LOC-N 79
WHELAN, Michael		
7	Michael Whelan's Works of Wonder	LOC-N 88
7	Michael Whelan's Works of Wonder	HUG-W 88
WHITE, James		
4	Custom Fitting	LOC-N 77
4	Custom Fitting	HUG-N 77
1	Escape Orbit	NEB-N 65
1	Hospital Station	NEB-N 62
3	Sanctuary	DAV-W 89
1	Second Ending	HUG-N 62
WHITE, Ted		
4	Peacock King, The	NEB-N 65
WIATER, Stanley		
7	Dark Dreamers	STO-W 91
WILDE, Kelley		
9	Suiting, The	STO-W 89
WILHELM, Kate		
2	April Fool's Day Forever	NEB-N 70
4	Baby, You Were Great	NEB-N 67
3	Brother to Dragons, A	HUG-N 75
4	Cold Night Dark With Snow, A	NEB-N 70
3	Encounter, The	NEB-N 71

AUTHOR		
CAT	T I T L E	AW W/N Y
WILHELM, Kate Continued...		
4	Forever Yours, Anna	HUG-N 88
4	Forever Yours, Anna	NEB-W 87
4	Forever Yours, Anna	SFC-N 88
3	Funeral, The	NEB-N 72
3	Girl Who Fell Into the Sky, The	NEB-W 86
2	Gorgon, The	NEB-N 85
2	Gorgon Field, The	WFA-N 86
2	Infinity Box, The	NEB-N 71
1	Juniper Time	NEB-N 79
1	Margaret and I	NEB-N 71
14	Nebula Award Stories 9	LOC-N 75
4	Planners, The	NEB-W 68
2	Plastic Abyss, The	NEB-N 71
4	Village, The	JUP-N 74
1	Where Late the Sweet Birds Sang	HUG-W 77
1	Where Late the Sweet Birds Sang	JWC-N 77
1	Where Late the Sweet Birds Sang	NEB-N 76
1	Where Late the Sweet Birds Sang	JUP-W 77
1	Where Late the Sweet Birds Sang	LOC-W 77
2	Winter Beach, The	NEB-N 81
2	With Thimbles, With Forks and Hope	HUG-N 82
WILLIAMS, John		
2	Witness	NEB-N 87
WILLIAMS, Paul		
7	Only Apparently Real: World of P K Dick	LOC-N 87
7	Only Apparently Real: World of P K Dick	HUG-N 87
WILLIAMS, Paul O		
9	Breaking of Northwall, The	LOC-N 82
WILLIAMS, Ralph		
4	Cat and Mouse	HUG-N 60
WILLIAMS, Tad		
9	Tailchaser's Song	LOC-N 86

AUTHOR		
CAT	TITLE	AW W/N Y
WILLIAMS, Walter Jon		
3	Dinausaurs	HUG-N 88
4	Dinosaurs	JWC-N 88
1	Knight Moves	DIC-N 86
2	Surfacing	DAV-N 89
2	Surfacing	LOC-N 89
2	Surfacing	NEB-N 88
2	Surfacing	HUG-N 89
WILLIAMSON, Chet		
1	Ash Wednesday	STO-N 88
2	Confession of St James, The	STO-N 90
4	From the Papers of Helmut Hecher	STO-N 91
4	Music of the Dark Time, The	STO-N 89
1	Reign	STO-N 91
6	Yore Skin's Jes' Soft'n' Purty, He Said	WFA-N 90
6	Yore Skin's Jes' Soft'n' Purty, He Said	STO-N 90
WILLIAMSON, J N		
5	Author's Choice Monthly #24	STO-N 92
6	Masques	WFA-N 85
6	Masques II	WFA-N 88
2	Night Seasons, The	WFA-N 87
WILLIAMSON, Jack		
7	Wonder's Child: My Life in S Fiction	HUG-W 85
7	Wonder's Child: My Life in S Fiction	LOC-N 85
WILLIS, Connie		
3	At the Rialto	LOC-N 90
3	At the Rialto	SFC-N 90
3	At the Rialto	HUG-N 90
3	At the Rialto	NEB-W 89
3	Blued Moon	LOC-N 85
3	Blued Moon	HUG-N 85
2	Chance	WFA-N 87
4	Cibola	LOC-N 91
4	Cibola	HUG-N 91
4	Cibola	SFC-N 91

	A U T H O R	
CAT	T I T L E	AW W/N Y
WILLIS, Connie Continued...		
4	Daisy, in the Sun	HUG-N 80
4	Dilemna	LOC-N 90
3	Fire Watch	SFC-W 83
3	Fire Watch	NEB-W 82
5	Fire Watch	LOC-N 86
3	Fire Watch	LOC-N 83
3	Fire Watch	HUG-W 83
4	In the Late Cretaceous	HUG-N 92
4	In the Late Cretaceous	LOC-N 92
2	Jack	NEB-N 92
2	Jack	SFC-N 92
2	Jack	LOC-N 92
2	Jack	HUG-N 92
2	Last of the Winnebagos, The	NEB-W 88
2	Last of the Winnebagos, The	DAV-W 89
2	Last of the Winnebagos, The	LOC-N 89
2	Last of the Winnebagos, The	SFC-N 89
2	Last of the Winnebagos, The	HUG-W 89
4	Letter From the Clearys, A	SFC-N 83
4	Letter From the Clearys, A	NEB-W 82
11	Lincoln's Dreams	LOC-N 88
1	Lincoln's Dreams	JWC-W 88
3	Miracle	HUG-N 92
3	Miracle	LOC-N 92
3	Schwarzschild Radius	NEB-N 87
3	Sidon in the Mirror, The	HUG-N 84
3	Sidon in the Mirror, The	NEB-N 83
2	Spice Pogrom	LOC-N 87
2	Spice Pogrom	HUG-N 87
2	Spice Pogrom	DAV-W 87
2	Time-Out	HUG-N 90
2	Time-Out	LOC-N 90
WILSON, Charles		
1	Hidden Place, A	COM-N 87

AUTHORS - Alphabetically

	A U T H O R	
CAT	T I T L E	AW W/N Y
	WILSON, F Paul	
2	Barrens, The	WFA-N 91
1	Black Wind	STO-N 89
4	Day-Tay-Vao	STO-N 88
2	Dydeetown Girl	NEB-N 86
2	Pelts	STO-N 91
6	Soft and Others	STO-N 90
4	Traps	STO-N 88
	WILSON, Richard	
4	Eight Billion, The	NEB-N 65
3	Mother of the World	NEB-W 68
3	Mother to the World	HUG-N 69
2	Story Writer, The	NEB-N 79
	WILSON, Robert Charles	
1	Bridge of Years	DIC-N 92
1	Hidden Place, A	AUR-N 87
9	Hidden Place, A	LOC-N 87
1	Hidden Place, A	DIC-N 87
	WILSON, Robin Scott	
13	Clarion 1	LOC-N 72
14	Those Who Can	LOC-N 74
	WINDLING, Terri	
6	Elsewhere	BFA-W 82
6	Elsewhere	WFA-W 82
6	Feary	WFA-N 86
	WINTER, Douglas E	
6	Black Wine	WFA-N 87
7	Faces of Fear: Encount W/t/Creat Mod Hor	HUG-N 86
7	Faces of Fear: Encount W/t/Creat Mod Hor	LOC-N 86
6	Prime Evil	WFA-N 89
4	Splatter: A Cautionary Tale	WFA-N 88

AUTHOR		
CAT	T I T L E	AW W/N Y
WOLF, Leonard		
7	Horror: A Connoisseur's Guide	STO-N 90
WOLFE, Gene		
4	Against the Lafayette Escadrille	NEB-N 72
4	Cabin on the Coast, A	LOC-N 85
4	Cabin on the Coast, A	NEB-N 84
1	Citadel of the Autarch, The	BSF-N 84
1	Citadel of the Autarch, The	SFC-N 84
1	Citadel of the Autarch, The	JWC-W 84
11	Citadel of the Autarch, The	LOC-N 83
1	Citadel of the Autarch, The	NEB-N 83
1	Claw of the Conciliator, The	NEB-W 81
1	Claw of the Conciliator, The	SFC-N 82
11	Claw of the Conciliator, The	LOC-W 82
1	Claw of the Conciliator, The	WFA-N 82
1	Claw of the Conciliator, The	HUG-N 82
3	Death of Doctor Island, The	JUP-N 74
2	Death of Doctor Island, The	NEB-W 73
2	Death of Doctor Island, The	HUG-N 74
2	Death of Doctor Island, The	LOC-W 74
5	Endangered Species	LOC-N 90
2	Eyeflash Miracles, The	NEB-N 76
2	Eyeflash Miracles, The	LOC-N 77
2	Fifth Head of Cerberus, The	HUG-N 73
2	Fifth Head of Cerberus, The	LOC-N 73
2	Fifth Head of Cerberus, The	NEB-N 72
1	Free, Live Free	BSF-N 86
1	Free, Live Free	NEB-N 86
5	Gene Wolfe's Book of Days	LOC-N 82
4	How I Lost the Second World War and ...	NEB-N 73
4	In The House of Gingerbread	WFA-N 88
5	Island of Dr. Death, The	LOC-N 81
4	Island of Dr. Death, The	NEB-N 70
1	Listeners, The	JWC-N 73
2	Seven American Nights	HUG-N 79
2	Seven American Nights	NEB-N 78
2	Seven American Nights	LOC-N 79
11	Shadow of the Torturer, The	LOC-N 81
1	Shadow of the Torturer, The	JWC-N 81
1	Shadow of the Torturer, The	WFA-W 81
1	Shadow of the Torturer, The	BSF-W 82
1	Shadow of the Torturer, The	NEB-N 80

	A U T H O R	
CAT	T I T L E	AW W/N Y
WOLFE, Gene Continued...		
11	Soldier of Arete	LOC-N 90
1	Soldier of Arete	WFA-N 90
11	Soldier of the Mist	LOC-W 87
1	Soldier of the Mist	NEB-N 87
1	Soldier of the Mist	WFA-N 87
5	Storeys From The Old Hotel	WFA-N 89
1	Sword of the Lichtor, The	SFC-W 83
1	Sword of the Lichtor, The	HUG-N 83
1	Sword of the Lichtor, The	WFA-N 83
11	Sword of the Lichtor, The	LOC-W 83
1	Sword of the Lichtor, The	NEB-N 82
1	Sword of the Lichtor, The	BSF-N 83
1	Sword of the Lichtor, The	BFA-W 83
11	There Are Doors	LOC-N 89
1	Urth of the New Sun, The	HUG-N 88
1	Urth of the New Sun, The	LOC-N 88
1	Urth of the New Sun, The	NEB-N 88
1	Urth of the New Sun, The	SFC-W 88
4	War Beneath the Tree	LOC-N 80
4	War Beneath the Tree	NEB-N 80
4	Woman the Unicorn Loved, The	HUG-N 82
WOLHEIM, Donald A		
14	1972 Annual World's Best SF	LOC-N 73
14	1973 Annual World's Best SF	LOC-N 74
14	1974 Annual World's Best SF	LOC-N 75
6	1978 Annual World's Best SF	LOC-N 79
6	1983 Annual World's Best SF	LOC-N 84
6	1984 Annual World's Best SF	LOC-N 85
6	1990 Annual World's Best SF	LOC-N 91
6	World's Best Science Fiction: 1970	LOC-N 71
14	World's Best Science Fiction: 1971	LOC-W 72
WOLVERTON, Dave		
1	On My Way To Paradise	DIC-N 90
9	On My Way to Paradise	LOC-N 90
WREN, Thomas (Thomas T Thomas)		
1	Doomsday Effect, The	COM-W 87

AUTHOR		
CAT	**T I T L E**	**AW W/N Y**
WRIGHTSON, Patricia		
1	Dark Bright Water, The	WFA-N 80
WU, William F		
4	Hong's Bluff	NEB-N 85
4	Hong's Bluff	HUG-N 86
4	Wong's Lost and Found Emporium	WFA-N 84
4	Wong's Lost and Found Emporium	HUG-N 84
4	Wong's Lost and Found Emporium	NEB-N 83
WYNDHAM, John		
1	Day of the Triffids, The	IFA-N 52
YARBRO, Chelsea Quinn		
1	Ariosto	WFA-N 81
4	Cabin 33	WFA-N 81
2	Dare I Eat A Peach	WFA-N 86
1	Palace, The	WFA-N 80
YOLEN, Jane		
2	Devil's Arithmetic, The	WFA-N 89
2	Devil's Arithmetic, The	NEB-N 88
6	Dragonfields	WFA-N 86
6	Merlin's Booke	WFA-N 87
1	Sister Light, Sister Dark	NEB-N 89
6	Tales of Wonder	WFA-N 84
11	White Jenna	LOC-N 90
1	White Jenna	NEB-N 91
YOUNG, Robert F		
4	Little Dog Gone	HUG-N 65
ZAHN, Timothy		
9	Blackcollar, The	LOC-N 84
2	Cascade Point	HUG-W 84
2	Cascade Point	LOC-N 84
3	Pawn's Gambit	HUG-N 83
3	Return to the Fold	HUG-N 85

AUTHORS - Alphabetically

	A U T H O R	
CAT	T I T L E	AW W/N Y
	ZEBROWSKI, George	
4	Eichman Variations, The	NEB-N 84
4	Heathen God	NEB-N 71
	ZELAZNY, Roger	
2	24 Views of Mount Fuji by Hokusai	LOC-N 86
2	24 Views of Mount Fuji by Hokusai	NEB-N 85
2	24 Views of Mount Fuji by Hokusai	HUG-W 86
11	Blood of Amber	LOC-N 87
11	Changeling	LOC-N 81
11	Changing Land, The	LOC-N 82
4	Comes Now the Power	HUG-N 67
2	Damnation Alley	HUG-N 68
4	Devil Car	NEB-N 65
5	Dilvish Be Damned	LOC-N 83
3	Doors of His Face...	NEB-W 65
1	Doorways in the Sand	NEB-N 75
1	Doorways in the Sand	HUG-N 76
4	Engine at Heartsprings Center, The	LOC-N 75
4	Engine at Heartsprings Center, The	NEB-N 74
4	Engine at Heartsprings Center, The	JUP-N 75
3	For A Breath I Tarry	HUG-N 67
5	Frost and Fire	LOC-N 90
2	He Who Shapes	NEB-W 65
2	Home is the Hangman	LOC-N 76
2	Home is the Hangman	NEB-W 75
2	Home is the Hangman	HUG-W 76
1	Isle of the Dead	NEB-N 69
1	Jack of Shadows	LOC-N 72
1	Jack of Shadows	HUG-N 72
3	Keys to December, The	NEB-N 67
5	Last Defender of Camelot	LOC-N 81
1	Lord of Light	HUG-W 68
1	Lord of Light	NEB-N 67
3	Moment of the Storm, This	NEB-N 66
3	Mortal Mountain, The	NEB-N 67
3	Permafrost	NEB-N 86
3	Permafrost	HUG-W 87
3	Permafrost	LOC-N 87
4	Rose for Ecclesiastes, A	HUG-N 64
11	Sign of Chaos	LOC-N 88
3	This Moment of the Storm	HUG-N 67
11	Trumps of Doom	LOC-W 86

	A U T H O R	
CAT	T I T L E	AW W/N Y
ZELAZNY, Roger	Continued...	
5	Unicorn Variations	LOC-W 84
3	Unicorn Variations	LOC-N 82
3	Unicorn Variations	HUG-W 82
ZINDELL, David		
1	Neverness	CLA-N 90

Part C   MAJOR SCIENCE FICTION AWARDS

Titles Listed Alphabetically

This section lists all the titles alphabetically. A listing will occur for each nomination or win.

A full description of all abbreviations used within these listings can be found on the next page.

HEADINGS:

CAT	T I T L E S	AW W/N Y	A U T H O R

EXPLANATIONS:

CAT   =   Category (length and type)

1 Novel	2 Novella	3 Novellette
4 Short Story	5 1-Author Collection	6 Collection/Anthology
7 Non-Fiction	8 Series	9 First Novel
10 Horror	11 Fantasy Novel	12 Magazine Article
13 Original Anthology	14 Reprint Anthology	

LENGTH OF WORK (from Locus Reader Awards)	
Novel	40,000 + words
Novella	17,500 - 40,000
Novellette	7,500 - 17,500
Short Story	up to 7,500

AW   =   Award

AUR	Aurora (Casper)
BFA	British Fantasy
BSF	British Science Fiction
CLA	Arthur C. Clarke
COM	Compton Crook
DAV	Davis Publications
DIC	Dick
DIT	Ditmar
HUG	Hugo
IFA	International Fantasy
JUP	Jupiter
JWC	J W Campbell
LOC	Locus Magazine
NEB	Nebula
SFC	SF Chronicle Magazine
STO	Bram Stoker
WFA	World Fantasy

W/N   =   winner or nominee

Y   =   year award presented

SECTION C: TITLES (Alphabetically)

CAT	T I T L E S	AW W/N Y	A U T H O R
3	102 H-Bombs	NEB-N 65	DISCH, Thomas M
14	1972 Annual World's Best SF	LOC-N 73	WOLHEIM, Donald A
14	1973 Annual World's Best SF	LOC-N 74	WOLHEIM, Donald A
14	1974 Annual World's Best SF	LOC-N 75	WOLHEIM, Donald A
6	1978 Annual World's Best SF	LOC-N 79	WOLHEIM, Donald A
6	1983 Annual World's Best SF	LOC-N 84	WOLHEIM, Donald A
6	1984 Annual World's Best SF	LOC-N 85	WOLHEIM, Donald A
6	1990 Annual World's Best SF	LOC-N 91	WOLHEIM, Donald A
3	1/72 nd Scale	NEB-N 91	MacLEOD, Ian
1	2010: Odyssey Two	SFC-N 83	CLARKE, Arthur C
1	2010: Odyssey Two	LOC-N 83	CLARKE, Arthur C
1	2010: Odyssey Two	HUG-N 83	CLARKE, Arthur C
2	24 Views of Mount Fuji by Hokusai	HUG-W 86	ZELAZNY, Roger
2	24 Views of Mount Fuji by Hokusai	LOC-N 86	ZELAZNY, Roger
2	24 Views of Mount Fuji by Hokusai	NEB-N 85	ZELAZNY, Roger
12	24th Century Medicine	DAV-N 89	DONALDSON, Thomas
1	334	NEB-N 74	DISCH, Thomas M
1	400 Billion Stars	DIC-N 89	McCAULEY, Paul J
6	900 Grandmothers	LOC-N 71	LAFFERTY, R A
4	Absent Thee From Felicity Awhile	HUG-N 82	SUCHARITKUL, SOMTOW
1	Across The Sea of Suns	LOC-N 85	BENFORD, Gregory
1	Acts of King Arthur & His Noble Knights	WFA-N 77	STEINBECK, John
4	Adinkra Cloth, The	NEB-N 89	ADRIDGE, Mary
3	Adrift, Just off t/Islets of Langerhans	LOC-W 75	ELLISON, Harlan
3	Adrift, Just off t/Islets of Langerhans	HUG-W 75	ELLISON, Harlan
4	Advent of Channel Twelve, The	HUG-N 59	KORNBLUTH, Cyril M
3	Adventure of the Extraterrestrial	NEB-N 65	REYNOLDS, Mack
2	Advocates	STO-N 92	CHARNAS, Suzy McKee
1	Aegypt	BFA-N 88	CROWLEY, John
1	Aegypt	WFA-N 88	CROWLEY, John
11	Aegypt	LOC-N 88	CROWLEY, John
1	Aegypt	CLA-N 88	CROWLEY, John
1	Affirmation, The	BSF-N 82	PRIEST, Christopher
1	Affirmation, The	DIT-W 82	PRIEST, Christopher
4	After Images	BSF-W 84	EDWARDS, Malcolm
4	After King Kong Fell	NEB-N 74	FARMER, Philip Jose
7	After Man	LOC-N 82	DIXON, Dougal
7	After Man	HUG-N 82	DIXON, Dougal
3	After the Dreamtime	HUG-N 75	LUPOFF, Richard A
6	After t/King:Stories Honor of Tolkien	WFA-N 92	GREENBERG, Martin H
1	After the Zap	COM-N 88	ARMSTRONG, Michael
6	Afterlives	LOC-N 87	SARGENT, Pamela
13	Again, Dangerous Visions	LOC-W 73	ELLISON, Harlan
1	Against Infinity	NEB-N 83	BENFORD, Gregory
4	Against the Lafayette Escadrille	NEB-N 72	WOLFE, Gene
1	Age of the Pussyfoot	NEB-N 69	POHL, Frederik
7	Age of Wonders: Exploring t/World of SF	LOC-N 85	HARTWELL, David
4	Air Raid	HUG-N 78	VARLEY, John (Herb BOEM)
4	Air Raid	NEB-N 77	VARLEY, John (Herb BOEM)
4	Air Raid	LOC-N 78	BOEM, Herb (VARLEY, John)
1	Al the Weyrs of Pern	LOC-N 92	McCAFFREY, Anne

SECTION C: TITLES (Alphabetically)

CAT	TITLES	AW W/N Y	AUTHOR
2	Alchemist, The	NEB-N 66	HARNESS, Chales L
3	Alchemist, The	HUG-N 67	HARNESS, Charles L
1	Alchemists, The	DIC-N 85	GRAVEL, Geary
8	Alien Blues	LOC-N 92	HIGHTOWER, Lynn S
13	Alien Condition, The	LOC-N 74	GOLDIN, Stephen
4	Alien Grafitti	LOC-N 87	BISHOP, Michael
6	Alien Sex	WFA-N 91	DATLOW, Ellen
6	Alien Sex	LOC-N 91	DATLOW, Ellen
4	Aliens Who Knew, I Mean Everything, The	HUG-N 85	EFFINGER, Alex
4	Aliens Who Knew, I Mean Everything, The	SFC-N 85	EFFINGER, George Alec
4	Aliens Who Knew, I Mean Everything, The	NEB-N 84	EFFINGER, Alec
4	Aliens Who Knew, I Mean Everything, The	LOC-N 85	EFFINGER, George Alec
5	All About Str'ge Monsters F/Recent Past	LOC-N 88	WALDROP, Howard
6	All About Str'ge Monsters F/Recent Past	STO-N 88	WALDROP, Howard
3	All Dracula's Children	LOC-W 92	SIMMONS, Dan
1	All Flesh is Grass	NEB-N 65	SIMAK, Clifford D
4	All the Last Wars at Once	LOC-N 72	EFFINGER, George Alec
4	All the Last Wars at Once	HUG-N 72	EFFINGER, George Alex
2	All the Lies That Are My Life	HUG-N 81	ELLISON, Harlan
4	All the Myriad Ways	HUG-N 69	NIVEN, Larry
1	All the Weyrs of Pern	SFC-N 92	McCAFFREY, Anne
1	All the Weyrs of Pern	HUG-N 92	McCAFFREY, Anne
1	All Times Possible	JUP-N 75	EKLUND, Gordon
4	Allamagoosa	HUG-W 55	RUSSELL, Eric Frank
4	Alley Man, The	HUG-N 60	FARMER, Philip Jose
3	All-consuming, The	NEB-N 92	SHEPARD, Lucius
14	Alpha 5	LOC-N 75	SILVERBERG, Robert
14	Alpha Three	LOC-N 73	SILVERBERG, Robert
1	Alteration, The	JWC-W 77	AMIS, Kingsley
1	Altered States	JWC-N 79	CHAYEFSKY, Paddy
6	Amazons!	LOC-N 80	SALMONSON, Jessica Amanda
6	Amazons!	WFA-W 80	SALMONSON, Jessica Amanda
3	America	LOC-N 88	CARD, Orson Scott
7	Amer Vampires:Fans,Victims,Practicioners	STO-N 90	DRESSER, Norine
2	Amnesia	NEB-N 81	DANN, Jack
9	An Abyss of Light	LOC-N 91	O'NEAL, Kathleen M
7	An Edge in My Voice	HUG-N 86	ELLISON, Harlan
13	An Exaltation of Stars	LOC-N 74	CARR, Terry
12	An Introduction to Psychohistory	DAV-W 89	FLYNN, Michael F
4	An Old Fashioned Girl	JUP-N 75	RUSS, Joanna
3	An Ornament to His Profession	NEB-N 66	HARNESS, Charles L
7	Anatomy of Wonder 2nd	LOC-N 82	BARRON, Neil
7	Anatomy of Wonder 2nd	HUG-N 82	BARRON, Neil
7	Anatomy of Wonder 3rd	LOC-N 88	BARRON, Neal
7	Anatomy of Wonder 3rd	HUG-N 88	BARRON, Neil
1	Ancient of Days	CLA-N 88	BISHOP, Michael
1	And Chaos Died	NEB-N 70	RUSS, Joanna
1	And Chaos Died	LOC-N 71	RUSS, Joanna
1	...And Having Writ	JWC-N 79	BENSEN, Donald R

SECTION C: TITLES (Alphabetically)

CAT	T I T L E S	AW W/N Y	A U T H O R
4	And He Not Busy Being Born	BSF-N 87	STABLEFORD, Brian
4	And I Awoke & Found Me Here t/Cold Hill'	HUG-N 73	TIPTREE, James Jr
4	And I Awoke & Found Me Here t/Cold Hill'	NEB-N 72	TIPTREE, James Jr
4	And I Awoke & Found Me Here t/Cold Hill'	LOC-N 73	TIPTREE, James Jr
3	...and Seven Times Never Kill Man	LOC-N 76	MARTIN, George R R
3	...and Seven Times Never Kill Man	HUG-N 76	MARTIN, George R R
5	And the Gods Laughed	LOC-N 88	BROWN, Fredric
2	And Wild For To Hold	LOC-N 92	KRESS, Nancy
2	And Wild To Hold	HUG-N 92	KRESS, Nancy
4	Angel	HUG-N 88	CADIGAN, Pat
4	Angel	SFC-N 88	CADIGAN, Pat
4	Angel	NEB-N 87	CADIGAN, Pat
4	Angel	LOC-W 88	CADIGAN, Pat
4	Angel	WFA-N 88	CADIGAN, Pat
3	Angel of Death, The	NEB-N 79	SHEA, Michael
4	Angels in Love	LOC-N 92	KOJA, Kathe
5	Angry Candy	LOC-W 89	ELLISON, Harlan
6	Angry Candy	STO-N 89	ELLISON, Harlan
5	Angry Candy	WFA-N 89	ELLISON, Harlan
3	Animal Fair, The	NEB-N 72	BESTER, Alfred
1	Annals of the HeeChee, The	LOC-N 88	POHL, Frederik
2	Another Orphan	NEB-W 82	KESSEL, John
2	Another Orphan	HUG-N 83	KESSEL, John
2	Another Orphan	SFC-N 83	KESSEL, John
4	Another World	BFA-N 88	CAMPBELL, Ramsey
4	Answering Service	NEB-N 67	LEIBER, Fritz
11	Anubis Gates, The	LOC-N 84	POWERS, Tim
1	Anubis Gates, The	BSF-N 86	POWERS, Tim
1	Anubis Gates, The	DIC-W 84	POWERS, Tim
1	Anubis Gates, The	SFC-W 84	POWERS, Tim
2	Anvil of Jove, The	LOC-N 77	BENFORD, Gregory
2	Apartheid,Superstr'gs & Modercai Thubana	NEB-N 92	BISHOP, Michael
2	Apartheid,Superstr'gs & Modercai Thubana	WFA-N 90	BISHOP, Michael
12	Ape-Man Within Us, The	DAV-W 90	De CAMP, L Sprague
3	Apology to Inky	NEB-N 66	GREEN, Robert M Jr
3	Apology to Inky	HUG-N 67	GREEN, Robert M Jr
2	April Fool's Day Forever	NEB-N 70	WILHELM, Kate
4	Apt Pupil	BFA-N 83	KING, Stephen
3	Aquila	HUG-N 83	SUCHARITKUL, Somtow
9	Arachne	LOC-N 91	MASON, Lisa
6	Arbor House Treasury of Modern SF	LOC-N 81	SILVERBERG, Robert
1	Archer's Goon	WFA-N 85	JONES, Diana Wynne
1	Architecture of Desire, The	BSF-N 92	GENTLE, Mary
6	Architecture of Fear	WFA-N 88	CRAMER, Kathryn
1	Ariosto	WFA-N 81	YARBRO, Chelsea Quinn
2	ARM	LOC-N 76	NIVEN, Larry
2	ARM	HUG-N 76	NIVEN, Larry
9	Armageddon Blues, The	LOC-N 89	MORAN, Daniel Keys
11	Armageddon Rag, The	LOC-N 84	MARTIN, George R R
1	Armageddon Rag, The	WFA-N 84	MARTIN, George R R
9	Arrows of the Queen	LOC-N 88	LACKEY, Mercedes

CAT	TITLES	AW W/N Y	AUTHOR
7	Art of Leo and Diane Dillon, The	LOC-N 82	PREISS, Byron
7	Art of Leo and Diane Dillon, The	HUG-N 82	PREISS, Byron
1	Artificial Things	DIC-N 87	FOWLER, Karen Joy
4	Ash of Memory, The Dust of Desire, The	STO-N 92	BRITE, Poppy Z
1	Ash Wednesday	STO-N 88	WILLIAMSON, Chet
3	Asian Shores	NEB-N 70	DISCH, Thomas M
2	Assault on a City	JUP-N 75	VANCE, Jack
2	Assault on a City	LOC-N 75	VANCE, Jack
2	Assault on a City	HUG-N 75	VANCE, Jack
13	Astounding	LOC-W 74	HARRISON, Harry
7	Astounding Days	HUG-N 90	CLARKE, Arthur C
7	Astounding Days	LOC-N 90	CLARKE, Arthur C
2	At First Just Ghostly	STO-N 90	WAGNER, Karl Edward
9	At the Eye of the Ocean	LOC-N 82	SCHENCK, Hilbert
3	At The Institute	NEB-N 65	KAGAN, Norman
3	At the Rialto	HUG-N 90	WILLIS, Connie
3	At the Rialto	NEB-W 89	WILLIS, Connie
3	At the Rialto	LOC-N 90	WILLIS, Connie
3	At the Rialto	SFC-N 90	WILLIS, Connie
7	Atlas of Pern, The	LOC-N 85	FONSTAD, Karen Wynn
4	Attachment	NEB-N 75	EISENSTEIN, Phyllis
2	Auk House	LOC-N 78	SIMAK, Clifford D
1	Aurelia	DIC-N 83	LAFFERTY, R A
4	Author of the Acacia Seeds, The	LOC-N 75	LeGUIN, Ursula K
5	Author's Choice Monthly #24	STO-N 92	WILLIAMSON, J N
3	Autopsy, The	HUG-N 81	SHEA, Michael
2	Autopsy, The	LOC-N 81	SHEA, Michael
2	Autopsy, The	NEB-N 80	SHEA, Michael
1	Autumn Angels	NEB-N 75	COVER, Arthur B
4	Autumn Land, The	LOC-N 72	SIMAK, Clifford
4	Autumn Land, The	HUG-N 72	SIMAK, Clifford D
4	Axiomatic	BSF-N 91	EGAN, Greg
4	Aye, and Gomorrah	NEB-W 67	DELANY, Samuel R
4	Aye, and Gomorrah	HUG-N 68	DELANY, Samuel R
3	Aymara	SFC-W 87	SHEPARD, Lucius
3	Aymara	NEB-N 86	SHEPARD, Lucius
2	Aztecs	NEB-N 77	McINTYRE, Vonda N
2	Aztecs	LOC-N 78	McINTYRE, Vonda N
2	Aztecs	HUG-N 78	McINTYRE, Vonda N
1	A.K.A.: A Cosmic Tale	BSF-N 80	SWIGART, Rob
1	Babel-17	HUG-N 67	DELANY, Samuel R
1	Babel-17	NEB-W 66	DELANY, Samuel R
1	Babel-17	HUG-N 66	DELANY, Samuel R
4	Baby, You Were Great	NEB-N 67	WILHELM, Kate
4	Back to the Stone Age	NEB-N 76	SAUNDERS, Jake
4	Back Windows	STO-N 91	TEM, Steve Rasnic
3	Bad Medicine	NEB-N 84	DANN, Jack
4	Bad Medicine	WFA-N 85	DANN, Jack
4	Bad Timing	BSF-W 92	BROWN, Molly
4	Bagful of Dreams	WFA-N 78	VANCE, Jack
7	Bakery Men Don't See Cookbook, The	HUG-N 92	GOMOLL, et al
4	Balance Ecology	NEB-N 65	SCHMITZ, James

CAT	T I T L E S	AW W/N Y	A U T H O R
2	Ballad of Beta-2	NEB-N 65	DELANY, Samuel R
2	Ballad of the Flexible Bullet, The	WFA-N 85	KING, Stephen
2	Ballad of the Flexible Bullet, The	LOC-N 85	KING, Stephen
3	Barbarian Princess, The	HUG-N 87	VINGE, Vernor
3	Barbie Murders, The	HUG-N 79	VARLEY, John
5	Barbie Murders, The	LOC-W 81	VARLEY, John
3	Barbie Murders, The	LOC-W 79	VARLEY, John
7	Bare Bones:Convers'ns on Terror w/S King	LOC-N 89	UNDERWOOD, Tim
7	Barlowe's Guide to Extraterrestials	HUG-N 80	BARLOWE, Wayne D
1	Barrayar	NEB-N 92	BUJOLD, Lois McMaster
1	Barrayar	HUG-N 92	BUJOLD, Lois McMaster
1	Barrayar	LOC-W 92	BUJOLD, Lois McMaster
1	Barrayar	SFC-N 92	BUJOLD, Lois McMaster
2	Barrens, The	WFA-N 91	WILSON, F Paul
2	Barrow Troll, The	WFA-N 76	DRAKE, David
3	Basilisk	HUG-N 73	ELLISON, Harlan
4	Basilisk	LOC-W 73	ELLISON, Harlan
3	Basilisk	NEB-N 72	ELLISON, Harlan
7	Battle of Brasil, The	HUG-N 88	MATHEWS, Jack
2	Battle of the Abaco Reefs, The	NEB-N 79	SCHENCK, Hilbert
2	Battle of the Abaco Reefs, The	LOC-N 80	SCHENCK, Hilbert
2	Battle of the Abaco Reefs, The	HUG-N 80	SCHENCK, Hilbert
4	Bear With the Knot on His Tail, The	HUG-N 72	TALL, Stephen
4	Bears Discover Fire	DAV-W 91	BISSON, Terry
4	Bears Discover Fire	NEB-N 91	BISSON, Terry
4	Bears Discover Fire	JWC-N 91	BISSON, Terry
4	Bears Discover Fire	HUG-W 91	BISSON, Terry
4	Bears Discover Fire	LOC-W 91	BISSON, Terry
4	Bears Discover Fire	WFA-N 91	BISSON, Terry
4	Bears Discover Fire	SFC-N 91	BISSON, Terry
4	Beast t/Shouted Love a/t/Heart o/t/World	HUG-W 69	ELLISON, Harlan
2	Beastchild	HUG-N 71	KOONTZ, Dean R
4	Beastchild	LOC-N 71	KOONTZ, Dean
3	Beatnik Bayou	HUG-N 81	VARLEY, John
3	Beatnik Bayou	NEB-N 80	WALDROP, Howard
3	Beatnik Bayou	LOC-N 81	VARLEY, John
2	Beautiful Uncut Hair of Graves	STO-W 92	MORRELL, David
11	Beauty	LOC-W 92	TEPPER, Sherri S
4	Becalmed in Hell	NEB-N 65	NIVEN, Larry
1	Becoming Alien	DIC-N 89	ORE, Rebecca Brown
4	Before I Wake	NEB-N 91	ROBINSON, Kim Stanley
14	Before the Golden Age	LOC-W 75	ASIMOV, Isaac
2	Beggars in Spain	LOC-N 92	KRESS, Nancy
2	Beggars in Spain	SFC-N 92	KRESS, Nancy
2	Beggars in Spain	HUG-W 92	KRESS, Nancy
2	Beggars in Spain	NEB-W 92	KRESS, Nancy
2	Behold the Man	NEB-W 67	MOORCOCK, Michael
1	Being Alien	DIC-N 90	ORE, Rebecca
2	Being There	NEB-N 71	KOSINSKI, Jerry
2	Belsen Express	WFA-N 76	LEIBER, Fritz
7	Benchmarks: Galaxy Bookshelf	HUG-N 86	BUDRYS, Algis
7	Benchmarks: Galaxy Bookshelf	LOC-W 86	BUDRYS, Algis

CAT	TITLES	AW W/N Y	AUTHOR
1	Benefits	DIC-N 84	FAIRBAIRNS, Zoe
2	Best Friends	WFA-N 88	McCAMMON, Robert R
14	Best From F&SF: 25th Anniversary	LOC-N 75	FERMAN, Ed
5	Best From Orbit 1-10	LOC-N 76	KNIGHT, Damon
6	Best New Horror	WFA-W 91	JONES, Stephen
6	Best New Horror	BFA-W 92	JONES, Stephen
6	Best of Cordwainer Smith, The	LOC-N 76	SMITH, Cordwainer
5	Best of Damon Knight, The	LOC-N 77	KNIGHT, Damon
6	Best of Henry Kuttner, The	LOC-N 76	KUTTNER, Henry
5	Best of James H. Schmitz, The	LOC-N 92	SCHMITZ, James H
6	Best of New Dimensions	LOC-N 80	SILVERBERG, Robert
14	Best Science Fiction of the Year # 2	LOC-W 74	CARR, Terry
14	Best Science Fiction of the Year # 3	LOC-N 75	CARR, Terry
5	Best Science Fiction of the Year # 4	LOC-N 76	CARR, Terry
14	Best Science Fiction of the Year # 5	LOC-W 77	CARR, Terry
6	Best Science Fiction of the Year # 7	LOC-W 79	CARR, Terry
6	Best Science Fiction of the Year # 8	LOC-N 80	CARR, Terry
6	Best Science Fiction of the Year # 9	LOC-N 81	CARR, Terry
6	Best Science Fiction of the Year #10	LOC-N 82	CARR, Terry
6	Best Science Fiction of the Year #11	LOC-W 83	CARR, Terry
6	Best Science Fiction of the Year #12	LOC-W 84	CARR, Terry
6	Best Science Fiction of the Year #13	LOC-N 85	CARR, Terry
6	Best Science Fiction of the Year #14	LOC-N 86	CARR, Terry
6	Best Science Fiction of the Year #15	LOC-N 87	CARR, Terry
14	Best Science Fiction of the Year: 1972	LOC-W 73	CARR, Terry
6	Best SF and Fantasy of the Year #16	LOC-N 88	CARR, Terry
2	Bestseller	STO-N 91	BLUMLEIN, Michael
4	Better Boy	WFA-N 92	BLAYLOCK, James P
4	Better Mousehold, A	NEB-N 65	PANGBORN, Edgar
4	Better Than Ever	NEB-N 65	KIRS, Alex
2	Beyond All Measure	WFA-W 83	WAGNER, Karl Edward
1	Beyond Apollo	JWC-W 73	MALZBERG, Barry N
9	Beyond Rejection	LOC-N 81	LEIBER, Fritz
1	Beyond The Blue Event Horizon	LOC-N 81	POHL, Frederik
1	Beyond the Blue Event Horizon	NEB-N 80	POHL, Frederik
1	Beyond the Blue Event Horizon	HUG-N 81	POHL, Frederik
1	Beyond the Blue Event Horizon	BSF-N 81	POHL, Frederik
4	Beyond the Dead Reef	LOC-W 84	TIPTREE, James Jr
4	Bible Stories For Adults #17 The Deluge	NEB-W 88	MORROW, James
3	Bicentennial Man, The	LOC-W 77	ASIMOV, Isaac
5	Bicentennial Man, The	LOC-N 77	ASIMOV, Isaac
3	Bicentennial Man, The	HUG-W 77	ASIMOV, Isaac
3	Bicentennial Man, The	NEB-W 76	ASIMOV, Isaac
1	Bid Time Return	WFA-W 76	MATHESON, Richard
3	Big Flash, The	NEB-N 69	SPINRAD, Norman
3	Big Front Yard, The	HUG-W 59	SIMAK, Clifford D
4	Big Spell, The	BFA-N 79	REAVES, Michael
1	Big Time, The	HUG-W 58	LEIBER, Fritz
7	Billion Year Spree	BSF-W 74	ALDISS, Brian W
7	Bio of an Ogre:Autobiog of Piers Anthony	LOC-N 89	ANTHONY, Piers
7	Biog Dictionary of SF & Fantasy Artists	HUG-N 89	WEINBERG, Robert
1	Birth of t/People's Republ of Antarctica	JWC-N 84	BATCHELOR, John C

SECTION C: TITLES (Alphabetically)

CAT	TITLES	AW W/N Y	AUTHOR
1	Birthgrave, The	NEB-N 75	LEE, Tanith
2	Black Air	WFA-W 84	ROBINSON, Kim Stanley
3	Black Air	SFC-W 84	ROBINSON, Kim Stanley
3	Black Air	NEB-N 83	ROBINSON, Kim Stanley
3	Black Air	HUG-N 84	ROBINSON, Kim Stanley
3	Black Air	LOC-N 84	ROBINSON, Kim Stanley
1	Black Castle, The	WFA-N 79	DANIELS, Lee
2	Black Cocktail	WFA-N 91	CARROLL, Jonathan
1	Black Easter	NEB-N 68	BLISH, James
1	Black Genesis	HUG-N 87	HUBBARD, L Ron
3	Black Glass	NEB-N 92	FOWLER, Karen Joy
3	Black Glass	LOC-N 92	FOWLER, Karen Joy
9	Black Snow Days	LOC-N 91	O'KEEFE, Claudia
6	Black Venus	WFA-N 86	CARTER, Angela
1	Black Wind	STO-N 89	WILSON, F Paul
6	Black Wine	WFA-N 87	WINTER, Douglas E
9	Blackcollar, The	LOC-N 84	ZAHN, Timothy
3	Bleeding Man, The	NEB-N 75	STRETE, Craig
2	Blind Geometer, The	SFC-N 88	ROBINSON, Kim Stanley
2	Blind Geometer, The	HUG-N 88	ROBINSON, Kim Stanley
2	Blind Geometer, The	LOC-N 88	ROBINSON, Kim Stanley
3	Blind Shemmy	SFC-N 84	DANN, Jack
3	Blind Shemmy	NEB-N 83	DANN, Jack
1	Blind Voices	BSF-N 80	REAMY, Tom
1	Blind Voices	LOC-N 79	REAMY, Tom
1	Blind Voices	NEB-N 78	REAMY, Tom
1	Blind Voices	HUG-N 79	REAMY, Tom
2	Blister, The	LOC-N 85	POHL, Frederik
6	Blood and Water and Other Tales	STO-N 89	McGRATH, Patrick
6	Blood is Not Enough	LOC-N 90	DATLOW, Ellen
6	Blood is Not Enough	WFA-N 90	DATLOW, Ellen
5	Blood Kiss, The	WFA-N 89	ETCHISON, Dennis
6	Blood Kiss, The	STO-N 89	ETCHISON, Dennis
3	Blood Music	SFC-N 84	BEAR, Greg
1	Blood Music	HUG-N 86	BEAR, Greg
1	Blood Music	NEB-N 85	BEAR, Greg
3	Blood Music	NEB-W 83	BEAR, Greg
3	Blood Music	HUG-W 84	BEAR, Greg
1	Blood Music	BSF-N 87	BEAR, Greg
3	Blood Music	LOC-N 84	BEAR, Greg
1	Blood Music	JWC-N 86	BEAR, Greg
11	Blood of Amber	LOC-N 87	ZELAZNY, Roger
9	Blood of the Children	STO-N 91	RODGERS, Alan
10	Blood Price	LOC-N 92	HUFF, Tanya
3	Bloodchild	HUG-W 85	BUTLER, Octavia E
3	Bloodchild	SFC-W 85	BUTLER, Octavia E
3	Bloodchild	NEB-W 84	BUTLER, Octavia E
3	Bloodchild	LOC-W 85	BUTLER, Octavia E
3	Blooded on Arachne	NEB-N 75	BISHOP, Michael
4	Blue Butter	JUP-N 75	STURGEON, Theodore
2	Blue Champagne	LOC-W 82	VARLEY, John
5	Blue Champagne	LOC-W 87	VARLEY, John
2	Blue Champagne	HUG-N 82	VARLEY, John

SECTION C: TITLES (Alphabetically)

CAT	TITLES	AW W/N Y	AUTHOR
5	Blue World and Other Stories	WFA-N 90	McCAMMON, Robert R
6	Blue World and Other Stories	STO-N 90	McCAMMON, Robert R
3	Blued Moon	LOC-N 85	WILLIS, Connie
3	Blued Moon	HUG-N 85	WILLIS, Connie
1	Boat of a Million Years	SFC-N 90	ANDERSON, Poul
1	Boat of a Million Years	NEB-N 89	ANDERSON, Poul
1	Boat of a Million Years	HUG-N 90	ANDERSON, Poul
1	Boat of a Million Years	LOC-N 90	ANDERSON, Poul
4	Bodies and Heads	STO-N 90	TEM, Steve Rasnic
1	Bone Dance	DIC-N 92	BULL, Emma
1	Bone Dance	NEB-N 92	BULL, Emma
1	Bone Dance	LOC-N 92	BULL, Emma
1	Bone Dance	HUG-N 92	BULL, Emma
1	Bone Dance	WFA-N 92	BULL, Emma
4	Bone Flute, The	NEB-W 81	TUTTLE, Lisa
5	Bone Forest, The	WFA-N 92	HOLDSTOCK, Robert
2	Bones	LOC-N 91	MURPHY, Pat
2	Bones	WFA-W 91	MURPHY, Pat
2	Bones	HUG-N 91	MURPHY, Pat
2	Bones	NEB-N 91	MURPHY, Pat
1	Bones of the Moon	BFA-N 88	CARROLL, Jonathan
4	Bones Wizard, The	WFA-W 85	RYAN, Alan
4	Boo Hoo Forest	BFA-N 91	PAVEY, Jack
4	Boobs	HUG-W 90	CHARNAS, Suzy McKee
4	Boobs	SFC-N 90	CHARNAS, Suzy McKee
4	Boobs	NEB-N 89	CHARNAS, Suzy McKee
4	Boobs	LOC-N 90	CHARNAS, Suzy McKee
11	Book of Kells, The	LOC-N 86	MacAVOY, R A
1	Book of Skulls, The	LOC-N 73	SILVERBERG, Robert
1	Book of Skulls, The	NEB-N 72	SILVERBERG, Robert
1	Book of Skulls, The	HUG-N 73	SILVERBERG, Robert
6	Book of the Dead	WFA-N 90	SKIPP, John
3	Borderland of Sol, The	HUG-W 76	NIVEN, Larry
2	Borderland of Sol, The	LOC-N 76	NIVEN, Larry
6	Borderlands	WFA-N 91	MONTELEONE, Thomas F
6	Borderlands	BFA-N 91	MONTELEONE, Thomas F
5	Borders of Infinity	LOC-N 90	BUJOLD, Lois McMaster
2	Born of the Winds	WFA-N 76	LUMLEY, Brian
2	Born With the Dead	JUP-N 75	SILVERBERG, Robert
2	Born With the Dead	LOC-W 75	SILVERBERG, Robert
2	Born With the Dead	HUG-N 75	SILVERBERG, Robert
2	Born With the Dead	NEB-W 74	SILVERBERG, Robert
3	Bound For Glory	LOC-N 90	SHEPARD, Lucius
2	Boy and His Dog, A	HUG-N 70	ELLISON, Harlan
2	Boy and His Dog, A	NEB-W 69	ELLISON, Harlan
2	Boy Who Came Back From the Dead, The	WFA-N 88	RODGERS, Alan
3	Boy Who Came Back From the Grave, The	STO-W 88	RODGERS, Alan
4	Boy Who Plaited Manes, The	HUG-N 87	SPRINGER, Nancy
4	Boy Who Plaited Manes, The	NEB-N 86	SPRINGER, Nancy
4	Boy Who Plaited Manes, The	LOC-N 87	SPRINGER, Nancy
4	Boy Who Plaited Manes, The	WFA-N 87	SPRINGER, Nancy
4	Boy Who Waterskied Forever, The	HUG-N 83	TIPTREE, James Jr
4	Boy Who Waterskied Forever, The	LOC-N 83	TIPTREE, James Jr

SECTION C: TITLES (Alphabetically)

CAT	TITLES	AW W/N Y	AUTHOR
1	Boy's Life	STO-W 92	McCAMMON, Robert R
1	Boy's Life	WFA-W 92	McCAMMON, Robert R
4	Braile Encyclopedia, The	STO-N 92	MORRISON, Grant
1	Brain Twister	HUG-N 60	PHILLIPS, Mark
2	Brainchild	HUG-N 83	DELANEY, Joseph H
6	Brains of Rats, The	STO-N 91	BLUMLEIN, Michael
4	Brains of Rats, The	WFA-N 87	BLUMLEIN, Michael
5	Brains of Rats, The	WFA-N 91	BLUMLEIN, Michael
2	Brave Little Toaster, The	NEB-N 80	DISCH, Thomas M
4	Brave Little Toaster, The	BSF-W 81	DISCH, Thomas M
2	Brave Little Toaster, The	HUG-N 81	DISCH, Thomas M
3	Brave Little Toaster, The	LOC-W 81	DISCH, Thomas M
3	Braver Thing, A	SFC-N 91	SHEFFIELD, Charles
3	Braver Thing, A	LOC-N 91	SHEFFIELD, Charles
3	Braver Thing, A	HUG-N 91	SHEFFIELD, Charles
4	Breaking Ball	AUR-W 92	SKEET, Michael
9	Breaking of Northwall, The	LOC-N 82	WILLIAMS, Paul O
4	Breathing Method, The	BFA-W 83	KING, Stephen
2	Breathing Method, The	WFA-N 83	KING, Stephen
1	Bridge of Birds	WFA-W 85	HUGHART, Barry
1	Bridge of Years	DIC-N 92	WILSON, Robert Charles
4	Bright Burning Tiger	LOC-N 85	LEE, Tanith
4	Brillo	HUG-N 71	BOVA, Ben
1	Brontomek?	BSF-W 77	CONEY, Michael G
3	Brother to Dragons, A	HUG-N 75	WILHELM, Kate
4	Brothers	SFC-N 84	COWPER, Richard
1	Buddy Holly is Alive & Well On Ganymede	JWC-W 92	DENTON, Bradley
4	Buffalo	JWC-N 92	KESSEL, John
4	Buffalo	NEB-N 92	KESSEL, John
4	Buffalo	LOC-W 92	KESSEL, John
4	Buffalo	HUG-N 92	KESSEL, John
2	Buffalo Gals, Won't You Come Out Tonight	WFA-W 88	LeGUIN, Ursula K
3	Buffalo Gals, Won't You Come Out Tonight	HUG-W 88	LeGUIN, Ursula K
3	Buffalo Gals, Won't You Come Out Tonight	LOC-N 88	LeGUIN, Ursula K
4	Buffalo Gals, Won't You Come Out Tonight	JWC-N 88	LeGUIN, Ursula K
3	Buffalo Gals, Won't You Come Out Tonight	NEB-N 87	LeGUIN, Ursula K
4	Bug House	LOC-N 81	TUTTLE, Lisa
1	Bug Jack Barrow	HUG-N 70	SPINRAD, Norman
1	Bug Jack Barrow	NEB-N 69	SPINRAD, Norman
2	Bully!	HUG-N 91	RESNICK, Mike
2	Bully!	NEB-N 91	RESNICK, Mike
2	Bully!	LOC-N 91	RESNICK, Mike
2	Bully!	SFC-N 91	RESNICK, Mike
2	Bully!	NEB-N 92	RESNICK, Mike
3	Burning Chrome	NEB-N 82	GIBSON, William
5	Burning Chrome	LOC-N 87	GIBSON, William
3	Burning Chrome	SFC-N 83	GIBSON, William
7	Bury My Heart at W.H. Smiths	HUG-N 91	ALDISS, Brian
7	Bury My Heart at W.H. Smiths	LOC-N 91	ALDISS, Brian
4	But You'll Never Follow Me	STO-N 91	WAGNER, Karl Edward
1	Butterfly Kid, The	HUG-N 68	ANDERSON, Chester
4	Button and What You Know, The	NEB-N 92	STEWART, W Gregory

SECTION C: TITLES (Alphabetically)

CAT	TITLES	AW W/N Y	AUTHOR
4	Button Molder, The	BFA-W 80	LEIBER, Fritz
4	Button Molder, The	WFA-N 80	LEIBER, Fritz
2	By Any Other Name	HUG-W 77	ROBINSON, Spider
6	By Bizarre Hands	STO-N 90	LANSDALE, Joe R
5	By Bizarre Hands	WFA-N 90	LANSDALE, Joe R
4	By the Falls	NEB-N 70	HARRISON, Harry
1	Byworlder	NEB-N 71	ANDERSON, Poul
5	Cabal	WFA-N 89	BARKER, CLive
4	Cabin 33	WFA-N 81	YARBRO, Chelsea Quinn
4	Cabin on the Coast, A	LOC-N 85	WOLFE, Gene
4	Cabin on the Coast, A	NEB-N 84	WOLFE, Gene
4	Cage for Death, A	BSF-N 82	WATSON, Ian
3	Call Him Lord	HUG-N 67	DICKSON, Gordon R
3	Call Him Lord	NEB-W 66	SPENCER, W
4	Calling, The	STO-W 91	SILVA, David
4	Calling All Gumdrops	BSF-N 84	SLADEK, John
4	Calling Dr. Clockwork	NEB-N 65	GOULART, Ron
2	Calvin Coolidge Home for Dead Comedians	NEB-N 88	DENTON, Bradley
2	Calvin Coolidge Home for Dead Comedians	HUG-N 89	DENTON, Bradley
4	Camera Obscura	NEB-N 77	MONTELEONE, Thomas F
1	Camp Concentration	DIT-W 69	DISCH, Thomas M
4	Camps	BSF-N 80	DANN, Jack
3	Camps	NEB-N 79	DANN, Jack
4	Can These Bones Live?	HUG-N 80	REYNOLDS, Ted
1	Canticle for Leibowitz	HUG-W 61	MILLER, Walter M Jr
11	Captive, The	LOC-N 82	STALLMAN, Robert
3	Captivity	HUG-N 59	HENDERSON, Zenna
4	Carpe Diem	AUR-W 90	KERNAGHAN, Eileen
10	Carrion Comfort	LOC-W 90	SIMMONS, Dan
1	Carrion Comfort	WFA-W 90	SIMMONS, Dan
1	Carrion Comfort	BFA-W 90	SIMMONS, Dan
1	Carrion Comfort	STO-W 90	SIMMONS, Dan
8	Carve the Sky	LOC-N 92	JABLOKOV, Alexander
2	Cascade Point	HUG-W 84	ZAHN, Timothy
2	Cascade Point	LOC-N 84	ZAHN, Timothy
3	Case and the Dreamer	NEB-N 73	STURGEON, Theodore
1	Case of Conscience, A	HUG-W 59	BLISH, James
4	Cassandra	NEB-N 78	CHERRYH, C J
4	Cassandra	HUG-W 79	CHERRYH, C J
4	Cassandra's Photographs	HUG-N 88	GOLDSTEIN, Lisa
4	Cassandra's Photographs	NEB-N 87	GOLDSTEIN, Lisa
11	Castle Roogna	LOC-N 80	ANTHONY, Piers
4	Cat and Mouse	HUG-N 60	WILLIAMS, Ralph
1	Cat Karina	BSF-N 84	CONEY, Michael
1	Cat Who Walks Through Walls, The	LOC-N 86	HEINLEIN, Robert A
4	Catch That Zeppelin	HUG-W 76	LEIBER, Fritz
4	Catch That Zeppelin	NEB-W 75	LEIBER, Fritz
4	Cathadonian Odyssey	HUG-W 75	BISHOP, Michael
9	Cats Have No Lord	LOC-N 86	SHETTERLY, Will
1	Cat's Cradle	HUG-N 64	VONNEGUT, Kurt Jr
1	Ceremonies, The	WFA-N 85	KLEIN, T E D
1	Ceremonies, The	BFA-W 85	KLEIN, T E D

SECTION C: TITLES (Alphabetically)

CAT	TITLES	AW W/N Y	AUTHOR
2	Chains of the Sea	JUP-N 74	DOZOIS, Gardner
2	Chains of the Sea	NEB-N 73	DOZOIS, Gardner
2	Chains of the Sea	HUG-N 74	DOZOIS, Gardner
2	Chains of the Sea	LOC-N 74	DOZOIS, Gardner
2	Chance	WFA-N 87	WILLIS, Connie
11	Changeling	LOC-N 81	ZELAZNY, Roger
4	Changer of Names, The	BFA-N 79	CAMPBELL, Ramsey
11	Changing Land, The	LOC-N 82	ZELAZNY, Roger
1	Chanur's Homecoming	LOC-N 87	CHERRYH, C J
1	Chanur's Venture	LOC-N 85	CHERRYH, C J
6	Charles Beaumont: Selected Stories	STO-W 89	BEAUMONT, Charles
5	Charles Beaumont: Selected Stories	WFA-N 89	ANKER, Roger
4	Checkout, The	BSF-N 82	ROBERTS, Keith
1	Child Across the Sky, A	WFA-N 90	CARROLL, Jonathan
1	Child Across the Sky, A	CLA-N 90	CARROLL, Jonathan
1	Child Garden, The	JWC-W 90	RYMAN, Geoff
4	Child of All Ages	NEB-N 75	PLAUGER, P J
4	Child of All Ages	LOC-N 76	PLAUGER, P J
4	Child of All Ages	HUG-N 76	PLAUGER, P J
1	Children of Dune	LOC-N 77	HERBERT, Frank
1	Children of Dune	HUG-N 77	HERBERT, Frank
1	Children of the Garden	CLA-W 90	RYMAN, Geoff
4	Children of the Kingdom	WFA-N 81	KLEIN, T E D
1	Choice of Gods, A	LOC-N 73	SIMAK, Clifford
1	Choice of Gods, A	HUG-N 73	SIMAK, Clifford D
4	Christmas Without Rodney	DAV-N 89	ASIMOV, Isaac
1	Chronicles o/Thomas Covenant t/Unbeleive	WFA-N 78	DONALDSON, Stephen R
1	Chronicles o/Thomas Covenant t/Unbeleive	BFA-W 79	DONALDSON, Stephen R
11	Chronicles o/Thomas Covenant t/Unbeleive	LOC-N 78	DONALDSON, Stephen R
6	Chrysalis 3	LOC-N 80	TORGESON, Roy
1	Chton	HUG-N 68	ANTHONY, Piers
1	Chton	NEB-N 67	ANTHONY, Piers
4	Cibola	HUG-N 91	WILLIS, Connie
4	Cibola	LOC-N 91	WILLIS, Connie
4	Cibola	SFC-N 91	WILLIS, Connie
3	Cicada Queen	NEB-N 83	STERLING, Bruce
6	Cinnabar	WFA-N 77	BRYANT, Edward
9	Cipher, The	STO-W 92	KOJA, Kathe
1	Cipher, The	DIC-N 92	KOJA, Kathe
8	Cipher, The	LOC-W 92	KOJA, Kathe
4	Circular Library of Stones	SFC-W 88	EMSHWILLER, Carol
4	Circus Horse, The	DAV-W 89	BECHTEL, Amy
1	Cirque	NEB-N 77	CARR, Terry
1	Citadel of the Autarch, The	SFC-N 84	WOLFE, Gene
11	Citadel of the Autarch, The	LOC-N 83	WOLFE, Gene
1	Citadel of the Autarch, The	BSF-N 84	WOLFE, Gene
1	Citadel of the Autarch, The	JWC-W 84	WOLFE, Gene
1	Citadel of the Autarch, The	NEB-N 83	WOLFE, Gene
9	Cities of the Dead	STO-N 89	PAINE, Michael
1	City	IFA-W 53	SIMAK, Clifford D
3	City on the Sand, The	HUG-N 74	EFFINGER, George Alec
13	Clarion 1	LOC-N 72	WILSON, Robin Scott
1	Clarke County, Space	DIC-N 91	STEELE, Alan
2	Clash of Star Kings	NEB-N 66	DAVIDSON, Avram

CAT	TITLES	AW W/N Y	AUTHOR
1	Claw of the Conciliator, The	HUG-N 82	WOLFE, Gene
1	Claw of the Conciliator, The	WFA-N 82	WOLFE, Gene
1	Claw of the Conciliator, The	NEB-W 81	WOLFE, Gene
11	Claw of the Conciliator, The	LOC-W 82	WOLFE, Gene
1	Claw of the Conciliator, The	SFC-W 82	WOLFE, Gene
6	Clive Barker's Books of Blood, Vols 1-3	WFA-W 85	BARKER, Clive
6	Clive Barker's Books of Blood, Vols 4-6	WFA-N 86	BARKER, Clive
5	Clive Barker's Books of Blood, Vols 4-6	LOC-N 86	BARKER, Clive
7	Clive Barker's Shadows in Eden	LOC-N 92	JONES, Stephen
7	Clive Barker's Shadows in Eden	STO-W 92	JONES, Stephen
7	Clive Barker's Shawows in Eden	HUG-N 92	JONES, Stephen
3	Cloak and the Staff, The	HUG-W 81	DICKSON, Gordon R
1	Clone, The	NEB-W 65	THOMAS, Theodore L
4	Code Three	HUG-N 64	RAPHAEL, Rick
4	Coin of the Realm	WFA-N 82	GRANT, Charles L
4	Coin of the Realm	BFA-N 82	GRANT, Charles L
6	Cold Chills	WFA-N 78	BLOCH, Robert
4	Cold Hands	HUG-N 81	DUNTEMANN, Jeff
4	Cold Night Dark With Snow, A	NEB-N 70	WILHELM, Kate
5	Collected Stories of Philip K Dick, The	LOC-N 88	DICK, Philip K
2	Collision	LOC-N 87	TIPTREE, James Jr
1	Colony	LOC-W 79	BOVA, Ben
2	Color of Neanderthal Eyes, The	LOC-N 89	TIPTREE, James Jr
4	Color Winter, The	NEB-N 88	POPKES, Steven
4	Come to Venus Melancholy	NEB-N 65	DISCH, Thomas M
4	Comes Now the Power	HUG-N 67	ZELAZNY, Roger
2	Companion, The	WFA-N 77	CAMPBELL, Ramsey
1	Company of Glory, The	JUP-N 75	PANGBORN, Edgar
1	Compass Rose, The	DIT-W 86	LeGUIN, Ursula K
5	Compass Rose, The	LOC-W 83	LeGUIN, Ursula K
1	Computer Connection, The	NEB-N 75	BESTER, Alfred
1	Computer Connection, The	HUG-N 76	BESTER, Alfred
1	Computer Connection, The	LOC-N 76	BESTER, Alfred
4	Computer Friendly	HUG-N 90	GUNN, Eileen
4	Computers Don't Argue	NEB-N 65	DICKSON, Gordon R
2	Confess the Seasons	WFA-W 83	GRANT, Charles L
2	Confession of St James, The	STO-N 90	WILLIAMSON, Chet
4	Conjure Man, The	WFA-N 92	DeLINT, Charles
7	Conquest of Space	IFA-W 51	LEY, Willy
4	Construction Shack	HUG-N 74	SIMAK, Clifford D
9	Contact	LOC-W 86	SAGAN, Carl
4	Continued on Next Rock	LOC-N 71	LAFFERTY, R A
3	Continued on Next Rock	NEB-N 70	LAFFERTY, R A
4	Continued on Next Rock	HUG-N 71	LAFFERTY, R A
5	Convergent Series	LOC-W 80	NIVEN, Larry
3	Coon Rolled Down and Ruptured...	NEB-N 91	HUGH, Dafydd ab
3	Coon Rolled Down and Ruptured...	HUG-N 91	HUGH, Dafydd ab
3	Coon Rolled Down and Ruptured...	LOC-N 91	HUGH, Dafydd ab
4	Corridors	NEB-N 82	MALZBERG, Barry N
7	Cosmic Connection, The	JWC-W 74	SAGAN, Carl
1	Cosmicomics	DIT-W 70	CALVINO, Italo
7	Cosmos	LOC-N 81	SAGAN, Carl
7	Cosmos	HUG-W 81	SAGAN, Carl

CAT	T I T L E S	AW W/N Y	A U T H O R
1	Count of Eleven, The	BFA-N 91	CAMPBELL, Ramsey
4	Count the Clock That Tells the Time	HUG-N 79	ELLISON, Harlan
4	Count the Clock That Tells the Time	LOC-W 79	ELLISON, Harlan
1	Count Zero	HUG-N 87	GIBSON, William
1	Count Zero	BSF-N 87	GIBSON, William
1	Count Zero	SFC-N 87	GIBSON, William
1	Count Zero	LOC-N 87	GIBSON, William
1	Count Zero	NEB-N 86	GIBSON, William
1	Courtship Rite	HUG-N 83	KINGSBURY, Donald
1	Courtship Rite	COM-W 83	KINGSBURY, Donald
1	Courtship Rite	HUG-N 83	KINGSBURY, Donald
1	Courtship Rite	LOC-N 83	KINGSBURY, Donald
9	Courtship Rite	LOC-W 83	KINGSBURY, Donald
4	Creation of Bennie Good, The	NEB-N 70	SALLIS, James
4	Croatoan	LOC-W 76	ELLISON, Harlan
4	Croatoan	HUG-N 76	ELLISON, Harlan
4	Crossing Into Cambodia	BSF-N 80	MOORCOCK, Michael
9	Crosstime Engineer, The	LOC-N 87	FRANKOWSKI, Leo
1	Crosstime Engineer, The	COM-N 87	FRANKOWSKI, Leo
4	Crouch End	BFA-N 81	KING, Stephen
4	Crowd of Shadows, A	HUG-N 77	GRANT, Charles L
4	Crowd of Shadows, A	LOC-N 77	GRANT, Charles L
4	Crowd of Shadows, A	NEB-W 76	GRANT, Charles L
5	Crown of Stars	LOC-N 89	TIPTREE, James Jr
4	Cryptic	NEB-N 83	McDEVITT, Jack
5	Crystal Express	LOC-N 90	STERLING, Bruce
4	Crystal Spheres, The	LOC-N 85	BRIN, David
4	Crystal Spheres, The	HUG-W 85	BRIN, David
4	Cube Root	BSF-W 86	LANGFORD, Dave
1	Cuckoo's Egg	HUG-N 86	CHERRYH, C J
1	Cujo	BFA-W 82	KING, Stephen
7	Culture Made Stupid	LOC-N 88	WELLER, Tom
3	Custer's Last Jump	NEB-N 76	UTLEY, Steven
2	Custodians, The	HUG-N 76	COWPER, Richard
3	Custodians, The	NEB-N 75	COWPER, Richard
2	Custodians, The	LOC-N 76	COWPER, Richard
4	Custom Fitting	HUG-N 77	WHITE, James
4	Custom Fitting	LOC-N 77	WHITE, James
6	Cutting Edge	WFA-N 87	ETCHISON, Dennis
4	Cyclops	NEB-N 65	LEIBER, Fritz
2	Cyclops	HUG-N 85	BRIN, David
1	Cyteen	SFC-W 89	CHERRYH, C J
1	Cyteen	LOC-W 89	CHERRYH, C J
1	Cyteen	HUG-W 89	CHERRYH, C J
4	Daisy, in the Sun	HUG-N 80	WILLIS, Connie
11	Damiano's Lute	LOC-N 85	MacAVOY, R A
2	Damnation Alley	HUG-N 68	ZELAZNY, Roger
9	Damnation Game, The	STO-N 88	BARKER, Clive
1	Damnation Game, The	WFA-N 86	BARKER, Clive
4	Dance of the Changer and the Three, The	NEB-N 68	CARR, Terry
4	Dance of the Changer and the Three, The	HUG-N 69	CARR, Terry
1	Dancers of Arun, The	WFA-N 80	LYNN, Elizabeth A
7	Dancing at the Edge of the World	HUG-N 90	LeGUIN, Ursula K
7	Dancing at the Edge of the World	LOC-N 90	LeGUIN, Ursula K

SECTION C: TITLES (Alphabetically)

CAT	TITLES	AW W/N Y	AUTHOR
2	Dangerous Games	LOC-N 81	RANDALL, Marta
2	Dangerous Games	NEB-N 80	RANDALL, Marta
7	Danse Macabre	LOC-W 82	KING, Stephen
7	Danse Macabre	HUG-W 82	KING, Stephen
2	Dare I Eat A Peach	WFA-N 86	YARBRO, Chelsea Quinn
3	Darfsteller, The	HUG-W 55	MILLER, Walter M Jr
4	Dark, The	NEB-N 92	FOWLER, Daren Joy
1	Dark Bright Water, The	WFA-N 80	WRIGHTSON, Patricia
4	Dark Country, The	WFA-W 82	ETCHISON, Dennis
4	Dark Country, The	BFA-W 82	ETCHISON, Dennis
1	Dark Crusade	WFA-N 77	WAGNER, Karl Edward
6	Dark Descent, The	WFA-N 88	HARTWELL, David G
6	Dark Descent, The	LOC-N 88	HARTWELL, David G
7	Dark Dreamers	STO-W 91	WIATER, Stanley
9	Dark Father	STO-N 91	PICCIRILLI, Tom
6	Dark Forces	LOC-N 81	McCAULEY, Kirby
6	Dark Forces	WFA-W 81	McCAULEY, Kirby
10	Dark Half, The	LOC-N 90	KING, Stephen
7	Dark Knight Returns, The	HUG-N 87	MILLER, Frank
4	Dark Land, The	BFA-W 91	SMITH, Michael Marshall
1	Dark Seeker	DIC-N 88	JETER, K W
1	Dark Towers III, The: The Waste Lands	STO-N 92	KING, Stephen
10	Dark Towers III, The: The Waste Lands	LOC-N 92	KING, Stephen
1	Dark Universe	HUG-N 62	GALOUYE, Daniel F
6	Dark Voices	BFA-N 91	SUTTON, David
6	Dark Voices 2	WFA-N 91	SUTTON, David
2	Dark Wings	WFA-N 77	LEIBER, Fritz
6	Darklands	BFA-W 91	BOYLE, Nicholson
4	Daughter Earth	LOC-N 92	MORROW, James
1	Davy	NEB-N 64	PANGBORN, Edgar
1	Davy	HUG-N 65	PANGBORN, Edgar
4	Day Before the Revolution, The	LOC-W 75	LeGUIN, Ursula K
4	Day Before the Revolution, The	NEB-W 74	LeGUIN, Ursula K
4	Day Before the Revolution, The	JUP-W 75	LeGUIN, Ursula K
4	Day Before the Revolution, The	HUG-N 75	LeGUIN, Ursula K
2	Day Beyond Forever, The	NEB-N 68	LAUMER, Keith
1	Day of the Minotaur	HUG-N 67	BURNETT, Thomas
1	Day of the Triffids, The	IFA-N 52	WYNDHAM, John
4	Days of Grass, Days of Straw	JUP-N 74	LAFFERTY, R A
4	Day-Tay-Vao	STO-N 88	WILSON, F Paul
2	Dead Image	WFA-N 86	MORRELL, David
4	Dead Men on TV	NEB-N 88	MURPHY, Pat
11	Dead Zone, The	LOC-N 80	KING, Stephen
3	Dear Aunt Annie	NEB-N 70	EKLUND, Gordon
2	Death and Designation Among the Asadi	NEB-N 73	BISHOP, Michael
2	Death and Designation Among the Asadi	HUG-N 74	BISHOP, Michael
2	Death Leaves an Echo	STO-N 92	DeLINT, Charles
4	Death of Cassandra Quebec, The	BSF-N 91	BROWN, Eric
3	Death of Doctor Island, The	JUP-N 74	WOLFE, Gene
2	Death of Doctor Island, The	HUG-N 74	WOLFE, Gene
2	Death of Doctor Island, The	LOC-W 74	WOLFE, Gene
2	Death of Doctor Island, The	NEB-W 73	WOLFE, Gene
4	Death of Princes, The	LOC-N 77	LEIBER, Fritz

SECTION C: TITLES (Alphabetically)

CAT	T I T L E S	AW W/N Y	A U T H O R
3	Deathbird, The	JUP-W 74	ELLISON, Harlan
4	Deathbird, The	LOC-W 74	ELLISON, Harlan
3	Deathbird, The	NEB-N 73	ELLISON, Harlan
3	Deathbird, The	HUG-W 74	ELLISON, Harlan
5	Deathbird Stories	WFA-N 76	ELLISON, Harlan
6	Deathbird Stories	LOC-N 76	ELLISON, Harlan
4	Deathtracks	WFA-N 83	ETCHISON, Dennis
1	Deathworld	HUG-N 61	HARRISON, Harry
1	Deathworld	HUG-N 60	HARRISON, Harry
4	Death's a Ware That Will Not Keep	NEB-N 76	MONTELEONE, Thomas F
1	Death's Master	BFA-W 80	LEE, Tanith
3	Decision Makers, The	NEB-N 65	GREEN, Joseph
4	Deep End, The	STO-W 88	McCAMMON, Robert R
3	Deeper Than the Darkness	NEB-N 69	BENFORD, Gregory
4	Deeper Than the Darkness	HUG-N 70	BENFORD, Gregory
2	Defenseless Dead, The	LOC-N 74	NIVEN, Larry
9	Deliver Us From Evil	STO-N 89	HARRIS, Alan Lee
4	Delta Sly Honey	LOC-N 88	SHEPARD, Lucius
4	Delusion for a Dragon Slayer	HUG-N 67	ELLISON, Harlan
1	Demolished Man	IFA-N 54	BESTER, Alfred
1	Demolished Man	HUG-W 53	BESTER, Alfred
1	Demon	LOC-N 85	VARLEY, John
9	Demon Night	STO-N 89	STRACZYNSKI, J Michael
2	Desert of Stolen Dreams, The	LOC-N 82	SILVERBERG, Robert
1	Deserted Cities of the Heart	NEB-N 88	SHINER, Louis
3	Deskful of Girls, A	HUG-N 59	LEIBER, Fritz
1	Desolation Road	CLA-N 90	McDONALD, Ian
9	Desolation Road	LOC-W 89	McDONALD, Ian
4	Devil Car	NEB-N 65	ZELAZNY, Roger
1	Devil is Dead, The	NEB-N 71	LAFFERTY, R A
3	Devil You Don't Know	LOC-N 79	ING, Dean
3	Devil You Don't Know	HUG-N 79	ING, Dean
3	Devil You Don't Know	NEB-N 78	ING, Dean
2	Devil's Arithmetic, The	WFA-N 89	YOLEN, Jane
2	Devil's Arithmetic, The	NEB-N 88	YOLEN, Jane
1	Dhalgren	LOC-N 76	DELANY, Samuel R
1	Dhalgren	NEB-N 75	DELANY, Samuel R
3	Diary of the Rose, The	HUG-N 77	LeGUIN, Ursula K
3	Diary of the Rose, The	LOC-N 77	LeGUIN, Ursula K
3	Diary of the Rose, The	JUP-W 77	LeGUIN, Ursula K
3	Diary of the Rose, The	NEB-N 76	LeGUIN, Ursula K
7	DiFate's Catalog of S Fiction Hardware	HUG-N 81	DiFATE, Vincent
1	Difference Engine, The	BSF-N 91	GIBSON, William
1	Difference Engine, The	LOC-N 91	GIBSON, William
1	Difference Engine, The	NEB-N 92	GIBSON, William
1	Difference Engine, The	JWC-N 92	GIBSON, William
5	Different Seasons	LOC-N 83	KING, Stephen
4	Dilemna	LOC-N 90	WILLIS, Connie
5	Dilvish Be Damned	LOC-N 83	ZELAZNY, Roger
3	Dinausaurs	HUG-N 88	WILLIAMS, Walter Jon
1	Dinner at Deviant's Place	NEB-N 85	POWERS, Tim
1	Dinner at Deviant's Place	DIC-W 86	POWERS, Tim

SECTION C: TITLES (Alphabetically)

CAT	T I T L E S	AW W/N Y	A U T H O R
4	Dinner in Audoghast	HUG-N 86	STERLING, Bruce
4	Dinner in Audoghast	LOC-N 86	STERLING, Bruce
4	Dinosaurs	JWC-N 88	WILLIAMS, Walter Jon
4	Direction of the Road	JUP-N 74	LeGUIN, Ursula K
4	Disciples	NEB-N 81	DOZOIS, Gardner
3	Dispatches from the Revolution	HUG-N 92	CADIGAN, Pat
1	Dispossessed, The	JWC-N 75	LeGUIN, Ursula K
1	Dispossessed, The	JUP-W 75	LeGUIN, Ursula K
1	Dispossessed, The	NEB-W 74	LeGUIN, Ursula K
1	Dispossessed, The	HUG-W 75	LeGUIN, Ursula K
1	Dispossessed, The	LOC-W 75	LeGUIN, Ursula K
4	Dissemblers, The	BSF-N 83	KILWORTH, Gary
1	Divine Invasion, The	BSF-N 83	DICK, Philip K
7	Divine Invasions	LOC-N 90	SUTIN, Lawrence
3	Djinn, No Chaser	LOC-W 83	ELLISON, Harlan
1	Do Androids Dream of Electric Sheep?	NEB-N 68	DICK, Philip K
4	Do the Dead Sing?	WFA-W 82	KING, Stephen
4	Do the Dead Sing?	BFA-W 82	KING, Stephen
3	Do Ya, Do Ya, Wanna Dance	HUG-N 89	WALDROP, Howard
3	Do Ya, Do Ya, Wanna Dance	LOC-N 89	WALDROP, Howard
3	Do Ya, Do Ya, Wanna Dance	NEB-N 88	WALDROP, Howard
4	Do Ya, Do Ya, Wanna Dance	JWC-N 89	WALDROP, Howard
3	Do Ya, Do Ya, Wanna Dance	SFC-N 89	WALDROP, Howard
4	Doctor, The	NEB-N 67	THOMAS, Theodore
1	Doctor Bloodmoney	NEB-N 65	DICK, Philip K
1	Doctor Rat	WFA-W 77	KOTZWINKLE, William
6	Dodd, Mead Gallery of Horrors, The	WFA-N 84	GRANT, Charles L
4	Dog Day Evening	HUG-N 78	ROBINSON, Spider
3	Dogfight	NEB-N 85	SWANWICK, Michael
3	Dogfight	LOC-N 86	SWANWICK, Michael
3	Dogfight	SFC-N 86	SWANWICK, Michael
3	Dogfight	HUG-N 86	SWANWICK, Michael
3	Dogwalker	HUG-N 90	CARD, Orson Scott
3	Dogwalker	LOC-W 90	CARD, Orson Scott
4	Dog's Life	NEB-N 92	SOUKUP, Martha
4	Dog's Life	HUG-N 92	SOUKUP, Martha
4	Doing Lennon	LOC-N 76	BENFORD, Gregory
4	Doing Lennon	NEB-N 75	BENFORD, Gregory
4	Doing Lennon	HUG-N 76	BENFORD, Gregory
1	Doll Who Ate His Mother, The	WFA-N 77	CAMPBELL, Ramsey
1	Doomsday Effect, The	COM-W 87	WREN, Thomas
1	Door Into Ocean	JWC-W 87	SLONCZEWSKI, Joan
3	Doors of His Face...	NEB-W 65	ZELAZNY, Roger
1	Doorways in the Sand	NEB-N 75	ZELAZNY, Roger
1	Doorways in the Sand	HUG-N 76	ZELAZNY, Roger
4	Dori Bangs	NEB-N 89	STERLING, Bruce
4	Dori Bangs	LOC-N 90	STERLING, Bruce
4	Dori Bangs	HUG-N 90	STERLING, Bruce
4	Dori Bangs	SFC-W 90	STERLING, Bruce
4	Dori Bangs	JWC-N 90	STERLING, Bruce
1	Double Star	HUG-W 56	HEINLEIN, Robert A
1	Dover Beach	DIC-N 88	BOWKER, Richard

SECTION C: TITLES (Alphabetically)

CAT	TITLES	AW W/N Y	AUTHOR
4	Down and Out in the Year 2000	LOC-N 87	ROBINSON, Kim Stanley
3	Down to a Sunless Sea	LOC-N 76	SMITH, Cordwainer
1	Downbelow Station	HUG-W 82	CHERRYH, C J
1	Downbelow Station	LOC-N 82	CHERRYH, C J
1	Downward to the Earth	LOC-N 71	SILVERBERG, Robert
3	Dowser	LOC-N 89	CARD, Orson Scott
3	Dowser	DAV-W 89	CARD, Orson Scott
2	Dozen Tough Jobs, A	WFA-N 90	WALDROP, Howard
2	Dozen Tough Jobs, A	NEB-N 89	WALDROP, Howard
2	Dozen Tough Jobs, A	LOC-N 90	WALDROP, Howard
1	Dragon and the George, The	WFA-N 77	DICKSON, Gordon R
1	Dragon and the George, The	BFA-W 77	DICKSON, Gordon R
4	Dragon Masters, The	HUG-W 63	VANCE, Jack
1	Dragon Prince	COM-N 89	RAWN, Melanie
9	Dragon Prince	LOC-N 89	RAWN, Melanie
1	Dragon Waiting, The	WFA-W 84	FORD, John M
6	Dragonfields	WFA-N 86	YOLEN, Jane
1	Dragonquest	HUG-N 72	McCAFFREY, Anne
1	Dragonquest	LOC-N 72	McCAFFREY, Anne
2	Dragonrider	HUG-N 69	McCAFFREY, Anne
2	Dragonrider	NEB-W 68	McCAFFREY, Anne
7	Dragons in Amber	IFA-N 52	LEY, Willy
6	Dragons of Light	WFA-N 81	CARD, Orson Scott
11	Dragonsbane	LOC-N 86	HAMBLY, Barbara
1	Dragon's Dawn	JWC-N 89	McCAFFREY, Anne
9	Dragon's Eggs	LOC-W 81	FORWARD, Dr. Robert L
2	Dramatic Mission	NEB-N 69	McCAFFREY, Anne
2	Dramatic Mission	HUG-N 70	McCAFFREY, Anne
2	Dread Empire	HUG-N 72	BRUNNER, John
4	Dream at Noonday, A	NEB-N 70	DOZOIS, Gardner
11	Dream Baby	LOC-N 90	McALLISTER, Bruce
3	Dream Baby	LOC-N 88	McALLISTER, Bruce
3	Dream Baby	NEB-N 87	McALLISTER, Bruce
3	Dream Baby	HUG-N 88	McALLISTER, Bruce
4	Dream Cargoes	SFC-N 92	BALLARD, J G
7	Dream Makers	HUG-N 81	PLATT, Charles
7	Dream Makers	LOC-N 81	PLATT, Charles
7	Dream Makers Vol 2	LOC-W 84	PLATT, Charles
7	Dream Makers Vol 2	HUG-N 84	PLATT, Charles
1	Dream Park	LOC-N 82	NIVEN, Larry
1	Dream Years, The	WFA-N 86	GOLDSTEIN, Lisa
1	Dreaming Dragon, The	JWC-N 81	BRODERICK, Damien
9	Dreamrider	LOC-N 83	MIESEL, Sandra
6	Dreams of Dark and Light	WFA-N 87	LEE, Tanith
1	Dreamsnake	HUG-W 79	McINTYRE, Vonda N
1	Dreamsnake	LOC-W 79	McINTYRE, Vonda N
1	Dreamsnake	NEB-W 78	McINTYRE, Vonda N
4	Driftglass	NEB-N 67	DELANY, Samuel R
14	Driftglass	LOC-N 72	DELANY, Samuel R
1	Drive-in, The	STO-N 89	LANSDALE, Joe R
1	Drive-in, The	WFA-N 89	LANSDALE, Joe R
1	Drowning Towers	NEB-N 88	TURNER, George

CAT	T I T L E S	AW W/N Y	A U T H O R
3	Dr. Pak's Preschool	HUG-N 91	BRIN, David
3	Dr. Pak's Preschool	LOC-N 91	BRIN, David
1	Dune	NEB-W 65	HERBERT, Frank
1	Dune	HUG-W 66	HERBERT, Frank
7	Dune Encyclopedia, The	LOC-N 85	McNELLY, Willis E Dr.
7	Dune Encyclopedia, The	HUG-N 85	McNELLY, Willis E Dr.
1	Dune World	HUG-N 64	HERBERT, Frank
9	Dwelling, The	STO-N 90	ELLIOT, Tom
3	Dybbuk Dolls, The	NEB-N 75	DANN, Jack
2	Dydeetown Girl	NEB-N 86	WILSON, F Paul
1	Dying Earth	HUG-N 64	VANCE, Jack
1	Dying Inside	NEB-N 72	SILVERBERG, Robert
1	Dying Inside	HUG-N 73	SILVERBERG, Robert
1	Dying Inside	LOC-N 73	SILVERBERG, Robert
1	Dying of the Light	BFA-N 79	MARTIN, George R R
1	Dying of the Light	HUG-N 78	MARTIN, George R R
4	Each Night, Each Year	STO-N 90	PTACEK, Kathryn
2	Ealdwood	WFA-N 82	CHERRYH, C J
14	Early Asimov, The	LOC-N 73	ASIMOV, Isaac
5	Early Long, The	WFA-N 76	LONG, Frank Belknap
1	Earth	LOC-N 91	BRIN, David
1	Earth	HUG-N 91	BRIN, David
1	Earth	SFC-N 91	BRIN, David
1	Earth Abides	IFA-W 51	STEWART, George R
5	Earth Book of Stormgate, The	LOC-N 79	ANDERSON, Poul
3	Earth Doth Like a Snake Renew, The	LOC-N 89	TIPTREE, James Jr
3	Earth Merchants, The	NEB-N 65	KAGAN, Norman
4	Earthwoman	NEB-N 67	BRETNOR, Reginald
4	Eat Me	STO-W 90	McCAMMON, Robert R
4	Edge of the Sea, The	HUG-N 59	BUDRYS, Algis
4	Edge of the World, The	WFA-N 90	SWANWICK, Michael
4	Edge of the World, The	HUG-N 90	SWANWICK, Michael
4	Edge of the World, The	LOC-N 90	SWANWICK, Michael
4	Edge of the World, The	JWC-W 90	SWANWICK, Michael
4	Eichman Variations, The	NEB-N 84	ZEBROWSKI, George
4	Eidolons	LOC-W 89	ELLISON, Harlan
3	Eifelheim	DAV-W 87	FLYNN, Michael F
2	Eifelheim	HUG-N 87	FLYNN, Michael F
4	Eight Billion, The	NEB-N 65	WILSON, Richard
11	Eight Skilled Gentlemen	LOC-N 92	HUGHART, Barry
1	Einstein Intersection	HUG-N 68	DELANY, Samuel R
1	Einstein Intersection	NEB-W 67	DELANY, Samuel R
2	Elementals	HUG-N 85	LANDIS, Geoffrey A
4	Elephant	JWC-N 87	PALWICK, Susan
4	Elle Est Trois	WFA-W 84	LEE, Tanith
6	Elsewhere	BFA-W 82	WINDLING, Terri
6	Elsewhere	WFA-W 82	WINDLING, Terri
1	Embedding, The	JWC-N 74	WATSON, Ian
1	Embedding, The	NEB-N 75	WATSON, Ian

SECTION C: TITLES (Alphabetically)

CAT	T I T L E S	AW W/N Y	A U T H O R
1	Emergence	COM-W 85	PALMER, David R
9	Emergence	LOC-N 85	PALMER, David R
1	Emergence	HUG-N 86	PALMER, David R
1	Emergence	DIC-N 85	PALMER, David R
2	Emergence	HUG-N 82	PALMER, David R
1	Emergence	HUG-N 85	PALMER, David R
5	Empire Dreams	LOC-N 89	McDONALD, Ian
1	Empire of Fear, The	CLA-N 89	STABLEFORD, Brian
1	Empire of the Sun	BSF-N 85	BALLARD, J G
9	Emprise	LOC-N 86	KUBE-McDOWELL, Michael P
3	Encounter, The	NEB-N 71	WILHELM, Kate
7	Encyclopedia of SF and Fantasy #2	LOC-N 79	TUCK, Donald H
7	Encyclopedia of SF and Fantasy #3	HUG-W 84	TUCK, Donald H
7	Encyclopedia of SF and Fantasy #3	LOC-N 84	TUCK, Donald H
4	End of the Whole Mess, The	WFA-N 87	KING, Stephen
5	Endangered Species	LOC-N 90	WOLFE, Gene
1	Ender's Game	HUG-W 86	CARD, Orson Scott
1	Ender's Game	NEB-W 85	CARD, Orson Scott
1	Ender's Game	LOC-N 86	CARD, Orson Scott
1	Ender's Game	SFC-W 86	CARD, Orson Scott
3	Ender's Game	HUG-N 78	CARD, Orson Scott
5	Ends of the Earth, The	WFA-N 92	SHEPARD, Lucius
2	Enemies of the System	HUG-N 79	ALDISS, Brian W
2	Enemy Mine	LOC-N 80	LONGYEAR, Barry B
2	Enemy Mine	NEB-W 79	LONGYEAR, Barry B
2	Enemy Mine	HUG-W 80	LONGYEAR, Barry B
1	Enemy Stars, The	HUG-N 59	ANDERSON, Poul
4	Engine at Heartsprings Center, The	JUP-N 75	ZELAZNY, Roger
4	Engine at Heartsprings Center, The	NEB-N 74	ZELAZNY, Roger
4	Engine at Heartsprings Center, The	LOC-N 75	ZELAZNY, Roger
1	Engine Summer	BSF-N 81	CROWLEY, John
1	Engine Summer	JWC-N 80	CROWLEY, John
7	Engines of the Night, The	LOC-W 83	MALZBERG, Barry N
7	Engines of the Night, The	HUG-N 83	MALZBERG, Barry N
5	Enquiries of Dr Eszterhazy	WFA-W 76	DAVIDSON, Avram
3	Enter a Soldier, Later Enter Another	LOC-N 90	SILVERBERG, Robert
3	Enter a Soldier, Later Enter Another	HUG-W 90	SILVERBERG, Robert
3	Enter a Soldier, Later Enter Another	NEB-N 89	SILVERBERG, Robert
1	Enterprise	DIC-N 86	KUBE-McDOWELL, Michael P
4	Entire and Perfect Chrysolite	NEB-N 70	LAFFERTY, R A
2	Entropy's Bed at Midnight	STO-N 91	SIMMONS, Dan
3	Entropy's Bed at Midnight	LOC-W 91	SIMMONS, Dan
1	Eon	CLA-N 87	BEAR, Greg
4	Episodes of the Argo	JWC-N 91	LAFFERTY, R A
5	Epoch	LOC-W 76	ELWOOD, Roger
2	Escape from Kathmandu	NEB-N 86	ROBINSON, Kim Stanley
2	Escape From Kathmandu	SFC-N 87	ROBINSON, Kim Stanley
2	Escape From Kathmandu	LOC-N 87	ROBINSON, Kim Stanley
2	Escape from Kathmandu	HUG-N 87	ROBINSON, Kim Stanley
1	Escape Orbit	NEB-N 65	WHITE, James
1	Escape Plans	CLA-N 87	JONES, Gwyneth

SECTION C: TITLES (Alphabetically)

CAT	TITLES	AW W/N Y	AUTHOR
1	Eskimo Invasion, The	NEB-N 67	HOWARD, Hayden
3	Eskimo Invasion, The	HUG-N 67	HOWARD, Hayden
3	Eskimo Invasion, The	NEB-N 66	HOWARD, Hayden
5	Essential Ellison, The	LOC-N 88	ELLISON, Harlan
6	Essential Ellison, The	STO-W 88	ELLISON, Harlan
2	Esterhazy and the Autogondola-Invention	NEB-N 83	DAVIDSON, Avram
1	Eternal Light	BSF-N 92	McAULEY, Paul J
1	Eternal Light	CLA-N 92	McAULEY, Paul J
1	Eternity	LOC-N 89	BEAR, Greg
4	Eurema's Dam	HUG-W 73	LAFFERTY, R A
3	Evening and the Morning and the Night	NEB-N 87	BUTLER, Octavia E
4	Evening and the Morning and the Night	JWC-N 88	BUTLER, Octavia E
3	Evening and the Morning and the Night	SFC-W 88	BUTLER, Octavia E
2	Events at Poroth Farm	WFA-N 75	KLEIN, T E D
3	Everyday Life in the Later Roman Empire	JUP-N 74	DISCH, Thomas
3	Everything But Honor	SFC-N 90	CARD, Orson Scott
3	Everything But Honor	HUG-N 90	EFFINGER, George Alec
9	Excavation	STO-N 88	TEM, Steve Rasnic
1	Exile Waiting, The	NEB-N 75	McINTYRE, Vonda N
7	Exploration of Space	IFA-W 52	CLARKE, Arthur C
3	Exploration Team	HUG-W 56	LEINSTER, Murray
4	Extraordinary Voyages of Amelie Bertrand	NEB-N 79	RUSS, Joanna
12	Extrat'l Intel & t/Interdict Hypothesis	DAV-N 89	FOGG, Martyn J
5	Extra(ordinary) People	LOC-N 85	RUSS, Joanna
3	Extreme Prejudice	HUG-N 75	POURNELLE, Jerry
2	Eye for Eye	LOC-N 88	CARD, Orson Scott
2	Eye for Eye	HUG-W 88	CARD, Orson Scott
11	Eye of the World, The	LOC-N 91	JORDON, Robert
2	Eyeflash Miracles, The	LOC-N 77	WOLFE, Gene
2	Eyeflash Miracles, The	NEB-N 76	WOLFE, Gene
4	Eyes Do More Than See	NEB-N 65	ASIMOV, Isaac
4	Eyes of Amber	LOC-N 78	VINGE, Joan D
5	Eyes of Amber	LOC-N 80	VINGE, Joan D
3	Eyes of Amber	HUG-W 78	VINGE, Joan D
6	Face of Chaos	LOC-N 84	ASPRIN, Robert
7	Faces of Fear: Encount W/t/Creat Mod Hor	LOC-N 86	WINTER, Douglas E
7	Faces of Fear: Encount W/t/Creat Mod Hor	HUG-N 86	WINTER, Douglas E
7	Faces of Science Fiction, The	HUG-N 85	PERRET, Patti
7	Faces of Science Fiction, The	LOC-N 85	PERRET, Patti
1	Fade	WFA-N 89	CORMIER, Robert
1	Faded Sun, The: Kesrith	NEB-N 78	CHERRYH, C J
1	Faded Sun, The: Kesrith	HUG-N 79	CHERRYH, C J
1	Faded Sun, The: Kesrith	LOC-N 79	CHERRYH, C J
10	Faerie Tale	LOC-N 89	FEIST, Raymond E
4	Fairy Tale	WFA-N 82	DANN, Jack
4	Fairy Tale	BFA-N 82	DANN, Jack
3	Faith of Our Fathers	HUG-N 68	DICK, Philip K
4	Faithful Companion, The	NEB-N 87	FOWLER, Karen Joy
4	Faithful Companion, The	HUG-N 88	FOWLER, Karen Joy
4	Faithful Companion at Forty, The	LOC-N 88	FOWLER, Karen Joy

SECTION C: TITLES (Alphabetically)

CAT	TITLES	AW W/N Y	AUTHOR
1	Fall of Hyperion, The	BSF-W 92	SIMMONS, Dan
1	Fall of Hyperion, The	SFC-N 91	SIMMONS, Dan
1	Fall of Hyperion, The	HUG-N 91	SIMMONS, Dan
1	Fall of Hyperion, The	NEB-N 91	SIMMONS, Dan
1	Fall of Hyperion, The	LOC-W 91	SIMMONS, Dan
1	Fall of Moondust, A	HUG-N 61	CLARKE, Arthur C
1	Fall of Moondust, A	HUG-N 63	CLARKE, Arthur C
1	Falling Free	HUG-N 89	BUJOLD, Lois McMaster
1	Falling Free	NEB-W 88	BUJOLD, Lois McMaster
1	Falling Woman, The	NEB-W 87	MURPHY, Pat
6	Famous Fantastic Mysteries	WFA-N 92	DZIEMIANOWICZ, Stefan R
1	Fancies and Goodnights	IFA-W 52	COLLIER, John
7	Fantasia: A Jack Vance Bibliography	LOC-N 79	LEVACK
7	Fantastic Art of Rowena	LOC-N 84	MORRILL, Rowena
7	Fantastic Art of Rowena	HUG-N 84	MORRILL, Rowena
6	Fantasy Annual 4	BFA-N 82	CARR, Terry
6	Fantasy Annual 4	WFA-N 82	CARR, Terry
6	Fantasy Annual 5	LOC-N 83	CARR, Terry
5	Far Lands, Other Days	WFA-N 76	PRICE, E Hoffman
1	Farewell Horizontal	JWC-N 90	JETER, K W
1	Farewell Horizontal	CLA-N 91	JETER, K W
2	Farmer's Tale, A	WFA-N 75	LANIER, Sterling
3	Fast Cars	NEB-N 89	RUSCH, Kristine
4	Fat Face	BFA-N 88	SHEA, Michael
2	Fatal Fulfillment, The	NEB-N 70	ANDERSON, Poul
2	Father of Stones, The	LOC-W 90	SHEPARD, Lucius
2	Father of Stones, The	WFA-N 90	SHEPARD, Lucius
2	Father of Stones, The	SFC-N 90	SHEPARD, Lucius
2	Father of Stones, The	HUG-N 90	SHEPARD, Lucius
9	Fear Book	STO-N 89	BYRNE, John L
7	Fear Itself:T/Horror Fiction of S King	LOC-N 83	UNDERWOOD,
7	Fear Itself:T/Horror Fiction of S King	HUG-N 83	UNDERWOOD, Tim
1	Fearful Symmetry, A	DIC-N 90	LUCENO, James
6	Feary	WFA-N 86	WINDLING, Terri
2	Feast of St. Dionysus, The	JUP-W 74	SILVERBERG, Robert
2	Feast of St. Dionysus, The	LOC-N 74	SILVERBERG, Robert
3	Feast of St. Janis, The	NEB-N 80	SWANWICK, Michael
1	Female Man, The	NEB-N 75	RUSS, Joanna
4	Fermi and Frost	HUG-W 86	POHL, Frederik
4	Fermi and Frost	LOC-N 86	POHL, Frederik
4	Fermi and Frost	SFC-N 86	POHL, Frederik
2	Fetish	STO-N 92	BRYANT, Edward
11	Fevre Dream	LOC-N 83	MARTIN, George R R
1	Fevre Dream	WFA-N 83	MARTIN, George R R
4	Few Kindred Spirits, A	NEB-N 65	CHRISTOPHER, John
1	Fiasco	CLA-N 88	LEM, Stanislaw
2	Fifth Head of Cerberus, The	LOC-N 73	WOLFE, Gene
2	Fifth Head of Cerberus, The	HUG-N 73	WOLGE, Gene
2	Fifth Head of Cerberus, The	NEB-N 72	WOLFE, Gene
3	Fin de Cycle	LOC-N 92	WALDROP, Howard
3	Fin de Cycle	HUG-N 92	WALDROP, Howard
6	Final Shadows	WFA-N 92	GRANT, Charles L

SECTION C: TITLES (Alphabetically)

CAT	T I T L E S	AW W/N Y	A U T H O R
3	Final Sighting of Fion Mac Cumhaill, The	NEB-N 75	GARRETT, Randall
5	Final Stage	LOC-N 76	FERMAN, Ed
3	Final War	NEB-N 68	O'DONNELL, K M
4	Find the Lady	NEB-N 75	FISK, Nicholas
1	Fire in the Sun, A	LOC-N 90	EFFINGER, George Alec
1	Fire in the Sun, A	HUG-N 90	EFFINGER, George Alec
1	Fire in the Sun, A	SFC-W 90	EFFINGER, George Alec
1	Fire Time	HUG-N 75	ANDERSON, Poul
5	Fire Watch	LOC-N 86	WILLIS, Connie
3	Fire Watch	NEB-W 82	WILLIS, Connie
3	Fire Watch	SFC-W 83	WILLIS, Connie
2	Fire When It Comes, The	WFA-W 82	GODWIN, Parke
6	Fire When It Comes, The	WFA-N 85	GODWIN, Parke
3	Fire When It Comes, The	NEB-N 81	GODWIN, Parke
3	Fireflood and Other Stories	HUG-N 80	McINTYRE, Vonda N
5	Fireflood and Other Stories	LOC-N 80	McINTYRE, Vonda N
3	Fireflood and Other Stories	LOC-N 80	McINTYRE, Vonda N
1	Firelord	WFA-N 81	GODWIN, Parkke
2	Fireship	LOC-N 79	VINGE, Joan D
2	Fireship	HUG-N 79	VINGE, Joan D
2	Fireship	NEB-N 79	VINGE, Joan D
1	Firestarter	BFA-N 81	KING, Stephen
4	Firestorm	WFA-N 83	TEM, Steve Rasnic
3	Firewatch	HUG-W 83	WILLIS, Connie
3	Firewatch	LOC-N 83	WILLIS, Connie
7	First Maitz	LOC-W 89	MAITZ, Don
7	First Maitz	HUG-N 89	MAITZ, Don
4	First Make Them Mad	BFA-N 80	COLE, Adrian
4	First Time, The	LOC-N 91	JETER, K W
3	Flash Crowd	JUP-N 74	NIVEN, Larry
4	Flash Kid, The	BSF-N 84	BRADFIELD, Scott
6	Flashing Swords #3	WFA-N 77	CARTER, Lin
6	Flashing Swords #5	LOC-N 82	CARTER, Lin
3	Flatlander	NEB-N 67	NIVEN, Larry
1	Flesh	STO-N 89	LAYMON, Richard
2	Flight	WFA-N 86	DICKINSON, Peter
4	Flipping	BFA-N 91	SILVA, David
4	Floating Dogs	BSF-N 92	McDONALD, Ian
1	Floating Dragons	BFA-W 84	STRAUB, Peter
1	Floating Gods, The	DIC-N 84	HARRISON, M John
1	Flow My Tears, The Policeman Said	LOC-N 75	DICK, Philip K
1	Flow My Tears, The Policeman Said	JWC-W 75	DICK, Philip K
1	Flow My Tears, The Policeman Said	NEB-N 74	DICK, Philip K
1	Flow My Tears, The Policeman Said	HUG-N 75	DICK, Philip K
1	Flowers for Algernon	HUG-N 67	KEYES, Daniel
1	Flowers for Algernon	NEB-W 66	KEYES, Daniel
4	Flowers for Algernon	HUG-W 60	KEYES, Daniel
3	FLowers of Edo	HUG-N 88	STERLING, Bruce
3	FLowers of Edo	NEB-N 87	STERLING, Bruce
3	Flowers of Edo	LOC-N 88	STERLING, Bruce
4	Flying Saucer Rock and Roll	NEB-N 85	WALDROP, Howard
4	Flying Saucer Rock and Roll	HUG-N 86	WALDROP, Howard
11	Folk of the Air, The	LOC-N 87	BEAGLE, Peter S

SECTION C: TITLES (Alphabetically)

CAT	TITLES	AW W/N Y	AUTHOR
5	Folk on the Fringe, The	LOC-N 90	CARD, Orson Scott
2	Fool to Believe	LOC-N 91	CADIGAN, Pat
2	Fool to Believe	HUG-N 91	CADIGAN, Pat
2	Fool to Believe	NEB-N 91	CADIGAN, Pat
1	Footfall	LOC-N 86	NIVEN, Larry
1	Footfall	HUG-N 86	NIVEN, Larry
3	For A Breath I Tarry	HUG-N 67	ZELAZNY, Roger
3	For A Single Yesterday	LOC-N 76	MARTIN, George R R
3	For I Have Touched the Sky	NEB-N 89	RESNICK, Mike
3	For I Have Touched the Sky	LOC-N 90	RESNICK, Mike
3	For I Have Touched the Sky	SFC-W 90	RESNICK, Mike
3	For I Have Touched the Sky	HUG-N 90	RESNICK, Mike
4	Forbidden, The	BFA-W 85	BARKER, Clive
1	Forbidden Tower (4): Darkover	HUG-N 78	BRADLEY, Marion Zimmer
2	Forest of Time, The	HUG-N 88	FLYNN, Michael
1	Forever War, The	NEB-W 75	HALDEMAN, Joe
1	Forever War, The	DIT-W 76	HALDEMAN, Joe
1	Forever War, The	LOC-W 76	HALDEMAN, Joe
1	Forever War, The	HUG-W 76	HALDEMAN, Joe
4	Forever Yours, Anna	NEB-W 87	WILHELM, Kate
4	Forever Yours, Anna	HUG-N 88	WILHELM, Kate
4	Forever Yours, Anna	SFC-N 88	WILHELM, Kate
1	Forge of God, The	LOC-N 88	BEAR, Greg
1	Forge of God, The	HUG-N 88	BEAR, Greg
1	Forge of God, The	NEB-N 87	BEAR, Greg
1	Forgotten Beast of Eld	WFA-W 75	McKILLIP, Patricia
4	Fort Moxie Branch, The	NEB-N 88	McDIVITT, Jack
4	Fort Moxie Branch, The	HUG-N 89	McDEVITT, Jack
8	Foundation	HUG-W 66	ASIMOV, Isaac
1	Foundation and Earth	LOC-N 87	ASIMOV, Isaac
8	Foundation Trilogy	HUG-W 66	ASIMOV, Isaac
1	Foundation's Edge	LOC-W 83	ASIMOV, Isaac
1	Foundation's Edge	HUG-W 83	ASIMOV, Isaac
1	Foundation's Edge	NEB-N 82	ASIMOV, Isaac
1	Foundation's Edge	SFC-N 83	ASIMOV, Isaac
6	Foundation's Friends	LOC-N 90	GREENBERG, Martin H
4	Founding Father	NEB-N 65	ASIMOV, Isaac
1	Fountains of Paradise, The	HUG-W 80	CLARKE, Arthur C
1	Fountains of Paradise, The	NEB-W 79	CLARKE, Arthur C
1	Fountains of Paradise, The	BSF-N 80	CLARKE, Arthur C
1	Fountains of Paradise, The	LOC-N 80	CLARKE, Arthur C
3	Four Ghosts in Hamlet	NEB-N 65	LEIBER, Fritz
5	Four Past Midnight	LOC-N 91	KING, Stephen
6	Four Past Midnight	STO-W 91	KING, Stephen
1	Fourth Mansions	NEB-N 70	LAFFERTY, R A
1	Fourth Mansions	LOC-N 71	LAFFERTY, R A
2	Fourth Profession	HUG-N 72	NIVEN, Larry
4	Four-Hour Fugue, The	LOC-N 75	BESTER, Alfred
4	Four-Hour Fugue, The	HUG-N 75	BESTER, Alfred
4	Frame of Reference	DAV-N 89	KRAUS, Stephen
1	Free, Live Free	BSF-N 86	WOLFE, Gene
1	Free, Live Free	NEB-N 86	WOLFE, Gene

CAT	T I T L E S	AW W/N Y	A U T H O R
1	Friday	HUG-N 83	HEINLEIN, Robert A
1	Friday	NEB-N 82	HEINLEIN, Robert A
1	Friday	LOC-N 83	HEINLEIN, Robert A
1	Friday	HUG-N 83	HEINLEIN, Robert A
1	Friendly Aliens	AUR-N 82	COLOMBO, Robert
4	Friend's Best Man	WFA-W 88	CARROLL, Jonathan
4	Friend's Best Man	STO-N 88	CARROLL, Jonathan
4	Friend's Best Man	BFA-N 88	CARROLL, Jonathan
6	Frights	WFA-W 77	McCAULEY, Kirby
3	Fringe, The	LOC-N 86	CARD, Orson Scott
3	Fringe, The	HUG-N 86	CARD, Orson Scott
3	Fringe, The	NEB-N 85	CARD, Orson Scott
5	From Earth's Pillow	WFA-N 75	COPPER, Basil
4	From the Papers of Helmut Hecher	STO-N 91	WILLIAMSON, Chet
1	Frontera	NEB-N 84	SHINER, Lewis
1	Frontera	DIC-N 85	SHINER, Lewis
5	Frost and Fire	LOC-N 90	ZELAZNY, Roger
4	Fruiting Bodies	BFA-W 89	LUMLEY, Brian
2	Fugue State	NEB-N 87	FORD, John M
6	Full Spectrum	LOC-W 89	ARONICA, Lou
6	Full Spectrum 2	LOC-N 90	ARONICA, Lou
6	Full Spectrum 3	LOC-W 92	ARONICA, Lou
3	Function of Dream Sleep, The	STO-N 89	ELLISON, Harlan
3	Function of Dream Sleep, The	LOC-W 89	ELLISON, Harlan
3	Function of Dream Sleep, The	HUG-N 89	ELLISON, Harlan
3	Funeral, The	NEB-N 72	WILHELM, Kate
1	Funeral For Eyes of Fire, A	NEB-N 75	BISHOP, Michael
1	Funland	STO-N 91	LAYMON, Richard
14	Future Power	LOC-N 77	DANN, Jack
1	Galapagos	JWC-N 86	VONNEGUT, Kurt
3	Galatea Galante	LOC-N 80	BESTER, Alfred
3	Galaxy Called Rome, A	NEB-N 75	MALZBERG, Barry N
3	Galaxy Called Rome, A	LOC-N 76	MALZBERG, Barry N
2	Gallery of His Dreams, The	LOC-W 92	RUSCH, Kristine Kathryn
2	Gallery of His Dreams, The	NEB-N 92	RUSCH, Kristine Kathryn
2	Gallery of His Dreams, The	HUG-N 92	RUSCH, Kristine Kathryn
2	Gallery of His Dreams, The	WFA-N 92	RUSCH, Kristine Kathryn
1	Game of Fox and Lion, The	COM-N 87	CHASE, Robert R
4	Games	NEB-N 65	BARTHELME, Donald
2	Gardener, The	WFA-N 89	TEPPER, Sheri S
3	Gate of Faces	NEB-N 92	ALDRIDGE, Ray
3	Gate of Faces	SFC-N 92	ALDRIDGE, Ray
9	Gates of Heaven, The	LOC-N 81	PREUSS, Paul
1	Gateway	HUG-W 78	POHL, Frederik
1	Gateway	LOC-W 78	POHL, Frederik
1	Gateway	JWC-W 78	POHL, Frederik
1	Gateway	NEB-W 77	POHL, Frederik
1	Geek Love	STO-N 90	DUNN, Katherine
10	Geek Love	LOC-N 90	DUNN, Katherine
5	Gene Wolfe's Book of Days	LOC-N 82	WOLFE, Gene
1	Genetic General (Dorsai)	HUG-N 60	DICKSON, Gordon R
1	Genocides, The	NEB-N 65	DISCH, Thomas M

SECTION C: TITLES (Alphabetically)

CAT	TITLES	AW W/N Y	AUTHOR
2	Geometer Blind, The	NEB-W 87	ROBINSON, Kim Stanley
4	Geometry of Narrative, The	NEB-N 83	SCHENCK, Hilbert
4	Geometry of Narrative, The	HUG-N 84	SCHENCK, Hilbert
3	Getting Real	NEB-N 92	SHWARTZ, Susan
3	Getting the Bugs Out	DAV-W 91	KAGAN, Janet
3	Getting Through University	HUG-N 69	ANTHONY, Piers
2	Ghastly Priest Doth Reign, The	WFA-N 76	WELLMAN, Manly Wade
5	Ghost Light, The	LOC-W 85	LEIBER, Fritz
4	Ghost Town	NEB-N 83	OLIVER, Chad
4	giANTS	NEB-W 79	BRYANT, Edward
4	giANTS	HUG-N 80	BRYANT, Edward
4	giANTS	LOC-N 80	BRYANT, Edward
4	Gift, The	JWC-N 88	FORDE, Pat
3	Gift, The	DAV-W 88	FORDE, Pat
3	Gift From the Graylanders, A	HUG-N 86	BISHOP, Michael
3	Gift From the Graylanders, A	NEB-N 85	BISHOP, Michael
7	Giger's Alien	LOC-N 90	GIGER, H R
11	Gilgamesh, The King	LOC-N 85	SILVERBERG, Robert
2	Gilgamesh in the Outback	SFC-N 87	SILVERBERG, Robert
2	Gilgamesh in the Outback	LOC-N 87	SILVERBERG, Robert
2	Gilgamesh in the Outback	HUG-W 87	SILVERBERG, Robert
2	Gilgamesh in the Outback	NEB-N 86	SILVERBERG, Robert
3	Ginny Sweethips' Flying Circus	NEB-N 88	BARRETT, Neal Jr
3	Ginny Sweethips' Flying Circus	HUG-N 89	BARRETT, Neal Jr
3	Ginungagap	NEB-N 80	VARLEY, John
3	Girl Who Fell Into the Sky, The	NEB-W 86	WILHELM, Kate
4	Girl Who Was Plugged In, The	LOC-N 74	TIPTREE, James Jr
3	Girl Who Was Plugged In, The	NEB-N 73	TIPTREE, James Jr
3	Girl Who Was Plugged In, The	JUP-N 74	TIPTREE, James Jr
2	Girl Who was Plugged In, The	HUG-W 74	TIPTREE, James Jr
4	Giving Plague, The	HUG-N 89	BRIN, David
4	Giving Plague, The	LOC-N 89	BRIN, David
3	Glacier	LOC-N 89	ROBINSON, Kim Stanley
3	Glacier	SFC-N 89	ROBINSON, Kim Stanley
1	Glamour, The	BSF-N 85	PRIEST, Christopher
2	Glass Cloud	LOC-N 88	KELLY, James Patrick
3	Glass Flower, The	LOC-N 87	MARTIN, George R R
4	Glassblower's Dragon, The	LOC-N 88	SHEPARD, Lucius
1	Gloriana	BFA-N 79	MOORCOCK, Michael
1	Gloriana	JWC-W 79	MOORCOCK, Michael
1	Gloriana	WFA-N 79	MOORCOCK, Michael
1	Glory Road	HUG-N 64	HEINLEIN, Robert A
3	Glow of Candles, a Unicorn's Eye, A	NEB-W 78	GRANT, C L
9	Goat Dance	STO-N 90	CLEGG, Douglas
4	Goat Song	LOC-N 73	ANDERSON, Poul
3	Goat Song	HUG-W 73	ANDERSON, Poul
3	Goat Song	NEB-W 72	ANDERSON, Poul
3	Goblin Night	NEB-N 65	SCHMITZ, James
2	God House, The	NEB-N 71	ROBERTS, Keith
4	Gods of Mars, The	NEB-N 85	DOZOIS, Gardner
1	Gods Themselves, The	LOC-W 73	ASIMOV, Isaac
1	Gods Themselves, The	NEB-W 72	ASIMOV, Isaac
1	Gods Themselves, The	DIT-W 73	ASIMOV, Isaac
1	Gods Themselves, The	HUG-W 73	ASIMOV, Isaac

SECTION C: TITLES (Alphabetically)

CAT	T I T L E S	AW W/N Y	A U T H O R
4	Godspeed	HUG-N 91	SHEFFIELD, Charles
4	Godspeed	LOC-N 91	SHEFFIELD, Charles
4	Godspeed	SFC-N 91	SHEFFIELD, Charles
1	Godwhale, The	NEB-N 74	BASS, T J
1	Godwhale, The	LOC-N 75	BASS, T J
4	God's Hooks	NEB-N 82	WALDROP, Howard
4	God's Hooks	LOC-N 83	WALDROP, Howard
4	Going Under	NEB-N 81	DANN, Jack
3	Gold	LOC-N 92	ASIMOV, Isaac
3	Gold	HUG-W 92	ASIMOV, Isaac
14	Gold at the Starbow's End, The	LOC-N 73	POHL, Frederik
2	Gold at the Starbow's End, The	HUG-N 73	POHL, Frederik
2	Gold at the Starbow's End, The	NEB-N 72	POHL, Frederik
2	Gold at the Starbow's End, The	LOC-W 73	POHL, Frederik
1	Gold Coast, The	LOC-N 89	ROBINSON, Kim Stanley
1	Gold Coast, The	JWC-N 89	ROBINSON, Kim Stanley
9	Golden Fleece	LOC-N 91	SAWYER, Robert J
1	Golden Fleece	AUR-W 92	SAWYER, Robert J
1	Golden Witchbreed	BSF-N 84	GENTLE, Mary
3	Gonna Roll Those Bones	NEB-W 67	LEIBER, Fritz
3	Gonna Roll Those Bones	HUG-W 68	LEIBER, Fritz
4	Good New Days, The	NEB-N 65	LEIBER, Fritz
1	Good News From Outer Space	JWC-N 90	KESSEL, John
1	Good News From Outer Space	NEB-N 89	KESSEL, John
4	Good News from the Vatican	NEB-W 71	SILVERBERG, Robert
4	Good Night's Sleep, A	WFA-N 79	DAVIDSON, Avram
1	Good Omens	WFA-N 91	PRATCHETT, Terry
11	Good Omens	LOC-N 91	PRATCHETT, Terry
11	Goodbody	LOC-N 87	STURGEON, Theodore
4	Gorgon, The	WFA-N 83	LEE, Tanith
4	Gorgon, The	WFA-W 83	LEE, Tanith
2	Gorgon, The	NEB-N 85	WILHELM, Kate
2	Gorgon Field, The	WFA-N 86	WILHELM, Kate
2	Gospel According to Gamaliel Crucis, The	NEB-N 83	BISHOP, Michael
3	Gotta Sing, Gotta Dance	HUG-N 77	VARLEY, John
3	Gotta Sing, Gotta Dance	LOC-N 77	VARLEY, John
7	Grand Tour, The	HUG-N 82	MILLER, Ron
7	Grand Tour, The	LOC-N 82	MILLER, Ron
1	Grass	LOC-N 90	TEPPER, Sheri S
1	Grass	HUG-N 90	TEPPER, Sheri S
4	Grave Angels, The	JWC-N 87	KEARNS, Richard
5	Gravity's Angels	LOC-N 92	SWANWICK, Michael
1	Gravity's Rainbow	JUP-N 74	PYNCHON, Thomas
1	Gravity's Rainbow	NEB-N 73	PYCHON, Thomas
10	Great and Secret Show	LOC-N 90	BARKER, Clive
6	Great SF Stories #21, The	LOC-N 91	ASIMOV, Isaac
1	Great Sky River	NEB-N 88	BENFORD, Gregory
2	Great Works of Time	SFC-N 90	CROWLEY, John
2	Great Works of Time	WFA-W 90	CROWLEY, John
2	Great Works of Time	NEB-N 89	CROWLEY, John
2	Green Days in Brunei	NEB-N 85	STERLING, Bruce

CAT	TITLES	AW W/N Y	AUTHOR
1	Green Eyes	CLA-N 87	SHEPARD, Lucius
1	Green Eyes	DIC-N 85	SHEPARD, Lucius
9	Green Eyes	LOC-N 85	SHEPARD, Lucius
1	Green Eyes	JWC-N 85	SHEPARD, Lucius
1	Green Gene, The	JWC-N 74	DICKINSON, Peter
2	Green Mars	HUG-N 86	ROBINSON, Kim Stanley
2	Green Mars	LOC-N 86	ROBINSON, Kim Stanley
2	Green Mars	SFC-N 86	ROBINSON, Kim Stanley
2	Greening of Bed-Stuy, The	NEB-N 84	POHL, Frederik
1	Grianne	CLA-N 88	ROBERTS, Keith
1	Grianne	BSF-W 88	ROBERTS, Keith
7	Griffin & Sabine	LOC-N 92	BANTOCK, Nick
2	Griffin's Egg	LOC-N 92	SWANWICK, Michael
2	Griffin's Egg	SFC-N 92	SWANWICK, Michael
2	Griffin's Egg	HUG-N 92	SWANWICK, Michael
5	Grimscribe: His Lives and Works	WFA-N 92	LIGOTTI, Thomas
4	Grotto of the Dancing Bear, The	NEB-W 80	SIMAK, Clifford D
4	Grotto of the Dancing Bear, The	HUG-W 81	SIMAK, Clifford D
4	Grotto of the Dancing Bear, The	LOC-W 81	SIMAK, Clifford D
1	Ground Ties	COM-N 92	FANCHER, Jane
4	Growing Up in Edge City	NEB-N 75	POHL, Frederik
7	Grumbles From the Grave	LOC-W 90	HEINLEIN, Robert A
7	Grumbles From the Grave	HUG-N 90	HEINLEIN, Robert A
4	Guardian	HUG-N 81	DUNTEMANN, Jeff
3	Guardians	HUG-N 82	MARTIN, George R R
3	Guardians	LOC-W 82	MARTIN, George R R
1	Guardsman, The	HUG-N 89	BEESE, P J
3	Guerilla Trees, The	NEB-N 68	HOLLIS, H H
1	Guernica Night	NEB-N 75	MALZBERG, Barry N
3	Guide Dog	NEB-W 92	CONNER, Mike
3	Guz's Place	DAV-N 89	PERPER, Timothy
2	Gwidion and the Dragon	WFA-N 92	CHERRYH, C J
3	Half a Loaf	NEB-N 65	FITZPATRICK, R C
1	Half Past Human	NEB-N 71	BASS, T J
8	Halo	LOC-N 92	MADDOX, Tom
1	Handmaid's Tale, The	NEB-N 86	ATWOOD, Margaret
1	Handmaid's Tale, The	CLA-W 87	ATWOOD, Margaret
1	Handmaid's Tale, The	LOC-N 87	ATWOOD, Margaret
1	Handmaid's Tale, The	SFC-N 87	ATWOOD, Margaret
4	Happy Dead, The	DAV-W 90	BECHTEL, Amy
4	Happy Man, The	JWC-N 92	LETHEM, Jonathan
3	Happy Man, The	NEB-N 92	LETHEM, Jonathan
2	Hardfought	LOC-N 84	BEAR, Greg
2	Hardfought	NEB-W 83	BEAR, Greg
2	Hardfought	HUG-N 84	BEAR, Greg
2	Hardfought	SFC-N 84	BEAR, Greg
7	Harlan Ellison's Watching	STO-W 90	ELLISON, Harlan
5	Harlan Ellison's Watching	WFA-N 90	ELLISON, Harlan
7	Harlan Ellison's Watching	HUG-N 90	ELLISON, Harlan
1	Harpist in the Wind	HUG-N 80	McKILLIP, Patricia A
11	Harpist in the Wind	LOC-W 80	McKILLIP, Patricia A
1	Harpist in the Wind	WFA-N 80	McKILLIP, Patricia A
1	Harpist in the Wind	BFA-N 80	McKILLIP, Patricia A

SECTION C: TITLES (Alphabetically)

CAT	TITLES	AW W/N Y	AUTHOR
9	Harvest Bride, The	STO-N 88	RICHARDS, Torvy
3	Hatrack River	LOC-N 87	CARD, Orson Scott
2	Hatrack River	WFA-W 87	CARD, Orson Scott
3	Hatrack River	HUG-N 87	CARD, Orson Scott
3	Hatrack River	SFC-N 87	CARD, Orson Scott
3	Hatrack River	NEB-N 86	CARD, Orson Scott
3	Haunted Tower, The	LOC-N 82	CHERRYH, C J
1	Have Space Suit-Will Travel	HUG-N 59	HEINLEIN, Robert A
2	Hawk Among The Sparrows	HUG-N 69	McLAUGHLIN, Dean
2	Hawk Among The Sparrows	NEB-N 68	McLAUGHLIN, Dean
2	Hawksbill Station	HUG-N 68	SILVERBERG, Robert
2	Hawksbill Station	NEB-N 67	SILVERBERG, Robert
3	He Fell Into a Dark Hole	HUG-N 74	POURNELLE, Jerry
2	He Who Shapes	NEB-W 65	ZELAZNY, Roger
2	Heads	LOC-N 91	BEAR, Greg
1	Healers War, The	NEB-W 89	SCARBOROUGH, Elizabeth
4	Hear Me Now, Sweet Abbey Rose	WFA-N 79	GRANT, Charles L
1	Heart of the Comet	LOC-N 87	BENFORD, Gregory
4	Heathen God	NEB-N 71	ZEBROWSKI, George
1	Heavenly Horse From the Outermost West,	COM-N 89	STANTON, Mary
1	Heechee Rendezvous	LOC-N 85	POHL, Frederik
6	Height of the Scream, The	WFA-N 77	CAMPBELL, Ramsey
4	Heirs of the Perisphere	NEB-N 85	WALDROP, Howard
2	Hellhound Heart	WFA-N 87	BARKER, Clive
2	Hellhound Project, The	JUP-N 74	GOULART, Ron
1	Helliconia Spring	LOC-N 83	ALDISS, Brian W
1	Helliconia Spring	BSF-W 83	ALDISS, Brian W
1	Helliconia Spring	BSF-N 84	ALDISS, Brian W
1	Helliconia Spring	NEB-N 82	ALDISS, Brian W
1	Helliconia Spring	JWC-W 83	ALDISS, Brian W
1	Helliconia Summer	SFC-N 84	ALDISS, Brian W
1	Helliconia Summer	LOC-N 84	ALDISS, Brian W
1	Helliconia Winter	SFC-N 86	ALDISS, Brian W
1	Helliconia Winter	NEB-N 85	ALDISS, Brian W
1	Helliconia Winter	BSF-W 86	ALDISS, Brian W
1	Helliconia Winter	LOC-N 86	ALDISS, Brian W
1	Hello America	BSF-N 82	BALLARD, J G
4	Hell-Bound Train, That	HUG-W 59	BLOCH, Robert
2	Hemingway Hoax, The	SFC-N 91	HALDEMAN, Joe
2	Hemingway Hoax, The	WFA-N 91	HALDEMAN, Joe
2	Hemingway Hoax, The	NEB-N 91	HALDEMAN, Joe
2	Hemingway Hoax, The	LOC-N 91	HALDEMAN, Joe
2	Hemingway Hoax, The	HUG-N 91	HALDEMAN, Joe
4	Her Furry Face	SFC-N 84	KENNEDY, Leigh
4	Her Furry Face	NEB-N 83	KENNEDY, Leigh
2	Her Habiline Husband	LOC-W 84	BISHOP, Michael
2	Her Habiline Husband	SFC-W 84	BISHOP, Michael
2	Her Habiline Husband	NEB-N 83	BISHOP, Michael
5	Her Smoke Rose Up Forever	LOC-N 91	TIPTREE, James Jr
9	Hercules Text, The	LOC-W 87	McDEVITT, Jack
1	Hercules Text, The	DIC-N 87	McDEVITT, Jack
11	Hereafter Gang, The	LOC-N 92	BARRETT, Neal Jr
1	Heritage Hastur (9):Darkover	NEB-N 75	BRADLEY, Marion Zimmer

SECTION C: TITLES (Alphabetically)

CAT	T I T L E S	AW W/N Y	A U T H O R
1	Heritage of Flight	DIC-N 90	SHWARTZ, Susan
1	Heritage of Stars	JUP-W 78	SIMAK, Clifford D
2	Hero	LOC-N 73	HALDEMAN, Joe
2	Hero	HUG-N 73	HALDEMAN, Joe
6	Heroes and Horror	WFA-N 79	LEIBER, Fritz
4	Heroics	JWC-N 88	KELLY, James Patrick
1	Herovit's World	JUP-N 74	MALZBERG, Barry
3	Hertford Manuscript, The	LOC-N 77	COWPER, Richard
1	Hidden Place, A	AUR-N 87	WILSON, Robert Charles
9	Hidden Place, A	LOC-N 87	WILSON, Robert Charles
1	Hidden Place, A	DIC-N 87	WILSON, Robert Charles
1	Hidden Place, A	COM-N 87	WILSON, Charles
1	High Crusade, The	HUG-N 60	ANDERSON, Poul
1	High Crusade, The	HUG-N 61	ANDERSON, Poul
7	High Kings, The	LOC-N 84	CHANT, Joy
7	High Kings, The	HUG-N 84	CHANT, Joy
6	High Spirits	WFA-W 84	DAVIES, Robinson
3	High Steel	LOC-N 83	HALDEMAN, Joe
4	High Steel	NEB-N 82	HALDEMAN, Jack C
3	His Hour Upon the Stage	NEB-N 76	CARRINGTON, Grant
4	Hiss of Dragon, A	LOC-N 79	BENFORD, Gregory
3	History of the 20th Century, A	SFC-N 92	ROBINSON, Kim Stanley
1	Hitchhiker's Guide to the Galaxy, The	DIT-W 80	ADAMS, Douglas
3	Hob, The	NEB-N 88	MOFFETT, Judith
3	Hob, The	DAV-N 89	MOFFATT, Judith
4	Hogfoot Right and Bird-Hands	WFA-N 88	KILWORTH, Garry
4	Hole Man, The	LOC-N 75	NIVEN, Larry
4	Hole Man, The	HUG-W 75	NIVEN, Larry
1	Hollow Lands, The	BFA-N 76	MOORCOCK, Michael
7	Hollywood Gothic	HUG-N 91	SKAL, David J
7	Hollywood Gothic	STO-N 91	SKAL, David J
7	Hollywood Gothic	LOC-N 91	SKAL, David J
2	Home is the Hangman	LOC-N 76	ZELAZNY, Roger
2	Home is the Hangman	NEB-W 75	ZELAZNY, Roger
2	Home is the Hangman	HUG-W 76	ZELAZNY, Roger
3	Homecoming	HUG-N 80	LONGYEAR, Barry
2	Homefaring	NEB-N 83	SILVERBERG, Robert
2	Homefaring	LOC-N 84	SILVERBERG, Robert
2	Homefaring	SFC-N 84	SILVERBERG, Robert
1	Homunculus	DIC-W 87	BLAYLOCK, James P
4	Hong's Bluff	HUG-N 86	WU, William F
4	Hong's Bluff	NEB-N 85	WU, William F
2	Horrible Imaginings (Death)	NEB-N 82	LEIBER, Fritz
2	Horrible Imaginings (Death)	LOC-N 83	LEIBER, Fritz
2	Horrible Imaginings (Death)	WFA-N 83	LEIBER, Fritz
2	Horrible Imaginings (Death)	SFC-N 83	LEIBER, Fritz
7	Horror Literature: A Reader's Guide	STO-N 91	BARRON, Neil
3	Horrorshow	STO-N 89	FARRIS, John
7	Horror: A Connoisseur's Guide	STO-N 90	WOLF, Leonard
7	Horror: The 100 Best Books	STO-N 90	JONES, Stephen
3	Horrus Errand, The	JUP-N 75	COCHRANE, William C
4	Horse of Air	NEB-N 71	DOZOIS, Gardner
1	Hospital Station	NEB-N 62	WHITE, James

SECTION C: TITLES (Alphabetically)

CAT	T I T L E S	AW W/N Y	A U T H O R
4	Hothouse Series, The	HUG-W 62	ALDISS, Brian W
1	Hour of the Oxrun Dead, The	WFA-N 78	GRANT, Charles L
4	House of the Temple, The	BFA-N 81	LUMLEY, Brian
4	House the Blakeneys Built, The	NEB-N 65	DAVIDSON, Avram
6	Houses Without Doors	STO-N 91	STRAUB, Peter
5	Houses Without Doors	WFA-N 91	STRAUB, Peter
2	Houston, Houston, Do You Read?	JUP-W 77	TIPTREE, James Jr
2	Houston, Houston, Do You Read?	LOC-N 77	TIPTREE, James Jr
2	Houston, Houston. Do You Read?	NEB-W 76	TIPTREE, James Jr
2	Houston, Houston. Do You Read?	HUG-W 77	TIPTREE, James Jr
4	How I Lost the Second World War and ...	NEB-N 73	WOLFE, Gene
7	How to Write Science Fiction and Fantasy	HUG-W 91	CARD, Orson Scott
7	How to Write Science Fiction and Fantasy	LOC-N 91	CARD, Orson Scott
5	Howard Who?	LOC-N 87	WALDROP, Howard
1	Hrolf Kraki's Saga	BFA-W 75	ANDERSON, Poul
14	Hugo Winners Vol 2	LOC-N 72	ASIMOV, Isaac
4	Hundred Year Christmas	WFA-N 84	MORRELL, David
1	Hungry Moon, The	BFA-W 88	CAMPBELL, Ramsey
3	Hunter's Moon	LOC-N 79	ANDERSON, Poul
3	Hunter's Moon	HUG-W 79	ANDERSON, Poul
1	Hunting the Ghost Dancer	WFA-N 92	ATTANASIO, A A
2	Hurricane Claude	HUG-N 84	SCHENCK, Hilbert
1	Hyperion	HUG-W 90	SIMMONS, Dan
1	Hyperion	BSF-N 91	SIMMONS, Dan
1	Hyperion	SFC-N 90	SIMMONS, Dan
1	Hyperion	LOC-W 90	SIMMONS, Dan
1	Hyperion Cantos	CLA-N 92	SIMMONS, Dan
2	Hypothetical Lizard, A	WFA-N 88	MOORE, Alan
7	H.P. Lovecraft	STO-N 90	CANNON, Peter
4	I Have no Mouth Yet I Must Scream	HUG-W 68	ELLISON, Harlan
4	I See You	JUP-W 77	KNIGHT, Damon
4	I See You	LOC-N 77	KNIGHT, Damon
4	I See You	HUG-N 77	KNIGHT, Damon
4	Idiot's Mate	NEB-N 68	TAYLOR, Robert
2	If All Men Were Brothers Would You Let..	NEB-N 67	STURGEON, Theodore
3	If the Stars are Gods	JUP-N 75	EKLUND, Gordon
3	If the Stars are Gods	NEB-W 74	BENFORD and EKLUND
4	Ike at the Mike	HUG-N 83	WALDROP, Howard
2	Ill Met in Lankhmar	NEB-W 70	LEIBER, Fritz
2	Ill Met in Lankhmar	HUG-W 71	LEIBER, Fritz
4	Illusionist, The	WFA-W 90	MILLHAUSER, Steven
1	Illustrated Man, The	IFA-N 52	BRADBURY, Ray
1	Illywacker	WFA-N 86	CAREY, Peter
6	Imaginary Lands	WFA-W 86	McKINLEY, Robin
6	Imaginary Lands	LOC-N 86	McKINLEY, Robin
7	Imagination: Art & Techn of David Cherry	HUG-N 88	CHERRY, David A
10	Imajica	LOC-N 92	BARKER, Clive
1	Imaro	AUR-N 82	SAUDERS, Charles
1	Immortality Inc	HUG-N 59	SHECKLEY, Robert
1	Imperial Earth	LOC-N 76	CLARKE, Arthur C
1	In A Dark Dream	WFA-N 90	GRANT, Charles L
1	In A Dark Stream	STO-N 90	GRANT, Charles L

SECTION C: TITLES (Alphabetically)

CAT	TITLES	AW W/N Y	AUTHOR
1	In Conquest Born	COM-N 88	FRIEDMAN, C S
9	In Conquest Born	LOC-N 88	FRIEDMAN, C S
7	In Joy Still Felt	HUG-N 81	ASIMOV, Isaac
7	In Joy Still Felt	LOC-W 81	ASIMOV, Isaac
7	In Memory Yet Green	HUG-N 80	ASIMOV, Isaac
7	In Memory Yet Green	LOC-N 80	ASIMOV, Isaac
4	In Our Block	NEB-N 65	LAFFERTY, R A
4	In the Bag	BFA-W 78	CAMPBELL, Ramsey
10	In the Blood	LOC-N 92	COLLINS, Nancy
9	In the Country of The Blind	LOC-W 91	FLYNN, Michael
1	In the Dark Lands	COM-N 92	SAGARA, Michelle
3	In the Deadlands	NEB-N 72	GERROLD, David
9	In the Drift	LOC-N 86	SWANWICK, Michael
2	In the Face of My Enemy	HUG-N 84	DELANEY, Joseph H
6	In the Field of Fire	LOC-N 88	DANN, Jeanne van Buren
6	In the Field of Fire	WFA-N 88	DANN, Jeanne Van Buren
2	In the Hall of the Martian Kings	JUP-W 78	VARLEY, John
2	In the Hall of the Martian Kings	HUG-N 78	VARLEY, John
7	In t/Heart Or In t/Head:Essay T/Travel	HUG-N 85	TURNER, George
4	In The House of Gingerbread	WFA-N 88	WOLFE, Gene
4	In the Late Cretaceous	HUG-N 92	WILLIS, Connie
4	In the Late Cretaceous	LOC-N 92	WILLIS, Connie
4	In the Midst of Life	LOC-N 88	TIPTREE, james Jr
1	In the Net of Dreams	COM-N 91	SIMMONS, Wm Mark
1	In the Ocean of the Night	NEB-N 77	BENFORD, Gregory
1	In the Ocean of the Night	LOC-N 78	BENFORD, Gregory
2	In The Problem Pit	JUP-N 74	POHL, Frederik
4	In the Queue	LOC-N 71	LAUMER, Keith
4	In the Queue	NEB-N 70	LAUMER, Keith
4	In the Queue	HUG-N 71	LAUMER, Keith
2	In The Sumerian Marshes	WFA-N 85	PEARLE, Gerald
2	In the Western Tradition	NEB-N 81	EISENSTEIN, Phyllis
2	In the Western Tradition	SFC-W 82	EISENSTEIN, Phyllis
2	In the Western Tradition	LOC-N 82	EISENSTEIN, Phyllis
2	In the Western Tradition	HUG-N 82	EISENSTEIN, Phyllis
4	In Transition	BSF-W 90	TUTTLE, Lisa
1	In Viriconium	BFA-N 83	HARRISON, M John
4	Inconstant Moon	HUG-W 72	NIVEN, Larry
7	Index to SF Anthologies and Collections	LOC-N 79	CONTENTO, William
7	Industrial Light & Magic: Special Effect	LOC-N 87	SMITH, Thomas G
7	Industrial Light & Magic: Special Effect	HUG-N 87	SMITH, Thomas G
1	Inferno	NEB-N 76	NIVEN, Larry
1	Inferno	HUG-N 76	NIVEN, Larry
5	Infinite Dreams	LOC-N 79	HALDEMAN, Joe
13	Infinity 2	LOC-N 72	HOSKINS, Robert
2	Infinity Box, The	NEB-N 71	WILHELM, Kate
11	Infinity Concerto, The	LOC-N 85	BEAR, Greg
1	Infinity Hold	DIC-N 90	LONGYEAR, Barry
1	Infinity's Web	COM-W 86	FINCH, Sheila
1	Influence, The	BFA-W 89	CAMPBELL, Ramsey
4	Ink Imp, The	BSF-N 81	LAMMING, R M
4	Inside Man	NEB-N 65	GOLD, H L

SECTION C: TITLES (Alphabetically)

CAT	T I T L E S	AW W/N Y	A U T H O R
1	Integral Trees, The	SFC-N 85	NIVEN, Larry
1	Integral Trees, The	LOC-W 85	NIVEN, Larry
1	Integral Trees, The	NEB-N 84	NIVEN, Larry
1	Integral Trees, The	HUG-N 85	NIVEN, Larry
1	Interior of Life, The	COM-N 91	BLAKE, Katherine
4	Into Whose Hands	WFA-N 84	WAGNER, Karl Edward
1	Inverted World, The	HUG-N 75	PRIEST, Christopher
1	Inverted World, The	LOC-N 75	PRIEST, Christopher
1	Invisible Cities	NEB-N 75	CALVINO, Italo
1	Iron Dream, The	NEB-N 72	SPINRAD, Norman
7	Isaac Asimov: The Foundations of SF	HUG-W 83	GUNN, James E
7	Isaac Asimov: The Foundations of SF	LOC-N 83	GUNN, James
5	Island of Dr. Death, The	LOC-N 81	WOLFE, Gene
4	Island of Dr. Death, The	NEB-N 70	WOLFE, Gene
1	Islands	NEB-N 76	RANDALL, Marta
1	Islands in the Net	JWC-W 89	STERLING, Bruce
1	Islands in the Net	LOC-N 89	STERLING, Bruce
1	Islands in the Net	SFC-N 89	STERLING, Bruce
1	Islands in the Net	HUG-N 89	STERLING, Bruce
1	Isle of the Dead	NEB-N 69	ZELAZNY, Roger
11	It	LOC-N 87	KING, Stephen
1	It	WFA-N 87	KING, Stephen
1	It	BFA-W 87	KING, Stephen
2	It Only Comes Out At Night	WFA-N 77	ETCHISON, Dennis
1	Ivory: Legend Past & Future	CLA-N 90	RESNICK, Mike
1	Ivory: Legend Past & Future	SFC-N 89	RESNICK, Michael
1	Ivory: Legend Past & Future	NEB-N 89	RESNICK, Mike
3	I'm Looking for Kadak	LOC-N 75	ELLISON, Harlan
2	Jack	NEB-N 92	WILLIS, Connie
2	Jack	SFC-N 92	WILLIS, Connie
2	Jack	HUG-N 92	WILLIS, Connie
2	Jack	LOC-N 92	WILLIS, Connie
1	Jack of Shadows	HUG-N 72	ZELAZNY, Roger
1	Jack of Shadows	LOC-N 72	ZELAZNY, Roger
1	Jack the Giant Killer	AUR-W 88	de LINT, Charles
7	Jack Vance	LOC-N 81	Underwood, Tim
4	Jack's Decline	STO-N 89	SHEPARD, Lucius
2	Jacqueline Ess: Her Will and Testament	WFA-N 85	BARKER, Clive
1	Jagged Orbit, The	BSF-W 71	BRUNNER, John
1	Jagged Orbit, The	NEB-N 69	BRUNNER, John
5	Jaguar Hunter, The	WFA-W 88	SHEPARD, Lucius
3	Jaguar Hunter, The	NEB-N 85	SHEPARD, Lucius
5	Jaguar Hunter, The	LOC-W 88	SHEPARD, Lucius
4	Jaguar Hunter, The	WFA-N 86	SHEPARD, Lucius
3	Jaguar Hunter, The	LOC-N 86	SHEPARD, Lucius
4	Jangling Geordie's Hole	BSF-N 87	WATSON, Ian
4	Jean Dupres	HUG-N 71	DICKSON, Gordon R
4	Jeffty is Five	LOC-W 78	ELLISON, Harlan
4	Jeffty is Five	BFA-W 79	ELLISON, Harlan
4	Jeffty is Five	WFA-N 78	ELLISON, Harlan
4	Jeffty is Five	NEB-W 77	ELLISON, Harlan
4	Jeffty is Five	JUP-W 78	ELLISON, Harlan
4	Jeffty is Five	HUG-W 78	ELLISON, Harlan

SECTION C: TITLES (Alphabetically)

CAT	T I T L E S	AW W/N Y	A U T H O R
1	JEM	HUG-N 80	POHL, Frederik
1	JEM	NEB-N 79	POHL, Frederik
1	JEM	LOC-N 80	POHL, Frederik
4	Jigsaw Man, The	HUG-N 68	NIVEN, Larry
1	Job: A Comedy of Justice	NEB-N 84	HEINLEIN, Robert A
1	Job: A Comedy of Justice	HUG-N 85	HEINLEIN, Robert A
11	Job: A Comedy of Justice	LOC-W 85	HEINLEIN, Robert A
7	Joe Bob Goes Back to the Drive-in	STO-N 91	BRIGGS, Joe Bob
7	Joe Bob Goes Back to the Drive-in	STO-N 88	BRIGGS, Joe Bob
5	John the Balladeer	LOC-N 89	WELLMAN, Manly Wade
7	John W Campbell Letters Vol 1, The	HUG-N 86	CHAPDELAINE, Perry
7	John W Campbell Letters Vol 1, The	LOC-N 87	CHAPDELAINE, Perry
4	Johny Mnemonic	NEB-N 81	GIBSON, William
1	Jonah Kit, The	BSF-W 78	WATSON, Ian
1	Journal of Nicholas the American	NEB-N 86	KENNEDY, L
2	Journals of the Plague Years, The	HUG-N 89	SPINRAD, Norman
2	Journals of the Plague Years, The	LOC-N 89	SPINRAD, Norman
2	Journals of the Plague Years, The	NEB-N 88	SPINRAD, Norman
2	Journals of the Plague Years, The	SFC-N 89	SPINRAD, Norman
1	Journey to Apriloth	AUR-W 85	KERNAGHAN, Eileen
1	Judgement of Dragons	AUR-W 82	GOTLIEB, Phyllis
2	Junction	NEB-N 73	DANN, Jack
1	Juniper Time	NEB-N 79	WILHELM, Kate
3	Juniper Tree, The	STO-N 89	STRAUB, Peter
14	Jupiter	LOC-N 74	POHL, Frederik
1	Jurassic Park	LOC-N 91	CRICHTON, Michael
4	Kaeti and the Hangman	BSF-W 87	ROBERTS, Keith
4	Kaeti and the Hangman	BFA-W 86	ROBERTS, Keith
1	Kairos	CLA-N 89	JONES, Gwyneth
2	Kalimantan	LOC-N 91	SHEPARD, Lucius
1	Kalki	NEB-N 78	VIDAL, Gore
4	Keep Them Happy	NEB-N 65	ROHRER, Robert
2	Ker Plop	HUG-N 80	REYNOLDS, Ted
3	Keys to December, The	NEB-N 67	ZELAZNY, Roger
4	Kibakusha Gallery, The	NEB-N 77	BRYANT, Edward
4	Kid Charlemagne	NEB-N 87	FILIPPO, Paul Di
1	Kill The Dead	BFA-N 81	LEE, Tanith
4	Killing Thought, The	BSF-W 82	SHAVER, Edward
3	Kindly Isle, The	LOC-N 85	POHL, Frederik
11	King of the Morning, Queen of Day	LOC-N 92	McDONALD, Ian
1	King of the Morning, Queen of Day	DIC-W 92	McDONALD, Ian
11	King of the Murgos	LOC-N 89	EDDINGS, David
1	King of the Swords, The	BFA-W 74	MOORCOCK, Michael
3	Kingdom By the Sea, A	HUG-N 73	DOZOIS, Gardner
3	Kingdom By the Sea, A	NEB-N 72	DOZOIS, Gardner
4	Kingdom by the Sea, A	LOC-N 73	DOZOIS, Gardner
9	King's Blood Four	LOC-N 84	TEPPER, Sheri S
11	King's Justice, The	LOC-N 86	KURTZ, Katherine
4	Kirinyaga	HUG-N 89	RESNICK, Mike
3	Kirinyaga	NEB-N 88	RESNICK, Mike
4	Kirinyaga	LOC-N 89	RESNICK, Mike
4	Kirinyaga	SFC-W 89	RESNICK, Mike

SECTION C: TITLES (Alphabetically)

CAT	TITLES	AW W/N Y	AUTHOR
4	Kitemaster	BSF-W 83	ROBERTS, Keith
4	Kitemistress	BSF-N 86	ROBERTS, Keith
1	Kiteworld	JWC-N 86	ROBERTS, Keith
1	Kiteworld	BSF-N 86	ROBERTS, Keith
5	Knight and the Knave of Swords, The	WFA-N 89	LEIBER, Fritz
5	Knight and the Knave of Swords, The	LOC-N 89	LEIBER, Fritz
1	Knight Moves	DIC-N 86	WILLIAMS, Walter John
1	Knight of the Swords, The	BFA-W 73	MOORCOCK, Michael
1	Koko	WFA-W 89	STRAUB, Peter
10	Koko	LOC-N 89	STRAUB, Peter
4	Kyrie	NEB-N 68	ANDERSON, Poul
4	La Carte du Tendre	AUR-W 87	VONARBURG, Elisabeth
2	Labyrinth	LOC-N 90	BUJOLD, Lois McMaster
3	Labyrinth	DAV-W 90	BUJOLD, Lois McMaster
4	Lady in White, The	BFA-N 79	DONALDSON, Stephen R
4	Lady Madonna	STO-W 92	HOLDER, Nancy
9	Lady of Light	LOC-N 83	PAXSON, Diana
5	Lafferty in Orbit	WFA-N 92	LAFFERTY, R A
7	Lands Beyond	IFA-W 53	LEY, Willy
2	Langoliers, The	STO-N 91	KING, Stephen
7	Language of the Night, The	LOC-N 80	LeGUIN, Ursula K
7	Language of the Night, The	HUG-N 80	LeGUIN, Ursula K
4	Last Answer, The	LOC-N 81	ASIMOV, Isaac
1	Last Call of Morning, The	WFA-N 80	GRANT, Charles L
2	Last Castle, The	NEB-W 66	VANCE, Jack
3	Last Castle, The	HUG-W 67	VANCE, Jack
11	Last Coin, The	LOC-N 89	BLAYLOCK, James P
1	Last Coin, The	WFA-N 89	BLAYLOCK, James P
5	Last Defender of Camelot	LOC-N 81	ZELAZNY, Roger
4	Last Feast of Harlequin, The	WFA-N 91	LIGOTTI, The
4	Last Flight of Dr. Ain, The	NEB-N 69	TIPTREE, James Jr
4	Last Ghost, The	NEB-N 71	GOLDIN, Stephen
2	Last of the Winnebagos, The	SFC-W 89	WILLIS, Connie
2	Last of the Winnebagos, The	LOC-N 89	WILIS, Connie
2	Last of the Winnebagos, The	NEB-W 88	WILLIS, Connie
2	Last of the Winnebagos, The	DAV-W 89	WILLIS, Connie
2	Last of the Winnebagos, The	HUG-W 89	WILLIS, Connie
4	Last Sad Love..., A	WFA-N 90	BRYANT, Edward
4	Last Sad Love..., A	STO-N 90	BRYANT, Edward
4	Late Shift, The	BFA-N 81	ETCHISON, Dennis
1	Lathe of Heaven, The	LOC-W 72	LeGUIN, Ursula K
1	Lathe of Heaven, The	NEB-N 71	LEGUIN, Ursula K
1	Lathe of Heaven, The	HUG-N 72	LeGUIN, Ursula K
3	Laugh Along With Franz	NEB-N 65	KAGAN, Norman
4	Lauralyn	HUG-N 78	GARRETT, Randall
9	Laying the Music to Rest	LOC-N 90	SMITH, Dean Wesley
9	Laying the Music to Rest	STO-N 90	SMITH, Dean Wesley
4	Leader For Yesterday, A	NEB-N 65	REYNOLDS, Mack
4	Leaks	BFA-W 88	TEM, Steve Rasnic
4	Learning To Be Me	BSF-N 91	EGAN, Greg
1	Leaves of October, The	COM-N 89	SAKERS, Don
1	Left Hand of Darkness, The	NEB-W 69	LEGUIN, Ursula K
1	Left Hand of Darkness, The	HUG-W 70	LEGUIN, Ursula K

CAT	T I T L E S	AW W/N Y	A U T H O R
5	Leiber Chronicles, The	WFA-N 91	LEIBER, Fritz
5	Leiber Chronicles, The	LOC-N 91	LEIBER, Fritz
4	Les Crabes des Venus	AUR-W 88	BERGERON, Alain
4	Letter From the Clearys, A	SFC-N 83	WILLIS, Connie
4	Letter From the Clearys, A	NEB-W 82	WILLIS, Connie
6	Liavek: The Players of Luck	WFA-N 87	SHETTERLEY, Will
9	Liege-Killer	LOC-N 88	HINZ, Christopher
1	Liege-Killer	COM-N 88	HINZ, Christopher
4	Lieserl	LOC-N 91	FOWLER, Karen Joy
4	Lieserl	NEB-N 91	FOWLER, Karen Joy
1	Life During Wartime	LOC-N 88	SHEPARD, Lucius
1	Life During Wartime	CLA-N 89	SHEPARD, Lucius
1	Life During Wartime	DIC-N 88	SHEPARD, Lucius
4	Life of Buddha	WFA-N 89	SHEPARD, Lucius
3	Life of Your Time, The	NEB-N 65	KARAGEORGE, Michael
1	Lifter	AUR-N 87	KILLIAN, Crawford
5	Light Fantastic, The	LOC-N 77	BESTER, Alfred
4	Light of Other Days	HUG-N 67	SHAW, Bob
4	Light of Other Days	NEB-N 66	SHAW, Bob
6	Light Years and Dark	LOC-W 85	BISHOP, Michael
9	Lilith Factor, The	STO-N 90	PAIVA, Jean
5	Limits	LOC-N 86	NIVEN, Larry
1	Lincoln's Dreams	JWC-W 88	WILLIS, Connie
11	Lincoln's Dreams	LOC-N 88	WILLIS, Connie
2	Lines of Power	NEB-N 68	DELANY, Samuel R
2	Lines of Power	HUG-N 69	DELANY, Samuel R
4	Lion Loose	HUG-N 62	SCHMITZ, James
2	Lion Time in Timbuctoo	LOC-N 91	SILVERBERG, Robert
4	Lions Are Asleep This Night, The	NEB-N 86	WALDROP, Howard
4	Lions Are Asleep This Night, The	JWC-N 87	WALDROP, Howard
3	Lirios: A Tale of The Quuintana Roo	NEB-N 81	TIPTREE, James Jr
1	Listeners, The	JWC-N 73	WOLFE, Gene
3	Listeners, The	NEB-N 68	GUNN, James E
3	Listening to Brahms	NEB-N 86	CHARNAS, Suzy McKee
1	Little Big	NEB-N 81	CROWLEY, John
1	Little Big	WFA-W 82	CROWLEY, John
1	Little Big	BSF-N 83	CROWLEY, John
11	Little Big	LOC-N 82	CROWLEY, John
1	Little Big	HUG-N 82	CROWLEY, John
11	Little Country, The	LOC-N 92	de LINT, Charles
1	Little Country, The	WFA-N 92	DeLINT, Charles
4	Little Dog Gone	HUG-N 65	YOUNG, Robert F
1	Little Fuzzy	HUG-N 63	PIPER, H Beam
1	Live Girls	STO-N 88	GARTON, Ray
3	Loch Moose Monster, The	DAV-W 90	KAGAN, Janet
3	Locusts, The	HUG-N 80	NIVEN, Larry
4	Loneliest Number, The	STO-N 91	BRYANT, Edward
6	Long After Midnight	WFA-N 77	BRADBURY, Ray
12	Long Stern Case: Speculative Exercise	DAV-W 87	COOK, Rick
4	Longest Voyage, The	HUG-W 61	ANDERSON, Poul
3	Loose Cannon	NEB-N 91	SHWARTZ, Susan
5	Lord Darcy Investigates	LOC-N 82	GARRETT, Randall
4	Lord Moon	NEB-N 65	BEAUCLERK, Jane

CAT	TITLES	AW W/N Y	AUTHOR
1	Lord of Light	HUG-W 68	ZELAZNY, Roger
1	Lord of Light	NEB-N 67	ZELAZNY, Roger
1	Lord of the Rings - Trilogy	IFA-W 57	TOLKIEN, J R R
1	Lord Valentine's Castle	HUG-N 81	SILVERBERG, Robert
11	Lord Valentine's Castle	LOC-W 81	SILVERBERG, Robert
3	Lordly Ones, The	HUG-N 81	ROBERTS, Keith
4	Lordly Ones, The	BSF-N 81	ROBERTS, Keith
4	Lost Boys	NEB-N 89	CARD, Orson Scott
4	Lost Boys	HUG-N 90	CARD, Orson Scott
4	Lost Boys	LOC-W 90	CARD, Orson Scott
4	Lost Boys	SFC-N 90	CARD, Orson Scott
2	Lost Dorsai	HUG-W 81	DICKSON, Gordon R
2	Lost Dorsai	NEB-N 80	DICKSON, Gordon R
4	Lost Kafoozalum, The	HUG-N 61	ASHWELL, Pauline
4	Love and Sex Among the Vertebrates	NEB-N 91	MURPHY, Pat
4	Love and Sex Among the Vertebrates	LOC-N 91	MURPHY, Pat
4	Love Doll: A Fable	STO-N 92	LANSDALE, Joe R
4	Love is the Plan, the Plan is Death	LOC-N 74	TIPTREE, James Jr
3	Love is the Plan, the Plan is Death	HUG-N 74	TIPTREE, James Jr
4	Love is the Plan, the Plan is Death	NEB-W 73	TIPTREE, James Jr
4	Love Sickness	BSF-W 88	RYMAN, Geoff
4	Love Song of Laura Morrison, The	DAV-W 88	OLTOIN, Jerry
4	Loveman's Comeback	WFA-N 78	CAMPBELL, Ramsey
1	Lucifer's Hammer	HUG-N 78	NIVEN, Larry
3	Lucky Strike, The	HUG-N 85	ROBINSON, Kim Stanley
3	Lucky Strike, The	SFC-N 85	ROBINSON, Kim Stanley
3	Lucky Strike, The	NEB-N 84	ROBINSON, Kim Stanley
3	Lucky Strike, The	LOC-N 85	ROBINSON, Kim Stanley
2	Lurking Duck, The	WFA-N 84	BAKER, Scott
1	Lyonesse	WFA-N 84	VANCE, Jack
1	Lyonesse	NEB-N 83	VANCE, Jack
11	Lyonesse	LOC-N 84	VANCE, Jack
1	Lyonesse: Madouc	WFA-W 90	VANCE, Jack
11	Lyonesse: Madouc	LOC-N 90	VANCE, Jack
11	Lyonesse: The Green Pearl	LOC-N 86	VANCE, Jack

SECTION C: TITLES (Alphabetically)

CAT	TITLES	AW W/N Y	AUTHOR
4	Ma Qui	JWC-N 92	BRENNERT, Alan
4	Ma Qui	NEB-W 92	BRENNERT, Alan
4	Macintosth Willy	WFA-W 80	CAMPBELL, Ramsey
1	Macroscope	HUG-N 70	ANTHONY, Piers
1	Macroscope	HUG-N 69	ANTHONY, Piers
6	Magazine of Fant & SF: A 30 Yr Retrospec	LOC-W 81	FERNAN, Edward L
4	Magic Goes Away, The	WFA-N 79	NIVEN, Larry
2	Magic Striptease, The	JUP-N 74	GARRETT, George
2	Magpie	STO-N 92	GALLAGHER, Stephen
3	Maiden Voyage	NEB-N 65	SCHUTZ, J W
5	Majipoor Chronicle	LOC-N 83	SILVERBERG, Robert
1	Malevil	JWC-W 74	MERLE, Robert
4	Man In His Time	NEB-N 66	ALDISS, Brian W
4	Man In His Time	HUG-N 67	ALDISS, Brian W
1	Man in the High Castle, The	HUG-W 63	DICK, Philip K
2	Man Opening a Door	NEB-N 92	ASH, Paul
1	Man Plus	HUG-N 77	POHL, Frederik
1	Man Plus	JWC-N 77	POHL, Frederik
1	Man Plus	NEB-W 76	POHL, Frederik
1	Man Plus	LOC-N 77	POHL, Frederik
4	Man Who Drew Cats, The	BFA-W 92	SMITH, Michael Marshall
1	Man Who Folded Himself, The	JUP-N 74	GERROLD, David
1	Man Who Folded Himself, The	NEB-N 73	GERROLD, David
1	Man Who Folded Himself, The	HUG-N 74	GERROLD, David
1	Man Who Folded Himself, The	LOC-N 74	GERROLD, David
3	Man Who Had No Idea, The	HUG-N 79	DISCH, Thomas M
4	Man Who Learned Loving, The	NEB-N 69	STURGEON, Theodore
4	Man Who Lost the Sea	HUG-N 60	STURGEON, Theodore
1	Man Who Melted, The	NEB-N 84	DANN, Jack
4	Man Who Met Picasso, The	WFA-N 83	SWANWICK, Michael
2	Man Who Painted the Dragon Griaule, The	WFA-N 85	SHEPARD, Lucius
4	Man Who Painted the Dragon Griaule, The	BSF-N 85	SHEPARD, Lucius
3	Man Who Painted the Dragon Griaule, The	SFC-N 85	SHEPARD, Lucius
3	Man Who Painted the Dragon Griaule, The	HUG-N 85	SHEPARD, Lucius
3	Man Who Painted the Dragon Griaule, The	NEB-N 84	SHEPARD, Lucius
3	Man Who Painted the Dragon Griaule, The	LOC-N 85	SHEPARD, Lucius
3	Manamouki, The	HUG-W 91	RESNICK, Mike
3	Manamouki, The	NEB-N 91	RESNICK, Mike
3	Manamouki, The	SFC-N 91	RESNICK, Mike
4	Manatee Gal, Ain't Ya Comin' Out Tonight	WFA-N 78	DAVIDSON, Avram
3	Manor of Roses, The	HUG-N 67	BURNETT, Thomas
9	Manse, The	STO-W 88	CANTRELL, Lisa W
1	Many-Colored Land, The	LOC-W 82	MAY, Julian
1	Many-Colored Land, The	NEB-N 81	MAY, Julian
1	Many-Colored Land, The	HUG-N 82	MAY, Julian
6	Man-Kzin Wars, The	LOC-N 89	NIVEN, Larry
6	Man-Kzin Wars IV	LOC-N 92	NIVEN, Larry
1	Maple Leaf Rag	AUR-W 86	SPENCER, Garth
5	Maps in a Mirror	LOC-W 91	CARD, Orson Scott
2	Marathon Photograph, The	LOC-N 75	SIMAK, Clifford D
1	Margaret and I	NEB-N 71	WILHELM, Kate
2	Marid Changes His Mind	NEB-N 89	EFFINGER, George

SECTION C: TITLES (Alphabetically)

CAT	TITLES	AW W/N Y	AUTHOR
1	Marooned in Real Time	HUG-N 87	VINGE, Vernor
2	Marrow Death	NEB-N 84	SWANWICK, Michael
2	Mars Masked	NEB-N 79	POHL, Frederik
2	Mars Masked	LOC-N 80	POHL, Frederik
2	Mars Ship, The	LOC-N 78	THURSTON, Robert
4	Mary Margaret Road-Grader	NEB-N 76	WALDROP, Howard
1	Mary Reilly	WFA-N 91	MARTIN, Valerie
1	Mary Reilly	NEB-N 91	MARTIN, Valerie
10	Mary Reilly	LOC-N 91	MARTIN, Valerie
7	Mary Shelley	STO-W 88	SPARKS, Muriel
3	Masculine Revolt, The	NEB-N 65	TENN, William
1	Mask For The General, A	CLA-N 90	GOLDSTEIN, Lisa
4	Masks	HUG-N 69	KNIGHT, Damon
4	Masks	NEB-N 68	KNIGHT, Damon
1	Masks of Time, The	NEB-N 68	SILVERBERG, Robert
3	Masque of the Red Shift	NEB-N 65	SABERHAGEN, Fred
6	Masques	WFA-N 85	WILLIAMSON, J N
6	Masques II	WFA-N 88	WILLIAMSON, J N
3	Matter's End	LOC-N 92	BENFORD, Gregory
6	Medea: Harlan's World	LOC-W 86	ELLISON, Harlan
4	Meeting, The	HUG-W 73	POHL and KORNBLUTH
4	Meeting With Medusa, A	LOC-N 72	CLARKE, Arthur C
2	Meeting With Medusa, A	HUG-N 72	CLARKE, Arthur C
2	Meeting With Medusa, A	NEB-W 72	CLARKE, Arthur C
5	Melancholy Elephants	LOC-N 86	ROBINSON, Spider
4	Melancholy Elephants	LOC-N 83	ROBINSON, Spider
4	Melancholy Elephants	HUG-W 83	ROBINSON, Spider
1	Memoirs of An Invisible Man	CLA-N 88	SAINT, H F
1	Memories	DIC-N 88	McQUAY, Mike
1	Memory of Whiteness, The	CLA-N 87	ROBINSON, Kim Stanley
4	Men Who Murdered Mohammed, The	HUG-N 59	BESTER, Alfred
4	Mengele	LOC-N 86	SHEPARD, Lucius
2	Mercenary, The	HUG-N 73	POURNELLE, Jerry
2	Mercuryman, The	NEB-N 65	MacAPP, C C
6	Merlin's Booke	WFA-N 87	YOLEN, Jane
1	Merlin's Ring	WFA-N 75	MUNN, H Warner
11	Merman's Children, The	LOC-N 80	ANDERSON, Poul
4	Metastasis	WFA-N 89	SIMMONS, Dan
9	Metrophage	LOC-N 89	KADREY, Richard
7	Michael Whelan's Works of Wonder	HUG-W 88	WHELAN, Michael
7	Michael Whelan's Works of Wonder	LOC-N 88	WHELAN, Michael
1	Michaelmas	LOC-N 78	BUDRYS, Algis
10	Midnight	LOC-N 90	KOONTZ, Dean R
1	Midnight	STO-N 90	KOONTZ, Dean R
3	Midnight by the Morphy Watch	HUG-N 75	LEIBER, Fritz
6	Midnight Pleasures	STO-N 88	BLOCH, Robert
1	Midnight Sun	BFA-W 92	CAMPBELL, Ramsey
1	Midplayers	DIC-N 88	CADIGAN, Pat
2	Midsummer Century	LOC-N 73	BLISH, James
4	Midsummer Night's Dream, A	WFA-N 91	GAIMAN, Neil
1	Midsummer Tempest, A	NEB-N 75	ANDERSON, Poul
1	Midsummer Tempest, A	WFA-N 75	ANDERSON, Poul

SECTION C: TITLES (Alphabetically)

CAT	TITLES	AW W/N Y	AUTHOR
4	Midwinter's Tale, A	LOC-N 89	SWANWICK, Michael
4	Midwinter's Tale, A	DAV-W 89	SWANWICK, Michael
3	Mikal's Songbird	LOC-N 79	CARD, Orson Scott
3	Mikal's Songbird	NEB-N 78	CARD, Orson Scott
3	Mikal's Songbird	HUG-N 79	CARD, Orson Scott
1	Millenium	LOC-N 84	VARLEY, John
1	Millenium	HUG-N 84	VARLEY, John
1	Millenium	DIC-N 84	VARLEY, John
1	Mindbridge	HUG-N 77	HALDEMAN, Joe
1	Mindbridge	LOC-N 77	HALDEMAN, Joe
9	Mindplayers	LOC-N 88	CADIGAN, Pat
1	Mine	STO-W 91	McCAMMON, Robert R
5	Mirabile	LOC-N 92	KAGAN, Janet
3	Miracle	LOC-N 92	WILLIS, Connie
3	Miracle	HUG-N 92	WILLIS, Connie
3	Miracle Workers	HUG-N 59	VANCE, Jack
1	Mirror for Observers, A	IFA-W 55	PANGBORN, Edgar
6	Mirrorshades: The Cyberpunk Anthology	LOC-N 87	STERLING, Bruce
4	Mischief Maker, The	NEB-N 65	OLIN, Richard
1	Misery	WFA-N 88	KING, Stephen
1	Misery	STO-W 88	KING, Stephen
1	Missing Man, The	NEB-N 75	MacLEAN, Katherine
2	Missing Man, The	NEB-W 71	MacLEAN, Katherine
1	Mission of Gravity	IFA-N 55	CLEMENT, Hal
1	Mist, The	WFA-N 81	KING, Stephen
11	Mists of Avalon, The	LOC-W 84	BRADLEY, Marion Zimmer
1	Mockingbird	NEB-N 80	TEVIS, Walter
1	Mojo and the Pickle Jar	DIC-N 92	BELL, Douglas
1	Molly Zero	BSF-N 81	ROBERTS, Keith
1	Moment of Eclipse, The	BSF-W 72	ALDISS, Brian W
3	Moment of the Storm, This	NEB-N 66	ZELAZNY, Roger
2	Momentary Taste of Being, A	NEB-N 75	TIPTREE, James Jr
1	Mona Lisa Overdrive	LOC-N 89	GIBSON, William
1	Mona Lisa Overdrive	NEB-N 88	GIBSON, William
1	Mona Lisa Overdrive	HUG-N 89	GIBSON, William
1	Mona Lisa Overdrive	AUR-W 89	GIBSON, William
3	Monkey Treatment, The	NEB-N 83	MARTIN, George R R
3	Monkey Treatment, The	LOC-W 84	MARTIN, George R R
3	Monkey Treatment, The	HUG-N 84	BEAR, Greg
2	Monkey's Bride, The	WFA-N 84	BISHOP, Michael
4	Monument	HUG-N 62	BIGGLE, Lloyd Jr
10	Moon Dance	LOC-N 91	SOMTOW, S P
2	Moon Goddess and the Son, The	HUG-N 80	KINGSBURY, Donald
1	Moon is a Harsh Mistress, The	HUG-N 66	HEINLEIN, Robert A
1	Moon is a Harsh Mistress, The	NEB-N 66	HEINLEIN, Robert A
1	Moon is a Harsh Mistress, The	HUG-W 67	HEINLEIN, Robert A
2	Moon of Ice	NEB-N 82	LINAWEAVER, Brad
1	Moonstar Odyssey	NEB-N 77	GERROLD, David
5	More Shapes Than One	WFA-N 92	CHAPPELL, Fred
1	More Than Human	IFA-W 54	STURGEON, Theodore
4	More Than The Sum of His Parts	NEB-N 85	HALDEMAN, Joe
1	Moreta	HUG-N 84	McCAFFREY, Anne
1	Moreta: Dragonlady of Pern	LOC-N 84	McCAFFREY, Anne

CAT	T I T L E S	AW W/N Y	A U T H O R
4	Morning Child	SFC-N 85	DOZOIS, Gardner
4	Morning Child	NEB-W 84	DOZOIS, Gardner
3	Mortal Mountain, The	NEB-N 67	ZELAZNY, Roger
1	Mote in God's Eye, The	JUP-N 75	NIVEN, Larry
1	Mote in God's Eye, The	LOC-N 75	NIVEN, Larry
1	Mote In God's Eye, The	NEB-N 75	NIVEN, Larry
1	Mote in God's Eye, The	HUG-N 75	NIVEN, Larry
2	Mother Goddess of the World	HUG-N 88	ROBINSON, Kim Stanley
2	Mother Goddess of the World	DAV-W 88	ROBINSON, Kim Stanley
2	Mother Goddess of the World	LOC-N 88	ROBINSON, Kim Stanley
3	Mother to the World	NEB-W 68	WILSON, Richard
3	Mother to the World	HUG-N 69	WILSON, Richard
4	Mother Trip, The	LOC-N 76	POHL, Frederik
7	Motion of Light in Water, The: Sex & SF	HUG-W 89	DELANY, Samuel R
7	Motion of Light in Water, The: Sex & SF	LOC-N 89	DELANY, Samuel R
3	Mount Charity	NEB-N 71	PANGBORN, Edgar
2	Mountains of Mourning, The	NEB-W 89	BUJOLD, Lois McMaster
2	Mountains of Mourning, The	LOC-N 90	BUJOLD, Lois McMaster
2	Mountains of Mourning, The	HUG-W 90	BUJOLD, Lois McMaster
2	Mountains of Mourning, The	SFC-W 90	BUJOLD, Lois McMaster
4	Mrs. Shummel Exits a Winner	NEB-N 88	KESSEL, John
2	Mr. Boy	DAV-W 91	KELLY, James Patrick
2	Mr. Boy	NEB-N 91	KELLY, James Patrick
2	Mr. Boy	LOC-N 91	KELLY, James Patrick
4	Mr. Fiddlehead	WFA-N 90	CARROLL, Jonathan
4	Mr. Jester	HUG-N 67	SABERHAGEN, Fred
4	Ms Found in an Abandoned Time Machine	LOC-N 74	SILVERBERG, Robert
4	Muffin Explains Technology to the World	AUR-W 91	GARDNER, James Alan
3	Mummer Kiss	SFC-W 82	SWANWICK, Michael
3	Mummer Kiss	NEB-N 81	SWANWICK, Michael
6	Mummy! A Chrestomathy of Crypt-ology	WFA-N 81	PRONZINI, Bill
6	Murgunstrumm and Others	WFA-W 78	CAVE, Hugh B
4	Music of the Dark Time, The	STO-N 89	WILLIAMSON, Chet
4	My Advice to the Civilized	JWC-N 91	BARNES, John
4	Myrrha	HUG-N 63	JENNINGS, Gary
3	Mystery of the Young Gentleman, The	NEB-N 82	RUSS, Joanna
3	Myth of the Near Future	LOC-N 83	BALLARD, J G
1	Mythago Wood	WFA-W 85	HOLDSTOCK, Robert
4	Mythago Wood	BSF-W 82	HOLDSTOCK, Robert
1	Mythago Wood	BSF-W 85	HOLDSTOCK, Robert
2	Mythago Wood	WFA-N 82	HOLDSTOCK, Robert
4	Myths of the Near Future	BSF-N 83	BALLARD, J G
3	Myths of the Near Future	NEB-N 82	BALLARD, J G
1	M.D., The	STO-N 92	DISCH, Thomas M
10	M.D., The	LOC-N 92	DISCH, Thomas M
2	Nadelman's God	WFA-W 86	KLEIN, T E D
4	Name and Number	BFA-N 83	LUMLEY, Brian
1	Nameless, The	WFA-N 82	CAMPBELL, Ramsey
12	Nanotechnology	DAV-W 88	PETERSON, Chris
4	Naples	WFA-W 79	DAVIDSON, Avram
14	Nebula Award Stories 9	LOC-N 75	WILHELM, Kate
6	Nebula Awards #24	LOC-N 91	BISHOP, Michael

SECTION C: TITLES (Alphabetically)

CAT	T I T L E S	AW W/N Y	A U T H O R
4	Need	HUG-N 61	STURGEON, Theodore
1	Needful Things	STO-N 92	KING, Stephen
4	Needle Men, The	LOC-N 82	MARTIN, George R R
4	Neither Brute Nor Human	BFA-W 84	WAGNER, Karl Edward
1	Neon Lotus	DIC-N 89	LAIDLAY, Marc
2	Nesting Instinct	WFA-N 88	BAKER, Scott
1	Nestling, The	WFA-N 83	GRANT, Charles L
9	Net, The	LOC-N 88	MacGREGOR, Loren J
1	Neuromancer	BSF-N 85	GIBSON, William
9	Neuromancer	LOC-N 85	GIBSON, William
1	Neuromancer	NEB-W 84	GIBSON, William
1	Neuromancer	HUG-W 85	GIBSON, William
1	Neuromancer	DIC-W 85	GIBSON, William
1	Neuromancer	SFC-W 85	GIBSON, William
1	Neuromancer	DIT-W 85	GIBSON, William
1	Neuromancer	JWC-N 85	GIBSON, William
4	Neutron Star, The	HUG-W 67	NIVEN, Larry
1	Neverness	CLA-N 90	ZINDELL, David
3	New Atlantis, The	LOC-W 76	LeGUIN, Ursula K
3	New Atlantis, The	HUG-N 76	LeGUIN, Ursula K
3	New Atlantis, The	NEB-N 75	LeGUIN, Ursula K
5	New Atlantis, The	LOC-N 76	SILVERBERG, Robert
13	New Dimensions 1	LOC-N 72	SILVERBERG, Robert
13	New Dimensions 2	LOC-N 73	SILVERBERG, Robert
13	New Dimensions 3	LOC-N 74	SILVERBERG, Robert
13	New Dimensions 4	LOC-N 75	SILVERBERG, Robert
5	New Dimensions 5	LOC-N 76	SILVERBERG, Robert
14	New Dimensions 6	LOC-N 77	SILVERBERG, Robert
6	New Dimensions 8	LOC-N 79	SILVERBERG, Robert
7	New Encyclopedia of Science Fiction, The	HUG-N 89	GUNN, James
7	New Encyclopedia of Science Fiction, The	LOC-N 89	GUNN, James
6	New Terrors 1	WFA-N 81	CAMPBELL, Ramsey
6	New Voices 4	LOC-N 82	MARTIN, George R R
14	New Worlds of Fantasy 3rd ed	LOC-N 72	CARR, Terry
2	Newton Sleep	NEB-N 86	BENFORD, Greg
4	Niche, A	AUR-W 92	WATTS, Peter
1	Nifft the Lean	WFA-W 83	SHEA, Michael
3	Night Flier, The	STO-N 89	KING, Stephen
2	Night Moves	WFA-N 87	POWERS, Tim
4	Night of the Cooters	HUG-N 88	WALDROP, Howard
5	Night of the Cooters: More Neat Stories	WFA-N 92	WALDROP, Howard
5	Night of the Cooters: More Neat Stories	LOC-W 92	WALDROP, Howard
2	Night Seasons, The	WFA-N 87	WILLIAMSON, J N
6	Night Shift	WFA-N 79	KING, Stephen
5	Night Sorceries	WFA-N 88	LEE, Tanith
4	Night They Missed the Horror Show, The	WFA-N 89	LANSDALE, Joe R
4	Night They Missed the Horror Show, The	STO-W 89	LANSDALE, Joe R
6	Night Visions 1	WFA-N 85	RYAN, Alan
6	Night Visions 2	WFA-N 86	GRANT, Charles L
6	Night Visions 3	WFA-N 87	MARTIN, George R R
6	Night Visions 4	WFA-N 88	Dark Harvest
6	Night Visions 6	WFA-N 89	ANON

SECTION C: TITLES (Alphabetically)

CAT	T I T L E S	AW W/N Y	A U T H O R
6	Night Winds	WFA-N 79	WAGNER, Karl Edward
9	Nightblood	STO-N 91	MARTINDALE, T Chris
4	Nightcrawlers	WFA-N 85	McCAMMON, Robert R
2	Nightflyers	LOC-W 81	MARTIN, George R R
5	Nightflyers	LOC-N 86	MARTIN, George R R
2	Nightflyers	HUG-N 81	MARTIN, George R R
3	Nightlife	HUG-N 83	EISENSTEIN, Phyllis
6	Nightmare Seasons	WFA-W 83	GRANT, Charles L
6	Nightmares	WFA-N 80	GRANT, Charles L
1	Nights At the Circus	BSF-N 85	CARTER, Angela
2	Nightwings	NEB-N 68	SILVERBERG, Robert
2	Nightwings	HUG-W 69	SILVERBERG, Robert
1	Night's Master	WFA-N 79	LEE, Tanith
2	Night's Swift Dragons	WFA-N 83	GRANT, Charles L
3	Nine Lives	NEB-N 69	LeGUIN, Ursula K
4	Nine Yards of Other Cloth	HUG-N 59	WELLMAN, Manly Wade
3	Ninth Symphony of Ludwig v/Beethoven...	NEB-N 77	SCHOLZ, Carter
3	Ninth Symphony of Ludwig v/Beethoven...	HUG-N 78	SCHOLZ, Carter
3	Nix Olypica	HUG-N 75	WALLING, William
1	No Enemy But Time	NEB-W 82	BISHOP, Michael
1	No Enemy But Time	BSF-N 83	BISHOP, Michael
1	No Enemy But Time	JWC-N 83	BISHOP, Michael
9	No Safe Place	LOC-N 87	MOROZ, Anne
4	No Truce with Kings	HUG-W 64	ANDERSON, Poul
4	Nobody Lives There Now	STO-N 89	ORLOCK, Carol
7	Noreascon Three Souvenir Book	HUG-N 90	THOKAR, Greg
1	Norstilia	JUP-N 75	SMITH, Cordwainer
11	Northern Girl, The	LOC-N 81	LYNN, Elizabeth A
4	Not Long Before the End	HUG-N 70	NIVEN, Larry
4	Not Long Before the End	NEB-N 69	NIVEN, Larry
4	Nothing Special	BSF-N 92	GREENLAND, Colin
1	Nova	HUG-N 69	DELANY, Samuel R
13	Nova 2	LOC-N 73	HARRISON, Harry
1	Nova Express	NEB-N 64	BURROUGHS, William S
1	Nova Express	NEB-N 65	BURROUGHS, William S
7	Novels of Philip K Dick, The	LOC-N 86	ROBINSON, Kim Stanley
5	Novelty	WFA-N 90	CRAWLEY, John
2	Nung Dimittis	WFA-N 84	LEE, Tanith
5	N-Space	LOC-N 91	NIVEN, Larry
4	Object of the Attack, The	BSF-N 85	BALLARD, J G
3	Ochrodinger's Kitten	NEB-W 88	EFFINGER, George Alec
4	Of Mist, and Grass, and Sand	LOC-N 74	McINTYRE, Vonda N
4	Of Mist, and Grass, and Sand	JUP-N 74	McINTYRE, Vonda N
3	Of Mist, and Grass, and Sand	HUG-N 74	McINTYRE, Vonda N
3	Of Mist, and Grass, and Sand	NEB-W 73	McINTYRE, Vonda N
4	Of One Mind	NEB-N 65	DURHAM, James
3	Of Space-Time and the River	LOC-N 87	BENFORD, Gregory
2	Old Folks At Home	LOC-N 79	BISHOP, Michael
4	Olympic Runner, The	BFA-W 87	ETCHISON, Dennis
4	Omnatidium Miniatures	NEB-N 89	BISHOP, Michael
9	On My Way to Paradise	LOC-N 90	WOLVERTON, Dave
1	On My Way To Paradise	DIC-N 90	WOLVERTON, Dave

SECTION C: TITLES (Alphabetically)

CAT	T I T L E S	AW W/N Y	A U T H O R
1	On Stranger Tides	WFA-N 88	POWERS, Tim
11	On Stranger Tides	LOC-N 88	POWERS, Tim
4	On the Downhill Side	NEB-N 72	ELLISON, Harlan
4	On t/Far Side of t/Cadillac Desert...	BFA-W 90	LANSDALE, Joe R
2	On t/Far Side of t/Cadillac Desert...	STO-W 90	LANSDALE, Joe R
2	On t/Far Side of t/Cadillac Desert...	WFA-W 90	LANSDALE, Joe R
2	On the Storm Planet	NEB-N 65	SMITH, Cordwainer
2	On the Street of the Serpents	NEB-N 74	BISHOP, Michael
3	On Venus, Have We Got A Rabbi	LOC-N 75	TENN, William
1	On Wings of Song	LOC-N 80	DISCH, Thomas M
1	On Wings of Song	HUG-N 80	DISCH, Thomas M
1	On Wings of Song	JWC-W 80	DISCH, Thomas M
1	On Wings of Song	NEB-N 79	DISCH, Thomas M
1	On Wings of Song	BSF-N 80	DISCH, Thomas M
4	Once A Cop	HUG-N 65	RAPHAEL, Rick
3	Once There Was a Giant	NEB-N 68	LAUMER, Keith
4	One Perfect Morning, With Jackals	SFC-N 92	RESNICK, Mike
4	One Perfect Morning, With Jackals	HUG-N 92	RESNICK, Mike
11	One Tree, The	LOC-N 83	DONALDSON, Stephen R
5	One Winter in Eden	LOC-N 85	BISHOP, Michael
4	Ones Who Walk Away from Omelas	JUP-N 74	LeGUIN, Ursula K
4	Ones Who Walk Away from Omelas	HUG-W 74	LeGUIN, Ursula K
4	Ones Who Walk Away from Omelas	LOC-N 74	LeGUIN, Ursula K
2	One-Wing	HUG-N 81	TUTTLE, Lisa
7	Only Apparently Real: World of P K Dick	HUG-N 87	WILLIAMS, Paul
7	Only Apparently Real: World of P K Dick	LOC-N 87	WILLIAMS, Paul
11	Only Begotten Daughter	LOC-N 91	MORROW, James
1	Only Begotten Daughter	JWC-N 91	MORROW, James
1	Only Begotten Daughter	NEB-N 91	MORROW, James
1	Only Begotten Daughter	WFA-W 91	MORROW, James
4	Only Death, The	LOC-N 82	CHERRYH, C J
2	Only Neat Thing To Do, The	NEB-N 85	TIPTREE, James Jr
2	Only Neat Thing To Do, The	SFC-W 86	TIPTREE, James Jr
2	Only Neat Thing To Do, The	HUG-N 86	TIPTREE, James Jr
2	Only Neat Thing To Do, The	LOC-W 86	TIPTREE, James Jr
4	Open to Me, My Sister (My Sis's Brother)	HUG-N 61	FARMER, Philip Jose
1	Opiuchi Hotline, The	LOC-N 78	VARLEY, John
3	Options	NEB-N 79	VARLEY, John
3	Options	LOC-N 80	VARLEY, John
3	Options	HUG-N 80	VARLEY, John
4	Or All The Seas With Oysters	HUG-W 58	DAVIDSON, Avram
3	Orange Is For Anguish, Blue For Insanity	STO-W 89	MORRELL, David
6	Orbit 6	LOC-N 71	KNIGHT, Damon
6	Orbit 7	LOC-N 71	KNIGHT, Damon
13	Orbit 10	LOC-N 73	KNIGHT, Damon
13	Orbit 11	LOC-N 73	KNIGHT, Damon
13	Orbit 12	LOC-N 74	KNIGHT, Damon
13	Orbit 14	LOC-N 75	KNIGHT, Damon
14	Orbit 18	LOC-N 77	KNIGHT, Damon
9	Orbital Decay	LOC-W 90	STEELE, Allan
1	Orbital Resonance	NEB-N 92	BARNES, John
1	Orbitsville	BSF-W 75	SHAW, Bob
4	Original Dr. Shade, The	BSF-W 91	NEWMAN, Kim

SECTION C: TITLES (Alphabetically)

CAT	T I T L E S	AW W/N Y	A U T H O R
3	Ornament of His Profession, An	HUG-N 67	HARNESS, Charles L
9	Orphan, The	LOC-N 81	STALLMAN, Robert
1	Orphan, The	NEB-N 80	STALLMAN, Robert
1	Orphan of Creation	DIC-N 89	ALLEN, Roger MacBride
5	Other Americas	LOC-N 89	SPINRAD, Norman
6	Other Edens	WFA-N 88	EVANS, Christopher
1	Our Lady of Darkness	WFA-W 78	LEIBER, Fritz
11	Our Lady of Darkness	LOC-N 78	LEIBER, Fritz
2	Our Lady of the Harbour	WFA-N 92	DeLINT, Charles
4	Our Lady of the Sauropods	HUG-N 81	SILVERBERG, Robert
4	Our Lady of the Sauropods	LOC-N 81	SILVERBERG, Robert
4	Our Neural Chernobyl	SFC-N 89	STERLING, Bruce
4	Our Neural Chernobyl	HUG-N 89	STERLING, Bruce
4	Out of All Them Bright Stars	NEB-W 85	KRESS, Nancy
3	Out of Everywhere	LOC-N 82	TIPTREE, James Jr
3	Out There Where the Big Ships Go	LOC-N 80	COWPER, Richard
1	Outside the Dog Museum	BFA-W 91	CARROLL, Jonathan
1	Outside the Dog Museum	WFA-N 92	CARROLL, Jonathan
3	Over the Long Haul	HUG-N 91	SOUKUP, Martha
3	Over the Long Haul	NEB-N 91	SOUKUP, Martha
4	Over the River and Through the Trees	NEB-N 65	SIMAK, Clifford D
4	Overture to a Midsummer Night's Dream	BSF-N 83	CARTER, Angela
1	Oxygen Barons	DIC-N 91	FEELEY, Gregory
4	O' Happy Day	BSF-N 86	RYMAN, Geoff
1	Pacific Edge	JWC-W 91	ROBINSON, Kim Stanley
2	Pageant Wagon	LOC-N 90	CARD, Orson Scott
2	Pages From A Young Girl's Diary	WFA-W 75	AICKMAN, Robert
4	Pain	WFA-N 87	STRIEBER, Whitley
3	Painwise	HUG-N 73	TIPTREE, James Jr
1	Palace, The	WFA-N 80	YARBRO, Chelsea Quinn
11	Paladin, The	LOC-N 89	CHERRYH, C J
3	Paladin of the Lost Hour	NEB-N 85	ELLISON, Harlan
3	Paladin of the Lost Hour	HUG-W 86	ELLISON, Harlan
3	Paladin of the Lost Hour	SFC-N 86	ELLISON, Harlan
3	Paladin of the Lost Hour	LOC-W 86	ELLISON, Harlan
7	Pale Shadow of Science, The	LOC-N 86	ALDISS, Brian
7	Pale Shadow of Science, The	HUG-N 86	ALDISS, Brian W
2	Palely Loitering	LOC-N 80	PRIEST, Christopher
3	Palely Loitering	HUG-N 80	PRIEST, Christopher
4	Palely Loitering	BSF-W 80	PRIEST, Christopher
3	Pamela's Get	STO-N 88	SCHOW, S P
4	Pamela's Get	WFA-N 88	SCHOW, David J
4	Paper Dragons	WFA-W 86	BLAYLOCK, James
4	Paper Dragons	SFC-W 86	BLAYLOCK, James P
4	Paper Dragons	NEB-N 85	BLAYLOCK, James P
1	Paper Grail, The	WFA-N 92	BLAYLOCK, James P
5	Particle Theory	LOC-N 82	BRYANT, Edward
3	Particle Theory	NEB-N 77	BRYANT, Edward
4	Passengers	NEB-W 69	SILVERBERG, Robert
4	Passengers	HUG-N 70	SILVERBERG, Robert
1	Past Master	HUG-N 69	LAFFERTY, R A
1	Past Master	NEB-N 68	LAFFERTY, R A
2	Patchwork Girl, The	LOC-N 81	NIVEN, Larry

SECTION C: TITLES (Alphabetically)

CAT	TITLES	AW W/N Y	AUTHOR
4	Patron of the Arts	LOC-N 73	ROTSLER, William
3	Patron of the Arts	HUG-N 73	ROTSLER, Bill
3	Patron of the Arts	NEB-N 72	ROTSLER, William
5	Patterns	LOC-W 90	CADIGAN, Pat
6	Patterns	STO-N 90	CADIGAN, Pat
2	Pavilion of Frozen Women, The	WFA-N 92	SOMTOW, S P
3	Pawn's Gambit	HUG-N 83	ZAHN, Timothy
1	Peace War, The	HUG-N 85	VINGE, Vernor
4	Peacemaker, The	SFC-W 84	DOZOIS, Gardner
4	Peacemaker, The	NEB-W 83	DOZOIS, Gardner
4	Peacemaker, The	LOC-N 84	DOZOIS, Gardner
4	Peacemaker, The	HUG-N 84	DOZOIS, Gardner
3	Peaches for Mad Molly	NEB-N 88	GOULD, Stephen
3	Peaches for Mad Molly	DAV-N 89	GOULD, Stephen
3	Peaches for Mad Molly	HUG-N 89	GOULD, Stephen
4	Peacock King, The	NEB-N 65	WHITE, Ted
2	Pear-Shaped Man, The	WFA-N 88	MARTIN, George R R
3	Pear-Shaped Man, The	STO-W 88	MARTIN, George R R
2	Pelts	STO-N 91	WILSON, F Paul
7	Penguin Encycl of Horror & Supernatural	LOC-N 87	SULLIVAN, Jack
4	People of the Precipice	BSF-N 86	WATSON, Ian
1	People of the Wind, The	HUG-N 74	ANDERSON, Poul
1	People of the Wind, The	NEB-N 73	ANDERSON, Poul
1	People of the Wind, The	LOC-N 74	ANDERSON, Poul
1	Perfume	WFA-W 87	SUSKIND, Patrick
3	Permafrost	LOC-N 87	ZELAZNY, Roger
3	Permafrost	NEB-N 86	ZELAZNY, Roger
3	Permafrost	HUG-W 87	ZELAZNY, Roger
6	Perpetual Light	LOC-N 83	RYAN, Alan
2	Persistence of Vision, The	HUG-W 79	VARLEY, John
2	Persistence of Vision, The	LOC-W 79	VARLEY, John
2	Persistence of Vision, The	NEB-W 78	VARLEY, John
1	Pet, The	WFA-N 87	GRANT, Charles L
1	Pet Sematary	WFA-N 84	KING, Stephen
4	Petey	WFA-N 80	KLEIN, T E D
4	Petra	NEB-N 82	BEAR, Greg
4	Petra	SFC-W 83	BEAR, Greg
4	Petra	WFA-N 83	BEAR, Greg
1	Phantom	WFA-N 83	TESSIER, Thomas
2	Phantom	STO-N 90	RUSCH, Kristine Katryn
3	Phantom of Kansas, The	LOC-N 77	VARLEY, John
3	Phantom of Kansas, The	HUG-N 77	VARLEY, John
4	Phargean Effect, The	BSF-N 91	BROWN, Eric
1	Philip K Dick Is Dead Alas	CLA-N 89	BISHOP, Michael
4	Phreak Encounter	DAV-W 87	ALLEN, Roger MacBride
4	Pi Man, The	HUG-N 60	BESTER, Alfred
1	Picnic on Paradise	HUG-N 69	RUSS, Joanna
7	Pictorial History of Science Fiction, A	BSF-W 77	KYLE, David A
2	Piper at the Gates of Dawn	LOC-N 77	COWPER, Richard
2	Piper at the Gates of Dawn	NEB-N 76	COWPER, Richard
2	Piper at the Gates of Dawn	HUG-N 77	COWPER, Richard
1	Pirates of Zan	HUG-N 60	LEINSTER, Murray
7	Pish, Posh, Said Hieronymous Bosch	LOC-N 92	DILLON, Leo

SECTION C: TITLES (Alphabetically)

CAT	T I T L E S	AW W/N Y	A U T H O R
4	Pity the Monsters	WFA-N 92	DeLINT, Charles
1	Plague of Demons, A	NEB-N 65	LAUMER, Keith
2	Plague Star, The	LOC-N 86	MARTIN, George R R
1	Planet Buyer, The	HUG-N 65	SMITH, Cordwainer
3	Planet of Forgetting	NEB-N 65	SCHMITZ, James
1	Planet of t/Damned (Sense of Obligation)	HUG-N 62	HARRISON, Harry
4	Planners, The	NEB-W 68	WILHELM, Kate
2	Plastic Abyss, The	NEB-N 71	WILHELM, Kate
1	Player Piano	IFA-N 53	VONNEGUT, Kurt Jr
5	Playgrounds of the Mind	LOC-N 92	NIVEN, Larry
5	Pohlstars	LOC-N 85	POHL, Frederik
1	Points of Departure	DIC-W 91	MURPHY, Pat
3	Polly Charms, The Sleeping Woman	NEB-N 75	DAVIDSON, Avram
5	Polyphemus	WFA-N 88	SHEA, Michael
3	Poor Man, Beggar Man	NEB-N 71	RUSS, Joanna
4	Pope of the Chimps, The	NEB-N 82	SILVERBERG, Robert
3	Portraits of His Children	SFC-W 86	MARTIN, George R R
5	Portraits of His Children	LOC-N 88	MARTIN, George R R
3	Portraits of His Children	NEB-W 85	MARTIN, George R R
3	Portraits of His Children	HUG-N 86	MARTIN, George R R
3	Portraits of His Children	LOC-N 86	MARTIN, George R R
1	Postman, The	NEB-N 85	BRIN, David
2	Postman, The	HUG-N 83	BRIN, David
1	Postman, The	HUG-N 86	BRIN, David
1	Postman, The	JWC-W 86	BRIN, David
1	Postman, The	SFC-N 86	BRIN, David
2	Postman, The	LOC-N 83	BRIN, David
1	Postman, The	LOC-W 86	BRIN, David
4	Power and the Passion, The	LOC-N 90	CADIGAN, Pat
4	Power and the Passion, The	NEB-N 91	CADIGAN, Pat
5	Prayers to Broken Stones	LOC-N 91	SIMMONS, Dan
5	Prayers to Broken Stones	STO-W 92	SIMMONS, Dan
6	Prayers to Broken Stones	STO-N 91	SIMMONS, Dan
5	Prayers to Broken Stones	WFA-N 91	SIMMONS, Dan
1	Prelude to Foundation	LOC-N 89	ASIMOV, Isaac
11	Prentice Alvin	LOC-W 90	CARD, Orson Scott
1	Prentice Alvin	HUG-N 90	CARD, Orson Scott
1	Prentice Alvin	NEB-N 89	CARD, Orson Scott
4	Press Ann	HUG-N 92	BISSON, Terry
4	Press Ann	LOC-N 92	BISSON, Terry
2	Press Enter	HUG-W 85	VARLEY, John
2	Press Enter	SFC-W 85	VARLEY, John
2	Press Enter	LOC-W 85	VARLEY, John
2	Press Enter	NEB-W 84	VARLEY, John
4	Pretty Boy Crossover	SFC-W 87	CADIGAN, Pat
4	Pretty Boy Crossover	NEB-N 86	CADIGAN, Pat
4	Pretty Boy Crossover	JWC-N 87	CADIGAN, Pat
3	Pretty Maggie Moneyeyes	NEB-N 67	ELLISON, Harlan
3	Pretty Maggie Moneyeyes	HUG-N 68	ELLISON, Harlan
3	Pre-Persons, The	LOC-N 75	DICK, Philip K
1	Pride of Chanur, The	LOC-N 83	CHERRYH, C J
1	Pride of Chanur, The	HUG-N 83	CHERRYH, C J

SECTION C: TITLES (Alphabetically)

CAT	TITLES	AW W/N Y	AUTHOR
6	Prime Evil	WFA-N 89	WINTER, Douglas E
3	Prince of Oranges, The	HUG-N 90	KRESS, Nancy
3	Prince of Oranges, The	LOC-N 90	KRESS, Nancy
7	Prism of the Night: Biography Anne Rice	STO-N 92	RAMSLAND, Katherine
3	Prismatica	HUG-N 78	DELANY, Samuel R
3	Prisoner of Chillon	DAV-W 87	KELLY, James Patrick
4	Privacy	LOC-N 90	BRIN, David
2	Probable Cause	NEB-N 69	HARNESS, Charles L
9	Prodigal	STO-W 92	TEM, Melanie
1	Productions of Time	NEB-N 67	BRUNNER, John
1	Project Pope	HUG-N 82	SIMAK, Clifford D
1	Project Pope	LOC-N 82	SIMAK, Clifford D
1	Prometheus Man, The	DIC-N 83	NELSON, Ray F
4	Prose Bowl	BSF-N 80	MALZBERG, Barry
1	Protector	HUG-N 74	NIVEN, Larry
1	Protector	LOC-N 74	NIVEN, Larry
1	Protector	DIT-W 75	NIVEN, Larry
13	Protostars	LOC-N 72	GERROLD, David
1	Psycho II	BFA-N 83	BLOCH, Robert
3	Psychologist Who Would'nt Do Awful Thing	LOC-N 77	TIPTREE, James Jr
4	Pusher, The	LOC-W 82	VARLEY, John
4	Pusher, The	HUG-W 82	VARLEY, John
4	Pusher, The	NEB-N 81	VARLEY, John
4	Pusher, The	SFC-W 82	VARLEY, John
1	Pyramids	BSF-W 90	PRATCHETT, Terry
6	Quark 1	LOC-N 71	DELANY,
2	Queen of Air and Darkness, The	HUG-W 72	ANDERSON, Poul
4	Queen of Air and Darkness, The	LOC-W 72	ANDERSON, Poul
3	Queen of Air and Darkness, The	NEB-W 71	ANDERSON, Poul
1	Queen of Angels	LOC-N 91	BEAR, Greg
1	Queen of Angels	HUG-N 91	BEAR, Greg
1	Queen of Angels	JWC-N 91	BEAR, Greg
10	Queen of the Damned	LOC-N 89	RICE, Anne
1	Queen of the Damned	STO-N 89	RICE, Anne
1	Queen of the States	BSF-N 87	SAXTON, Josephine
1	Queen of the States	CLA-N 87	SAXTON, Josephine
1	Quest of the White Witch, The	BFA-N 79	LEE, Tanith
3	Quickening, The	HUG-N 82	BISHOP, Michael
3	Quickening, The	NEB-W 81	BISHOP, Michael
4	Quiet, The	HUG-N 82	FLORANCE-GUTHRIDGE, George
4	Quiet, The	NEB-N 81	FLORANCE-GUTHRIDGE, George
1	Quiet Pools, The	LOC-N 91	KUBE-McDOWELL, Michael
1	Quiet Pools, The	HUG-N 91	KUBE-McDOWELL, Michael
4	Quiet Revolution For Death	NEB-N 78	DANN, Jack
4	Quietus	LOC-N 80	CARD, Orson Scott
2	Quincux of Time, The	JUP-N 74	BLISH, James
2	R & R	LOC-W 87	SHEPARD, Lucius
2	R & R	SFC-W 87	SHEPARD, Lucius
2	R & R	HUG-N 87	SHEPARD, Lucius
2	R & R	NEB-W 86	SHEPARD, Lucius

SECTION C: TITLES (Alphabetically)

CAT	T I T L E S	AW W/N Y	A U T H O R
3	Rachel in Love	NEB-W 87	MURPHY, Pat
3	Rachel in Love	LOC-W 88	MURPHY, Pat
4	Rachel in Love	JWC-W 88	MURPHY, Pat
3	Rachel in Love	DAV-W 88	MURPHY, Pat
3	Rachel in Love	SFC-N 88	MURPHY, Pat
3	Rachel in Love	HUG-N 88	MURPHY, Pat
9	Radix	LOC-N 82	ATTANASIO, A A
1	Radix	NEB-N 81	ATTANASIO, A A
8	Raft	LOC-N 92	BAXTER, Stephen
1	Raft	CLA-N 92	BAXTER, S M
1	Ragged Astronauts, The	HUG-N 87	SHAW, Bob
1	Ragged Astronauts, The	CLA-N 87	SHAW, Bob
1	Ragged Astronauts, The	BFA-W 86	SHAW, Bob
1	Ragged Astronauts, The	BSF-W 87	SHAW, Bob
2	Ragthorn, The	WFA-N 92	HOLDSTOCK, Robert
1	Ragtime	NEB-N 75	DOCTOROW, E L
11	Rainbow Abyss, The	LOC-N 92	HAMBLY, Barbara
1	RAMA II	LOC-N 90	CLARKE, Arthur C
11	Raphael	LOC-N 85	MacAVOY, R A
4	Rat	SFC-N 87	KELLY, James Patrick
4	Rat	HUG-N 87	KELLY, James Patrick
4	Rat	LOC-N 87	KELLY, James Patrick
4	Rat	NEB-N 86	KELLY, James Patrick
3	Rat in the Skull	HUG-N 59	PHILLIPS, Rog
4	Rat Race	HUG-N 67	JONES, Raymond F
1	Rats and Gargoyles	CLA-N 91	GENTLE, Mary
1	Rats and Gargoyles	BSF-N 91	GENTLE, Mary
4	Rautavaara's Case	BSF-N 81	DICK, Philip K
6	Razored Saddles	WFA-N 90	LANSDALE, Joe R
6	Razored Saddles	LOC-N 90	LANSDALE, Joe R
7	Reader's Guide to Fantasy, A	LOC-N 83	SEARLES, Baird
7	Reader's Guide to Fantasy, A	HUG-N 83	SEARLES, Baird
7	Reader's Guide to SF, A	LOC-N 80	SEARLES, Baird
3	Reap the Dark Tide (Shark Ship)	HUG-N 59	KORNBLUTH, Cyril M
6	Red As Blood	WFA-N 84	LEE, Tanith
4	Red As Blood	NEB-N 79	LEE, Tanith
5	Red As Blood	LOC-N 84	LEE, Tanith
4	Red As Blood	BFA-N 80	LEE, Tanith
2	Red Hawk, The	WFA-N 84	LYNN, Elizabeth A
4	Red Light	WFA-W 87	SCHOW, David J
9	Red Magician, The	LOC-N 83	GOLDSTEIN, Lisa
11	Red Prophet	LOC-W 89	CARD, Orson Scott
1	Red Prophet	NEB-N 88	CARD, Orson Scott
1	Red Prophet	HUG-N 89	CARD, Orson Scott
1	Red Spider, White Web	CLA-N 91	MISHA
4	Redeemer	LOC-N 80	BENFORD, Gregory
1	Redshift Rendezvous	NEB-N 91	STITH, John E
1	Redshift Rendezvous	LOC-N 91	STITH, John E
6	Redward, Edward Papers, The	WFA-N 79	DAVIDSON, Avram
1	Reefsong	COM-W 92	SEVERANCE, Carol
4	Region Between, The	LOC-W 71	ELLISON, Harlan
2	Region Between, The	HUG-N 71	ELLISON, Harlan
2	Region Between, The	NEB-N 70	ELLISON, Harlan

SECTION C: TITLES (Alphabetically)

CAT	T I T L E S	AW W/N Y	A U T H O R
1	Reign	STO-N 91	WILLIAMSON, Chet
5	Remaking History	LOC-N 92	ROBINSON, Kim Stanley
1	Remaking of Sigmund Freud, The	NEB-N 85	MALZBERG, Barry N
1	Remaking of Sigmund Freud, The	DIC-N 86	MALZBERG, Barry
4	Remembering Melody	LOC-N 82	MARTIN, George R R
1	Rendezvous	DIC-N 89	SMITH, D Alexander
1	Rendezvous with Rama	JWC-W 74	CLARKE, Arthur C
1	Rendezvous with Rama	BSF-W 74	CLARKE, Arthur C
1	Rendezvous with Rama	NEB-W 73	CLARKE, Arthur C
1	Rendezvous with Rama	LOC-W 74	CLARKE, Arthur C
1	Rendezvous with Rama	JUP-W 74	CLARKE, Arthur C
1	Rendezvous with Rama	HUG-W 74	CLARKE, Arthur C
4	Repent Harlequin Said The Ticktockman	NEB-W 65	ELLISON, Harlan
4	Repent Harlequin Said The Ticktockman	HUG-W 66	ELLISON, Harlan
1	Replay	CLA-N 88	GRIMWOOD, Ken
1	Replay	WFA-W 88	GRIMWOOD, Ken
2	Research Alpha	NEB-N 65	VAN VOGT, A E
3	Rest Is Silence, The	NEB-N 74	GRANT, C L
3	Resurrec Tech	STO-N 88	SOMTOW, S P
9	Resurrection Inc.	STO-N 89	ANDERSON, Kevin J
3	Retrograde Summer	NEB-N 75	VARLEY, John
3	Retrograde Summer	LOC-N 76	VARLEY, John
4	Return of the Dust Vampire	WFA-N 86	FARBER, Sharon
4	Return of William Proxmire, The	HUG-N 90	NIVEN, Larry
3	Return to the Fold	HUG-N 85	ZAHN, Timothy
9	Revelation, The	STO-W 91	LITTLE, Bentley
6	Richard Matheson: Collected Stories	STO-W 90	MATHESON, Richard
5	Richard Matheson: Collected Stories	WFA-W 90	MATHESON, Richard
4	Richard's Head	STO-N 92	SARRANTONIO, Al
1	Riddley Walker	NEB-N 81	HOBAN, Russell
1	Riddley Walker	DIT-W 83	HOBAN, Russell
1	Riddley Walker	JWC-W 82	HOBAN, Russell
2	Riders of the Purple Wage	NEB-N 67	FARMER, Philip Jose
2	Riders of the Purple Wage	HUG-W 68	FARMER, Philip Jose
4	Ridge Running	LOC-N 85	ROBINSON, Kim Stanley
4	Ridge Running	HUG-N 85	ROBINSON, Kim Stanley
2	Riding the Torch	JUP-W 75	SPINRAD, Norman
2	Riding the Torch	LOC-N 75	SPINRAD, Norman
2	Riding the Torch	HUG-N 75	SPINRAD, Norman
1	Rimrunners	LOC-N 90	CHERRYH, C J
1	Ringworld	HUG-W 71	NIVEN, Larry
1	Ringworld	NEB-W 70	NIVEN, Larry
1	Ringworld	DIT-W 72	NIVEN, Larry
1	Ringworld	LOC-W 71	NIVEN, Larry
1	Ringworld Engineers, The	LOC-N 81	NIVEN, Larry
1	Ringworld Engineers, The	HUG-N 81	NIVEN, Larry
4	Ripples in the Dirac Sea	NEB-W 89	LANDIS, Geoffrey A
4	Ripples in the Dirac Sea	DAV-N 89	LANDIS, Geoffrey A
4	Ripples in the Dirac Sea	SFC-N 89	LANDIS, Geoffrey A
4	Ripples in the Dirac Sea	HUG-N 89	LANDIS, Geoffrey A
4	Rise and Fall of Father Alex, The	WFA-N 87	NAEGELE, Amyas
1	Rite of Passage	NEB-W 68	PANSHIN, Alexei
1	Rite of Passage	HUG-N 69	PANSHIN, Alexei

SECTION C: TITLES (Alphabetically)

CAT	TITLES	AW W/N Y	AUTHOR
4	Rite of Spring, A	LOC-N 78	LEIBER, Fritz
3	Rite of Spring, A	NEB-N 77	LEIBER, Fritz
2	River of Night's Dreaming	WFA-N 82	WAGNER, Karl Edward
5	River of Time, The	LOC-N 87	BRIN, David
5	Riverworlds and Other Stories	LOC-N 80	FARMER, Philip Jose
1	Road to Corlay, The	NEB-N 79	COWPER, Richard
1	Road to Corlay, The	BFA-N 79	COWPER, Richard
4	Robot Dreams	NEB-N 86	ASIMOV, Isaac
4	Robot Dreams	SFC-N 87	ASIMOV, Isaac
4	Robot Dreams	DAV-W 87	ASIMOV, Isaac
4	Robot Dreams	HUG-N 87	ASIMOV, Isaac
4	Robot Dreams	LOC-W 87	ASIMOV, Isaac
1	Robots and Empire	LOC-N 86	ASIMOV, Isaac
1	Robots of Dawn	HUG-N 84	ASIMOV, Isaac
1	Robots of Dawn	LOC-N 84	ASIMOV, Isaac
3	Rockabye Baby	NEB-N 85	SYKES, S C
7	Rockets,Jets,Guided Missls & Spaceships	IFA-N 52	COGGINS, Jack
1	Roderick	DIC-N 83	SLADEK, John
1	Rogue Dragon	NEB-N 65	DAVIDSON, Avram
2	Rogue Dragon	NEB-N 65	DAVIDSON, Avram
1	Rogue Moon	HUG-N 61	BUDRYS, Algis
4	Rogue Tomato	HUG-N 76	BISHOP, Michael
4	Rory	HUG-N 85	GOULD, Steven
4	Rose for Ecclesiastes, A	HUG-N 64	ZELAZNY, Roger
9	Rumor of Angels, A	LOC-N 84	KELLOGG, M Bradley
1	Rumours of Spring	CLA-N 89	GRANT, Richard
4	Rump-Titty-Titty-Tum-TAH-Tee	HUG-N 59	LEIBER, Fritz
11	Rusalka	LOC-N 90	CHERRYH, C J
4	Sail the Tide of Mourning	NEB-N 75	LUPOFF, Richard A
4	Sail the Tide of Mourning	HUG-N 76	LUPOFF, Richard A
4	Sail the Tide of Mourning	LOC-N 76	LUPOFF, Richard A
2	Sailing to Byzantium	NEB-W 85	SILVERBERG, Robert
2	Sailing to Byzantium	HUG-N 86	SILVERBERG, Robert
2	Sailing to Byzantium	LOC-N 86	SILVERBERG, Robert
2	Sailing to Byzantium	SFC-N 86	SILVERBERG, Robert
1	Sailor on the Seas of Fate, The	WFA-N 77	MOORCOCK, Michael
3	Saint Theresa of the Aliens	NEB-N 84	KELLY, James Patrick
1	Salem's Lot	WFA-N 76	KING, Stephen
2	Saliva Tree	NEB-W 65	ALDISS, Brian W
4	Salvador	HUG-N 85	SHEPARD, Lucius
4	Salvador	NEB-N 84	SHEPARD, Lucius
4	Salvador	LOC-W 85	SHEPARD, Lucius
4	Salvador	SFC-W 85	SHEPARD, Lucius
2	Samurai and the Willows, The	HUG-N 77	BISHOP, Michael
2	Samurai and the Willows, The	NEB-N 76	BISHOP, Michael
2	Samurai and the Willows, The	LOC-W 77	BISHOP, Michael
5	San Diego Lightfoot Sue	LOC-N 81	REAMY, Tom
3	San Diego Lightfoot Sue	HUG-N 76	REAMY, Tom
3	San Diego Lightfoot Sue	NEB-W 75	REAMY, Tom
3	Sanctuary	DAV-W 89	WHITE, James

SECTION C: TITLES (Alphabetically)

CAT	T I T L E S	AW W/N Y	A U T H O R
3	Sandkings	NEB-W 79	MARTIN, George R R
3	Sandkings	LOC-W 80	MARTIN, George R R
3	Sandkings	HUG-W 80	MARTIN, George R R
5	Sandkings	LOC-W 82	MARTIN, George R R
1	Saraband of Lost Time	DIC-N 86	GRANT, Richard
4	Saturday's Shadow	WFA-N 80	NOLAN, William F
2	Saturn Game, The	HUG-W 82	ANDERSON, Poul
2	Saturn Game, The	LOC-N 82	ANDERSON, Poul
2	Saturn Game, The	NEB-W 81	ANDERSON, Poul
4	Savage Pellucidar	HUG-N 64	BURROUGHS, Edgar Rice
3	Savage Planet, The	HUG-N 81	LONGYEAR, Barry
1	Savage Season	STO-N 91	LANSDALE, Joe R
2	Scalehunter's Beautiful Daughter, The	SFC-N 89	SHEPARD, Lucius
2	Scalehunter's Beautiful Daughter, The	DAV-N 89	SHEPARD, Lucius
2	Scalehunter's Beautiful Daughter, The	NEB-N 88	SHEPARD, Lucius
2	Scalehunter's Beautiful Daughter, The	WFA-N 89	SHEPARD, Lucius
2	Scalehunter's Beautiful Daughter, The	HUG-N 89	SHEPARD, Lucius
2	Scalehunter's Beautiful Daughter, The	LOC-W 89	SHEPARD, Lucius
2	Scapegoat, The	LOC-N 85	CHERRYH, C J
2	Scapegoat, The	LOC-N 86	CHERRYH, C J
2	Scapegoat, The	HUG-N 86	CHERRYH, C J
6	Scare Tactics	STO-N 89	FARRIS, John
6	Scared Stiff, Tales of Sex & Death	STO-N 88	CAMPBELL, Ramsey
5	Scared Stiff, Tales of Sex & Death	WFA-N 88	CAMPBELL, Ramsey
1	Schismatrix	NEB-N 85	STERLING, Bruce
1	Schismatrix	BSF-N 87	STERLING, Bruce
1	Schizogenic Man, The	DIC-N 91	HARRIS, Raymond
4	Schrodinger's Kitten	JWC-W 89	EFFINGER, George Alec
3	Schrodinger's Kitten	HUG-W 89	EFFINGER, George Alec
3	Schrodinger's Kitten	SFC-W 89	EFFINGER, George Alec
3	Schrodinger's Kitten	LOC-N 89	EFFINGER, George Alec
4	Schwartz Between The Galaxies	LOC-N 75	SILVERBERG, Robert
4	Schwartz Between The Galaxies	HUG-N 75	SILVERBERG, Robert
3	Schwarzschild Radius	SFC-N 88	SHWARTZ, Susan
3	Schwarzschild Radius	NEB-N 87	WILLIS, Connie
7	Science Fiction, Fantasy and Horror	HUG-N 89	BROWN, Charles N
14	Science Fiction Argosy, A	LOC-N 73	KNIGHT, Damon
7	Science Fiction Encyclopedia, The	HUG-W 80	NICHOLS, Peter
7	Science Fiction Encyclopedia, The	LOC-W 80	NICHOLLS, Peter
6	Science Fiction Hall of Fame Vol 1	LOC-W 71	SILVERBERG, Robert
14	Science Fiction Hall of Fame Vol 2a & 2b	LOC-N 74	BOVA, Ben
7	Science Fiction in Print 1985	LOC-N 87	BROWN, Charles N
7	Science Fiction in Print 1985	HUG-N 87	BROWN, Charles N
7	Science Fiction in the Real World	HUG-N 91	SPINRAD, Norman
7	Science Fiction in the Real World	LOC-N 91	SPINRAD, Norman
7	Science Fiction: The 100 Best Novels	LOC-N 86	PRINGLE, David
7	Science Made Stupid	HUG-W 86	WELLER, Tom
7	Science Made Stupid	LOC-N 86	WELLER, Tom
7	Science-Fantasy Publishers, The	HUG-N 92	CHALKER, Jack
4	Scraping of the Bones, A	NEB-N 75	BUDRYS, Algis
4	Screwfly Solution, The	LOC-N 78	SHELDON, Raccoona
3	Screwfly Solution, The	HUG-N 78	SHELDON, Raccoona
3	Screwfly Solution, The	NEB-W 77	SHELDON, Raccoona

SECTION C: TITLES (Alphabetically)

CAT	T I T L E S	AW W/N Y	A U T H O R
4	Scylla's Daughter	HUG-N 62	LEIBER, Fritz
1	Sea and Summer, The	CLA-W 88	TURNER, George
3	Sea Changeling	NEB-N 81	BROXON, Midlred Downey
1	Sea In Summer, The	JWC-N 88	TURNER, George
1	Second Ending	HUG-N 62	WHITE, James
3	Second Game (Cosmic Checkmate)	HUG-N 59	MacLEAN, Katherine
3	Second Inquisition, The	NEB-N 70	RUSS, Joanna
4	Secret Place, The	NEB-W 66	McKENNA, Richard
4	Secret Place, The	HUG-N 67	McKENNA, Richard
2	Secret Sharer, The	SFC-W 88	SILVERBERG, Robert
2	Secret Sharer, The	NEB-N 87	SILVERBERG, Robert
2	Secret Sharer, The	HUG-N 88	SILVERBERG, Robert
2	Secret Sharer, The	LOC-W 88	SILVERBERG, Robert
4	Secrets of the Heart	NEB-N 80	GRANT, Charles L
4	Seeing	LOC-N 77	ELLISON, Harlan
2	Seeking	LOC-N 84	PALMER, David
2	Seeking	HUG-N 84	PALMER, David
5	Sentinel, The	LOC-N 84	CLARKE, Arthur C
4	Serpent's Teeth	LOC-N 82	ROBINSON, Spider
4	Servant of the People	HUG-N 84	POHL, Frederik
4	Servant of the People	LOC-N 84	POHL, Frederik
2	Seven American Nights	LOC-N 79	WOLFE, Gene
2	Seven American Nights	NEB-N 78	WOLFE, Gene
2	Seven American Nights	HUG-N 79	WOLFE, Gene
3	Seventeen Virgins	JUP-W 75	VANCE, Jack
1	Seventh Son	DIT-W 89	CARD, Orson Scott
1	Seventh Son	HUG-N 88	CARD, Orson Scott
1	Seventh Son	WFA-N 88	CARD, Orson Scott
11	Seventh Son	LOC-W 88	CARD, Orson Scott
4	Sex Pirates of the Blood Asteroid	BSF-N 80	LANGFORD, David
5	Sexpunks and Savage Sagas	STO-N 92	SUTPHIN, Richard
7	SF, Fantasy & Horror 1986	LOC-N 88	BROWN, Charles N
7	SF, Fantasy & Horror 1986	HUG-N 88	BROWN, Charles N
7	SF, Fantasy & Horror 1988	LOC-N 90	BROWN, Charles N
7	SF, Fantasy & Horror 1990	LOC-N 92	BROWN, Charles N
7	SF and Fantasy Authors	LOC-N 81	CURREY, L W
7	SF and Heroic Fantasy Index	LOC-N 79	WELLS, Stuart W III
7	SFWA Handbook: The Prof Writer's Guide	HUG-N 91	RUSCH, Kristine Kathryn
7	SFWA Handbook: The Prof Writer's Guide	LOC-W 91	RUSCH and SMITH
7	SF: The Early Years	LOC-W 92	BLEILER, Everett F
7	SF: The Early Years	HUG-N 92	BLEILER, Everett F
3	Shades	LOC-N 88	SHEPARD, Lucius
2	Shades	WFA-N 88	SHEPARD, Lucius
1	Shadow Land	WFA-N 81	STRAUB, Peter
1	Shadow of the Torturer, The	NEB-N 80	WOLFE, Gene
1	Shadow of the Torturer, The	WFA-W 81	WOLFE, Gene
1	Shadow of the Torturer, The	BSF-W 82	WOLFE, Gene
11	Shadow of the Torturer, The	LOC-N 81	WOLFE, Gene
1	Shadow of the Torturer, The	JWC-N 81	WOLFE, Gene

CAT	T I T L E S	AW W/N Y	A U T H O R
6	Shadows	WFA-W 79	GRANT, Charles L
6	Shadows 2	WFA-N 80	GRANT, Charles L
6	Shadows 3	WFA-N 81	GRANT, Charles L
6	Shadows 4	BFA-N 82	GRANT, Charles L
6	Shadows 4	WFA-N 82	GRANT, Charles L
6	Shadows 6	WFA-N 84	GRANT, Charles L
6	Shadows of Sanctuary	LOC-W 82	ASPRIN, Robert
1	Shadrach in the Furnace	LOC-N 77	SILVERBERG, Robert
1	Shadrach in the Furnace	HUG-N 77	SILVERBERG, Robert
1	Shadrach in the Furnace	NEB-N 76	SILVERBERG, Robert
4	Shaffery Among the Immortals	NEB-N 72	POHL, Frederik
3	Shaker Revival	NEB-N 70	JONAS, Gerald
3	Shall We Have a Little Talk?	NEB-N 65	SHECKLEY, Robert
7	Shape Under t/Street:Compl Encycl S King	STO-N 92	SPIGNESI, Stephen J
1	Shards of Honor	COM-N 87	BUJOLD, Lois McMaster
9	Shards of Honor	LOC-N 87	BUJOLD, Lois McMaster
3	Sharing of Flesh, The	NEB-N 68	ANDERSON, Poul
3	Sharing of Flesh, The	HUG-W 69	ANDERSON, Poul
4	Shark	NEB-N 73	BRYANT, Edward
4	Shark	JUP-N 74	BRYANT, Edward
6	Shatterday	WFA-N 81	ELLISON, Harlan
5	Shatterday	LOC-N 81	ELLISON, Harlan
4	Shatterday	NEB-N 75	ELLISON, Harlan
4	Shattered Like a Glass Goblin	NEB-N 69	ELLISON, Harlan
1	Sheep Look Up, The	NEB-N 72	BRUNNER, John
1	Sheep Look Up, The	LOC-N 73	BRUNNER, John
1	Sheepfarmer's Daughter	COM-W 89	MOON, Elizabeth
9	Sheepfarmer's Daughter	LOC-N 89	MOON, Elizabeth
4	She's A Yng Thing & C'not Leave H/Mother	STO-N 89	ELLISON, Harlan
11	Shining, The	LOC-N 78	KING, Stephen
1	Shining Falcon, The	COM-W 90	SHERMAN, Josepha
2	Ship of Shadows	NEB-N 69	LEIBER, Fritz
2	Ship of Shadows	HUG-W 70	LEIBER, Fritz
1	Ship Sailed the Time Stream	NEB-N 65	EDMONDSON, G C
3	Shipwrecked Hotel, The	NEB-N 65	BLISH, James
3	Shobie's Story, The	HUG-N 91	LeGUIN, Ursula K
3	Shobie's Story, The	LOC-N 91	LeGUIN, Ursula K
3	Shobie's Story, The	NEB-N 91	LeGUIN, Ursula K
1	Shockwave Rider, The	LOC-N 76	BRUNNER, John
2	Short, Sharp, Shock, A	LOC-W 91	ROBINSON, Kim Stanley
2	Short, Sharp, Shock, A	SFC-N 91	ROBINSON, Kim Stanley
2	Short, Sharp, Shock, A	HUG-N 91	ROBINSON, Kim Stanley
3	Sidon in the Mirror, The	HUG-N 84	WILLIS, Connie
3	Sidon in the Mirror, The	NEB-N 83	WILLIS, Connie
4	Sierra Maestra	LOC-N 76	SPINRAD, Norman
11	Sign of Chaos	LOC-N 88	ZELAZNY, Roger
2	Silent Eyes of Time, The	HUG-N 76	BUDRYS, Algis
1	Silence of the Lambs, The	STO-W 89	HARRIS, Thomas
1	Silence of the Lambs, The	WFA-N 89	HARRIS, Thomas
10	Silence of the Lambs, The	LOC-N 89	HARRIS, Thomas
4	Silent Cradle	WFA-N 84	KENNEDY, Leigh
2	Silent Eyes of Time, The	LOC-N 76	BUDRYS, Algis

SECTION C: TITLES (Alphabetically)

CAT	TITLES	AW W/N Y	AUTHOR
1	Silicon Man, The	JWC-N 92	PLATT, Charles
3	Silicon Muse	HUG-N 85	SCHENCK, Hilbert
11	Silmarillion	LOC-W 78	TOLKIEN, J R R
4	Silver Lady and the Fortyish Man, The	JWC-N 90	LINDHOLM, Megan
3	Silver Lady and the Fortyish Man, The	NEB-N 89	LINDHOLM, Megan
6	Silver Scream	WFA-N 89	SCHOW, David J
1	Simarillion, The	DIT-W 78	TOLKIEN, J R R
4	Siren	DAV-N 89	AUSTIN, A J
1	Sirens of Titan, The	HUG-N 60	VONNEGET, Kurt
1	Sister Light, Sister Dark	NEB-N 89	YOLEN, Jane
3	Sisters	NEB-N 89	BEAR, Greg
3	Sisters	LOC-N 90	BEAR, Greg
12	Sixty Astounding Years	DAV-W 91	FLYNN, Michael F
5	Skeleton Crew	LOC-W 86	KING, Stephen
6	Skeleton Crew	WFA-N 86	KING, Stephen
2	Sketches Among the Ruins of My Mind	LOC-N 74	FARMER, Philip Jose
2	Skin Trade, The	WFA-W 89	MARTIN, George R R
3	Skin Trade, The	STO-N 89	MARTIN, George R R
2	Skull City	LOC-N 91	SHEPARD, Lucius
4	Sky	HUG-N 72	LAFFERTY, R A
1	Skylark Dusquenes	HUG-N 66	SMITH, E E "Doc"
1	Slaughterhouse-Five	NEB-N 69	VONNEGET, Kurt
1	Slaughterhouse-Five	HUG-N 70	VONNEGET, Kurt
4	Sleeping Dogs	JUP-N 75	ELLISON, Harlan
4	Sleeping in a Box	AUR-W 89	DORSEY, Candas Jane
1	Sleeping in Flame	WFA-N 89	CARROLL, Jonathan
7	Sleepless Nights in the Procrustean Bed	HUG-N 85	ELLISON, Harlan
7	Sleepless Nights in the Procrustean Bed	LOC-W 85	ELLISON, Harlan
9	Slob	STO-N 88	MILLER, Rex
4	Slovo Stove, The	WFA-N 86	DAVIDSON, Avram
3	Slow Birds	LOC-N 84	WATSON, Ian
3	Slow Birds	HUG-N 84	WATSON, Ian
3	Slow Birds	NEB-N 83	WATSON, Ian
4	Slow Sculpture	LOC-N 71	STURGEON, Theodore
4	Slow Sculpture	HUG-W 71	STURGEON, Theodore
3	Slow Sculpture	NEB-W 70	STURGEON, Theodore
4	Slow Tuesday Night	NEB-N 65	LAFFERTY, R A
3	Small One	NEB-N 65	McCARTY, E Clayton
2	Snark in the Night, A	LOC-N 78	BENFORD, Gregory
2	Snark in the Night, A	HUG-N 78	BENFORD, Gregory
4	Snow	LOC-N 86	CROWLEY, John
4	Snow	NEB-N 85	CROWLEY, John
4	Snow	HUG-N 86	CROWLEY, John
1	Snow Queen, The	HUG-W 81	VINGE, Joan D
1	Snow Queen, The	NEB-N 80	VINGE, Joan D
1	Snow Queen, The	LOC-W 81	VINGE, Joan D
4	Snow Women, The	LOC-N 71	LEIBER, Fritz
2	Snow Women, The	HUG-N 71	LEIBER, Fritz
6	Soft and Others	STO-N 90	WILSON, F Paul
1	Software	DIC-W 83	RUCKER, Rudy
4	Soldier, Ask Not	HUG-W 65	DICKSON, Gordon R

SECTION C: TITLES (Alphabetically)

CAT	TITLES	AW W/N Y	AUTHOR
1	Soldier of Arete	WFA-N 90	WOLFE, Gene
11	Soldier of Arete	LOC-N 90	WOLFE, Gene
1	Soldier of the Mist	NEB-N 87	WOLFE, Gene
11	Soldier of the Mist	LOC-W 87	WOLFE, Gene
1	Soldier of the Mist	WFA-N 87	WOLFE, Gene
1	Soldiers of Paradise	CLA-N 90	PAUL, Park
4	Solitario's Eyes	WFA-N 84	SHEPARD, Lucius
4	Somewhere Doors, The	WFA-N 92	CHAPPELL, Fred
2	Son of the Morning	NEB-N 72	GOTLIEB, Phyllis
5	Song for Lya, A	LOC-W 77	MARTIN, George R R
2	Song for Lya, A	NEB-N 74	MARTIN, George R R
2	Song for Lya, A	LOC-N 75	MARTIN, George R R
2	Song for Lya, A	JUP-N 75	MARTIN, George R R
2	Song for Lya, A	HUG-W 75	MARTIN, George R R
1	Song of Kali	WFA-W 86	SIMMONS, Dan
6	Songbird of Pain, The	WFA-N 85	KILWORTH, Garry
2	Songhouse	LOC-N 80	CARD, Orson Scott
2	Songhouse	HUG-N 80	CARD, Orson Scott
1	Sorcerer's Son	BFA-N 80	EISENSTEIN, Phyllis
2	Souls	LOC-W 83	RUSS, Joanna
2	Souls	SFC-W 83	RUSS, Joanna
2	Souls	HUG-W 83	RUSS, Joanna
2	Souls	NEB-N 82	RUSS, Joanna
1	Sound At Midnight, The	WFA-N 79	GRANT, Charles L
4	Souvenir	NEB-N 65	BALLARD, J G
1	Space Machine, The	DIT-W 77	PRIEST, Christopher
4	Space to Swing a Cat	HUG-N 59	MULLEN, Stanley
1	Speaker for the Dead	NEB-W 86	CARD, Orson Scott
1	Speaker for the Dead	SFC-W 87	CARD, Orson Scott
1	Speaker for the Dead	LOC-W 87	CARD, Orson Scott
1	Speaker for the Dead	JWC-N 87	CARD, Orson Scott
1	Speaker for the Dead	HUG-W 87	CARD, Orson Scott
2	Special Kind of Morning	HUG-N 72	DOZOIS, Gardner
3	Special Kind of Morning	NEB-N 71	DOZOIS, Gardner
4	Speech Sounds	HUG-W 84	BUTLER, Octavia
4	Speech Sounds	LOC-N 84	BUTLER, Octavia E
1	Spell for Chameleon, A	BFA-W 78	ANTHONY, Piers
4	Spending A Day at the Lottery Fair	LOC-N 84	POHL, Frederik
2	Spice Pogrom	DAV-W 87	WILLIS, Connie
2	Spice Pogrom	LOC-N 87	WILLIS, Connie
2	Spice Pogrom	HUG-N 87	WILLIS, Connie
4	Spider Rose	LOC-N 83	STERLING, Bruce
4	Spider Rose	HUG-N 83	STERLING, Bruce
4	Spidersong	HUG-N 81	PETREY, Susan C
4	Spiral Winds	BSF-N 85	KILWORTH, Garry
4	Splatter: A Cautionary Tale	WFA-N 88	WINTER, Douglas E
1	Squares of the City, The	HUG-N 66	BRUNNER, John
4	Stable Strategies for Middle Management	HUG-N 89	GUNN, Eileen
4	Stains	BFA-W 81	AICKMAN, Robert
4	Stairs	JWC-N 89	BARRETT, Neil Jr
5	Stalking the Nightmare	LOC-N 83	ELLISON, Harlan
1	Stand, The	WFA-N 79	KING, Stephen
10	Stand, The: The Complete, Uncut Edition	LOC-N 91	KING, Stephen

SECTION C: TITLES (Alphabetically)

CAT	T I T L E S	AW W/N Y	A U T H O R
1	Stand on Zanzibar	HUG-W 69	BRUNNER, John
1	Stand on Zanzibar	BSF-W 70	BRUNNER, John
1	Stand on Zanzibar	NEB-N 68	BRUNNER, John
3	Standing in Line with Mister Jimmy	NEB-N 92	KELLY, James Patrick
4	Star, The	HUG-W 56	CLARKE, Arthur C
1	Star Fox	NEB-N 65	ANDERSON, Poul
5	Star Light, Star Bright	LOC-N 77	BESTER, Alfred
2	Star of the Sea	LOC-N 92	ANDERSON, Poul
2	Star Pit, The	HUG-N 68	DELANY, Samuel R
2	Stardance	LOC-W 78	ROBINSON, Spider
1	Stardance	LOC-N 80	ROBINSON, Spider
2	Stardance	NEB-W 77	ROBINSON, Spider & Jeanne
2	Stardance	HUG-W 78	ROBINSON, Spider & Jeanne
1	Starlight	HUG-N 71	CLEMENT, Hal
9	Starrigger	LOC-N 84	DeCHANCIE, John
5	Stars Are the Styx, The	LOC-N 80	STURGEON, Theodore
1	Stars in My Pocket Like Grains of Sand	LOC-N 85	DELANY, Samuel R
1	Stars in My Pocket Like Grains of Sand	CLA-N 87	DELANY, Samuel R
9	Starship and Haiku	LOC-W 82	SOMTOW, S P
1	Starship Troopers	HUG-W 60	HEINLEIN, Robert A
5	Start of the End of It All...	WFA-W 91	EMSHWILLER, Carol
1	Startide Rising	NEB-W 83	BRIN, David
1	Startide Rising	LOC-W 84	BRIN, David
1	Startide Rising	SFC-N 84	BRIN, David
1	Startide Rising	HUG-W 84	BRIN, David
1	Stations of the Tide	NEB-W 92	SWANWICK, Michael
1	Stations of the Tide	SFC-N 92	SWANWICK, Michael
1	Stations of the Tide	LOC-N 92	SWANWICK, Michael
1	Stations of the Tide	HUG-N 92	SWANWICK, Michael
1	Stations of the Tide	JWC-N 92	SWANWICK, Michael
4	Status Quo	HUG-N 62	REYNOLDS, Mack
7	Staying Alive: A Writer's Guide	HUG-N 84	SPINRAD, Norman
7	Staying Alive: A Writer's Guide	LOC-N 84	SPINRAD, Norman
1	Steel Crocodile, The	NEB-N 70	COMPTON, D G
4	Steiger Effect, The	HUG-N 69	CURTIS, Betsy
13	Stellar 1	LOC-N 75	del REY, Judy-Lynn
14	Stellar 2	LOC-N 77	Del REY, Judy-Lynn
6	Stellar 4	LOC-N 79	del REY, Judy Lynn
4	Stephen	WFA-N 91	MASSIE, Elizabeth
2	Stephen	STO-W 91	MASSIE, Elizabeth
2	Sticks	WFA-N 75	WAGNER, Karl Edward
4	Sticks	BFA-W 75	WAGNER, Karl Edward
5	Still I Persist in Wondering	LOC-N 79	PANGBORN, Edgar
4	Still Life	HUG-N 87	GARNETT, David
4	Still Life With Scorpion	WFA-W 85	BAKER, Scott
1	Stinger	STO-N 89	McCAMMON, Robert R
10	Stinger	LOC-N 89	McCAMMON, Robert R
1	Stochastic Man, The	HUG-N 76	SILVERBERG, Robert
1	Stochastic Man, The	LOC-N 76	SILVERBERG, Robert
1	Stochastic Man, The	NEB-N 75	SILVERBERG, Robert
4	Stone	NEB-W 78	BRYANT, Edward
4	Stone	HUG-N 79	BRYANT, Edward
4	Stone	LOC-N 79	BRYANT, Edward

SECTION C: TITLES (Alphabetically)

CAT	T I T L E S	AW W/N Y	A U T H O R
4	Stone Circle	NEB-N 76	TUTTLE, Lisa
3	Stone City, The	NEB-N 77	MARTIN, George R R
5	Storeys From The Old Hotel	WFA-N 89	WOLFE, Gene
1	Storm of Wings, A	BFA-N 81	HARRISON, M John
6	Storm Season	LOC-N 83	ASPRIN, Robert Lynn
2	Storms of Windhaven, The	NEB-N 75	TUTTLE, Lisa
2	Storms of Windhaven, The	HUG-N 76	MARTIN, George R R
2	Storms of Windhaven, The	LOC-W 76	MARTIN, George R R
4	Story Child	NEB-N 91	RUSCH, Kristine Kathryn
2	Story Writer, The	NEB-N 79	WILSON, Richard
9	Strange Invasion	LOC-N 90	KANDEL, Michael
1	Strange Toys	DIC-W 88	GEARY, Patricia
5	Strange Wine	LOC-N 79	ELLISON, Harlan
1	Stranger in a Strange Land	HUG-W 62	HEINLEIN, Robert A
2	Strangers	HUG-N 75	DOZOIS, Gardner
1	Strangers	NEB-N 78	DOZOIS, Gardner
2	Strangers	LOC-N 75	DOZOIS, Gardner
1	Strangers	WFA-N 87	KOONTZ, Dean R
2	Strangers	JUP-N 75	DOZOIS, Gardner
3	Strata	NEB-N 80	BRYANT, Edward
3	Strata	LOC-N 81	BRYANT, Edward
3	Street Meat	LOC-N 84	SPINRAD, Norman
11	Stress of Her Regard, The	LOC-N 90	POWERS, Tim
1	Stress of Her Regard, The	WFA-N 90	POWERS, Tim
7	Strokes: Essays and Reviews 1966-1986	LOC-N 89	CLUTE, John
14	Sturgeon is Alive and Well	LOC-N 72	STURGEON, Theodore
1	Subterranean Gallery	CLA-N 92	RUSSO, Richard Paul
1	Subturranean Gallery	DIC-W 90	RUSSO, Richard Paul
9	Suiting, The	STO-W 89	WILDE, Kelley
1	Summer of Night	STO-N 92	SIMMONS, Dan
1	Summer of Night	BFA-N 91	SIMMONS, Dan
10	Summer of Night	LOC-W 92	SIMMONS, Dan
1	Summer Queen, The	LOC-N 92	VINGE, Joan D
1	Summer Queen, The	HUG-N 92	VINGE, Joan D
2	Summer Solstice	HUG-N 85	HARNESS, Charles L
9	Summer Tree, The	LOC-N 86	KAY, Guy Gavriel
4	Sunday Visit, A	NEB-N 80	STRETE, Craig
9	Sundiver	LOC-N 81	BRIN, David
5	Sunfall	LOC-N 82	CHERRYH, C J
9	Sunglasses After Dark	LOC-N 90	COLLINS, Nancy A
9	Sunglasses After Dark	STO-N 90	COLLINS, Nancy
4	Sunken Gardens	NEB-N 84	STERLING, Bruce
2	Sunrise West	NEB-N 75	CARLSON, William K
6	Superhorror	WFA-N 77	CAMPBELL, Ramsey
2	Superwine	LOC-N 88	TURTLEDOVE, Harry
4	Supplicant in Space, A	JUP-W 74	SHECKLEY, Robert
4	Sur	LOC-W 83	LeGUIN, Ursula K
4	Sur	HUG-N 83	LeGUIN, Ursula K
4	Sur	SFC-N 83	LeGUIN, Ursula K
2	Surfacing	NEB-N 88	WILLIAMS, Walter Jon
2	Surfacing	LOC-N 89	WILLIAMS, Walter Jon
2	Surfacing	DAV-N 89	WILLIAMS, Walter Jon
2	Surfacing	HUG-N 89	WILLIAMS, Walter Jon

SECTION C: TITLES (Alphabetically)

CAT	T I T L E S	AW W/N Y	A U T H O R
3	Survivability	JUP-N 74	TUNING, William
4	Surviving	JWC-W 87	MOFFETT, Judith
3	Surviving	NEB-N 86	MOFFETT, Judith
1	Swan Song	WFA-N 88	McCAMMON, Robert R
1	Swan Song	STO-W 88	McCAMMON, Robert R
3	Swanilda's Song	LOC-N 79	POHL, Frederik
3	Swarm	NEB-N 82	STERLING, Bruce
3	Swarm	HUG-N 83	STERLING, Bruce
2	Swarmer, Skimmer	NEB-N 81	BENFORD, Gregory
4	Sword Game	NEB-N 68	HOLLIS, H H
1	Sword of Aldones(10): Darkover	HUG-N 63	BRADLEY, Marion Zimmer
1	Sword of Aldones(10): Darkover	HUG-N 62	BRADLEY, Marion Zimmer
11	Sword of Shannara, The	LOC-N 78	BROOKS, Terry
1	Sword of the Demon	NEB-N 77	LUPOFF, Richard A
1	Sword of the Lichtor, The	WFA-N 83	WOLFE, Gene
1	Sword of the Lichtor, The	BSF-N 83	WOLFE, Gene
1	Sword of the Lichtor, The	BFA-W 83	WOLFE, Gene
11	Sword of the Lichtor, The	LOC-W 83	WOLFE, Gene
1	Sword of the Lichtor, The	SFC-W 83	WOLFE, Gene
1	Sword of the Lichtor, The	HUG-N 83	WOLFE, Gene
1	Sword of the Lichtor, The	NEB-N 82	WOLFE, Gene
1	Swordpoint	SFC-N 88	KUSHNER, Ellen
6	Swords and Ice Magic	WFA-N 78	LEIBER, Fritz
1	Sylva	HUG-N 63	VERCORS
4	Symphony for a Lost Traveler	HUG-N 85	KILLOUGH, Lee
1	Synners	CLA-W 92	CADIGAN, Pat
1	Synners	NEB-N 92	CADIGAN, Pat
9	Tailchaser's Song	LOC-N 86	WILLIAMS, Tad
1	Take Back Plenty	BSF-W 91	GREENLAND, Colin
1	Take Back Plenty	CLA-W 91	GREENLAND, Colin
1	Takeoff	IFA-N 53	KORNBLUTH, Cyril M
2	Tale of Gorgik, The	NEB-N 79	DELANY, Samuel R
2	Tale of Rumor and Desire, The	SFC-N 88	DELANY, Samuel R
6	Tales From the Nightside	BFA-N 82	GRANT, Charles L
6	Tales From the Nightside	WFA-N 82	GRANT, Charles L
6	Tales of Known Space	LOC-N 76	NIVEN, Larry
11	Tales of Neveryon	LOC-N 80	DELANY, Samuel R
6	Tales of the Quintana Roo	WFA-W 87	TIPTREE, James Jr
6	Tales of the Vulgar Unicorn	LOC-N 81	ASPRIN, Robert Lynn
6	Tales of Wonder	WFA-N 84	YOLEN, James
11	Talisman, The	LOC-N 85	KING, Stephen
1	Talisman, The	WFA-N 85	STRAUB, Peter
1	Talking Man	WFA-N 87	BISSON, Terry
5	Tamastara	LOC-N 85	LEE, Tanith
4	Tangents	NEB-W 86	BEAR, Greg
5	Tangents	LOC-N 90	BEAR, Greg
4	Tangents	LOC-N 87	BEAR, Greg
4	Tangents	HUG-W 87	BEAR, Greg
4	Tangents	SFC-N 87	BEAR, Greg
2	Tango Charlie and Foxtrot Romeo	LOC-N 87	VARLEY, John
1	Tau Zero	HUG-N 71	ANDERSON, Poul

SECTION C: TITLES (Alphabetically)

CAT	T I T L E S	AW W/N Y	A U T H O R
1	Tea With The Black Dragon	WFA-N 84	MacAVOY, R A
1	Tea With The Black Dragon	DIC-N 84	MacAVOY, R A
9	Tea With The Black Dragon	LOC-W 84	MacAVOY, R A
1	Tea With The Black Dragon	HUG-N 84	MacAVOY, R A
1	Tea With The Black Dragon	NEB-N 83	MacAVOY, R A
1	Tehanu: The Last Book of Earthsea	NEB-W 91	LeGUIN, Ursula K
11	Tehanu: The Last Book of Earthsea	LOC-W 91	LeGUIN, Ursula K
4	Temple to a Minor Goddess	NEB-N 87	SHWARTZ, Susan
10	Tempter	LOC-N 91	COLLINS, A
14	Ten Thousand Light Years From Home	LOC-N 74	TIPTREE, James Jr
1	Terrarium	DIC-N 86	SANDERS, Scott Russell
6	Terry's Universe	LOC-N 89	MEECHAM, Beth
3	That Thou Art Mindful of Him	HUG-N 75	ASIMOV, Isaac
3	That Thou Art Mindful of Him	LOC-N 75	ASIMOV, Isaac
1	The City, Not Long After	CLA-N 91	MURPHY, Pat
3	The Fire When it Comes	HUG-N 82	GODWIN, Parker
1	Them Bones	DIC-N 85	WALDROP, Howard
9	Them Bones	LOC-N 85	WALDROP, Howard
4	Theory of Rocketry	HUG-N 59	KORNBLUTH, Cyril M
11	There Are Doors	LOC-N 89	WOLFE, Gene
2	There Beneath the Silky Trees...	NEB-N 80	DAVIDSON, Avram
1	There Will be Time	HUG-N 73	ANDERSON, Poul
2	There's A Long, Long Trail A-Winding	WFA-W 77	KIRK, Russell
3	Thermals of August, The	LOC-N 82	BRYANT, Edward
3	Thermals of August, The	HUG-N 82	BRYANT, Edward
3	Thermals of August, The	NEB-N 81	BRYANT, Edward
2	Thesme and the Ghayrog	LOC-N 83	SILVERBERG, Robert
1	They'd Rather Be Right	HUG-W 55	CLIFTON, Mark
4	They're Coming For You	WFA-N 87	DANIELS, Les
4	They're Made Out of Meat	NEB-N 92	BISSON, Terry
4	They've Been Working On...	HUG-N 59	BAKER, Anton Lee
6	Thieve's World	WFA-N 80	ASPRIN, Robert
6	Thieve's World #7: The Dead of Winter	LOC-N 86	ASPRIN, Robert Lynn
4	Thing At the Top of the Stairs, The	STO-N 89	BRADBURY, Ray
2	Thing in the Stone, The	HUG-N 71	SIMAK, Clifford D
2	Thing in the Stone, The	NEB-N 70	SIMAK, Clifford D
4	Thing of Beauty, A	NEB-N 73	SPINRAD, Norman
4	Thing of Beauty, A	JUP-N 74	SPINRAD, Norman
4	Third Test, The	BSF-N 83	WEINER, Andrew
1	This Is the Way The World Ends	JWC-N 87	MORROW, James
1	This Is the Way the World Ends	NEB-N 86	MORROW, James
3	This Moment of the Storm	HUG-N 67	ZELAZNY, Roger
4	This Old Man	STO-N 88	GRANT, Charles L
11	Thomas the Rhymer	LOC-N 91	KUSHNER, Ellen
1	Thomas the Rhymer	WFA-W 91	KUSHNER, Ellen
3	Thor Meets Captain America	LOC-W 87	BRIN, David
3	Thor Meets Captain America	SFC-N 87	BRIN, David
3	Thor Meets Captain America	HUG-N 87	BRIN, David
1	Thorns	HUG-N 67	SILVERBERG, Robert
1	Thorns	NEB-N 67	SILVERBERG, Robert
14	Those Who Can	LOC-N 74	WILSON, Robin Scott
10	Those Who Hunt the Night	LOC-W 89	HAMBLY, Barbara
4	Though A Sparrow Fall	NEB-N 65	NICHOLS, Scott

CAT	T I T L E S	AW W/N Y	A U T H O R
13	Threads of Time	LOC-N 75	SILVERBERG, Robert
1	Three Stigmata Palmer Eldritch	NEB-N 65	DICK, Philip K
9	Tides of God, The	LOC-N 90	REYNOLDS, Ted
1	Tides of Light	LOC-N 90	BENFORD, Gregory
11	Tigana	LOC-N 91	KAY, Guy Gavriel
1	Tigana	WFA-N 91	KAY, Guy Gavriel
1	Tigana	AUR-W 91	KAY, Guy Gavriel
2	Tiger Sweater, The	NEB-N 87	ROBERTS, Keith
4	Tight Little Stitches in Dead Man's Back	WFA-N 87	LANSDALE, Joe R
1	Tik-Tok	JWC-N 84	SLADEK, John
1	Tik-Tok	BSF-W 84	SLADEK, John
4	Time Considered as a Helix..	HUG-W 70	DELANY, Samuel R
3	Time Considered as a Helix...	NEB-W 69	DELANY, Samuel R
4	Time Deer	NEB-N 75	STRETE, Craig
1	Time Enough For Love	NEB-N 73	HEINLEIN, Robert A
1	Time Enough For Love	LOC-N 74	HEINLEIN, Robert A
1	Time Enough For Love	HUG-N 74	HEINLEIN, Robert A
1	Time Enough For Love	JUP-N 74	HEINLEIN, Robert A
3	Time For Every Purpose, A	NEB-N 91	RUSCH, Kristine Kathryn
1	Time is the Simplest Thing (Fisherman)	HUG-N 62	SIMAK, Clifford D
1	Time of Changes, A	LOC-N 72	SILVERBERG, Robert
1	Time of Changes, A	NEB-W 71	SILVERBERG, Robert
1	Time of Changes, A	HUG-N 72	SILVERBERG, Robert
3	Time Storm	JUP-W 78	DICKSON, Gordon R
1	Time Storm	LOC-N 78	DICKSON, Gordon R
1	Time Storm	HUG-N 78	DICKSON, Gordon R
1	Timescape	LOC-N 81	BENFORD, Gregory
1	Timescape	NEB-W 80	BENFORD, Gregory
1	Timescape	JWC-W 81	BENFORD, Gregory
1	Timescape	BSF-W 81	BENFORD, Gregory
1	Timescape	DIT-W 81	BENFORD, Gregory
1	Timeservers, The	DIC-N 86	GRIFFIN, Russell
4	Time's Rub	SFC-N 86	BENFORD, Gregory
4	Time's Rub	LOC-N 86	BENFORD, Gregory
2	Time-Out	LOC-N 90	WILLIS, Connie
2	Time-Out	HUG-N 90	WILLIS, Connie
4	Time-Sharing Angel	HUG-N 78	TIPTREE, James Jr
3	Tin Soldier	JUP-N 75	VINGE, Joan
4	Tin Woodsman	NEB-N 77	BAILEY, Dennis
3	Tinker	HUG-N 76	POURNELLE, Jerry
2	Tiny Tango	NEB-N 89	MOFFETT, Judith
2	Tiny Tango	HUG-N 90	MOFFETT, Judith
2	Tiny Tango	LOC-N 90	MOFFETT, Judith
1	Titan	LOC-W 80	VARLEY, John
1	Titan	NEB-N 79	VARLEY, John
1	Titan	HUG-N 80	VARLEY, John
4	Tithonian Factor, The	BSF-N 84	COWPER, Richard
2	To Become A Sorcerer	WFA-N 92	SCHWEITZER, Darrell
2	To Jorslem	NEB-N 69	SILVERBERG, Robert
2	To Jorslem	HUG-N 70	SILVERBERG, Robert
2	To Leave a Mark	HUG-N 83	ROBINSON, Kim Stanley
1	To Wake the Dead	BFA-W 81	CAMPBELL, Ramsey

SECTION C: TITLES (Alphabetically)

CAT	T I T L E S	AW W/N Y	A U T H O R
1	To Your Scattered Bodies Go	HUG-W 72	FARMER, Philip Jose
1	To Your Scattered Bodies Go	LOC-N 72	FARMER, Philip Jose
1	Too Many Magicians	HUG-N 67	GARRETT, Randall
3	Total Environment	HUG-N 69	ALDISS, Brian W
3	Total Environment	NEB-N 68	ALDISS, Brian W
2	Touch of Lavender, A	DAV-W 90	LINDHOLM, Megan
2	Touch of Lavender, A	NEB-N 89	LINDHOLM, Megan
2	Touch of Lavender, A	HUG-N 90	LINDHOLM, Megan
3	Tower of Babylon	HUG-N 91	CHIANG, Ted
3	Tower of Babylon	SFC-N 91	CHIANG, Ted
3	Tower of Babylon	LOC-N 91	CHIANG, Ted
3	Tower of Babylon	NEB-N 91	CHIANG, Ted
1	Tower of Glass, The	LOC-N 71	SILVERBERG, Robert
1	Tower of Glass, The	HUG-N 71	SILVERBERG, Robert
1	Tower of Glass, The	NEB-N 70	SILVERBERG, Robert
6	Toynbee Convector, The	STO-N 89	BRADBURY, Ray
1	Transfigurations	BSF-N 81	BISHOP, Michael
2	Transit	NEB-N 83	McINTYRE, Vonda N
1	Transmigration of Timothy Archer, The	NEB-N 82	DICK, Philip K
11	Transmigration of Timothy Archer, The	LOC-N 83	DICK, Philip K
4	Traps	STO-N 88	WILSON, F Paul
2	Traveler's Tale, A	LOC-N 85	SHEPARD, Lucius
2	Traveler's Tale, A	NEB-N 84	SHEPARD, Lucius
2	Traveler's Tale, A	SFC-N 85	SHEPARD, Lucius
4	Treading the Maze	BSF-N 82	TUTTLE, Lisa
4	Tricentennial	LOC-W 77	HALDEMAN, Joe
4	Tricentennial	NEB-N 76	HALDEMAN, Joe
4	Tricentennial	HUG-W 77	HALDEMAN, Joe
1	Tricksters, The	WFA-N 87	MAHY, Margaret
4	Triggerman	HUG-N 59	BONE, J F
7	Trillion Year Spree	HUG-W 87	ALDISS, Brian
7	Trillion Year Spree	LOC-W 87	ALDISS, Brian W
2	Trinity	NEB-N 84	KRESS, Nancy
2	Trinity	SFC-N 85	KRESS, Nancy
2	Trinity	LOC-N 85	KRESS, Nancy
1	Triton	NEB-N 76	DELANY, Samuel R
3	Trojan Horse	NEB-N 84	SWANWICK, Michael
2	True Names	NEB-N 81	VINGE, Vernor
2	True Names	HUG-N 82	VINGE, Vernor
1	Trullion Alastor	LOC-N 74	VANCE, Jack
11	Trumps of Doom	LOC-W 86	ZELAZNY, Roger
5	Tuf Voyaging	LOC-N 87	MARTIN, George R R
3	Twig	LOC-N 75	DICKSON, Gordon R
3	Twilla	NEB-N 74	REAMY, Tom
11	Twisting The Rope	LOC-N 87	MacAVOY, R A
2	Two Suns Setting	WFA-N 77	WAGNER, Karl Edward
4	Two Suns Setting	BFA-W 77	WAGNER, Karl Edward
3	Ugly Chickens, The	LOC-N 81	WALDROP, Howard
4	Ugly Chickens, The	WFA-W 81	WALDROP, Howard
3	Ugly Chickens, The	HUG-N 81	WALDROP, Howard
3	Ugly Chickens, The	NEB-W 80	WALDROP, Howard
4	Unaccompanied Sonata	HUG-N 80	CARD, Orson Scott
4	Unaccompanied Sonata	NEB-N 79	CARD, Orson Scott
1	Unassigned Territory	STO-N 88	NUNN, Ken

SECTION C: TITLES (Alphabetically)

CAT	TITLES	AW W/N Y	AUTHOR
4	Uncollected Works	NEB-N 65	CARTER, Lin
4	Unconquered Country, The	BSF-W 85	RYMAN, Geoff
2	Unconquered Country, The	WFA-W 85	RYMAN, Geoff
2	Unconquered Country, The	NEB-N 87	RYMAN, Geoff
1	Unconquered Country, The	JWC-N 88	RYMAN, Geoff
3	Under Siege	LOC-N 86	MARTIN, George R R
3	Under the Covenant Stars	DAV-N 89	BARNES, John
2	Under Two Moons	NEB-N 65	POHL, Frederik
3	Understand	HUG-N 92	CHIANG, Ted
3	Understanding Human Behavior	SFC-W 83	DISCH, Thomas M
3	Understanding Human Behavior	NEB-N 82	DISCH, Thomas M
9	Unearthed	STO-N 92	McCONNELL, Ashley
3	Unfinished Portrait of the King of Pain	NEB-N 88	McDonald, Ian
4	Unholy Grail, The	HUG-N 63	LEIBER, Fritz
11	Unicorn Mountain	LOC-N 89	BISHOP, Michael
4	Unicorn Tapestry	WFA-N 81	CHARNAS, Suzy McKee
2	Unicorn Tapestry	NEB-N 80	CHARNAS, Suzy McKee
3	Unicorn Variations	LOC-N 82	ZELAZNY, Roger
3	Unicorn Variations	HUG-W 82	ZELAZNY, Roger
5	Unicorn Variations	LOC-W 84	ZELAZNY, Roger
13	Universe 1	LOC-W 72	CARR, Terry
6	Universe 1	LOC-N 91	CARR, Terry
13	Universe 2	LOC-N 73	CARR, Terry
13	Universe 3	LOC-N 74	CARR, Terry
13	Universe 4	LOC-W 75	CARR, Terry
14	Universe 6	LOC-N 77	CARR, Terry
6	Universe 8	LOC-N 79	CARR, Terry
6	Universe 9	LOC-W 80	CARR, Terry
6	Universe 11	LOC-N 82	CARR, Terry
6	Universe 12	LOC-N 83	CARR, Terry
6	Universe 13	LOC-N 84	CARR, Terry
6	Universe 14	LOC-N 85	CARR, Terry
6	Universe 15	LOC-N 86	CARR, Terry
6	Universe 16	LOC-N 87	CARR, Terry
6	Universe 17	LOC-N 88	CARR, Terry
1	Unlimited Dream Company, The	JWC-N 80	BALLARD, J G
1	Unlimited Dream Company, The	BSF-W 80	BALLARD, J G
4	Unmistakably the Finest	BSF-N 85	BRADFIELD, Scott
1	Unquenchable Fire	CLA-W 89	POLLACK, Richard
1	Unsleeping Eye, The	LOC-N 75	COMPTON, D G
2	Unsound Variations	NEB-N 82	MARTIN, George R R
2	Unsound Variations	HUG-N 83	MARTIN, George R R
2	Unsound Variations	LOC-N 83	MARTIN, George R R
3	Unwilling to School	HUG-N 59	ASHWELL, Pauline
1	Up the Line	NEB-N 69	SILVERBERG, Robert
1	Up the Line	HUG-N 70	SILVERBERG, Robert
1	Up the Walls of the World	HUG-N 79	TIPTREE, James Jr
1	Uplift War, The	NEB-N 87	BRIN, David
1	Uplift War, The	HUG-W 88	BRIN, David
1	Uplift War, The	LOC-W 88	BRIN, David

SECTION C: TITLES (Alphabetically)

CAT	TITLES	AW W/N Y	AUTHOR
1	Urth of the New Sun, The	SFC-W 88	WOLFE, Gene
1	Urth of the New Sun, The	HUG-N 88	WOLFE, Gene
1	Urth of the New Sun, The	LOC-N 88	WOLFE, Gene
1	Urth of the New Sun, The	NEB-N 88	WOLFE, Gene
1	Use of Weapons	CLA-N 91	BANKS, Iain M
1	Use of Weapons	BSF-N 91	BANKS, Iain M
4	Utility Man, The	LOC-N 91	REED, Robert
4	Utility Man, The	HUG-N 91	REED, Rober
4	Utopia of a Tired Man	NEB-N 75	BORGES, Jorge Luis
2	Valentina	HUG-N 85	DELANEY, Joseph H
9	Valentina: Soul in Sapphire	LOC-N 85	DELANEY, Joseph H
1	Valley of Lights	BFA-N 88	GALLAGHER, Stephen
1	Vampire Lestat, The	WFA-N 86	RICE, Anne
11	Vampire Lestat, The	LOC-N 86	RICE, Anne
1	Vampire Tapestry, The	NEB-N 81	CHARNAS, Suzy McKee
7	Vampires Among Us	STO-N 92	GUILLEN, Rosemary Ellen
3	Vanishing Point	NEB-N 65	BRAND, Jonathan
4	Varicose Worms	WFA-N 90	BAKER, Scott
4	Vaster Than Empires and More Slow	HUG-N 72	LeGUIN, Ursula K
4	Venice Drowned	NEB-N 81	ROBINSON, Kim Stanley
1	Venus Pluz X	HUG-N 61	STURGEON, Theodore
1	Vergil in Averno	NEB-N 87	DAVIDSON, Avram
4	Vernalfest	NEB-N 79	BISHOP, Michael
4	Very Slow Time Machine, The	HUG-N 79	WATSON, Ian
4	View From A Height	LOC-N 79	VINGE, Joan D
4	View From a Height	HUG-N 79	VINGE, Joan D
4	Village, The	JUP-N 74	WILHELM, Kate
4	Vinland the Dream	LOC-N 92	ROBINSON, Kim Stanley
4	Vinland the Dream	SFC-N 92	ROBINSON, Kim Stanley
6	Viriconium Nights	WFA-N 85	HARRISON, M John
4	Virra	LOC-N 79	CARR, Terry
5	Visible Light	LOC-N 87	CHERRYH, C J
7	Visions From the Edge	AUR-N 82	BELL, John
4	Voices of the Kill	NEB-N 88	DISCH, Thomas
1	Void Captain's Tale, The	LOC-N 84	SPINRAD, Norman
1	Void Captain's Tale, The	NEB-N 83	SPINRAD, Norman
1	Vor Game, The	SFC-N 91	BUJOLD, Lois McMaster
1	Vor Game, The	LOC-N 91	BUJOLD, Lois McMaster
1	Vor Game, The	HUG-W 91	BUJOLD, Lois McMaster
1	Voyage to the Red Planet	LOC-N 91	BISSON, Ted
1	Voyager in Night	DIC-N 85	CHERRYH, C J
4	VRM-547	HUG-N 91	THOMPSON, W R
4	VRM-547	DAV-W 91	THOMPSON, W R
4	VRM-547	LOC-N 91	THOMPSON, W R
1	Waiting for the Barbarians	DIC-N 83	COETZEE, J M
4	Walk in the Sun, A	HUG-W 92	LANDIS, Geoffrey A
9	Walkabout Woman	LOC-N 89	ROESSNER, Michaela
5	Walking Nightmares	STO-N 92	CAMPBELL, Ramsey
6	Walls of Fear	WFA-N 91	CRAMER, Kathryn
1	Wanderer, The	HUG-W 65	LEIBER, Fritz
1	Wandering Fire, The	AUR-W 87	KAY, Guy Gavriel
13	Wandering Stars	LOC-N 75	DANN, Jack
1	Wandering Unicorn, The	WFA-N 84	LAINEZ, Manuel Mujica

CAT	TITLES	AW W/N Y	AUTHOR
4	War Beneath the Tree	LOC-N 80	WOLFE, Gene
4	War Beneath the Tree	NEB-N 80	WOLFE, Gene
1	War for Eternity, The	COM-W 84	ROWLEY, Christopher
1	War for the Oaks	COM-W 88	BULL, Emma
9	War for the Oaks	LOC-W 88	BULL, Emma
9	War Games	LOC-N 82	HANSEN, Karl
11	War Hounds and the World's Pain, The	LOC-N 82	MOORCOCK, Michael
1	War Hounds and the World's Pain, The	WFA-N 82	MOORCOCK, Michael
7	Warhoon 28 Walter A Willis	HUG-N 81	BERGERON, Richard
3	Warlord of Saturn's Moons, The	NEB-N 75	ARNASON, Eleanor
6	Warm Worlds and Otherwise	LOC-N 76	TIPTREE, James Jr
1	Warrior Who Carried Life, The	BSF-N 86	RYMAN, Geoff
2	Watched, The	LOC-N 79	PRIEST, Christopher
2	Watched, The	HUG-N 79	PRIEST, Christopher
7	Watchmen	LOC-W 88	MOORE, Alan
1	Watchtower	WFA-W 80	LYNN, Elizabeth A
4	Way of Cross and Dragon, The	LOC-W 80	MARTIN, George R R
4	Way of Cross and Dragon, The	HUG-W 80	MARTIN, George R R
4	Way of Cross and Dragon, The	NEB-N 79	MARTIN, George R R
3	Way Station, The	LOC-N 81	KING, Stephen
3	Way Station, The	NEB-N 80	KING, Stephen
1	Way Station (Here Gather Stars)	HUG-W 64	SIMAK, Clifford
7	Way the Future Was, The	LOC-N 79	POHL, Frederik
3	Ways of Love, The	NEB-N 79	ANDERSON, Poul
2	We All Die Naked	HUG-N 70	BLISH, James
2	We Are for the Dark	LOC-N 89	SILVERBERG, Robert
2	Weather War	LOC-N 77	COCHRANE, William E
2	Weatherman	NEB-N 91	BUJOLD, Lois McMaster
2	Weatherman	LOC-N 91	BUJOLD, Lois McMaster
2	Weatherman	DAV-W 91	BUJOLD, Lois McMaster
1	Weaveworld	WFA-N 88	BARKER, Clive
11	Weaveworld	LOC-N 88	BARKER, Clive
1	Weaveworld	BFA-N 88	BARKER, Clive
2	Web of the Magi, The	LOC-N 81	COWPER, Richard
4	Web of the Magi, The	BSF-N 81	COWPER, Richard
7	Weird Tale, The	STO-N 91	JOSHI, S T
10	Werewolves of London	LOC-N 91	STABLEFORD, Brian M
1	West of January	AUR-W 90	DUNCAN, Dave
1	Wetware	DIC-W 89	RUCKER, Rudy
2	Weyr Search	NEB-N 67	McCAFFREY, Anne
2	Weyr Search	HUG-N 68	McCAFFREY, Anne
3	What Continues, What Fails	SFC-N 92	BRIN, David
1	What Entropy Means to Me	NEB-N 72	EFFINGER, George Alec
2	What Is Life	WFA-N 77	SHECKLEY, Robert
6	What Might Have Been Vol 2	LOC-N 90	BENFORD, Gregory
6	What Might Have Been Vol 3: Alt Wars	LOC-N 92	BENFORD, Gregory
4	Wheels	LOC-N 72	THURSTON, Robert
4	When All the Children Call My Name	WFA-N 78	GRANT, Charles L
1	When Gravity Fails	SFC-N 88	EFFINGER, George Alec
1	When Gravity Fails	HUG-N 88	EFFINGER, George Alec
1	When Gravity Fails	LOC-N 88	EFFINGER, George Alec
1	When Gravity Fails	NEB-N 87	EFFINGER, George Alec

SECTION C: TITLES (Alphabetically)

CAT	T I T L E S	AW W/N Y	A U T H O R
1	When Harlie Was One	NEB-N 72	GERROLD, David
1	When Harlie Was One	LOC-N 73	GERROLD, David
1	When Harlie Was One	HUG-N 73	GERROLD, David
4	When It Changed	LOC-N 73	RUSS, Joanna
4	When It Changed	HUG-N 73	RUSS, Joanna
4	When It Changed	NEB-W 72	RUSS, Joanna
6	When The Music is Over	WFA-N 92	SHINER, Lewis
4	When We Went to See the End of the World	HUG-N 73	SILVERBERG, Robert
4	When You Care, When You Love	HUG-N 63	STURGEON, Theodore
4	Where is the Bird of Fire?	HUG-N 63	SWANN, Thomas Burnett
1	Where Late the Sweet Birds Sang	NEB-N 76	WILHELM, Kate
1	Where Late the Sweet Birds Sang	HUG-W 77	WILHELM, Kate
1	Where Late the Sweet Birds Sang	LOC-W 77	WILHELM, Kate
1	Where Late the Sweet Birds Sang	JWC-N 77	WILHELM, Kate
1	Where Late the Sweet Birds Sang	JUP-W 77	WILHELM, Kate
1	Where Time Winds Blow	BSF-N 82	HOLDSTOCK, Robert
6	Whisper of Blood, A	WFA-N 92	DATLOW, Ellen
6	Whisper of Blood, A	LOC-N 92	DATLOW, Ellen
6	Whispers	WFA-N 78	SCHIFF, Stuart David
6	Whispers 2	WFA-N 80	SCHIFF, Stuart David
6	Whispers 3	WFA-N 82	SCHIFF, Stuart David
6	Whispers 3	BFA-N 82	SCHIFF, Stuart David
6	Whispers 4	LOC-N 84	SCHIFF, Stuart David
6	Whispers 5	WFA-N 86	SCHIFF, Stuart David
4	White Creatures	NEB-N 75	BENFORD, Gregory
1	White Dragon, The	HUG-N 79	McCAFFREY, Anne
1	White Dragon, The	DIT-W 79	McCAFFREY, Anne
1	White Dragon, The	LOC-N 79	McCAFFREY, Anne
11	White Gold Wielder	LOC-N 84	DONALDSON, Stephen R
1	White Hotel, The	WFA-N 82	THOMAS, D M
11	White Jenna	LOC-N 90	YOLEN, Jane
1	White Jenna	NEB-N 91	YOLEN, Jane
8	White Mists of Power, The	LOC-N 92	RUSCH, Kristine Kathryn
2	White Otters of Childhood, The	NEB-N 73	BISHOP, Michael
2	White Otters of Childhood, The	HUG-N 74	BISHOP, Michael
2	White Otters of Childhood, The	LOC-N 74	BISHOP, Michael
1	White Queen	CLA-N 92	JONES, Gwyneth
4	White Wolf Calling	NEB-N 75	GRANT, C L
1	Who	HUG-N 59	BUDRYS, Algis
3	Who Steals My Purse	JUP-N 74	BRUNNER, John
1	Whole Man, The	HUG-N 65	BRUNNER, John
1	Whores of Babylon	CLA-N 89	WATSON, Ian
4	Why I Left Harry's All-Night Hamburgers	DAV-W 88	WATT-EVANS, Lawrence
4	Why I Left Harry's All-Night Hamburgers	HUG-W 88	WATT-EVANS, Lawrence
4	Why I Left Harry's All-Night Hamburgers	NEB-N 87	WATT-EVANS, Lawrence
4	Why I Left Harry's All-Night Hamburgers	LOC-N 88	WATT-EVANS, Lawrence
5	Why Not You and I?	WFA-N 88	WAGNER, Karl Edward
6	Why Not You and I?	STO-N 88	WAGNER, Karl Edward
3	Wigher, The	HUG-N 85	VINICOFF, Eric
4	Wild, Wild Horses	LOC-N 89	WALDROP, Howard
6	Wild Cards	LOC-N 87	MARTIN, George R R
6	Wild Cards IV: Aces Abroad	LOC-N 89	MARTIN, George R R

CAT	T I T L E S	AW W/N Y	A U T H O R
9	Wild Shore, The	LOC-W 85	ROBINSON, Kim Stanley
1	Wild Shore, The	SFC-N 85	ROBINSON, Kim Stanley
1	Wild Shore, The	NEB-N 84	ROBINSON, Kim Stanley
1	Wild Shore, The	DIC-N 85	ROBINSON, Kim Stanley
9	Wilderness	STO-N 92	DANVERS, Dennis
3	Willow	LOC-N 83	CHERRYH, C J
5	Wind From A Burning Woman	LOC-N 84	BEAR, Greg
1	Windhaven	LOC-N 82	MARTIN, George R R
9	Windhover Tapes, The	LOC-N 83	NORWOOD, Warren
4	Window	LOC-N 81	LEMAN, Bob
4	Window	NEB-N 80	LEMAN, Bob
4	Windwagon Smith and the Martians	DAV-W 90	WATT-EVANS, Lawrence
6	Wind's Twelve Quarters	LOC-W 76	LeGUIN, Ursula K
4	Wings	HUG-N 74	McINTYRE, Vonda N
4	Wings	NEB-N 73	McINTYRE, Vonda N
6	Wings of Omen	LOC-N 85	ASPRIN, Robert Lynn
4	Winning	BSF-N 91	McDONALD, Ian
2	Winter Beach, The	NEB-N 81	WILHELM, Kate
1	Winter King	WFA-N 86	HAZEL, Paul
3	Winter Market, The	SFC-N 87	GIBSON, William
3	Winter Market, The	LOC-N 87	GIBSON, William
3	Winter Market, The	HUG-N 87	GIBSON, William
4	Winter Market, The	BSF-N 87	GIBSON, William
3	Winter Market, The	NEB-N 86	GIBSON, William
9	Winter Scream	STO-N 92	CURRY, Chris
4	Winter Solstice	HUG-N 92	RESNICK, Mike
4	Winter Solstice, Camelot Station	WFA-W 89	FORD, John M
1	Wintersong	DIC-N 91	HAND, Elizabeth
9	Wintersong	LOC-N 91	HAND, Elizabeth
4	Winter's King	HUG-N 70	LeGUIN, Ursula K
1	Witch World	HUG-N 63	NORTON, Andre
1	Witch World	HUG-N 64	NORTON, Andre
1	Witches of Karres	HUG-N 67	SCHMITZ, James H
10	Witching Hour, The	LOC-W 91	RICE, Anne
3	With A Little Help From Her Friends	LOC-N 85	BISHOP, Michael
2	With Delicate Mad Hands	LOC-N 82	TIPTREE, James Jr
4	With Morning Comes Mistfall	NEB-N 73	MARTIN, George R R
4	With Morning Comes Mistfall	HUG-N 74	MARTIN, George R R
2	With t/Bentfin Boomer Boys on Little Old	LOC-N 73	LUPOFF, Dick
2	With t/Bentfin Boomer Boys on Little Old	NEB-N 72	LUPOFF, Richard A
2	With Thimbles, With Forks and Hope	HUG-N 82	WILHELM, Kate
4	With Virgil Oddum at the East Pole	LOC-W 86	ELLISON, Harlan
4	Within the Walls of Tyre	WFA-N 79	BISHOP, Michael
4	Within the Walls of Tyre	BFA-N 79	BISHOP, Michael
2	Witness	NEB-N 87	WILLIAMS, John
1	Wizard	LOC-N 81	VARLEY, John
1	Wizard	HUG-N 81	VARLEY, John
7	Wizardry and Wild Romance	LOC-N 88	MOORCOCK, Michael
3	Wizard's World	HUG-N 68	NORTON, Andre
4	Wolf Winter	STO-N 92	O'CALLAGHAN, Maxine
10	Wolf's Hour, The	LOC-N 90	McCAMMON, Robert R
1	Wolf's Hour, The	STO-N 90	McCAMMON, Robert R

SECTION C: TITLES (Alphabetically)

CAT	T I T L E S	AW W/N Y	A U T H O R
1	Woman of the Iron People, A	JWC-N 92	ARNASON, Eleanor
4	Woman the Unicorn Loved, The	HUG-N 82	WOLFE, Gene
3	Women Men Don't See	JUP-N 75	TIPTREE, James Jr
4	Women Who Loved the Moon	WFA-W 80	LYNN, Elizabeth A
2	Wonderful Secret, The	HUG-N 78	LAUMER, Keith
7	Wonderworks	HUG-N 80	DONNING, Whelan
7	Wonder's Child: My Life in S Fiction	LOC-N 85	WILLIAMSON, Jack
7	Wonder's Child: My Life in S Fiction	HUG-W 85	WILLIAMSON, Jack
4	Wong's Lost and Found Emporium	WFA-N 84	WU, William F
4	Wong's Lost and Found Emporium	HUG-N 84	WU, William F
4	Wong's Lost and Found Emporium	NEB-N 83	WU, William F
2	Word for World is Forest, The	LOC-N 73	LeGUIN, Ursula K
2	Word for World is Forest, The	HUG-W 73	LeGUIN, Ursula K
2	Word for World is Forest, The	NEB-N 72	LeGUIN, Ursula K
1	World Between, A	BSF-N 81	SPINRAD, Norman
7	World Beyond the Hill, The	LOC-N 90	PANSHIN, Alexei & Cory
7	World Beyond the Hill, The	HUG-W 90	PANSHIN, Alexei & Cory
1	World Inside, The	HUG-N 72	SILVERBERG, Robert
7	World of Charles Addams, The	HUG-W 92	ADDAMS, Charles
7	World of Charles Addams, The	LOC-N 92	ADDAMS, Charles
7	World of SF 1926-76	LOC-N 80	del REY, Lester
7	World of the Dark Crystal, The	LOC-N 83	FROUD, Brian
7	World of the Dark Crystal, The	HUG-N 83	FROUD, Brian
1	World Out of Time, A	LOC-N 77	NIVEN, Larry
2	World Outside, The	HUG-N 71	SILVERBERG, Robert
4	World SF Convention of 2080, The	BSF-N 81	WATSON, Ian
5	Worlds of Fritz Leiber, The	LOC-N 77	LEIBER, Fritz
6	Worlds of Wonder	LOC-N 88	SILVERBERG, Robert
14	World's Best Science Fiction: 1971	LOC-W 72	WOLHEIM, Donald A
6	World's Best Science Fiction: 1970	LOC-N 71	WOLHEIM, Donald A
5	Worse Things Waiting	WFA-W 75	WELLMAN, Manly Wade
4	Wound, The	BFA-N 88	TUTTLE, Lisa
11	Wounded Land, The	LOC-N 81	DONALDSON, Stephen R
1	Wounded Land, The	BFA-N 81	DONALDSON, Stephen R
9	Wrack & Roll	LOC-N 87	DENTON, Bradley
4	Wrong-Way Street	NEB-N 65	NIVEN, Larry
1	Xenocide	HUG-N 92	CARD, Orson Scott
1	Xenocide	LOC-N 92	CARD, Orson Scott
4	Yadjine et la Mort	AUR-W 86	SERMINE, Daniel
1	Yarrow	AUR-N 87	de LINT, Charles
1	Year of the Quiet Sun	HUG-N 71	TUCKER, Wilson
1	Year of the Quiet Sun	LOC-N 71	TUCKER, Wilson
1	Year of the Quiet Sun	NEB-N 70	TUCKER, Wilson
1	Years of the City, The	JWC-W 85	POHL, Frederik
5	Years of the City, The	LOC-N 85	POHL, Frederik

SECTION C: TITLES (Alphabetically)

CAT	T I T L E S	AW W/N Y	A U T H O R
6	Year's Best Fantasy and Horror 1st	WFA-W 89	DATLOW, Ellen
6	Year's Best Fantasy and Horror 1st	LOC-N 89	DATLOW, Ellen
6	Year's Best Fantasy and Horror 2nd	LOC-N 90	DATLOW, Ellen
6	Year's Best Fantasy and Horror 2nd	WFA-W 90	DATLOW, Ellen
6	Year's Best Fantasy and Horror 3rd	LOC-N 91	DATLOW, Ellen
6	Year's Best Fantasy and Horror 4th	LOC-N 92	DATLOW, Ellen
6	Year's Best Fantasy and Horror 4th	WFA-N 91	DATLOW, Ellen
6	Year's Best Fantasy and Horror 4th	WFA-N 92	DATLOW, Ellen
6	Year's Best Horror Stories # 5	WFA-N 78	PAGE, Gerald W
6	Year's Best Horror Stories # 6	WFA-N 79	PAGE, Gerald W
6	Year's Best Horror Stories #15	WFA-N 88	WAGNER, Karl Edward
6	Year's Best Science Fiction, 1st	LOC-N 85	DOZOIS, Gardner
6	Year's Best Science Fiction, 2nd	LOC-N 86	DOZOIS, Gardner
6	Year's Best Science Fiction, 3rd	LOC-W 87	DOZOIS, Gardner
6	Year's Best Science Fiction, 4th	LOC-W 88	DOZOIS, Gardner
4	Year's Best Science Fiction, 5th	LOC-N 89	DOZOIS, Gardner
4	Year's Best Science Fiction, 6th	LOC-W 90	DOZOIS, Gardner
2	Year's Best Science Fiction, 7th	LOC-W 91	DOZOIS, Gardner
4	Year's Best Science Fiction, 8th	LOC-N 92	DOZOIS, Gardner
4	Year's Finest Fantasy Vol 2	WFA-N 80	CARR, Terry
6	Yore Skin's Jes' Soft'n' Purty, He Said	STO-N 90	WILLIAMSON, Chet
6	Yore Skin's Jes' Soft'n' Purty, He Said	WFA-N 90	WILLIAMSOM, Chet
6	Young Doctor Esterhazy	NEB-N 84	DAVIDSON, Avram
6	Young Man's Journey to Viriconium, A	BSF-N 86	HARRISON, M John
6	Youthful Folly	LOC-N 89	SHEPARD, Lucius
5	Zanzibar Cat, The	LOC-N 84	RUSS, Joanna
4	Zeke Timothy	NEB-N 81	SULLIVAN, Robert
1	Zen Gun, The	DIC-N 84	BAYLEY, Barrington J
7	Zombies That Ate Pittsburgh	STO-N 88	GAGNE, Paul A

Part D MAJOR SCIENCE FICTION AWARDS

Award Winners Listed Annually

In this section, all award winners are listed, annually. Readers may identify trends in these awards, from year-to-year.

A full description of all abbreviations used within these listings can be found on the next page.

SECTION D: AWARD WINNERS ONLY - (By Year)

HEADINGS:

CAT	T I T L E	AW W/N Y	A U T H O R

EXPLANATIONS:

CAT = Category (length and type)

1 Novel	2 Novella	3 Novellette
4 Short Story	5 1-Author Collection	6 Collection/Anthology
7 Non-Fiction	8 Series	9 First Novel
10 Horror	11 Fantasy Novel	12 Magazine Article
13 Original Anthology	14 Reprint Anthology	

LENGTH OF WORK (from Locus Reader Awards)	
Novel	40,000 + words
Novella	17,500 - 40,000
Novellette	7,500 - 17,500
Short Story	up to 7,500

AW = Award

AUR	Aurora (Casper)
BFA	British Fantasy
BSF	British Science Fiction
CLA	Arthur C. Clarke
COM	Compton Crook
DAV	Davis Publications
DIC	Dick
DIT	Ditmar
HUG	Hugo
IFA	International Fantasy
JUP	Jupiter
JWC	J W Campbell
LOC	Locus Magazine
NEB	Nebula
SFC	SF Chronicle Magazine
STO	Bram Stoker
WFA	World Fantasy

W/N = winner or nominee

Y = year award presented

SECTION D: AWARD WINNERS ONLY - (By Year)

CAT	TITLE	AW W/N Y	AUTHOR
1	Earth Abides	IFA-W 51	STEWART, George
7	Conquest of Space	IFA-W 51	LEY, Willy
1	Fancies and Goodnights	IFA-W 52	COLLIER, John
7	Exploration of Space	IFA-W 52	CLARKE, Arthur C
1	City	IFA-W 53	SIMAK, Clifford D
1	Demolished Man	HUG-W 53	BESTER, Alfred
7	Lands Beyond	IFA-W 53	LEY, Willy
1	More Than Human	IFA-W 54	STURGEON, Theodore
1	Mirror for Observers, A	IFA-W 55	PANGBORN, Edgar
1	They'd Rather Be Right	HUG-W 55	CLIFTON, Mark
3	Darfsteller, The	HUG-W 55	MILLER, Walter M Jr
4	Allamagoosa	HUG-W 55	RUSSELL, Eric Frank
1	Double Star	HUG-W 56	HEINLEIN, Robert A
3	Exploration Team	HUG-W 56	LEINSTER, Murray
4	Star, The	HUG-W 56	CLARKE, Arthur C
1	Lord of the Rings - Trilogy	IFA-W 57	TOLKIEN, J R R
1	Big Time, The	HUG-W 58	LEIBER, Fritz
4	Or All The Seas With Oysters	HUG-W 58	DAVIDSON, Avram
1	Case of Conscience, A	HUG-W 59	BLISH, James
3	Big Front Yard, The	HUG-W 59	SIMAK, Clifford D
4	Hell-Bound Train, That	HUG-W 59	BLOCH, Robert
1	Starship Troopers	HUG-W 60	HEINLEIN, Robert A
4	Flowers for Algernon	HUG-W 60	KEYES, Daniel
1	Canticle for Leibowitz	HUG-W 61	MILLER,
4	Longest Voyage, The	HUG-W 61	ANDERSON, Poul
1	Stranger in a Strange Land	HUG-W 62	HEINLEIN, Robert A
4	Hothouse Series, The	HUG-W 62	ALDISS, Brian W

SECTION D: AWARD WINNERS ONLY - (By Year)

CAT	TITLE	AW W/N Y	AUTHOR
1	Man in the High Castle, The	HUG-W 63	DICK, Philip K
4	Dragon Masters, The	HUG-W 63	VANCE, Jack
1	Way Station (Here Gather Stars)	HUG-W 64	SIMAK, Clifford
4	No Truce with Kings	HUG-W 64	ANDERSON, Poul
1	Wanderer, The	HUG-W 65	LEIBER, Fritz
2	He Who Shapes	NEB-W 65	ZELAZNY, Roger
2	Saliva Tree	NEB-W 65	ALDISS, Brian W
3	Doors of His Face...	NEB-W 65	ZELAZNY, Roger
4	Soldier, Ask Not	HUG-W 65	DICKSON, Gordon R
1	Babel-17	NEB-W 66	DELANY, Samuel R
1	Dune	NEB-W 65	HERBERT, Frank
1	Dune	HUG-W 66	HERBERT, Frank
1	Flowers for Algernon	NEB-W 66	KEYES, Daniel
3	Call Him Lord	NEB-W 66	SPENCER, W
4	Repent Harlequin Said The Ticktockman	NEB-W 65	ELLISON, Harlan
4	Repent Harlequin Said The Ticktockman	HUG-W 66	ELLISON, Harlan
4	Secret Place, The	NEB-W 66	McKENNA, Richard
8	Foundation Trilogy	HUG-W 66	ASIMOV, Isaac
8	Foundation	HUG-W 66	ASIMOV, Isaac
1	Einstein Intersection	NEB-W 67	DELANY, Samuel R
1	Moon is a Harsh Mistress	HUG-W 67	HEINLEIN, Robert A
2	Behold the Man	NEB-W 67	MOORCOCK, Michael
2	Last Castle, The	NEB-W 66	VANCE, Jack
3	Last Castle, The	HUG-W 67	VANCE, Jack
4	Aye, and Gomorrah	NEB-W 67	DELANY, Samuel R
4	Neutron Star, The	HUG-W 67	NIVEN, Larry
1	Lord of Light	HUG-W 68	ZELAZNY, Roger
1	Rite of Passage	NEB-W 68	PANSHIN, Alexei
2	Dragonrider	NEB-W 68	McCAFFREY, Ann
2	Riders of the Purple Wage	HUG-W 68	FARMER, Philip Jose
2	Weyr Search	HUG-W 68	McCAFFREY, Anne
3	Gonna Roll Those Bones	HUG-W 68	LEIBER, Fritz
3	Gonna Roll Those Bones	NEB-W 67	LEIBER, Fritz
3	Mother of the World	NEB-W 68	WILSON, Richard
4	I Have no Mouth..	HUG-W 68	ELLISON, Harlan
4	Planners, The	NEB-W 68	WILHELM, Kate

SECTION D: AWARD WINNERS ONLY - (By Year)

CAT	TITLE	AW W/N Y	AUTHOR
1	Camp Concentration	DIT-W 69	DISCH, Thomas M
2	Boy and His Dog, A	NEB-W 69	ELLISON, Harlan
2	Nightwings	HUG-W 69	SILVERBERG, Robert
3	Sharing of Flesh, The	HUG-W 69	ANDERSON, Poul
4	Beast t/Shouted Love a/t/Heart o/t/World	HUG-W 69	ELLISON, Harlan
4	Passengers	NEB-W 69	SILVERBERG, Robert
1	Cosmicomics	DIT-W 70	CALVINO, Italo
1	Left Hand of Darkness	HUG-W 70	LEGUIN, Ursula K
1	Left Hand of Darkness	NEB-W 69	LEGUIN, Ursula K
1	Stand on Zanzibar	HUG-W 69	BRUNNER, John
1	Stand on Zanzibar	BSF-W 70	BRUNNER, John
2	Ship of Shadows	HUG-W 70	LEIBER, Fritz
3	Time Considered as a Helix...	NEB-W 69	DELANY, Samuel R
4	Time Considered as a Helix..	HUG-W 70	DELANY, Samuel R
1	Jagged Orbit, The	BSF-W 71	BRUNNER, John
1	Ringworld	NEB-W 70	NIVEN, Larry
1	Ringworld	LOC-W 71	NIVEN, Larry
1	Ringworld	HUG-W 71	NIVEN, Larry
1	Ringworld	DIT-W 72	NIVEN, Larry
1	Time of Changes, A	NEB-W 71	SILVERBERG, Robert
2	Ill Met in Lankhmar	NEB-W 70	LEIBER, Fritz
2	Ill Met in Lankhmar	HUG-W 71	LEIBER, Fritz
2	Missing Man, The	NEB-W 71	MacLEAN, Katherine
4	Good News from the Vatican	NEB-W 71	SILVERBERG, Robert
4	Region Between, The	LOC-W 71	ELLISON, Harlan
3	Slow Sculpture	NEB-W 70	STURGEON, Theodore
4	Slow Sculpture	HUG-W 71	STURGEON, Theodore
6	Science Fiction Hall of Fame Vol 1	LOC-W 71	SILVERBERG, Robert
1	Lathe of Heaven, The	LOC-W 72	LeGUIN, Ursula K
1	Moment of Eclipse, The	BSF-W 72	ALDISS, Brian W
1	To Your Scattered Bodies Go	HUG-W 72	FARMER, Philip Jose
2	Meeting with Medusa, A	NEB-W 72	CLARKE, Arthur C
3	Queen of Air and Darkness, The	NEB-W 71	ANDERSON, Poul
2	Queen of Air and Darkness, The	HUG-W 72	ANDERSON, Poul
4	Queen of Air and Darkness, The	LOC-W 72	ANDERSON, Poul
4	Inconstant Moon	HUG-W 72	NIVEN, Larry
4	When it Changed	NEB-W 72	RUSS, Joanna
13	Universe 1	LOC-W 72	CARR, Terry
14	World's Best Science Fiction: 1971	LOC-W 72	WOLDHEIM, Donald A

SECTION D: AWARD WINNERS ONLY - (By Year)

CAT	TITLE	AW W/N Y	AUTHOR
1	Beyond Apollo	JWC-W 73	MALZBERG, Barry N
1	Gods Themselves, The	NEB-W 72	ASIMOV, Isaac
1	Gods Themselves, The	LOC-W 73	ASIMOV, Isaac
1	Gods Themselves, The	DIT-W 73	ASIMOV, Isaac
1	Gods Themselves, The	HUG-W 73	ASIMOV, Isaac
1	Knight of the Swords, The	BFA-W 73	MOORCOCK, Michael
2	Gold at the Starbow's End, The	LOC-W 73	POHL, Frederik
2	Word for World is Forest, The	HUG-W 73	LeGUIN, Ursula
3	Goat Song	NEB-W 72	ANDERSON, Poul
3	Goat Song	HUG-W 73	ANDERSON, Poul
3	Of Mist, and Grass, and Sand	NEB-W 73	McINTYRE, Vonda
4	Basilisk	LOC-W 73	ELLISON, Harlan
4	Eurema's Dam	HUG-W 73	LAFFERTY, R A
4	Love is the Plan, the Plan is Death	NEB-W 73	TIPTREE, James Jr
4	Meeting, The	HUG-W 73	POHL and KORNBLUTH
13	Again, Dangerous Visions	LOC-W 73	ELLISON, Harlan
14	Best Science Fiction of the Year: 1972	LOC-W 73	CARR, Terry
1	King of the Swords, The	BFA-W 74	MOORCOCK, Michael
1	Malevil	JWC-W 74	MERLE, Robert
1	Rendezvous with Rama	HUG-W 74	CLARKE, Arthur C
1	Rendezvous with Rama	JUP-W 74	CLARKE, Arthur C
1	Rendezvous with Rama	NEB-W 73	CLARKE, Arthur C
1	Rendezvous with Rama	LOC-W 74	CLARKE, Arthur C
1	Rendezvous with Rama	BSF-W 74	CLARKE, Arthur C
1	Rendezvous with Rama	JWC-W 74	CLARKE, Arthur C
2	Death of Doctor Island, The	LOC-W 74	WOLFE, Gene
2	Death of Doctor Island, The	NEB-W 73	WOLFE, Gene
2	Feast of St. Dionysus, The	JUP-W 74	SILVERBERG, Robert
2	Girl Who was Plugged In, The	HUG-W 74	TIPTREE, James Jr
3	Deathbird, The	JUP-W 74	ELLISON, Harlan
3	Deathbird, The	HUG-W 74	ELLISON, Harlan
4	Deathbird, The	LOC-W 74	ELLISON, Harlan
3	If the Stars are Gods	NEB-W 74	BENFORD and EKLUND
4	Ones Who Walk Away from Omelas	HUG-W 74	LeGUIN, Ursula
4	Supplicant in Space, A	JUP-W 74	SHECKLEY, Robert
7	Billion Year Spree	BSF-W 74	ALDISS, Brian W
7	Cosmic Connection, The	JWC-W 74	SAGAN, Carl
13	Astounding	LOC-W 74	HARRISON, Harry
14	Best Science Fiction of the Year # 2	LOC-W 74	CARR, Terry

SECTION D: AWARD WINNERS ONLY - (By Year)

CAT	TITLE	AW W/N Y	AUTHOR
1	Dispossessed, The	JUP-W 75	LeGUIN, Ursula K
1	Dispossessed, The	LOC-W 75	LeGUIN, Ursula K
1	Dispossessed, The	NEB-W 74	LeGUIN, Ursula K
1	Dispossessed, The	HUG-W 75	LeGUIN, Ursula K
1	Flow My Tears, The Policeman Said	JWC-W 75	DICK, Philip K
1	Forgotten Beast of Eld	WFA-W 75	McKILLIP, Patricia
1	Hrolf Kraki's Saga	BFA-W 75	ANDERSON, Poul
1	Orbitsville	BSF-W 75	SHAW, Bob
1	Protector	DIT-W 75	NIVEN, Larry
2	Born with the Dead	LOC-W 75	SILVERBERG, Robert
2	Born with the Dead	NEB-W 74	SILVERBERG, Robert
2	Pages From A Young Girl's Diary	WFA-W 75	AICKMAN, Robert
2	Riding the Torch	JUP-W 75	SPINRAD, Norman
2	Song For Lya, A	HUG-W 75	MARTIN, George R R
3	Adrift, Just off t/Islets of Langerhans	HUG-W 75	ELLISON, Harlan
3	Adrift, Just off t/Islets of Langerhans	LOC-W 75	ELLISON, Harlan
3	San Diego Lightfoot Sue	NEB-W 75	REAMY, Tom
3	Seventeen Virgins	JUP-W 75	VANCE, Jack
4	Day Before the Revolution, The	JUP-W 75	LeGUIN, Ursula K
4	Day Before the Revolution, The	NEB-W 74	LeGUIN, Ursula K
4	Day Before the Revolution, The	LOC-W 75	LeGUIN, Ursula K
4	Hole Man, The	HUG-W 75	NIVEN, Larry
4	Sticks	BFA-W 75	WAGNER, Karl Edward
5	Worse Things Waiting	WFA-W 75	WELLMAN, Manly Wade
13	Universe 4	LOC-W 75	CARR, Terry
14	Before the Golden Age	LOC-W 75	ASIMOV, Isaac
1	Bid Time Return	WFA-W 76	MATHESON, Richard
1	Forever War, The	LOC-W 76	HALDEMAN, Joe
1	Forever War, The	NEB-W 75	HALDEMAN, Joe
1	Forever War, The	HUG-W 76	HALDEMAN, Joe
1	Forever War, The	DIT-W 76	HALDEMAN, Joe
1	Hollow Lands, The	BFA-W 76	MOORCOCK, Michael
1	Man Plus	NEB-W 76	POHL, Frederik
2	Belsen Express	WFA-W 76	LEIBER, Fritz
2	Home is the Hangman	HUG-W 76	ZELAZNY, Roger
2	Home is the Hangman	NEB-W 75	ZELAZNY, Roger
2	Storms of Windhaven, The	LOC-W 76	MARTIN, George R R
3	Borderland of Sol, The	HUG-W 76	NIVEN, Larry
3	New Atlantis, The	LOC-W 76	LeGUIN, Ursula K

SECTION D: AWARD WINNERS ONLY - (By Year)

CAT	TITLE	AW W/N Y	AUTHOR
4	Catch That Zeppelin	HUG-W 76	LEIBER, Fritz
4	Catch That Zeppelin	NEB-W 75	LEIBER, Fritz
4	Croatoan	LOC-W 76	ELLISON, Harlan
4	Crowd of Shadows, A	NEB-W 76	GRANT, Charles L
5	Enquiries of Dr Eszterhazy	WFA-W 76	DAVIDSON, Avram
5	Epoch	LOC-W 76	ELWOOD, Roger
6	Wind's Twelve Quarters	LOC-W 76	LeGUIN, Ursula K
1	Alteration, The	JWC-W 77	AMIS, Kingsley
1	Brontomek?	BSF-W 77	CONEY, Michael G
1	Doctor Rat	WFA-W 77	KOTZWINKLE, William
1	Dragon and the George, The	BFA-W 77	DICKSON, Gordon R
1	Space Machine, The	DIT-W 77	PRIEST, Christopher
1	Where Late the Sweet Birds Sang	HUG-W 77	WILHELM, Kate
1	Where Late the Sweet Birds Sang	LOC-W 77	WILHELM, Kate
1	Where Late the Sweet Birds Sang	JUP-W 77	WILHELM, Kate
2	By Any Other Name	HUG-W 77	ROBINSON, Spider
2	Houston, Houston. Do You Read?	HUG-W 77	TIPTREE, James Jr
2	Houston, Houston. Do You Read?	NEB-W 76	TIPTREE, James Jr
2	Houston, Houston, Do You Read?	JUP-W 77	TIPTREE, James Jr
2	Samurai and the Willows, The	LOC-W 77	BISHOP, Michael
2	There's A Long, Long Trail A-Winding	WFA-W 77	KIRK, Russell
3	Bicentennial Man, The	LOC-W 77	ASIMOV, Isaac
3	Bicentennial Man, The	HUG-W 77	ASIMOV, Isaac
3	Bicentennial Man, The	NEB-W 76	ASIMOV, Isaac
3	Diary of the Rose, The	JUP-W 77	LeGUIN, Ursula K
3	Screwfly Solution, The	NEB-W 77	SHELDON, Raccoona(Tiptree)
4	I See You	JUP-W 77	KNIGHT, Damon
4	Tricentennial	LOC-W 77	HALDEMAN, Joe
4	Tricentennial	HUG-W 77	HALDEMAN, Joe
4	Two Suns Setting	BFA-W 77	WAGNER, Karl Edward
5	Song for Lya, A	LOC-W 77	MARTIN, George R R
6	Frights	WFA-W 77	McCAULEY, Kirby
7	Pictorial History of Science Fiction, A	BSF-W 77	KYLE, David A
14	Best Science Fiction of the Year # 5	LOC-W 77	CARR, Terry
1	Gateway	JWC-W 78	POHL, Frederik
1	Gateway	NEB-W 77	POHL, Frederik
1	Gateway	LOC-W 78	POHL, Frederik
1	Gateway	HUG-W 78	POHL, Frederik
1	Heritage of Stars	JUP-W 78	SIMAK, Clifford D
1	Jonah Kit, The	BSF-W 78	WATSON, Ian
1	Our Lady of Darkness	WFA-W 78	LEIBER, Fritz
1	Simarillion, The	DIT-W 78	TOLKIEN, J R R
1	Spell for Chameleon, A	BFA-W 78	ANTHONY, Piers

SECTION D: AWARD WINNERS ONLY - (By Year)

CAT	T I T L E	AW W/N Y	A U T H O R
2	In the Hall of the Martian Kings	JUP-W 78	VARLEY, John
2	Stardance	HUG-W 78	ROBINSON, Spider & Jeanne
2	Stardance	LOC-W 78	ROBINSON, Spider & Jeanne
2	Stardance	NEB-W 77	ROBINSON, Spider & Jeanne
3	Eyes of Amber	HUG-W 78	VINGE, Joan
3	Glow of Candles, a Unicorn's Eye, A	NEB-W 78	GRANT, C L
3	Time Storm	JUP-W 78	DICKSON, Gordon R
4	In the Bag	BFA-W 78	CAMPBELL, Ramsey
4	Jeffty is Five	HUG-W 78	ELLISON, Harlan
4	Jeffty is Five	LOC-W 78	ELLISON, Harlan
4	Jeffty is Five	JUP-W 78	ELLISON, Harlan
4	Jeffty is Five	NEB-W 77	ELLISON, Harlan
4	Jeffty is Five	BFA-W 79	ELLISON, Harlan
4	Stone	NEB-W 78	BRYANT, Edward
6	Murgunstrumm and Others	WFA-W 78	CAVE, Hugh B
11	Silmarillion	LOC-W 78	TOLKIEN, J R R
1	Chronicles o/Thomas Covenant t/Unbeleive	BFA-W 79	DONALDSON, Stephen R
1	Dreamsnake	LOC-W 79	McINTYRE, Vonda N
1	Dreamsnake	NEB-W 78	McINTYRE, Vonda N
1	Dreamsnake	HUG-W 79	McINTYRE, Vonda N
1	Gloriana	JWC-W 79	MOORCOCK, Michael
1	Gloriana	WFA-W 79	MOORCOCK, Michael
1	White Dragon, The	DIT-W 79	McCAFFREY, Anne
2	Persistence of Vision, The	HUG-W 79	VARLEY, John
2	Persistence of Vision, The	NEB-W 78	VARLEY, John
2	Persistence of Vision, The	LOC-W 79	VARLEY, John
3	Hunter's Moon	HUG-W 79	ANDERSON, Poul
4	Count the Clock That Tells the Time	LOC-W 79	ELLISON, Harlan
4	Cassandra	HUG-W 79	CHERRYH, C J
4	giANTS	NEB-W 79	BRYANT, Edward
4	Naples	WFA-W 79	DAVIDSON, Avram
6	Best Science Fiction of the Year # 7	LOC-W 79	CARR, Terry
6	Shadows	WFA-W 79	GRANT, Charles L
7	Way the Future Was, The	LOC-W 79	POHL, Frederik
1	Death's Master	BFA-W 80	LEE, Tanith
1	Fountains of Paradise, The	HUG-W 80	CLARKE, Arthur C
1	Fountains of Paradise, The	NEB-W 79	CLARKE, Arthur C
1	Hitchhiker's Guide to the Galaxy, The	DIT-W 80	ADAMS, Douglas
1	On Wings of Song	JWC-W 80	DISCH, Thomas M
1	Titan	LOC-W 80	VARLEY, John
1	Unlimited Dream Company, The	BSF-W 80	BALLARD, J G
1	Watchtower	WFA-W 80	LYNN, Elizabeth A

CAT	TITLE	AW W/N Y	AUTHOR
2	Enemy Mine	LOC-W 80	LONGYEAR, Barry
2	Enemy Mine	HUG-W 80	LONGYEAR, Barry
2	Enemy Mine	NEB-W 79	LONGYEAR, Barry
2	Unicorn Tapestry	NEB-W 80	CHARNAS, Suzy McKee
3	Sandkings	HUG-W 80	MARTIN, George R R
3	Sandkings	NEB-W 79	MARTIN, George R R
3	Sandkings	LOC-W 80	MARTIN, George R R
4	Button Molder, The	BFA-W 80	LEIBER, Fritz
4	Macintosth Willy	WFA-W 80	CAMPBELL, Ramsey
4	Palely Loitering	BSF-W 80	PRIEST, Christopher
4	Way of Cross and Dragon, The	LOC-W 80	MARTIN, George R R
4	Way of Cross and Dragon, The	HUG-W 80	MARTIN, George R R
4	Women Who Loved the Moon	WFA-W 80	LYNN, Elizabeth A
5	Convergent Series	LOC-W 80	NIVEN, Larry
6	Amazons!	WFA-W 80	SALMONSON, Jessica Amanda
6	Universe 9	LOC-W 80	CARR, Terry
7	Science Fiction Encyclopedia, The	LOC-W 80	NICHOLS, Peter
7	Science Fiction Encyclopedia, The	HUG-W 80	NICHOLS, Peter
11	Harpist in the Wind	LOC-W 80	McKILLIP, Patricia
1	Shadow of the Torturer, The	BSF-W 82	WOLFE, Gene
1	Shadow of the Torturer, The	WFA-W 81	WOLFE, Gene
1	Snow Queen, The	HUG-W 81	VINGE, Joan D
1	Snow Queen, The	LOC-W 81	VINGE, Joan D
1	Timescape	JWC-W 81	BENFORD, Gregory
1	Timescape	DIT-W 81	BENFORD, Gregory
1	Timescape	BSF-W 81	BENFORD, Gregory
1	Timescape	NEB-W 80	BENFORD, Gregory
1	To Wake the Dead	BFA-W 81	CAMPBELL, Ramsey
2	Lost Dorsai	HUG-W 81	DICKSON, Gordon R
2	Nightflyers	LOC-W 81	MARTIN, George R R
3	Brave Little Toaster, The	LOC-W 81	DISCH, Thomas M
3	Cloak and the Staff, The	HUG-W 81	DICKSON, Gordon R
3	Quickening, The	NEB-W 81	BISHOP, Michael
4	Bone Flute, The	NEB-W 81	TUTTLE, Lisa
4	Brave Little Toaster, The	BSF-W 81	DISCH, Thomas M
4	Grotto of the Dancing Bear, The	NEB-W 80	SIMAK, Clifford D
4	Grotto of the Dancing Bear, The	HUG-W 81	SIMAK, Clifford D
4	Grotto of the Dancing Bear, The	LOC-W 81	SIMAK, Clifford D
4	Stains	BFA-W 81	AICKMAN, Robert
3	Ugly Chickens, The	NEB-W 80	WALDROP, Howard
4	Ugly Chickens, The	WFA-W 81	WALDROP, Howard
5	Barbie Murders, The	LOC-W 81	VARLEY, John
3	Barbie Murders, The	LOC-W 79	VARLEY, John
6	Dark Forces	WFA-W 81	McCAULEY, Kirby
6	Magazine of Fant & SF: A 30 Yr Retrospec	LOC-W 81	FERNAN, Edward L

SECTION D: AWARD WINNERS ONLY - (By Year)

CAT	T I T L E	AW W/N Y	A U T H O R
7	Cosmos	HUG-W 81	SAGAN, Carl
7	In Joy Still Felt	LOC-W 81	ASIMOV, Isaac
9	Dragon's Eggs	LOC-W 81	FORWARD, Dr. Robert L
11	Lord Valentine's Castle	LOC-W 81	SILVERBERG, Robert
1	Affirmation, The	DIT-W 82	PRIEST, Christopher
1	Cujo	BFA-W 82	KING, Stephen
1	Claw of the Conciliator, The	NEB-W 81	WOLFE, Gene
1	Claw of the Conciliator, The	SFC-W 82	WOLFE, Gene
1	Downbelow Station	HUG-W 82	CHERRYH, C J
1	Judgement of Dragons	AUR-W 82	GOTLIEB, Phyllis
1	Little Big	WFA-W 82	CROWLEY, John
1	Many Colored Land, The	LOC-W 82	MAY, Julian
1	No Enemy But Time	NEB-W 82	BISHOP, Michael
2	Another Orphan	NEB-W 82	KESSEL, John
2	Blue Champagne	LOC-W 82	VARLEY, John
2	Fire When It Comes, The	WFA-W 82	GODWIN, Parke
2	In the Western Tradition	SFC-W 82	EISENSTEIN, Phyllis
2	Saturn Game, The	NEB-W 81	ANDERSON, Poul
2	Saturn Game, The	HUG-W 82	ANDERSON, Poul
3	Guardians	LOC-W 82	MARTIN, George R R
3	Mummer Kiss	SFC-W 82	SWANWICK, Michael
3	Unicorn Variations	HUG-W 82	Zelazny, Roger
4	Dark Country, The	WFA-W 82	ETCHISON, Dennis
4	Dark Country, The	BFA-W 82	ETCHISON, Dennis
4	Do the Dead Sing?	BFA-W 82	KING, Stephen
4	Do the Dead Sing?	WFA-W 82	KING, Stephen
4	Letter From the Clearys, A	NEB-W 82	WILLIS, Connie
4	Mythago Wood	BSF-W 82	HOLDSTOCK, Robert
4	Pusher, The	LOC-W 82	VARLEY, John
4	Pusher, The	HUG-W 82	VARLEY, John
4	Pusher, The	SFC-W 82	VARLEY, John
5	Sandkings	LOC-W 82	MARTIN, George R R
6	Elsewhere	BFA-W 82	WINDLING, Terri
6	Elsewhere	WFA-W 82	WINDLING, Terri
6	Shadows of Sanctuary	LOC-W 82	ASPRIN, Robert
7	Danse Macabre	HUG-W 82	KING, Stephen
7	Danse Macabre	LOC-W 82	KING, Stephen
9	Starship and Haiku	LOC-W 82	SOMTOW, S P
11	Claw of the Conciliator, The	LOC-W 82	WOLFE, Gene

SECTION D: AWARD WINNERS ONLY - (By Year)

CAT	TITLE	AW W/N Y	AUTHOR
1	Courtship Rite	COM-W 83	KINGSBURY, Donald
1	Foundation's Edge	HUG-W 83	ASIMOV, Isaac
1	Foundation's Edge	LOC-W 83	ASIMOV, Isaac
1	Helliconia Spring	JWC-W 83	ALDISS, Brian W
1	Helliconia Spring	BSF-W 83	ALDISS, Brian W
1	Nifft the Lean	WFA-W 83	SHEA, Michael
1	Riddley Walker	JWC-W 82	HOBAN, Russell
1	Riddley Walker	DIT-W 83	HOBAN, Russell
1	Software	DIC-W 83	RUCKER, Rudy
1	Sword of the Lichtor, The	BFA-W 83	WOLFE, Gene
1	Sword of the Lichtor, The	SFC-W 83	WOLFE, Gene
2	Beyond All Measure	WFA-W 83	WAGNER, Karl Edward
2	Confess the Seasons	WFA-W 83	GRANT, Charles L
2	Hardfought	NEB-W 83	BEAR, Greg
2	Souls	HUG-W 83	RUSS, Joanna
2	Souls	SFC-W 83	RUSS, Joanna
2	Souls	LOC-W 83	RUSS, Joanna
3	Djinn, No Chaser	LOC-W 83	ELLISON, harlan
3	Fire Watch	HUG-W 83	WILLIS, Connie
3	Fire Watch	NEB-W 82	WILLIS, Connie
3	Fire Watch	SFC-W 83	WILLIS, Connie
3	Understanding Human Behavior	SFC-W 83	DISCH, Thomas M
4	Gorgon, The	WFA-W 83	LEE, Tanith
4	Breathing Method, The	BFA-W 83	KING, Stephen
4	Kitemaster	BSF-W 83	ROBERTS, Keith
4	Melancholy Elephants	HUG-W 83	ROBINSON, Spider
4	Peacemaker, The	NEB-W 83	DOZOIS, Gardner
4	Petra	SFC-W 83	BEAR, Greg
4	Sur	LOC-W 83	LeGUIN, Ursula K
5	Compass Rose, The	LOC-W 83	LeGUIN, Ursula K
6	Best Science Fiction of the Year #11	LOC-W 83	CARR, Terry
6	Nightmare Seasons	WFA-W 83	GRANT, Charles L
7	Engines of the Night, The	LOC-W 83	MALZBERG, Barry N
7	Isaac Asimov: The Foundations of SF	HUG-W 83	GUNN, James E
9	Courtship Rite	LOC-W 83	KINGSBURY, Donald
11	Sword of the Lichtor, The	LOC-W 83	WOLFE, Gene

SECTION D: AWARD WINNERS ONLY - (By Year)

CAT	TITLE	AW W/N Y	AUTHOR
1	Anubis Gates, The	SFC-W 84	POWERS, Tim
1	Anubis Gates, The	DIC-W 84	POWERS, Tim
1	Citadel of the Autarch, The	JWC-W 84	WOLFE, Gene
1	Dragon Waiting, The	WFA-W 84	FORD, John M
1	Floating Dragons	BFA-W 84	STRAUB, Peter
1	Startide Rising	LOC-W 84	BRIN, David
1	Startide Rising	NEB-W 83	BRIN, David
1	Startide Rising	HUG-W 84	BRIN, David
1	Tik-Tok	BSF-W 84	SLADEK, John
1	War for Eternity, The	COM-W 84	ROWLEY, Christopher
2	Cascade Point	HUG-W 84	ZAHN, Timothy
2	Her Habiline Husband	SFC-W 84	BISHOP, Michael
2	Her Habiline Husband	LOC-W 84	BISHOP, Michael
2	Black Air	WFA-W 84	ROBINSON, Kim Stanley
3	Black Air	SFC-W 84	ROBINSON, Kim Stanley
3	Blood Music	HUG-W 84	BEAR, Greg
3	Blood Music	NEB-W 83	BEAR, Greg
3	Monkey Treatment, The	LOC-W 84	MARTIN, George R R
4	After Images	BSF-W 84	EDWARDS, Malcolm
4	Beyond the Dead Reef	LOC-W 84	TIPTREE, James Jr
4	Elle Est Trois	WFA-W 84	LEE, Tanith
4	Morning Child	NEB-W 84	DOZOIS, Gardner
4	Neither Brute Nor Human	BFA-W 84	WAGNER, Karl Edward
4	Peacemaker, The	SFC-W 84	DOZOIS, Gardner
4	Speech Sounds	HUG-W 84	BUTLER, Octavia
5	Unicorn Variations	LOC-W 84	ZELAZNY, Roger
6	Best Science Fiction of the Year #12	LOC-W 84	CARR, Terry
6	High Spirits	WFA-W 84	DAVIES, Robinson
7	Dream Makers Vol 2	LOC-W 84	PLATT, Charles
7	Encyclopedia of SF and Fantasy #3	HUG-W 84	TUCK, Donald H
9	Tea with the Black Dragon	LOC-W 84	MacAVOY, R A
11	Mists of Avalon, The	LOC-W 84	BRADLEY, Marion Zimmer
1	Bridge of Birds	WFA-W 85	HUGHART, Barry
1	Ceremonies, The	BFA-W 85	KLEIN, T.E.D.
1	Emergence	COM-W 85	PALMER, David R
1	Integral Trees, The	LOC-W 85	NIVEN, Larry
1	Journey to Apriloth	AUR-W 85	KERNAGHAN, Eileen
1	Mythago Wood	BSF-W 85	HOLDSTOCK, Robert
1	Mythago Wood	WFA-W 85	HOLDSTOCK, Robert
1	Neuromancer	DIT-W 85	GIBSON, William
1	Neuromancer	NEB-W 84	GIBSON, William
1	Neuromancer	DIC-W 85	GIBSON, William
1	Neuromancer	HUG-W 85	GIBSON, William
1	Neuromancer	SFC-W 85	GIBSON, William
1	Years of the City, The	JWC-W 85	POHL, Frederik

SECTION D: AWARD WINNERS ONLY - (By Year)

CAT	T I T L E	AW W/N Y	A U T H O R
2	Press Enter	LOC-W 85	VARLEY, John
2	Press Enter	HUG-W 85	VARLEY, John
2	Press Enter	NEB-W 84	VARLEY, John
2	Press Enter	SFC-W 85	VARLEY, John
2	Sailing To Byzantium	NEB-W 85	SILVERBERG, Robert
2	Unconquered Country, The	WFA-W 85	RYMAN, Geoff
3	Bloodchild	HUG-W 85	BUTLER, Octavia E
3	Bloodchild	NEB-W 84	BUTLER, Octavia E
3	Bloodchild	LOC-W 85	BUTLER, Octavia E
3	Bloodchild	SFC-W 85	BUTLER, Octavia E
4	Bones Wizard, The	WFA-W 85	RYAN, Alan
4	Crystal Spheres, The	HUG-W 85	BRIN, David
4	Forbidden, The	BFA-W 85	BARKER, Clive
4	Out of All Them Bright Stars	NEB-W 85	KRESS, Nancy
4	Salvador	SFC-W 85	SHEPARD, Lucius
4	Salvador	LOC-W 85	SHEPARD, Lucius
4	Still Life With Scorpion	WFA-W 85	BAKER, Scott
4	Unconquered Country, The	BSF-W 85	RYMAN, Geoff
5	Ghost Light, The	LOC-W 85	LEIBER, Fritz
6	Clive Barker's Books of Blood, Vols 1-3	WFA-W 85	BARKER, Clive
6	Light Years and Dark	LOC-W 85	BISHOP, Michael
7	Sleepless Nights in the Procrustean Bed:	LOC-W 85	ELLISON, Harlan
7	Wonder's Child: My Life in S Fiction	HUG-W 85	WILLIAMSON, Jack
9	Wild Shore, The	LOC-W 85	ROBINSON, Kim Stanley
11	Job: A Comedy of Justice	LOC-W 85	HEINLEIN, Robert A
1	Compass Rose, The	DIT-W 86	LeGUIN, Ursula K
1	Dinner at Deviant's Place	DIC-W 86	POWERS, Tim
1	Ender's Game	SFC-W 86	CARD, Orson Scott
1	Ender's Game	HUG-W 86	CARD, Orson Scott
1	Ender's Game	NEB-W 85	CARD, Orson Scott
1	Helliconia Winter	BSF-W 86	ALDISS, Brian W
1	Infinity's Web	COM-W 86	FINCH, Sheila
1	Maple Leaf Rag	AUR-W 86	SPENCER, Garth
1	Song of Kali	WFA-W 86	SIMMONS, Dan
1	Postman, The	JWC-W 86	BRIN, David
1	Postman, The	LOC-W 86	BRIN, David
2	24 Views of Mount Fuji by Hokusai	HUG-W 86	ZELAZNY, Roger
2	Nadelman's God	WFA-W 86	KLEIN, T E D
2	Only Neat Thing To Do, The	LOC-W 86	TIPTREE, James Jr
2	Only Neat Thing to Do, The	SFC-W 86	TIPTREE, James Jr
3	Girl Who Fell Into the Sky, The	NEB-W 86	WILHELM, Kate
3	Paladin of the Lost Hour	HUG-W 86	ELLISON, Harlan
3	Paladin of the Lost Hour	LOC-W 86	ELLISON, Harlan
3	Portraits of His Children	NEB-W 85	MARTIN, George R R
3	Portraits of His Children	SFC-W 86	MARTIN, George R R

SECTION D: AWARD WINNERS ONLY - (By Year)

CAT	TITLE	AW W/N Y	AUTHOR
4	Cube Root	BSF-W 86	LANGFORD, Dave
4	Fermi and Frost	HUG-W 86	POHL, Frederik
4	Paper Dragons	WFA-W 86	BLAYLOCK, James P
4	Paper Dragons	SFC-W 86	BLAYLOCK, James P
4	With Virgil Oddum at the East Pole	LOC-W 86	ELLISON, Harlan
4	Yadjine et la Mort	AUR-W 86	SERMINE, Daniel
5	Skeleton Crew	LOC-W 86	KING, Stephen
6	Imaginary Lands	WFA-W 86	McKINLEY, Robin
6	Medea: Harlan's World	LOC-W 86	ELLISON, Harlan
7	Benchmarks: Galaxy Bookshelf	LOC-W 86	BUDRYS, Algis
7	Science Made Stupid	HUG-W 86	WELLER, Tom
9	Contact	LOC-W 86	SAGAN, Carl
11	Trumps of Doom	LOC-W 86	ZELAZNY, Roger
1	Doomsday Effect, The	COM-W 87	WREN, Thomas
1	Door Into Ocean	JWC-W 87	SLONCZEWSKI, Joan
1	Falling Woman, The	NEB-W 87	MURPHY, Pat
1	Handmaid's Tale, The	CLA-W 87	ATWOOD, Margaret
1	Homunculus	DIC-W 87	BLAYLOCK, James P
1	It	BFA-W 87	KING, Stephen
1	Perfume	WFA-W 87	SUSKIND, Patrick
1	Ragged Astronauts, The	BSF-W 87	SHAW, Bob
1	Ragged Astronauts, The	BFA-W 86	SHAW, Bob
1	Speaker for the Dead	SFC-W 87	CARD, Orson Scott
1	Speaker for the Dead	LOC-W 87	CARD, Orson Scott
1	Speaker for the Dead	NEB-W 86	CARD, Orson Scott
1	Speaker for the Dead	HUG-W 87	CARD, Orson Scott
1	Wandering Fire, The	AUR-W 87	KAY, Guy Gavriel
2	Geometer Blind, The	NEB-W 87	ROBINSON, Kim Stanley
2	Gilgamesh in the Outback	HUG-W 87	SILVERBERG, Robert
2	Hatrack River	WFA-W 87	CARD, Orson Scott
2	R & R	NEB-W 86	SHEPARD, Lucius
2	R & R	SFC-W 87	SHEPARD, Lucius
2	R & R	LOC-W 87	SHEPARD, Lucius
2	Spice Pogrom	DAV-W 87	WILLIS, Connie
3	Aymara	SFC-W 87	SHEPARD, Lucius
3	Eifelheim	DAV-W 87	FLYNN, Michael F
3	Permafrost	HUG-W 87	ZELAZNY, Roger
3	Prisoner of Chillon	DAV-W 87	KELLY, James Patrick
3	Thor Meets Captain America	LOC-W 87	BRIN, David

CAT	TITLE	AW W/N Y	AUTHOR
4	Forever Yours, Anna	NEB-W 87	WILHELM, Kate
4	Kaeti and the Hangman	BSF-W 87	ROBERTS, Keith
4	Kaeti and the Hangman	BFA-W 86	ROBERTS, Keith
4	La Carte du Tendre	AUR-W 87	VONARBURG, Elisabeth
4	Olympic Runner, The	BFA-W 87	ETCHISON, Dennis
4	Phreak Encounter	DAV-W 87	ALLEN, Roger MacBride
4	Pretty Boy Crossover	SFC-W 87	CADIGAN, Pat
4	Red Light	WFA-W 87	SCHOW, David J
4	Robot Dreams	DAV-W 87	ASIMOV, Isaac
4	Robot Dreams	LOC-W 87	ASIMOV, Isaac
4	Surviving	JWC-W 87	MOFFETT, Judith
4	Tangents	HUG-W 87	BEAR, Greg
4	Tangents	NEB-W 86	BEAR, Greg
5	Blue Champagne	LOC-W 87	VARLEY, John
6	Tales of the Quintana Roo	WFA-W 87	TIPTREE, James Jr
6	Year's Best Science Fiction, 3rd	LOC-W 87	DOZOIS, Gardner
7	Trillion Year Spree	HUG-W 87	ALDISS, Brian W
7	Trillion Year Spree	LOC-W 87	ALDISS, Brian W
9	Hercules Text, The	LOC-W 87	McDEVITT, Jack
11	Soldier of the Mist	LOC-W 87	WOLFE, Gene
12	Long Stern Case: Speculative Exercise	DAV-W 87	COOK, Rick
1	Falling Free	NEB-W 88	BUJOLD, Lois McMaster
1	Grianne	BSF-W 88	ROBERTS, Keith
1	Hungry Moon, The	BFA-W 88	CAMPBELL, Ramsey
1	Jack the Giant Killer	AUR-W 88	de LINT, Charles
1	Lincoln's Dreams	JWC-W 88	WILLIS, Connie
1	Misery	STO-W 88	KING, Stephen
1	Replay	WFA-W 88	GRIMWOOD, Ken
1	Sea and Summer, The	CLA-W 88	TURNER, George
1	Strange Toys	DIC-W 88	GEARY, Patricia
1	Swan Song	STO-W 88	McCAMMON, Robert R
1	Uplift War, The	HUG-W 88	BRIN, David
1	Uplift War, The	LOC-W 88	BRIN, David
1	Urth of the New Sun, The	SFC-W 88	WOLFE, Gene
2	Buffalo Gals, Won't You Come Out Tonight	WFA-W 88	LeGUIN, Ursula K
2	Eye for Eye	HUG-W 88	CARD, Orson Scott
2	Last of the Winnebagos, The	NEB-W 88	WILLIS, Connie
2	Mother Goddess of the World	DAV-W 88	ROBINSON, Kim Stanley
2	Secret Sharer, The	SFC-W 88	SILVERBERG, Robert
2	Secret Sharer, The	LOC-W 88	SILVERBERG, Robert
3	Boy Who Came Back From the Grave, The	STO-W 88	RODGERS, Alan
3	Buffalo Gals, Won't You Come Out Tonight	HUG-W 88	LeGUIN, Ursula K
3	Evening and the Morning and the Night	SFC-W 88	BUTLER, Octavia E
3	Gift, The	DAV-W 88	FORDE, Pat
3	Ochrodinger's Kitten	NEB-W 88	EFFINGER, George Alec
3	Pear-Shaped Man, The	STO-W 88	MARTIN, George R R
3	Rachel in Love	NEB-W 87	MURPHY, Pat
3	Rachel in Love	LOC-W 88	MURPHY, Pat
3	Rachel in Love	DAV-W 88	MURPHY, Pat

SECTION D: AWARD WINNERS ONLY - (By Year)

CAT	TITLE	AW W/N Y	AUTHOR
4	Angel	LOC-W 88	CADIGAN, Pat
4	Bible Stories For Adults #17 The Deluge	NEB-W 88	MORROW, James
4	Circular Library of Stones	SFC-W 88	EMSHWILLER, Carol
4	Deep End, The	STO-W 88	McCAMMON, Robert R
4	Friend's Best Man	WFA-W 88	CARROLL, Jonathan
4	Leaks	BFA-W 88	TEM, Steve Rasnic
4	Les Crabes des Venus	AUR-W 88	BERGERON, Alain
4	Love Sickness	BSF-W 88	RYMAN, Geoff
4	Love Song of Laura Morrison, The	DAV-W 88	OLTOIN, Jerry
4	Rachel in Love	JWC-W 88	MURPHY, Pat
4	Why I Left Harry's All-Night Hamburgers	HUG-W 88	WATT-EVANS, Lawrence
4	Why I Left Harry's All-Night Hamburgers	DAV-W 88	WATT-EVANS, Lawrence
5	Jaguar Hunter, The	LOC-W 88	SHEPARD, Lucius
5	Jaguar Hunter, The	WFA-W 88	SHEPARD, Lucius
6	Essential Ellison, The	STO-W 88	ELLISON, Harlan
6	Year's Best Science Fiction, 4th	LOC-W 88	DOZOIS, Gardner
7	Mary Shelley	STO-W 88	SPARKS, Muriel
7	Michael Whelan's Works of Wonder	HUG-W 88	WHELAN, Michael
7	Watchmen	LOC-W 88	MOORE, Alan
9	Manse, The	STO-W 88	CANTRELL, Lisa W
9	War for the Oaks	LOC-W 88	BULL, Emma
12	Nanotechnology	DAV-W 88	PETERSON, Chris
1	Cyteen	LOC-W 89	CHERRYH, C J
1	Cyteen	SFC-W 89	CHERRYH, C J
1	Cyteen	HUG-W 89	CHERRYH, C J
1	Healers War, The	NEB-W 89	SCARBOROUGH, Elizabeth
1	Influence, The	BFA-W 89	CAMPBELL, Ramsey
1	Islands in the Net	JWC-W 89	STERLING, Bruce
1	Koko	WFA-W 89	STRAUB, Peter
1	Mona Lisa Overdrive	AUR-W 89	GIBSON, William
11	Seventh Son	LOC-W 88	CARD, Orson Scott
1	Seventh Son	DIT-W 89	CARD, Orson Scott
1	Sheepfarmer's Daughter	COM-W 89	MOON, Elizabeth
1	Silence of the Lambs, The	STO-W 89	HARRIS, Thomas
1	Unquenchable Fire	CLA-W 89	POLLACK, Richard
1	Wetware	DIC-W 89	RUCKER, Rudy
2	Last of the Winnebagos, The	DAV-W 89	WILLIS, Connie
2	Last of the Winnebagos, The	SFC-W 89	WILLIS, Connie
2	Last of the Winnebagos, The	HUG-W 89	WILLIS, Connie
2	Scalehunter's Beautiful Daughter, The	LOC-W 89	SHEPARD, Lucius
2	Skin Trade, The	WFA-W 89	MARTIN, George R R

SECTION D: AWARD WINNERS ONLY - (By Year)

CAT	TITLE	AW W/N Y	AUTHOR
3	At the Rialto	NEB-W 89	WILLIS, Connie
3	Dowser	DAV-W 89	CARD, Orson Scott
3	Function of Dream Sleep, The	LOC-W 89	ELLISON, Harlan
3	Orange Is For Anguish, Blue For Insanity	STO-W 89	MORRELL, David
3	Sanctuary	DAV-W 89	WHITE, James
3	Schrodinger's Kitten	HUG-W 89	EFFINGER, George Alec
3	Schrodinger's Kitten	SFC-W 89	EFFINGER, George Alec
4	Schrodinger's Kitten	JWC-W 89	EFFINGER, George Alec
4	Circus Horse, The	DAV-W 89	BECHTEL, Amy
4	Eidolons	LOC-W 89	ELLISON, Harlan
4	Fruiting Bodies	BFA-W 89	LUMLEY, Brian
4	Kirinyaga	SFC-W 89	RESNICK, Mike
4	Kirinyaga	HUG-W 89	RESNICK, Mike
4	Midwinter's Tale, A	DAV-W 89	SWANWICK, Michael
4	Night They Missed the Horror Show, The	STO-W 89	LANSDALE, Joe
4	Ripples in the Dirac Sea	NEB-W 89	LANDIS, Geoffrey
4	Sleeping in a Box	AUR-W 89	DORSEY, Candas Jane
4	Winter Solstice, Camelot Station	WFA-W 89	FORD, John M
5	Angry Candy	LOC-W 89	ELLISON, Harlan
6	Charles Beaumont: Selected Stories	STO-W 89	BEAUMONT, Charles
6	Full Spectrum	LOC-W 89	ARONICA, Lou
6	Year's Best Fantasy and Horror 1st	WFA-W 89	DATLOW, Ellen
7	First Maitz	LOC-W 89	MAITZ, Don
7	Motion of Light in Water, The: Sex & SF	HUG-W 89	DELANY, Samuel R
9	Desolation Road	LOC-W 89	McDONALD, Ian
9	Suiting, The	STO-W 89	WILDE, Kelley
10	Those Who Hunt the Night	LOC-W 89	HAMBLY, Barbara
11	Red Prophet	LOC-W 89	CARD, Orson Scott
12	An Introduction to Psychohistory	DAV-W 89	FLYNN, Michael F
1	Carrion Comfort	BFA-W 90	SIMMONS, Dan
1	Carrion Comfort	STO-W 90	SIMMONS, Dan
1-	Child Garden, The	JWC-W 90	RYMAN, Geoff
1	Children of the Garden	CLA-W 90	RYMAN, Geoff
1	Fire in the Sun, A	SFC-W 90	EFFINGER, George Alec
1	Hyperion	HUG-W 90	SIMMONS, Dan
1	Hyperion	LOC-W 90	SIMMONS, Dan
1	Lyonesse: Madouc	WFA-W 90	VANCE, Jack
1	Pyramids	BSF-W 90	PRATCHETT, Terry
1	Subturranean Gallery	DIC-W 90	RUSSO, Richard Paul
1	Shining Falcon, The	COM-W 90	SHERMAN, Josepha
1	West of January	AUR-W 90	DUNCAN, Dave

SECTION D: AWARD WINNERS ONLY - (By Year)

CAT	TITLE	AW W/N Y	AUTHOR
2	Great Works of Time	WFA-W 90	CROWLEY, John
2	Father of Stones, The	LOC-W 90	SHEPARD, Lucius
2	Mountains of Mourning, The	HUG-W 90	BUJOLD, Lois McMaster
2	Mountains of Mourning, The	SFC-W 90	BUJOLD, Lois McMaster
2	Mountains of Mourning, The	NEB-W 89	BUJOLD, Lois
2	On t/Far Side of t/Cadillac Desert...	STO-W 90	LANSDALE, Joe R
2	Touch of Lavender, A	DAV-W 90	LINDHOLM, Megan
3	Dogwalker	LOC-W 90	CARD, Orson Scott
3	Enter a Soldier, Later Enter Another	HUG-W 90	SILVERBERG, Robert
3	For I Have Touched the Sky	SFC-W 90	RESNICK, Mike
3	Labyrinth	DAV-W 90	BUJOLD, Lois McMaster
3	Loch Moose Monster, The	DAV-W 90	KAGAN, Janet
4	Boobs	HUG-W 90	CHARNAS, Suzy McKee
4	Dori Bangs	SFC-W 90	STERLING, Bruce
4	Carpe Diem	AUR-W 90	KERNAGHAN, Eileen
4	Eat Me	STO-W 90	McCAMMON, Robert R
4	Edge of the World, The	JWC-W 90	SWANWICK, Michael
4	Happy Dead, The	DAV-W 90	BECHTEL, Amy
4	Illusionist, The	WFA-W 90	MILLHAUSER, Steven
4	In Transition	BSF-W 90	TUTTLE, Lisa
4	Lost Boys	LOC-W 90	CARD, Orson Scott
4	On t/Far Side of t/Cadillac Desert...	BFA-W 90	LANSDALE, Joe R.
4	Windwagon Smith and the Martians	DAV-W 90	WATT-EVANS, Lawrence
4	Year's Best Science Fiction, 6th	LOC-W 90	DOZOIS, Gardner
5	Patterns	LOC-W 90	CADIGAN, Pat
5	Richard Matheson: Collected Stories	WFA-W 90	MATHESON, Richard
6	Richard Matheson: Collected Stories	STO-W 90	MATHESON, Richard
6	Year's Best Fantasy and Horror 2nd	WFA-W 90	DATLOW, Ellen
7	Harlan Ellison's Watching	STO-W 90	ELLISON, Harlan
7	Grumbles From the Grave	LOC-W 90	HEINLEIN, Robert A
7	World Beyond the Hill, The	HUG-W 90	PANSHIN, Alexei and Cory
9	Orbital Decay	LOC-W 90	STEELE, Allan
9	Sunglasses After Dark	STO-W 90	COLLINS, Nancy
10	Carrion Comfort	LOC-W 90	SIMMONS, Dan
11	Prentice Alvin	LOC-W 90	CARD, Orson Scott
12	Ape-Man Within Us, The	DAV-W 90	De CAMP, L Sprague
1	Mine	STO-W 91	McCAMMON, Robert R
1	Only Begotten Daughter	WFA-W 91	MORROW, James
1	Outside the Dog Museum	BFA-W 91	CARROLL, Jonathan
1	Pacific Edge	JWC-W 91	ROBINSON, Kim Stanley
1	Points of Departure	DIC-W 91	MURPHY, Pat
1	Take Back Plenty	CLA-W 91	GREENLAND, Colin
1	Take Back Plenty	BSF-W 91	GREENLAND, Colin
1	Tehanu: The Last Book of Earthsea	NEB-W 91	LeGUIN, Ursula K
1	Thomas the Rhymer	WFA-W 91	KUSHNER, Ellen
1	Tigana	AUR-W 91	KAY, Guy Gavriel
1	Vor Game, The	HUG-W 91	BUJOLD, Lois McMaster

CAT	T I T L E	AW W/N Y	A U T H O R
2	Bones	WFA-W 91	MURPHY, Pat
2	Hemingway Hoax, The	HUG-W 91	HALDEMAN, Joe
2	Mr. Boy	DAV-W 91	KELLY, James Patrick
2	Short, Sharp, Shock, A	LOC-W 91	ROBINSON, Kim Stanley
2	Stephen	STO-W 91	MASSIE, Elizabeth
2	Weatherman	DAV-W 91	BUJOLD, Lois McMaster
2	Year's Best Science Fiction, 7th	LOC-W 91	DOZOIS, Gardner
3	Entropy's Bed at Midnight	LOC-W 91	SIMMONS, Dan
3	Getting the Bugs Out	DAV-W 91	KAGAN, Janet
3	Manamouki, The	HUG-W 91	RESNICK, Mike
4	Bears Discover Fire	HUG-W 91	BISSON, Terry
4	Bears Discover Fire	JWC-W 91	BISSON, Terry
4	Bears Discover Fire	LOC-W 91	BISSON, Terry
4	Bears Discover Fire	DAV-W 91	BISSON, Terry
4	Calling, The	STO-W 91	SILVA, David
4	Dark Land, The	BFA-W 91	SMITH, Michael Marshall
4	Midsummer Night's Dream, A	WFA-W 91	GAIMAN, Neil
4	Muffin Explains Technology to the World	AUR-W 91	GARDNER, James Alan
4	Original Dr. Shade, The	BSF-W 91	NEWMAN, Kim
4	VRM-547	DAV-W 91	THOMPSON, W R
5	Maps in a Mirror	LOC-W 91	CARD, Orson Scott
5	Start of the End of It All...	WFA-W 91	EMSHWILLER, Carol
6	Darklands	BFA-W 91	BOYLE, Nicholson
6	Four Past Midnight	STO-W 91	KING, Stephen
7	Dark Dreamers	STO-W 91	WIATER, Stanley
7	How to Write Science Fiction and Fantasy	HUG-W 91	CARD, Orson Scott
7	SFWA Handbook: The Prof Writer's Guide	LOC-W 91	RUSCH & SMITH
9	In the Country of The Blind	LOC-W 91	FLYNN, Michael
9	Revelation, The	STO-W 91	LITTLE, Bentley
10	Witching Hour, The	LOC-W 91	RICE, Anne
11	Tehanu: The Last Book of Earthsea	LOC-W 91	LeGUIN, Ursula K
12	Sixty Astounding Years	DAV-W 91	FLYNN, Michael F
1	Barrayar	HUG-W 92	BUJOLD, Lois McMaster
1	Barrayar	LOC-W 92	BUJOLD, Lois McMaster
1	Boy's Life	STO-W 92	McCAMMON, Robert R
1	Boy's Life	WFA-W 92	McCAMMON, Robert R
1	Buddy Holly is Alive & Well On Ganymede	JWC-W 92	DENTON, Bradley
1	Fall of Hyperion, The	LOC-W 91	SIMMONS, Dan
1	Fall of Hyperion, The	BSF-W 92	SIMMONS, Dan
1	Golden Fleece	AUR-W 92	SAWYER, Robert J
1	King of the Morning, Queen of Day	DIC-W 92	McDONALD, Ian
1	Midnight Sun	BFA-W 92	CAMPBELL, Ramsey
1	Reefsong	COM-W 92	SEVERANCE, Carol
1	Stations of the Tide	NEB-W 92	SWANWICK, Michael
1	Synners	CLA-W 92	CADIGAN, Pat

SECTION D: AWARD WINNERS ONLY - (By Year)

CAT	TITLE	AW W/N Y	AUTHOR
2	Beautiful Uncut Hair of Graves	STO-W 92	MORRELL, David
2	Beggars in Spain	HUG-W 92	KRESS, Nancy
2	Beggars in Spain	NEB-W 92	KRESS, Nancy
2	Gallery of His Dreams, The	LOC-W 92	RUSCH, Kristine Kathryn
3	All Dracula's Children	LOC-W 92	SIMMONS, Dan
3	Gold	HUG-W 92	ASIMOV, Isaac
3	Guide Dog	NEB-W 92	CONNER, Mike
4	Bad Timing	BSF-W 92	BROWN, Molly
4	Breaking Ball	AUR-W 92	SKEET, Michael
4	Buffalo	JWC-W 92	KESSEL, John
4	Buffalo	LOC-W 92	KESSEL, John
4	Lady Madonna	STO-W 92	HOLDER, Nancy
4	Ma Qui	NEB-W 92	BRENNERT, Alan
4	Man Who Drew Cats, The	BFA-W 92	SMITH, Michael Marshall
4	Niche, A	AUR-W 92	WATTS, Peter
4	Walk in the Sun, A	HUG-W 92	LANDIS, Geoffrey A
5	Night of the Cooters: More Neat Stories	LOC-W 92	WALDROP, Howard
5	Prayers to Broken Stones	STO-W 92	SIMMONS, Dan
6	Best New Horror	WFA-W 91	JONES, Stephen
6	Best New Horror	BFA-W 92	JONES, Stephen
6	Full Spectrum 3	LOC-W 92	ARONICA, Lou
7	Clive Barker's Shadows of Eden	STO-W 92	JONES, Stephen
7	SF: The Early Years	LOC-W 92	BLEILER, Everett F
7	World of Charles Addams, The	HUG-W 92	ADDAMS, Charles
8	Cipher, The	LOC-W 92	KOJA, Kathe
9	Cipher, The	STO-W 92	KOJA, Kathe
9	Prodigal	STO-W 92	TEM, Melanie
10	Summer of Night	LOC-W 92	SIMMONS, Dan
11	Beauty	LOC-W 92	TEPPER, Sherri S

Part E BEST OF THE BEST

Explanatory Notes

A weighting system has been applied to all titles; higher points for winners than nominees and higher points for the more important awards (see table below).

Some titles may have won or been nominated for a number of Awards, thus they will carry the combined "weight" of all their wins and nominations. Finally, the titles with the highest indeces, thus the Best of the Best, are listed by categories: novels, shorter works, collection/anthologies, horror and fantasy.

Science Fiction Awards – Weights

The following Science Fiction Awards have been weighted according to their influence and longevity. The major awards received 5 points for a win and 4 points for a nomination. The remaining awards received lesser weights.

Explanation:

HUG-W = a Hugo
award winner will
receive 5 pts.

HUG-N = a Hugo
nominee will
receive 4 pts.

For a lesser award,
i.e. the Arthur C.
Clarke Award,
winners and
nominees would
receive the
following:

CLA-W = the winner
would receive 2 pts.

CLA-N = a nominee
would receive 1 pt.

Abbreviations				Points	
Winner	Nominee	Award Name	1st Year	Win	Nom
HUG-W	HUG-N	Hugo	1953	5	4
IFA-W	IFA-N	International Fantasy	1951	5	4
NEB-W	NEB-N	Nebula	1962	5	4
BFA-W	BFA-W	British Fantasy	1971	4	3
BSF-W	BSF-W	British Science Fiction	1970	4	3
JWC-W	JWC-N	J W Campbell	1973	4	3
LOC-W	LOC-N	Locus Magazine	1971	4	3
WFA-W	WFA-N	World Fantasy	1975	4	3
AUR-W	AUR-N	Aurora	1980	3	2
COM-W	COM-N	Compton Crook	1983	3	2
DIC-W	DIC-N	Dick, Philip K	1983	3	2
SFC-W	SFC-N	SF Chronicle Magazine	1982	3	2
CLA-W	CLA-N	Arthur C. Clarke	1987	2	1
DAV-W	DAV-N	Davis Publications	1987	2	1
DIT-W	DIT-N	Ditmar	1969	2	1
JUP-W	JUP-N	Jupiter	1974	2	1
STO-W	STO-N	Bram Stoker	1988	2	1

The weighted-points total is calculated by adding together all of the points awarded to the title, that is, for each nomination and win.

Example: If a story won the Hugo award (5 points), was nominated for a Nebula (4 points) and won the Dick Award (3 points) then, the total weighted-points allocated is 12.

A full description of all abbreviations used within these listings can be found on the next page.

SECTION E: "BEST OF BEST" BY GROUP

HEADINGS:

RANK	CAT	T I T L E	YR	A U T H O R	PTS

EXPLANATIONS:

RANK = Ranking (the work recieving the greatest number of points, ranks #1)

CAT = Category (length and type)

1 Novel	2 Novella	3 Novellette
4 Short Story	5 1-Author Collection	6 Collection/Anthology
7 Non-Fiction	8 Series	9 First Novel
10 Horror	11 Fantasy Novel	12 Magazine Article
13 Original Anthology	14 Reprint Anthology	

LENGTH OF WORK (from Locus Reader Awards)	
Novel	40,000 + words
Novella	17,500 - 40,000
Novellette	7,500 - 17,500
Short Story	up to 7,500

AW = Award

AUR	Aurora (Casper)
BFA	British Fantasy
BSF	British Science Fiction
CLA	Arthur C. Clarke
COM	Compton Crook
DAV	Davis Publications
DIC	Dick
DIT	Ditmar
HUG	Hugo
IFA	International Fantasy
JUP	Jupiter
JWC	J W Campbell
LOC	Locus Magazine
NEB	Nebula
SFC	SF Chronicle Magazine
STO	Bram Stoker
WFA	World Fantasy

YR = year award presented

PTS = Total weighted points

The categories are grouped as follows:

1: Novels, Novellas, First Novels	4: Non-Fiction, Mag Articles
2: Novellettes, Short Stories	5: Horror
3: Author Coll, Coll/Anth, Orig/Reprint Anth	6: Fantasy Novel

RANK	CAT	TITLE	YR	AUTHOR	PTS
Group 1:	Novels (1), Novellas (2), First Novels (9)				
1	1	Neuromancer	85	GIBSON, William	28
2	1	Sword of the Lichtor, The	82	WOLFE, Gene	26
3	1	Postman, The	86	BRIN, David	26
4	1	Rendezvous with Rama	74	CLARKE, Arthur C	24
5	1	Ender's Game	86	CARD, Orson Scott	21
6	1	Speaker for the Dead	87	CARD, Orson Scott	21
7	1	Emergence	85	PALMER, David	20
8	1	Claw of the Conciliator, The	82	WOLFE, Gene	20
9	2	Last of the Winnebagos, The	89	WILLIS, Connie	19
10	1	Dispossessed, The	75	LeGUIN, Ursula K	19
11	1	Fall of Hyperion, The	91	SIMMONS, Dan	19
12	2	Scalehunter's Beautiful Daughter, The	89	SHEPARD, Lucius	19
13	1	Timescape	81	BENFORD, Gregory	18
14	1	Little Big	82	CROWLEY, John	18
15	2	Bully!	92	RESNICK, Mike	18
16	1	Gateway	77	POHL, Frederik	18
17	2	Press Enter	84	VARLEY, John	18
18	1	Where Late the Sweet Birds Sang	77	WILHELM, Kate	18
19	1	Helliconia Spring	83	ALDISS, Brian W	18
20	1	Courtship Rite	83	KINGSBURY, Donald	18
21	2	Escape from Kathmandu	87	ROBINSON, Kim Stanley	18
22	1	On Wings of Song	80	DISCH, Thomas M	18
23	1	Stations of the Tide	92	SWANWICK, Michael	18
24	1	Shadow of the Torturer, The	81	WOLFE, Gene	18
25	2	Hemingway Hoax, The	91	HALDEMAN, Joe	18
26	1	Startide Rising	84	BRIN, David	17
27	1	Count Zero	86	GIBSON, William	17
28	1	Tea With the Black Dragon	83	MacAVOY, R R	17
29	2	Song For Lya, A	75	MARTIN, George R R	17
30	2	Souls	82	RUSS, Joanna	17
31	2	Mountains of Mourning, The	90	BUJOLD, Lois McMaster	17
32	1	Citadel of the Autarch, The	83	WOLFE, Gene	17
33	2	Stardance	78	ROBINSON, Spider & Jeanne	17
34	2	R & R	86	SHEPARD, Lucius	17
35	1	Foundation's Edge	83	ASIMOV, Isaac	16
36	1	Ringworld	71	NIVEN, Larry	16
37	1	Forever War, The	76	HALDEMAN, Joe	16
38	2	Only Neat Thing To Do, The	86	TIPTREE, James Jr	16
39	1	Fountains of Paradise, The	80	CLARKE, Arthur C	16
40	2	Beggars in Spain	92	KRESS, Nancy	16
41	1	Bone Dance	92	BULL, Emma	16
42	1	Barrayar	92	BUJOLD, Lois McMaster	16
43	1	Gods Themselves, The	73	ASIMOV, Isaac	16
44	2	Secret Sharer, The	88	SILVERBERG, Robert	16
45	1	Friday	83	HEINLEIN, Robert A	15

SECTION E: "BEST OF BEST" BY GROUP

RANK	CAT	TITLE	YR	AUTHOR	PTS
		Group 1: Novels (1), Novellas (2), First Novels (9)			
46	1	Urth of the New Sun, The	88	WOLFE, Gene	15
47	2	Hardfought	84	BEAR, Greg	15
48	2	Gilgamesh in the Outback	86	SILVERBERG, Robert	15
49	2	Gallery of His Dreams, The	92	RUSCH, Kristine Kathryn	15
50	2	Gold at the Starbow's End, The	73	POHL, Frederik	15
51	1	Hyperion	90	SIMMONS, Dan	15
52	2	Sailing to Byzantium	86	SILVERBERG, Robert	15
53	1	Flow My Tears, The Policeman Said	75	DICK, Philip K	15
54	2	Bones	91	MUURPHY, Pat	15
55	2	Mythago Wood	82	HOLDSTOCK, Robert	15
56	2	Houston, Houston. Do You Read?	77	TIPTREE, James Jr	15
57	1	Integral Trees, The	85	NIVEN, Larry	15
58	1	Unconquered Country, The	88	RYMAN, Geoff	15
59	1	Man Plus	77	POHL, Frederik	15
60	2	In the Western Tradition	82	EISENSTEIN, Phyllis	15
61	1	When Gravity Fails	87	EFFINGER, George Alec	14
62	2	Death of Doctor Island, The	73	WOLFE, Gene	14
63	1	Harpist in the Wind	80	McKILLIP, Patricia	14
64	2	Journals of the Plague Years, The	89	SPINRAD, Norman	14
65	1	Islands in the Net	89	STERLING, Bruce	14
66	2	Jack	92	WILLIS, Connie	14
67	1	Mona Lisa Overdrive	89	GIBSON, William	14
68	2	Persistence of Vision, The	78	VARLEY, John	14
69	1	Blind Voices	79	REAMY, Tom	14
70	1	Only Begotten Daughter	91	MORROW, James	14
71	1	Boat of A Million Years	90	ANDERSON, Poul	14
72	2	Born with the Dead	74	SILVERBERG, Robert	14
73	1	Beyond the Blue Event Horizon	81	POHL, Frederik	14
74	2	Father of Stones, The	90	SHEPARD, Lucius	14
75	1	Blood Music	86	BEAR, Greg	14
76	1	Flowers for Algernon	67	KEYES, Daniel	14
77	1	Dreamsnake	78	McINTYRE, Vonda N	14
78	2	Enemy Mine	80	LONGYEAR, Barry	14
79	1	Helliconia Winter	86	ALDISS, Brian	14
80	1	Anubis Gates, The	84	POWERS, Tim	13
81	1	Stand on Zanzibar	68	BRUNNER, John	13
82	1	Moon is a Harsh Mistress	67	HEINLEIN, Robert A	13
83	1	Ragged Astronauts, The	87	Shaw, Bob	13
84	1	Wild Shore, The	85	ROBINSON, Kim Stanley	13
85	1	Babel-17	66	DELANY, Samuel R	13
86	2	Saturn Game, The	81	ANDERSON, Poul	13
87	1	Uplift War, The	88	BRIN, David	13
88	1	Carrion Comfort	90	SIMMONS, Dan	13
89	1	Cyteen	89	CHERRYH, C J	13
90	2	Home is the Hangman	76	ZELAZNY, Roger	13

SECTION E: "BEST OF BEST" BY GROUP

Group 1: Novels (1), Novellas (2), First Novels (9)					
RANK	CAT	T I T L E	YR	A U T H O R	PTS
91	1	Difference Engine, The	92	GIBSON, William	13
92	2	Horrible Imaginings (Death)	83	LEIBER, Fritz	13
93	1	Snow Queen, The	81	VINGE, Joan D	13
94	1	Titan	80	VARLEY, John	12
95	2	Storms of Windhaven, The	76	MARTIN, George R R	12
96	2	24 Views of Mount Fuji by Hokusai	85	ZELAZNY, Roger	12
97	2	Samurai and the Willows, The	77	BISHOP, Michael	12
98	1	Many-Colored Land, The	82	MAY, Julian	12
99	2	Strangers	75	DOZOIS, Gardner	12
100	2	Her Habiline Husband	83	BISHOP, Michael	12
101	2	Surfacing	89	WILLIAMS, Walter Jon	12
102	1	Red Prophet	89	CARD, Orson Scott	12
103	2	Meeting with Medusa, A	72	CLARKE, Arthur C	12
104	1	Man Who Folded Himself, The	74	GERROLD, David	12
105	2	Another Orphan	83	KESSEL, John	12
106	1	Mote in God's Eye, The	75	NIVEN, Larry	12
107	2	Region Between, The	70	ELLISON, Harlan	12
108	1	Time of Changes, A	72	SILVERBERG, Robert	12
109	2	Blue Champagne	82	VARLEY, John	12
110	1	Handmaid's Tale, The	87	ATWOOD, Margaret	12
111	2	Chains of the Sea	74	DOZOIS, Gardner	12
112	1	Prentice Alvin	89	CARD, Orson Scott	12
113	1	Job: A Comedy of Justice	84	HEINLEIN, Robert A	12
114	1	Lathe of Heaven, The	72	LeGUIN, Ursula K	12
115	2	Word for World is Forest, The	72	LeGUIN, Ursula K	12
116	1	Computer Connection, The	76	BESTER, Alfred	11
117	1	Fire in the Sun, A	90	EFFINGER, George Alec	11
118	1	People of the Wind, The	74	ANDERSON, Poul	11
119	2	Short, Sharp, Shock, A	91	ROBINSON, Kim Stanley	11
120	2	Battle of the Abaco Reefs, The	80	SCHENCK, Hilbert	11
121	2	Fool to Believe	91	CADIGAN, Pat	11
122	1	Vor Game, The	91	BUJOLD, Lois McMaster	11
123	2	Unsound Variations	83	MARTIN, George	11
124	1	Year of the Quiet Sun	70	TUCKER, Wilson	11
125	2	Piper at the Gates of Dawn	77	COWPER, Richard	11
126	1	Tower of Glass, The	70	SILVERBERG, Robert	11
127	2	White Otters of Childhood, The	74	BISHOP, Michael	11
128	1	Book of Skulls, The	73	SILVERBERG, Robert	11
129	2	Fifth Head of Cerberus, The	72	WOLFE, Gene	11
130	1	Soldier of the Mist	87	WOLFE, Gene	11
131	2	Custodians, The	76	COWPER, Richard	11
132	1	Faded Sun, The: Kesrith	79	CHERRYH, C J	11
133	1	Gloriana	79	MOORCOCK, Michael	11
134	1	JEM.	80	POHL, Frederik	11
135	2	Great Works of Time	89	CROWLEY, John	11

SECTION E: "BEST OF BEST" BY GROUP

RANK	CAT	TITLE	YR	AUTHOR	PTS

Group 1: Novels (1), Novellas (2), First Novels (9)

RANK	CAT	TITLE	YR	AUTHOR	PTS
136	1	Dying Inside	73	SILVERBERG, Robert	11
137	2	Seven American Nights	79	WOLFE, Gene	11
138	1	Forge of God, The	87	BEAR, Greg	11
139	2	Tiny Tango	90	MOFFETT, Judith	11
140	1	Stochastic Man, The	75	SILVERBERG, Robert	11
141	2	Aztecs	78	McINTYRE, Vonda N	11
142	1	No Enemy But Time	83	BISHOP, Michael	11
143	2	Nightflyers	81	MARTIN, George R R	11
144	2	Autopsy, The	80	SHEA, Michael	11
145	1	When Harlie Was One	73	GERROLD, David	11
146	1	Shadrach in the Furnace	76	SILVERBERG, Robert	11
147	2	Griffin's Egg	92	SWANWICK, Michael	10
148	1	Earth	91	BRIN, David	10
149	1	Aegypt	88	CROWLEY, John	10
150	2	Trinity	85	KRESS, Nancy	10
151	2	Traveler's Tale, A	85	SHEPARD, Lucius	10
152	1	2010: Odyssey Two	83	CLARKE, Arthur C	10
153	2	Touch of Lavender, A	90	LINDHOLM, Megan	10
154	1	Lyonesse	84	VANCE, Jack	10
155	2	Scapegoat, The	86	CHERRYH, C J	10
156	1	Left Hand of Darkness	70	LEGUIN, Ursula K	10
157	2	Homefaring	84	SILVERBERG, Robert	10
158	2	Blind Geometer, The	88	ROBINSON, Kim Stanley	10
159	2	Green Mars	86	ROBINSON, Kim Stanley	10
160	1	Queen of Angels	91	BEAR, Greg	10
161	2	Dozen Tough Jobs, A	90	WALDROP, Howard	10
162	1	It	87	KING, Stephen	10
163	1	Riddley Walker	82	HOBAN, Russell	10
164	1	Dune	66	HERBERT, Frank	10
165	2	Ill Met in Lankhmar	71	LEIBER, Fritz	10
166	1	Rite of Passage	69	PANSHIN, Alexei	9
167	1	Einstein Intersection	67	DELANY, Samuel R	9
168	2	On t/Far Side of t/Cadillac Desert w/Dea	90	LANSDALE, Joe R	9
169	1	Falling Free	88	BUJOLD, Lois McMaster	9
170	2	Ship of Shadows	70	LEIBER, Fritz	9
171	1	White Dragon, The	79	McCAFFREY, Anne	9
172	2	Boy and His Dog, A	69	ELLISON, Harlan	9
173	2	Riding the Torch	75	SPINRAD, Norman	9
174	2	Mother Goddess of the World	88	ROBINSON, Kim Stanley	9
175	2	Nightwings	69	SILVERBERG, Robert	9
176	2	Dragonrider	68	McCAFFREY, Ann	9
177	2	Missing Man, The	71	MacLEAN, Katherine	9
178	2	Riders of the Purple Wage	68	FARMER, Philip Jose	9
179	2	Mr. Boy	91	KELLY, James Patrick	9
180	1	Protector	75	NIVEN, Larry	9

SECTION E: "BEST OF BEST" BY GROUP

Group 1: Novels (1), Novellas (2), First Novels (9)

RANK	CAT	TITLE	YR	AUTHOR	PTS
181	1	Weaveworld	88	BARKER, Clive	9
182	1	Green Eyes	85	SHEPARD, Lucius	9
183	1	Tigana	91	KAY, Guy Gavriel	9
184	1	Hidden Place, A	87	WILSON, Robert Charles	9
185	2	Weyr Search	68	McCAFFREY, Anne	9
186	1	Millenium	84	VARLEY, John	9
187	2	Weatherman	91	BUJOLD, Lois McMaster	9
188	1	Lord of Light	67	ZELAZNY, Roger	9
189	2	Lost Dorsai	80	DICKSON, Gordon R	9
190	1	Time Storm	78	DICKSON, Gordon R	9
191	2	Spice Pogrom	87	WILLIS, Connie	9
192	1	Demolished Man	53	BESTER, Alfred	9
193	1	High Crusade, The	61	ANDERSON, Poul	8
194	1	Downbelow Station	82	CHERRYH, C J	8
195	1	Inferno	76	NIVEN, Larry	8
196	2	Rogue Dragon	65	DAVIDSON, Avram	8
197	1	Bug Jack Barrow	69	SPINRAD, Norman	8
198	2	Dramatic Mission	70	McCAFFREY, Anne	8
199	1	Up the Line	70	SILVERBERG, Robert	8
200	2	Cascade Point	84	ZAHN, Timothy	8
201	1	Deathworld	60	HARRISON, Harry	8
202	2	Unicorn Tapestry	80	CHARNAS, Suzy McKee	8
203	1	Slaughterhouse-Five	70	VONNEGET, Kurt	8
204	2	To Jorslem	70	SILVERBERG, Robert	8
205	1	Witch World	64	NORTON, Andre	8
206	2	Eye for Eye	88	CARD, Orson Scott	8
207	1	Lord Valentine's Castle	81	SILVERBERG, Robert	8
208	1	Sword of Aldones(10): Darkover	62	BRADLEY, Marion Zimmer	8
209	1	Macroscope	69	ANTHONY, Piers	8
210	1	To Your Scattered Bodies Go	72	FARMER, Philip Jose	8
211	1	Thorns	67	SILVERBERG, Robert	8
212	1	Jagged Orbit, The	69	BRUNNER, John	8
213	2	Hawksbill Station	67	SILVERBERG, Robert	8
214	2	Thing in the Stone, The	70	SIMAK, Clifford D	8
215	1	Time Enough For Love	74	HEINLEIN, Robert A	8
216	2	Assault on a City	75	VANCE, Jack	8
217	1	Nova Express	65	BURROUGHS, William	8
218	2	True Names	82	VINGE, Vernor	8
219	1	Past Master	68	LAFFERTY, R A	8
220	1	Davy	65	PANGBORN, Edgar	8
221	1	Doorways in the Sand	76	ZELAZNY, Roger	8
222	2	Hawk Among The Sparrows	68	McLAUGHLIN, Dean	8
223	2	Death and Designation Among the Asadi	74	BISHOP, Michael	8
224	2	Borderland of Sol, The	76	NIVEN, Larry	8
225	1	Ivory: Legend Past & Future	89	RESNICK, Mike	8

RANK	CAT	TITLE	YR	AUTHOR	PTS
		Group 1: Novels (1), Novellas (2), First Novels (9)			
226	1	Fall of Moondust, A	63	CLARKE, Arthur C	8
227	2	Lines of Power	69	DELANY, Samuel R	8
228	2	Calvin Coolidge Home for Dead Comedians	89	DENTON, Bradley	8
229	1	Chton	67	ANTHONY, Piers	8
230	1	Free, Live Free	86	WOLFE, Gene	7
231	1	Lincoln's Dreams	88	WILLIS, Connie	7
232	1	Schismatrix	87	STERLING, Bruce	7
233	2	Seeking	84	PALMER, David	7
234	1	In the Ocean of the Night	78	BENFORD, Gregory	7
235	2	And Wild For To Hold	92	KRESS, Nancy	7
236	1	Ceremonies, The	85	KLEIN, T.E.D.	7
237	2	Watched, The	79	PRIEST, Christopher	7
238	1	Moreta: Dragonlady of Pern	84	McCAFFREY, Anne	7
239	2	Time-Out	90	WILLIS, Connie	7
240	1	Project Pope	82	SIMAK, Cliffor D	7
241	2	Eyeflash Miracles, The	76	WOLFE, Gene	7
242	1	Void Captain's Tale, The	83	SPINRAD, Norman	7
243	2	Snow Women, The	71	LEIBER, Fritz	7
244	1	Embedding, The	75	WATSON, Ian	7
245	2	Snark in the Night, A	78	BENFORD, Gregory	7
246	1	Road to Corley, The	79	COWPER, Richard	7
247	2	Apartheid,Superstr'gs & Modercai Thubana	90	BISHOP, Michael	7
248	1	Dhalgren	75	DELANY, Samuel R	7
249	9	Valentina: Soul in Sapphire	85	DELANEY, Joseph H	7
250	1	Inverted World, The	75	PRIEST, Christopher	7
251	1	Children of Dune	77	HERBERT, Frank	7
252	1	Orphan, The	80	STALLMAN, Robert	7
253	1	Summer Queen, The	92	VINGE, Joan D	7
254	1	Lyonesse: Madouc	90	VANCE, Jack	7
255	1	Sheep Look Up, The	73	BRUNNER, John	7
256	1	All the Weyrs of Pern	92	McCAFFREY, Anne	7
257	1	Outside the Dog Museum	92	CARROLL, Jonathan	7
258	1	Grass	90	TEPPER, Sheri S	7
259	1	Wizard	81	VARLEY, John	7
260	1	Ringworld Engineers, The	81	NIVEN, Larry	7
261	1	Dying of the Light	78	MARTIN, George R R	7
262	1	Robots of Dawn	84	ASIMOV, Isaac	7
263	1	Thomas the Rhymer	91	KUSHNER, Ellen	7
264	1	Jack of Shadows	72	ZELAZNY, Roger	7
265	2	Dangerous Games	80	RANDALL, Marta	7
266	1	Pride of Chanur, The	83	CHERRYH, C J	7
267	2	Fireship	79	VINGE, Joan D	7
268	1	Koko	89	STRAUB, Peter	7
269	2	With t/Bentfin Boomer Boys on Little Old	72	LUPOFF, Richard A	7
270	1	Tik-Tok	84	SLADEK, John	7

SECTION E: "BEST OF BEST" BY GROUP

RANK	CAT	TITLE	YR	AUTHOR	PTS
Group 1: Novels (1), Novellas (2), First Novels (9)					
271	2	Songhouse	80	CARD, Orson Scott	7
272	1	Godwhale, The	75	BASS, T J	7
273	1	Xenocide	92	CARD, Orson Scott	7
274	1	Unlimited Dream Company, The	80	BALLARD, J G	7
275	1	Dragon and the George, The	77	DICKSON, Gordon R	7
276	1	Good News From Outer Space	89	KESSEL, John	7
277	1	Mindbridge	77	HALDEMAN, Joe	7
278	1	Radix	81	ATTANASIO, A A	7
279	1	And Chaos Died	71	RUSS, Joanna	7
280	1	Choice of Gods, A	73	SIMAK, Clifford D	7
281	2	Mars Masked	80	POHL, Frederik	7
282	1	Dragonquest	72	McCAFFREY, Anne	7
283	2	Devil's Arithmetic, The	88	YOLEN, Jane	7
284	1	Dinner at Deviant's Place	86	POWERS, Tim	7
285	1	Quiet Pools, The	91	KUBE-McDOWELL, Michael	7
286	1	Midsummer Tempest, A	75	ANDERSON, Poul	7
287	1	Fourth Mansions	71	LAFFERTY, R A	7
288	1	Redshift Rendezvous	91	STITH, John E	7
289	2	Hero	73	HALDEMAN, Joe	7
290	1	Footfall	86	NIVEN, Larry	7
291	1	White Jenna	91	YOLEN, Jane	7
292	2	ARM	76	NIVEN, Larry	7
293	2	Breathing Method, The	83	KING, Stephen	7
294	1	This is the Way the World Ends	86	MORROW, James	7
295	1	Life During Wartime	88	SHEPARD, Lucius	6
296	1	Good Omens	91	PRATCHETT, Terry	6
297	1	Remaking of Sigmund Freud, The	86	MALZBERG, Barry	6
298	1	Simarillion, The	78	TOLKIEN, J R R	6
299	1	Little Country, The	92	DeLINT, Charles	6
300	9	War for the Oaks	88	BULL, Emma	6
301	1	Stress of Her Regard, The	90	POWERS, Tim	6
302	1	King of the Morning, Queen of Day	92	McDONALD, Ian	6
303	1	Helliconia Summer	84	ALDISS, Brian	6
304	2	Eifelheim	87	FLYNN, Michael	6
305	1	Golden Fleece	92	SAWYER, Robert J	6
306	2	Ballad of the Flexible Bullet, The	85	KING, Stephen	6
307	1	Frontera	85	SHINER, Lewis	6
308	1	Engine Summer	80	CROWLEY, John	6
309	1	Wounded Land, The	81	DONALDSON, Stephen R	6
310	1	Synners	92	CADIGAN, Pat	6
311	1	Talisman, The	85	STRAUB, Peter	6
312	9	Sheepfarmer's Daughter	89	MOON, Elizabeth	6
313	1	Gold Coast, The	89	ROBINSON, Kim Stanley	6
314	2	In the Hall of the Martian Kings	78	VARLEY, John	6
315	1	Hercules Text, The	87	McDEVITT, Jack	6

SECTION E: "BEST OF BEST" BY GROUP

RANK	CAT	TITLE	YR	AUTHOR	PTS
		Group 1: Novels (1), Novellas (2), First Novels (9)			
316	1	Take Back Plenty	91	GREENLAND, Colin	6
317	1	Armageddon Rag, The	84	MARTIN, George R R	6
318	1	Kiteworld	86	ROBERTS, Keith	6
319	1	Fevre Dream	83	MARTIN, George R R	6
320	2	Shades	88	SHEPARD, Lucius	6
321	1	War Hounds and the World's Pain, The	82	MOORCOCK, Michael	6
322	1	Last Coin, The	89	BLAYLOCK, James P	6
323	1	Boy's Life	92	McCAMMON, Robert R	6

SECTION E: "BEST OF BEST" BY GROUP

RANK	CAT	T I T L E	YR	A U T H O R	PTS
		Group 2: Novellettes (3), Short Stories (4)			
1	4	Bears Discover Fire	91	BISSON, Terry	25
2	4	Jeffty is Five	78	ELLISON, Harlan	23
3	3	Rachel in Love	88	MURPHY, Pat	22
4	3	Man Who Painted the Dragon Griaule, The	85	SHEPARD, Lucius	20
5	3	Black Air	84	ROBINSON, Kim Stanley	19
6	3	Portraits of His Children	86	MARTIN, George R R	19
7	4	Tangents	87	BEAR, Greg	19
8	3	Buffalo Gals, Won't You Come Out Tonight	87	LeGUIN, Ursula K	19
9	3	Bloodchild	85	BUTLER, Octavia E	18
10	3	Hatrack River	86	CARD, Orson Scott	18
11	4	Angel	88	CADIGAN, Pat	18
12	3	Jaguar Hunter, The	86	SHEPARD, Lucius	18
13	4	Dori Bangs	90	STERLING, Bruce	18
14	3	Do Ya, Do Ya, Wanna Dance	89	WALDROP, Howard	17
15	4	Pusher, The	82	VARLEY, John	17
16	3	Bicentennial Man, The	76	ASIMOV, Isaac	17
17	4	Robot Dreams	87	ASIMOV, Isaac	17
18	3	Winter Market, The	86	GIBSON, William	17
19	3	Schrodinger's Kitten	89	EFFINGER, George Alec	16
20	3	Brave Little Toaster, The	81	DISCH, Thomas M	16
21	3	Blood Music	84	BEAR, Greg	16
22	4	Buffalo	92	KESSEL, John	16
23	4	Kirinyaga	89	RESNICK, Mike	16
24	3	Paladin of the Lost Hour	86	ELLISON, Harlan	16
25	4	Peacemaker, The	84	DOZOIS, Gardner	16
26	3	Ugly Chickens, The	80	WALDROP, Howard	16
27	3	Deathbird, The	74	ELLISON, Harlan	15
28	3	At the Rialto	90	WILLIS, Connie	15
29	4	Boobs	90	CHARNAS, Suzy McKee	15
30	4	Lost Boys	90	CARD, Orson Scott	15
31	4	Day Before the Revolution, The	75	LeGUIN, Ursula K	15
32	3	For I Have Touched the Sky	90	RESNICK, Mike	15
33	3	Lucky Strike, The	85	ROBINSON, Kim Stanley	14
34	3	Tower of Babylon	91	CHIANG, Ted	14
35	4	Edge of the World, The	90	SWANWICK, Michael	14
36	4	Grotto of the Dancing Bear, The	81	SIMAK, Clifford D	14
37	3	Dream Baby	88	McALLISTER, Bruce	14
38	4	Salvador	85	SHEPARD, Lucius	14
39	3	Queen of Air and Darkness, The	71	ANDERSON, Poul	14
40	4	Boy Who Plaited Manes, The	87	SPRINGER, Nancy	14
41	4	Why I Left Harry's All-Night Hamburgers	88	WATT-EVANS, Lawrence	14
42	3	Dogfight	86	SWANWICK, Michael	14
43	4	Rat	86	KELLY, James Patrick	14
44	4	Aliens Who Knew, I Mean Everything, The	85	EFFINGER, George Alec	14
45	3	Goat Song	72	ANDERSON, Poul	13

RANK	CAT	TITLE	YR	AUTHOR	PTS
		Group 2: Novellettes (3), Short Stories (4)			
46	4	Tricentennial	77	HALDEMAN, Joe	13
47	3	Diary of the Rose, The	76	LeGUIN, Ursula K	13
48	4	Girl Who Was Plugged In, The	74	TIPTREE, James Jr	13
49	4	Red As Blood	80	LEE, Tanith	13
50	3	Slow Sculpture	70	STURGEON, Theodore	13
51	4	Ripples in the Dirac Sea	89	LANDIS, Geoffrey A	13
52	4	Way of Cross and Dragon, The	79	MARTIN, George R R	13
53	3	Of Mist, and Grass, and Sand	73	McINTYRE, Vonda	13
54	3	Monkey Treatment, The	84	BEAR, Greg	12
55	3	Fire Watch	83	WILLIS, Connie	12
56	3	Eskimo Invasion, The	66	HOWARD, Hayden	12
57	4	giANTS	80	BRYANT, Edward	12
58	3	San Diego Lightfoot Sue	75	REAMY, Tom	12
59	4	Love is the Plan, the Plan is Death	73	TIPTREE, James Jr	12
60	3	Permafrost	87	ZELAZNY, Roger	12
61	4	Stone	79	BRYANT, Edward	12
62	3	Enter a Soldier, Later Enter Another	89	SILVERBERG, Robert	12
63	3	Basilisk	72	ELLISON, Harlan	12
64	3	Barbie Murders, The	79	VARLEY, John	12
65	4	When it Changed	72	RUSS, Joanna	12
66	3	Screwfly Solution, The	77	SHELDON, Raccoona(Tiptree)	12
67	4	Paper Dragons	85	BLAYLOCK, James P	12
68	4	Crowd of Shadows, A	76	GRANT, Charles L	12
69	4	Forever Yours, Anna	88	WILHELM, Kate	12
70	3	Manamouki, The	91	RESNICK, Mike	12
71	3	Options	80	VARLEY, John	11
72	3	Slow Birds	83	WATSON, Ian	11
73	3	Thor Meets Captain America	87	BRIN, David	11
74	4	Pretty Boy Crossover	87	CADIGAN, Pat	11
75	3	Coon Rolled Down and Ruptured...	91	HUGH, Dafydd A B	11
76	4	Doing Lennon	76	BENFORD, Gregory	11
77	3	Thermals of August, The	81	BRYANT, Edward	11
78	4	Palely Loitering	80	PRIEST, Christopher	11
79	3	Mikal's Songbird	79	CARD, Orson Scott	11
80	4	Child of All Ages	76	PLAUGER, P J	11
81	3	Devil You Don't Know	78	ING, Dean	11
82	4	Continued on Next Rock	71	LAFFERTY, R A	11
83	3	Flowers of Edo	88	STERLING, Bruce	11
84	4	In the Queue	71	LAUMER, Keith	11
85	3	Eyes of Amber	78	VINGE, Joan	11
86	3	Fringe, The	85	CARD, Orson Scott	11
87	3	Patron of the Arts	72	ROTSLER, William	11
88	4	Fermi and Frost	86	POHL, Frederik	11
89	3	Shobie's Story, The	91	LeGUIN, Ursula K	11
90	4	Kingdom by the Sea, A	73	DOZOIS, Gardner	11

Group 2: Novellettes (3), Short Stories (4)

RANK	CAT	TITLE	YR	AUTHOR	PTS
91	3	Beatnik Bayou	81	VARLEY, John	11
92	4	Sur	83	LeGUIN, Ursula K	11
93	3	Fire When it Comes, The	81	GODWIN, Parke	11
94	4	Wong's Lost and Found Emporium	83	WU, William F	11
95	3	Evening and the Morning and the Night	88	BUTLER, Octavia E	11
96	4	Petra	83	BEAR, Greg	11
97	4	Snow	86	CROWLEY, John	11
98	4	Air Raid	78	VARLEY, John	11
99	4	Sail the Tide of Mourning	76	LUPOFF, Richard	11
100	4	And I Awoke & Found Me Here t/Cold Hill'	73	TIPTREE, James Jr	11
101	4	Melancholy Elephants	83	ROBINSON, Spider	11
102	3	Fireflood and Other Stories	80	McINTYRE, Vonda N	10
103	3	Burning Chrome	83	GIBSON, William	10
104	3	Time Considered as a Helix...	69	DELANY, Samuel R	10
105	4	Cibola	91	WILLIS, Connie	10
106	3	Braver Thing, A	91	SHEFFIELD, Charles	10
107	4	Shatterday	75	ELLISON, Harlan	10
108	3	Last Castle, The	67	VANCE, Jack	10
109	4	Repent Harlequin...	66	ELLISON, Harlan	10
110	4	Catch That Zeppelin	75	LEIBER, Fritx	10
111	4	Godspeed	91	SHEFFIELD, Charles	10
112	3	Gonna Roll Those Bones	68	LEIBER, Fritz	10
113	3	Mother to the World	69	WILSON, Richard	9
114	4	Cassandra	79	CHERRYH, C J	9
115	3	Call Him Lord	67	DICKSON, Gordon R	9
116	4	Secret Place, The	67	McKENNA, Richard	9
117	3	Adrift, Just off t/Islets of Langerhans	75	ELLISON, Harlan	9
118	4	I See You	77	KNIGHT, Damon	9
119	4	Ones Who Walk Away from Omelas	74	LeGUIN, Ursula K	9
120	4	VRM-547	91	THOMPSON, W R	9
121	4	Passengers	70	SILVERBERG, Robert	9
122	3	Sharing of Flesh, The	69	ANDERSON, Poul	9
123	3	Peaches for Mad Molly	89	GOULD, Stepehn	9
124	3	Function of Dream Sleep, The	89	ELLISON, Harlan	9
125	4	Aye, and Gomorrah	68	DELANY, Samuel R	9
126	3	Quickening, The	81	BISHOP, Michael	9
127	4	Flying Saucer Rock and Roll	86	WALDROP, Howard	8
128	4	Hole Man, The	75	NIVEN, Larry	8
129	4	Dance of the Changer and the Three, The	69	CARR, Terry	8
130	4	With Morning Comes Mistfall	74	MARTIN, George R R	8
131	4	Dark Country, The	82	ETCHISON, Dennis	8
132	4	Ma Qui	92	BRENNERT, Alan	8
133	4	Light of Other Days	66	SHAW, Bob	8
134	4	Dog's Life	92	SOUKUP, Martha	8
135	4	Man In His Time	67	ALDISS, Brian W	8

SECTION E: "BEST OF BEST" BY GROUP

RANK	CAT	TITLE	YR	AUTHOR	PTS
Group 2:		Novellettes (3), Short Stories (4)			
136	3	Mummer Kiss	81	SWANWICK, Michael	8
137	4	Masks	68	KNIGHT, Damon	8
138	3	Swarm	83	STERLING, Bruce	8
139	4	Wings	73	McINTYRE, Vonda N	8
140	3	Over the Long Haul	91	SOUKUP, Martha	8
141	4	Speech Sounds	84	BUTLER, Octavia E	8
142	3	Guardians	82	MARTIN, George R R	8
143	4	Hong's Bluff	85	WU, William F	8
144	3	Understanding Human Behavior	82	DISCH, Thomas M	8
145	4	Unaccompanied Sonata	79	CARD, Orson Scott	8
146	3	Surviving	86	MOFFETT, Judith	8
147	4	Morning Child	84	DOZOIS, Gardner	8
148	3	Gift From the Graylanders, A	85	BISHOP, Michael	8
149	4	Not Long Before the End	69	NIVEN, Larry	8
150	3	Firewatch	83	WILLIS, Connie	8
151	4	Friend's Best Man	88	CARROLL, Jonathan	8
152	3	Total Environment	68	ALDISS, Brian W	8
153	4	Kaeti and the Hangman	86	ROBERTS, Keith	8
154	3	Special Kind of Morning	71	DOZOIS, Gardner	8
155	4	Do the Dead Sing?	82	KING, Stephen	8
156	3	Alchemist, The	67	HARNESS, Charles L	8
157	4	Count the Clock That Tells the Time	79	ELLISON, Harlan	8
158	3	Pretty Maggie Moneyeyes	68	ELLISON, Harlan	8
159	4	Croatoan	76	ELLISON, Harlan	8
160	3	Aymara	86	SHEPARD, Lucius	8
161	4	Deeper Than the Darkness	70	BENFORD, Gregory	8
162	3	Sidon in the Mirror, The	83	WILLIS, Connie	8
163	4	Crystal Spheres, The	85	BRIN, David	8
164	3	Apology to Inky	67	GREEN, Robert M Jr	8
165	4	Geometry of Narrative, The	84	SCHENCK, Hilbert	8
166	3	Ninth Symphony of Ludwig v/Beethoven...	78	SCHOLZ, Carter	8
167	4	Engine at Heartsprings Center, The	75	ZELAZNY, Roger	8
168	3	Ginny Sweethips' Flying Circus	89	BARRETT, Neal Jr	8
169	4	Letter From the Clearys, A	82	WILLIS, Connie	8
170	3	Gold	92	ASIMOV, Isaac	8
171	4	Cassandra's Photographs	87	GOLDSTEIN, Lisa	8
172	3	Dogwalker	90	CARD, Orson Scott	8
173	4	Fort Moxie Branch, The	89	McDEVITT, Jack	8
174	4	Quiet, The	81	FLORANCE-GUTHRIDGE, George	8
175	4	Faithful Companion, The	88	FOWLER, Karen Joy	8
176	3	Hunter's Moon	79	ANDERSON, Poul	8
177	4	Cabin on the Coast, A	84	WOLFE, Gene	7
178	4	Button Molder, The	80	LEIBER, Fritz	7
179	4	Giving Plague, The	89	BRIN, David	7
180	4	Two Suns Setting	77	WAGNER, Karl Edward	7

RANK	CAT	TITLE	YR	AUTHOR	PTS
		Group 2: Novellettes (3), Short Stories (4)			
181	4	Driftglass	67	DELANY, Samuel R	7
182	4	Lieserl	91	FOWLER, Karen Joy	7
183	3	Myths of the Near Future	82	BALLARD, J G	7
184	4	Utility Man, The	91	REED, Rober	7
185	3	Everything but Honor	90	EFFINGER, George Alec	7
186	4	Four-Hour Fugue, The	75	BESTER, Alfred	7
187	3	Blued Moon	85	WILLIS, Connie	7
188	4	Beastchild	71	KOONTZ, Dean	7
189	3	Dr. Pak's Preschool	91	BRIN, David	7
190	4	Window	80	LEMAN, Bob	7
191	3	Black Glass	92	FOWLER, Karen Joy	7
192	4	All the Last Wars at Once	72	EFFINGER, George Alex	7
193	3	Galaxy Called Rome, A	76	MALZBERG, Barry	7
194	4	Spider Rose	83	STERLING, Bruce	7
195	3	That Thou Art Mindful of Him	75	ASIMOV, Isaac	7
196	4	Her Furry Face	83	KENNEDY, Leigh	7
197	3	Blind Shemmy	83	DANN, Jack	7
198	4	Schwartz Between the Galaxies	75	SILBERBERG, Robert	7
199	3	...and Seven Times Never Kill Man	76	MARTIN, George R R	7
200	4	Lordly Ones, The	81	ROBERTS, Keith	7
201	3	Way Station, The	80	KING, Stephen	7
202	4	Our Lady of the Sauropods	81	SILVERBERG, Robert	7
203	3	Sisters	90	BEAR, Greg	7
204	4	War Beneath the Tree	80	WOLFE, Gene	7
205	4	Servant of the People	84	POHL, Frederik	7
206	4	In the Late Cretaceous	92	WILLIS, Connie	7
207	4	Our Neural Chernobyl	89	STERLING, Bruce	7
208	4	Custom Fitting	77	WHITE, James	7
209	4	Gorgon, The	83	LEE, Tanith	7
210	4	Island of Dr. Death, The	70	WOLFE, Gene	7
211	3	Particle Theory	77	BRYANT, Edward	7
212	3	Retrograde Summer	76	VARLEY, John	7
213	3	Schwarzschild Radius	87	WILLIS, Connie	7
214	4	Power and the Passion, The	91	CADIGAN, Pat	7
215	3	Miracle	92	WILLIS, Connie	7
216	4	Ridge Running	85	ROBINSON, Kim Stanley	7
217	3	Rite of Spring, A	77	LEIBER, Fritz	7
218	4	Happy Man, The	92	LETHEM, Jonathan	7
219	3	Gate of Faces	92	ALDRIDGE, Ray	7
220	4	God's Hooks	83	WALDROP, Howard	7
221	4	View From a Height	79	VINGE, Joan D	7
222	4	Boy Who Waterskied Forever, The	83	TIPTREE, James Jr	7
223	4	Press Ann	92	BISSON, Terry	7
224	4	Sticks	75	WAGNER, Karl Edward	7
225	3	Silver Lady and the Fortyish Man, The	89	LINDHOLM, Megan	7

RANK	CAT	TITLE	YR	AUTHOR	PTS
		Group 2: Novellettes (3), Short Stories (4)			
226	4	Bad Medicine	85	DANN, Jack	7
227	3	Phantom of Kansas, The	77	VARLEY, John	7
228	4	Love and Sex Among the Vertebrates	91	MURPHY, Pat	7
229	3	Gotta Sing, Gotta Dance	77	VARLEY, John	7
230	4	Autumn Land, The	72	SIMAK, Clifford D	7
231	4	One Perfect Morning, With Jackals	92	RESNICK, Mike	7
232	4	Dinner in Audoghast	86	STERLING, Bruce	7
233	3	Fin de Cycle	92	WALDROP, Howard	7
234	3	Strata	81	BRYANT, Edward	7
235	4	Lions Are Asleep This Night, The	87	WALDROP, Howard	7
236	4	High Steel	82	HALDEMAN, Jack C	7
237	3	Glacier	89	ROBINSON, Kim Stanley	6
238	4	Within the Walls of Tyre	79	BISHOP, Michael	6
239	3	If the Stars are Gods	74	BENFORD and EKLUND	6
240	4	Web of the Magi, The	81	COWPER, Richard	6
241	4	Time's Rub	86	BENFORD, Gregory	6
242	4	Vinland the Dream	92	ROBINSON, Kim Stanley	6
243	4	Coin of the Realm	82	GRANT, Charles L	6
244	4	Fairy Tale	82	DANN, Jack	6

SECTION E: "BEST OF BEST" BY GROUP

RANK	CAT	T I T L E	YR	A U T H O R	PTS
		Group 3: Author Coll (5), Coll/Anth (6), Orig Anth (13), Reprint Anth (14)			
1	5	Sandkings	82	MARTIN, George R R	18
2	5	New Atlantis, The	76	SILVERBERG, Robert	15
3	5	Unicorn Variations	84	ZELAZNY, Roger	12
4	5	Prayers to Broken Stones	91	SIMMONS, Dan	9
5	5	Angry Candy	89	ELLISON, Harlan	8
6	6	Elsewhere	82	WINDLING, Terri	8
7	6	Universe 1	91	CARR, Terry	7
8	6	Amazons!	80	SALMONSON, Jessica Amanda	7
9	6	Year's Best Fantasy and Horror 2nd	90	DATLOW, Ellen	7
10	6	Skeleton Crew	86	KING, Stephen	7
11	5	Night of the Cooters: More Neat Stories	92	WALDROP, Howard	7
12	6	Year's Best Fantasy and Horror 1st	89	DATLOW, Ellen	7
13	6	Dark Forces	81	McCAULEY, Kirby	7
14	5	Brains of Rats, The	91	BLUMLEIN, Michael	7
15	5	Years of the City, The	85	POHL, Frederik	7
16	6	Imaginary Lands	86	McKINLEY, Robin	7
17	6	Dark Descent, The	88	HARTWELL, David	6
18	6	Whispers 3	82	SCHIFF, Stuart David	6
19	6	Tales From the Nightside	82	GRANT, Charles L	6
20	5	Leiber Chronicles, The	91	LEIBER, Fritz	6
21	6	In the Field of Fire	88	DANN, Jeanne Van Buren	6
22	5	Compass Rose, The	83	LeGUIN, Ursula K	6
23	6	Deathbird Stories	76	ELLISON, Harlan	6
24	6	Razored Saddles	90	LANSDALE,	6
25	5	Knight and the Knave of Swords, The	89	LEIBER, Fritz	6
26	6	Year's Best Fantasy and Horror 4th	92	DATLOW, Ellen	6
27	6	Alien Sex	91	DATLOW, Ellen	6
28	6	Year's Best Fantasy and Horror 4th	91	DATLOW, Ellen	6
29	6	Fantasy Annual 4	82	CARR, Terry	6
30	6	Whisper of Blood, A	92	DATLOW, Ellen	6
31	6	Blood is Not Enough	90	DATLOW, Ellen	6
32	6	Shadows 4	82	GRANT, Charles L	6
33	6	Borderlands	91	MONTELEONE, Thomas	6
34	5	Clive Barker's Books of Blood, Vols 4-6	86	BARKER, Clive	6
35	5	Richard Matheson: Collected Stories	90	MATHESON, Richard	6
36	5	Charles Beaumont: Selected Stories	89	ANKER, Roger	5
37	6	Essential Ellison, The	88	ELLISON, Harlan	5
38	6	Four Past Midnight	91	KING, Stephen	5
39	6	Patterns	90	CADIGAN, Pat	5
40	6	Best New Horror	91	JONES, Stephen	4
41	6	Murgunstrumm and Others	78	CAVE, Hugh B	4
42	6	Yore Skin's Jes' Soft'n' Purty, He Said	90	WILLIAMSOM, Chet	4
43	6	Best New Horror	92	JONES, Stephen	4
44	6	Frights	77	McCAULEY, Kirby	4
45	6	Best Science Fiction of the Year # 7	79	CARR, Terry	4

SECTION E: "BEST OF BEST" BY GROUP

Group 3:	Author Coll (5), Coll/Anth (6), Orig Anth (13), Reprint Anth (14)				
RANK	CAT	T I T L E	YR	A U T H O R	PTS
46	6	Shadows	79	GRANT, Charles L	4
47	6	Shadows of Sanctuary	82	ASPRIN, Robert	4
48	6	Wind's Twelve Quarters	76	LeGUIN, Ursula K	4
49	6	Medea: Harlan's World	86	ELLISON, Harlan	4
50	6	Why Not You and I?	88	WAGNER, Karl Edwards	4
51	13	Astounding	74	HARRISON, Harry	4
52	6	Science Fiction Hall of Fame Vol 1	71	SILVERBERG, Robert	4
53	13	Again, Dangerous Visions	73	ELLISON, Harlan	4
54	6	Clive Barker's Books of Blood, Vols 1-3	85	BARKER, Clive	4
55	13	Universe 4	75	CARR, Terry	4
56	6	Year's Best Science Fiction, 4th	88	DOZOIS, Gardner	4
57	14	Best Science Fiction of the Year # 2	74	CARR, Terry	4
58	6	Full Spectrum	89	ARONICA, Lou	4
59	14	World's Best Science Fiction: 1971	72	WOLDHEIM, Donald A	4
60	6	Young Doctor Esterhazy	84	DAVIDSON, Avram	4
61	14	Before the Golden Age	75	ASIMOV, Isaac	4
62	6	Year's Best Science Fiction, 3rd	87	DOZOIS, Gardner	4
63	14	Best Science Fiction of the Year # 5	77	CARR, Terry	4
64	6	Full Spectrum 3	92	ARONICA, Lou	4
65	14	Best Science Fiction of the Year: 1972	73	CARR, Terry	4
66	6	Blue World and Other Stories	90	McCAMMON, Robert R	4
67	5	Maps in a Mirror	91	CARD, Orson Scott	4
68	6	All About Str'ge Monsters F/Recent Past	88	WALDROP, Howard	4
69	5	Epoch	76	ELWOOD, Roger	4
70	6	Magazine of Fant & SF: A 30 Yr Retrospec	81	FERNAN, Edward L	4
71	5	By Bizarre Hands	90	LANSDALE, Joe R	4
72	6	Best Science Fiction of the Year #12	84	CARR, Terry	4
73	5	Houses Without Doors	91	STRAUB, Peter	4
74	6	High Spirits	84	DAVIES, Robinson	4
75	5	Enquiries of Dr Eszterhazy	76	DAVIDSON, Avram	4
76	6	Light Years and Dark	85	BISHOP, Michael	4
77	5	Worse Things Waiting	75	WELLMAN, Manly Wade	4
78	6	Best Science Fiction of the Year #11	83	CARR, Terry	4
79	5	Convergent Series	80	NIVEN, Larry	4
80	6	Blood Kiss, The	89	ETCHISON, Dennis	4
81	5	Scared Stiff, Tales of Sex & Death	88	CAMPBELL, Ramsey	4
82	6	Nightmare Seasons	83	GRANT, Charles L	4
83	5	Ghost Light, The	85	LEIBER, Fritz	4
84	6	Universe 9	80	CARR, Terry	4
85	6	Tales of the Quintana Roo	87	TIPTREE, James Jr	4
86	6	Darklands	91	BOYLE, Nicholson	4
87	5	Start of the End of It All...	91	EMSHWILLER, Carol	4

RANK	CAT	TITLE	YR	AUTHOR	PTS
		Group 4: Non-Fiction (7), Magazine Articles (12)			
1	7	Encyclopedia of SF and Fantasy #3	84	TUCK, Donald H	11
2	7	Harlan Ellison's Watching	90	ELLISON, Harlan	9
3	7	Science Fiction Encyclopedia, The	80	NICHOLLS, Peter	9
4	7	Clive Barker's Shawows in Eden	92	JONES, Stephen	9
5	7	Danse Macabre	82	KING, Stephen	9
6	7	Trillion Year Spree	87	ALDISS, Brian W	9
7	7	In Joy Still Felt	81	ASIMOV, Isaac	8
8	7	SF: The Early Years	92	BLEILER, Everett F	8
9	7	Grumbles from the Grave	90	HEINLEIN, Robert A	8
10	7	SFWA Handbook: The Prof Writer's Guide	91	RUSCH & SMITH	8
11	7	First Maitz	89	MAITZ, Don	8
12	7	Sleepless Nights in the Procrustean Bed:	85	ELLISON, Harlan	8
13	7	Hollywood Gothic	91	SKAL, David J	8
14	7	Dream Makers Vol 2	84	PLATT, Charles	8
15	7	Benchmarks: Galaxy Bookshelf	86	BUDRYS, Algis	8
16	7	Michael Whelan's Works of Wonder	88	WHELAN, Michael	8
17	7	Science Made Stupid	86	WELLER, Tom	8
18	7	Cosmos	81	SAGAN, Carl	8
19	7	Isaac Asimov: The Foundations of SF	83	GUNN, James	8
20	7	How to Write Science Fiction and Fantasy	91	CARD, Orson Scott	8
21	7	World Beyond the Hill, The	90	PANSHIN, Alexei & Cory	8
22	7	Motion of Light in Water, The: Sex & SF	89	DELANY, Samuel R	8
23	7	Wonder's Child: My Life in S Fiction	85	WILLIAMSON, Jack	8
24	7	World of Charles Addams, The	92	ADDAMS, Charles	8
25	7	Engines of the Night, The	83	MALZBERG, Barry N	8
26	7	John W Campbell Letters Vol 1, The	87	CHAPDELAINE, Perry A Sr.	7
27	7	Fantastic Art of Rowena	84	MORRILL, Rowena	7
28	7	Staying Alive: A Writer's Guide	84	SPINRAD, Norman	7
29	7	Anatomy of Wonder 3rd	88	BARRON, Neil	7
30	7	Anatomy of Wonder 2nd	82	BARRON, Neil	7
31	7	Dream Makers	81	PLATT, Charles	7
32	7	Art of Leo and Diane Dillon, The	82	PREISS, Byron	7
33	7	SF, Fantasy & Horror 1986	88	BROWN, Charles N	7
34	7	Pale Shadow of Science, The	86	ALDISS, Brian W	7
35	7	Science Fiction in the Real World	91	SPINRAD, Norman	7
36	7	Bury My Heart at W.H. Smiths	91	ALDISS, Brian	7
37	7	Language of the Night, The	80	LeGUIN, Ursula K	7
38	7	Fear Itself:T/Horror Fiction of S King	83	UNDERWOOD, Tim	7
39	7	After Man	82	DIXON, Dougal	7
40	7	Dancing at the Edge of the World	90	LeGUIN, Ursula K	7
41	7	Grand Tour, The	82	MILLER, Ron	7
42	7	World of the Dark Crystal, The	83	FROUD, Brian	7
43	7	In Memory Yet Green	80	ASIMOV, Isaac	7
44	7	Industrial Light & Magic: Special Effect	87	SMITH, Thomas G	7
45	7	High Kings, The	84	CHANT, Joy	7

SECTION E: "BEST OF BEST" BY GROUP

Group 4:	Non-Fiction (7), Magazine Articles (12)				
RANK	**CAT**	**T I T L E**	**YR**	**A U T H O R**	**PTS**
46	7	Dune Encyclopedia, The	85	McNELLY, Dr. Willis E	7
47	7	Reader's Guide to Fantasy, A	83	SEARLES, Baird	7
48	7	Faces of Fear: Encount W/t/Creat Mod Hor	86	WINTER, Douglas E	7
49	7	Faces of Science Fiction, The	85	PERRET, Patti	7
50	7	New Encyclopedia of Science Fiction, The	89	GUNN, James	7
51	7	Astounding Days	90	CLARKE, Arthur C	7
52	7	Only Apparently Real: World of P K Dick	87	WILLIAMS, Paul	7
53	7	Science Fiction in Print 1985	87	BROWN, Charlie	7
54	7	Conquest of Space	51	LEY, Willy	5
55	7	Lands Beyond	53	LEY, Willy	5
56	7	Exploration of Space	52	CLARKE, Arthur C	5
57	7	Imagination: Art & Techn of David Cherry	88	CHERRY, David A	4
58	7	Way the Future Was, The	79	POHL, Frederik	4
59	7	Pictorial History of Science Fiction, A	77	KYLE, David A	4
60	7	Anatomy of Wonder 2nd	82	BARRON, Neil	4
61	7	An Edge in My Voice	86	ELLISON, Harlan	4
62	7	Dark Knight Returns, The	87	MILLER, Frank	4
63	7	Warhoon 28 Walter A Willis	81	BERGERON, Richard	4
64	7	Barlowe's Guide to Extraterrestials	80	BARLOWE, Wayne D	4
65	7	In t/Heart Or In t/Head:Essay T/Travel	85	TURNER, George	4
66	7	Rockets,Jets,Guided Missls & Spaceships	52	COGGINS, Jack	4
67	7	Dragons in Amber	52	LEY, Willy	4
68	7	Bakery Men Don't See Cookbook, The	92	GOMOLL, et al	4
69	7	Noreascon Three Souvenir Book	90	THOKAR, Greg	4
70	7	Cosmic Connection, The	74	SAGAN, Carl	4
71	7	Biog Dictionary of SF & Fantasy Artists	89	WEINBERG, Robert	4
72	7	Science-Fantasy Publishers, The	92	CHALKER, Jack	4
73	7	Science Fiction, Fantasy and Horror	89	BROWN, Charles N	4
74	7	Battle of Brasil, The	88	MATHEWS, Jack	4
75	7	DiFate's Catalog of S Fiction Hardware	81	DiFATE, Vincent	4
76	7	Wonderworks	80	DONNING, Whelan	4
77	7	Billion Year Spree	74	ALDISS, Brian W	4
78	7	Watchmen	88	MOORE, Alan	4
79	7	Age of Wonders: Exploring t/World of SF	85	HARTWELL, David	3
80	7	Wizardry and Wild Romance	88	MOORCOCK, Michael	3
81	7	Fantasia: A Jack Vance Bibliography	79	LEVACK,	3
82	7	Index to SF Anthologies and Collections	79	CONTENTO, William	3
83	7	SF, Fantasy & Horror 1990	92	BROWN, Charles N	3
84	7	Atlas of Pern, The	85	FONSTAD, Karen Wynn	3
85	7	SF and Fantasy Authors	81	CURREY, L W	3
86	7	Penguin Encycl of Horror & Supernatural	87	SULLIVAN, Jack	3
87	7	Science Fiction: The 100 Best Novels	86	PRINGLE, David	3
88	7	Giger's Alien	90	GIGER, H R	3
89	7	Novels of Philip K Dick, The	86	ROBINSON, Kim Stanley	3
90	7	Divine Invasions	90	SUTIN, Lawrence	3

RANK	CAT	TITLE	YR	AUTHOR	PTS
		Group 4: Non-Fiction (7), Magazine Articles (12)			
91	7	Culture Made Stupid	88	WELLER, Tom	3
92	7	Reader's Guide to SF, A	80	SEARLES, Baird	3
93	7	Bare Bones:Convers'ns on Terror w/S King	89	UNDERWOOD, Tim	3
94	7	World of SF 1926-76	80	del REY, Lester	3
95	7	SF and Heroic Fantasy Index	79	WELLS, Stuart W III	3
96	7	Jack Vance	81	Underwood, Tim	3
97	7	Strokes: Essays and Reviews 1966-1986	89	CLUTE, John	3
98	7	Bio of an Ogre:Autobiog of Piers Anthony	89	ANTHONY, Piers	3
99	7	Griffin & Sabine	92	BANTOCK, Nick	3
100	7	Pish, Posh, Said Hieronymous Bosch	92	DILLON, Leo	3
101	7	SF, Fantasy & Horror 1988	90	BROWN,	3

SECTION E: "BEST OF BEST" BY GROUP

RANK	CAT	T I T L E	YR	A U T H O R	PTS
\- Group 5: Horror (10)					
1	10	Mary Reilly	91	MARTIN, Valerie	10
2	10	Silence of the Lambs, The	89	HARRIS, Thomas	8
3	10	Summer of Night	92	SIMMONS, Dan	8
4	10	Stand, The: The Complete, Uncut Edition	91	KING, Stephen	6
5	10	M.D., The	92	DISCH, Thomas M	4
6	10	Stinger	89	McCAMMON, Robert E	4
7	10	Witching Hour, The	91	RICE, Anne	4
8	10	Those Who Hunt the Night	89	HAMBLY, Barbara	4
9	10	Faerie Tale	89	FEIST, Raymond E	3
10	10	Moon Dance	91	SOMTOW, S P	3
11	10	Great and Secret Show	90	BARKER, Clive	3
12	10	Imajica	92	BARKER, Clive	3
13	10	Tempter	91	COLLINS, A	3
14	10	In the Blood	92	COLLINS, Nancy	3
15	10	Blood Price	92	HUFF, Tanya	3
16	10	Werewolves of London	91	STABLEFORD, Brian M	3
17	10	Dark Half, The	90	KING, Stephen	3

SECTION E: "BEST OF BEST" BY GROUP

Group 6:	Fantasy Novel (11)				
RANK	CAT	T I T L E	YR	A U T H O R	PTS
1	11	Seventh Son	88	CARD, Orson Scott	13
2	11	Chronicles o/Thomas Covenant t/Unbeleive	78	DONALDSON, Stephen R	10
3	11	Tehanu: The Last Book of Earthsea	91	LeGUIN, Ursula K	9
4	11	Our Lady of Darkness	78	LEIBER, Fritz	7
5	11	Transmigration of Timothy Archer, The	83	DICK, Philip K	7
6	11	Vampire Lestat, The	86	RICE, Anne	6
7	11	Soldier of Arete	90	WOLFE, Gene	6
8	11	On Stranger Tides	88	POWERS, Tim	6
9	11	Mists of Avalon, The	84	BRADLEY, Marion Zimmer	4
10	11	Beauty	92	TEPPER, Sherri S	4
11	11	Trumps of Doom	86	ZELAZNY, Roger	4
12	11	Captive, The	82	STALLMAN, Robert	3
13	11	Gilgamesh, The King	85	SILVERBERG, Robert	3
14	11	Blood of Amber	87	ZELAZNY, Roger	3
15	11	Eye of the World, The	91	JORDON, Robert	3
16	11	White Gold Wielder	84	DONALDSON, Stephen R	3
17	11	Dead Zone, The	80	KING, Stephen	3
18	11	Northern Girl, The	81	LYNN, Elizabeth A	3
19	11	Twisting The Rope	87	MacAVOY, R A	3
20	11	Changeling	81	ZELAZNY, Roger	3
21	11	Paladin, The	89	CHERRYH, C J	3
22	11	Sword of Shannara, The	78	BROOKS, Terry	3
23	11	Damiano's Lute	85	MacAVOY, R A	3
24	11	Castle Roogna	80	ANTHONY, Piers	3
25	11	Dragonsbane	86	HAMBLY, Barbara	3
26	11	Hereafter Gang, The	92	BARRETT, Neal Jr	3
27	11	King's Justice, The	86	KURTZ, Katherine	3
28	11	There Are Doors	89	WOLFE, Gene	3
29	11	Goodbody	87	STURGEON, Theodore	3
30	11	Eight Skilled Gentlemen	92	HUGHART, Barry	3
31	11	King of the Murgos	89	EDDINGS, David	3
32	11	Infinity Concerto, The	85	BEAR, Greg	3
33	11	Raphael	85	MacAVOY, R A	3
34	11	Lyonesse: The Green Pearl	86	VANCE, Jack	3
35	11	Rusalka	90	CHERRYH, C J	3
36	11	One Tree, The	83	DONALDSON, Stephen R	3
37	11	Folk of the Air, The	87	BEAGLE, Peter S	3
38	11	Changing Land, The	82	ZELAZNY, Roger	3
39	11	Book of Kells, The	86	MacAVOY, R A	3
40	11	Sign of Chaos	88	ZELAZNY, Roger	3
41	11	Rainbow Abyss, The	92	HAMBLY, Barbara	3
42	11	Tales of Neveryon	80	DELANY, Samuel R	3
43	11	Unicorn Mountain	89	BISHOP, Michael	3
44	11	Merman's Children, The	80	ANDERSON, Poul	3
45	11	Shining, The	78	KING, Stephen	3

Part F   BEST OF THE BEST

Explanatory Notes

The purpose of this section is to give chronological significance to the Best of the Best selections (from Section E), that is, to list titles earning at least 5 weighted points, on a year-to-year basis. Thus, the reader will note which were the most important books or stories in each year.

SECTION F: "BEST OF BEST" BY YEAR

HEADINGS:

CAT	TITLE	YR	AUTHOR	PTS

EXPLANATIONS:

CAT = Category (length and type)

1 Novel	2 Novella	3 Novellette
4 Short Story	5 1-Author Collection	6 Collection/Anthology
7 Non-Fiction	8 Series	9 First Novel
10 Horror	11 Fantasy Novel	12 Magazine Article
13 Original Anthology	14 Reprint Anthology	

LENGTH OF WORK (from Locus Reader Awards)	
Novel	40,000 + words
Novella	17,500 - 40,000
Novellette	7,500 - 17,500
Short Story	up to 7,500

YR = year award presented

PTS = Total weighted points

CAT	T I T L E	YR	A U T H O R	PTS
7	Conquest of Space	51	LEY, Willy	5
1	Earth Abides	51	STEWART, George R	5
7	Exploration of Space	52	CLARKE, Arthur C	5
1	Fancies and Goodnights	52	COLLIER, John	5
1	Demolished Man	53	BESTER, Alfred	9
1	City	53	SIMAK, Clifford D	5
7	Lands Beyond	53	LEY, Willy	5
1	More Than Human	54	STURGEON, Theodore	5
1	They'd Rather Be Right	55	CLIFTON, Mark	5
4	Allamagoosa	55	RUSSELL, Eric Frank	5
1	Mirror for Observers, A	55	PANGBORN, Edgar	5
3	Darfsteller, The	55	MILLER, Walter M Jr	5
1	Double Star	56	HEINLEIN, Robert A	5
3	Exploration Team	56	LEINSTER, Murray	5
4	Star, The	56	CLARKE, Arthur C	5
1	Lord of the Rings - Trilogy	57	TOLKIEN, J R R	5
1	Big Time, The	58	LEIBER, Fritz	5
4	Or All The Seas With Oysters	58	DAVIDSON, Avram	5
4	Hell-Bound Train, That	59	BLOCH, Robert	5
1	Case of Conscience, A	59	BLISH, James	5
3	Big Front Yard, The	59	SIMAK, Clifford D	5
1	Deathworld	60	HARRISON, Harry	8
1	Starship Troopers	60	HEINLEIN, Robert A	5
1	High Crusade, The	61	ANDERSON, Poul	8
4	Longest Voyage, The	61	ANDERSON, Poul	5
1	Canticle for Leibowitz	61	MILLER, Walter M Jr	5
1	Sword of Aldones(10): Darkover	62	BRADLEY, Marion Zimmer	8
4	Hothouse Series, The	62	ALDISS, Brian W	5
1	Stranger in a Strange Land	62	HEINLEIN, Robert A	5
1	Fall of Moondust, A	63	CLARKE, Arthur C	8
1	Man in the High Castle, The	63	DICK, Philip K	5
4	Dragon Masters, The	63	VANCE, Jack	5
1	Witch World	64	NORTON, Andre	8
4	No Truce with Kings	64	ANDERSON, Poul	5
1	Way Station (Here Gather Stars)	64	SIMAK, Clifford	5
2	Rogue Dragon	65	DAVIDSON, Avram	8
1	Davy	65	PANGBORN, Edgar	8
1	Nova Express	65	BURROUGHS, William	8
2	Saliva Tree	65	ALDISS, Brian W	5
4	Soldier, Ask Not	65	DICKSON, Gordon R	5
2	He Who Shapes	65	ZELAZNY, Roger	5
1	Wanderer, The	65	LEIBER, Fritz	5
3	Doors of His Face...	65	ZELAZNY, Roger	5

SECTION F: "BEST OF BEST" BY YEAR

CAT	TITLE	YR	AUTHOR	PTS
By Year (5 points or better)				
1	Babel-17	66	DELANY, Samuel R	13
3	Eskimo Invasion, The	66	HOWARD, Hayden	12
1	Dune	66	HERBERT, Frank	10
4	Repent Harlequin...	66	ELLISON, Harlan	10
4	Light of Other Days	66	SHAW, Bob	8
8	Foundation	66	ASIMOV, Isaac	5
8	Foundation Trilogy	66	ASIMOV, Isaac	5
1	Flowers for Algernon	67	KEYES, Daniel	14
1	Moon is a Harsh Mistress	67	HEINLEIN, Robert A	13
3	Last Castle, The	67	VANCE, Jack	10
4	Secret Place, The	67	McKENNA, Richard	9
3	Call Him Lord	67	DICKSON, Gordon R	9
1	Einstein Intersection	67	DELANY, Samuel R	9
1	Lord of Light	67	ZELAZNY, Roger	9
4	Man In His Time	67	ALDISS, Brian W	8
3	Alchemist, The	67	HARNESS, Charles L	8
1	Thorns	67	SILVERBERG, Robert	8
1	Chton	67	ANTHONY, Piers	8
3	Apology to Inky	67	GREEN, Robert M Jr	8
2	Hawksbill Station	67	SILVERBERG, Robert	8
4	Driftglass	67	DELANY, Samuel R	7
2	Behold the Man	67	MOORCOCK, Michael	5
4	Neutron Star, The	67	NIVEN, Larry	5
1	Stand on Zanzibar	68	BRUNNER, John	13
3	Gonna Roll Those Bones	68	LEIBER, Fritz	10
2	Dragonrider	68	McCAFFREY, Ann	9
2	Weyr Search	68	McCAFFREY, Anne	9
4	Aye, and Gomorrah	68	DELANY, Samuel R	9
2	Riders of the Purple Wage	68	FARMER, Philip Jose	9
3	Total Environment	68	ALDISS, Brian W	8
4	Masks	68	KNIGHT, Damon	8
2	Hawk Among The Sparrows	68	McLAUGHLIN, Dean	8
3	Pretty Maggie Moneyeyes	68	ELLISON, Harlan	8
1	Past Master	68	LAFFERTY, R A	8
4	I Have no Mouth..	68	ELLISON, Harlan	5
4	Planners, The	68	WILHELM, Kate	5
3	Time Considered as a Helix...	69	DELANY, Samuel R	10
2	Boy and His Dog, A	69	ELLISON, Harlan	9
3	Mother to the World	69	WILSON, Richard	9
3	Sharing of Flesh, The	69	ANDERSON, Poul	9
1	Rite of Passage	69	PANSHIN, Alexei	9
2	Nightwings	69	SILVERBERG, Robert	9
1	Bug Jack Barrow	69	SPINRAD, Norman	8
1	Macroscope	69	ANTHONY, Piers	8
1	Jagged Orbit, The	69	BRUNNER, John	8
2	Lines of Power	69	DELANY, Samuel R	8

SECTION F: "BEST OF BEST" BY YEAR

CAT	TITLE	YR	AUTHOR	PTS
\multicolumn{5}{l}{By Year (5 points or better)}

CAT	TITLE	YR	AUTHOR	PTS
4	Not Long Before the End	69	NIVEN, Larry	8
4	Dance of the Changer and the Three, The	69	CARR, Terry	8
4	Beast t/Shouted Love a/t/Heart o/t/World	69	ELLISON, Harlan	5
3	Slow Sculpture	70	STURGEON, Theodore	13
2	Region Between, The	70	ELLISON, Harlan	12
1	Year of the Quiet Sun	70	TUCKER, Wilson	11
1	Tower of Glass, The	70	SILVERBERG, Robert	11
1	Left Hand of Darkness	70	LEGUIN, Ursula K	10
2	Ship of Shadows	70	LEIBER, Fritz	9
4	Passengers	70	SILVERBERG, Robert	9
2	To Jorslem	70	SILVERBERG, Robert	8
4	Deeper Than the Darkness	70	BENFORD, Gregory	8
1	Up the Line	70	SILVERBERG, Robert	8
2	Thing in the Stone, The	70	SIMAK, Clifford D	8
2	Dramatic Mission	70	McCAFFREY, Anne	8
1	Slaughterhouse-Five	70	VONNEGET, Kurt	8
4	Island of Dr. Death, The	70	WOLFE, Gene	7
1	Ringworld	71	NIVEN, Larry	16
3	Queen of Air and Darkness, The	71	ANDERSON, Poul	14
4	Continued on Next Rock	71	LAFFERTY, R A	11
4	In the Queue	71	LAUMER, Keith	11
2	Ill Met in Lankhmar	71	LEIBER, Fritz	10
2	Missing Man, The	71	MacLEAN, Katherine	9
3	Special Kind of Morning	71	DOZOIS, Gardner	8
4	Beastchild	71	KOONTZ, Dean	7
1	And Chaos Died	71	RUSS, Joanna	7
2	Snow Women, The	71	LEIBER, Fritz	7
1	Fourth Mansions	71	LAFFERTY, R A	7
4	Good News from the Vatican	71	SILVERBERG, Robert	5
3	Goat Song	72	ANDERSON, Poul	13
1	Time of Changes, A	72	SILVERBERG, Robert	12
2	Word for World is Forest, The	72	LeGUIN, Ursula K	12
2	Meeting with Medusa, A	72	CLARKE, Arthur C	12
3	Basilisk	72	ELLISON, Harlan	12
1	Lathe of Heaven, The	72	LeGUIN, Ursula K	12
4	When it Changed	72	RUSS, Joanna	12
3	Patron of the Arts	72	ROTSLER, William	11
2	Fifth Head of Cerberus, The	72	WOLFE, Gene	11
1	To Your Scattered Bodies Go	72	FARMER, Philip Jose	8
4	All the Last Wars at Once	72	EFFINGER, George Alex	7
1	Jack of Shadows	72	ZELAZNY, Roger	7
4	Autumn Land, The	72	SIMAK, Clifford D	7
1	Dragonquest	72	McCAFFREY, Anne	7
2	With t/Bentfin Boomer Boys on Little Old	72	LUPOFF, Richard A	7
4	Inconstant Moon	72	NIVEN, Larry	5

SECTION F: "BEST OF BEST" BY YEAR

CAT	T I T L E	YR	A U T H O R	PTS
	By Year (5 points or better)			
1	Gods Themselves, The	73	ASIMOV, Isaac	16
2	Gold at the Starbow's End, The	73	POHL, Frederik	15
2	Death of Doctor Island, The	73	WOLFE, Gene	14
3	Of Mist, and Grass, and Sand	73	McINTYRE, Vonda N	13
4	Love is the Plan, the Plan is Death	73	TIPTREE, James Jr	12
1	When Harlie Was One	73	GERROLD, David	11
1	Book of Skulls, The	73	SILVERBERG, Robert	11
4	And I Awoke & Found Me Here t/Cold Hill'	73	TIPTREE, James Jr	11
4	Kingdom by the Sea, A	73	DOZOIS, Gardner R	11
1	Dying Inside	73	SILVERBERG, Robert	11
4	Wings	73	McINTYRE, Vonda N	8
1	Sheep Look Up, The	73	BRUNNER, John	7
1	Choice of Gods, A	73	SIMAK, Clifford D	7
2	Hero	73	HALDEMAN, Joe	7
1	Gravity's Rainbow	73	PYCHON, Thomas	5
4	Eurema's Dam	73	LAFFERTY, R A	5
4	Meeting, The	73	POHL and KORNBLUTH	5
1	Rendezvous with Rama	74	CLARKE, Arthur C	24
3	Deathbird, The	74	ELLISON, Harlan	15
2	Born with the Dead	74	SILVERBERG, Robert	14
4	Girl Who Was Plugged In, The	74	TIPTREE, James Jr	13
2	Chains of the Sea	74	DOZOIS, Gardner	12
1	Man Who Folded Himself, The	74	GERROLD, David	12
2	White Otters of Childhood, The	74	BISHOP, Michael	11
1	People of the Wind, The	74	ANDERSON, Poul	11
4	Ones Who Walk Away from Omelas	74	LeGUIN, Ursula K	9
4	With Morning Comes Mistfall	74	MARTIN, George R R	8
2	Death and Designation Among the Asadi	74	BISHOP, Michael	8
1	Time Enough For Love	74	HEINLEIN, Robert A	8
3	If the Stars are Gods	74	BENFORD and EKLUND	6
4	Thing of Beauty, A	74	SPINRAD, Norman	5
2	Feast of St. Dionysus, The	74	SILVERBERG, Robert	5
4	Shark	74	BRYANT, Edward	5
1	Dispossessed, The	75	LeGUIN, Ursula K	19
2	Song For Lya, A	75	MARTIN, George R R	17
4	Day Before the Revolution, The	75	LeGUIN, Ursula K	15
1	Flow My Tears, The Policeman Said	75	DICK, Philip K	15
2	Strangers	75	DOZOIS, Gardner	12
3	San Diego Lightfoot Sue	75	REAMY, Tom	12
1	Mote in God's Eye, The	75	NIVEN, Larry	12
1	Stochastic Man, The	75	SILVERBERG, Robert	11
4	Catch That Zeppelin	75	LEIBER, Fritz	10
4	Shatterday	75	ELLISON, Harlan	10
2	Riding the Torch	75	SPINRAD, Norman	9
3	Adrift, Just off t/Islets of Langerhans	75	ELLISON, Harlan	9
1	Protector	75	NIVEN, Larry	9
2	Assault on a City	75	VANCE, Jack	8
4	Engine at Heartsprings Center, The	75	ZELAZNY, Roger	8

SECTION F: "BEST OF BEST" BY YEAR

CAT	TITLE	YR	AUTHOR	PTS
	By Year (5 points or better)			
4	Hole Man, The	75	NIVEN, Larry	8
1	Midsummer Tempest, A	75	ANDERSON, Poul	7
3	That Thou Art Mindful of Him	75	ASIMOV, Isaac	7
4	Schwartz Between the Galaxies	75	SILBERBERG, Robert	7
1	Godwhale, The	75	BASS, T J	7
4	Sticks	75	WAGNER, Karl Edward	7
1	Inverted World, The	75	PRIEST, Christopher	7
1	Dhalgren	75	DELANY, Samuel R	7
1	Embedding, The	75	WATSON, Ian	7
4	Four-Hour Fugue, The	75	BESTER, Alfred	7
3	Bicentennial Man, The	76	ASIMOV, Isaac	17
1	Forever War, The	76	HALDEMAN, Joe	16
5	New Atlantis, The	76	SILVERBERG, Robert	15
3	Diary of the Rose, The	76	LeGUIN, Ursula K	13
2	Home is the Hangman	76	ZELAZNY, Roger	13
2	Storms of Windhaven, The	76	MARTIN, George R R	12
4	Crowd of Shadows, A	76	GRANT, Charles L	12
2	Custodians, The	76	COWPER, Richard	11
4	Child of All Ages	76	PLAUGER, P J	11
1	Computer Connection, The	76	BESTER, Alfred	11
4	Doing Lennon	76	BENFORD, Gregory	11
4	Sail the Tide of Mourning	76	LUPOFF, Richard	11
1	Shadrach in the Furnace	76	SILVERBERG, Robert	11
4	Croatoan	76	ELLISON, Harlan	8
2	Borderland of Sol, The	76	NIVEN, Larry	8
1	Inferno	76	NIVEN, Larry	8
1	Doorways in the Sand	76	ZELAZNY, Roger	8
2	Eyeflash Miracles, The	76	WOLFE, Gene	7
3	...and Seven Times Never Kill Man	76	MARTIN, George R R	7
3	Galaxy Called Rome, A	76	MALZBERG, Barry	7
3	Retrograde Summer	76	VARLEY, John	7
2	ARM	76	NIVEN, Larry	7
6	Deathbird Stories	76	ELLISON, Harlan	6
1	Where Late the Sweet Birds Sang	77	WILHELM, Kate	18
1	Gateway	77	POHL, Frederik	18
2	Houston, Houston. Do You Read?	77	TIPTREE, James Jr	15
1	Man Plus	77	POHL, Frederik	15
4	Tricentennial	77	HALDEMAN, Joe	13
2	Samurai and the Willows, The	77	BISHOP, Michael	12
3	Screwfly Solution, The	77	SHELDON, Raccoona(Tiptree)	12
2	Piper at the Gates of Dawn	77	COWPER, Richard	11
4	I See You	77	KNIGHT, Damon	9
1	Mindbridge	77	HALDEMAN, Joe	7
3	Rite of Spring, A	77	LEIBER, Fritz	7
4	Two Suns Setting	77	WAGNER, Karl Edward	7
1	Dragon and the George, The	77	DICKSON, Gordon R	7
4	Custom Fitting	77	WHITE, James	7
3	Phantom of Kansas, The	77	VARLEY, John	7

SECTION F: "BEST OF BEST" BY YEAR

CAT	TITLE	YR	AUTHOR	PTS
	By Year (5 points or better)			
1	Children of Dune	77	HERBERT, Frank	7
3	Gotta Sing, Gotta Dance	77	VARLEY, John	7
3	Particle Theory	77	BRYANT, Edward	7
2	By Any Other Name	77	ROBINSON, Spider	5
4	Jeffty is Five	78	ELLISON, Harlan	23
2	Stardance	78	ROBINSON, Spider & Jeanne	17
1	Dreamsnake	78	McINTYRE, Vonda N	14
2	Persistence of Vision, The	78	VARLEY, John	14
4	Air Raid	78	VARLEY, John	11
3	Devil You Don't Know	78	ING, Dean	11
3	Eyes of Amber	78	VINGE, Joan	11
2	Aztecs	78	McINTYRE, Vonda N	11
11	Chronicles o/Thomas Covenant t/Unbeleive	78	DONALDSON, Stephen R	10
1	Time Storm	78	DICKSON, Gordon R	9
3	Ninth Symphony of Ludwig v/Beethoven...	78	SCHOLZ, Carter	8
1	Dying of the Light	78	MARTIN, George R R	7
2	Snark in the Night, A	78	BENFORD, Gregory	7
11	Our Lady of Darkness	78	LEIBER, Fritz	7
1	In the Ocean of the Night	78	BENFORD, Gregory	7
2	In the Hall of the Martian Kings	78	VARLEY, John	6
1	Simarillion, The	78	TOLKIEN, J R R	6
3	Glow of Candles, a Unicorn's Eye, A	78	GRANT, C L	5
1	Blind Voices	79	REAMY, Tom	14
4	Way of Cross and Dragon, The	79	MARTIN, George R R	13
4	Stone	79	BRYANT, Edward	12
3	Barbie Murders, The	79	VARLEY, John	12
3	Mikal's Songbird	79	CARD, Orson Scott	11
1	Gloriana	79	MOORCOCK, Michael	11
2	Seven American Nights	79	WOLFE, Gene	11
1	Faded Sun, The: Kesrith	79	CHERRYH, C J	11
4	Cassandra	79	CHERRYH, C J	9
1	White Dragon, The	79	McCAFFREY, Anne	9
4	Unaccompanied Sonata	79	CARD, Orson Scott	8
3	Hunter's Moon	79	ANDERSON, Poul	8
4	Count the Clock That Tells the Time	79	ELLISON, Harlan	8
4	View From a Height	79	VINGE, Joan D	7
2	Fireship	79	VINGE, Joan D	7
1	Road to Corley, The	79	COWPER, Richard	7
2	Watched, The	79	PRIEST, Christopher	7
4	Within the Walls of Tyre	79	BISHOP, Michael	6
1	On Wings of Song	80	DISCH, Thomas M	18
1	Fountains of Paradise, The	80	CLARKE, Arthur C	16
3	Ugly Chickens, The	80	WALDROP, Howard	16
2	Enemy Mine	80	LONGYEAR, Barry	14
1	Harpist in the Wind	80	McKILLIP, Patricia	14

SECTION F: "BEST OF BEST" BY YEAR

CAT	TITLE	YR	AUTHOR	PTS
	By Year (5 points or better)			
4	Red As Blood	80	LEE, Tanith	13
4	giANTS	80	BRYANT, Edward	12
1	Titan	80	VARLEY, John	12
3	Options	80	VARLEY, John	11
4	Palely Loitering	80	PRIEST, Christopher	11
2	Battle of the Abaco Reefs, The	80	SCHENCK, Hilbert	11
1	JEM	80	POHL, Frederik	11
2	Autopsy, The	80	SHEA, Michael	11
3	Fireflood and Other Stories	80	McINTYRE, Vonda N	10
2	Lost Dorsai	80	DICKSON, Gordon R	9
7	Science Fiction Encyclopedia, The	80	NICHOLLS, Peter	9
2	Unicorn Tapestry	80	CHARNAS, Suzy McKee	8
1	Orphan, The	80	STALLMAN, Robert	7
2	Mars Masked	80	POHL, Frederik	7
3	Way Station, The	80	KING, Stephen	7
7	In Memory Yet Green	80	ASIMOV, Isaac	7
7	Language of the Night, The	80	LeGUIN, Ursula K	7
2	Songhouse	80	CARD, Orson Scott	7
2	Dangerous Games	80	RANDALL, Marta	7
4	Button Molder, The	80	LEIBER, Fritz	7
6	Amazons!	80	SALMONSON, Jessica Amanda	7
1	Unlimited Dream Company, The	80	BALLARD, J G	7
4	Window	80	LEMAN, Bob	7
4	War Beneath the Tree	80	WOLFE, Gene	7
1	Engine Summer	80	CROWLEY, John	6
1	Shadow of the Torturer, The	81	WOLFE, Gene	18
1	Timescape	81	BENFORD, Gregory	18
3	Brave Little Toaster, The	81	DISCH, Thomas M	16
1	Beyond the Blue Event Horizon	81	POHL, Frederik	14
4	Grotto of the Dancing Bear, The	81	SIMAK, Clifford D	14
2	Saturn Game, The	81	ANDERSON, Poul	13
1	Snow Queen, The	81	VINGE, Joan D	13
3	Beatnik Bayou	81	VARLEY, John	11
3	Thermals of August, The	81	BRYANT, Edward	11
2	Nightflyers	81	MARTIN, George R R	11
3	Fire When it Comes, The	81	GODWIN, Parke	11
3	Quickening, The	81	BISHOP, Michael	9
3	Mummer Kiss	81	SWANWICK, Michael	8
7	In Joy Still Felt	81	ASIMOV, Isaac	8
7	Cosmos	81	SAGAN, Carl	8
4	Quiet, The	81	FLORANCE-GUTHRIDGE, George	8
1	Lord Valentine's Castle	81	SILVERBERG, Robert	8
1	Wizard	81	VARLEY, John	7
4	Lordly Ones, The	81	ROBERTS, Keith	7
6	Dark Forces	81	McCAULEY, Kirby	7

SECTION F: "BEST OF BEST" BY YEAR

CAT	T I T L E	YR	A U T H O R	PTS
4	Our Lady of the Sauropods	81	SILVERBERG, Robert	7
1	Radix	81	ATTANASIO, A A	7
7	Dream Makers	81	PLATT, Charles	7
3	Strata	81	BRYANT, Edward	7
1	Ringworld Engineers, The	81	NIVEN, Larry	7
1	Wounded Land, The	81	DONALDSON, Stephen R	6
4	Web of the Magi, The	81	COWPER, Richard	6
4	Bone Flute, The	81	TUTTLE, Lisa	5
3	Cloak and the Staff, The	81	DICKSON, Gordon R	5
1	Sword of the Lichtor, The	82	WOLFE, Gene	26
1	Claw of the Conciliator, The	82	WOLFE, Gene	20
5	Sandkings	82	MARTIN, George R R	18
1	Little Big	82	CROWLEY, John	18
4	Pusher, The	82	VARLEY, John	17
2	Souls	82	RUSS, Joanna	17
2	Mythago Wood	82	HOLDSTOCK, Robert	15
2	In the Western Tradition	82	EISENSTEIN, Phyllis	15
2	Blue Champagne	82	VARLEY, John	12
1	Many-Colored Land, The	82	MAY, Julian	12
1	Riddley Walker	82	HOBAN, Russell	10
7	Danse Macabre	82	KING, Stephen	9
4	Dark Country, The	82	ETCHISON, Dennis	8
4	Letter From the Clearys, A	82	WILLIS, Connie	8
3	Understanding Human Behavior	82	DISCH, Thomas M	8
3	Guardians	82	MARTIN, George R R	8
2	True Names	82	VINGE, Vernor	8
4	Do the Dead Sing?	82	KING, Stephen	8
1	Downbelow Station	82	CHERRYH, C J	8
6	Elsewhere	82	WINDLING, Terri	8
4	High Steel	82	HALDEMAN, Jack C	7
3	Myths of the Near Future	82	BALLARD, J G	7
7	After Man	82	DIXON, Dougal	7
1	Project Pope	82	SIMAK, Cliffor D	7
7	Anatomy of Wonder 2nd	82	BARRON, Neil	7
7	Grand Tour, The	82	MILLER, Ron	7
7	Art of Leo and Diane Dillon, The	82	PREISS, Byron	7
4	Fairy Tale	82	DANN, Jack	6
6	Fantasy Annual 4	82	CARR, Terry	6
6	Tales From the Nightside	82	GRANT, Charles L	6
6	Whispers 3	82	SCHIFF, Stuart David	6
1	War Hounds and the World's Pain, The	82	MOORCOCK, Michael	6
6	Shadows 4	82	GRANT, Charles L	6
4	Coin of the Realm	82	GRANT, Charles L	6
1	Affirmation, The	82	PRIEST, Christopher	5

SECTION F: "BEST OF BEST" BY YEAR

	By Year (5 points or better)			
CAT	T I T L E	YR	A U T H O R	PTS
1	Courtship Rite	83	KINGSBURY, Donald	18
1	Helliconia Spring	83	ALDISS, Brian W	18
1	Tea With the Black Dragon	83	MacAVOY, R R	17
1	Citadel of the Autarch, The	83	WOLFE, Gene	17
1	Foundation's Edge	83	ASIMOV, Isaac	16
1	Friday	83	HEINLEIN, Robert A	15
2	Horrible Imaginings (Death)	83	LEIBER, Fritz	13
3	Fire Watch	83	WILLIS, Connie	12
2	Another Orphan	83	KESSEL, John	12
2	Her Habiline Husband	83	BISHOP, Michael	12
2	Unsound Variations	83	MARTIN, George	11
4	Sur	83	LeGUIN, Ursula K	11
4	Petra	83	BEAR, Greg	11
1	No Enemy But Time	83	BISHOP, Michael	11
4	Wong's Lost and Found Emporium	83	WU, William F	11
4	Melancholy Elephants	83	ROBINSON, Spider	11
3	Slow Birds	83	WATSON, Ian	11
3	Burning Chrome	83	GIBSON, William	10
1	2010: Odyssey Two	83	CLARKE, Arthur C	10
3	Firewatch	83	WILLIS, Connie	8
3	Swarm	83	STERLING, Bruce	8
7	Isaac Asimov: The Foundations of SF	83	GUNN, James	8
7	Engines of the Night, The	83	MALZBERG, Barry N	8
3	Sidon in the Mirror, The	83	WILLIS, Connie	8
4	God's Hooks	83	WALDROP, Howard	7
7	Reader's Guide to Fantasy, A	83	SEARLES, Baird	7
4	Gorgon, The	83	LEE, Tanith	7
7	World of the Dark Crystal, The	83	FROUD, Brian	7
3	Blind Shemmy	83	DANN, Jack	7
2	Breathing Method, The	83	KING, Stephen	7
1	Pride of Chanur, The	83	CHERRYH, C J	7
7	Fear Itself:T/Horror Fiction of S King	83	UNDERWOOD, Tim	7
4	Boy Who Waterskied Forever, The	83	TIPTREE, James Jr	7
4	Her Furry Face	83	KENNEDY, Leigh	7
4	Spider Rose	83	STERLING, Bruce	7
1	Void Captain's Tale, The	83	SPINRAD, Norman	7
11	Transmigration of Timothy Archer, The	83	DICK, Philip K	7
5	Compass Rose, The	83	LeGUIN, Ursula K	6
1	Fevre Dream	83	MARTIN, George R R	6
3	Black Air	84	ROBINSON, Kim Stanley	19
2	Press Enter	84	VARLEY, John	18
1	Startide Rising	84	BRIN, David	17
4	Peacemaker, The	84	DOZOIS, Gardner	16
3	Blood Music	84	BEAR, Greg	16

SECTION F: "BEST OF BEST" BY YEAR

	By Year (5 points or better)			
CAT	T I T L E	YR	A U T H O R	PTS
2	Hardfought	84	BEAR, Greg	15
1	Anubis Gates, The	84	POWERS, Tim	13
3	Monkey Treatment, The	84	BEAR, Greg	12
1	Job: A Comedy of Justice	84	HEINLEIN, Robert A	12
5	Unicorn Variations	84	ZELAZNY, Roger	12
7	Encyclopedia of SF and Fantasy #3	84	TUCK, Donald H	11
1	Lyonesse	84	VANCE, Jack	10
2	Homefaring	84	SILVERBERG, Robert	10
1	Millenium	84	VARLEY, John	9
4	Geometry of Narrative, The	84	SCHENCK, Hilbert	8
4	Morning Child	84	DOZOIS, Gardner	8
7	Dream Makers Vol 2	84	PLATT, Charles	8
2	Cascade Point	84	ZAHN, Timothy	8
4	Speech Sounds	84	BUTLER, Octavia E	8
2	Seeking	84	PALMER, David	7
4	Servant of the People	84	POHL, Frederik	7
4	Cabin on the Coast, A	84	WOLFE, Gene	7
7	Fantastic Art of Rowena	84	MORRILL, Rowena	7
1	Moreta: Dragonlady of Pern	84	McCAFFREY, Anne	7
1	Tik-Tok	84	SLADEK, John	7
1	Robots of Dawn	84	ASIMOV, Isaac	7
7	Staying Alive: A Writer's Guide	84	SPINRAD, Norman	7
7	High Kings, The	84	CHANT, Joy	7
1	Helliconia Summer	84	ALDISS, Brian	6
1	Armageddon Rag, The	84	MARTIN, George R R	6
1	Neuromancer	85	GIBSON, William	28
3	Man Who Painted the Dragon Griaule, The	85	SHEPARD, Lucius	20
1	Emergence	85	PALMER, David	20
3	Bloodchild	85	BUTLER, Octavia E	18
1	Integral Trees, The	85	NIVEN, Larry	15
3	Lucky Strike, The	85	ROBINSON, Kim Stanley	14
4	Aliens Who Knew, I Mean Everything, The	85	EFFINGER, George Alec	14
4	Salvador	85	SHEPARD, Lucius	14
1	Wild Shore, The	85	ROBINSON, Kim Stanley	13
2	24 Views of Mount Fuji by Hokusai	85	ZELAZNY, Roger	12
4	Paper Dragons	85	BLAYLOCK, James P	12
3	Fringe, The	85	CARD, Orson Scott	11
2	Trinity	85	KRESS, Nancy	10
2	Traveler's Tale, A	85	SHEPARD, Lucius	10
1	Green Eyes	85	SHEPARD, Lucius	9
4	Crystal Spheres, The	85	BRIN, David	8
7	Wonder's Child: My Life in S Fiction	85	WILLIAMSON, Jack	8
4	Hong's Bluff	85	WU, William F	8
3	Gift From the Graylanders, A	85	BISHOP, Michael	8
7	Sleepless Nights in the Procrustean Bed:	85	ELLISON, Harlan	8

SECTION F: "BEST OF BEST" BY YEAR

CAT	T I T L E	YR	A U T H O R	PTS
	By Year (5 points or better)			
3	Blued Moon	85	WILLIS, Connie	7
1	Ceremonies, The	85	KLEIN, T.E.D.	7
4	Bad Medicine	85	DANN, Jack	7
7	Dune Encyclopedia, The	85	McNELLY, Dr. Willis E	7
5	Years of the City, The	85	POHL, Frederik	7
4	Ridge Running	85	ROBINSON, Kim Stanley	7
7	Faces of Science Fiction, The	85	PERRET, Patti	7
9	Valentina: Soul in Sapphire	85	DELANEY, Joseph H	7
2	Ballad of the Flexible Bullet, The	85	KING, Stephen	6
1	Talisman, The	85	STRAUB, Peter	6
1	Frontera	85	SHINER, Lewis	6
4	Out of All Them Bright Stars	85	KRESS, Nancy	5
9	Them Bones	85	WALDROP, Howard	5
1	Postman, The	86	BRIN, David	26
1	Ender's Game	86	CARD, Orson Scott	21
3	Portraits of His Children	86	MARTIN, George R R	19
3	Jaguar Hunter, The	86	SHEPARD, Lucius	18
3	Hatrack River	86	CARD, Orson Scott	18
2	R & R	86	SHEPARD, Lucius	17
1	Count Zero	86	GIBSON, William	17
3	Winter Market, The	86	GIBSON, William	17
3	Paladin of the Lost Hour	86	ELLISON, Harlan	16
2	Only Neat Thing To Do, The	86	TIPTREE, James Jr	16
2	Sailing to Byzantium	86	SILVERBERG, Robert	15
2	Gilgamesh in the Outback	86	SILVERBERG, Robert	15
3	Dogfight	86	SWANWICK, Michael	14
4	Rat	86	KELLY, James Patrick	14
1	Helliconia Winter	86	ALDISS, Brian	14
1	Blood Music	86	BEAR, Greg	14
4	Snow	86	CROWLEY, John	11
4	Fermi and Frost	86	POHL, Frederik	11
2	Scapegoat, The	86	CHERRYH, C J	10
2	Green Mars	86	ROBINSON, Kim Stanley	10
3	Aymara	86	SHEPARD, Lucius	8
7	Benchmarks: Galaxy Bookshelf	86	BUDRYS, Algis	8
4	Kaeti and the Hangman	86	ROBERTS, Keith	8
7	Science Made Stupid	86	WELLER, Tom	8
3	Surviving	86	MOFFETT, Judith	8
4	Flying Saucer Rock and Roll	86	WALDROP, Howard	8
4	Dinner in Audoghast	86	STERLING, Bruce	7
1	This is the Way the World Ends	86	MORROW, James	7
7	Faces of Fear: Encount W/t/Creat Mod Hor	86	WINTER, Douglas E	7
7	Pale Shadow of Science, The	86	ALDISS, Brian W	7
6	Imaginary Lands	86	McKINLEY, Robin	7
1	Footfall	86	NIVEN, Larry	7
1	Dinner at Deviant's Place	86	POWERS, Tim	7
1	Free, Live Free	86	WOLFE, Gene	7
6	Skeleton Crew	86	KING, Stephen	7

SECTION F: "BEST OF BEST" BY YEAR

CAT	TITLE	YR	AUTHOR	PTS
By Year (5 points or better)				
1	Remaking of Sigmund Freud, The	86	MALZBERG, Barry	6
1	Kiteworld	86	ROBERTS, Keith	6
4	Time's Rub	86	BENFORD, Gregory	6
5	Clive Barker's Books of Blood, Vols 4-6	86	BARKER, Clive	6
11	Vampire Lestat, The	86	RICE, Anne	6
3	Girl Who Fell Into the Sky, The	86	WILHELM, Kate	5
1	Speaker for the Dead	87	CARD, Orson Scott	21
3	Buffalo Gals, Won't You Come Out Tonight	87	LeGUIN, Ursula K	19
2	Escape from Kathmandu	87	ROBINSON, Kim Stanley	18
4	Robot Dreams	87	ASIMOV, Isaac	17
4	Boy Who Plaited Manes, The	87	SPRINGER, Nancy	14
1	When Gravity Fails	87	EFFINGER, George Alec	14
1	Ragged Astronauts, The	87	Shaw, Bob	13
3	Permafrost	87	ZELAZNY, Roger	12
3	Thor Meets Captain America	87	BRIN, David	11
1	Soldier of the Mist	87	WOLFE, Gene	11
1	Forge of God, The	87	BEAR, Greg	11
4	Pretty Boy Crossover	87	CADIGAN, Pat	11
1	It	87	KING, Stephen	10
1	Hidden Place, A	87	WILSON, Robert Charles	9
7	Trillion Year Spree	87	ALDISS, Brian W	9
2	Spice Pogrom	87	WILLIS, Connie	9
4	Cassandra's Photographs	87	GOLDSTEIN, Lisa	8
3	Schwarzschild Radius	87	WILLIS, Connie	7
7	Industrial Light & Magic: Special Effect	87	SMITH, Thomas G	7
4	Lions Are Asleep This Night, The	87	WALDROP, Howard	7
7	Only Apparently Real: World of P K Dick	87	WILLIAMS, Paul	7
1	Schismatrix	87	STERLING, Bruce	7
7	John W Campbell Letters Vol 1, The	87	CHAPDELAINE, Perry A Sr.	7
7	Science Fiction in Print 1985	87	BROWN, Charlie	7
2	Eifelheim	87	FLYNN, Michael	6
1	Hercules Text, The	87	McDEVITT, Jack	6
9	Shards of Honor	87	BUJOLD, Lois McMaster	5
2	Geometer Blind, The	87	ROBINSON, Kim Stanley	5
1	Falling Woman, The	87	MURPHY, Pat	5
1	Crosstime Engineer, The	87	FRANKOWSKI, Leo	5
3	Rachel in Love	88	MURPHY, Pat	22
4	Angel	88	CADIGAN, Pat	18
2	Secret Sharer, The	88	SILVERBERG, Robert	16
1	Unconquered Country, The	88	RYMAN, Geoff	15
1	Urth of the New Sun, The	88	WOLFE, Gene	15
4	Why I Left Harry's All-Night Hamburgers	88	WATT-EVANS, Lawrence	14
3	Dream Baby	88	McALLISTER, Bruce	14
1	Uplift War, The	88	BRIN, David	13
11	Seventh Son	88	CARD, Orson Scott	13
4	Forever Yours, Anna	88	WILHELM, Kate	12

CAT	T I T L E	YR	A U T H O R	PTS
By Year (5 points or better)				
3	Flowers of Edo	88	STERLING, Bruce	11
3	Evening and the Morning and the Night	88	BUTLER, Octavia E	11
2	Blind Geometer, The	88	ROBINSON, Kim Stanley	10
1	Aegypt	88	CROWLEY, John	10
2	Mother Goddess of the World	88	ROBINSON, Kim Stanley	9
1	Falling Free	88	BUJOLD, Lois McMaster	9
1	Weaveworld	88	BARKER, Clive	9
2	Eye for Eye	88	CARD, Orson Scott	8
7	Michael Whelan's Works of Wonder	88	WHELAN, Michael	8
4	Faithful Companion, The	88	FOWLER, Karen Joy	8
4	Friend's Best Man	88	CARROLL, Jonathan	8
7	Anatomy of Wonder 3rd	88	BARRON, Neil	7
7	SF, Fantasy & Horror 1986	88	BROWN, Charles N	7
2	Devil's Arithmetic, The	88	YOLEN, Jane	7
1	Lincoln's Dreams	88	WILLIS, Connie	7
9	War for the Oaks	88	BULL, Emma	6
1	Life During Wartime	88	SHEPARD, Lucius	6
11	On Stranger Tides	88	POWERS, Tim	6
6	Dark Descent, The	88	HARTWELL, David	6
6	In the Field of Fire	88	DANN, Jeanne Van Buren	6
2	Shades	88	SHEPARD, Lucius	6
3	Gift, The	88	FORDE, Pat	5
1	Grianne	88	ROBERTS, Keith	5
1	Replay	88	GRIMWOOD, Ken	5
3	Ochrodinger's Kitten	88	EFFINGER, George Alec	5
6	Essential Ellison, The	88	ELLISON, Harlan	5
3	Boy Who Came Back From the Grave, The	88	RODGERS, Alan	5
1	Misery	88	KING, Stephen	5
1	Swan Song	88	McCAMMON, Robert R	5
1	Liege-Killer	88	HINZ, Christopher	5
1	In Conquest Born	88	FRIEDMAN, C S	5
4	Bible Stories For Adults #17 The Deluge	88	MORROW, James	5
3	Pear-Shaped Man, The	88	MARTIN, George R R	5
2	Scalehunter's Beautiful Daughter, The	89	SHEPARD, Lucius	19
2	Last of the Winnebagos, The	89	WILLIS, Connie	19
3	Do Ya, Do Ya, Wanna Dance	89	WALDROP, Howard	17
4	Kirinyaga	89	RESNICK, Mike	16
3	Schrodinger's Kitten	89	EFFINGER, George Alec	16
2	Journals of the Plague Years, The	89	SPINRAD, Norman	14
1	Mona Lisa Overdrive	89	GIBSON, William	14
1	Islands in the Net	89	STERLING, Bruce	14
4	Ripples in the Dirac Sea	89	LANDIS, Geoffrey A	13
1	Cyteen	89	CHERRYH, C J	13
3	Enter a Soldier, Later Enter Another	89	SILVERBERG, Robert	12
1	Red Prophet	89	CARD, Orson Scott	12
2	Surfacing	89	WILLIAMS, Walter Jon	12
1	Prentice Alvin	89	CARD, Orson Scott	12
2	Great Works of Time	89	CROWLEY, John	11

By Year (5 points or better)				
CAT	TITLE	YR	AUTHOR	PTS
3	Peaches for Mad Molly	89	GOULD, Stepehn	9
3	Function of Dream Sleep, The	89	ELLISON, Harlan	9
5	Angry Candy	89	ELLISON, Harlan	8
2	Calvin Coolidge Home for Dead Comedians	89	DENTON, Bradley	8
4	Fort Moxie Branch, The	89	McDEVITT, Jack	8
1	Ivory: Legend Past & Future	89	RESNICK, Mike	8
7	Motion of Light in Water, The: Sex & SF	89	DELANY, Samuel R	8
10	Silence of the Lambs, The	89	HARRIS, Thomas	8
7	First Maitz	89	MAITZ, Don	8
3	Ginny Sweethips' Flying Circus	89	BARRETT, Neal Jr	8
4	Giving Plague, The	89	BRIN, David	7
7	New Encyclopedia of Science Fiction, The	89	GUNN, James	7
4	Our Neural Chernobyl	89	STERLING, Bruce	7
3	Silver Lady and the Fortyish Man, The	89	LINDHOLM, Megan	7
6	Year's Best Fantasy and Horror 1st	89	DATLOW, Ellen	7
1	Good News From Outer Space	89	KESSEL, John	7
1	Koko	89	STRAUB, Peter	7
1	Last Coin, The	89	BLAYLOCK, James P	6
3	Glacier	89	ROBINSON, Kim Stanley	6
9	Sheepfarmer's Daughter	89	MOON, Elizabeth	6
5	Knight and the Knave of Swords, The	89	LEIBER, Fritz	6
1	Gold Coast, The	89	ROBINSON, Kim Stanley	6
3	Hob, The	89	MOFFATT, Judith	5
3	Skin Trade, The	89	MARTIN, George R R	5
4	Night They Missed the Horror Show, The	89	LANSDALE, Joe	5
1	Healers War, The	89	SCARBOROUGH, Elizabeth	5
5	Charles Beaumont: Selected Stories	89	ANKER, Roger	5
3	Dowser	89	CARD, Orson Scott	5
9	Dragon Prince	89	RAWN, Melanie	5
9	Desolation Road	89	McDONALD, Ian	5
4	Midwinter's Tale, A	89	SWANWICK, Michael	5
4	Dori Bangs	90	STERLING, Bruce	18
2	Mountains of Mourning, The	90	BUJOLD, Lois McMaster	17
4	Boobs	90	CHARNAS, Suzy McKee	15
3	At the Rialto	90	WILLIS, Connie	15
4	Lost Boys	90	CARD, Orson Scott	15
1	Hyperion	90	SIMMONS, Dan	15
3	For I Have Touched the Sky	90	RESNICK, Mike	15
2	Father of Stones, The	90	SHEPARD, Lucius	14
4	Edge of the World, The	90	SWANWICK, Michael	14
1	Boat of A Million Years	90	ANDERSON, Poul	14
1	Carrion Comfort	90	SIMMONS, Dan	13
1	Fire in the Sun, A	90	EFFINGER, George Alec	11
2	Tiny Tango	90	MOFFETT, Judith	11
2	Touch of Lavender, A	90	LINDHOLM, Megan	10
2	Dozen Tough Jobs, A	90	WALDROP, Howard	10

SECTION F: "BEST OF BEST" BY YEAR

CAT	TITLE	YR	AUTHOR	PTS
	By Year (5 points or better)			
7	Harlan Ellison's Watching	90	ELLISON, Harlan	9
2	On t/Far Side of t/Cadillac Desert w/Dea	90	LANSDALE, Joe R	9
7	Grumbles from the Grave	90	HEINLEIN, Robert A	8
3	Dogwalker	90	CARD, Orson Scott	8
7	World Beyond the Hill, The	90	PANSHIN, Alexei & Cory	8
2	Apartheid,Superstr'gs & Modercai Thubana	90	BISHOP, Michael	7
7	Astounding Days	90	CLARKE, Arthur C	7
1	Lyonesse: Madouc	90	VANCE, Jack	7
2	Time-Out	90	WILLIS, Connie	7
6	Year's Best Fantasy and Horror 2nd	90	DATLOW, Ellen	7
3	Sisters	90	BEAR, Greg	7
3	Everything but Honor	90	EFFINGER, George Alec	7
7	Dancing at the Edge of the World	90	LeGUIN, Ursula K	7
1	Grass	90	TEPPER, Sheri S	7
5	Richard Matheson: Collected Stories	90	MATHESON, Richard	6
1	Stress of Her Regard, The	90	POWERS, Tim	6
11	Soldier of Arete	90	WOLFE, Gene	6
6	Razored Saddles	90	LANSDALE,	6
6	Blood is Not Enough	90	DATLOW, Ellen	6
6	Patterns	90	CADIGAN, Pat	5
9	Sunglasses After Dark	90	COLLINS, Nancy	5
3	Labyrinth	90	BUJOLD, Lois McMaster	5
1	On My Way To Paradise	90	WOLVERTON, Dan	5
4	Bears Discover Fire	91	BISSON, Terry	25
1	Fall of Hyperion, The	91	SIMMONS, Dan	19
2	Hemingway Hoax, The	91	HALDEMAN, Joe	18
2	Bones	91	MUURPHY, Pat	15
1	Only Begotten Daughter	91	MORROW, James	14
3	Tower of Babylon	91	CHIANG, Ted	14
3	Manamouki, The	91	RESNICK, Mike	12
2	Fool to Believe	91	CADIGAN, Pat	11
3	Shobie's Story, The	91	LeGUIN, Ursula K	11
3	Coon Rolled Down and Ruptured...	91	HUGH, Dafydd A B	11
2	Short, Sharp, Shock, A	91	ROBINSON, Kim Stanley	11
1	Vor Game, The	91	BUJOLD, Lois McMaster	11
1	Earth	91	BRIN, David	10
10	Mary Reilly	91	MARTIN, Valerie	10
1	Queen of Angels	91	BEAR, Greg	10
4	Cibola	91	WILLIS, Connie	10
4	Godspeed	91	SHEFFIELD, Charles	10
3	Braver Thing, A	91	SHEFFIELD, Charles	10
4	VRM-547	91	THOMPSON, W R	9
2	Weatherman	91	BUJOLD, Lois McMaster	9

SECTION F: "BEST OF BEST" BY YEAR

CAT	TITLE	YR	AUTHOR	PTS
By Year (5 points or better)				
11	Tehanu: The Last Book of Earthsea	91	LeGUIN, Ursula K	9
1	Tigana	91	KAY, Guy Gavriel	9
5	Prayers to Broken Stones	91	SIMMONS, Dan	9
2	Mr. Boy	91	KELLY, James Patrick	9
7	Hollywood Gothic	91	SKAL, David J	8
7	SFWA Handbook: The Prof Writer's Guide	91	RUSCH & SMITH	8
3	Over the Long Haul	91	SOUKUP, Martha	8
7	How to Write Science Fiction and Fantasy	91	CARD, Orson Scott	8
3	Dr. Pak's Preschool	91	BRIN, David	7
1	Thomas the Rhymer	91	KUSHNER, Ellen	7
4	Utility Man, The	91	REED, Rober	7
5	Brains of Rats, The	91	BLUMLEIN, Michael	7
7	Science Fiction in the Real World	91	SPINRAD, Norman	7
1	Quiet Pools, The	91	KUBE-McDOWELL, Michael	7
4	Power and the Passion, The	91	CADIGAN, Pat	7
4	Lieserl	91	FOWLER, Karen Joy	7
4	Love and Sex Among the Vertebrates	91	MURPHY, Pat	7
6	Universe 1	91	CARR, Terry	7
7	Bury My Heart at W.H. Smiths	91	ALDISS, Brian	7
1	White Jenna	91	YOLEN, Jane	7
1	Redshift Rendezvous	91	STITH, John E	7
1	Take Back Plenty	91	GREENLAND, Colin	6
6	Year's Best Fantasy and Horror 4th	91	DATLOW, Ellen	6
5	Leiber Chronicles, The	91	LEIBER, Fritz	6
6	Alien Sex	91	DATLOW, Ellen	6
6	Borderlands	91	MONTELEONE, Thomas	6
1	Good Omens	91	PRATCHETT, Terry	6
10	Stand, The: The Complete, Uncut Edition	91	KING, Stephen	6
3	Entropy's Bed at Midnight	91	SIMMONS, Dan	5
6	Four Past Midnight	91	KING, Stephen	5
9	Wintersong	91	HAND, Elizabeth	5
2	Stephen	91	MASSIE, Elizabeth	5
1	Stations of the Tide	92	SWANWICK, Michael	18
2	Bully!	92	RESNICK, Mike	18
1	Barrayar	92	BUJOLD, Lois McMaster	16
4	Buffalo	92	KESSEL, John	16
1	Bone Dance	92	BULL, Emma	16
2	Beggars in Spain	92	KRESS, Nancy	16
2	Gallery of His Dreams, The	92	RUSCH, Kristine Kathryn	15
2	Jack	92	WILLIS, Connie	14
1	Difference Engine, The	92	GIBSON, William	13
2	Griffin's Egg	92	SWANWICK, Michael	10

SECTION F: "BEST OF BEST" BY YEAR

CAT	TITLE	YR	AUTHOR	PTS
	By Year (5 points or better)			
7	Clive Barker's Shawows in Eden	92	JONES, Stephen	9
7	SF: The Early Years	92	BLEILER, Everett F	8
8	Cipher, The	92	KOJA, Kathe	8
4	Dog's Life	92	SOUKUP, Martha	8
10	Summer of Night	92	SIMMONS, Dan	8
7	World of Charles Addams, The	92	ADDAMS, Charles	8
3	Gold	92	ASIMOV, Isaac	8
4	Ma Qui	92	BRENNERT, Alan	8
1	Outside the Dog Museum	92	CARROLL, Jonathan	7
3	Gate of Faces	92	ALDRIDGE, Ray	7
3	Fin de Cycle	92	WALDROP, Howard	7
1	Xenocide	92	CARD, Orson Scott	7
2	And Wild For To Hold	92	KRESS, Nancy	7
3	Black Glass	92	FOWLER, Karen Joy	7
5	Night of the Cooters: More Neat Stories	92	WALDROP, Howard	7
1	All the Weyrs of Pern	92	McCAFFREY, Anne	7
4	Press Ann	92	BISSON, Terry	7
4	Happy Man, The	92	LETHEM, Jonathan	7
4	One Perfect Morning, With Jackals	92	RESNICK, Mike	7
3	Miracle	92	WILLIS, Connie	7
1	Summer Queen, The	92	VINGE, Joan D	7
4	In the Late Cretaceous	92	WILLIS, Connie	7
1	Boy's Life	92	McCAMMON, Robert R	6
1	Golden Fleece	92	SAWYER, Robert J	6
6	Year's Best Fantasy and Horror 4th	92	DATLOW, Ellen	6
6	Whisper of Blood, A	92	DATLOW, Ellen	6
4	Vinland the Dream	92	ROBINSON, Kim Stanley	6
1	Synners	92	CADIGAN, Pat	6
1	Little Country, The	92	DeLINT, Charles	6
1	King of the Morning, Queen of Day	92	McDONALD, Ian	6
4	Walk in the Sun, A	92	LANDIS, Geoffrey A	5
3	Guide Dog	92	CONNER, Mike	5

APPENDIX

A P P E N D I X

| CHRONOLOGY OF AWARDS
From the beginning, including, 1992 |||||
AWARDED From To	TOTAL YEARS	CODE	NAME	
1951 1957	7	IFA	International Fantasy	
1953 1992	40	HUG	Hugo	
1962 1992	31	NEB	Nebula	
1970 1992	23	BSF	British Science Fiction	
1971 1992	22	BFA	British Fantasy	
1971 1992	22	LOC	Locus Magazine	
1973 1992	20	JWC	J W Campbell	
1974 ? 19		JUP	Jupiter	
1975 1992	18	WFA	World Fantasy	
1979 ? 19		GAN	Gandalf?	
1980 1992	13	AUR	Aurora	
1982 1992	11	SFC	SF Chronicle Magazine	
1983 1992	10	COM	Compton Crook	
1983 1992	10	DIC	Dick	
1986 1992	7	WOF	Writers of the Future	
1987 1992	6	DAV	Davis Publications	
1987 1992	6	CLA	Arthur C. Clarke	
1988 1992	5	STO	Bram Stoker	
1992 1992	1	TIP	James Tiptree Jr	

A P P E N D I X

CHRONOLOGY OF MAJOR SCIENCE FICTION AWARDS

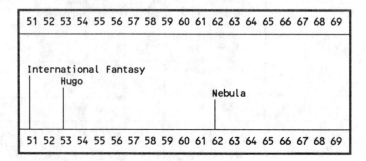

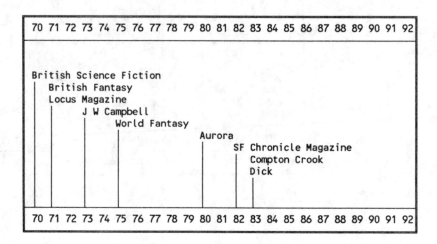

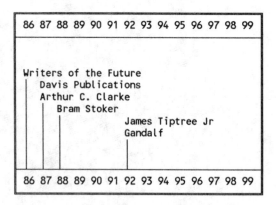

Note: Not all awards shown in this chronology are included in the text. A few lesser awards have been added for clarity of context.

REFERENCES

R E F E R E N C E S

BOOKS:

REGINALD'S SCIENCE FICTION AND FANTASY AWARDS
2nd Edition
MALLETT, Daryl Furumi and REGINALD, Robert
San Bernardino, California 1991
Borgo Press

A HISTORY OF THE HUGO, NEBULA AND INTERNATIONAL FANTASY AWARDS
2nd Edition
FRANSON, Donald and DeVORE, Howard
Misfit Press 1987

MAGAZINES:

LOCUS: THE NEWSPAPER OF THE SCIENCE FICTION FIELD
Charles N. Brown, Editor
Locus Publications
Box 13305
Oakland, CA 94661

SCIENCE FICTION CHRONICLE: THE MONTHLY SF AND FANTASY NEWSMAGAZINE
Andrew I. Porter, Editor
Algol Press
Box 4175
New York, NY 10163